Essentials of Economics

Dirk Mateer
University of Arizona

Lee Coppock
University of Virginia

Brian O'Roark
Robert Morris University

W • W • NORTON
NEW YORK • LONDON

W. W. Norton & Company has been independent since its founding in 1923, when William Warder Norton and Mary D. Herter Norton first published lectures delivered at the People's Institute, the adult education division of New York City's Cooper Union. The firm soon expanded its program beyond the Institute, publishing books by celebrated academics from America and abroad. By midcentury, the two major pillars of Norton's publishing program—trade books and college texts—were firmly established. In the 1950s, the Norton family transferred control of the company to its employees, and today—with a staff of four hundred and a comparable number of trade, college, and professional titles published each year—W. W. Norton & Company stands as the largest and oldest publishing house owned wholly by its employees.

Printed in the United States of America.
First Edition

Editor: Jack Repcheck

Developmental Editor: Steven Rigolosi

Manuscript Editor: Alice Vigliani

Project Editors: Rebecca Homiski, Diane Cipollone, Katie Callahan

Media Editor: Carson Russell

Associate Media Editor: Stefani Wallace

Media Editorial Assistant: Kerishma Panigrahi

Editorial Assistants: Lindsey Osteen, Theresia Kowara

Marketing Manager, Economics: Janise Turso

Production Manager: Eric Pier-Hocking

Photo Editor and Researcher: Trish Marx

Permissions Manager: Megan Jackson

Text Design: Lisa Buckley

Art Director: Rubina Yeh

Cover Design: Kiss Me I'm Polish

Composition: Jouve

Manufacturing: Webcrafters, Inc.

Library of Congress Cataloging-in-Publication Data

Mateer, G. Dirk.

Essentials of economics / Dirk Mateer, University of Arizona, Lee Coppock, University of Virginia, J. Brian O'Roark, Robert Morris University. — First Edition.

pages cm

Includes index.

ISBN 978-0-393-26458-6 (pbk.)

1. Economics. I. Title.

HB171.5.M434 2016

330—dc23

2015030231

W. W. Norton & Company, Inc., 500 Fifth Avenue, New York, NY 10110-0017
wwnorton.com

W. W. Norton & Company Ltd., Castle House, 75/76 Wells Street, London W1T 3QT
1 2 3 4 5 6 7 8 9 0

To my father, who gave up a successful career in business and found his passion teaching finance. Thanks for encouraging me to become a teacher as well.

D.M.

To Krista: Many women do noble things, but you surpass them all.—Proverbs 31:29

L.C.

To Christie: This life is more amazing because of you.

B.O.

BRIEF CONTENTS

PART I Introduction

PART II Microeconomics

PART III Macroeconomics

Appendix

CONTENTS

PART II Microeconomics

PART III Macroeconomics

APPENDIX

PREFACE

We are teachers of economics. That is what we do. We teach students of all majors and interest levels, and have done so for, well . . . a very long time.

The Mateer/Coppock *Principles of Economics* text, on which this book is based, has been a resounding success. It has been adopted widely because it is a book by teachers for teachers, and it has a strong student focus. The task of adapting this text for the survey level has followed the same recipe for success.

The one-semester survey course presents unique challenges to instructors. For most students, this course is unrelated to their major. It will be the only economics course that they will ever take, and many approach it with trepidation, perhaps even genuine fear.

While this challenge is very real, there are also unique opportunities. Beyond this course, students will likely have no further formal education on many of the important issues that arise in this class, such as why the price of college keeps rising, why wages are stagnant, how monetary policy and fiscal policy affect them, and why credit-card debt can be a very serious problem. Economics and the economic way of thinking are extremely important for students, even if they don't yet know that. Teaching this subject to non-business students is an opportunity to help them learn about topics that will affect their lives far beyond graduation.

Thus, the survey course is not the same thing as a principles course, mainly because it is terminal. It needs to be taught differently from the principles course, and a survey text needs to be fundamentally different from a principles text. When we reviewed the existing survey books, we found that most are slimmed-down versions of existing principles texts. While that approach to writing a survey text helps to ensure that relevant topics are covered, simply transferring material from a principles book is not an effective approach for helping students learn economics in the survey course.

Why? Simply condensing a principles textbook doesn't take into account the areas that students consistently find problematic. Understanding cost curves is important for business and economics students, but survey students do not need to cover this topic in the same detail. They need to see graphs, but these graphs should be streamlined and easy to read, with no extraneous information. Similarly, while it is important for a business or economics major to know the minutiae of the market-structure models, a basic knowledge of the differences between competition and monopoly is more than sufficient for students who are getting the broader picture that comes in the survey course—which is, after all, a *survey* of economics.

Our years of experience in the classroom—both the principles classroom and the survey classroom—have taught us an important lesson: when ideas resonate with students, and stick with them through reinforcement, students are more likely to carry the basic ideas of economics into their lives beyond the classroom. In transforming the Mateer/Coppock principles text into a survey text, we had one key goal in mind: to write a textbook that connects to students where they are. No other text that we know of uses the experiences of modern students to reinforce new terminology with examples from everyday life in everyday language. While they may not know it, students are key participants in the economy and their experiences should be the platform from which our instruction begins. *Essentials of Economics* uses examples that resonate in students' lives (for instance, the market for cell phones, student-loan and credit-card payments, computing devices, ride-sharing).

So, ultimately, we wanted to develop a textbook that would engage students, one that is enjoyable to read week in and week out, a concise presentation of the discipline that encourages students to think about how economics affects their lives. As economists, we know that the "dismal science" isn't really dismal at all; rather, it's full of insights that help us better understand ourselves and the events going on around us. *Essentials of Economics* will help your students learn to think like economists by showing them how to make better choices in the workplace, their personal investments, their long-term planning, their voting—indeed, in all their critical choices. We hope that *Essentials of Economics* will be your partner in success in helping your students live more fulfilled and satisfying lives.

What does this classroom-inspired, student-centered text look like?

A Simple Narrative

First and foremost, we keep the narrative simple. We always bear in mind all those office-hour conversations with students where we searched for some way to make sense of this foreign language—for them—that is economics. It is incredibly satisfying when you find the right expression, explanation, or example that creates the "Oh, now I get it . . ." moment with your student. We have filled the narrative with those successful "now I get it" passages.

Trade-offs are important at many levels. For instance, there is a trade-off between security and convenience. When you use your credit card or shop online, there is the possibility that your personal information will be compromised. Companies store your personal data electronically when they issue credit cards. It's a fact of life in the information age: whenever data is stored, that data needs to be protected. If it isn't, it can be stolen.

Swipe a credit card, compromise your financial data?

There have been many news stories about breaches of information security. In late 2013, hackers stole financial information for over 70 million Target customers by compromising credit-card readers with a malicious software code, sometimes called malware. When the credit card was swiped, the customers' information was made available to the hackers. This lapse in security cost Target over $200 million in public-relations expenses, damage control, and updated technology, not to mention an untold loss of sales as customers worried that the company hadn't fixed the problem. However, Target could have easily prevented the problem. If Target had accepted only cash for transactions, there would have been no credit-card information to steal. Taking down the company's web site would have prevented hackers from stealing information via the Internet. Target could have then advertised itself as the most secure major retailer in America. No hacker could ever steal customers' financial information from Target simply because Target wouldn't have that information. However, taking down its web site or not accepting credit cards would severely harm Target's bottom line. Customers who are used to the convenience of using credit cards would stop patronizing the store. Online shoppers would surf to another store's web site and buy there instead. In the current environment, customers are willing to trade off security for convenience. How do we know this? They keep shopping on the Internet, and many customers have returned to Target.

Examples and Cases That Resonate and Therefore Stick: Economics in the Real World

Nothing makes this material stick for students like good examples and cases, and we have peppered our book with them. They are not in boxed inserts. They are part of the narrative, set off with an **Economics in the Real World** heading.

ECONOMICS IN THE REAL WORLD

Why LeBron James Has Someone Else Help Him Move

LeBron James is a pretty big guy—6′8″ and roughly 250 pounds. In the summer of 2014, he decided to move from Miami to Cleveland to play with his hometown basketball team. Given his size and strength, you might think that LeBron would have moved his household himself. But despite the fact that he could replace two or more ordinary movers, he kept playing basketball and hired movers. Let's examine the situation to see if this was a wise decision.

Will LeBron ever ask his teammates, "Guys . . . can you help me move this weekend?"

LeBron has an absolute advantage in both playing basketball and moving furniture. But, as we have seen, an absolute advantage doesn't mean that he should do both tasks himself. Even though his move happened during the off-season, taking time away from his practice and workout schedule is an opportunity cost he has to face (not to mention the possibility of injury). The movers, with a much lower opportunity cost of their time, have a comparative advantage in moving—so LeBron made a smart decision to hire them!

However, when LeBron retires, the value of his time will be lower. If the opportunity cost of his time becomes low enough, it's conceivable that the next time he changes residence, he'll move himself rather than pay movers. ✷

ECONOMICS IN THE REAL WORLD

General Motors Sales Up in China, but Down in Europe

General Motors, one of the world's largest car manufacturers, now sells over 250,000 vehicles per month in China. GM announced in November 2014 that it had already sold more than 3 million vehicles in China, well ahead of its 2013 numbers. Sales of the Cadillac line were particularly strong, rising 58% from 2013. This trend is contrary to the growth of the luxury car's performance in the United States, where 2014 sales were slightly down from 2013.

In China, people say that they would rather drive a Buick.

GM's Buick product line does exceptionally well in China. Buick now sells about four times as many cars in China as in the United States. This sales growth for GM is thanks in large part to the growing incomes of many Chinese citizens.

The bad news for GM comes from Europe. Increased sales in China have been offset by slowing sales in Europe, where many economies were recovering from recessions, but only mildly. By mid-2014, GM was continuing to see declining sales of its cars in Europe. ✷

Reinforcers: Practice What You Know

Practice What You Know exercises allow students to self-assess while reading and provide a bit of hand-holding; they ask questions and then provide worked-out solutions. While other survey texts have in-chapter questions, no other book consistently frames these exercises within real-world situations to which students relate.

PRACTICE WHAT YOU KNOW

Externalities: Fracking

In 2003, energy companies began using a process known as hydraulic fracturing, or fracking, to extract underground reserves of natural gas in certain states, including Pennsylvania, Texas, West Virginia, and Wyoming. Fracking involves injecting water, chemicals, and sand into rock formations more than a mile deep. This process taps the natural gas that is trapped in those rocks, allowing it to escape up the well. The gas comes to the surface along with much of the water and chemical mixture, which now must be disposed of. Unfortunately, the chemicals in the mix make the water toxic. Consequently, as fracking activities have expanded to more areas, controversy has grown about the potential environmental effects of the process.

How would a natural gas well affect your local area?

Question: What negative externalities might fracking generate?

Answer: People who live near wells worry about the amount of pollutants in the water mixture and the potential for them to leach into drinking water supplies. Additionally, the drilling of a well is a noisy process. Drilling occurs 24 hours a day for a period of a few weeks. This noise pollution affects anyone who lives close by. Another issue is that the gas has to be transported away from the well in trucks. Additional truck traffic can potentially damage local roads.

Question: What positive externalities might fracking generate?

Answer: Fracking has brought tremendous economic growth to the areas where it is occurring. The resulting jobs have employed many people, providing them with a good income. Local hotels and restaurants have seen an increase in business as temporary employees move from one area to another. As permanent employees take over well operation, housing prices climb as a result of increasing demand. Rising house prices benefit local homeowners.

PRACTICE WHAT YOU KNOW

Value of the Marginal Product of Labor: Flower Barrettes

Question: Penny can make five flower barrettes each hour. She works eight hours each day. Penny is paid $75.00 a day. The firm can sell the barrettes for $1.99 each. What is Penny's VMP of labor? What is the barrette firm's marginal profit from hiring her?

Answer: In eight hours, Penny can make 40 barrettes. Since each barrette sells for $1.99, her value of the marginal product of labor, or VMP_{labor}, is $40 \times \$1.99$, or $79.60. Since her VMP_{labor} is greater than the daily wage she receives, the marginal profit from hiring her is $79.60 – $75, or $4.60.

How many flower barrettes could you make in an hour?

Additional Reinforcers: Economics for Life, Economics in the Media

Two additional elements will help to reinforce the material with your students. The first, **Economics for Life**, appears near the end of each chapter and applies economic reasoning to important decisions that your students will face in their early adulthood, such as buying or leasing a car. The second, **Economics in the Media**, analyze classic scenes from movies and TV shows that deal directly with economics. One of us has written the book (literally!) on economics in the movies, and we have used these clips year after year to make economics stick with students.

Recession-Proof Your Job

ECONOMICS FOR LIFE

Recessions are hard on almost everyone in an economy, but there are ways you can shield yourself from unemployment.

The first thing you need is a college degree. In October 2014, the U.S. national unemployment rate was 5.9% for the entire labor force, but just 3.1% for college graduates.

Unemployment can occur in the macroeconomy when wages are sticky, meaning that they don't respond to changes in the economy. This outcome applies to individuals too. If you do happen to lose your job, you may need to consider accepting a lower wage or even a change of career so as to obtain another job. The more flexible your wage range, the less likely you are to experience long-term unemployment.

Finally, if you lose your job, be sure to take advantage of all the modern job-search tools available today. There are millions of jobs available, even when unemployment rates are very high—you just need to know how to find those jobs. For example, the web site indeed.com turns up thousands of job vacancies for almost any job description. As of November 2014, searching for either "accountant" or "CPA" yielded nearly 39,000 results, a search for "civil engineer" yielded 13,732 results, and "marketing" yielded 289,884 results.

Don't let this happen to you!

How Does a Criminal Get a Loan?

ECONOMICS IN THE MEDIA

Despicable Me

In the movie *Despicable Me* (2010), we find the aging villain Gru trying to compete with other, younger villains. His plan to steal the moon would get him back in the criminal headlines, but he doesn't have the finances to put his plan into action. Like any entrepreneur looking to get his business venture off the ground, Gru goes to the bank hoping to secure a loan. Being a villain, he goes to the Bank of Evil (Formerly Lehman Brothers) and presents his business plan. While impressed with his audacity, Mr. Perkins, the bank manager, insists on seeing more progress before extending the loan. Gru has financed other schemes through the bank that haven't panned out, and Mr. Perkins is understandably reluctant to lend Gru more money when the return on investment is so uncertain. Mr. Perkins also informs Gru that there are better risks in the market—villains with more recent successes who are also seeking funding. Therefore, Mr. Perkins demands to see the shrink ray, which Gru will use in his plot to steal the moon, as a form of collateral.

This animated version of the lending process isn't all that far off from what happens in the real world. Banks do want to lend to businesses, but they want to make sure a new business has a chance of success. Otherwise, the borrower will be less likely to repay the loans, and that is bad for the bank—even an evil bank.

Gru: Evil villain, motivated entrepreneur, or both?

Bonus Chapter: Personal Finance

Too many students (and adults) have little to no understanding of the massive debts they can incur via student loans and credit-card debt. Chapter 19, "Personal Finance," is a primer on student and consumer borrowing, interest rates, personal debt, and home purchases. The chapter covers both the short run and the long run: Students who read this chapter will think twice before making their next credit-card purchase while also thinking about the decision to rent vs. buy and how to save for retirement.

The Costs and Benefits of Home Ownership

Home ownership is expensive. There is homeowner's insurance to pay and property taxes to pay. If there is damage to your home or property, you have to pay to have it fixed. Leaks in the basement need to be repaired, the driveway needs to be cleared during the winter, the grass needs to be cut, occasional broken windows need to be replaced—and the homeowner pays for (or does) all of this. Homeowners also have to pay for utilities—water, sewer, electric, cable, and trash pick-up. That adds up!

As a homeowner, fixing this is your responsibility.

If you're a renter, many of these headaches go away. You pay a fixed amount for your rent, which may include some of your utilities and almost always provides for snow removal and lawn care. In addition, you don't have to pay property taxes directly (although your rent does pay part of them) or pay for homeowner's insurance (although you might want to buy renter's insurance to guard against theft or fire).

Why do so many people want to own a home when there are so many added costs associated with the purchase? Much of this decision has to do with building equity. There are also tax implications to owning your own home. Let's look at both of these issues.

How Do Interest Rates Affect Borrowers?

Now we'll return to your credit card bill. Let's say that the **minimum payment**, the smallest amount the credit card company requires you to pay each month so as not to damage your credit score, is $2. "Fine," you say to yourself. "That means it'll take about five months to pay off my $10.50 Blake Shelton music purchase." You calculate that $2 a month for five months equals $10, and if you add 50 cents to the last payment you're free and clear. That would be the case if interest payments weren't included; however, there are interest payments to make, and you need to take that into consideration. But here is where you can get yourself into real trouble if you make only the minimum payment every month: the interest *compounds*. In the context of borrowing, **compounding** means that interest is added to your balance, so you end up paying interest on the increasingly higher balance.

On the saver's side, compounding interest can be a very good thing. When you're saving money, compounding interest helps you save more. (We'll see how this type of compounding works a little later in this chapter.) Unfortunately, when you're borrowing money, compounding interest can cause your repayment plan to drag on and on and on.

The **minimum payment** is the smallest amount that a lender requires a borrower to pay each month so as not to damage the borrower's credit score.

Compounding of interest (in the context of borrowing money) means that interest is added to an account balance so that the borrower ends up paying interest on an increasingly higher balance. In the context of saving, compounding means that interest is added to your total savings: you get paid interest on your savings plus any prior interest earned.

Big-Picture Pedagogy

Chapter-Opening Misconceptions

When we first started teaching we assumed that most of our students were taking economics for the first time and were therefore blank slates on which we could draw. We were wrong. We now realize that students come to our classes with a number of strongly held misconceptions about economics and the economy, so we begin each chapter recognizing these misconceptions and then establishing what we will do to help students onto the path of accurate knowledge.

CHAPTER **4** **Market Efficiency**

MISCONCEPTION

The minimum wage helps everyone earn a living wage.

You are probably familiar with the minimum wage, which is an example of a *price control*. If you've ever worked for the minimum wage, you probably think that raising it sounds like a great idea. You may support minimum-wage legislation because you believe it will help struggling workers to make ends meet. After all, it seems reasonable that firms should pay a living wage to cover necessities.

Price controls are not a new idea. The first recorded attempt to control prices was four thousand years ago in ancient Babylon, when King Hammurabi decreed how much corn a farmer could pay for a cow. Similar attempts to control prices occurred in ancient Egypt, Greece, and Rome. Each attempt ended badly. In Egypt, farmers revolted against tight price controls and intrusive inspections, eventually causing the economy to collapse. In Greece, the Athenian government set the price of grain at a very low level. Predictably, the quantity of grain supplied dried up. In 301 CE, the Roman government under Emperor Diocletian prescribed the maximum price of beef, grains, clothing, and many other items. Almost immediately, markets for these goods disappeared.

History has shown us that price controls generally do not work. Why? Because they disrupt the normal functioning of the market. By the end of this chapter, we hope you will understand the importance of market efficiency and how price controls (such as minimum-wage laws) erode that efficiency. Higher wages or lower prices may sound good on the surface, but there are always trade-offs. However, interfering with markets can lead to unintended consequences.

Big Questions

After the opening misconception, we present the learning goals for the chapter in the form of **Big Questions**. We come back to the Big Questions in the conclusion to the chapter with a summary titled **Answering the Big Questions**.

BIG QUESTIONS

* **What are the roles of profits?**
* **How are profits and losses calculated?**
* **How much should a firm produce?**

ANSWERING THE BIG QUESTIONS

What are the roles of profits?

* Profits provide the financial incentive for entrepreneurs to enter a business. Without the prospect of financial gain, very few people would take the risk of starting a business.
* Profits also direct (allocate) resources to businesses that are producing things consumers want. If you don't make a profit, it's difficult to afford the inputs necessary to continue production.
* Profits determine which companies stay in business and which ones do not. A company that isn't making profits isn't covering its costs and will have to shut down.

How are profits and losses calculated?

* Profits and losses are determined by calculating the difference between expenses and revenue.
* Economists break cost into two components: explicit costs, which are easy to calculate, and implicit costs, which are hard to calculate. Economic profit accounts for both explicit costs and implicit costs. If a business has an economic profit, its revenues are larger than the combination of its explicit and implicit costs.

Solved Problems

We conclude each chapter with a full set of problems, including at least two fully solved problems that appear on the last page of the chapter.

SOLVED PROBLEMS

6. There is a two-part answer here. The first graph shows the monopolist making a profit:

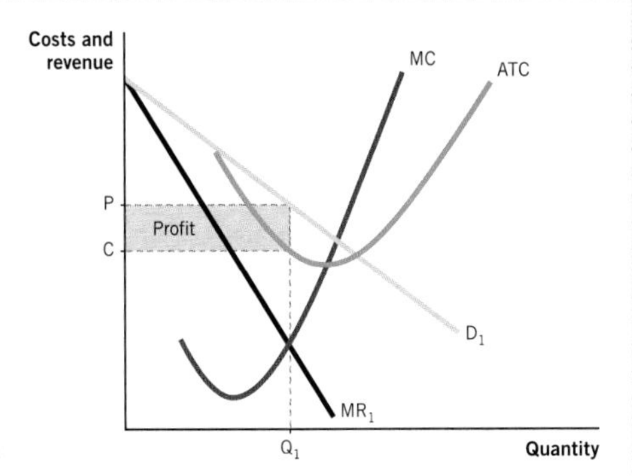

Now we show what happens if demand falls:

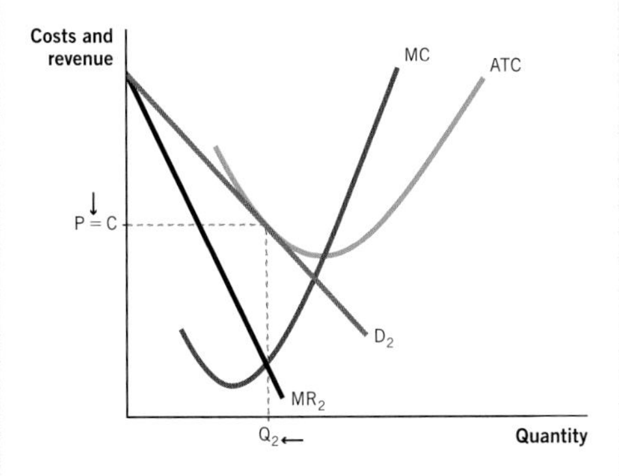

Lower demand causes the price to fall, the output to decline, and the profit to disappear. Note: When the demand curve falls, the marginal revenue curve falls as well.

9. The cardboard firm manufactures a product that is a component used mostly by other firms that need to package final products for sale. As a result, any efforts at advertising will only raise costs without increasing the demand for cardboard. This contrasts with the bookseller, who advertises to attract consumers to the store. More traffic means more purchases of books and other items sold in the store. The bookstore has some market power. In this case, it pays to advertise. A cardboard manufacturing firm sells exactly the same product as other cardboard producers, so it has no monopoly power, and any advertising expenses will only make its cost higher than its rivals'.

Essentials of Economics: Structure and Content

Essentials of Economics is structured as a typical survey text, with microeconomic topics preceding macroeconomics. The order of chapters will also appear familiar, but the similarities end there. This book has been specifically designed to meet the needs of students who will not be taking another course on economics. Therefore, the content focuses not only on understanding the basics, but also on how economics applies to life.

The first half of the text covers microeconomics. Basic introductory chapters address four ways to think like an economist (opportunity cost, marginal thinking, incentives, and trade creates value) and how economists approach the subject. These chapters explain what economics is all about and lay the groundwork for the rest of the book.

We then discuss markets, emphasizing the importance of markets as mechanisms for distributing goods. To avoid muddying the waters too much, we provide two appendixes, one on multiple demand and supply shifts, and another explaining basic concepts of elasticity. These topics can be addressed or not, depending on instructor preference.

While we have certainly not abandoned the use of graphs, we have minimized their complexity, especially when examining a firm's costs. The focus is on marginal decision-making, as this is the most important concept in the choices that businesses make. Market structure is streamlined to a single chapter. Including competitive and monopolistic firms in one chapter forced us to target the basics of market structure and be judicious with our use of graphs.

Following the discussion of market structures, we include a chapter on behavioral economics and game theory. An understanding of these topics is helpful to students who major in a number of areas (including psychology and political science) and the topics themselves have become quite popular as areas of research and discussion within the economics profession.

The labor chapter emphasizes the factors that affect wages. Students are paying a tremendous amount of money to attend college and if they hope to repay their student loans, an understanding of what and why people get paid will be of great use.

The chapter on the role of government helps students to consider the consequences of government action. In most survey texts, if this topic is covered at all, the solutions to market failure are deemed to be governmental in nature with few or no potential side effects. We highlight the idea that even the best intentions have costs and consequences.

The macro section of the text condenses the mundane measurements of the macroeconomy, providing an opportunity to explore how different parts of the macroeconomy work. We introduce GDP, unemployment, and inflation (the key macro variables) in the opening macro chapter, and then devote a single chapter to the measurement of all three variables.

The aggregate demand and supply chapter appears earlier in this text than in most. One reason for this decision is the idea that students will still recall how the basic market model works. With the usual tweaks, the aggregate model works in a similar fashion. Additionally, understanding the AD/AS tool before they learn about growth and policy will allow students to more effectively analyze the changes in the three major macro variables. Combining AD/AS with a discussion of business cycles also helps students understand the rationale behind policies designed to increase growth, when these policies should be adopted, and the problems with timing. In short, macroeconomic policy has a direct effect on students' lives, and a better understanding of policymakers' intentions will help students better understand government policies.

Students need to be aware that economics is always evolving. The tools we use are different today than those we used in the past. Bits of economic history are woven throughout the pages of this text, showing students how the great thinkers and past events influence modern economics. Adam Smith informs the role of government. Reference to the classical and Keynesian debates illustrates the difficulty that macro policymakers encounter when trying to reach consensus. The post–World War II change to activist policy, along with some background on the Fed, also provides context regarding how we arrived at our current state of economic understanding. Providing history and perspective is also a way to engage students from a variety of majors, from the liberal arts through the social sciences and beyond.

Because it is vitally important for students to have some idea of basic finance, the final chapter focuses on personal finance. The question arises: Why include such a chapter? The answer: When students think about economics, their first thoughts are not usually centered on GDP, market structure, or even incentives. Rather, they think of the stock market and money. Students who are not business oriented, and even some who are, expect that they will learn a little something about finance when they sign up for an economics class. And why shouldn't they? We say we want students to make better choices. Many of the bad choices people make involve their finances. So, let's provide them with some context to help them make better choices. The personal finance chapter does exactly that.

Supplements and Media

InQuizitive

InQuizitive isn't your average homework assignment. InQuizitive is a new formative, adaptive learning tool that improves student understanding of important learning objectives. Students progress through three different levels in each activity, are never allowed to give up on a question, and wager points as they go. Personalized quiz questions, game-like elements, and rich answer-specific feedback engage and motivate students as they learn.

InQuizitive for *Essentials of Economics* includes a variety of dynamic question types beyond basic multiple-choice. Image-click, numeric entry, and various graph-interpretation questions build economic skills and better prepare students for lectures, quizzes, and exams. The efficacy of formative assessment is backed by education and psychology research. Performance-specific feedback, varied question types, and gaming elements built into InQuizitive have been shown to increase student retention of material and student engagement. For more information on research supporting formative assessment, visit inquizitive.wwnorton.com.

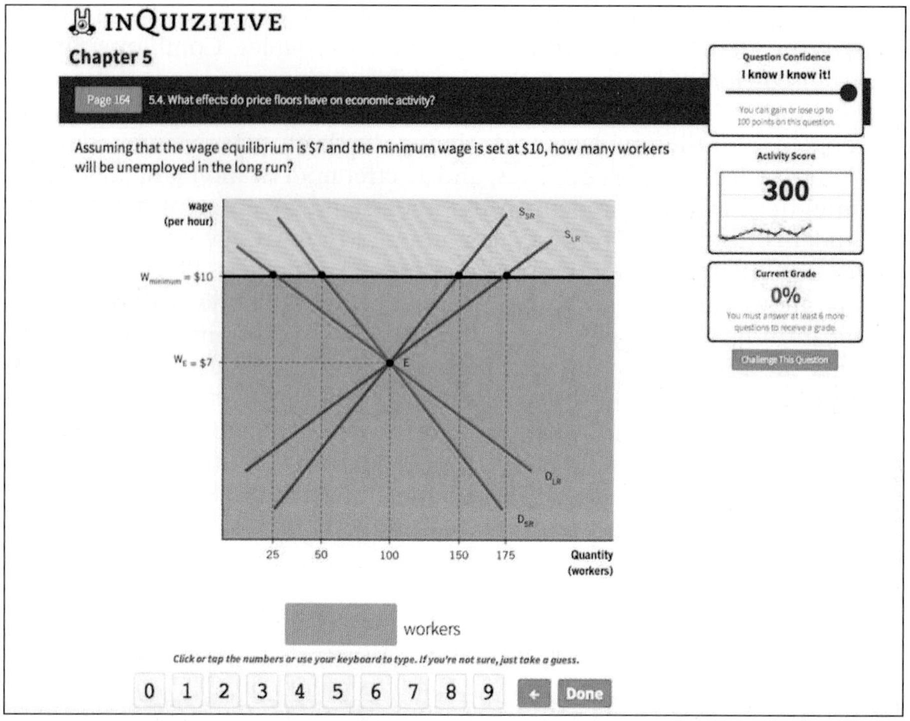

Norton Coursepack

Bring tutorial videos, assessment, and other online teaching resources directly into your new or existing online course with the Norton Coursepack. It's easily customizable and available for all major learning management systems including Blackboard, Desire2Learn, Angel, Moodle, and Canvas.

The Norton Coursepack for *Essentials of Economics* includes:

- Concept Check quizzes
- Homework quizzes
- Office Hours video tutorials
- Interactive Scratch Paper modules
- Flashcards
- Links to the eBook
- Links to InQuizitive activities
- Test Bank

Enhanced eBook

The electronic version of *Essentials of Economics* provides an enhanced reading experience for both students and instructors. The eBook includes dynamic and engaging features such as embedded video, expandable and collapsible sections, flashcards, and dynamic graphs. Instructors can focus student reading by sharing notes with their classes, including embedded images and video. Students can read their eBook on all computers and devices while using intuitive highlighting, note-taking, and bookmarking features that those who dog-ear their printed texts will love.

The Ultimate Guide to Teaching Essentials of Economics

The Ultimate Guide to Teaching Essentials of Economics isn't just a guide to using *Essentials of Economics,* it's a guide to becoming a better teacher. Combining more than 50 years of teaching experience, authors Dirk Mateer, Lee Coppock, Brian O'Roark, Wayne Geerling (Pennsylvania State University), and Kim Holder (University of West Georgia) have compiled hundreds of teaching tips into one essential teaching resource. The *Ultimate Guide* is thoughtfully designed, making it easy for new instructors to incorporate best teaching practices into their courses and for veteran teachers to find new inspiration to enliven their lectures.

The hundreds of tips in *The Ultimate Guide* include:

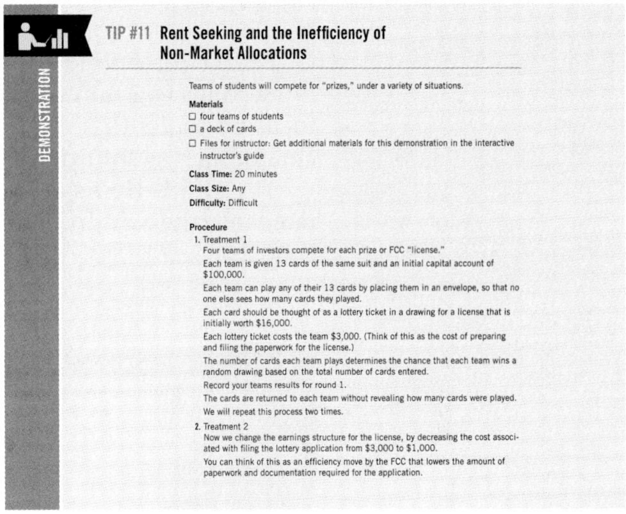
DEMONSTRATION

TIP #11 **Rent Seeking and the Inefficiency of Non-Market Allocations**

Teams of students will compete for "prizes," under a variety of situations.

Materials
- ☐ four teams of students
- ☐ a deck of cards
- ☐ Files for instructor: Get additional materials for this demonstration in the interactive instructor's guide

Class Time: 20 minutes
Class Size: Any
Difficulty: Difficult

Procedure
1. Treatment 1
   Four teams of investors compete for each prize or FCC "license."
   Each team is given 13 cards of the same suit and an initial capital account of $100,000.
   Each team can play any of their 13 cards by placing them in an envelope, so that no one else sees how many cards they played.
   Each card should be thought of as a lottery ticket in a drawing for a license that is initially worth $16,000.
   Each lottery ticket costs the team $3,000. (Think of this as the cost of preparing and filing the paperwork for the license.)
   The number of cards each team plays determines the chance that each team wins a random drawing based on the total number of cards entered.
   Record your teams results for round 1.
   The cards are returned to each team without revealing how many cards were played.
   We will repeat this process two times.
2. Treatment 2
   Now we change the earnings structure for the license, by decreasing the cost associated with filing the lottery application from $3,000 to $1,000.
   You can think of this as an efficiency move by the FCC that lowers the amount of paperwork and documentation required for the application.

- Think-pair-share activities to promote small-group discussion and active learning
- "Recipes" for in-class activities and demonstrations that include descriptions of the activity, required materials, estimated length of time, estimated difficulty, recommended class size, and instructions. Ready-to-use worksheets are also available for select activities.
- Descriptions of movie clips, TV shows, commercials, and other videos that can be used in class to illustrate economic concepts
- Clicker questions
- Ideas for music examples that can be used as lecture starters
- Suggestions for additional real-world examples to engage students

In addition to the teaching tips, each chapter begins with an introduction by one of the textbook authors, highlighting important concepts to teach in the chapter and pointing out his favorite tips. Each chapter ends with solutions to the unsolved end-of-chapter problems in the textbook.

Interactive Instructor's Guide

The Interactive Instructor's Guide (IIG) brings all the great content from *The Ultimate Guide* into a searchable online database that can be filtered by topic and resource type. Subscribing instructors will be alerted by email as new resources are made available.

In order to make it quick and easy for instructors to incorporate the tips from *The Ultimate Guide,* the IIG includes:

- Links for video tips when an online video is available
- Links to news articles for real-world examples when an article is available
- Downloadable versions of student worksheets for activities and demonstrations
- Downloadable PowerPoint slides for clicker questions
- Additional teaching resources from dirkmateer.com and leecoppock.com

Office Hours Video Tutorials

This collection of videos brings the office-hour experience online. Each video explains a fundamental concept and was conceived by and filmed with the textbook authors.

Perfect for online courses, each Office Hours video tutorial is succinct (90 seconds to 2 minutes) and mimics the office-hour experience. The videos focus on topics that are typically difficult to explain just in writing (or over email), such as shifting supply and demand curves.

The Office Hours videos have been integrated into the eBook, incorporated into the Norton Coursepack, and are available in the Instructor Resource Folder.

Test Bank

Every question in the *Essentials of Economics* test bank has been author reviewed and approved. Each chapter includes between 100 and 150 questions and incorporates graphs and images where appropriate.

The test bank has been developed using the Norton Assessment Guidelines. Each chapter of the test bank consists of three question types classified according to Bloom's taxonomy of knowledge types (Remembering, Understanding, Applying, Analyzing, Evaluating, and Creating). Questions are further classified by section and difficulty, making it easy to construct tests and quizzes that are meaningful and diagnostic.

Presentation Tools

Norton offers a variety of presentation tools so new instructors and veteran instructors alike can find the resources that are best suited for their teaching style. All of the following presentation tools are ADA compliant.

Enhanced Lecture PowerPoint Slides. These comprehensive, "lecture-ready" slides are perfect for new instructors and instructors who have limited time to prepare for lecture. In addition to conceptual content, the slides also include images from the book, stepped-out versions of in-text graphs, additional examples not included in the chapter, and clicker questions.

Art Slides and Art .JPEGs. For instructors who simply want to incorporate in-text art into their existing slides, all pieces of art from the book (tables, graphs, figures, and photos) are available in both PowerPoint and .jpeg formats. Stepped-out versions of in-text graphs are also available and have been optimized for screen projection.

Instructor Resource Folder

The Instructor Resource Folder includes the following resources in an all-in-one folder:

- The test bank in ExamView format on a CD
- Instructor's Resource Disc: PDFs of *The Ultimate Guide to Teaching Essentials of Economics,* PowerPoints (enhanced lecture slides, art slides, art .jpegs)
- Office Hours video tutorial DVD

dirkmateer.com & leecoppock.com

Visit dirkmateer.com to find a library of hundreds of recommended movie and TV clips, along with links to online video sources to use in class.

Lee Coppock blogs about the macroeconomy at leecoppock.com. Visit Lee's blog to read analysis of the latest macroeconomic events, to help connect what is taught in the course with current economic issues.

ACKNOWLEDGMENTS

We would like to thank the literally hundreds of fellow instructors who have helped us refine our vision and the actual words on the page for both this text and the first edition of *Principles of Economics*. Without your help, we would never have gotten to the finish line. We hope that the result is the economics teacher's text that we set out to write.

Reviewers of *Essentials of Economics*:

Casey Abington, Northwest Missouri State University
Kenneth Baker, University of Tennessee
Joseph Calhoun, Florida State University
Michael Enz, Roanoke College
Karl Geisler, New Mexico State University
Linda Kinney, Shepherd University
Randall Methenitis, Dallas County Community College
Cheryl Morrow, The University of Alabama at Birmingham
Anne-Marie Ryan-Guest, Normandale Community College
Tom Scheiding, St. Norbert College

Class testers of *Principles of Economics*:

Jennifer Bailly, California State University, Long Beach
Mihajlo Balic, Harrisburg Community College
Erol Balkan, Hamilton College
Susan Bell, Seminole State College
Scott Benson, Idaho State University
Joe DaBoll-Lavoie, Nazareth College
Michael Dowell, California State University, Sacramento
Abdelaziz Farah, State University of New York, Orange
Shelby Frost, Georgia State University
Karl Geisler, University of Nevada, Reno
Nancy Griffin, Tyler Junior College
Lauren Heller, Berry College
John Hilston, Brevard Community College
Kim Holder, University of West Georgia
Todd Knoop, Cornell College
Katharine W. Kontak, Bowling Green State University
Daniel Kuester, Kansas State University
Herman Li, University of Nevada, Las Vegas
Gary Lyn, University of Massachusetts, Lowell
Kyle Mangum, Georgia State University
Shah Mehrabi, Montgomery College
Sean Mulholland, Stonehill College
Vincent Odock, State University of New York, Orange
Michael Price, Georgia State University
Matthew Rousu, Susquehanna University
Tom Scales, Southside Virginia Community College
Tom Scheiding, University of Wisconsin, Stout
Clair Smith, St. John Fisher College
Tesa Stegner, Idaho State University
James Tierney, State University of New York, Plattsburgh
Nora Underwood, University of Central Florida
Michael Urbancic, University of Oregon
Marlon Williams, Lock Haven University

Our reviewers and advisors from focus groups for the first edition of *Principles of Economics*:

Mark Abajian, California State University, San Marcos
Teshome Abebe, Eastern Illinois University
Rebecca Achee Thornton, University of Houston
Mehdi Afiat, College of Southern Nevada
Seemi Ahmad, State University of New York, Dutchess
Abdullah Al-Bahrani, Bloomsburg University
Frank Albritton, Seminole State College
Rashid Al-Hmoud, Texas Tech University
Tom Andrews, West Chester University
Becca Arnold, San Diego Mesa College
Lisa Augustyniak, Lake Michigan College
Dennis Avola, Bentley University
Roberto Ayala, California State University, Fullerton
Ron Baker, Millersville University
Kuntal Banerjee, Florida Atlantic University
Jude Bayham, Washington State University
Mary Beal-Hodges, University of North Florida
Stacie Beck, University of Delaware
Jodi Beggs, Northeastern University
Richard Beil, Auburn University
Doris Bennett, Jacksonville State University
Karen Bernhardt-Walther, The Ohio State University
Prasun Bhattacharjee, East Tennessee State University
Richard Bilas, College of Charleston
Kelly Blanchard, Purdue University
Inácio Bo, Boston College
Michael Bognanno, Temple University
Donald Boudreaux, George Mason University
Austin Boyle, Pennsylvania State University
Elissa Braunstein, Colorado State University
Kristie Briggs, Creighton University
Stacey Brook, University of Iowa
Bruce Brown, California State Polytechnic University, Pomona
John Brown, Clark University
Vera Brusentsev, Swarthmore College
Laura Maria Bucila, Texas Christian University
Richard Burkhauser, Cornell University
W. Jennings Byrd, Troy University
Joseph Calhoun, Florida State University
Charles Callahan, State University of New York, Brockport
Douglas Campbell, University of Memphis
Giorgio Canarella, University of Nevada, Las Vegas
Semih Cekin, Texas Tech University
Sanjukta Chaudhuri, University of Wisconsin, Eau Claire
Shuo Chen, State University of New York, Geneseo
Monica Cherry, State University of New York, Buffalo
Larry Chisesi, University of San Diego
Steve Cobb, University of North Texas
Rhonda Collier, Portland Community College
Glynice Crow, Wallace State Community College
Chad D. Cotti, University of Wisconsin, Oshkosh
Damian Damianov, University of Texas, Pan American
Ribhi Daoud, Sinclair Community College
Kacey Douglas, Mississippi State University
William Dupor, The Ohio State University
Harold W. Elder, University of Alabama
Diantha Ellis, Abraham Baldwin Agricultural College
Tisha Emerson, Baylor University
Lucas Englehardt, Kent State University
Erwin Erhardt, University of Cincinnati
Molly Espey, Clemson University
Patricia Euzent, University of Central Florida
Brent Evans, Mississippi State University
Carolyn Fabian Stumph, Indiana University–Purdue University, Fort Wayne
Leila Farivar, The Ohio State University
Roger Frantz, San Diego State University
Gnel Gabrielyan, Washington State University
Craig Gallet, California State University, Sacramento
Wayne Geerling, Pennsylvania State University
Elisabetta Gentile, University of Houston
Menelik Geremew, Texas Tech University
Dipak Ghosh, Emporia State University
J. Robert Gillette, University of Kentucky
Rajeev Goel, Illinois State University
Bill Goffe, State University of New York, Oswego
Michael Gootzeit, University of Memphis
Paul Graf, Indiana University, Bloomington
Jeremy Groves, Northern Illinois University
Dan Hamermesh, University of Texas, Austin
Mehdi Haririan, Bloomsburg University
Oskar Harmon, University of Connecticut

David Harrington, The Ohio State University
Darcy Hartman, The Ohio State University
John Hayfron, Western Washington University
Jill Hayter, East Tennessee State University
Marc Hellman, Oregon State University
Wayne Hickenbottom, University of Texas, Austin
Mike Hilmer, San Diego State University
Lora Holcombe, Florida State University
Charles Holt, University of Virginia
James Hornsten, Northwestern University
Yu-Mong Hsiao, Campbell University
Alice Hsiaw, College of the Holy Cross
Yu Hsing, Southeastern Louisiana University
Paul Johnson, University of Alaska, Anchorage
David Kalist, Shippensburg University of Pennsylvania
Ara Khanjian, Ventura College
Frank Kim, University of San Diego
Colin Knapp, University of Florida
Mary Knudson, University of Iowa
Ermelinda Laho, LaGuardia Community College
Carsten Lange, California State Polytechnic University, Pomona
Tony Laramie, Merrimack College
Paul Larson, University of Delaware
Teresa Laughlin, Palomar College
Eric Levy, Florida Atlantic University
Charles Link, University of Delaware
Delores Linton, Tarrant County College
Xuepeng Liu, Kennesaw State University
Monika Lopez-Anuarbe, Connecticut College
Bruce Madariaga, Montgomery College
Brinda Mahalingam, University of California, Riverside
Chowdhury Mahmoud, Concordia University
Mark Maier, Glendale Community College
Daniel Marburger, Arkansas State University
Cara McDaniel, Arizona State University
Scott McGann, Grossmont College
Christopher McIntosh, University of Minnesota, Duluth
Evelina Mengova, California State University, Fullerton
William G. Mertens, University of Colorado, Boulder
Ida Mirzaie, The Ohio State University
Michael A. Mogavero, University of Notre Dame
Moon Moon Haque, University of Memphis
Mike Nelson, Oregon State University
Boris Nikolaev, University of South Florida
Caroline Noblet, University of Maine
Fola Odebunmi, Cypress College
Paul Okello, Tarrant County College
Stephanie Owings, Fort Lewis College
Caroline Padgett, Francis Marion University
Kerry Pannell, DePauw University
R. Scott Pearson, Charleston Southern University
Andrew Perumal, University of Massachusetts, Boston
Rinaldo Pietrantonio, West Virginia University
Irina Pritchett, North Carolina State University
Sarah Quintanar, University of Arkansas at Little Rock
Ranajoy Ray-Chaudhuri, The Ohio State University
Mitchell Redlo, Monroe Community College
Debasis Rooj, Northern Illinois University
Jason Rudbeck, University of Georgia
Naveen Sarna, Northern Virginia Community College
Noriaki Sasaki, McHenry County College
Jessica Schuring, Central College
Robert Schwab, University of Maryland
James Self, Indiana University, Bloomington
Gina Shamshak, Goucher College
Neil Sheflin, Rutgers University
Brandon Sheridan, North Central College
Joe Silverman, Mira Costa College
Brian Sloboda, University of Phoenix
Todd Sorensen, University of California, Riverside
Liliana Stern, Auburn University
Joshua Stillwagon, University of New Hampshire
Burak Sungu, Miami University
Vera Tabakova, East Carolina University
Yuan Emily Tang, University of California, San Diego
Anna Terzyan, Loyola Marymount University
Henry Thompson, Auburn University
Mehmet Tosun, University of Nevada, Reno
Robert Van Horn, University of Rhode Island
Adel Varghese, Texas A&M University
Marieta Velikova, Belmont University
Will Walsh, Samford University
Ken Woodward, Saddleback College
Jadrian Wooten, Washington State University
Anne York, Meredith College
Arindra Zainal, Oregon State University
Erik Zemljic, Kent State University
Kent Zirlott, University of Alabama

All of the individuals listed on the preceding pages helped us to improve the text and ancillaries, but a smaller group of them offered us extraordinary insight and support. They went above and beyond, and we would like them to know just how much we appreciate it. In particular, we want to recognize Alicia Baik (University of Virginia), Jodi Beggs (Northeastern University), Dave Brown (Penn State University), Jennings Byrd (Troy University), Douglas Campbell (University of Memphis), Shelby Frost (Georgia State University), Wayne Geerling (Penn State University), Paul Graf (Indiana University), Oskar Harmon (University of Connecticut), Jill Hayter (East Tennessee State University), John Hilston (Brevard Community College), Kim Holder (University of West Georgia), Todd Knoop (Cornell College), Katie Kontak (Bowling Green State University), Brendan LaCerda (University of Virginia), Paul Larson (University of Delaware), Ida Mirzaie (Ohio State University), Charles Newton (Houston Community College), Boris Nikolaev (University of South Florida), Andrew Perumal (University of Massachusetts, Boston), Irina Pritchett (North Carolina State University), Matt Rousu (Susquehanna College), Tom Scheiding (Cardinal Stritch University), Brandon Sheridan (North Central College), Clair Smith (Saint John Fisher College), James Tierney (SUNY Plattsburgh), Nora Underwood (University of Central Florida), Joseph Whitman (University of Florida), Erik Zemljic (Kent State University), and Zhou Zhang (University of Virginia).

We would also like to thank our partners at W. W. Norton & Company, who have been as committed to this text as we've been. They have been a pleasure to work with and we hope that we get to work together for many years. We like to call them Team Econ: Hannah Bachman, Theresia Kowara, Lindsey Osteen, Jack Borrebach, Diane Cipollone, Rebecca Homiski, Katie Callahan, Cassie del Pilar, Dan Jost, Lorraine Klimowich, John Kresse, Janise Turso, Pete Lesser, Sasha Levitt, Jack Repcheck, Spencer Richardson-Jones, Megan Jackson, Rubina Yeh, Mateus Teixeira, Carson Russell, Nicole Sawa, Stefani Wallace, and Kerishma Panigrahi. Our development editors, Becky Kohn and Steven Rigolosi, were a big help, as was our copy editor, Alice Vigliani. The visual appeal of the book is the result of our photo researchers, Dena Digilio Betz, Nelson Colón, and Trish Marx, and the team at Kiss Me I'm Polish who created the front cover: Agnieszka Gasparska, Andrew Janik, and Annie Song. Thanks to all—it's been a wonderful adventure.

Finally, from Dirk: I'd like to thank my colleagues at Penn State—especially Dave Brown and Wayne Geerling—for their hard work on the supplements, my friends from around the country for the encouragement to write a textbook, and my family for their patience as the process unfolded. In addition, I want to thank the thousands of former students who provided comments, suggestions, and other insights that helped shape the book.

Finally, from Lee: First, I'd like to acknowledge Krista, my excellent wife, who consistently sacrificed to enable me to write this book. I'd also like to thank Jack Repcheck, who had the vision and the will to make this project a reality; we can't thank him enough. Finally, I'd also like to acknowledge Ken Elzinga, Charlie Holt, and Mike Shaub: three great professors who are my role models in the academy and beyond.

Finally, from Brian: I am incredibly grateful to my colleagues at Robert Morris University—chiefly Pat Litzinger—for comments and insight they don't even know they provided. Many thanks to the authors in my life who have encouraged me to write and provided inspiration. To the great teachers whom I have learned from and continue to learn from, without your gifts I wouldn't be where I am. And finally, thanks to my family, my parents and especially Christie, Emily, Katie, and Maggie, who through the countless hours of work have supported the fanciful task of writing a book.

ABOUT THE AUTHORS

Dirk Mateer has a Ph.D. from Florida State University and is the Senior Lecturer and Gerald Swanson Chair of Economic Education at the University of Arizona. Dirk has been teaching Principles of Economics for over twenty years; he specializes in the Principles of Microeconomics. Before moving to the University of Arizona, Dirk spent 1 year at the University of Kentucky developing their online Principles courses and 15 years at Penn State, where he taught very large classes (700+ students per lecture), developing a reputation as one of the most effective and creative instructors of Principles of Economics in the country; for this, he was recently featured in *Businessweek*.

Lee Coppock has a Ph.D. from George Mason University and is Associate Professor of Economics at the University of Virginia. Like Dirk, Lee has been teaching Principles of Economics for over twenty years; he specializes in the Principles of Macroeconomics. Lee has been at UVA for more than ten years, where he teaches very large classes (600+ students per lecture) and has become a local legend. He is especially well known for cutting through the jargon and "econ speak" that plagues so many economics courses and texts, and patiently explaining the lessons of modern economics in terms that his students readily understand.

Brian O'Roark has a Ph.D. from George Mason University and is University Professor of Economics at Robert Morris University in Pittsburgh. He is the Co-Director of the Robert Morris Center for Economics Education. In 2014, Brian was given the Undergraduate Teaching Innovation Award by the Middle Atlantic Association of Colleges of Business Administration. He teaches the Survey of Economics course, and Principles of Micro and Macro Economics, every semester.

Essentials of Economics

PART

I

INTRODUCTION

CHAPTER 1

Thinking Like an Economist

MISCONCEPTION

Economics is the dismal science.

Perhaps you have heard of the "dismal science"? This derogatory term was first used by historian and essayist Thomas Carlyle in the nineteenth century. He called economics the dismal science after he read a prediction from economist Thomas Malthus stating that because our planet had limited resources, continued population growth would ultimately lead to widespread starvation.

Malthus was a respected thinker, but he was unduly pessimistic. The world population was one billion in 1800, and it's over seven billion today. One of the things that Malthus did not take into account was increases in technology and productivity. Today, the efficiency of agricultural production enables more than seven billion people to live on this planet. Far from being the dismal science, economics in the twenty-first century is a vital social science that helps world leaders improve their citizens' lives.

This textbook will provide the tools you need to be able to make your own assessments about the economy. What other discipline helps you discover how the world works, how to be an informed citizen, and how to live your life to the fullest? Economics can improve your understanding of the stock market and help you make better personal finance decisions. If you're interested in learning more about the job market, the answers are here. Economics provides answers to all of these questions and much more.

In this chapter, you will learn about four ways to think like an economist—opportunity cost, marginal thinking, incentives, and the principle that trade creates value. You will find that many of the more complex problems presented later in the text are based on one of these principles. Think of this chapter as a road map that provides a broad overview of your journey into economics. Let's get started!

Predicting the future is a tough business.

BIG QUESTIONS

- What is economics?
- What are four ways to think like an economist?

What Is Economics?

Economists study how decisions are made. Examples of economic decisions include whether or not you should buy or lease a car, sublet your apartment, and whether to buy that Gibson guitar you've been eyeing. And, just as individuals must choose what to buy within the limits of the income they possess, society as a whole must determine what to produce from its limited set of resources.

Scarcity refers to the limited nature of society's resources, given society's unlimited wants and needs.

Economics is the study of how people allocate their limited resources to satisfy their nearly unlimited wants.

Of course, life would be a lot easier if we could have whatever we wanted whenever we wanted it. Unfortunately, life doesn't work that way. Our wants and needs are nearly unlimited, but the resources available to satisfy these wants and needs are always limited. The term used to describe the limited nature of society's resources is **scarcity**. Even the most abundant resources, like the water we drink and the air we breathe, aren't always abundant enough everywhere to meet the wants and needs of every person. So how do individuals and societies make decisions about scarce resources? This is the basic question economists seek to answer. **Economics** is the study of how people allocate their limited resources to satisfy their nearly unlimited wants.

Microeconomics is the study of the individual units that make up the economy.

Macroeconomics is the study of the overall aspects and workings of an economy.

Microeconomics and Macroeconomics

The study of economics is divided into two subfields: microeconomics and macroeconomics. **Microeconomics** is the study of the individual units that make up the economy. **Macroeconomics** is the study of the overall aspects

Water is scarce . . .

. . . and so are diamonds!

and workings of an economy, such as inflation, growth, employment, interest rates, and the productivity of the economy as a whole. To see if you understand the difference, consider a worker who gets laid off and becomes unemployed. Is this an issue that would be addressed in microeconomics or macroeconomics? The question seems to fit parts of both definitions. The worker is an individual, which is micro, but employment is one of the broad areas of concern for economists, which is macro. However, since only one worker is laid off, this is a micro issue. If many workers had been laid off and

PRACTICE WHAT YOU KNOW

Microeconomics and Macroeconomics: The Big Picture

This mosaic of the flag illustrates the difference between micro and macro.

Identify whether each of the following statements identifies a microeconomic or a macroeconomic issue.

The national savings rate is less than 2% of disposable income.

Answer: The national savings rate is a statistic based on the average amount each household saves as a percentage of income. As such, this is a broad measure of savings and something that describes a macroeconomic issue.

Jim was laid off from his last job and is currently unemployed.

Answer: Jim's personal financial circumstances constitute a microeconomic issue.

Apple decides to open up 100 new stores.

Answer: Even though Apple is a very large corporation and 100 new stores will create many new jobs, Apple's decision is a microeconomic issue because the basis for its decision is best understood as part of a single firm's competitive strategy.

The government passes a jobs bill designed to stabilize the economy during a recession.

Answer: A *recession* is a downturn in economic activity and performance. You might be tempted to ask how many jobs are created before deciding on your answer, but that isn't relevant to this question. The key part of the statement refers to "stabiliz[ing] the economy during a recession." This is an example of a *fiscal policy*, in which the government uses taxing and spending activity to take an active role in managing the economy. Therefore, it is a macroeconomic issue.

mass layoffs led to a higher unemployment rate across the entire economy, the issue would be broad enough to be studied by macroeconomists.

What Are Four Ways to Think Like an Economist?

The study of economics can be complicated, but we can make it very accessible by helping you to think like an economist. You have probably engaged in some of these ways of thinking without even knowing it. Almost every economic subject can be analyzed through the prism of one of these ways of thinking. By mastering these tools, you will be on your way to succeeding in this course and thinking like an economist.

You can think like an economist by remembering four key principles: (1) all choices entail opportunity costs; (2) decisions are made at the margin; (3) incentives matter; and (4) trade creates value. Each of these, explained in the following sections, will reappear throughout the book and enable you to solve complex problems.

Opportunity cost
Marginal thinking
Incentives
Trade creates value

Every time you encounter one of these ways of thinking like an economist, you'll see an icon of a house to remind you of what you have learned. As you become more adept at economic analysis, it will not be uncommon to use two or more of these foundational ideas to explain the economic world around us.

All Choices Entail Opportunity Costs

Opportunity cost

We live in a world of scarcity. We cannot have everything we want because there isn't enough of everything and Earth doesn't have an unlimited store of resources. Even Bill Gates, the founder of Microsoft, faces a limit on his resources. One of the objectives of Gates's nonprofit organization, the Gates Foundation, is to help provide inoculations against diseases in developing countries. Yet the Gates Foundation realizes that it does not have the resources necessary to meet its goals. It says as much on its web site: "Because our resources alone are not enough to advance the causes we care about, we engage in advocacy efforts to promote public policies that advance our work. . . ."

Due to scarcity, the Gates Foundation must make choices. How will it allocate its scarce resources to the causes to which it is devoted? Inoculating children in Pakistan against polio takes resources away from providing food for families in Sudan. Making any choice means making a trade-off between possible options because nobody has enough resources to do everything—not even Bill Gates.

You face trade-offs in your daily life as well. Should you hit the snooze bar and sleep through your 8:00 class? You can't be in two places at one time, so you have to choose. Should you have Lucky Charms or Cheerios for breakfast? Should you ask out Emily or Katie, Jack or Steve? You can't afford to take them both to the movies (and they might not appreciate the competition, either). As you live your life, you have to make choices, and choices involve trade-offs.

The existence of so many choices requires making hard decisions. Choosing one thing means giving up something else. Suppose that you receive two invitations—the first to spend the day hiking, and the second to go to a concert—and both events occur at the same time. No matter which event you choose, you'll have to sacrifice the other option. In this example, you can think of the cost of going to the concert as the lost opportunity to be on the hike. Likewise, the cost of going hiking is the lost opportunity to go to the concert. No matter what choice you make, there is an opportunity cost, or next-best alternative, that must be sacrificed. **Opportunity cost** is the highest-valued alternative that must be sacrificed in order to get something else.

Opportunity cost is the highest-valued alternative that must be sacrificed in order to get something else.

Every time we make a choice, we experience an opportunity cost. The key to making the best possible decision is to minimize your opportunity cost by selecting the option that gives you the largest benefit. If you prefer going to a concert, you should go to the concert. What you give up, the hike, has less value to you than the concert; so it has a lower opportunity cost.

Do you have the moves like Jagger?

The hiking/concert choice is a simple and clear example of opportunity cost. Usually, it takes deliberate effort to see the world through the opportunity-cost prism. But thinking in terms of opportunity cost is worthwhile because it will help you make better decisions. For example, when there is a large pile-up on the highway, medics are flown to the scene. They have to make split-second decisions about who needs care the most, a system called triage. Someone with a scrape on an arm shouldn't be treated prior to someone with massive head trauma. The opportunity cost of making the wrong decision could be someone's life. Economists (and some doctors) would say that the question after the accident should be: *Could more*

PRACTICE WHAT YOU KNOW

The Opportunity Cost of Attending College

Question: What is the opportunity cost of attending college?

Answer: When people think about the cost of attending college, they usually think of tuition, room and board, textbooks, and travel-related expenses. While those expenses are indeed a part of going to college, they are not its full opportunity cost. The opportunity cost is the next-best alternative that is sacrificed. This means that the opportunity cost—or what you potentially could have done if you were not in college—includes the lost income you could have earned working a full-time job. If you take the cost of attending college plus the forgone income lost while in college, it is a very expensive proposition. Setting aside the question of how much more you might have to pay for room and board at college rather than elsewhere, consider the costs of tuition and books. Those fees can be $50,000 or more at many of the nation's most expensive colleges. Add those out-of-pocket expenses to the forgone income from a full-time job that might pay $40,000, and your four years in college can easily cost over a quarter of a million dollars.

Spending thousands on college expenses? You could be working instead!

lives have been saved by doing something differently? Individuals often ask: *Could I be using my time, talents, or energy on another activity that would be more profitable for me?*

Mick Jagger did just that. Before joining the Rolling Stones, he had been attending the London School of Economics. For Mick, the opportunity cost of becoming a musician was forgoing a degree in economics. Given the success of the Rolling Stones, it is hard to fault his decision!

ECONOMICS IN THE REAL WORLD

Breaking the Curse of the Bambino: How Opportunity Cost Causes a Drop in Hospital Visits While the Red Sox Play

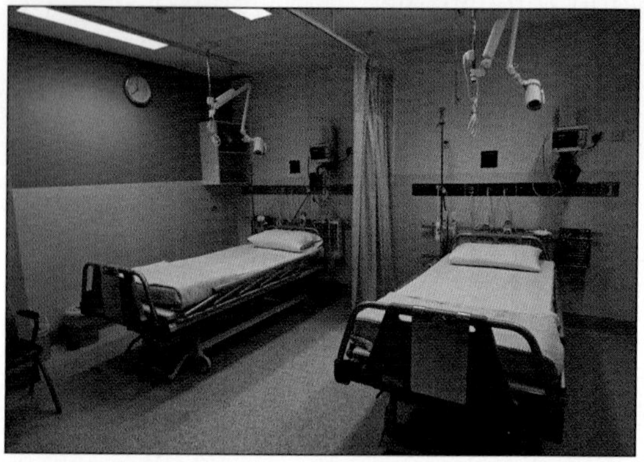

Emergency room beds are empty. Are the Sox playing?

If you're injured or severely ill, you head straight to the emergency room, right? Not so fast! A 2005 study published in the *Annals of Emergency Medicine* found that visits to the ER in the Boston area fell by as much as 15% when the Red Sox were playing games in the 2004 playoffs. Part of the decline is attributable to more people sitting inside at home—presumably watching the ballgame—instead of engaging in activities that might get them hurt. But the study also determined that this didn't explain the entire decline in emergency-room visits. It turns out that a surprising number of people are willing to put off seeking medical attention for a few hours. Apparently, for some people the opportunity cost of seeking medical attention is high enough to postpone care until after the Red Sox game. ✷

Trade-offs are important at many levels. For instance, there is a trade-off between security and convenience. When you use your credit card or shop online, there is the possibility that your personal information will be compromised. Companies store your personal data electronically when they issue credit cards. It's a fact of life in the information age: whenever data is stored, that data needs to be protected. If it isn't, it can be stolen.

Swipe a credit card, compromise your financial data?

There have been many news stories about breaches of information security. In late 2013, hackers stole financial information for over 70 million Target customers by compromising credit-card readers with a malicious software code, sometimes called malware. When the credit card was swiped, the customers' information was made available to the hackers. This lapse in security cost Target over $200 million in public-relations expenses, damage control, and updated technology, not to mention an untold loss of sales as customers worried that the company hadn't fixed the problem. However, Target could have easily prevented the problem. If Target had accepted only cash for transactions, there would have been no credit-card information to steal. Taking down the company's web site would have prevented hackers from stealing information via the Internet. Target could have then advertised itself as the most secure major retailer in America. No hacker could ever steal customers' financial information from Target simply because Target wouldn't have that information. However, taking down its web site or not accepting credit cards would severely harm Target's bottom line. Customers who are used to the convenience of using credit cards would stop patronizing the store. Online shoppers would surf to another store's web site and buy there instead. In the current environment, customers are willing to trade off security for convenience. How do we know this? They keep shopping on the Internet, and many customers have returned to Target.

Decisions Are Made at the Margin

Marginal thinking

If choices always involve costs, how do people make choices that will generate the best results for themselves? Economists systematically evaluate a course of action through a process called economic thinking. **Economic thinking involves a purposeful evaluation of the available opportunities to make the best decision possible.** In this context, economic thinkers use a process called *marginal analysis* to break down decisions into smaller parts. Often, the choice is not between doing and not doing something, but between doing more or less of something. For instance, if you take on a part-time job while in school, you probably wrestle with the question of how many hours to work. If you work a little more, you can earn additional income. If you work a little less, you have more time to study. Working more has a tangible benefit (more money) and a tangible cost (poor grades). All of this should sound familiar from our earlier discussion about opportunity costs. The cost of working more is what you have to give up—in this case, a higher grade. Studying more entails giving up more income.

Economic thinking requires a purposeful evaluation of the available opportunities to make the best decision possible.

An economist would say that your decision—weighing how much money you want against the grades you want—is a decision at the *margin*. What exactly does the word "margin" mean? There are many different definitions. To a reader, the margin is the blank space bordering a page. A "margin" can also be thought of as the size of a victory. In economics, **marginal thinking requires decision-makers to evaluate whether the benefit of one more unit of something is greater than its cost.** Understanding how to analyze decisions at the margin is essential to becoming a good economist.

Marginal thinking requires decision-makers to evaluate whether the benefit of one more unit of something is greater than its cost.

For example, have you ever wondered why people straighten their places, vacuum, dust, scrub their bathrooms, clean out their garages, and wash their windows, but leave dust bunnies under the refrigerator? The answer lies in thinking at the margin. Moving the refrigerator out from the wall to clean requires a significant effort for a small benefit. Guests who enter the kitchen can't see under the refrigerator. So most of us ignore the dust bunnies and just clean the visible areas of our homes. In other words, when economists say that you should think at the margin, what they really mean is that you should weigh the costs and benefits of your actions and choose to do the things with the greatest payoff. For most of us, that means being willing to live with dust bunnies. The *marginal cost* of cleaning under the refrigerator (or on top of the cabinets, or behind the sofa cushions) is too high and the added value of making the effort, or the *marginal benefit*, is too low to justify the additional cleaning.

ECONOMICS IN THE REAL WORLD

Why Buying and Selling Your Textbooks Benefits You at the Margin

New textbooks are expensive. The typical textbook purchasing pattern works as follows: you buy a textbook at the start of the term, often at full price, and sell it back at the end of the term for half the price you paid. Ouch. Nobody likes to make a bad investment, and textbooks depreciate the moment that students buy them. Even non-economists know not to buy high and sell low—but that is the textbook cycle for most students.

One solution would be to avoid buying textbooks in the first place. But that isn't practical, nor is it a good decision. To understand why, let's use marginal analysis to break the decision into two separate components: the decision to buy and the decision to resell.

Let's start with the decision to buy. A rational buyer will purchase a textbook only if the expected value of the information included in the book is greater than the cost. For instance, say the book contains mandatory assignments or information that is useful for your major, and you decide that the book is worth \$200 to you. If you're able to purchase the book for \$100, the gain from buying the textbook would be \$100. But what if the book is supplemental reading and you think it's worth only \$50? If you value the book at \$50 and it costs \$100, purchasing the book would entail a \$50 loss. If students buy only the books from which they receive gains, every textbook bought will increase someone's welfare.

Why do students buy and sell textbooks?

A similar logic applies to the resale of textbooks. At the end of the course, once you have learned the information inside the book, the value of hanging on to the textbook is low. You might think it's worth \$20 to keep the textbook for future reference, but if you can sell it for \$50, the difference represents a gain of \$30. In this case, you would decide to sell.

We have seen that buying and selling are two separate decisions made at the margin. If you combine these two decisions and argue that the purchase price (\$100) and resale price (\$50) are related, as most students typically think they are, you will arrive at a faulty conclusion that you have made a poor decision. That is simply not true.

Textbooks may not be cheap, but they create value twice—once when bought and again when sold. This is a win-win outcome. Since we assume that decision-makers will not make choices that leave them worse off, the only way to explain why students buy textbooks and sell them again later is because the students benefit at the margin from both sides of the transaction. ✷

Incentives Matter

Incentives

By using marginal thinking, you can make better decisions. But the conditions under which decisions are made don't always stay the same. Sometimes circumstances change, which calls for a change in your decision. When you're faced with making a decision, you usually make the choice that you think will most improve your situation. In making your decision, you respond to **incentives**—factors that motivate you to act or to exert effort. For example, the choice to study for an exam you have tomorrow instead of spending the evening with your friends is based on the belief that doing well on the exam will provide a greater benefit. You are incentivized to study because you know that an A in the course will raise your grade-point average and make you a more attractive candidate on the job market when you are finished with school. We can further divide incentives into two paired categories: positive and negative, and direct and indirect.

Incentives are factors that motivate a person to act or exert effort.

Positive and Negative Incentives

Positive incentives encourage action. For example, end-of-the-year bonuses motivate employees to work hard throughout the year, higher oil prices cause suppliers to extract more oil, and tax rebates encourage citizens to spend more money. Negative incentives also encourage action. For instance, the fear of receiving a speeding ticket keeps motorists from driving too fast, and the dread of a trip to the dentist motivates people to brush their teeth regularly. In each case, a potential negative consequence spurs individuals to action.

Conventional wisdom tells us that "learning is its own reward," but try telling that to most students. Teachers are aware that incentives, both positive and negative, create additional interest among their students to learn the course material. Positive incentives include bonus points, gold stars, public praise, and extra credit. Many students respond to these encouragements by studying more. However, positive incentives are not enough. Suppose that your instructor never gave any grade lower than an A. Your incentive to participate actively in the course, do assignments, or earn bonus points would be small. For positive incentives to work, they generally need to be coupled with negative incentives. This is why instructors require students to complete assignments, take exams, and write papers. Students know that if they don't complete these requirements, they will get a lower grade and perhaps even fail the class.

Direct and Indirect Incentives

In addition to being positive or negative, incentives can be direct or indirect. For instance, if one gas station lowers its prices, it most likely will get business from customers who would not usually stop there. This is a direct incentive. Lower gasoline prices also work as an indirect incentive, since lower prices might encourage consumers to use more gas.

Direct incentives are easy to recognize. "Cut my grass and I'll pay you \$30" is an example of a direct incentive. Indirect incentives are much harder to recognize. But learning to recognize them is one of the keys to mastering economics. For instance, consider the indirect incentives at work in welfare

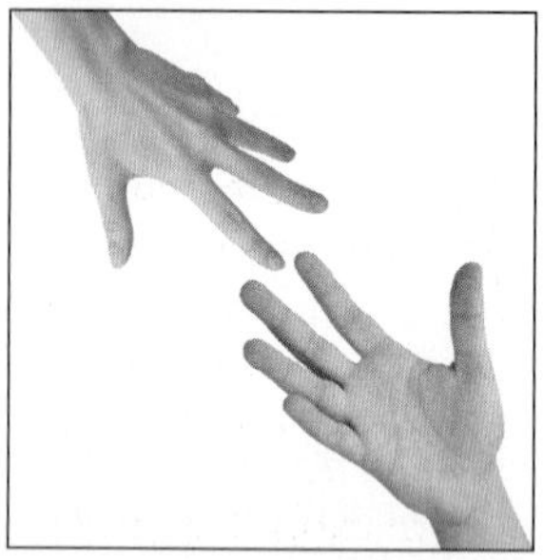

Public assistance: a hand in time of need, or an incentive not to work?

programs. Almost everyone agrees that societies should provide a safety net for those without employment or whose income isn't enough to meet basic needs. Thus, a society has a direct incentive to alleviate suffering caused by poverty. But how does a society provide this safety net without taking away the incentive to work? In other words, if the amount of welfare a person receives is higher than the amount that person can hope to make from a job, the welfare recipient might decide to stay on welfare rather than go to work. The indirect incentive to stay on welfare creates an unintended consequence—people who were supposed to use government assistance as a safety net until they can find a job use it instead as a permanent source of income.

Policymakers have the tough task of deciding how to balance such conflicting incentives. To decrease the likelihood that a person will stay on welfare, policymakers could cut benefits. But doing so might leave some people without enough money to live on. For this reason, many government programs specify limits on the amount of time people can receive benefits. Ideally, this system allows the welfare programs to continue to meet basic needs while creating incentives that encourage recipients to search for jobs and acquire skills that will enable them to do better in the workforce.

ECONOMICS IN THE REAL WORLD

How Incentives Create Unintended Consequences

Let's look at an example of how incentives operate in the real world and how they can lead to consequences no one envisioned. Two Australian researchers noted a large spike in births on July 1, 2004, as shown in Figure 1.1. The sudden spike was not an accident. Australia, like many other developed countries, has seen the fertility rate fall below the replacement level, which is the birthrate necessary to keep the population from declining. In response to falling birthrates, the Australian government decided to enact a "baby bonus" of $3,000 for all babies born on or after July 1, 2004. (One Australian dollar equals roughly one U.S. dollar.)

The policy was designed to provide a direct incentive for couples to have children and, in part, to compensate them for lost pay and the added costs of raising a newborn. However, this direct incentive had an indirect incentive attached to it, too—the couples found a way to delay the birth of their children until after July 1, perhaps jeopardizing the health of both the infants and the mothers. This was clearly an unintended consequence. Despite reassurances from the government that would-be parents would not put financial gain over their newborns' welfare, over 1,000 births were switched from late June to early July through a combination of additional bed rest and pushing scheduled caesarian sections back a few days. This behavior is testament to the power of incentives.

On a much smaller scale, the same dynamic exists in the United States. Parents can claim a tax credit for the entire year, whether their child is born in January or in December. This tax credit gives parents an incentive to ask for labor to be induced or for a caesarian section to be performed late in December so they can have their child before January 1 and thereby capitalize on

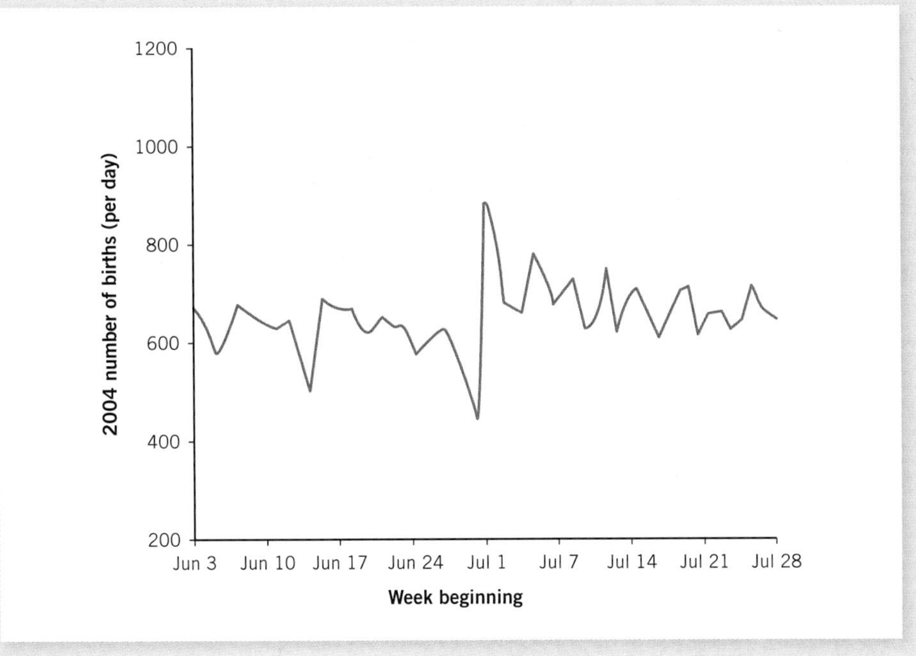

FIGURE 1.1

Australian Births by Week in 2004

The plunge and spike in births are evidence of an unintended consequence.

Source: Joshua S. Gans and Andrew Leigh, "Born on the First of July: An (un)natural experiment in birth timing," *Journal of Public Economics* 93 (2009): 246–263.

the tax advantages. Ironically, hospitals and newspapers often celebrate the arrival of the first baby of the new year even though his or her parents might actually be financially worse off because of the infant's January 1 birthday. ✷

Incentives Are Everywhere

There are many sides to incentives. However, financial gain almost always plays a prominent role. In the film *All the President's Men*, the story of the Watergate scandal that led to the unraveling of the Nixon administration in the early 1970s, a secret source called Deep Throat tells Bob Woodward, an investigative reporter at the *Washington Post*, to "follow the money." Woodward responds, "What do you mean? Where?" Deep Throat responds, "Just . . . follow the money." That is exactly what Woodward did. He eventually pieced everything together and followed the "money" trail all the way to President Nixon.

Understanding the incentives that caused the participants in the Watergate scandal to do what they did led Bob Woodward to the truth. Economists use the same process to explain how people make decisions, how firms operate, and how the economy functions. In fact, understanding incentives, from positive to negative and direct to indirect, is the key to understanding economics. If you remember only one concept from this course, it should be that incentives matter!

ECONOMICS IN THE MEDIA

Incentives

Ferris Bueller's Day Off

Many people believe that the study of economics is boring. In *Ferris Bueller's Day Off* (1986), Ben Stein plays a high school economics teacher who sedates his class with a monotone voice while referring to many abstract economic theories and uttering the unforgettable "Anyone, anyone?" while trying to engage his students. In fact, the movie is really about incentives and trade-offs.

Was this your first impression of economics?

Trade Creates Value

Trade creates value

Markets bring buyers and sellers together to exchange goods and services.

Trade is the voluntary exchange of goods and services between two or more parties.

Imagine trying to find food in a world without grocery stores. The task of getting what you need to eat each day would require visiting many separate locations. Traditionally, this need to bring buyers and sellers together was met by weekly markets, or bazaars, in central locations like town squares. **Markets** bring buyers and sellers together to exchange goods and services. As commerce spread throughout the ancient world, trade routes developed. Markets grew from infrequent gatherings, where exchange involved trading goods and services for other goods and services, into more sophisticated systems that use cash, credit, and other financial instruments. Today, when we think of markets we often think of eBay or Craigslist, where goods can be transferred from one person to another with the click of a mouse. For instance, if you want to find a rare DVD of season 1 of *Entourage*, there is no better place to look than eBay, which allows users to search for just about any product, bid on it, and then have it sent directly to their homes.

Trade is the voluntary exchange of goods and services between two or more parties. Voluntary trade among rational individuals creates value for everyone involved. Imagine you are on your way home from class and you want to pick up a gallon of milk. You know that milk will be more expensive at a convenience store than it will be at the grocery store five miles away, but you're in a hurry to study for your economics exam and are willing to pay up to $5.00 for the convenience of getting it quickly. At the store, you find that the price is $4.00, and you happily purchase the milk. This ability to buy the milk for less than the price you're willing to pay provides a positive incentive to make the purchase. But what about the seller? If the store owner paid $3.00 to buy the milk from a supplier, and you're willing to pay the $4.00 price that he has set in order to make a profit, the store owner has an incentive to sell. This simple voluntary transaction has made both sides better off.

By fostering the exchange of goods, trade helps to create additional growth through specialization. **Specialization** occurs when someone focuses his or her skills to become an expert in a particular area. Specialization is demonstrated through comparative advantage. **Comparative advantage** refers to the situation in which an individual, business, or country can produce at a lower opportunity cost than a competitor can. As a result, it is possible to be a physician, teacher, or plumber and not worry about how to do everything yourself. The physician becomes proficient at dispensing medical advice, the teacher at helping students, and the plumber at fixing leaks. The physician and the teacher call the plumber when they need work on their plumbing. The teacher and the plumber see the doctor when they are sick. The physician and the plumber send their children to school to learn from the teacher. On a broader scale, this type of trading of services increases the welfare of everyone in society. Trade creates gains for everyone involved.

Specialization occurs when someone focuses his or her skills to become an expert in a particular area.

Comparative advantage refers to the situation in which an individual, business, or country can produce at a lower opportunity cost than a competitor can.

The same process is at work among businesses. For instance, Starbucks specializes in making coffee and Honda in making automobiles. You wouldn't want to get your morning cup of joe at Honda any more than you would want to buy a car from Starbucks!

Sports teams also have specialists to help increase their productivity. In baseball, there are pitchers and position players. Even among pitchers, some are starters and some are relievers. Relief pitchers may pitch many innings or just one. Closers are usually only called into action to pitch games in the final inning when their team is ahead. You will also be specializing at some point. Your choice of major is a form of specialization.

Specialization exists at the country level as well. Some countries have highly developed workforces capable of managing and solving complex processes. Other countries have large pools of relatively unskilled labor. As a result, businesses that need skilled labor gravitate to countries where they can easily find the workers they need. Likewise, firms with production processes that rely on unskilled labor look for employees in less-developed countries. By harnessing the power of increased specialization, global companies and economies create value through increased production and growth.

However, globalized trade is not without controversy. When goods and jobs are free to move across borders, not everyone benefits equally. Consider the case of an American worker who loses her job when her position is outsourced to a call center in India. The jobless worker now has to find new employment—a process that will require significant time and energy. In contrast, the new position in the call center in India provides a job and an income that improve the life of another worker. Also, the American firm enjoys the advantage of being able to hire lower-cost labor elsewhere. The firm's lower costs often

Our economy depends on specialization.

ECONOMICS FOR LIFE

Midcareer Earnings by Selected Majors

A 2012 study by PayScale surveyed full-time employees across the United States who possessed a bachelor's degree but no advanced degree. Twenty popular subject areas are listed in the graph below.

Not all majors are created equal, and by choosing one major over another you are facing opportunity costs. However, the majors that produce more income initially do not necessarily keep their advantage a decade or two later. This means that today's newly minted economics majors, with a median starting salary of $48,500, will likely surpass those who majored in civil engineering in earnings by the time they reach midcareer. The same holds true for political science majors, who have a lower starting salary than business majors but eventually surpass them. In the long run, pay growth matters to income level as much as, if not more than, starting salary. In terms of salary, any decision about what to major in that looks only at starting pay is misleading. How much you make over your whole career is what matters!

Will you make more by majoring in economics or finance?

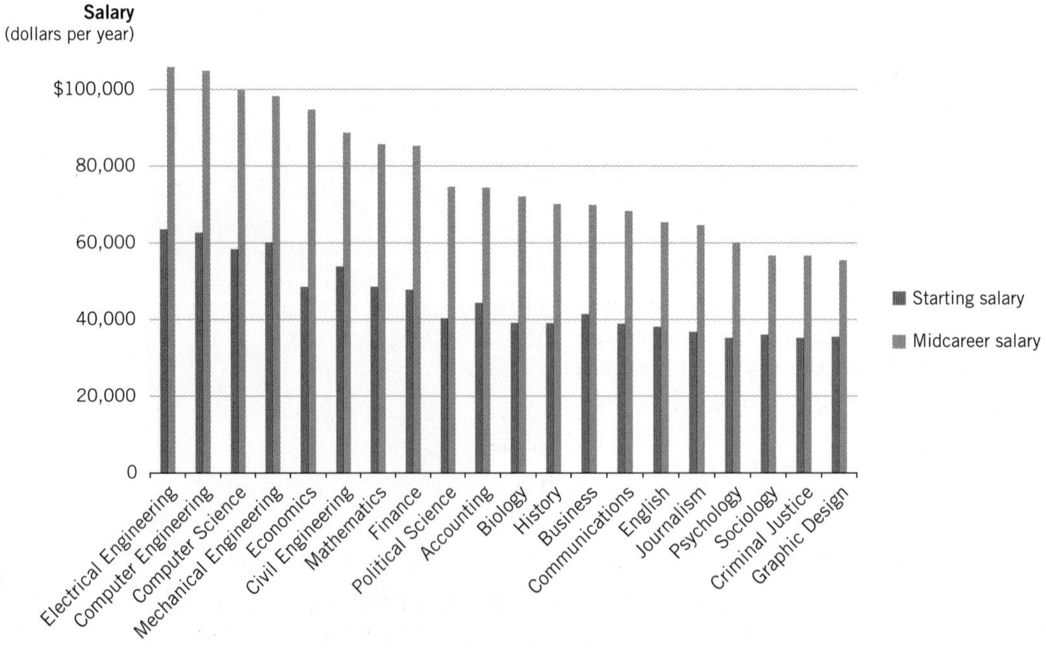

translate into lower prices for domestic consumers. None of those advantages make the outsourcing of jobs any less painful for affected workers, but it is an important component of economic growth in the long run.

Conclusion

Is economics the dismal science?

We began this chapter by discussing this misconception. Now that you have begun your exploration of economics, you know that this is not true. Economists ask, and answer, big questions about life. This is what makes the study of economics so fascinating. Understanding how an entire economy operates and functions may seem like a daunting task, but it's not nearly as hard as it sounds. If you remember the first time you drove a car, the process is similar. When you're learning to drive, everything seems difficult and unfamiliar. Learning economics is the same way. However, once you learn a few key principles and practice them, you can become a good driver quite quickly. In the next chapter, we will take our first look at the tools economists use.

ANSWERING THE BIG QUESTIONS

What is economics?

* Economics is the study of how people allocate their limited resources to satisfy their nearly unlimited wants. Because of the limited nature of society's resources, even the most abundant resources are not always plentiful enough everywhere to meet the wants and needs of every person. So how do individuals and societies make decisions about how to use the scarce resources at our disposal? This is the basic question economists seek to answer.

What are four ways to think like an economist?

* You can think like an economist by remembering these four key principles: (1) all choices entail opportunity costs; (2) decisions are made at the margin; (3) incentives matter; and (4) trade creates value.
* Each time you make a choice, you make a trade-off and experience an opportunity cost, or a lost chance to do something else.
* Marginal thinking requires you to weigh the extra benefits against the extra costs of a decision.
* Incentives matter because they help explain how decisions are made.
* Trade creates value because participants in markets are able to specialize in the production of goods and services in which they have a comparative advantage.

CONCEPTS YOU SHOULD KNOW

comparative advantage (p. 17)
economics (p. 6)
economic thinking (p. 11)
incentives (p. 13)
macroeconomics (p. 6)
marginal thinking (p. 11)
markets (p. 16)
microeconomics (p. 6)
opportunity cost (p. 9)
scarcity (p. 6)
specialization (p. 17)
trade (p. 16)

QUESTIONS FOR REVIEW

1. How would you respond if your instructor gave daily quizzes on the course readings? Would this be a positive or a negative incentive?
2. Explain why many seniors often earn lower grades in their last semester before graduation. **Hint:** this is an incentive problem.
3. What is the opportunity cost of reading this textbook?
4. Evaluate the following statement: "Trade is like football: one team wins and the other loses."
5. Give a personal example of how pursuing your self-interest has made society better off.

STUDY PROBLEMS (**solved at the end of the section*)

* 1. What role do incentives play in each of the following situations?
   a. You learn that you can resell a ticket to next week's homecoming game for twice what you paid.
   b. A state government announces a "sales tax holiday" for back-to-school shopping during one week each August.

2. Compare your standard of living with that of your parents when they were the same age as you are now. Ask them or somebody you know around their age to recall where they were living and what they owned. What has happened to the average standard of living over the last 25 years? Explain your answer.

3. By referencing events in the news or something from your personal experiences, describe one example of each of the four key principles involved in thinking like an economist.

* 4. Suppose that Colombia is good at growing coffee but not very good at making computer software, and that Canada is good at making computer software but not very good at growing coffee. The two countries decide to trade with each other. If Colombia decided to grow only coffee and Canada made only computer software, would both countries be better or worse off? Can you think of a similar example from your life?

5. After some consideration, you decide to hire someone to help you move. Wouldn't it be cheaper to move yourself? Do you think this is a rational choice? Explain your response.

* 6. Suppose that 20 students from your economics class each pay $20 to enter a grades-based contest. This would create a $400 prize pool. An equal share of the $400 pot is awarded at the end of the term to each contestant who earns an A in the course. If four students earn A's, they each receive $100. If only one student earns an A, that person gets the entire $400 pot. What economic concept is this contest harnessing in order to encourage participants to learn more?

SOLVED PROBLEMS

1.a. Since your tickets are worth more than you paid for them, you have a direct positive incentive to resell them.

b. The "sales tax holiday" is a direct positive incentive to buy more clothes during the back-to-school period. An unintended consequence of this policy is that people are likely to make fewer purchases both before and after the tax holiday.

4. If Colombia decided to specialize in the production of coffee, it could trade coffee to Canada in exchange for computer software. This process illustrates gains from specialization and trade. Both countries have a comparative advantage in producing one particular good. Colombia has ideal coffee-growing conditions, and Canada has a workforce that is more adept at writing software. Since each country specializes in what it does best, both countries are able to produce more value than what they could produce by trying to make both products on their own.

6. The contest is using the power of incentives to motivate learning. Earning a letter grade is a positive motivation to do well, or a penalty—or negative incentive—when you do poorly. This scenario takes incentives one step further, as the student who earns an A also receives a small cash payment—a positive incentive. This incentive provides extra motivation to study hard and achieve an A, since it pays cash, as opposed to earning a B or lower.

CHAPTER 2 Economic Models and Gains from Trade

MISCONCEPTION

Trade always results in winners and losers.

When most people think about trade, they consider it as a game with winners and losers. For instance, suppose that you and your friends are playing Magic. Players collect cards with special powers in order to assemble decks to play the game. Magic players love to trade their cards, and novice players often don't know which cards are the most powerful or rare. When a novice unknowingly swaps one of the desirable cards, the other player is probably getting a much better deal. In other words, there is a winner and a loser.

Now think about international trade, in which countries exchange goods and services. Many people believe that rich countries exploit the natural resources of poor countries and even steal their most talented workers. In this view, the rich countries are winners and the poor countries are losers. Others think of trade as the redistribution of goods. If you trade your kayak for a friend's bicycle, no new goods are created. But, some people think, someone must have come out ahead in the trade.

In this chapter, we will see that trade is not an imbalanced equation of winners and losers. To explain the benefits of trade, the discussion will make several simplifying assumptions and use the scientific method to help explain the world we live in. These foundations will serve as the tools we need to explore why trade creates value.

Trade is vital to Magic players, and vital to the economy.

BIG QUESTIONS

- **How do economists study the economy?**
- **What is a production possibilities frontier?**
- **What are the benefits of specialization and trade?**
- **How does the economy work?**

How Do Economists Study the Economy?

Economics is a social science that uses the scientific method to develop economic *models*. To create these models, economists make many assumptions to simplify reality. These models help economists understand the key relationships that drive economic decisions.

The Scientific Method in Economics

On the television show *MythBusters*, Jamie Hyneman and Adam Savage put popular myths to the test. In Savage's words, "We replicate the circumstances, then duplicate the results." The entire show is dedicated to scientific testing of the myths. At the end of each episode, the myth is confirmed, decreed plausible, or busted. For instance, in a memorable episode Hyneman and Savage explored the reasons behind the *Hindenburg* disaster. The *Hindenburg* was a German passenger airship, or zeppelin, that caught fire and became engulfed in flames as it attempted to dock in New Jersey on May 6, 1937. Thirty-six people died.

The scientific method was used to discover why the *Hindenburg* caught fire.

Some people have claimed that the fire was sparked by the painted fabric used to wrap the zeppelin. Others have suggested that the hydrogen used to give the airship lift was the primary cause of the disaster. To test the hypothesis that the paint used on the fabric was to blame, Hyneman and Savage built two small-scale models. The first model was filled with hydrogen and had a non-flammable skin; the second model used a replica of the original fabric for the skin but did not contain any hydrogen. Hyneman and Savage then compared their models' burn times with the original footage of the disaster.

After examining the results, they "busted" the myth that the paint was to blame. Why? The model containing the hydrogen burned twice as fast as the one with just the painted fabric skin. It seems reasonable to conclude that hydrogen caused the disaster, not paint.

Economists work in much the same way as Hyneman and Savage: they use the scientific method to answer questions about observable phenomena and to explain how the world works. The scientific method consists of several steps:

- First, researchers observe a phenomenon that interests them.
- Next, based on these observations, researchers develop a *hypothesis*, which is a proposed explanation for the phenomenon.
- Then they construct a model to test the hypothesis.
- Finally, they design experiments to test how well the model (which is based on the hypothesis) works. After collecting data from the experiments, they can verify, revise, or refute the hypothesis.

The economist's laboratory is the world around us, and it ranges from the economy as a whole to the decisions made by firms and individuals. As a result, economists cannot always design experiments to test their hypotheses. Often, they must gather historical data or wait for real-world events to take place—for example, the Great Recession of 2007–2009—to better understand the economy.

Positive and Normative Analysis

As scientists, economists strive to approach their subject with objectivity. This means that they rigorously avoid letting personal beliefs and values influence the outcome of their analysis. To be as objective as possible, economists deploy positive analysis. A **positive statement** can be tested and validated. Each positive statement can be thought of as a description of "what is." For instance, the statement "the unemployment rate is 7.0%" is a positive statement because it can be tested by gathering data. In contrast, a **normative statement** cannot be tested or validated; it is about "what ought to be." For instance, the statement "an unemployed worker should receive financial assistance to help make ends meet" is a matter of opinion. One can reasonably argue that financial assistance to the unemployed is beneficial for society as a whole because it helps eliminate poverty. However, many would argue that financial assistance to the unemployed provides the wrong incentives. If the financial assistance provides enough to meet basic needs, workers may end up spending more time remaining unemployed than they otherwise would. Neither opinion is right or wrong; they are differing viewpoints based on values, beliefs, and opinions.

A **positive statement** can be tested and validated; it describes "what is."

A **normative statement** is an opinion that cannot be tested or validated; it describes "what ought to be."

Economists are concerned with positive analysis. In contrast, normative statements are the realm of policymakers, voters, and philosophers. For example, if the unemployment rate rises, economists try to understand the conditions that created the situation. Economics does not attempt to determine who should receive unemployment assistance, which involves normative analysis. Economics, done properly, is confined to positive analysis.

PRACTICE WHAT YOU KNOW

Positive versus Normative Statements

Question: Which of the following statements are positive, and which ones are normative?

1. Winters in Arkansas are too cold.
2. Everyone should work at a bank to learn the true value of money.
3. On average, people save 15% on their car insurance when they switch to Geico.
4. Everyone ought to have a life insurance policy.
5. University of Virginia graduates earn more than Duke University graduates.
6. The average temperature in Fargo, North Dakota, in January is 56 degrees Fahrenheit.
7. You should eat five servings of fruit or vegetables each day.

Answers

1. The phrase "too cold" is a matter of opinion. This is a normative statement.
2. While working at a bank might give someone an appreciation for the value of money, the word "should" indicates an opinion. This is a normative statement.
3. The Geico insurance company makes this claim in many of its commercials. It is a positive statement because it is a testable claim. If you had the data from Geico, you could determine if the statement is correct or not.
4. This sounds like a true statement, or at least a very sensible one. However, the word "ought" makes it an opinion. This is a normative statement.
5. You can look up the data and see which university's graduates earn more. This is a positive statement.
6. This is a positive statement, but the statement is wrong. The average January temperature in North Dakota is lower than 56 degrees Fahrenheit. The data can be verified (or, in this case, proven wrong) by climate data.
7. This is a normative statement. It offers an opinion regarding what you should do.

Economic Models

Thinking like an economist means learning how to analyze complex issues and problems. Many economic topics—such as international trade, Social Security, job loss, and inflation—are complicated. To analyze these phenomena and to determine the effect of various government-policy options related to them, economists use *models*, which are simplified versions of reality. Models help us analyze the parts of the economy.

A good model should be simple, flexible, and useful for making accurate predictions. Let's consider one of the most famous models in history, designed by Wilbur and Orville Wright. Before the Wright brothers made their famous first flight in 1903, they built a small wind tunnel out of a six-foot-long wooden box. Inside the box they placed a device to measure aerodynamics, and at one end they attached a small fan to supply the wind. The brothers then tested over 200 different wing configurations to determine the lifting properties of each design. Using the data they collected, the Wright brothers were able to determine the best type of wing to use on their aircraft.

The Wright brothers' wind tunnel

Similarly, economic models provide frameworks that help us to predict the effects of changes in things like prices, production processes, and government policies on real-life behavior.

Ceteris Paribus

Using a controlled setting that held many other variables constant enabled the Wright brothers to experiment with different wing designs. By altering only a single element—for example, the angle of the wing—they could test whether the change in design was advantageous. The process of examining a change in one variable while holding everything else constant involves assuming a condition of ***ceteris paribus***, from the Latin meaning "other things being equal."

Ceteris paribus means "other things being equal" and is used to build economic models. It allows economists to examine a change in one variable while holding everything else constant.

The *ceteris paribus* assumption is central to model building. If the Wright brothers had changed many design elements simultaneously and found that a new version of the wing worked better, they would have had no way of knowing which change was responsible for the improved performance. For this reason, engineers generally modify only one design element at a time and test only that one element before testing additional elements.

Like the Wright brothers, economists start with a simplified version of reality. Economists build models, change one variable at a time, and ask whether the change in the variable had a positive or negative impact on performance. Perhaps the best-known economic model is supply and demand, which economists use to explain how markets function. We'll get to supply and demand in Chapter 3.

What Is a Production Possibilities Frontier?

Now it's time to build our first economic model.

In Chapter 1, we learned that economics is about the trade-offs that individuals and societies face every day. For instance, you may frequently have to decide between spending more time studying to get better grades or hanging out with your friends. The more time you study, the less time you have for your friends. Similarly, a society has to determine how to allocate its resources. The decision to build new roads will mean there is less money available for new schools, and vice versa.

A **production possibilities frontier** is a model that illustrates the combinations of outputs that a society can produce if all of its resources are being used efficiently.

A **production possibilities frontier** is a model that illustrates the combinations of outputs that a society can produce if all of its resources are being used efficiently. To preserve *ceteris paribus*, we assume that the technology available for production and the quantity and quality of resources used in the production process remain constant. These assumptions allow us to model trade-offs more clearly.

Let's begin by imagining a society that produces only two goods—steel and ketchup. This may not seem like a very realistic assumption, since a real economy produces millions of different goods and services, but this approach helps us understand trade-offs by keeping the analysis simple.

Table 2.1 shows the production possibilities for our simplified economy. Options A through F are all possible with existing resources and technology. If we take this data and plot it in a graph, we will have the production possibilities frontier (PPF) shown in Figure 2.1(a).

If the economy uses all of its resources to produce steel, it can produce 100 bars of steel and 0 bottles of ketchup. If it uses all of its resources to produce ketchup, it can make 300 bottles of ketchup and 0 bars of steel. These outcomes are represented by points A and F, respectively, on the production possibilities frontier. It is unlikely that the society will choose either of these extreme outcomes; human beings tend to like variety.

Still looking at Figure 2.1(a), if our theoretical society decides to spend some of its resources producing steel and some of its resources making ketchup, its economy will end up with a combination of steel and ketchup that can be placed somewhere along the production possibilities frontier between points A and F. At point C, for example, the society would deploy its resources to produce 70 bars of steel and 200 bottles of ketchup. At point D, the combination would be 50 bars of steel and 250 bottles of ketchup. Each point along the production possibilities frontier represents a possible set of outcomes that the society can choose if it uses all of its resources *efficiently*. That is, at any combination of steel and ketchup along the production possibilities frontier, the society is using all of its resources in the most productive way possible.

TABLE 2.1

Production Possibilities

OPTIONS	KETCHUP (bottles)	STEEL (bars)
A	0	100
B	120	90
C	200	70
D	250	50
E	280	30
F	300	0

FIGURE 2.1

The Production Possibilities Frontier and Opportunity Cost

(a) The production possibilities frontier (PPF) shows the trade-off between producing steel and producing ketchup. Any combination of steel and ketchup is possible along or inside the curve. Combinations of steel and ketchup beyond the production possibilities frontier—for example, at point G—are not possible with the current set of resources. Point H and any other points located in the shaded region are inefficient.

(b) To make more steel bars, the society will have to use workers who are increasingly less skilled at making them. As a result, as we move up along the PPF, the opportunity cost of producing an extra 20 steel bars rises from 30 bottles of ketchup between points E and D to 80 bottles of ketchup between points C and B.

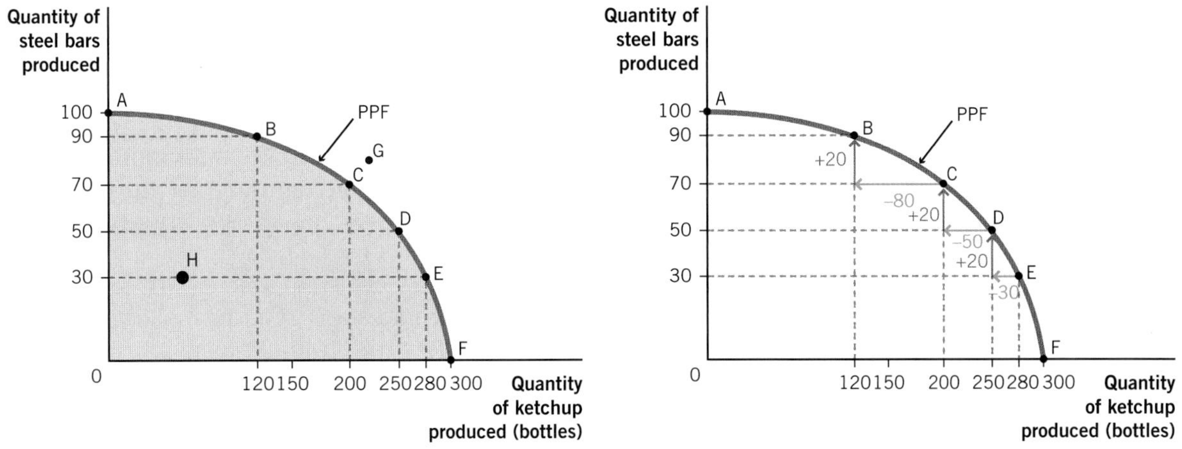

(a) The Production Possibilities Frontier (PPF)

(b) The PPF and Opportunity Cost

Notice that some combinations of steel and ketchup cannot be produced. This is because resources within the society are scarce. Our theoretical society would like to produce at point G because compared to point C you get more of both goods; but given the available resources, it cannot produce that output level. Points beyond the production possibilities frontier are desirable but not feasible, given the available resources and technology.

What about point H and any other points that are located in the shaded region in Figure 2.1(a)? These points represent outcomes inside the production possibilities frontier. They indicate an inefficient use of the society's resources. Consider, for example, labor resources. If employees spend many hours surfing the Web instead of doing their jobs, the output of steel and ketchup will drop and the outcome will no longer be efficient. As long as workers use all of their time efficiently, they will produce the maximum amount of steel and ketchup, and output will lie somewhere on the production possibilities frontier.

Whenever society is producing on the production possibilities frontier, the only way to get more of one good is to accept less of another. Because an economy operating at a point on the frontier will be efficient, economists do not favor one point over another. But a society may favor one particular point over another because it prefers that combination of goods. For example, in our theoretical two-good society, if ketchup is suddenly viewed as more important, the movement from point C to point D will represent a desirable trade-off. The society will produce 20 fewer steel bars (decreasing from 70 to 50) but 50 additional bottles of ketchup (increasing from 200 to 250).

The Production Possibilities Frontier and Opportunity Cost

Opportunity cost

Because our two-good society produces only steel and ketchup, the trade-offs that occur along the production possibilities frontier represent the opportunity cost of producing one good instead of the other. As we saw in Chapter 1, an opportunity cost is the highest-valued alternative given up to pursue another course of action. As Figure 2.1(b) shows, when society moves from point C to point D, it gives up 20 steel bars to produce 50 more bottles of ketchup; this is the opportunity cost of producing more ketchup. Going in reverse, the movement from point D to point C has an opportunity cost of 50 bottles of ketchup to produce 20 more steel bars.

Not all resources in our theoretical society are perfectly adaptable for use in making steel and ketchup. Some workers are good at making steel, and others are not so good. When the society tries to make as much steel as possible, it will be using both types of workers. That is, to get more steel, the society will have to use workers who are increasingly less skilled at making steel bars. This means that steel production will not expand at a constant rate. To understand why, look again at Table 2.1 and Figure 2.1(b).

Since resources are not perfectly adaptable, production does not expand at a constant rate. For example, to produce 20 extra steel bars, the society can move from point E (30 steel bars) to point D (50 steel bars). But moving from point E (280 bottles of ketchup) to point D (250 bottles of ketchup) means giving up 30 bottles of ketchup. Thus, moving from E to D has an opportunity cost of 30 bottles of ketchup. Now suppose that the society decides it wants even more steel and moves from point D (50 steel bars) to point C (70 steel bars). Now the opportunity cost of more steel is 50 bottles of ketchup, because ketchup production declines from 250 to 200. If the society decides that 70 steel bars are not enough, it can expand steel production from point C (70 steel bars) to point B (90 steel bars). Now the society gives up 80 bottles of ketchup. (Use Table 2.1 to verify that this is true.) Notice that as we move up along the PPF from point E to point B, the opportunity cost of producing 20 more steel bars rises from 30 bottles of ketchup to 80 bottles of ketchup. This increased trade-off is necessary to produce more steel bars.

The bowed-out shape of the production possibilities frontier in Figure 2.1(b) reflects the increasing opportunity cost of production. This figure illustrates the **law of increasing relative cost**, which states that the opportunity cost of producing a good rises as a society produces more of it. Changes in relative cost mean that a society faces a significant trade-off if it tries to produce an extremely large amount of a single good.

The **law of increasing relative cost** states that the opportunity cost of producing a good rises as a society produces more of it.

The Production Possibilities Frontier and Economic Growth

So far, we have modeled the production possibilities frontier based on the resources available to society at a particular moment in time. However, most societies hope to create economic growth. *Economic growth* is the process that enables a society to produce more output in the future. (We discuss economic growth in detail in Chapter 13.)

We can use the production possibilities frontier to explore economic growth. For example, we can ask what would happen to the PPF if our two-good society developed a new technology (let's say a new assembly line for the production of steel) that increases efficiency and, therefore, productivity. Suppose that this new technology improves the steel-production process and that the development of the new technology does not require the use of more of the society's resources. This development would allow the society to make more steel with the same number of workers. Or it would allow the same amount of steel to be made with fewer workers. Either way, the society has expanded its resource base. Figure 2.2 shows this change. Note that the maximum output of ketchup remains the same, but the maximum output of steel has increased.

With the new technology, it becomes possible to produce 120 steel bars using the same number of workers and in the same amount of time that it previously took to produce 100 steel bars. Although the society's ability to produce bottles of ketchup hasn't changed, the new steel-making technology causes the production possibilities frontier to expand outward from PPF_1 to PPF_2. PPF_1 corresponds to the data in Table 2.1, but PPF_2 shows a completely

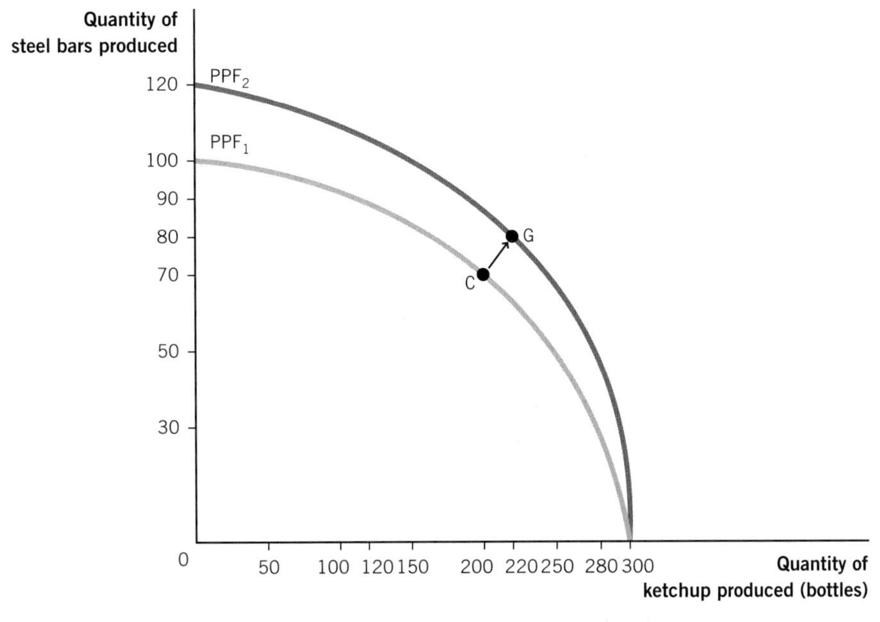

FIGURE 2.2

A Shift in the Production Possibilities Frontier

A new steel assembly line that improves the productive capacity of steel-makers shifts the PPF upward from PPF_1 to PPF_2. As a result, more steel bars can be produced.

PRACTICE WHAT YOU KNOW

The Production Possibilities Frontier: Bicycles and Cars

Question: Are the following statements true or false? Base your answers on the PPF shown below.

There is a trade-off between making bicycles and cars.

1. Point A represents a possible amount of cars and bicycles that can be sold.
2. The movement along the curve from point A to point B shows the opportunity cost of producing more bicycles.
3. If the economy experiences high unemployment, the PPF shifts inward.
4. If an improved process for manufacturing cars is introduced, the entire PPF will shift outward.

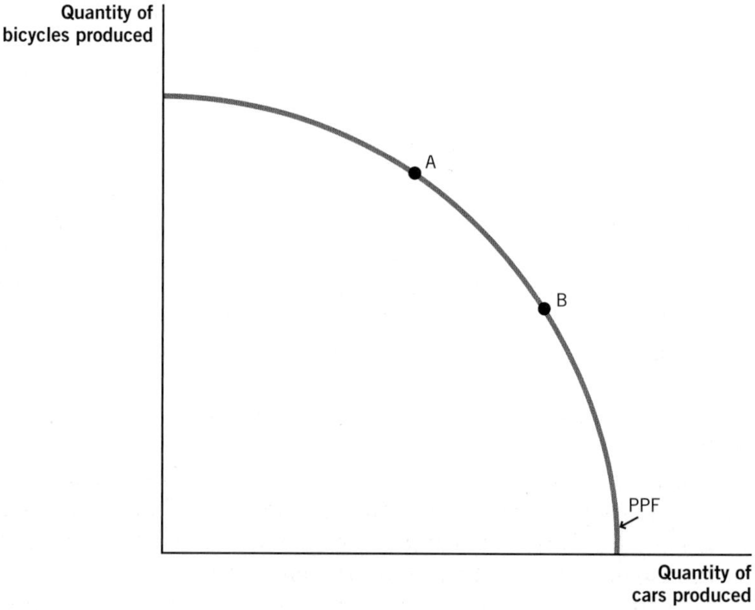

Answers

1. False. Point A represents a number of cars and bicycles that can be *produced*, not sold.
2. False. Moving from point A to point B shows the opportunity cost of producing more cars, not more bicycles.
3. False. Unemployment does not shift the curve inward, because the PPF is the maximum that can be produced when all resources are being used efficiently. More unemployment would locate society at a point inside the PPF, because some people who could help produce more cars or bicycles would not be working.
4. False. The PPF will shift outward along the car axis, but it will not shift upward along the bicycle axis.

FIGURE 2.3

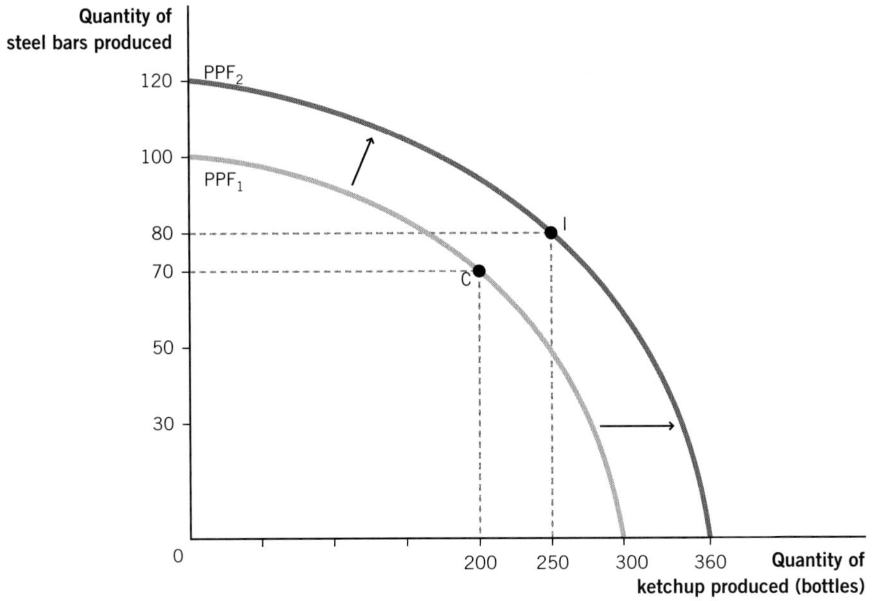

More Resources (Workers) Expand the Production Possibilities Frontier

When more resources (for example, workers) are available for the production of either steel or ketchup, the entire PPF shifts upward and outward. This makes point I, along PPF_2, possible.

new production possibilities frontier. It is now possible for the society to move from point C to point G, where it can produce more steel bars and ketchup (80 steel bars and 220 bottles of ketchup) compared to point C (70 steel bars and 200 bottles of ketchup). Why can the society produce more of both goods? Because the improvement in steel-making technology allows a redeployment of the labor force that also increases the production of ketchup. Improvements in technology make point G possible when previously it was beyond the PPF.

The production possibilities frontier will also expand if the population grows. A larger population means more workers to help make steel and ketchup. Figure 2.3 illustrates what happens when the labor force increases. With more workers, the society is able to produce more steel bars and ketchup than before. This causes the PPF to shift from PPF_1 to PPF_2, expanding up along the steel (vertical) axis and out along the ketchup (horizontal) axis. Like improvements in technology, additional resources expand the frontier and enable the society to reach a point—in this case, I—that was not possible before. The extra workers have pushed the entire frontier out—not just one end, as the steel assembly line did in Figure 2.2.

What Are the Benefits of Specialization and Trade?

We have seen that improving technology and adding resources make an economy more productive. A third way to create gains for society is through specialization and trade. Determining what to specialize in is an important part of this process. Every worker, business, or country is relatively good at producing certain products or services. Suppose that you decide to learn about information technology. You earn a certificate or degree and find an employer who hires you for your specialized skills. Your information-technology skills determine your salary. As a result, you can use your salary to purchase other goods and services that you desire and that you wouldn't be able to make for yourself.

In the next section, we will explore why specializing and exchanging your expertise with others makes gains from trade possible.

Gains from Trade

Trade creates value

Let's return to our two-good economy. Now we'll make the further assumption that this economy has only two people. One person is better at making steel bars, and the other is better at making ketchup. When this is the case, the potential gains from trade are clear. Each person will specialize in what he or she is better at producing and then will trade in order to acquire some of the good produced by the other person.

Figure 2.4 shows the production potential of the two people in our economy, Andy and Henry. (Andy is named after steel magnate Andrew Carnegie, and Henry is named after ketchup magnate Henry J. Heinz.) As the chart in the figure shows, if Andy devotes all of his work time to making steel bars, he can produce 120 steel bars. If he doesn't spend any time making steel bars, he can make 120 bottles of ketchup. In contrast, Henry can spend all his time on producing 25 steel bars, or all his time producing 100 bottles of ketchup.

The graphs in Figure 2.4(a) and (b) illustrate the number of steel bars and bottles of ketchup that each person produces daily. Ketchup production is plotted on the x (horizontal) axis, and steel production on the y (vertical) axis. Each of the production possibilities frontiers is drawn from data in the chart at the top of the figure.

Since Andy and Henry can choose to produce at any point along their production possibilities frontiers, let's assume they each want some of both goods. When this is the case, Andy produces 60 steel bars and 60 bottles of ketchup, while Henry produces 20 steel bars and 20 bottles of ketchup. Because Andy is more productive in general, he produces more of each good. Andy has an **absolute advantage,** meaning that he has the ability to produce more with the same quantity of resources than Henry can produce.

Absolute advantage refers to the ability of one producer to make more than another producer with the same quantity of resources.

At first glance, it would appear that Andy should produce some of each good and have nothing to do with Henry. But consider what happens if Andy and Henry both specialize and then trade. Table 2.2 compares production with and without specialization and trade. Without trade, Andy and Henry have a combined production of 80 units of steel and 80 bottles of ketchup (Andy's 60 + Henry's 20, respectively). As shown in the table, they both consume only what they produce. But when Andy specializes and produces only steel, his production is 120 bars. In this case, his individual steel output is greater than the combined output of 80 steel bars (Andy's 60 + Henry's 20). Similarly, if Henry specializes in ketchup, he is able to make 100 bottles. His individual ketchup output is greater than their combined output of 80 bottles of ketchup (Andy's 60 + Henry's 20). Specialization has resulted in the production of 40 additional steel bars and 20 additional bottles of ketchup.

FIGURE 2.4

The Production Possibilities Frontier with No Trade

Andy (panel a) can produce more steel and more bottles of ketchup than Henry (panel b). Since Andy is more productive in general, he produces more of each good. If Andy and Henry each want to produce an equal number of steel bars and bottles of ketchup on their own, Andy makes 60 units of each and Henry makes 20 units of each.

Person	Daily production: Steel (bars)	Daily production: Ketchup (bottles)
Andy	120	120
Henry	25	100

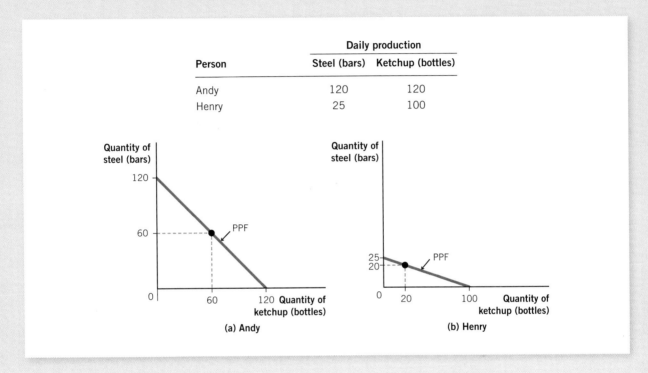

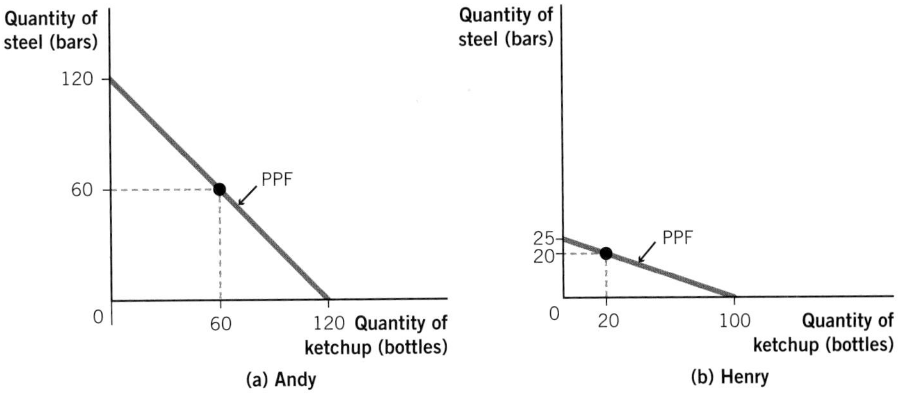

Specialization leads to greater productivity. But Andy and Henry would like to have both steel and ketchup. So if they specialize and then trade with each other, they will both benefit. If Andy gives Henry 25 steel bars in exchange for 75 bottles of ketchup, they are each better off than if they tried to produce each good on their own. Andy has 95 steel bars remaining

TABLE 2.2

The Gains from Trade

		Without trade		With specialization and trade		
Person	**Good**	**Production**	**Consumption**	**Production**	**Consumption**	**Gains from trade**
Andy	Steel bars	60	60	120	95 (keeps)	+ 35
	Bottles of ketchup	60	60	0	75 (from Henry)	+ 15
Henry	Steel bars	20	20	0	25 (from Andy)	+ 5
	Bottles of ketchup	20	20	100	25 (keeps)	+ 5

FIGURE 2.5

The Production Possibilities Frontier with Trade

(a) If Andy produces only steel, he will have 120 steel bars, shown at point A. If he does not specialize, he will produce 60 steel bars and 60 bottles of ketchup (point B). If he specializes and trades with Henry, he will have 95 steel bars and 75 bottles of ketchup (point C).

(b) If Henry produces only bottles of ketchup, he will have 100 bottles of ketchup (point A). If he does not specialize, he will produce 20 steel bars and 20 bottles of ketchup (point B). If he specializes and trades with Andy, he can have 25 steel bars and 25 bottles of ketchup (point C).

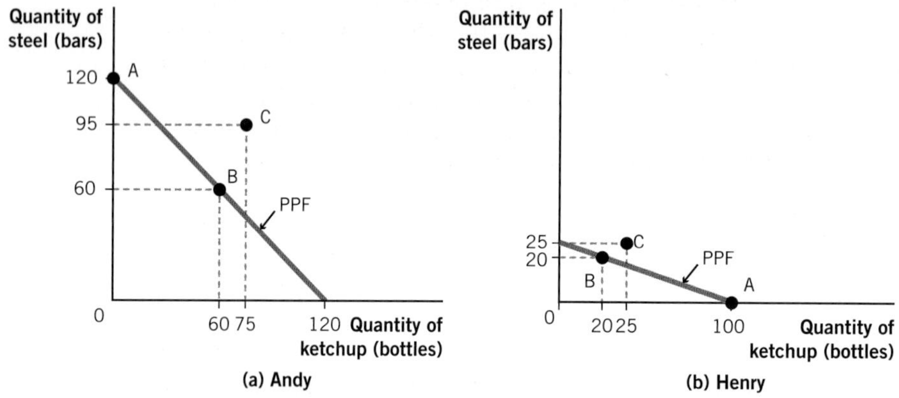

(instead of 60), and Henry has 25 steel bars (instead of 20). This result is evident in the Consumption (With specialization and trade) column of Table 2.2 and at point C in Figure 2.5 (a and b).

In Figure 2.5(a), at point A Andy produces 120 steel bars and 0 bottles of ketchup. If he does not specialize, he produces 60 steel bars and 60 bottles of ketchup, as shown at point B. If he specializes and then trades with Henry, he can have 95 steel bars and 75 bottles of ketchup, shown at point C. His value gained from trade is 35 steel bars and 15 bottles of ketchup. In Figure 2.5(b), we see a similar benefit for Henry. If he produces only bottles of ketchup, he will have 100 bottles of ketchup, shown at point A. If he does not specialize, he produces 20 steel bars and 20 bottles of ketchup, shown at point B. If he specializes and trades with Andy, he can have 25 steel bars and 25 bottles of ketchup, shown at point C. His value gained from trade is 5 steel bars and 5 bottles of ketchup.

Notice that Andy and Henry are now able to consume beyond their ability to produce individually. While each can only produce some combination of goods on the PPF, by specializing and trading they can have more of both products than if they produced these things on their own. In spite of Andy's absolute advantage in making both steel bars and ketchup, he is still better off trading with Henry. This amazing result occurs because of specialization.

When Andy and Henry spend their time on what they do best, they are able to produce more collectively and then divide the gain.

Comparative Advantage

We have seen that specialization enables workers to enjoy gains from trade. The concept of opportunity cost provides us with a second way of validating the principle that trade creates value. Recall that opportunity cost is the highest-valued alternative that is sacrificed to pursue something else. Assume that Andy and Henry each face a constant trade-off between producing steel and producing ketchup. Andy can produce 120 steel bars or 120 bottles of ketchup; this means his trade-off between producing steel and bottles of ketchup is fixed at 1:1 (the equivalent of a ratio of 120:120; divide both sides by 120). If he gives up 60 steel bars he can produce 60 bottles of ketchup (a 1:1 ratio), and this puts him at point B on the curve in Figure 2.5(a). Henry can produce 25 steel bars or 100 bottles of ketchup. His trade-off between producing steel bars and bottles of ketchup is fixed at 1:4 (a ratio of 25:100; divide both sides by 25). If Henry began by choosing to produce 25 steel bars and no ketchup and gave up 5 steel bars, he gets 20 bottles of ketchup ($5 \times 4 = 20$). This means he has 20 steel bars and 20 bottles of ketchup, placing him at point B on the curve in Figure 2.5(b). These trade-offs are summarized in Table 2.3. You can see that in order to produce 1 more steel bar Andy must give up producing 1 bottle of ketchup. We can say that the opportunity cost of 1 steel bar is 1 bottle of ketchup. We can also reverse the observation and say that the opportunity cost of 1 bottle of ketchup is 1 steel bar. In Henry's case, each steel bar he produces means giving up the production of 4 bottles of ketchup. In other words, the opportunity cost for him to produce 1 steel bar is 4 bottles of ketchup. In reverse, we can say that when he produces 1 bottle, he gives up $\frac{1}{4}$ of a steel bar.

Recall from Chapter 1 that *comparative advantage* is the ability to make a good at a lower cost than another producer. Looking at Table 2.3, you can see that Andy has a lower opportunity cost of producing steel bars than Henry. Andy gives up 1 bottle of ketchup for each steel bar he produces, while Henry gives up 4 bottles of ketchup for each steel bar he produces. In other words, Andy has a comparative advantage in producing steel bars. However, Andy does not have a comparative advantage in producing ketchup. For Andy to produce 1 bottle of ketchup, he would have to give up production of 1 steel

TABLE 2.3

The Opportunity Cost of Steel and Ketchup

	Opportunity cost	
Person	**1 Steel Bar**	**1 Bottle of Ketchup**
Andy	1 bottle of ketchup	1 steel bar
Henry	4 bottles of ketchup	$\frac{1}{4}$ steel bar

PRACTICE WHAT YOU KNOW

Opportunity Cost

Question: Imagine that you're traveling to visit your family in Chicago. You can take a train or a plane. The plane ticket costs $300, and traveling by air takes 2 hours each way. The train ticket costs $200, and traveling by rail takes 12 hours each way. Which form of transportation should you choose?

Will you travel by plane or train?

Answer: The key to answering the question is learning to value time. The simplest way to do this is to calculate the financial cost savings of taking the train and compare that to the value of the time you would save if you took the plane.

Cost savings with train	Round-trip time saved with plane
$300 − $200 = $100	24 hours − 4 hours = 20 hours
(plane) − (train)	(train) − (plane)

A person who takes the train can save $100, but it will cost 20 hours to do so. At an hourly rate, the savings would be $100/20 hours = $5/hour. If you value your time at exactly $5 an hour, you'll be indifferent between plane and train travel (that is, you'll be equally satisfied with both options). If your time is worth more than $5 an hour, you should take the plane. If your time is worth less than $5 an hour, you should take the train.

Opportunity cost

It is important to note that this approach to calculating opportunity cost gives us a more realistic answer than simply observing ticket prices. The train has a lower ticket price, but very few people ride the train instead of flying because the opportunity cost of their time is worth more to them than the difference in the ticket prices. This is why most business travelers fly—it saves valuable time. Good economists learn to examine the full opportunity cost of their decisions, which must include both the financial part of each decision and the cost of time.

We have examined this question by holding everything else constant (that is, applying the principle of *ceteris paribus*). In other words, at no point did we discuss possible side issues such as the fear of flying, sleeping arrangements on the train, or anything else that might be relevant to someone making the decision.

bar. Henry, in contrast, gives up $\frac{1}{4}$ of a steel bar each time he produces 1 bottle of ketchup. So Andy's opportunity cost for producing bottles of ketchup is higher than Henry's. Because Henry is the low-opportunity-cost producer of ketchup, he has a comparative advantage in producing it. Recall that Andy has an absolute advantage in the production of steel bars and ketchup; he is better at making both. However, from this example we see that he cannot have a comparative advantage in making both goods.

Opportunity cost

Applying the concept of opportunity cost helps us see why specialization enables people to produce more. Andy's opportunity cost of producing steel bars (he gives up making 1 bottle of ketchup for every bar) is less than Henry's opportunity cost of producing steel bars (he gives up 4 bottles of ketchup for every bar). Therefore, Andy should specialize in producing steel bars. If you want to double-check this result, consider who should produce ketchup. Andy's opportunity cost of producing bottles of ketchup (he gives up 1 steel bar for every bottle of ketchup he makes) is more than Henry's opportunity cost of producing bottles of ketchup (he gives up $\frac{1}{4}$ of a steel bar for every bottle he makes). Therefore, Henry should specialize in producing ketchup.

ECONOMICS IN THE MEDIA

Opportunity Cost

Saving Private Ryan

Saving one life means sacrificing another.

In most war movies, the winner is quite apparent. One side wins if it loses fewer airplanes, tanks, or soldiers during the course of the conflict or attains a strategic objective worth the cost. These casualties of war are the trade-off that is necessary to achieve victory. The movie *Saving Private Ryan* (1998) is different because in its plot the calculus of war does not add up: the mission is to save a single man. Private Ryan is one of four brothers who are all fighting on D-Day (June 6, 1944), the day the Allies landed in Normandy, France, to liberate Europe from Nazi occupation. In a twist of fate, all three of Ryan's brothers are killed. As a result, the general in charge believes that the family has sacrificed enough and sends orders to find Ryan and return him home.

The catch is that in order to save Private Ryan the army needs to send a small group of soldiers to find him. A patrol led by Captain Miller loses many good men in the process, and those who remain begin to doubt the mission. Captain Miller says to the sergeant, "This Ryan better be worth it. He better go home and cure a disease or invent a longer-lasting light bulb." Captain Miller hopes that saving Private Ryan will be worth the sacrifices they are making. That is how he rationalizes the decision to try to save him.

The opportunity cost of saving Private Ryan ends up being the lives that the patrol loses—lives that otherwise could have been pursuing a strategic military objective. In that sense, the entire film is about opportunity cost.

Finding the Right Price to Facilitate Trade

We have seen that Andy and Henry will do better if they specialize and then trade. But how many bottles of ketchup should it cost to buy a steel bar? How many steel bars for a bottle of ketchup? In other words, what trading price will benefit both parties? To answer this question, we need to return to opportunity cost. For context, think of the process you likely went through when trading lunch food with friends in grade school. Perhaps you wanted a friend's apple and he wanted a few of your Oreos. If you agreed to trade three Oreos for the apple, the exchange benefited both parties because you valued your three cookies less than your friend's apple and your friend valued your three cookies more than his apple.

In our example, Andy and Henry will benefit from exchanging a good at a price that is lower than the opportunity cost of producing it. Recall that Andy's opportunity cost is 1 steel bar (S) per 1 bottle of ketchup (K). We can express this as a ratio of 1S:1K. This means that any exchange that yields Andy more than 1 bottle of ketchup for 1 steel bar will be beneficial to Andy, since he ends up with more steel and bottles of ketchup than he had without trade. Henry's opportunity cost is 1 steel bar per 4 bottles of ketchup, or a ratio of 1S:4K. For trade to be mutually beneficial, the ratio of the amount exchanged must fall between the ratio of Andy's opportunity cost of 1S:1K and the ratio of Henry's opportunity cost of 1S:4K. If the ratio falls outside of that range, Andy and Henry will be better off without trade, since the price of trading (which is the ratio in this case) will not be attractive to both parties. In the example shown in Table 2.4, Andy trades 25 steel bars for 75 bottles of ketchup. The ratio of 25S:75K or 1S:3K (dividing each side by 25) falls between Andy's and Henry's opportunity costs.

Trade creates value

As long as the terms of trade fall between the trading partners' opportunity costs, the trade benefits both sides. (You can test this by trying a trade of 1 steel bar for 2 bottles of ketchup.) But if Henry insists on a trading ratio of 1 steel bar for 1 bottle of ketchup, which would be a good deal for him, Andy will refuse to trade because he will be better off producing both goods on his own. Likewise, if Andy insists on receiving 4 bottles of ketchup for every steel bar he gives to Henry, Henry will refuse to trade with him because Henry will be better off producing both goods on his own.

TABLE 2.4

Gaining from Trade

Person	Opportunity cost	Ratio (steel to ketchup)
Andy	1 steel bar equals 1 bottle of ketchup	1:1
[Terms of trade]	1 steel bar for 3 bottles of ketchup	1:3
Henry	1 steel bar equals 4 bottles of ketchup	1:4

ECONOMICS IN THE REAL WORLD

Why LeBron James Has Someone Else Help Him Move

Will LeBron ever ask his teammates, "Guys . . . can you help me move this weekend?"

LeBron James is a pretty big guy—6′8″ and roughly 250 pounds. In the summer of 2014, he decided to move from Miami to Cleveland to play with his hometown basketball team. Given his size and strength, you might think that LeBron would have moved his household himself. But despite the fact that he could replace two or more ordinary movers, he kept playing basketball and hired movers. Let's examine the situation to see if this was a wise decision.

LeBron has an absolute advantage in both playing basketball and moving furniture. But, as we have seen, an absolute advantage doesn't mean that he should do both tasks himself. Even though his move happened during the off-season, taking time away from his practice and workout schedule is an opportunity cost he has to face (not to mention the possibility of injury). The movers, with a much lower opportunity cost of their time, have a comparative advantage in moving—so LeBron made a smart decision to hire them!

However, when LeBron retires, the value of his time will be lower. If the opportunity cost of his time becomes low enough, it's conceivable that the next time he changes residence, he'll move himself rather than pay movers. ✷

How Does the Economy Work?

Models are useful in explaining individual behavior, but they can also illustrate interactions between larger groups. Let's consider how the economy as a whole works in the context of what economists call the circular flow model.

The Circular Flow Model

The **circular flow model** is a model that shows how resources and final goods and services flow through the economy. In the model there are two groups, households and firms, that want to trade with each other. *Households* are the people we usually think of as consumers. *Firms* are businesses. Households want the goods and services produced by the firms, and firms want the resources owned by the households in order to make goods and provide services. The model shows how households get the things firms produce and how firms acquire the resources to produce those things. Both of these trades happen in a market.

The **circular flow model** is a model that shows how resources and final goods and services flow through the economy.

A **market** is a place or system that brings buyers and sellers together to exchange goods and services.

A **market** is a place or a system that brings buyers and sellers together to exchange goods and services. Markets can take different forms, such as a local grocery store, a Walmart, or a garage sale. Amazon, eBay, and the iTunes Store are all examples of Internet marketplaces. Every group of people throughout history has established markets of some sort to help them deal with scarcity.

Without money, what would you trade for this coffee and bagel?

The circular flow model contains two markets. The first market is the *product market*. In this market, households are the buyers and firms are the sellers. This is the type of market you're probably most familiar with. When you go to the gas station or the mall, you're acting as a buyer. The store is the seller.

The second market is the *resource market*, and here the roles are reversed. In this market, the household acts as the seller and the firm is the buyer. The market for labor is a resource market. When you go on the job market, you are basically selling yourself. Firms are looking for employees to help them produce goods and services. They are buying labor.

Figure 2.6(a) shows the circular flow model. The households and firms are the actors. They interact in the two different markets. The arrows show the flow of goods, services, and

FIGURE 2.6

The Circular Flow Model

(a) *Circular Flow Model:* Goods and services move counterclockwise from one part of the economy to another. Firms produce goods and services and send them to the product market. Households barter with firms to acquire goods and services in the product market. Households provide the inputs necessary to make goods and services. Firms barter with households to acquire these resources and turn them into goods and services.

(b) *Circular Flow Model with Money:* Instead of bartering for goods and services, people use money to make the transactions much easier. Money acts as a medium of exchange, enabling the economy to avoid the double-coincidence-of-wants problem.

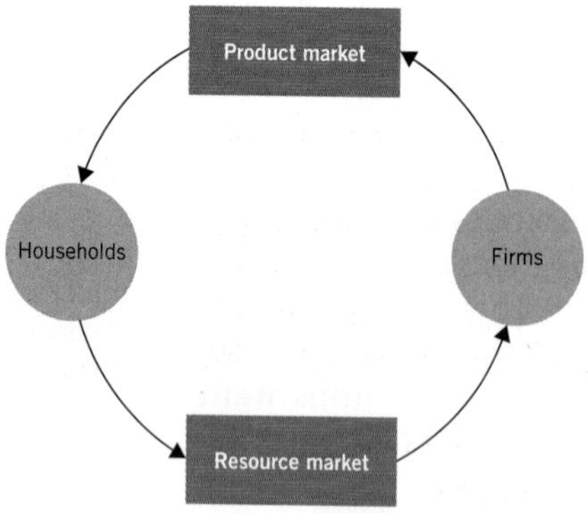

(a) Circular Flow Model

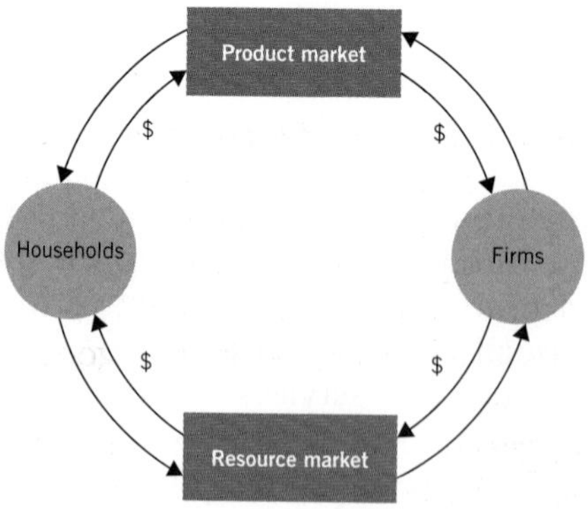

(b) Circular Flow Model with Money

resources through the economy. This basic view of how things work is actually incredibly accurate. However, we can add one more thing to make the picture of economic activity more complete. At this point, we are assuming that the households and the firms trade goods for resources. In other words, they barter. **Barter** involves individuals trading a good they already have or providing a service in exchange for something they want. The problem is that barter requires a **double coincidence of wants**, in which each party in an exchange transaction has what the other party desires. A double coincidence of wants is pretty unusual. Consider how you would get what you want in a barter economy. Let's say you are hungry. To get something to eat, you go get a job at a Subway restaurant. At the end of the day, you get paid. You eagerly choose a foot-long meatball sub as payment for your day's work. Satisfied, you walk home, where you find that your landlord is demanding payment for the rent you owe him. You agree to pay him with a six-inch turkey sub every other day for the next month. Fortunately, the landlord likes Subway sandwiches. In this situation, there is a double coincidence of wants. Unfortunately for you, when you get upstairs there's a message from the cable company. It needs to be paid as well. You call the company and offer food from Subway, but the company doesn't want food. Instead, it wants to be paid with gasoline because its service trucks don't run on sandwiches. To pay your cable bill, you need to find someone who will trade sandwiches for gasoline so you can trade gasoline for cable TV.

Barter involves individuals trading a good they already have or providing a service in exchange for something they want.

A **double coincidence of wants** occurs when each party in an exchange transaction has what the other party desires.

You probably see where this is going, and you probably already understand what's missing in our simple model: money. We'll discuss money extensively in Chapter 15, but for now it's clear that having some common commodity that buyers and sellers both want will increase the efficiency of the market. Thus, we see societies develop some form of money. Adding money to our model, as we do in Figure 2.6(b), makes it look more like reality. Money flows in the opposite direction of the goods, services, and resources, illustrating that money serves as a medium of exchange. Now we have two flows—one of goods and services, and one of money—moving in a circle. Hence, the term "circular flow."

Conclusion

Does trade create winners and losers? After reading this chapter, you should know the answer: trade creates value. We have dispelled the misconception that many first-time learners of economics begin with—that every trade results in a winner and a loser. The simple yet powerful idea that trade creates value has far-reaching consequences for society. Voluntary trades will maximize society's wealth by redistributing goods and services to people who value them the most.

Trade creates value

We have also developed two key economic models, the production possibilities frontier and the circular flow model. The production possibilities model illustrates the benefits of trade and helps us describe ways to grow the economy. Trade and growth rest on a fundamental idea—specialization. When producers specialize, they focus their efforts on those goods and services for which they have the lowest opportunity cost; they then trade with

ECONOMICS FOR LIFE

Models Aren't Perfect: Failure to Account for Unexpected Events When Making Predictions

Models help economists make predictions, but those predictions are often based on past experiences and current observations. Many of the least accurate predictions fail to take into account the extent to which technological change influences the economy. Here we repeat a few predictions as a cautionary reminder that technology doesn't remain constant.

PREDICTION: "There is no reason anyone would want a computer in their home." Said in 1977 by Ken Olson, founder of Digital Equipment Corp. (DEC), a maker of mainframe computers.
FAIL: Over 80% of all American households have a computer today.

PREDICTION: "There will never be a bigger plane built." Said in 1933 by a Boeing engineer referring to the 247, a twin-engine plane that holds 10 people.
FAIL: Today, the Airbus A380 can hold more than 800 people.

PREDICTION: "The wireless music box has no imaginable commercial value. Who would pay for a message sent to no one in particular?" Said by people in the communications industry when David Sarnoff (founder of NBC) wanted to invest in the radio.
FAIL: Radio programs quickly captured the public's imagination.

PREDICTION: "The world potential market for copying machines is five thousand at most." Said in 1959 by executives of IBM to the people who founded Xerox.
FAIL: Today, a combination printer, fax machine, and copier costs less than $100. There are tens of millions of copiers in use throughout the United States.

PREDICTION: "The Americans have need of the telephone, but we do not. We have plenty of messenger boys." Said in 1878 by Sir William Preece, chief engineer, British Post Office.
FAIL: Today, almost everyone in Britain has a telephone.

These predictions may seem funny to us today, but note the common feature: they didn't account for how the new technology would affect consumer demand and behavior. Nor did these predictions anticipate how improvements in technology through time would make future versions of new products substantially better. The lesson: don't count on the status quo. Models are very useful tools, but no model can anticipate changes that the people using them don't see coming.

Source: Listverse.com, "Top 30 Failed Technology Predictions."

Epic fail: planes have continued to get larger despite predictions to the contrary.

others who are good at making something else. To have something valuable to trade, each producer, in effect, must find its comparative advantage. As a result, trade creates value and contributes to an improved standard of living in society.

The circular flow model illustrates how the economy functions. The economy is a very complex thing, but by simplifying it to two general markets (the market for products and the market for resources) and two broadly defined actors (households and firms) and then adding money to the mix we have a pretty good idea of what takes place. In the next chapter, we look to expand our understanding of markets. The major economies of the world rely on markets to set prices and distribute goods. If we want to understand how economics works, this is a logical next step.

ANSWERING THE BIG QUESTIONS

How do economists study the economy?

- Economists design hypotheses and then test them by collecting real data. The economist's laboratory is the world around us.
- A good model should be simple, flexible, and useful for making accurate predictions. A model is both more realistic and harder to understand when it involves many variables. To keep models simple, economists often use the concept of *ceteris paribus*, or "other things being equal." Maintaining a positive (as opposed to normative) framework is crucial for economic analysis because it allows decision-makers to observe the facts objectively.

What is a production possibilities frontier?

- A production possibilities frontier is a model that illustrates the combinations of outputs that a society can produce if all of its resources are being used efficiently. Economists use this model to illustrate trade-offs and to explain opportunity costs and the role of additional resources and technology in creating economic growth.

What are the benefits of specialization and trade?

- Society is better off if individuals and firms specialize and trade on the basis of the principle of comparative advantage.
- Parties that are better at producing goods and services than their potential trading partners (and thus hold an absolute advantage) still benefit from trade. Trade allows them to specialize and trade what they produce for other goods and services that they are not as skilled at making.

- As long as the terms of trade fall between the opportunity costs of the trading partners, the trade benefits both sides.

How does the economy work?

- Parties trade with each other to get the things they want. The circular flow model shows us that in the product and resource markets, households and firms use money to facilitate exchange. Without money, we would have to barter for the things we want and need.

CONCEPTS YOU SHOULD KNOW

absolute advantage (p. 34)
barter (p. 43)
ceteris paribus (p. 27)
circular flow model (p. 41)
double coincidence of wants (p. 43)
law of increasing relative cost (p. 30)
market (p. 42)
normative statement (p. 25)
positive statement (p. 25)
production possibilities frontier (p. 28)

QUESTIONS FOR REVIEW

1. What is a positive economic statement? What is a normative economic statement? Provide an example of each.
2. Is it important to build completely realistic economic models? Explain your response.
3. Draw a production possibilities frontier curve. Illustrate the set of points that is feasible, the set of points that is efficient, and the set of points that is not feasible.
4. Why does the production possibilities frontier bow outward? Give an example of two goods for which this would be the case.
5. Does having an absolute advantage mean that you should undertake everything on your own? Why or why not?
6. What criteria would you use to determine which of two workers has a comparative advantage in performing a task?
7. Why does comparative advantage matter more than absolute advantage for trade?
8. What factors are most important for economic growth?
9. Which two markets make up the circular flow model? Who are the actors in the circular flow model?
10. What function does money play in an economy?

STUDY PROBLEMS (* *solved at the end of the section*)

* 1. Michael and Angelo live in a small town in Italy. They work as artists. Michael is the more productive artist. He can produce 10 small sculptures each day but only 5 paintings. Angelo can produce 6 sculptures each day but only 2 paintings.

	Output per day	
	Sculptures	Paintings
Michael	10	5
Angelo	6	2

a. What is the opportunity cost of a painting for each artist?
b. Based on your answer in part a, who has a comparative advantage in producing paintings?
c. If the two men decide to specialize, who should produce the sculptures and who should produce the paintings?

* 2. The following table shows scores that a student can earn on two upcoming exams according to the amount of time devoted to study:

Hours spent studying for economics	Economics score	Hours spent studying for history	History score
10	100	0	40
8	96	2	60
6	88	4	76
4	76	6	88
2	60	8	96
0	40	10	100

a. Plot the production possibilities frontier.
b. Does the production possibilities frontier exhibit the law of increasing relative cost?
c. If the student wishes to move from a grade of 60 to a grade of 88 in economics, what is the opportunity cost?

3. Think about comparative advantage when answering this question: Should your professor, who has highly specialized training in economics, take time out of his or her teaching schedule to mow his or her lawn? Defend your answer.

* 4. Are the following statements positive or normative?
   a. My dog weighs 75 pounds.
   b. Dogs are required by law to have rabies shots.
   c. You should take your dog to the veterinarian once a year for a check-up.
   d. Chihuahuas are cuter than bulldogs.
   e. Leash laws for dogs are a good idea because they reduce injuries.

* 5. Suppose that an amazing new fertilizer doubles the production of potatoes. How would this discovery affect the production possibilities frontier between potatoes and carrots? Would it now be possible to produce more potatoes *and* more carrots, or only more potatoes?

6. Suppose that a politician tells you about a plan to create two expensive but necessary programs to build more production facilities for solar power and wind power. At the same time, the politician is unwilling to cut any other programs. Use the production possibilities frontier graph below to explain if this is possible.

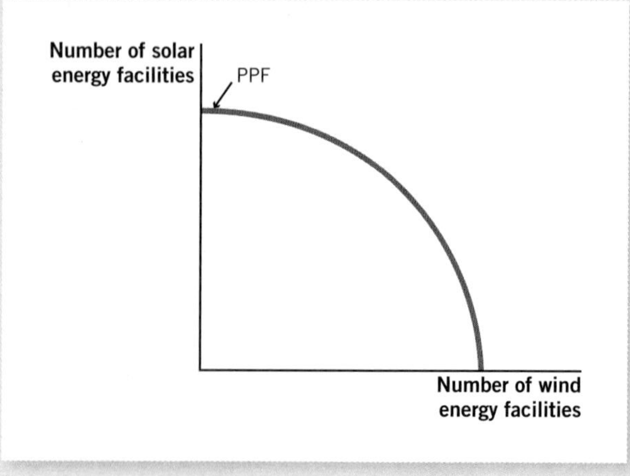

* 7. Two friends, Rachel and Joey, enjoy baking bread and making apple pies. Rachel takes 2 hours to bake a loaf of bread and 1 hour to make a pie. Joey takes 4 hours to bake a loaf of bread and 4 hours to make a pie.
   a. What are Joey's and Rachel's opportunity costs of baking bread?
   b. Who has the absolute advantage in making bread?
   c. Who has a comparative advantage in making bread?
   d. If Joey and Rachel decide to specialize in order to increase their joint production, what should Joey produce? What should Rachel produce?
   e. The price of a loaf of bread can be expressed in terms of an apple pie. If Joey and Rachel are specializing in production and decide to trade with each other, what range of ratios of bread and apple pie would allow both parties to benefit from trade?

8. Where would you plot unemployment on a production possibilities frontier? Where would you plot full employment on a production possibilities frontier? Now suppose that in a time of crisis everyone pitches in and works much harder than usual. What happens to the production possibilities frontier?

SOLVED PROBLEMS

1.a. Michael's opportunity cost is 2 sculptures for each painting he produces. How do we know this? If he devotes all of his time to sculptures, he can produce 10. If he devotes all of his time to paintings, he can produce 5. The ratio 10:5 is the same as 2:1. Michael is therefore twice as fast at producing sculptures as he is at producing paintings. Angelo's opportunity cost is 3 sculptures for each painting he produces. If he devotes all of his time to sculptures, he can produce 6. If he devotes all of his time to paintings, he can produce 2. The ratio 6:2 is the same as 3:1.

b. For this question, we need to compare Michael's and Angelo's relative strengths. Michael produces 2 sculptures for every painting, and Angelo produces 3 sculptures for every painting. Since Michael is only twice as good at producing sculptures, his opportunity cost of producing each painting is 2 sculptures instead of 3. Therefore, Michael is the low-opportunity-cost producer of paintings. He has a comparative advantage in producing paintings.

c. If they specialize, Michael should paint and Angelo should sculpt. You might be tempted to argue that Michael should just work alone; but if Angelo does the sculptures, Michael can concentrate on the paintings. This is what comparative advantage is all about.

2.a.

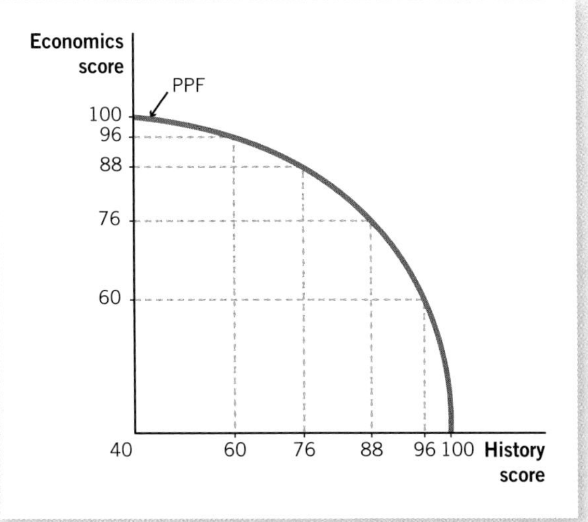

b. Yes, since it is not a straight line.

c. The opportunity cost is that the student's grade falls from 96 to 76 in history.

4.a. Positive.

b. Positive.

c. Normative.

d. Normative.

e. Normative.

5. A new fertilizer that doubles potato production will shift the entire PPF out along the potato axis but not along the carrot axis. Nevertheless, the added ability to produce more potatoes means that less acreage will have to be planted in potatoes and more land can be used to produce carrots. This makes it possible to produce more potatoes and carrots at many points along the production possibilities frontier. Figure 2.3 has a nice illustration if you are unsure how this works.

7.a. Rachel gives up 2 pies for every loaf she makes. Joey gives up 1 pie for every loaf he makes.

b. Rachel has the absolute advantage.

c. Joey has a comparative advantage.

d. Joey should make the bread and Rachel the pies.

e. Rachel makes 2 pies per loaf and Joey makes 1 pie per loaf. So any trade between 2:1 and 1:1 would benefit them both.

CHAPTER 3

The Market at Work

Supply and Demand

MISCONCEPTION

Demand matters more than supply.

What do Starbucks, Nordstrom, and Microsoft have in common? If you guessed that they all have headquarters in Seattle, that's true. But even more interesting is that each company supplies a product much in demand by consumers. Starbucks supplies coffee from coast to coast and seems to be everywhere someone wants a cup of coffee. Nordstrom, a giant retailer with hundreds of department stores, supplies fashion apparel to meet a broad spectrum of individual demand, from the basics to designer collections. Microsoft supplies software for customers all over the world. Demand for Microsoft products has made large fortunes for founder Bill Gates and other investors in the company.

Notice the two recurring words in the previous paragraph: "supply" and "demand." Economists consistently use these words when describing how an economy functions. Many people think that demand matters more than supply. This occurs because most people have much more experience as buyers than as sellers. Often, our first instinct is to wonder how much something costs to buy rather than how much it costs to produce. This one-sided impression of the market undermines our ability to fully appreciate how prices are determined. To help correct this misconception, this chapter describes how markets work and the nature of competition. To shed light on the process, we will introduce the formal model of demand and supply. We'll begin by looking at demand and supply separately. Then we'll combine them to see how they interact to establish the market price and determine how much is produced.

Black Friday crush at Target.

BIG QUESTIONS

- **What are the fundamentals of a market economy?**
- **What determines demand?**
- **What determines supply?**
- **How do supply and demand shifts affect a market?**

What Are the Fundamentals of a Market Economy?

Have you ever wondered why stores have what you want? You've probably never told the Starbucks management team to add a new latte to the menu. You haven't had discussions with executives at Nordstrom about the newest fashions. Bill Gates has never had you over to his house to talk about improvements to Microsoft Windows. Nevertheless, products are made and people buy them. In Chapter 1, we talked about scarcity and how pervasive it is. Yet other than a few times a year (usually around Christmas), there are plenty of lattes, designer dresses, and copies of Windows to go around. Why is that? The answer has to do with how a country decides to distribute goods and services. Markets are the primary method used by developed countries to distribute goods.

In a **market economy**, resources are allocated among households and firms with little or no government interference.

Markets bring trading partners together to create order out of chaos. Companies supply goods and services, and customers want to obtain the goods and services that companies supply. In a **market economy**, resources are allocated among households and firms with little or no government interference. Adam Smith, the founder of modern economics, described the dynamic best: "It is not from the benevolence of the butcher, the brewer, or the baker, that we expect our dinner, but from their regard to their own interest."* In other words, producers earn a living by selling the products that consumers want. Consumers are also motivated by self-interest; they must decide how to use their money to select the goods that they need or want the most. According to Adam Smith, this *invisible hand* guides resources to their highest-valued use. So even though no one is directing the economy, the goods and services that consumers want get produced. Sellers are guided by what seems to be an invisible hand to make things that consumers want. If they don't, those sellers go out of business.

The exchange of goods and services in a market economy happens through prices that are established in markets. Those prices change according to the level of demand for a product and how much is supplied. For instance, hotel

---

*Adam Smith, *Wealth of Nations*, 5th ed., ed. Edwin Cannan (London: Methuen & Co., 1904), bk. 1, chap. 2.

Peak season is expensive . . .

. . . but off-season is a bargain.

rates near Disney World are reduced in the fall when demand is low, and they peak in March during spring break. If spring break takes you to a ski resort instead, you'll find lots of company and high prices there, too. But if you're looking for an outdoor adventure during the summer, ski resorts have plenty of lodging available at great rates.

Similarly, many parents know how hard it is to find a reasonably priced hotel room in a college town on graduation weekend. Likewise, a pipeline break or unsettled political conditions in the Middle East can disrupt the supply of oil and cause the price of gasoline to spike overnight. When higher gas prices continue over a period of time, consumers respond by changing their driving habits or buying more fuel-efficient cars.

Why does all of this happen? Demand and supply tell the story. To have a market, you must have both demand and supply. To understand markets and prices completely, we need to understand these two sides of the market.

What Determines Demand?

Demand exists when an individual or a group wants something badly enough to pay or trade for it. How much an individual or a group actually buys will depend on the **price**. In a market economy, prices are set by the interaction of demand and supply. Again, we need both sides to set a price. The price helps guide goods and services (and, as we'll discuss later, the resources to produce these goods and services) to the people who value them the most. In economics, the amount of a good or service purchased at the current price is known as the **quantity demanded**.

When the price of a good increases, consumers often respond by purchasing less of the good or buying something else. For instance, many consumers who would buy salmon at $5.00 per pound would likely buy something else if the price rose to $20.00 per pound, even if they really, really love salmon. Therefore, as price goes up, quantity demanded goes down. Similarly, as price goes down, quantity demanded goes up. This relationship between the price and the quantity demanded is referred to as the law of demand. The **law of demand** states that, other things being equal, the quantity demanded falls

The **price** is the market-determined opportunity cost of a good or service. It is the key determinant of how market economies allocate goods and services.

The **quantity demanded** is the amount of a good or service that buyers are willing and able to purchase at the current price.

The **law of demand** states that, other things being equal, quantity demanded falls when prices rise, and rises when prices fall.

when the price rises, and the quantity demanded rises when the price falls. This holds true over a wide range of goods and settings.

The Demand Curve

In economics, graphs can help us explain the relationship between two variables or two sets of data. Once we draw the graph, we can then manipulate it to demonstrate how outcomes in the economy will change under different circumstances. Demand and supply are easy to represent in a graph. This graph then enables us to determine prices in the market and see how those prices would change under different circumstances. First, however, we need some data to work with.

A **demand schedule** is a table that shows the relationship between the price of a good and the quantity demanded.

A table that shows the relationship between the price of a good and the quantity demanded is known as a **demand schedule**. Table 3.1 shows Ryan Seacrest's hypothetical demand schedule for salmon. When the price is $20.00 or more per pound, Ryan will not purchase any salmon. However, below $20.00 the amount that Ryan purchases is *inversely* related to the price. (That is, quantity demanded and price move in opposite directions.) For instance, at a price of $10.00, Ryan's quantity demanded is 4 pounds per month. If the price rises to $12.50 per pound, his quantity demanded is 3 pounds. Every time the price increases, Ryan buys less salmon. In contrast, every time the price falls, he buys more. If the price falls to zero, Ryan would demand 8 pounds. That is, even if the salmon is free, there is a limit to how much he demands because he would grow tired of eating the same thing.

A **demand curve** is a graph of the relationship between the prices in the demand schedule and the quantity demanded at those prices.

The numbers in Ryan's demand schedule from Table 3.1 are plotted on a graph, known as a *demand curve* (D), in Figure 3.1. A **demand curve** is a graph of the relationship between the prices in the demand schedule and the quantity demanded at those prices. For simplicity, the demand "curve" is often drawn as a straight line. When economists talk about *demand*, they mean the

TABLE 3.1

Ryan's Demand Schedule for Salmon

Price of salmon (per pound)	Pounds of salmon demanded (per month)
$20.00	0
$17.50	1
$15.00	2
$12.50	3
$10.00	4
$ 7.50	5
$ 5.00	6
$ 2.50	7
$ 0.00	8

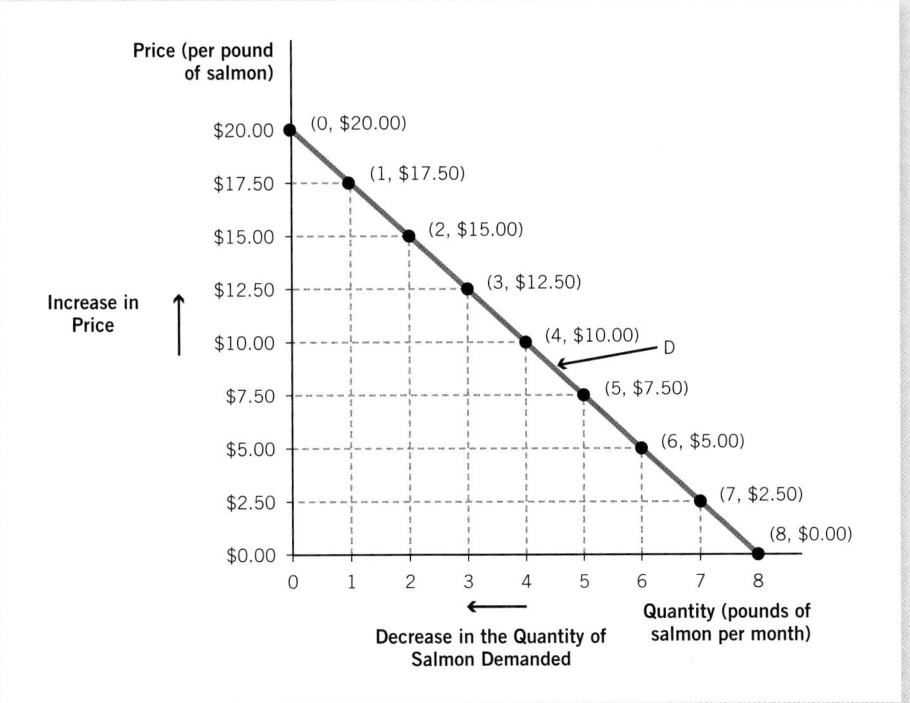

FIGURE 3.1

Ryan's Demand Curve for Salmon

Ryan's demand curve for salmon plots the data from Table 3.1. When the price of salmon is $10.00 per pound, he buys 4 pounds. If the price rises to $12.50 per pound, Ryan reduces the quantity that he buys to 3 pounds. The figure illustrates the law of demand by showing a negative relationship between price and the quantity demanded.

amounts people are willing and able to buy at particular prices. Essentially, they're talking about the relationship between price and quantity demanded as illustrated by the demand curve.

Market Demand

Thus far, we have been looking at one person's demand, but markets are made up of many different buyers. In this section, we will examine the collective demand of all of the buyers in a given market.

The **market demand** is the sum of all the individual quantities demanded by each buyer in a market at each price. During a typical day at Pike Place Market (a public market in Seattle), over 100 individuals buy salmon. However, to make our analysis simpler, let's assume that our market consists of only two buyers, Jeannie and Ryan, both of whom enjoy eating salmon. Figure 3.2 shows individual demand schedules for the two people in this market, a combined market demand schedule, and the corresponding graphs. At a price of $10.00 per pound, Jeannie buys 2 pounds a month ($D_{Jeannie}$), while Ryan buys 4 pounds (D_{Ryan}). To determine the market demand, we add Jeannie's 2 pounds to Ryan's 4 for a total of 6 pounds. As you can see in the table within Figure 3.2, by adding Jeannie and Ryan's demand we arrive at the combined market demand, or D_{Market}.

Market demand is the sum of all the individual quantities demanded by each buyer in the market at each price.

FIGURE 3.2

Calculating Market Demand

To calculate the market demand for salmon, we add Jeannie's demand and Ryan's demand.

Price of salmon (per pound)	Jeannie's demand (per month)	Ryan's demand (per month)	Combined market demand
$20.00	0	0	0
$17.50	0.5	1	1.5
$15.00	1	2	3
$12.50	1.5	3	4.5
$10.00	2	4	6
$ 7.50	2.5	5	7.5
$ 5.00	3	6	9
$ 2.50	3.5	7	10.5
$ 0.00	4	8	12

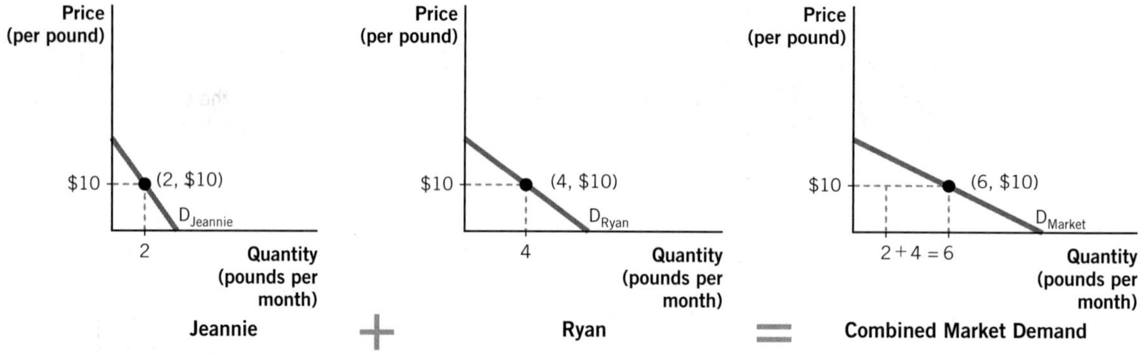

Shifts in the Demand Curve

We have examined the relationship between price and quantity demanded. This relationship, described by the law of demand, shows us that when price changes, consumers respond by altering the amount they purchase. The law of demand is shown on any demand curve (individual or market) with movements up or down the curve that reflect the effect of a price change on the quantity demanded of the good or service. Only a change in price can cause a movement along a demand curve. In addition to price, many other variables influence how much of a good or service is purchased. For instance, news about the possible risks or benefits associated with the consumption of a good or service can change overall demand.

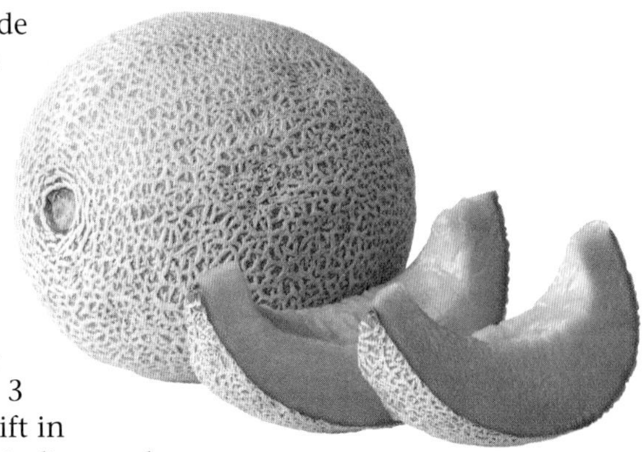

Suppose that the government issues a nationwide safety warning that cautions against eating cantaloupe because of a recent discovery of *Listeria* bacteria in some melons. The government warning would cause consumers to buy fewer cantaloupes at any given price, and overall demand would decline. Looking at Figure 3.3, we see that an overall decline in demand will cause the entire demand curve to shift to the left of the original curve, from D_1 to D_2. Note that although the price remains at $5 per cantaloupe, quantity demanded has moved from 6 melons (on D_1) to 3 (on D_2). Figure 3.3 also shows what does *not* cause a shift in demand curve: the price. The orange arrow along D_1 indicates that the quantity demanded will rise or fall in response to a price change. *A price change causes a movement along a given demand curve, but it cannot cause a shift in the demand curve.*

This may sound like semantics, but it's an important distinction. If price changes, you stay on the same demand curve. *Shifting* demand means that you're moving the entire curve either to the left or to the right. At each

If a new medical study indicates that eating more cantaloupe lowers cholesterol, would this finding cause a shift in demand or a movement along the demand curve?

FIGURE 3.3

A Shift in the Demand Curve

When the price changes, the quantity demanded changes along the existing demand curve (D_1) in the direction of the orange arrow. A shift in the demand curve from D_1 to D_2 or D_3, indicated by the black arrows, occurs when something other than price affects demand.

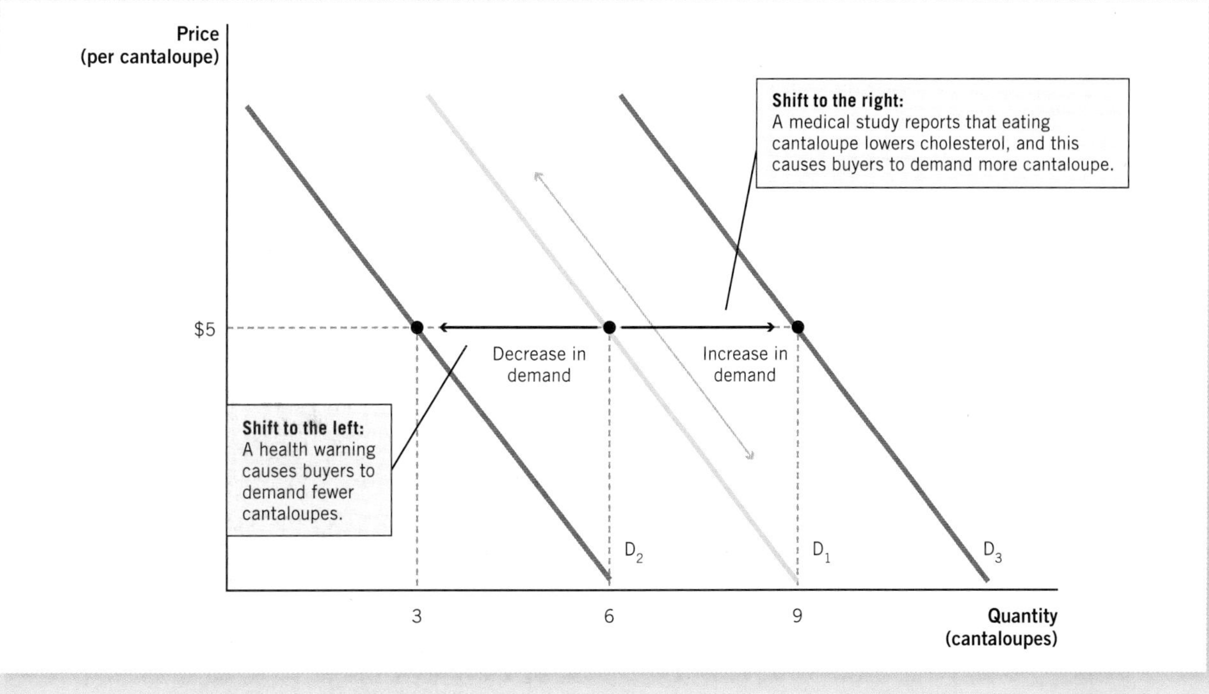

price, there is an entirely new and different quantity demanded. This means that the new demand curve is based on the data in a totally different (new) demand table. However, if price is the only factor that changes, you can use the original demand table and thus the same demand curve. All you need to do is move to a different price and quantity combination on the original demand curve. The demand curve itself does not have to move.

A decrease in overall demand causes the demand curve to shift to the left. But what happens when a variable causes overall demand to *increase*? Suppose that the news media have just announced the results of a medical study indicating that cantaloupe contains a natural substance that lowers cholesterol. Because of the newly discovered health benefit of cantaloupe, overall demand for it will increase. This increase in demand would shift the demand curve to the right, from D_1 to D_3, as Figure 3.3 shows.

Anything that causes a shift in demand impacts buyer behavior. In fact, many different variables can shift demand. These include changes in buyers' income, the price of related goods, changes in buyers' taste and preferences, expectations regarding the future price, and the number of buyers.

Figure 3.4 provides an overview of the variables or factors that can shift demand. The easiest way to keep all of these elements straight is to ask yourself

FIGURE 3.4

Factors That Shift the Demand Curve

The demand curve shifts to the left when a factor adversely affects (decreases) demand. The demand curve shifts to the right when a factor positively affects (increases) demand. (*Note*: a change in price does not cause a shift. Price changes cause movements along the demand curve.)

Factors That Shift Demand to the Left (Decrease Demand)

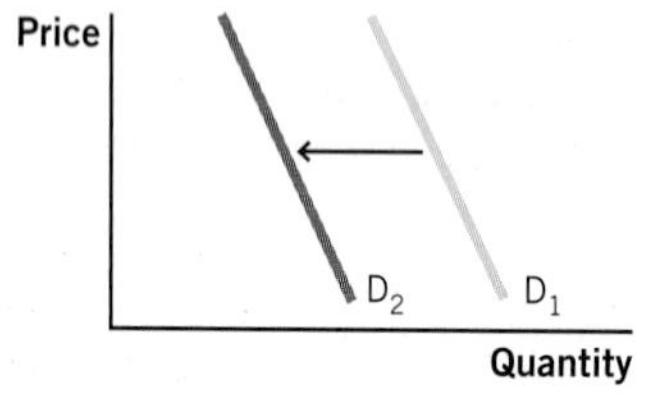

- Income falls (demand for a normal good).
- Income rises (demand for an inferior good).
- The price of a substitute good falls.
- The price of a complementary good rises.
- The good falls out of style.
- There is a belief that the future price of the good will decline.
- The number of buyers in the market falls.

Factors That Shift Demand to the Right (Increase Demand)

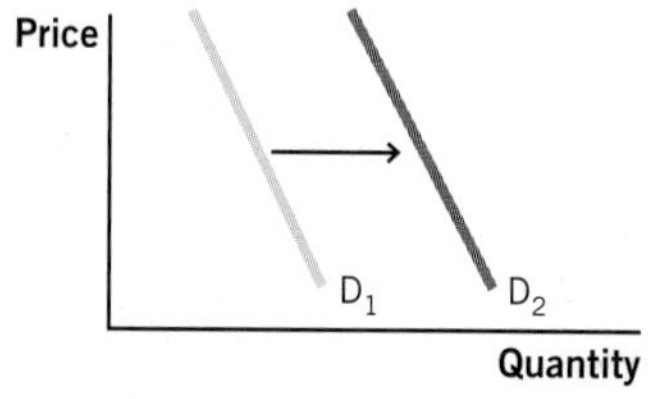

- Income rises (demand for a normal good).
- Income falls (demand for an inferior good).
- The price of a substitute good rises.
- The price of a complementary good falls.
- The good is currently in style.
- There is a belief that the future price of the good will rise.
- The number of buyers in the market increases.

a simple question: *Would this change cause me to buy more or less of the good?* If the change reduces how much you would buy at any given price, you shift the demand curve to the left. If the change increases how much you would buy at any given price, you shift the curve to the right.

Changes in Buyers' Income

When your income goes up, you have more to spend. Assuming that prices don't change, individuals with higher incomes are able to buy more of what they want. Similarly, when your income declines, your purchasing power (how much you can afford) falls. In either case, the amount of income you make affects your overall demand.

When economists look at how consumers spend, they often differentiate between two types of goods: normal and inferior. A consumer will buy more of a **normal good** as his or her income goes up. An example is a meal at a restaurant. When income goes up, the demand for restaurant meals increases and the demand curve shifts to the right. Similarly, if income falls and the demand for restaurant meals goes down, the demand curve shifts to the left.

Consumers buy more of a **normal good** as income rises, holding other things constant.

While a consumer with an increase in income may purchase more of some things, the additional purchasing power will mean that he or she purchases less of other things. A consumer will buy more of an **inferior good** as his or her income falls. Examples include used cars (as opposed to new cars), rooms in boarding houses (as opposed to one's own apartment or house), and Ramen noodles (as opposed to just about any other kind of food). As income goes up, consumers buy less of an inferior good because they can afford something better. Within a specific product market, you can often find examples of inferior and normal goods in the form of different brands. For instance, store brands of cereal, soda, and juice are usually considered inferior to name brands.

Consumers buy more of an **inferior good** as their income falls, holding other things constant.

The Price of Related Goods

Another factor that can shift the demand curve is the price of related goods. Certain goods directly influence the demand for other goods. **Complements** are two goods that are used together. **Substitutes** are two goods that are used in place of each other.

Complements are two goods that are used together, such as color ink cartridges and photo paper. When the price of a complementary good rises, the demand for the related good goes down.

Substitutes are two goods that are used in place of each other, such as butter and margarine. When the price of a substitute good rises, the quantity demanded falls and the demand for the related good goes up.

Consider this pair of complementary goods: color ink cartridges and photo paper. You need both to print a photo in color. What happens when the price of color ink cartridges rises? As you would expect, the quantity demanded of ink cartridges goes down. But demand for its complement, photo paper, also goes down because people are not likely to use one without the other.

Substitute goods work in the opposite way. When the price of a substitute good increases, the quantity demanded declines and the demand for the alternative good increases. For example, if the price of the PlayStation 4 goes up and the price of Microsoft's Xbox remains unchanged, the demand for the Xbox will increase while the quantity demanded of the PlayStation 4 will decline.

In both cases, notice that it's the price of the *related good* that changes, not the price of the good you're examining. If you're looking at the market for the Xbox and the price of the PlayStation 4 goes up, then the demand for the Xbox would rise. If the price of the Xbox goes down, the *quantity demanded* for the Xbox would change, not the demand.

ECONOMICS IN THE MEDIA

Shifting the Demand Curve

The Hudsucker Proxy

This 1994 film chronicles the introduction of the hula hoop, a toy that set off one of the greatest fads in U.S. history. According to Wham-O, the manufacturer of the hoop, when the toy was first introduced in the late 1950s over 25 million were sold in four months.

One scene from the movie clearly illustrates the difference between movements along the demand curve and a shift of the entire demand curve.

The Hudsucker Corporation has decided to sell the hula hoop for $1.79. We see the toy-store owner leaning next to the front door waiting for customers to enter. But business is slow. The movie cuts to the president of the company, played by Tim Robbins, sitting behind a big desk waiting to hear about sales of the new toy. It's not doing well. So the store lowers the price, first to $1.59, then to $1.49, and so on, until finally the hula hoop is "free with any purchase." But even this isn't enough to attract consumers, so the toy-store owner throws the unwanted hula hoops into the alley behind the store.

One of the unwanted toys rolls across the street and around the block before landing at the foot of a boy who is skipping school. He picks up the hula hoop and tries it out. He's a natural. When school lets out, a throng of students rounds the corner and sees him playing with the hula hoop. Suddenly, everyone wants a hula hoop and there is a run on the toy store. Now preferences have changed, and the overall demand has increased. The hula hoop craze is born. In economic terms, we can say that the increased demand has shifted the entire demand curve to the right. The toy store responds by ordering new hula hoops and raising the price to $3.99—the new market price after the increase, or shift, in demand.

This scene reminds us that changes in price cannot shift the demand curve. Shifts in demand can happen only when an outside event influences human behavior. The graph below uses demand curves to show us the effect.

First part of the scene: The price drops from $1.79 to "free with any purchase." Demand doesn't change—we only move downward along the demand curve (D_1), resulting in a negligible increase in the quantity demanded.

Second part of the scene: The hula hoop craze begins, and kids run to the toy store. The sudden change in behavior is evidence of a change in tastes, which shifts the demand curve to the right (D_2).

How did the hula hoop craze start?

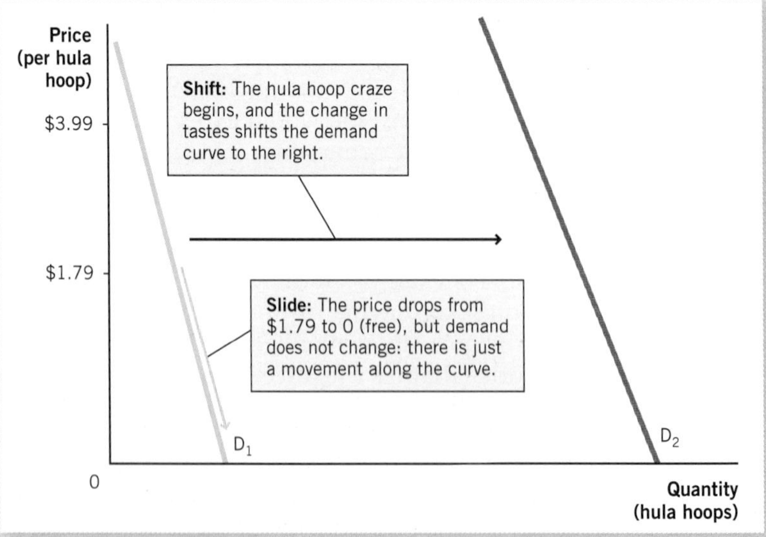

Changes in Tastes and Preferences

Will you be wearing these next year?

In fashion, types of apparel go in and out of style quickly. Walk into Nordstrom or another clothing retailer, and you'll see that fashion changes from season to season and year to year. For instance, what do you think of Chuck Taylor Converse All Star shoes? They were popular 25 years ago and they may be popular again now, but it's safe to assume that Chucks won't be in style forever. While something is popular, demand increases. As soon as the item is no longer in favor, you can expect demand for it to fall. Tastes and preferences can change quickly, and this fluctuation alters the demand for a particular good.

Although changes in fashion trends are usually purely subjective, other changes in preferences are often the result of new information about the goods and services that we buy. Recall our example of shifting demand for cantaloupe as the result of either the *Listeria* contamination or a new positive medical finding. This is one example of how information can influence consumers' preferences. Contamination would cause a decrease in demand because people would no longer want to eat cantaloupe. However, if people learn that eating cantaloupe lowers cholesterol, their demand for the melon will go up.

Price Expectations

Have you ever waited to purchase a sweater because warm weather was right around the corner and you expected the price to come down? Conversely, have you ever purchased an airline ticket well in advance because you figured that the price would rise as the flight filled up? In both cases, expectations about the future influenced your current demand. If we expect a price to be higher tomorrow, we're likely to buy more today to beat the price increase. The result is an increase in current demand. Likewise, if you expect a price to decline soon, you might delay your purchases to try to get a lower price in the future. An expectation of a lower price in the future will therefore decrease current demand.

Pay attention to the fact that we're talking about expectations. The price hasn't changed, but it might. Price might even go in the opposite direction. That's why the demand curve shifts, not the quantity demanded. This particular cause of shifting demand helps explain why people buy and sell stock. Demand rises today on the speculation that price will rise in the future.

The Number of Buyers

Recall that the market demand curve is the sum of all individual demand curves. Therefore, another way to increase overall demand is for more individual buyers to enter the market. For example, the United States adds 3 million people each year to its population through immigration and births. All these new people have needs and wants, just as the existing population of 319 million does. Collectively, immigration and births add about 1% annually to the overall size of many existing markets.

PRACTICE WHAT YOU KNOW

Shift or Movement?

Suppose that a local pizza place likes to run a "late-night special" after 11 p.m. The owners have contacted you for some advice. One of the owners tells you, "We want to increase the demand for our pizza." He proposes two marketing ideas to accomplish this goal:

1. Reduce the price of large pizzas.
2. Reduce the price of a complementary good—for example, offer two half-priced bottles or cans of soda with every large pizza ordered.

Question: Which strategy will you recommend?

Cheap pizza or . . .

. . . cheap drinks?

Answer: First, consider why "late-night specials" exist in the first place. Since most people prefer to eat dinner early in the evening, the pizzeria has to encourage late-night patrons to buy pizzas by stimulating demand. "Specials" of all sorts are held during periods of low demand when regular prices would leave the establishment largely empty.

Next, look at what the question asks. The owners want to know which option would "increase demand" more. The question is very specific; it's looking for something that will increase (or shift) demand.

Consider the first option, a reduction in the price of pizzas. Let's look at this graphically (see below). A reduction in the price of a large pizza causes a movement along the demand curve, or a change in the quantity demanded.

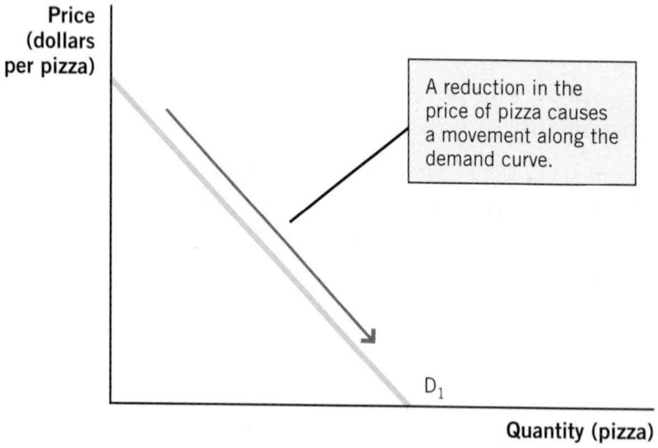

Now consider the second option, a reduction in the price of a complementary good. Let's look at this graphically (see below). A

(CONTINUED)

(CONTINUED)

reduction in the price of a complementary good (like soda) causes the entire demand curve to shift. This is the correct answer, since the question asks which marketing idea would increase (or shift) demand more.

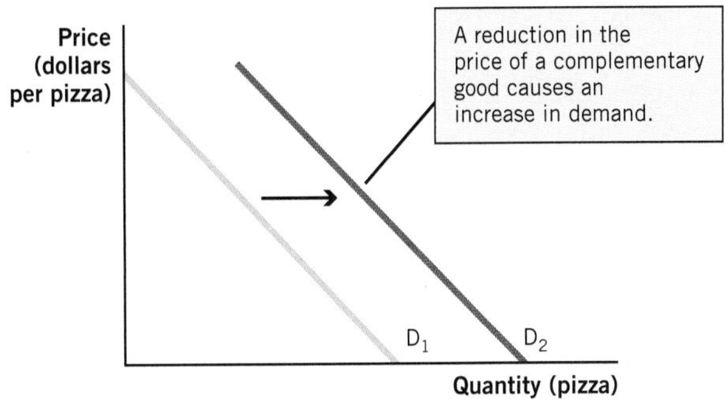

Recall that a reduction in the price of a complementary good shifts the demand curve to the right. This is the correct answer by definition! The other answer, cutting the price of pizzas, will cause an increase in the quantity demanded, or a movement along the existing demand curve.

If you move along a curve instead of shifting it, you'll analyze the problem incorrectly.

The number of buyers also varies by age. Consider two markets—one for baby equipment, such as diapers, high chairs, and strollers, and the other for health care, including medicine, cancer treatments, hip replacement surgery, and nursing facilities. In countries with aging populations (for example, in Italy, where the birthrate has plummeted over several generations), the demand for baby equipment will decline and the demand for health care will expand. Therefore, demographic changes in society are another source of shifts in demand. In many markets, ranging from movie-theater attendance to home ownership, population trends play an important role in determining whether the market is expanding or contracting.

What Determines Supply?

Even though we have learned a great deal about demand, our understanding of markets is incomplete without also analyzing supply. Remember, you can't have a market unless you have both demand and supply. Let's start by focusing on the behavior of producers interested in selling fresh salmon at Pike Place Market.

With demand, price and output are negatively related. With supply, however, the price level and quantity supplied are *positively* related. (That is, they move in the same direction.) For instance, few producers would sell salmon if the market price was $2.50 per pound, but many would sell it if the price was $20.00 per pound. (At $20.00, producers earn more profit than they do at a price of $2.50.) The **quantity supplied** is the amount of a good or service that producers are willing and able to sell at the current price. Higher prices cause the quantity supplied to increase. Conversely, lower prices cause the quantity supplied to decrease.

The **quantity supplied** is the amount of a good or service that producers are willing and able to sell at the current price.

When price increases, producers often respond by offering more for sale. As price goes down, quantity supplied also goes down. This direct relationship between price and quantity supplied is referred to as the law of supply. The **law of supply** states that, other things being equal, the quantity supplied increases when the price rises, and the quantity supplied falls when the price falls. This law holds true over a wide range of goods and settings.

The **law of supply** states that, other things being equal, the quantity supplied of a good rises when the price of the good rises, and falls when the price of the good falls.

The Supply Curve

A **supply schedule** is a table that shows the relationship between the price of a good and the quantity supplied.

A **supply schedule** is a table that shows the relationship between the price of a good and the quantity supplied. The supply schedule for salmon in Table 3.2 shows how many pounds of salmon Sol Amon, owner of Pure Food Fish, would sell each month at different prices. (Pure Food Fish is a fish stand that sells all kinds of freshly caught seafood.) When the market price is $20.00 per pound, Sol is willing to sell 800 pounds. At $12.50, Sol's quantity offered is 500 pounds. If the price falls to $10.00, he offers 400 pounds. Every time the price falls, Sol offers less salmon. This means he is constantly adjusting the amount he offers. As the price of salmon falls, so does Sol's profit from selling

TABLE 3.2

Pure Food Fish's Supply Schedule for Salmon

Price of salmon (per pound)	Pounds of salmon supplied (per month)
$20.00	800
$17.50	700
$15.00	600
$12.50	500
$10.00	400
$ 7.50	300
$ 5.00	200
$ 2.50	100
$ 0.00	0

FIGURE 3.5

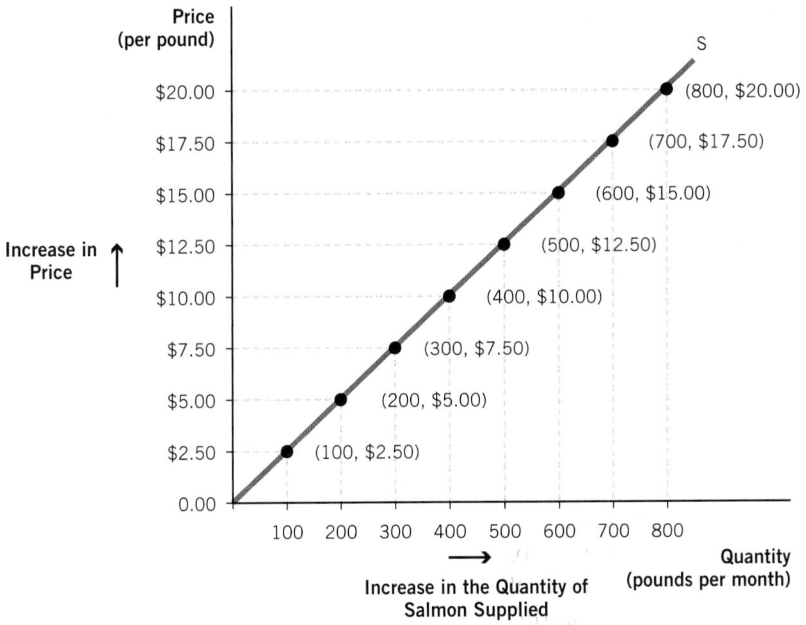

Pure Food Fish's Supply Curve for Salmon

Pure Food Fish's supply curve for salmon plots the data from Table 3.2. When the price of salmon is $10.00 per pound, Pure Food Fish supplies 400 pounds. If the price rises to $12.50 per pound, Pure Food Fish increases its quantity supplied to 500 pounds. The figure illustrates the law of supply by showing a positive relationship between price and the quantity supplied.

it. Since Sol's livelihood depends on selling seafood, he has to find a way to compensate for the lost income. So he might offer more cod instead.

Sol and the other seafood vendors must respond to price changes by adjusting what they offer for sale in the market. This is why Sol offers more salmon when the price rises, and less salmon when the price declines.

When we plot the supply schedule in Table 3.2, we get the *supply curve* (S) shown in Figure 3.5. A **supply curve** is a graph of the relationship between the prices in the supply schedule and the quantity supplied at those prices. When economists refer to *supply,* they mean the amounts that firms are willing and able to produce at particular prices. The supply curve illustrates this relationship.

A **supply curve** is a graph of the relationship between the prices in the supply schedule and the quantity supplied at those prices.

As you can see in Figure 3.5, this relationship produces an upward-sloping curve. By *upward-sloping* we mean the curve moves from the lower-left side of the graph to the upper-right side. Sellers are more willing to supply the market when prices are high, since high prices generate more profits for the business. The upward-sloping curve illustrates a positive relationship between the price and the quantity offered for sale. For instance, when the price of salmon increases from $10.00 to $12.50 per pound, Pure Food Fish will increase the quantity it supplies to the market from 400 to 500 pounds.

Market Supply

Sol Amon is not the only vendor selling fish at the Pike Place Market. The **market supply** is the sum of the quantities supplied by each seller in the market

Market supply is the sum of the quantities supplied by each seller in the market at each price.

at each price. However, to make our analysis simpler, let's assume that our market consists of just two sellers, City Fish and Pure Food Fish, each of which sells salmon. Figure 3.6 shows supply schedules for those two fish sellers and the combined, total-market supply schedule and the corresponding graphs.

Looking at the supply schedule (the table within the figure), you can see that at a price of $10.00 per pound, City Fish supplies 100 pounds of salmon and Pure Food Fish supplies 400. To determine the total (combined) market supply, we add City Fish's 100 pounds ($S_{City\ Fish}$) to Pure Food Fish's 400 ($S_{Pure\ Food\ Fish}$) for a total market supply (S_{Total}) of 500 pounds.

FIGURE 3.6

Calculating Market Supply

Market supply is calculated by adding together the amount supplied by individual vendors. Each vendor's supply, listed in the second and third columns of the table, is illustrated graphically below. The total supply, shown in the last column of the table, is illustrated in the Combined Market Supply graph below.

Price of salmon (per pound)	City Fish's supply (per month)	Pure Food Fish's supply (per month)	Combined market supply (pounds of salmon)
$20.00	200	800	1000
$17.50	175	700	875
$15.00	150	600	750
$12.50	125	500	625
$10.00	100	400	500
$ 7.50	75	300	375
$ 5.00	50	200	250
$ 2.50	25	100	125
$ 0.00	0	0	0

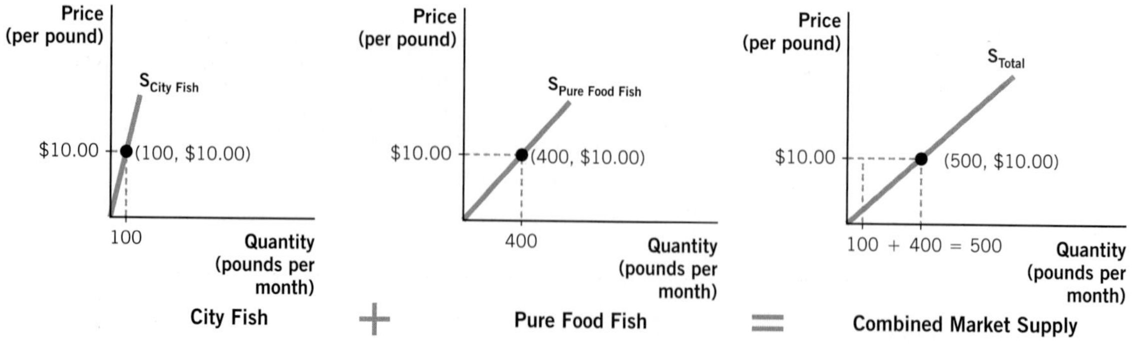

Shifts in the Supply Curve

When a variable that affects a seller's behavior (other than the price) changes, the entire supply curve shifts. For instance, suppose that beverage scientists at Starbucks discover a new way to brew a richer coffee at half the cost. The new process would increase the company's profits because its costs of supplying a cup of coffee would go down. The increased profits as a result of lower costs motivate Starbucks to sell more coffee and open new stores. Therefore, overall supply increases. Looking at Figure 3.7, we see that the supply curve shifts to the right of the original curve, from S_1 to S_2. Note that the retail price of coffee ($3 per cup) hasn't changed. When we shift the curve, we assume that price is constant and that something else has changed. In this case, the new brewing process, which has reduced the cost of producing coffee, has stimulated additional supply—that is, still at a price of $3, quantity rises from Q_1 to Q_2.

We have just seen that an increase in supply causes the supply curve (S) to shift to the right. But what happens when a variable causes supply to decrease? Suppose that a hurricane devastates the coffee crop in Colombia

FIGURE 3.7

A Shift in the Supply Curve

When price changes, the quantity supplied changes along the existing supply curve, illustrated here by the orange arrow. A shift in supply occurs when something other than price changes, illustrated by the black arrows.

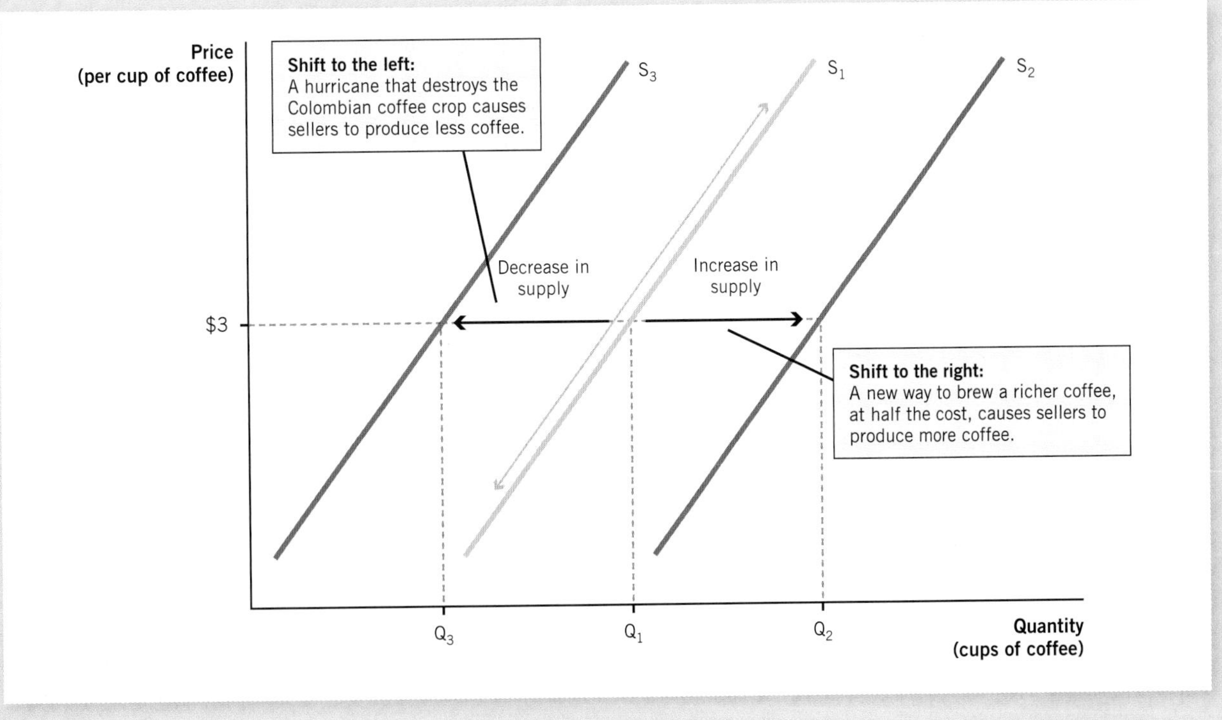

and reduces world supply of coffee beans by 10% for that year. There is no way to make up for the destroyed coffee crop, and for the rest of the year at least, the quantity of coffee supplied will be less than the previous year. This decrease in supply shifts the supply curve in Figure 3.7 to the left, from S_1 to S_3. Thus, still at a price of \$3, quantity falls from Q_1 to Q_3.

It is important to make sure you shift the curve in the proper direction. As we will see shortly, these shifts help us make predictions about the direction of prices and even explain why prices have changed. Just like decreases in demand, decreases in supply are always shown as a movement to the left. An increase is shown as a movement to the right.

Many variables can shift supply, but Figure 3.7 also reminds us of what does *not* cause a shift in supply: the price. Recall that price is the variable that causes the supply curve to slope upward. The orange arrow along S_1 indicates that the quantity supplied will rise or fall in response to a price change. *A price change causes a movement along the supply curve, not a shift in the curve.*

Factors that shift the supply curve include the cost of inputs, changes in technology or the production process, taxes and subsidies, the number of

FIGURE 3.8

Factors That Shift the Supply Curve

The supply curve shifts to the left when a factor negatively affects (decreases) supply. The supply curve shifts to the right when a factor positively affects (increases) supply. (*Note*: a change in price does not cause a shift. Price changes cause movements along the supply curve.)

Factors That Shift Supply to the Left (Decrease Supply)

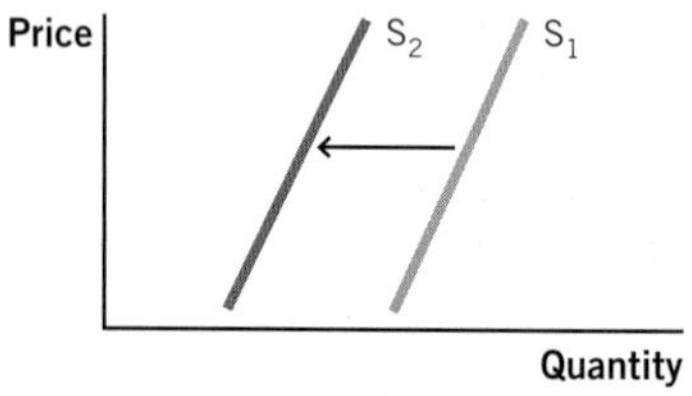

- The cost of an input rises.
- The business adopts inefficient production processes or technology.
- Business taxes increase or subsidies decrease.
- The number of sellers decreases.
- The price of the product is anticipated to rise in the future.

Factors That Shift Supply to the Right (Increase Supply)

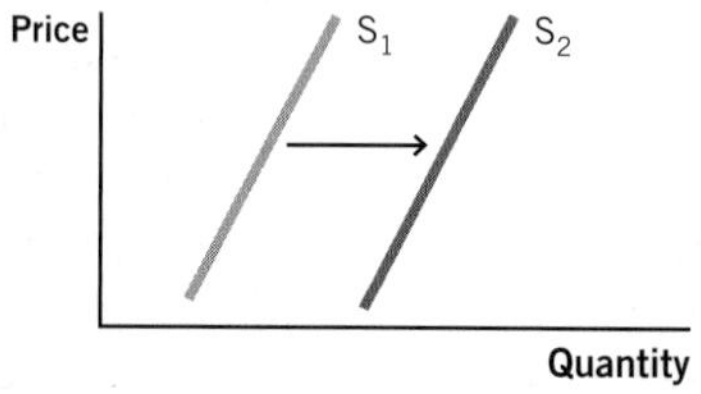

- The cost of an input falls.
- The business deploys more efficient technology.
- Business taxes decrease or subsidies increase.
- The number of sellers increases.
- The price of the product is expected to fall in the future.

firms in the industry, and price expectations. Figure 3.8 provides an overview of the variables that shift the supply curve. The easiest way to keep them all straight is to ask yourself a simple question: *Would the change cause a business to produce more or less of the good?* If the change would reduce the amount of a good or service that a business is willing and able to supply at every given price, the supply curve shifts to the left. If the change would increase the amount of the good or service that a business is willing and able to supply at every given price, the supply curve shifts to the right.

The Cost of Inputs

Inputs are resources used in the production process.

Inputs are resources used in the production process. Inputs can take a number of forms and may include workers, equipment, raw materials, and buildings. Each of these resources is critical to the production process. When the prices of inputs change, so does the seller's profit margin. If the cost of inputs declines, profit margins improve. Improved profit margins make the firm more willing to supply the good. So, for example, if Starbucks is able to purchase coffee beans at a significantly reduced price, it will want to supply more coffee. Conversely, higher input costs reduce profits. For instance, the salaries of Starbucks store employees, or baristas as they are commonly called, are a large part of the production cost. An increase in the minimum wage would require Starbucks to pay its workers more. This would raise the cost of making coffee, cut into Starbucks' profits, and make Starbucks less willing to supply coffee at the same price. (We discuss the minimum wage in more detail in Chapter 4.)

Baristas' wages make up a large share of the cost of selling coffee.

Changes in Technology or the Production Process

Technology encompasses knowledge that producers use to make their products. An improvement in technology enables a producer to increase output with the same resources or to produce a given level of output with fewer resources. For example, if a new espresso machine works twice as fast as the old technology, Starbucks could serve its customers more quickly, reduce long lines, and increase the number of sales it makes. As a result, Starbucks would be willing to produce and sell more espressos at each price in its established menu. In other words, if the producers of a good discover a new and improved technology or a better production process, there will be an increase in supply; that is, the supply curve for the good will shift to the right. If a firm utilizes an inefficient production process, the supply curve will shift to the left. However, firms that make such decisions either quickly return to their original production processes or go out of business.

Taxes and Subsidies

Sometimes, the changes that affect the production process come from outside normal market events. When government steps into markets, things usually change. When government places taxes on suppliers, these taxes become added costs of doing business. For example, the cost of doing business increases when property taxes go up. A firm may attempt to pass along the tax to consumers through higher prices, but higher prices will discourage sales. So, in some cases, the firm will simply have to accept the taxes as an added cost of doing business. Either way, a tax makes the firm less profitable. Lower profits make the firm less willing to supply the product; thus, the tax shifts the supply curve to the left and the overall supply declines.

A **subsidy** is a payment made by the government to encourage the consumption or production of a good or service.

The reverse is true for a **subsidy**, which is a payment made by the government to encourage the consumption or production of a good or service. Consider a hypothetical example in which the government wants to promote flu shots for high-risk groups like the young and the elderly. One approach would be to offer large subsidies to clinics and hospitals, thereby offsetting those firms' costs of immunizing the targeted groups. The subsidy changes the firms' incentives to produce by essentially paying the firms' production costs. The supply curve of immunizations shifts to the right under the subsidy.

The Number of Firms in the Industry

We saw that an increase in total buyers shifts the demand curve to the right. A similar dynamic happens with an increase in the number of sellers in an industry. Each additional firm that enters the market increases the available supply of a good. In graphic form, the supply curve shifts to the right to reflect the increased production. By the same reasoning, if the number of firms in the industry decreases, the supply curve will shift to the left.

Changes in the number of firms in a market are a regular part of business. For example, if a new pizza joint opens up nearby, more pizzas can be produced and supply expands. Conversely, if a pizzeria closes, the number of pizzas produced falls and supply contracts.

Price Expectations

A seller who expects a higher price for a product in the future may wish to delay sales until a time when it will bring a higher price. For instance, florists know that the demand for roses spikes on Valentine's Day and Mother's Day. Because of higher demand, they can charge higher prices. In order to sell more flowers during times of peak demand, many florists work longer hours and hire temporary employees. This enables them to make more deliveries and, therefore, increase their ability to supply flowers while the price is high.

Likewise, the expectation of lower prices in the future will cause sellers to offer more while prices are still relatively high. This effect is particularly noticeable in the electronics sector, where newer—and much better—products are constantly being developed and released. Sellers know that their current offerings will soon be replaced by something better and that consumer demand for the existing technology will then plummet. This means that prices typically fall when a product has been on the market for a time. Since producers know that the price will fall, they supply as many of the new models as possible before the next wave of innovation cuts the price that they can charge.

ECONOMICS IN THE REAL WORLD

Why Are Prices for Tiger Parts Rising?

Of the many animals on the endangered species list, perhaps none is as recognizable as the tiger. One reason for the demise of tiger populations is the demand for their body parts for use in traditional medicines in Asian countries. Everyone acknowledges that continued hunting of the tiger will lead to the elimination of the species, yet the market for tiger parts continues to grow. Why? Supply and demand tell the story.

Two factors seem to be driving demand in this market. First, as countries in Asia have become more prosperous, the income of the average person has risen. As incomes rise, demand for normal goods rises as well. Traditional medicines must be normal goods for enough people in Asia such that the demand keeps rising.

Second, tastes are changing. In parts of the West, some people have begun experimenting with alternative approaches to medicine. A shift toward medical techniques used in places like China has spurred an interest in medications that include tiger parts, leading to a market that by some estimations is worth as much as $6 billion annually.

Despite laws and agreements between countries prohibiting the trade of tiger parts, the market continues to grow. The reason also relates to demand and supply. As demand rises, price goes up, and the new equilibrium price raises the opportunity cost for not participating in this market. At these higher prices, penalties for violating the law are much smaller than the rewards of successfully poaching a tiger. There may only be a limited number of tigers, but if demand continues to increase, higher prices will make hunting them more profitable notwithstanding what the current laws say. ✴

Understanding markets helps explain prices for goods, even when buying and selling things is illegal.

PRACTICE WHAT YOU KNOW

The Supply of and Demand for Ice Cream

Question: Which one of the following will increase the demand for ice cream?

a. a decrease in the price of the butterfat used to make ice cream

b. a decrease in the price of ice cream

c. an increase in the price of the milk used to make ice cream

d. an increase in the price of frozen yogurt, a substitute for ice cream

I scream, you scream, we all scream for ice cream.

Answer: If you answered (b), you made a common mistake. A change in the price of a good cannot change overall market demand; it can only cause a movement along an existing curve. So, as important as price changes are, they are not the right answer. First, you need to look for an event that shifts the entire curve.

Answers (a) and (c) refer to the prices of butterfat and milk. Since these are the inputs of production for ice cream, a change in those input prices will shift the supply curve, not the demand curve. That leaves answer (d) as the only possibility. Answer (d) is correct because the increase in the price of frozen yogurt will cause consumers to look elsewhere. Consumers will substitute away from frozen yogurt and toward ice cream. This shift in consumer behavior will result in an increase in the demand for ice cream even though its price remains the same.

Question: Which one of the following will decrease the supply of chocolate ice cream?

a. a medical report finding that consuming chocolate prevents cancer

b. a decrease in the price of chocolate ice cream

c. an increase in the price of chocolate, an ingredient used to make chocolate ice cream

d. an increase in the price of whipped cream, a complementary good

Answer: Option (b) cannot be the answer because a change in the price of the good cannot change supply; it can only cause a movement along an existing curve. Answers (a) and (d) would both cause a change in demand without affecting the supply curve. That leaves answer (c) as the only possibility. Chocolate is a necessary ingredient used in the production process. Whenever the price of an input rises, profits are squeezed. The result is a decrease in supply at the existing price.

How Do Supply and Demand Shifts Affect a Market?

We have examined supply and demand separately. Now it's time to see how the two interact. The real power and potential of supply-and-demand analysis is in how well it predicts prices and output in the entire market. By summing all of the individual demand and supply curves, we can determine what price and quantity will be set in the market.

Supply, Demand, and Equilibrium

Let's consider the market for salmon again. In Figure 3.9, we see that when the price of salmon fillets is $10.00 per pound, consumers demand 500 pounds and producers supply 500 pounds. This situation is represented graphically at point E, known as the point of **equilibrium**, where the demand curve and the supply curve intersect. At this point, supply and demand are perfectly balanced.

Notice that at $10.00 per fillet, the quantity demanded equals the quantity supplied. At this price, and only at this price, every buyer who wants salmon is able to find some and every producer is able to sell his or her entire stock. We say that $10.00 is the **equilibrium price** because the quantity supplied equals the quantity demanded. Similarly, there is also an **equilibrium quantity** of 500 pounds, at which the quantity supplied equals the quantity

Equilibrium occurs at the point where the demand curve and the supply curve intersect. At equilibrium, supply and demand are perfectly balanced.

The **equilibrium price** is the price at which the quantity supplied is equal to the quantity demanded.

The **equilibrium quantity** is the amount at which the quantity supplied is equal to the quantity demanded.

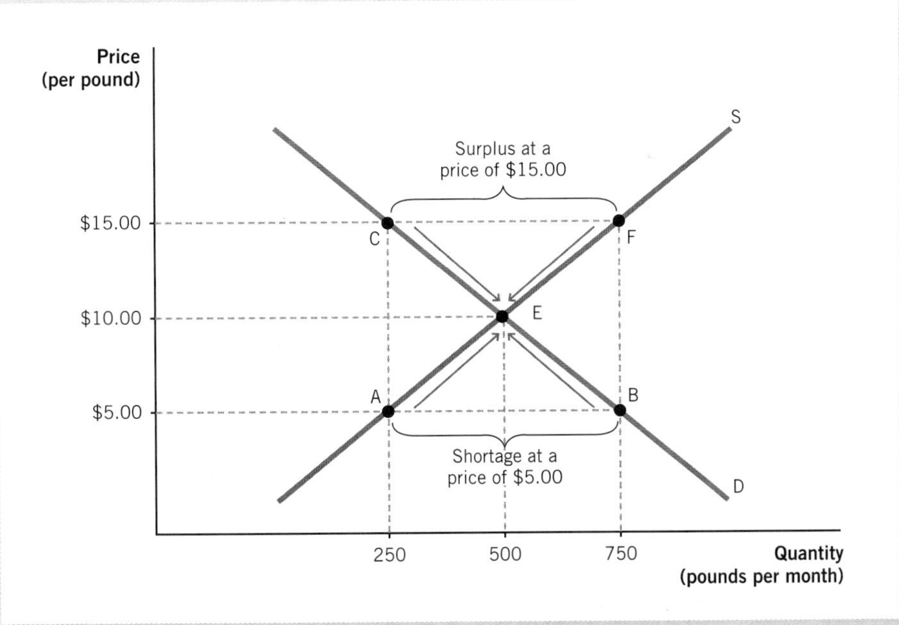

FIGURE 3.9

The Salmon Market

At the equilibrium point, E, quantity supplied and quantity demanded are perfectly balanced. At prices above the equilibrium price, a surplus of goods exists. At prices below the equilibrium price, a shortage of goods exists.

demanded. When the market is in equilibrium, we sometimes say tha *market clears* or that *the price clears the market.*

The equilibrium point has a special place in economics because m ments away from that point throw the market out of balance. The pro ss of getting to equilibrium is so powerful that it is often referred to as the law of supply and demand. According to the **law of supply and demand**, the market price of any good will adjust to bring the quantity supplied and the quantity demanded into balance.

The **law of supply and demand** states that the market price of any good will adjust to bring the quantity supplied and the quantity demanded into balance.

Shortages and Surpluses

How does the market respond when it is not in equilibrium? Let's look at two other prices for salmon shown on the *y* axis in Figure 3.9: \$5.00 and \$15.00 per pound.

At a price of \$5.00 per pound, salmon is quite attractive to buyers but not very profitable to sellers—the quantity demanded is 750 pounds, represented by point B on the demand curve (D). However, the quantity supplied, which is represented by point A on the supply curve (S), is only 250 pounds. So at \$5.00 per pound there is an excess quantity of 750 − 250 = 500 pounds demanded. This excess demand creates disequilibrium in the market.

When there is more demand for a product than sellers are willing or able to supply, we say there is a shortage. A **shortage**, or excess demand**,** occurs whenever the quantity supplied is less than the quantity demanded. New shipments of salmon fly out the door. This provides a strong signal for sellers to raise the price. As the market price increases in response to the shortage, sellers continue to increase the quantity that they offer. You can see this on the graph in Figure 3.9 by following the upward-sloping arrow from point A to point E. At the same time, as the price rises, buyers will demand an increasingly smaller quantity, represented by the upward-sloping arrow from point B to point E along the demand curve. Eventually, when the price reaches \$10.00, the quantity supplied and the quantity demanded will be equal. The market will be in equilibrium.

A **shortage** (also called excess demand) occurs whenever the quantity supplied is less than the quantity demanded.

What happens when the price is set above the equilibrium point—say, at \$15.00 per pound? At this price, salmon is quite profitable for sellers but not very attractive to buyers. The quantity demanded, represented by point C on the demand curve, is 250 pounds. However, the quantity supplied, represented by point F on the supply curve, is 750. In other words, sellers provide 500 pounds more than buyers wish to purchase. This excess supply creates disequilibrium in the market. This situation is known as a surplus. A **surplus**, or excess supply, occurs whenever the quantity supplied is greater than the quantity demanded.

A **surplus** (also called excess supply) occurs whenever the quantity supplied is greater than the quantity demanded.

When there is a surplus, sellers realize that salmon has been oversupplied. This provides a strong signal to lower the price. As the market price decreases in response to the surplus, more buyers enter the market and purchase salmon. Figure 3.9 represents this by the downward-sloping arrow moving from point C to point E along the demand curve. At the same time, sellers reduce output, represented by the downward-sloping arrow moving from point F to point E on the supply curve. As long as the surplus persists, the price will continue o fall. Eventually, the price will reach $10.00 per pound. At this point, the uantity supplied and the quantity demanded will be equal and the market will be in equilibrium again.

When markets work properly, surpluses and shortages are resolved through the process of price adjustment. Buyers who are unable to find enough salmon at $5.00 per pound compete to find the available stocks; this drives the price up. Likewise, businesses that cannot sell their product at $15.00 per pound must lower their prices to reduce inventories; this drives the price down.

Every seller and buyer has a vital role to play in the market. Venues like the Pike Place Market bring buyers and sellers together. Amazingly, all of this happens spontaneously, without the need for government planning to ensure an adequate supply of the goods that consumers want or need. You might think that a decentralized system would create chaos, but nothing could be further from the truth. Markets work because buyers and sellers can rapidly adjust to changes in prices. These adjustments bring balance.

How do markets respond to additional demand? In the case of the bowling cartoon shown here, the increase in demand comes from an unseen customer who wants to use a bowling lane favored by another patron. An increase in the number of buyers causes an increase in demand. The lane is valued by two buyers, instead of just one, so the owner is contemplating a price increase! This is how markets work. Price is a mechanism to determine which buyer wants the good or service the most.

Figure 3.10 provides four examples of what happens when either the supply or the demand curve shifts. As you study these, you should develop a sense for how price and quantity are affected by changes in supply and demand. When one curve shifts, we can make a definitive statement about how price and quantity will change. In Appendix 3A, we consider what happens when supply and demand change at the same time. There you will discover the challenges in simultaneously determining price and quantity when more than one variable changes. In Appendix 3B we examine an extension of demand called elasticity. Now that you know about the law of demand, you know that when price changes quantity demanded changes in the opposite direction. Elasticity focuses on how much the quantity demanded changes in reaction to a change in price.

FIGURE 3.10

Price and Quantity When Either Supply or Demand Changes

Change | **Illustration** | **Impact on price and quantity**

1. Demand increases; supply does not change.

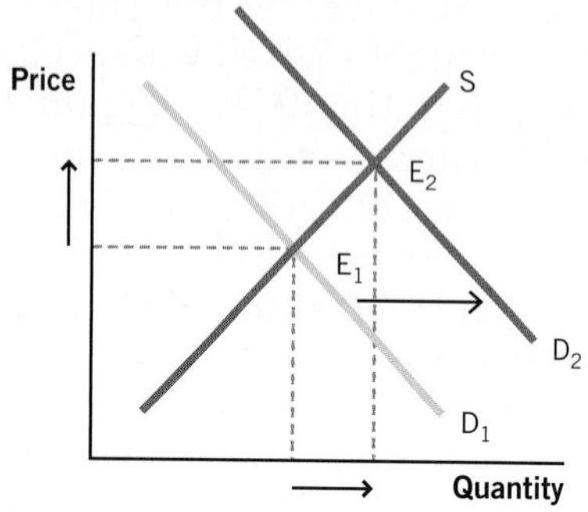

The demand curve shifts to the right. As a result, the equilibrium price and the equilibrium quantity increase.

2. Supply increases; demand does not change.

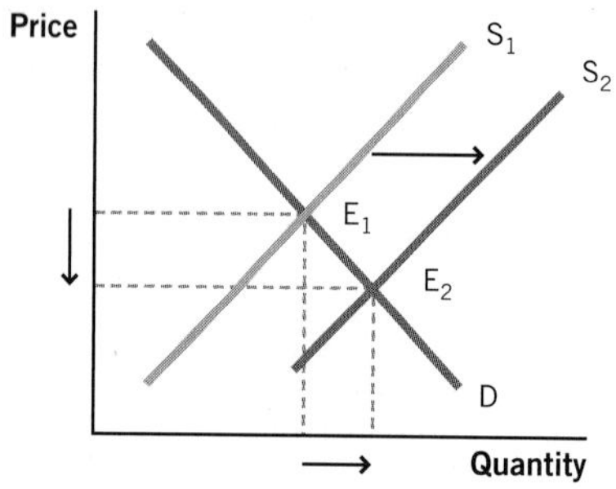

The supply curve shifts to the right. As a result, the equilibrium price decreases and the equilibrium quantity increases.

3. Demand decreases; supply does not change.

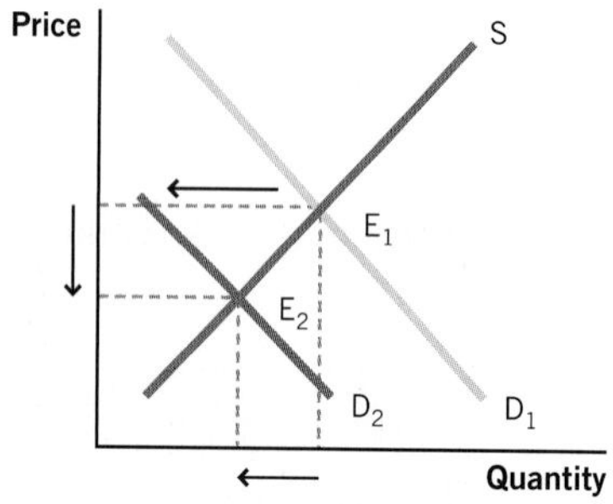

The demand curve shifts to the left. As a result, the equilibrium price and the equilibrium quantity decrease.

4. Supply decreases; demand does not change.

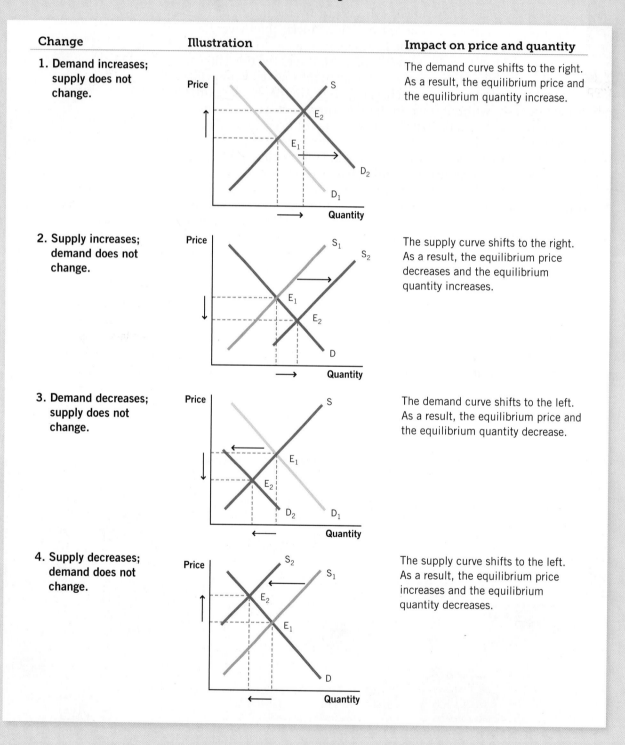

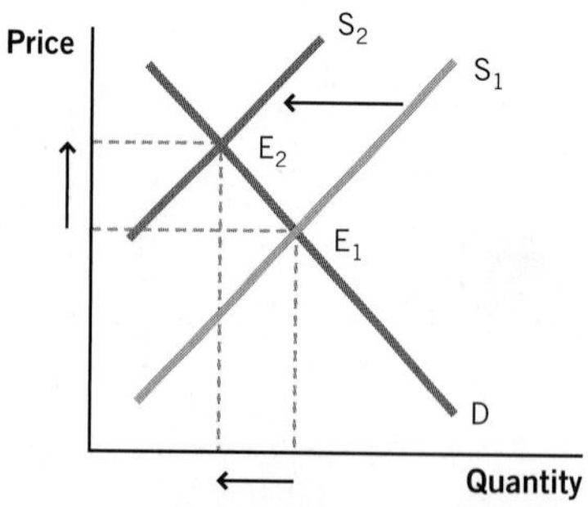

The supply curve shifts to the left. As a result, the equilibrium price increases and the equilibrium quantity decreases.

ECONOMICS FOR LIFE

Bringing Supply and Demand Together: Advice for Buying Your First Home

There is an old adage in real estate: "location, location, location." Why does location matter so much? Simple. Supply and demand. There are only so many places to live in any given location—that is the supply. The most desirable locations have many buyers who'd like to purchase in that area—that is the demand.

Consider for a moment all of the variables that can influence where you want to live. As you're shopping for your new home, you may want to consider proximity to where you work, your favorite restaurants, and public transportation, as well as the quality of the public schools. You'll also want to pay attention to the crime rate, local tax rates, traffic concerns, noise issues, and zoning restrictions. In addition, many communities have restrictive covenants that limit how owners can use their property. Smart buyers determine how the covenants work and whether they would be happy to give up some freedom in order to maintain an attractive neighborhood. Finally, it's always a good idea to visit the neighborhood in the evening or on the weekend to meet your future neighbors before you buy. All of these variables determine the demand for any given property.

Once you've done your homework and settled on a neighborhood, you will find that property values can vary tremendously across very short distances. A home along a busy street may sell for half the price of a similar property that backs up to a quiet park a few blocks away. Properties near a subway line command a premium, as do properties with views or close access to major employers and amenities (such as parks, shopping centers, and places to eat). Here is the main point to remember, even if some of these things aren't important to you: when it comes time to sell, the location of the home will always matter. The number of potential buyers depends on the characteristics of your neighborhood and the size and condition of your property. If you want to be able to sell your place easily, you'll have to consider not only where you want to live now but who might want to live there later.

All of this discussion brings us back to supply and demand. The best locations are in short supply and high demand. The combination of low supply and high demand causes property values in those areas to rise. Likewise, less desirable locations have lower property values because demand is relatively low and the supply is relatively high. Since first-time buyers often have wish lists that far exceed their budgets, considering the costs and benefits will help you find the best available property.

A popular HGTV show called *Property Virgins* follows first-time buyers through the process of buying their first home. If you've never seen the show, watching an episode is one of the best lessons in economics you'll ever get. Check it out, and remember that even though you may be new to buying property, you still can get a good deal if you use some basic economics to guide your decision.

Where you buy is more important than *what* you buy.

Conclusion

Does demand matter more than supply? As you learned in this chapter, the answer is no. Demand and supply contribute equally to the functioning of markets. Five years from now, if someone asks you what you remember about your course in economics, you'll probably respond with two words: "supply" and "demand." These two opposing forces enable economists to model market behavior through prices. Supply and demand help establish the market equilibrium, or the price at which quantity supplied and quantity demanded are in balance. At the equilibrium point, every good and service produced has a corresponding buyer who wants to purchase it. When the market is out of equilibrium, a shortage or surplus exists. These conditions persist until buyers and sellers have a chance to adjust the quantity they demand and the quantity they supply, respectively.

In the next chapter, we will extend our understanding of supply and demand by examining how artificially imposed controls on prices affect markets and equilibrium.

ANSWERING THE BIG QUESTIONS

What are the fundamentals of a market economy?

- In a market economy, resources are allocated among households and firms with little or no government interference.
- Supply and demand interact through the invisible hand.
- An understanding of demand and supply is essential to understanding how markets function.

What determines demand?

- The law of demand states that, other things being equal, quantity demanded falls when prices rise, and rises when prices fall.
- A price change causes a movement along the demand curve, not a shift in the curve.
- Changes in something other than price (including changes in buyers' income, the price of related goods, changes in tastes and preferences, price expectations, and the number of buyers) cause the demand curve to shift.
- The demand curve is downward sloping.

What determines supply?

- The law of supply states that, other things being equal, the quantity supplied of a good rises when the price of the good rises, and falls when the price of the good falls.
- A price change causes a movement along the supply curve, not a shift in the curve.
- Changes in something other than price (the cost of inputs, changes in technology or the production process, taxes and subsidies, the number of firms in the industry, and price expectations) cause the original supply curve to shift.
- The supply curve is upward sloping.

How do supply and demand shifts affect a market?

- Together, supply and demand lead to equilibrium, the balancing point between the two forces. The market-clearing price and output are determined at the equilibrium point, where quantity demanded equals quantity supplied.
- When the price is above the equilibrium point, a surplus exists and inventories build up. Suppliers will lower their price in an effort to sell the unwanted goods. The process continues until the equilibrium price is reached.
- When the price is below the equilibrium point, a shortage exists and inventories are depleted. Suppliers will raise the price until the equilibrium point is reached.

CONCEPTS YOU SHOULD KNOW

complements (p. 59)
demand curve (p. 54)
demand schedule (p. 54)
equilibrium (p. 73)
equilibrium price (p. 73)
equilibrium quantity (p. 73)
inferior good (p. 59)
inputs (p. 69)
law of demand (p. 53)
law of supply (p. 64)
law of supply and demand (p. 74)
market demand (p. 55)
market supply (p. 65)
market economy (p. 52)
normal good (p. 59)
price (p. 53)
quantity demanded (p. 53)
quantity supplied (p. 64)
shortage (p. 74)
subsidy (p. 70)
substitutes (p. 59)
supply curve (p. 65)
supply schedule (p. 64)
surplus (p. 74)

QUESTIONS FOR REVIEW

1. Why does the demand curve slope downward?
2. Does a price change cause a movement along a demand curve or a shift of the entire curve? What factors cause the entire demand curve to shift?
3. Describe the difference between inferior and normal goods.
4. Why does the supply curve slope upward?
5. Does a price change cause a movement along a supply curve or a shift of the entire curve? What factors cause the entire supply curve to shift?
6. Describe the process that leads the market toward equilibrium.
7. What happens in a competitive market when the price is above or below the equilibrium price?
8. What roles do shortages and surpluses play in the market?

STUDY PROBLEMS (*✱ solved at the end of the section*)

1. In the song "Money, Money, Money" by ABBA, one of the lead singers, Anni-Frid Lyngstad, is tired of the hard work life requires and plans to marry a wealthy man. If she is successful, how would this marriage change her demand for goods? Illustrate this change using a demand curve. Be sure to explain what is happening in the diagrams. (*Note:* you can find the full lyrics for the song by Googling the song title and "ABBA"; for inspiration, try listening to the song while you solve the problem.)
2. For each of the following scenarios, determine if there is an increase or a decrease in demand for the good in *italics*.
   a. The price of *oranges* increases.
   b. The cost of producing *tires* increases.
   c. Samantha Brown, who is crazy about *air travel*, gets fired from her job.
   d. A local community has an unusually wet spring and a subsequent problem with mosquitoes, which can be deterred with *citronella*.
   e. Many motorcycle enthusiasts enjoy riding without *helmets* (in states where this is permitted by law). The price of new motorcycles rises.
3. For each of the following scenarios, determine if there is an increase or a decrease in supply for the good in *italics*.
   a. The price of *silver* increases.
   b. Growers of *tomatoes* experience an unusually good growing season.
   c. New medical evidence reports that consumption of *organic products* reduces the incidence of cancer.
   d. The wages of low-skill workers, a resource used to help produce *clothing*, increase.
   e. A new *streaming movie service* enters the market to compete with Netflix.
4. Are laser pointers and cats complements or substitutes? (Not sure? Search for videos of cats and laser pointers online.) Discuss.

✱ 5. The market for ice cream has the following demand and supply schedules:

Price (per quart)	Quantity demanded (quarts)	Quantity supplied (quarts)
$2	100	30
$3	80	45
$4	60	60
$5	40	75
$6	20	90

a. What are the equilibrium price and equilibrium quantity in the ice cream market? Confirm your answer by graphing the demand and supply curves.

b. If the actual price was $3 per quart, what would drive the market toward equilibrium?

6. Starbucks Entertainment announced in a 2007 news release that the Dave Matthews Band's *Live Trax* CD was available only at the company's coffee shops in the United States and Canada. The compilation features recordings of the band's performances dating back to 1995. Why would Starbucks and Dave Matthews have agreed to partner in this way? To come up with an answer, think about the nature of complementary goods and how both sides can benefit from this arrangement.

7. The Baltimore Orioles baseball team wants to determine the equilibrium price for seats for each of the next two seasons. The supply of seats at the ballpark is fixed at 45,000.

Price (per seat)	Quantity demanded in year 1	Quantity demanded in year 2	Quantity supplied
$25	75,000	60,000	45,000
$30	60,000	55,000	45,000
$35	45,000	50,000	45,000
$40	30,000	45,000	45,000
$45	15,000	40,000	45,000

Draw the supply curve and each of the demand curves for years 1 and 2. What are the equilibrium prices in these two years?

✱ 8. Demand and supply curves can also be represented with equations. Suppose that the quantity demanded, Q_D, is represented by the following equation:

$$Q_D = 90 - 2P$$

The quantity supplied, Q_S, is represented by the equation:

$$Q_S = P$$

a. Find the equilibrium price and quantity. **Hint**: Set $Q_D = Q_S$ and solve for the price, P, and then plug your result back into either of the original equations to find Q.

b. Suppose that the price is $20. Determine Q_D and Q_S.

c. At a price of $20, is there a surplus or a shortage in the market?

d. Given your answer in part (c), will the price rise or fall in order to find the equilibrium point?

SOLVED PROBLEMS

5.

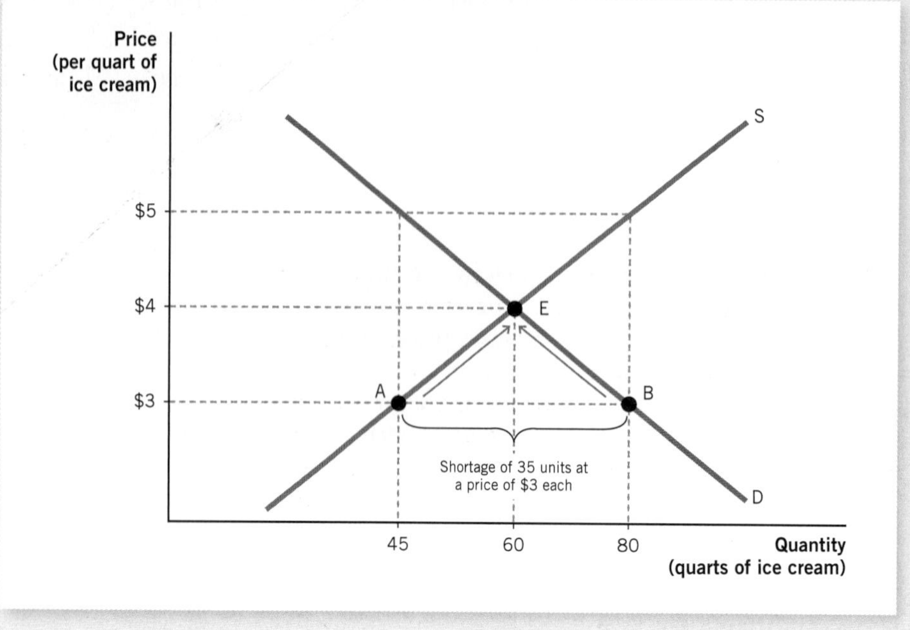

a. The equilibrium price is \$4 and quantity is 60 units (quarts). The next step is to graph the curves. This is done above.

b. A shortage of 35 units of ice cream exists at \$3; therefore, there is excess demand. Ice cream sellers will raise their price as long as excess demand exists—that is, as long as the price is below \$4. It is not until \$4 that the equilibrium point is reached and the shortage is resolved.

8.a. The first step is to set $Q_D = Q_S$. Doing so gives us $90 - 2P = P$. Solving for price, we find that $90 = 3P$, or $P = 30$. Once we know that $P = 30$, we can plug this value back into either of the original equations, $Q_D = 90 - 2P$ or $Q_S = P$. Beginning with Q_D, we get $90 - 2(30) = 90 - 60 = 30$, or we can plug it into $Q_S = P$, so $Q_S = 30$. Since we get a quantity of 30 for both Q_D and Q_S, we know that the price of \$30 is correct.

b. In this part, we plug \$20 into Q_D. This yields $90 - 2(20) = 50$. Now we plug \$20 into Q_S. This yields 20.

c. Since $Q_D = 50$ and $Q_S = 20$, there is a shortage of 30 units.

d. Whenever there is a shortage of a good, the price will rise in order to find the equilibrium point.

Changes in Both Demand and Supply

APPENDIX

3A

We have considered what would happen if supply *or* demand changed. But life is often more complex than that. To provide a more realistic analysis, we need to examine what happens when supply and demand both shift at the same time. Doing this adds considerable uncertainty to the analysis.

Suppose that a major drought hits the northwestern United States. The water shortage reduces both the amount of farmed salmon and the ability of wild salmon to spawn in streams and rivers. Figure 3A.1(a) shows the ensuing decline in the salmon supply, from S_1 progressively leftward, represented by the dotted supply curves. At the same time, a medical journal reports that people who consume at least four pounds of salmon a month live five years longer than those who consume an equal amount of cod. Figure 3A.1(b) shows the ensuing rise in the demand for salmon, from D_1 progressively rightward, represented by the dotted demand curves. This scenario leads to a twofold change. Because of the water shortage, the supply of salmon shrinks. At the same time, new information about the health benefits of eating salmon causes demand for salmon to increase.

It is impossible to predict exactly what happens to the equilibrium point when both supply and demand are shifting. We can, however, determine a region where the resulting equilibrium point must reside.

In this situation, we have a simultaneous decrease in supply and increase in demand. Since we do not know the magnitude of the supply reduction or the demand increase, the overall effect on the equilibrium quantity cannot be determined. This result is evident in the shaded purple region in Figure 3A.1(c). The points where supply and demand cross within this area represent the set of possible new market equilibriums. Since each of the possible points of intersection in the purple region occurs at prices greater than $10.00 per pound, we know that the price must rise. However, the left half of the purple region produces equilibrium quantities less than 500 pounds of salmon, while the right half of the purple region results in equilibrium quantities greater than 500. Therefore, the equilibrium quantity may rise or fall.

The world we live in is complex, and often more than one variable will change simultaneously. When this occurs, it's not possible to be as definitive as when only one variable—supply or demand—changes. You should think of the new equilibrium not as a single point but as a range of outcomes represented by the shaded purple area in Figure 3A.1(c). Therefore, we cannot be exactly sure at what point the new price *and* quantity will settle. For a closer look at four possibilities, see Figure 3A.2.

FIGURE 3A.1

A Shift in Supply and Demand

When supply and demand both shift, the resulting equilibrium can no longer be identified as an exact point. This result is shown in panel (c), which combines the supply shift in panel (a) with the demand shift in panel (b). When supply decreases and demand increases, the result is that the price must rise, but the equilibrium quantity can either rise or fall.

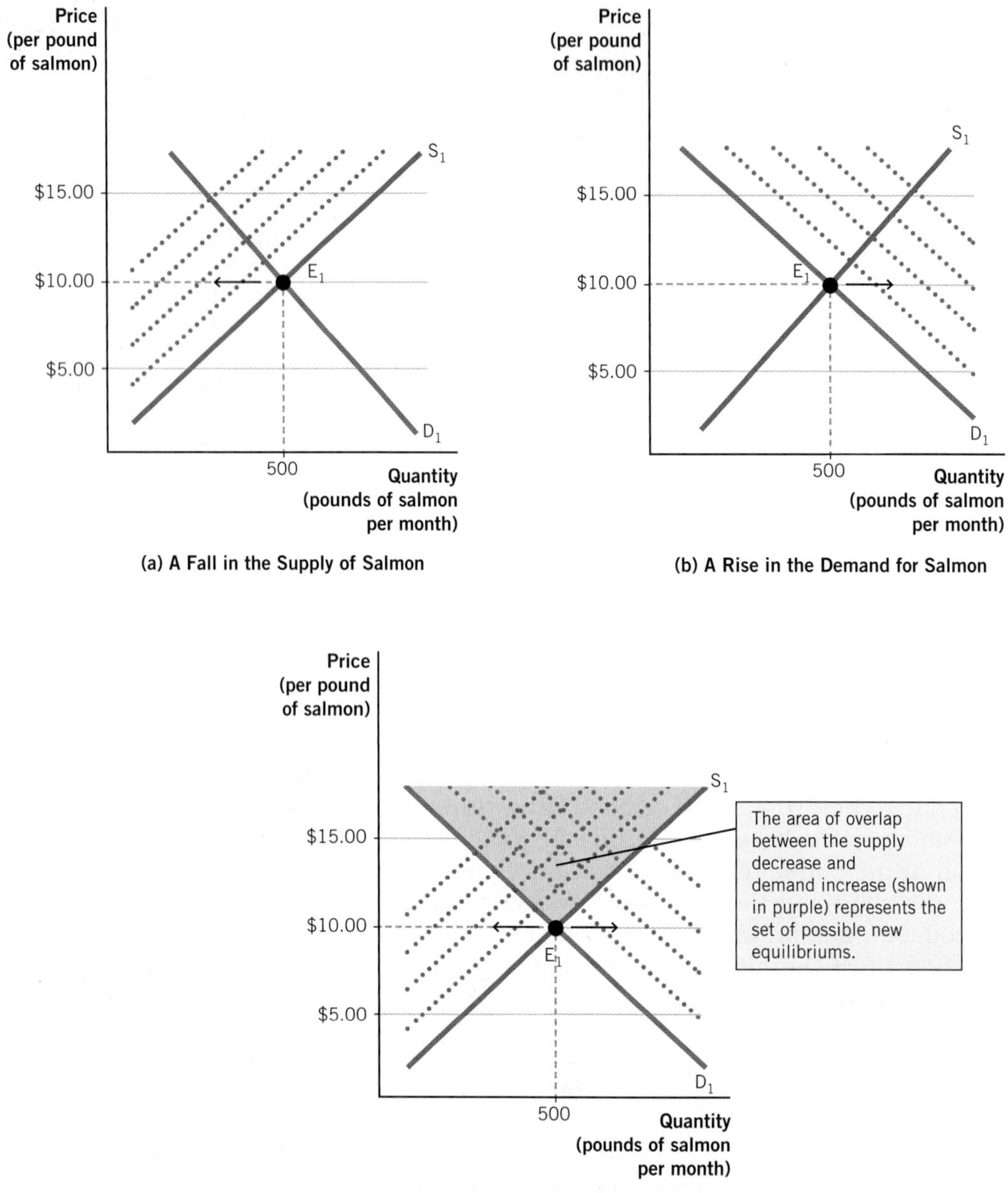

(c) Possible Equilibriums after Supply Decreases and Demand Increases

FIGURE 3A.2

Price and Quantity When Demand and Supply Both Change

Change | **Illustration** | **Impact on price and quantity**

1. Demand and supply both increase.

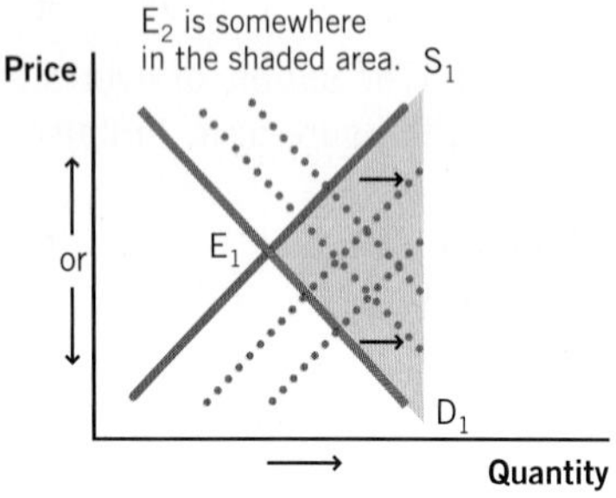

The demand and supply curves shift to the right. The shifts reinforce each other with respect to quantity, which increases, but they act as countervailing forces along the Price axis. Price could be either higher or lower.

2. Demand and supply both decrease.

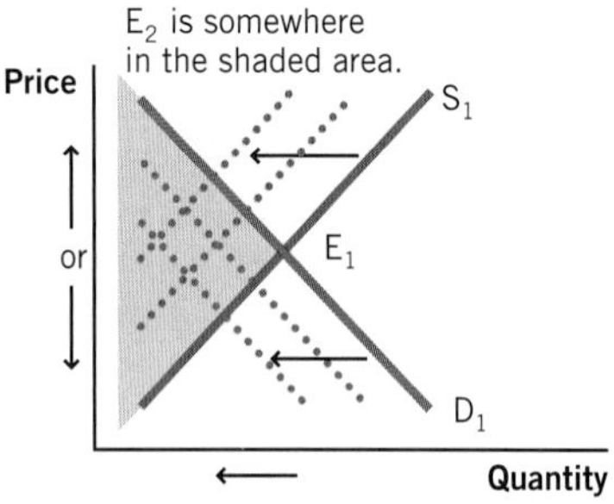

The demand and supply curves shift to the left. The shifts reinforce each other with respect to quantity, which decreases, but they act as countervailing forces along the Price axis. Price could be either higher or lower.

3. Demand increases and supply decreases.

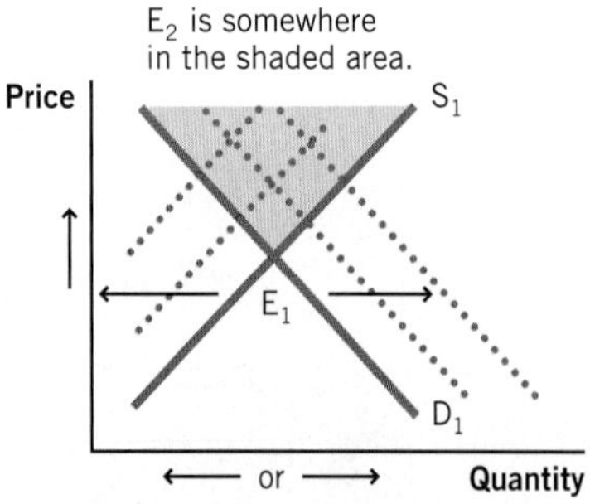

The demand curve shifts to the right and the supply curve shifts to the left. The shifts reinforce each other with respect to price, which increases, but they act as countervailing forces along the Quantity axis. Quantity could be either higher or lower.

4. Demand decreases and supply increases.

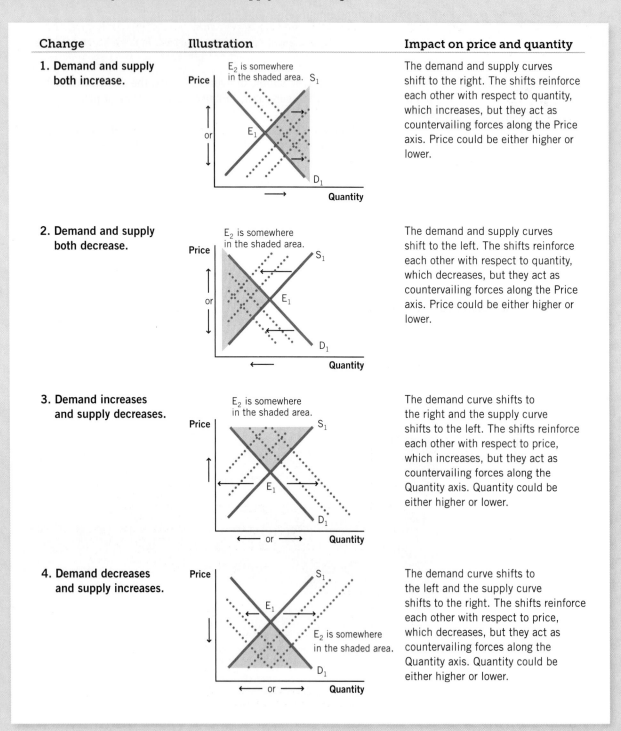

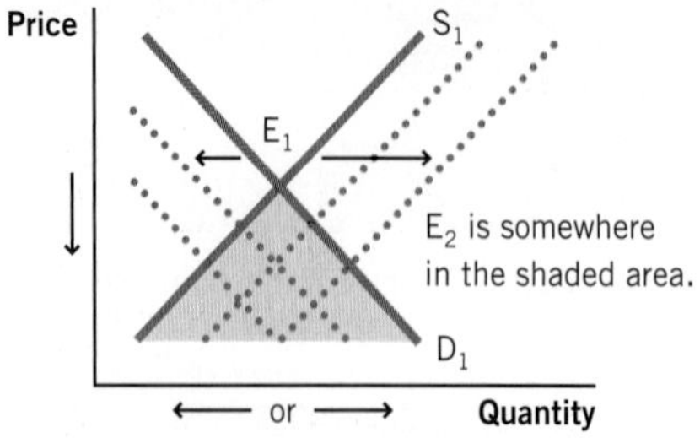

The demand curve shifts to the left and the supply curve shifts to the right. The shifts reinforce each other with respect to price, which decreases, but they act as countervailing forces along the Quantity axis. Quantity could be either higher or lower.

PRACTICE WHAT YOU KNOW

When Supply and Demand Both Change: Hybrid Cars

Question: At lunch, two friends engage in a heated argument. Their exchange goes like this:

The first friend begins, "The supply of hybrid cars and the demand for hybrid cars will both increase, I'm sure of it. I'm also sure the price of hybrids will go down."

The second friend interrupts, "I agree with the first part of your statement, but I'm not sure about the price. In fact, I'm pretty sure that hybrid prices will rise."

They go back and forth endlessly, each unable to convince the other, so they turn to you for advice. What do you say to them?

Answer: Either of your friends could be correct. In this case, supply and demand both shift out to the right, so we know that the quantity bought and sold will increase. However, an increase in supply would normally lower the price, and an increase in demand would typically raise the price. Without knowing which of these two effects on price is stronger, you can't predict how the price will change. The overall price will rise if the increase in demand is larger than the increase in supply. However, if the increase in supply is larger than the increase in demand, the price will fall. But your two friends don't know which condition will be true—so they're locked in an argument that neither can win!

Hybrid cars are becoming increasingly common.

QUESTIONS FOR REVIEW

1. What happens to price and quantity when supply and demand change at the same time?
2. Is there more than one potential equilibrium point when supply and demand change at the same time?

STUDY PROBLEM

1. Check out the short video at abcnews.com called "Crude Oil Slumps to a 6-Year Low" from 2015 (http://abcnews.go.com/Business/video/crude-oil-slumps-year-low-29666552). Using your understanding of the market forces of supply and demand, explain how the market works. Add in a global economic slowdown to illustrate how decreasing global demand for oil has impacted the equilibrium price.

APPENDIX

3B Elasticity

We know how a change in price affects how much we buy. If the price goes up, we typically buy less. If the price falls, we usually buy more. But we don't react to all price changes in the same proportion. For example, pasta fans may prefer linguini to spaghetti or angel hair, but all three taste about the same and can be substituted for one another in a pinch. With goods such as pasta, for which consumers can easily purchase a substitute, we think of demand as being *responsive* to changes in price. That is, a small change in price will likely cause many people to switch from one good to a substitute.

In contrast, many things in life are irreplaceable or have few good substitutes. Examples include insulin and a hospital emergency room visit. A significant rise in price for either of these items would probably not cause you to consume a smaller quantity. If the price of insulin goes up and you're diabetic, you need the insulin. You could try to treat a serious medical crisis without a visit to the ER—but the consequences of making a mistake would likely be disastrous. In these cases, we say that consumers are *unresponsive*, or unwilling to change their behavior, even when the price of the good or service changes.

The responsiveness of buyers and sellers to changes in price or income is known as **elasticity**. In general, demand is **elastic** when it is responsive to price changes. When demand is elastic and price rises, buyers end up purchasing a lot less because they react to the price change. Demand is **inelastic** when it is less responsive to price changes. When demand is inelastic and price rises, consumers will buy less, but not a lot less because they don't react much to a change in price. Elasticity is a useful concept because it allows us to measure how much consumers and producers change their behavior when prices or income change. In the next section, we look at the factors that determine the elasticity of demand.

Elasticity is a measure of the buyers' and sellers' responsiveness to changes in price or income.

Elastic describes a demand condition in which consumers are responsive to a change in price.

Inelastic describes a demand condition in which consumers are not very responsive to a change in price.

Determinants of the Price Elasticity of Demand

The **price elasticity of demand** measures the responsiveness of quantity demanded to a change in price.

The **price elasticity of demand** is a measure of the responsiveness of quantity demanded to a change in price.

Four determinants play a crucial role in influencing the price elasticity of demand. These are the existence of substitutes, the share of the budget spent on a good, whether the good is a necessity or a luxury good, and the time available to adjust to a price change.

The Existence of Substitutes

The most important determinant of price elasticity is the number of substitutes available. When substitutes are plentiful, market forces tilt in favor of the consumer. For example, imagine that an unexpected freeze in Florida reduces the supply of oranges. As a result, the supply of orange juice shifts to the left. Since demand remains unchanged, the price of orange juice rises. However, the consumer of orange juice can find many good substitutes. Since cranberries, grapes, and apple crops are unaffected by the Florida freeze, prices for juices made with those fruits remain unchanged. Thus, consumers have a choice: they can continue to buy orange juice at a higher price or choose to pay a lower price for a fruit juice that may not be their first choice but is nonetheless acceptable. Faced with higher orange juice prices, some consumers will switch. How quickly this switch takes place, and to what extent consumers are willing to replace one product with another, determines whether demand is elastic or inelastic. Since many substitutes for orange juice exist, the price elasticity of demand for orange juice is elastic, or responsive to price changes.

Beyoncé is irreplaceable.

What if there are no good substitutes? Disneyland is billed as the "happiest place on Earth." Kids dream of going to see Mickey and Minnie at Disneyland because they can't see those two famous mice in person anywhere else (well, maybe at Disney World). While there are many other amusement parks in the United States, the Disney parks have established themselves as unique places with no close substitutes; this makes demand for Disney park visits more inelastic, or less responsive to price changes.

To some degree, the price elasticity of demand depends on consumer preferences. For instance, sports fans are often willing to shell out big bucks to follow their passions. Amateur golfers can play the same courses that professional golfers do. But the opportunity to golf where the professionals play doesn't come cheaply. A round of golf at Pebble Beach, a famous course in California, costs close to $500. Why are some golfers willing to pay that much? For an avid golfer with the financial means, the experience of living out the same shots seen on television tournaments is worth $500. In this case, demand is inelastic—the avid golfer doesn't view other golf courses as good substitutes. However, a less enthusiastic golfer, or one without the financial resources, is happy to golf on a less expensive course. When less expensive courses serve as good substitutes, the price tag makes demand elastic. Ultimately, whether demand is inelastic or elastic depends on buyers' preferences and resources.

The Share of the Budget Spent on the Good

Despite the example above of an avid golfer, in most cases the price is a critical element in determining what we can afford and what we'll choose to buy. If you plan to purchase a 70-inch-screen TV, which can cost as much as $3,000, you'll probably be willing to take the time to find the best deal. Because of the high price, even a

Saving 10% on this purchase adds up to hundreds of dollars.

Saving 10% on this purchase amounts to a few pennies.

small-percentage discount in the price can cause a relatively large change in consumer demand. A "10% off sale" may not sound like much, but when purchasing a big-ticket item like a big-screen TV, it can mean hundreds of dollars in savings. In this case, the willingness to shop for the best deal indicates that the price matters, so demand is elastic.

The price elasticity of demand is much more inelastic for inexpensive items on sale. For example, if a candy bar is discounted 10%, the price falls by pennies. The savings from switching candy bars isn't enough to make a difference in what you can afford elsewhere. Therefore, the incentive to switch is small. Most consumers still buy their favorite candy since the price difference is so insignificant. In this case, demand is inelastic because the savings gained by purchasing a less desirable candy bar are small in comparison to the consumer's budget.

Incentives

Necessities versus Luxury Goods

A big-screen TV and a candy bar are both luxury goods. You don't need to have either one. But some goods are necessities. For example, you have to pay your rent and water bill, purchase gasoline for your car or fares for public transportation, and eat. When a consumer purchases a necessity, he or she is generally thinking about the need, not the price. When the need trumps the price, we expect demand to be relatively inelastic. Therefore, the demand for things like emergency room visits, sunscreen at the beach, and electricity all tend to have inelastic demand.

The Time Available to Adjust to a Price Change

When the market price changes, consumers respond. But that response does not remain the same over time. As time passes, consumers are able to find substitutes. To understand these different market responses, economists consider time. Specifically, how much time do you have to respond to a change in price?

If you need something immediately, there is no time for you as a consumer to adjust your behavior. Consider the demand for gasoline. When the gas tank is empty, you have to stop at the nearest gas station and pay the posted price. Filling up as soon as possible is more important than driving around searching for the lowest price. Inelastic demand exists whenever price is secondary to the desire to attain a certain amount of the good. So in the case of an empty tank, the demand for gasoline is inelastic.

But what if your tank isn't empty? If you have some time before running out of gas, you can search for a better price. When consumers have some time to make a purchase, they gain flexibility. They can shop for lower prices at the pump, carpool to save gas, or even change how often they drive. In the short run, flexibility reduces the demand for expensive gasoline and makes consumer demand more elastic.

TABLE 3B.1

Developing Intuition for the Price Elasticity of Demand

Example	Discussion	Overall elasticity
Football tickets for a true fan 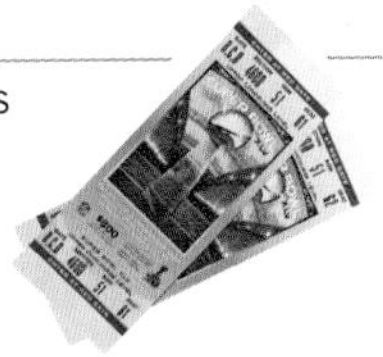	Being able to watch a game live and go to pre- and post-game tailgate parties is a unique experience. For many fans, the experience of going to the game has few close substitutes; therefore, the demand is relatively inelastic.	Tends to be relatively inelastic
Assigned textbooks for a class 	The information inside a textbook is valuable. Substitutes such as older editions and free online resources are not exactly the same. As a result, most students buy the required course materials. The fact that a textbook is needed in the short run (for a few months while taking a class) also tends to make the demand inelastic.	Tends to be inelastic
A slice of pizza from Domino's 	In most locations, many pizza competitors exist, so there are many close substitutes. This tends to make the demand for a particular brand of pizza elastic.	Tends to be elastic
A silver Ford Escape 	There are many styles, makes, and colors of cars to choose from. With large purchases, consumers are sensitive to smaller percentages of savings. Moreover, people typically plan their car purchases many months or years in advance. The combination of all these factors makes the demand for any particular model and color relatively elastic.	Tends to be relatively elastic.

We have looked at four determinants of elasticity of demand—substitutes, the share of the budget spent on the good, necessities versus luxury goods, and time. Each is significant, but the number of substitutes tends to be the most influential factor and dominates the others. Table 3B.1 will help you develop your intuition about how different market situations influence the overall elasticity of demand.

Computing the Price Elasticity of Demand

Until this point, our discussion of elasticity has been descriptive. However, to apply the concept of elasticity in decision-making, we need to be able to view it in a more quantitative way. For example, if the owner of a business is trying to decide whether to put a good on sale, he or she needs to be able to estimate how many new customers would purchase the good at the sale price. Or if a government is considering a new tax, it needs to know how much revenue that tax would generate. These are questions about elasticity that we can evaluate by using a mathematical formula.

The Price Elasticity of Demand Formula

Consider an owner of a pizzeria who is trying to attract more customers. For one month, he lowers the price by 10% and is pleased to find that sales jump by 30%.

Here is the formula for the price elasticity of demand (E_D):

(Equation 3B.1) $$\text{Price elasticity of demand} = E_D = \frac{\text{percentage change in the quantity demanded}}{\text{percentage change in price}}$$

Using the data from the pizzeria example, we can calculate the price elasticity of demand as follows:

$$\text{Price elasticity of demand} = E_D = \frac{30\%}{-10\%} = -3$$

How do we read this equation? The price elasticity of demand, –3 in this case, is expressed as a coefficient with a specific sign (it has a minus in front of it). The coefficient, 3, tells us how much the quantity demanded changed (30%) compared to the price change (10%). In this case, the percentage change in the quantity demanded is three times the percentage change in the price. Whenever the percentage change in the quantity demanded is larger than the percentage change in price, we say that demand is *elastic*. In other words, the price drop made a big difference in how much pizza consumers purchased from the pizzeria. If the opposite occurs and a price drop makes a small difference in the quantity that consumers purchase, we say that demand is *inelastic*.

The negative (minus) sign in front of the coefficient is equally important. Recall that the law of demand describes an inverse relationship between the price of a good and the quantity demanded; when price rises, the quantity demanded falls. The E_D coefficient reflects this inverse relationship with a negative sign. In other words, the pizzeria drops its price and consumers buy more pizza. Since pizza prices and consumer purchases of pizza generally move in opposite directions, the sign of the price elasticity of demand is almost always negative.

CONCEPTS YOU SHOULD KNOW

elastic (p. 88)
elasticity (p. 88)
inelastic (p. 88)
price elasticity of demand (p. 88)

QUESTIONS FOR REVIEW

1. Define the price elasticity of demand.
2. What are the four determinants of the price elasticity of demand?
3. Give an example of a good that has elastic demand. Also give an example of a good that has inelastic demand.

STUDY PROBLEMS (*✱ solved at the end of the section*)

1. Search YouTube for the video titled *Black Friday 2006—Best Buy Line*. Do the early shoppers appear to have elastic or inelastic demand on Black Friday? Explain your response.
2. College logo T-shirts priced at \$15 sell at a rate of 25 per week, but when the bookstore marks them down by 33%, it finds that it can sell twice as many T-shirts per week. What is the price elasticity of demand for the logo T-shirts?
3. Characterize each of the following goods as relatively elastic or relatively inelastic.
   a. a life-saving medication
   b. photocopies at a copy shop, when all competing shops charge 10 cents per copy
   c. a fast-food restaurant located in the food court of a shopping mall
   d. the water bill you pay
4. Do customers who visit convenience stores at 3 a.m. have a price elasticity of demand that is more or less elastic than those who visit at 3 p.m.?
5. ✱ One of the gas stations in your town begins selling gas at 5% below the price of every other station. As a result, you increase your purchase of gas at that station by 25%. What is your price elasticity of demand for gas from this station? Is this demand elastic or inelastic?

SOLVED PROBLEM

5. In this question, the gas station is dropping its price by 5%. Your quantity demanded increases by 25%. To determine the price elasticity of demand, you put these values into equation (3B.1):

$$\text{Price elasticity of demand} = E_D = \frac{\text{percentage change in quantity demanded}}{\text{percentage change in price}}$$

$$E_D = 25\% \div (-5\%) = -5$$

Since the percentage change in quantity demanded is greater than the percentage change in price, demand for gas from this station is elastic.

CHAPTER

4 Market Efficiency

MISCONCEPTION

The minimum wage helps everyone earn a living wage.

You are probably familiar with the minimum wage, which is an example of a *price control.* If you've ever worked for the minimum wage, you probably think that raising it sounds like a great idea. You may support minimum-wage legislation because you believe it will help struggling workers to make ends meet. After all, it seems reasonable that firms should pay a living wage to cover necessities.

Price controls are not a new idea. The first recorded attempt to control prices was four thousand years ago in ancient Babylon, when King Hammurabi decreed how much corn a farmer could pay for a cow. Similar attempts to control prices occurred in ancient Egypt, Greece, and Rome. Each attempt ended badly. In Egypt, farmers revolted against tight price controls and intrusive inspections, eventually causing the economy to collapse. In Greece, the Athenian government set the price of grain at a very low level. Predictably, the quantity of grain supplied dried up. In 301 CE, the Roman government under Emperor Diocletian prescribed the maximum price of beef, grains, clothing, and many other items. Almost immediately, markets for these goods disappeared.

History has shown us that price controls generally do not work. Why? Because they disrupt the normal functioning of the market. By the end of this chapter, we hope you will understand the importance of market efficiency and how price controls (such as minimum-wage laws) erode that efficiency. Higher wages or lower prices may sound good on the surface, but there are always trade-offs. However, interfering with markets can lead to unintended consequences.

The Code of Hammurabi established the first known price controls.

BIG QUESTIONS

- What are consumer surplus and producer surplus?
- When is a market efficient?
- When do price ceilings matter?
- What effects do price ceilings have on economic activity?
- When do price floors matter?
- What effects do price floors have on economic activity?

What Are Consumer Surplus and Producer Surplus?

Markets create value by bringing together buyers and sellers so that consumers and producers can mutually benefit from trade. As a result of trade, both parties are better off and economic well-being is enhanced. In competitive markets, the equilibrium price is simultaneously low enough to attract consumers and high enough to encourage producers. This balance between demand and supply enhances the well-being of society. That is not to say that society's well-being depends solely on markets. People also find satisfaction in many non-market settings, including spending time with their families and friends, and doing hobbies and charity work. Unfortunately, these non-market aspects are difficult to measure. For this reason, we will look at how markets directly measure value using two new concepts: consumer surplus and producer surplus.

Consumer Surplus

How much will they pay for an economics textbook?

Consider three students: Frank, Beanie, and Mitch. (You may recognize these names from the movie *Old School*.) Like students everywhere, each one has a maximum price he's willing to pay for a new economics textbook. This is the highest price he would pay if he couldn't get the book any other way. Beanie owns a successful business, so for him the cost of a new textbook doesn't present a financial hardship. Mitch is a business major who really wants to do well in economics. Frank is not serious about his studies and will buy the book only if it's relatively

TABLE 4.1

Willingness to Pay for a New Economics Textbook

Buyer	Willingness to pay
Beanie	$200
Mitch	$150
Frank	$100

inexpensive. Table 4.1 shows the maximum value that each student places on the textbook. This value, called the **willingness to pay**, or *reservation price*, is the maximum price a consumer will pay for a good. In an auction or a negotiation, the willingness to pay (reservation price) is the price beyond which the consumer decides to walk away from the transaction.

Willingness to pay is the maximum price a consumer will pay for a good. Also called the reservation price.

Consider what happens when the price of the book is $151. If Beanie purchases the book at $151, he pays $49 less than the $200 maximum he was willing to pay. He values the textbook at $49 more than the purchase price, so buying the book will make him better off.

Consumer surplus is the difference between the willingness to pay for a good and the price that is paid to get it. While Beanie gains $49 in consumer surplus, a price of $151 is more than either Mitch or Frank is willing to pay. Since Mitch is willing to pay only $150, if he purchases the book he will experience a consumer loss of $1. Frank's willingness to pay is $100, so if he buys the book for $151 he will experience a consumer loss of $51. Whenever the price is greater than the willingness to pay, a rational consumer will decide not to buy in order to avoid the consumer loss.

Consumer surplus is the difference between the willingness to pay for a good and the price that is paid to get it.

Using Demand Curves to Illustrate Consumer Surplus

In the previous section, we discussed consumer surplus as a dollar figure or amount. We can also illustrate it graphically with a demand curve. Figure 4.1 shows the demand curve drawn from the data in Table 4.1. Notice that the curve looks like a staircase with three steps—one for each additional textbook purchase. Each point on a market demand curve corresponds to one unit sold, so if we added more consumers into our example, the "steps" would become narrower and the demand curve would become smoother.

At any price above $200, none of the students wants to purchase a textbook. This relationship is evident on the *x* axis where the quantity demanded is 0. At any price between $151 and $200, Beanie is the only buyer, so the quantity demanded is 1. At prices between $101 and $150, Beanie and Mitch are each willing to buy the textbook, so the quantity demanded is 2. Finally, if the price is $100 or less, all three students are willing to buy the textbook, so the quantity demanded is 3. As the price falls, the quantity demanded increases.

We can measure the total extent of consumer surplus by examining the area under the demand curve for each of our three consumers, as shown in

FIGURE 4.1

Demand Curve for an Economics Textbook

The demand curve has a step for each additional textbook purchase. As the price goes down, more students buy the textbook.

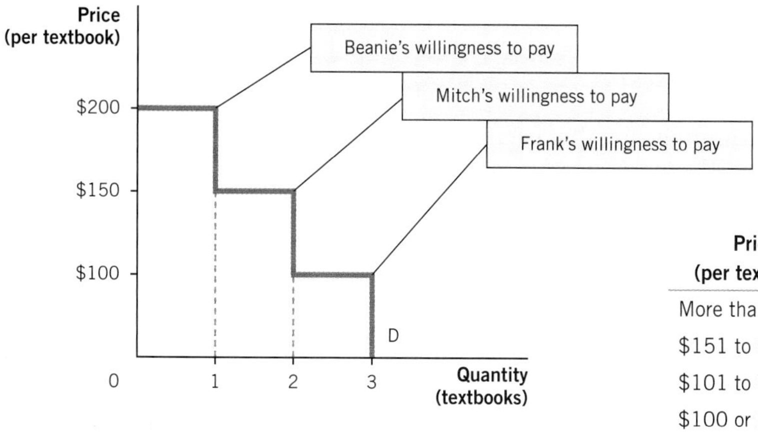

Price (per textbook)	Buyers	Quantity demanded (textbooks)
More than $200	None	0
$151 to $200	Beanie	1
$101 to $150	Mitch, Beanie	2
$100 or less	Frank, Mitch, and Beanie	3

FIGURE 4.2

Determining Consumer Surplus from a Demand Curve

(a) At a price of $175, Beanie is the only buyer, so the quantity demanded is 1. (b) At a price of $125, Beanie and Mitch are each willing to buy the textbook, so the quantity demanded is 2.

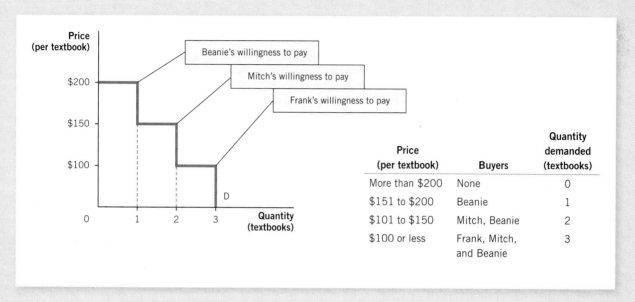

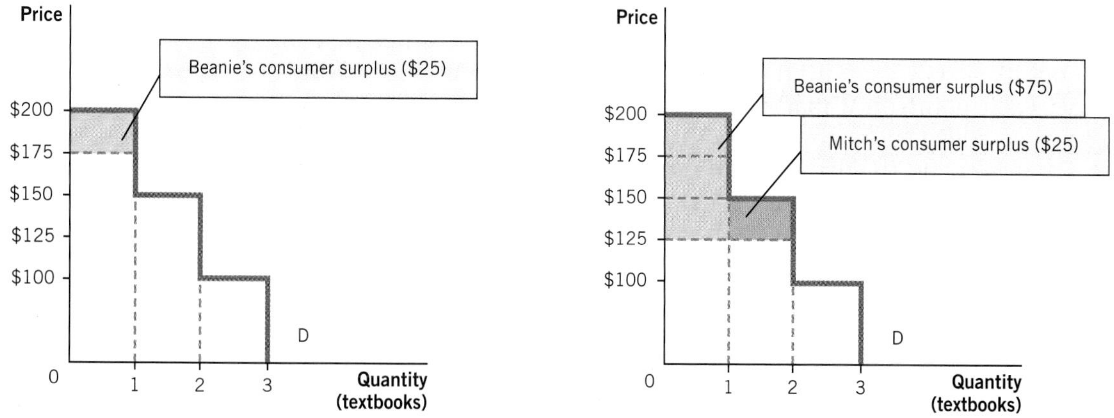

(a) $175 per Book

(b) $125 per Book

Figure 4.2. In Figure 4.2(a) the price is $175, and only Beanie decides to buy. Since his willingness to pay is $200, he is better off by $25; this is his consumer surplus. The green-shaded area under the demand curve and above the price represents the added benefit Beanie receives from purchasing a textbook at a price of $175. When the price drops to $125, as shown in Figure 4.2(b), Mitch also decides to buy a textbook. Now the total quantity demanded is 2 textbooks. Mitch's willingness to pay is $150, so his consumer surplus, represented by the red-shaded area, is $25. However, since Beanie's willingness to pay is $200, his consumer surplus rises from $25 to $75. So a textbook price of $125 raises the total consumer surplus to $100 ($75 for Beanie + $25 for Mitch). In other words, lower prices create more consumer surplus in this market—and in any other market.

Producer Surplus

Like buyers, sellers also benefit from market transactions. In this section, our three students discover that they are good at economics and decide to go into the tutoring business. They don't want to provide this service for free, but each has a different minimum price, or willingness to sell. The **willingness to sell** is the minimum price a seller will accept to sell a good or service. Table 4.2 shows each tutor's willingness to sell his services.

Willingness to sell is the minimum price a seller will accept to sell a good or service.

Consider what happens at a tutoring price of $25 per hour. Since Frank is willing to tutor for $10 per hour, every hour that he tutors at $25 per hour earns him $15 more than his willingness to sell. This extra $15 per hour is his producer surplus. **Producer surplus** is the difference between the willingness to sell a good and the price that the seller receives. Mitch is willing to tutor for $20 per hour and earns a $5 producer surplus for every hour he tutors. Finally, Beanie's willingness to tutor, at $30 per hour, is more than the market price of $25. If he tutors, he will have a producer loss of $5 per hour. In other words, at a price of $25 Beanie should do something else with his time to avoid that loss.

Producer surplus is the difference between the willingness to sell a good and the price that the seller receives.

How do producers determine their willingness to sell? They must consider two factors: (1) the direct costs of producing the good and (2) the indirect costs, or opportunity costs. We'll talk more about the direct costs of running a business (things like paying employees, buying materials, and paying the electric bill) in Chapter 5. We've already discussed the idea of indirect costs. These costs refer to the opportunity costs to the producer. While opportunity costs are more difficult to quantify, they are still important when deciding whether to produce a good or service. In the case of tutoring, the direct costs

Opportunity cost

TABLE 4.2

Willingness to Sell Tutoring Services

Seller	Willingness to sell
Beanie	$30/hr
Mitch	$20/hr
Frank	$10/hr

are minimal. Maybe Frank needs to travel to the buyer of the tutoring service, but there isn't much else to pay for. Opportunity costs, however, might be rather large. At a price of $25, Beanie should clearly do something else with this time. Why? Because Beanie owns his own business, the time spent tutoring is time that he could have spent running his business. Mitch is a business student who might otherwise be studying to get better grades. Frank is neither a businessman nor a serious student, so the $10 he can earn in an hour of tutoring is not taking the place of other earning opportunities or studying more to get better grades.

Using Supply Curves to Illustrate Producer Surplus

Continuing our example, the supply curve in Figure 4.3 shows the relationship between the price for an hour of tutoring and the quantity of tutors who are willing to work. As you can see on the supply schedule (the table within the figure), at any price less than $10 per hour no one wants to tutor. At prices between $10 and $19 per hour, Frank is the only tutor, so the quantity

FIGURE 4.3

Supply Curve for Economics Tutoring

The supply curve has three steps, one for each additional student who is willing to tutor. Higher prices will induce more students to become tutors.

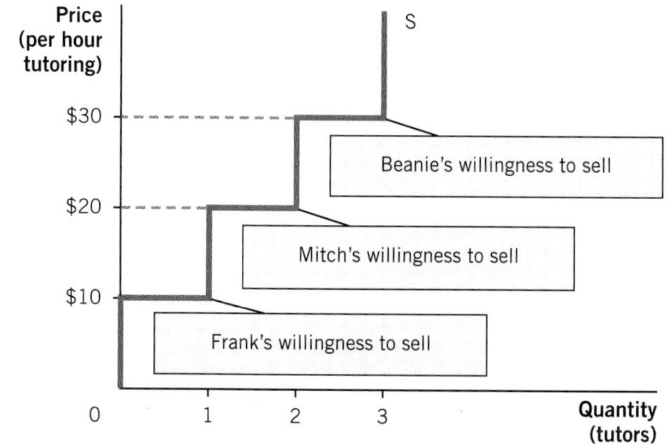

Price (per hour tutoring)	Sellers	Quantity supplied (tutors)
$30 or more	Frank, Mitch, and Beanie	3
$20 to 29	Frank, Mitch	2
$10 to 19	Frank	1
Less than $10	None	0

supplied is 1. Between $20 and $29 per hour, Frank and Mitch are willing to tutor, so the quantity supplied rises to 2. Finally, if the price is $30 or more per hour, all three friends are willing to tutor, so the quantity supplied is 3. As the price they receive for tutoring rises above certain levels, the number of tutors increases from 1 to 3.

What do these relationships between price and supply tell us about producer surplus? Let's turn to Figure 4.4. By examining the area above the supply curve, we can measure the extent of producer surplus. In Figure 4.4(a), the price of an hour of tutoring is $15. At that price, only Frank decides to tutor. Since he would be willing to tutor even if the price were as low as $10 per hour, he is $5 better off per hour tutoring. Frank's producer surplus is represented by the red-shaded area above the supply curve and below the price of $15. Since Beanie and Mitch do not tutor when the price is $15, they do not receive any producer surplus. In Figure 4.4(b), the price for tutoring is $25 per hour. At this price, Mitch also decides to tutor. He is willing to tutor at $20 per hour, so when the price is $25 per hour his producer surplus is $5 per hour, represented by the blue-shaded area. Since Frank is willing to tutor for $10 per hour, at $25 per hour his producer surplus rises to $15 per hour. By looking at the shaded boxes in Figure 4.4(b), we see that an increase in the price of tutoring raises the combined producer surplus of Frank and Mitch to $20 per hour ($15 per hour for Frank + $5 per hour for Mitch). In other words, higher prices create more producer surplus in this market—and in any other market.

FIGURE 4.4

Determining Producer Surplus from a Supply Curve

(a) The price of an hour of tutoring is $15. At this price, only Frank decides to tutor. (b) The price for tutoring is $25 per hour. At this price, Mitch also decides to tutor.

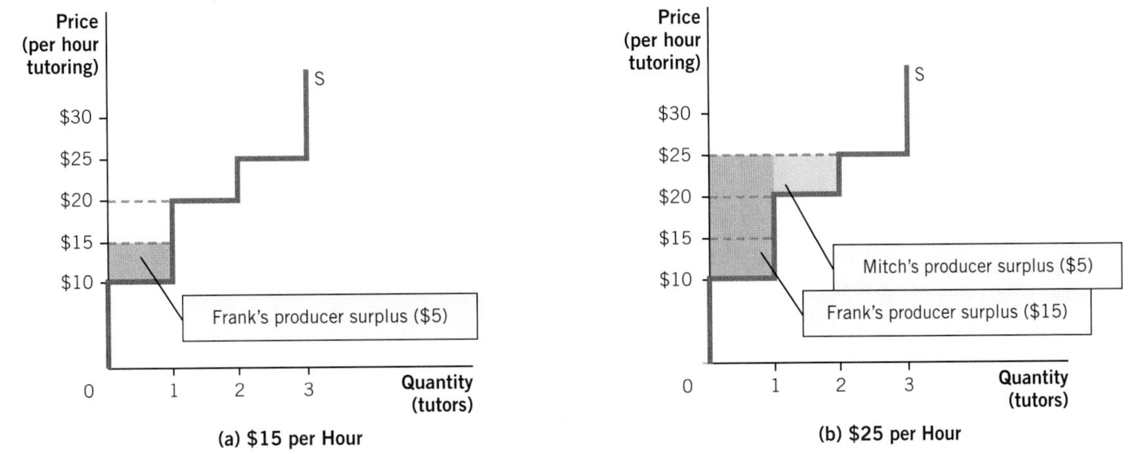

PRACTICE WHAT YOU KNOW

Consumer and Producer Surplus: Trendy Fashion

Dolce & Gabbana (D&G) has put a jacket on sale to clear out inventory. The company is willing to sell at a price no lower than $80. Leah decides to buy the new jacket from D&G for $80. She was willing to pay $100. When her friend Becky sees the jacket, she loves it and thinks it's worth $150. So she offers Leah $125 for the jacket, and Leah accepts. Leah and Becky are both thrilled with the exchange.

Rachel Bilson wearing a D&G jacket

Question: What is the total surplus from the original purchase and the additional surplus generated by the resale of the jacket?

Answer: Since D&G's willingness to sell is $80, there is no producer surplus. Leah was willing to pay $100 and the jacket cost $80, so she keeps the difference, or $20, as consumer surplus. Therefore, total surplus is $20. When Leah resells the jacket to Becky for $125, she earns $25 in producer surplus ($125 minus the $100 at which she values the jacket). At the same time, Becky receives $25 in consumer surplus, since she was willing to pay Leah up to $150 for the jacket but Leah sells it to her for $125. The resale thus generates an additional $50 in surplus ($25 consumer surplus + $25 producer surplus).

When Is a Market Efficient?

Total surplus is the sum of consumer surplus and producer surplus.

We have seen how consumers benefit from lower prices and how producers benefit from higher prices. When we combine the concepts of consumer and producer surplus, we can build a complete picture of the well-being of buyers and sellers. Adding consumer and producer surplus gives us **total surplus** because it measures the benefit of market transactions to society. Total surplus is the best way economists have to measure the benefits that markets create.

Figure 4.5 illustrates the relationship between consumer and producer surplus for coconut cream pie. The demand curve shows that some customers are willing to pay more for a slice of pie than others. Likewise, some sellers (producers) are willing to sell pie for less than other sellers.

Trade creates value

Let's say that Russ is willing to pay $7.00 per slice of pie, but when he gets to the store he finds it for $4.00 per slice. The difference between the price he's willing to pay (represented by point A) and the price he actually pays (represented by E, the equilibrium price) is $3.00 in consumer surplus. This surplus is indicated by the arrow showing the distance from $4.00 to $7.00. Russ's friend Audrey is willing to pay $5.00 for a slice of coconut cream pie, but, like Russ, she finds it for $4.00. Therefore, she receives $1.00 in consumer

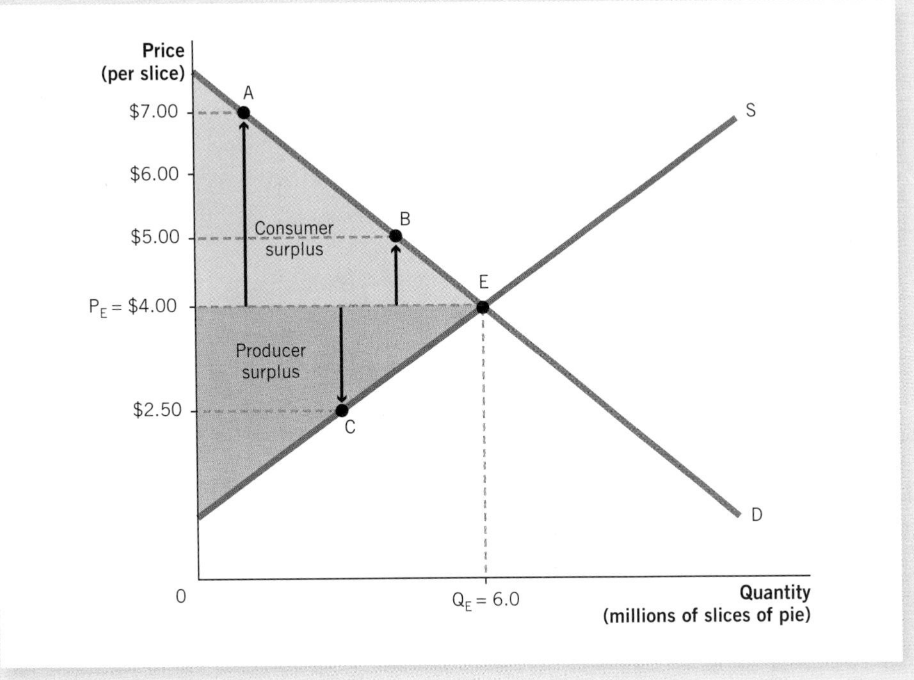

FIGURE 4.5

Consumer and Producer Surplus for Coconut Cream Pie

Consumer surplus is the difference between the willingness to pay along the demand curve and the equilibrium price, P_E. It is illustrated by the blue-shaded triangle. Producer surplus is the difference between the willingness to produce along the supply curve and the equilibrium price. It is illustrated by the red-shaded triangle.

surplus, indicated by the arrow at point B showing the distance from $4.00 to $5.00. In fact, all consumers who are willing to pay more than $4.00 per slice are better off when they purchase a slice of pie at $4.00. We can show this total area of consumer surplus on the graph as the blue-shaded triangle bordered by the demand curve, the *y* axis, and the equilibrium price (P_E). At every point in this area, the consumers who are willing to pay more than the equilibrium price for a slice of coconut cream pie will be better off.

Continuing with Figure 4.5, producer surplus follows a similar process. Suppose that Crazy Eddie's Pie Barn is willing to sell coconut cream pie for $2.50 per slice, represented by point C. Since the equilibrium price is $4.00, the business makes $1.50 in producer surplus for each slice of pie sold. This is indicated by the arrow at point C showing the distance from $4.00 to $2.50. If we think of the supply curve as representing the costs of many different sellers, we can calculate the total producer surplus as the red-shaded triangle bordered by the supply curve, the *y* axis, and the equilibrium price. The shaded blue triangle (consumer surplus) and the shaded red triangle (producer surplus) illustrate the total surplus, or social well-being, created by the production and exchange of the good at the equilibrium price. At the equilibrium quantity of 6 million slices

The buyer and seller each benefit from this exchange.

ECONOMICS IN THE MEDIA

Efficiency

Old School

In the 2003 movie *Old School*, Frank tries to give away a bread maker he received as a wedding present. First, he offers it to a friend as a housewarming gift, but it turns out that this is the friend who originally gave him the bread maker. Ouch! Later in the movie, we see Frank giving the bread maker to a small boy at a birthday party. Both efforts at re-gifting fail miserably.

Frank re-gifts a bread maker.

From an economic perspective, giving the wrong gift makes society poorer. If you spend $50 on a gift and give it to someone who thinks it's worth only $30, you've lost $20 in value. Whenever you receive a shirt that's the wrong size or style, a fruitcake you won't eat, or something that's worth less to you than what the gift-giver spent on it, an economic inefficiency has occurred. Until now, we have thought of the market as enhancing efficiency by increasing the total surplus in society. But we can also think of the billions of dollars spent on mismatched gifts as a failure to maximize the total surplus involved in exchange. In other words, we can think of the efficiency of the gift-giving process as less than 100 percent.

Given what we have learned so far about economics, you might be tempted to argue that cash is the best gift you can give. When you give cash, it's never the wrong size or color, and the recipients can use it to buy whatever they want. However, very few people actually give cash (unless it is requested). Considering the advantages of cash, why don't more people give it instead of gifts? One reason is that cash seems impersonal. Another reason is that cash communicates exactly how much the giver spent. To avoid both problems, most people rarely give cash. Instead, they buy personalized gifts to communicate how much they care, while making it hard for the recipient to determine exactly how much they spent.

One way that society overcomes inefficiency in gifting is through the dissemination of information. For instance, wedding registries provide a convenient way for people who may not know the newlyweds very well to give them what they want. Similarly, prior to holidays many people tell each other what they would like to receive. By purchasing gifts that others want, givers can exactly match what the recipients would have purchased if they had received a cash transfer. This eliminates any potential inefficiency. At the same time, the giver conveys affection—an essential part of giving. To further reduce the potential inefficiencies associated with giving, many large families practice holiday gift exchanges. And another interesting mechanism for eliciting information involves Santa Claus. Children throughout the world send Santa Claus wish lists for Christmas, never realizing that the parents who help to write and send the lists are the primary beneficiaries.

To economists, the strategies of providing better information, having gift exchanges, and sending wish lists to Santa Claus are just a few examples of how society tries to get the most out of the giving process—and that is something to be joyful about!

of pie, output and consumption reach the largest possible combination of producer and consumer surplus.

When an allocation of resources maximizes total surplus, the result is said to demonstrate **efficiency**. Efficiency occurs at point E in Figure 4.5 when the market is in equilibrium. To think about why the market creates the largest possible total surplus, or social well-being, it is important to recall how the market allocates resources. Consumers who are willing to pay more than the equilibrium price will buy the good because they will enjoy the consumer surplus. Producers who are willing to sell the good for less than the market-equilibrium price will enjoy the producer surplus. In addition, consumers with a low willingness to buy (less than \$4.00 per slice) and producers with a high willingness to sell (more than \$4.00 per slice) do not participate in the market since they would be worse off. Therefore, the equilibrium output at point E maximizes the total surplus and is also an efficient allocation of resources.

An outcome demonstrates **efficiency** when an allocation of resources maximizes total surplus.

The Efficiency-Equity Debate

When we model behavior, we assume that participants in a market are rational decision-makers. We assume that producers will always operate in the region of the triangle that represents producer surplus and that consumers will always operate in the region of the triangle that represents consumer surplus. We do not, for example, expect Russ to pay more than \$7.00 for a piece of pie or Crazy Eddie's Pie Barn to sell a slice of pie for less than \$2.50. In other words, for the market to work efficiently, voluntary instances of consumer loss must be rare. We assume that self-interest helps to ensure that all participants will benefit from an exchange.

Efficiency only requires that the pie gets eaten. Equity is a question of dividing the pie equally or fairly.

However, the fact that both parties benefit from an exchange does not mean that each benefits equally. Economists are also interested in the distribution of the gains. **Equity** refers to the fairness of the distribution of the benefits within the society. In a world where no one cared about equity, only efficiency would matter. The objective would be to maximize the total surplus, and no particular division would be preferred. Another way of thinking about fairness versus efficiency is to consider a pie—coconut cream or otherwise. If our only concern is efficiency, we'll simply want to make sure that none of the pie goes to waste. In this scenario, we can think of efficiency as the entire pie being eaten. However, if we care about equity, we'll also want to make sure that the pie is divided equally. Russ and Audrey get the same size piece of pie as everyone else.

Equity refers to the fairness of the distribution of the benefits within the society.

Up to this point, we have assumed that markets produce efficient outcomes. But in the real world, efficiency is not guaranteed. What if the market-clearing price isn't the actual price, and what if there was no way to get to that market price? This is what happens when governments institute price controls.

PRACTICE WHAT YOU KNOW

Total Surplus: How Would Lower Income Affect Urban Outfitters?

Question: If a drop in consumer income occurs, what will happen to the consumer surplus that customers enjoy at Urban Outfitters? What will happen to the amount of producer surplus that Urban Outfitters receives? Illustrate your answer by shifting the demand curve appropriately and labeling the new and old areas of consumer and producer surplus.

Does less income affect total surplus?

Answer: Since the items sold at Urban Outfitters are normal goods, a drop in income causes the demand curve (D) to shift to the left. The arrow shows the leftward shift in graph (b) below. When you compare the area of consumer surplus (in blue) before and after the drop in income—that is, graphs (a) and (b)—you can see that it shrinks. The same is true when comparing the area of producer surplus (in red) before and after the shift in demand.

Your intuition might already confirm what the graphs tell us. Since consumers have less income, they buy fewer clothes at Urban Outfitters—so consumer surplus falls. Likewise, since fewer customers buy the store's clothes, Urban Outfitters sells less—so producer surplus falls. This is also evident in graph (b), since $Q_2 < Q_1$.

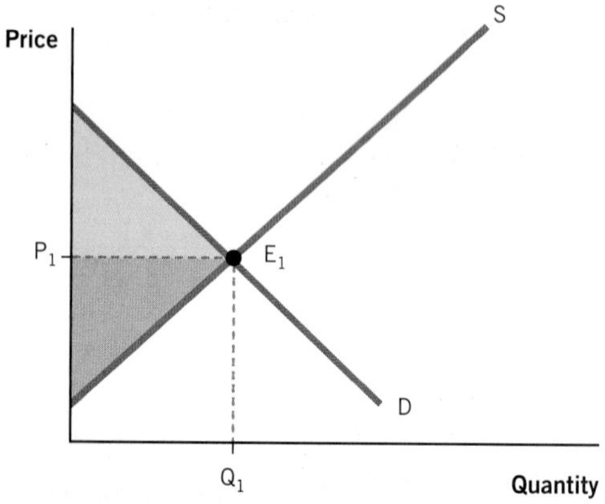

(a) Before the Drop in Income

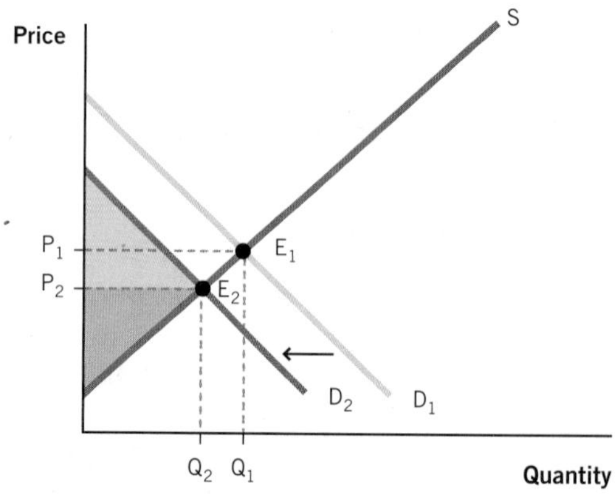

(b) After the Drop in Income

A **price control** attempts to set prices through govern-ment involvement in the market.

A **price ceiling** is a legally established maximum price for a good or service.

A **price floor** is a legally established minimum price for a good or service.

When Do Price Ceilings Matter?

Price controls are an attempt to set prices through government involvement in the market. In most cases, and certainly in the United States, price controls are enacted by government to ease perceived burdens on society. There are two types of price controls: price ceilings and price floors. A **price ceiling** creates a legally established maximum price for a good or service. A **price floor** creates a legally established minimum price for a good or service. By preventing the market price from being established, price controls create many unintended effects that policymakers rarely acknowledge.

Understanding Price Ceilings

To understand how price ceilings work, let's try a simple thought experiment. Suppose that the government is concerned about the price of gasoline. As the price rises, more and more of a household's income is spent to fill gas tanks. To help those harmed by the rise in gas prices, legislators pass a law stating that no one can charge more than $2.00 for a gallon of regular gasoline. What happens? Does the new law accomplish its goal?

Lines at the pumps? A sign of a shortage.

The law of supply and demand tells us that if the price drops, the quantity that consumers demand will increase. At the same time, the quantity supplied will fall because producers will be receiving lower profits for their efforts. This twin dynamic of increased quantity demanded and reduced quantity supplied will cause a shortage of gasoline.

On the demand side, consumers will want more gas than is available at the legal price. There will be long lines for gas, and many people won't be able to get the gas they want. On the supply side, producers will look for ways to maintain their profits. They can close their stations early. They can raise the price of items in the convenience store attached to the gas station. They might even stop selling higher grades of gasoline that are now unprofitable to produce. They could even tinker with the pumps so that what registers as a gallon pumped is actually just a little bit less. This is definitely illegal, but price controls can and do cause buyers and sellers to alter their behavior to avoid the price control.

Incentives

Black markets are illegal markets that arise where either illegal goods are sold or legal goods are sold at illegal prices.

When normal market mechanisms are prevented, black markets will develop to help supply meet demand. **Black markets** are illegal markets that arise where either illegal goods are sold or legal goods are sold at illegal prices. For instance, in the 1970s the U.S. government imposed price controls on gasoline in reaction to significant cuts in production by Middle Eastern countries. The result was a shortage and long lines at the pumps. In some cases, fights broke out as gas stations couldn't keep enough gasoline on hand. People who didn't want to wait in line and were willing to pay resorted to illegal means to obtain gasoline. Similarly, in the aftermath of Superstorm Sandy, a devastating storm that impacted the New York–New Jersey region in 2012, the black market price for a gallon of gas in the storm-affected region ranged between $8.00 and $20.00 despite price controls on gasoline!

Table 4.3 summarizes the likely outcome of price controls on gasoline.

The Effect of Price Ceilings

Now that we have some understanding of how a price ceiling works, we can transfer that knowledge into the supply and demand model for a deeper analysis of how price ceilings affect the market.

If you can touch the ceiling, you can't go any higher. A binding price ceiling stops prices from rising.

Remember what the purpose of a price ceiling is. Someone has deemed the market price to be too high, so the price must be forced down. If gasoline is $4.00 a gallon and a policymaker thinks that price is too high, the policymaker certainly wouldn't advocate for a $5.00 price ceiling, which wouldn't accomplish the goal of lowering the price of gasoline. Therefore, a *binding*

TABLE 4.3

A Price Ceiling on Gasoline

Question	Answer / Explanation		Result
Will there be more or less gas for sale?	Consumers will want to buy more since the price is lower (the law of demand), but producers will manufacture less (the law of supply). The net result will be a shortage of gas.		Stations shut down early because they have no gasoline left to sell.
Will the size of a gallon change?	Since the price is capped at $2.00 per gallon, manufacturers may try to maintain profits by selling a slightly smaller gallon.		You get less than you paid for.
Will the quality change?	Since the price is capped, producers will use cheaper ingredients, and many expensive brands and varieties will no longer be profitable to produce. Thus, the quality of available gas will decline.		High-octane gas will disappear.
Will the opportunity cost of finding gas change?	The opportunity cost of finding gas will rise. This means that consumers will spend significant resources going from station to station to see if a gas shipment has arrived and waiting in line for a chance to get some.		Gas lines will become the norm.
Will people have to break the law to buy gas?	Since gas will be hard to find and people will still need it, a black market will develop. Those selling and buying on the black market will be breaking the law.		Black-market gas dealers will help reduce the shortage.

price ceiling, one that effectively lowers the price, must be set below the equilibrium price. The problem for the market is that this binding constraint prevents supply and demand from clearing the market. (When a price ceiling is *nonbinding*, it is above the equilibrium price and does not impact the market price.)

In Figure 4.6, the price ceiling for gas is set at $2.00 per gallon. Since $2.00 is well below the equilibrium price of $4.00, this price ceiling is binding. Notice that at a price of $2.00, the quantity demanded (Q_D) is greater than the quantity supplied (Q_S)—in other words, a shortage exists. Shortages typically cause prices to rise, but the imposed price ceiling prevents that from happening. A price ceiling of $2.00 allows only the prices in the green area. The market cannot reach the equilibrium point E at $4.00 per gallon because it is located above the price ceiling, in the red area.

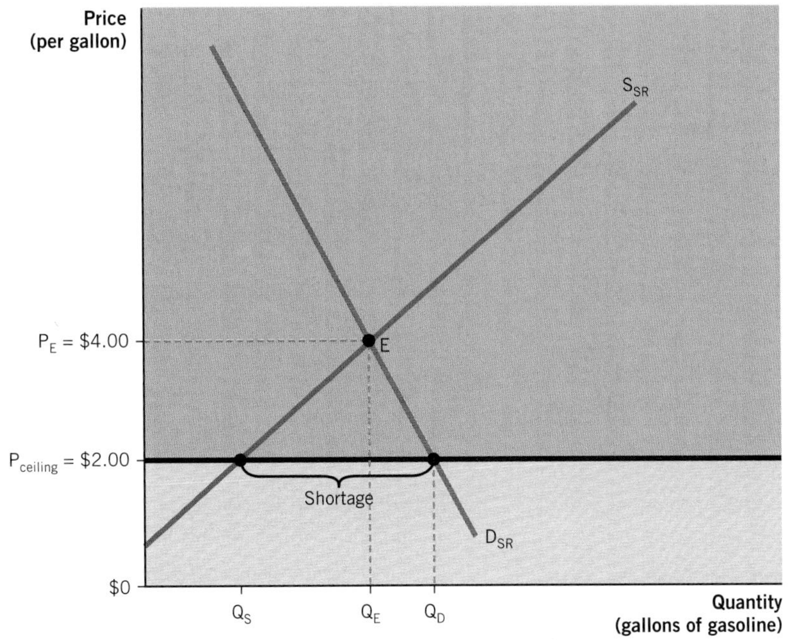

FIGURE 4.6

A Binding Price Ceiling for Gasoline

A binding price ceiling prevents sellers from increasing the price and causes them to reduce the quantity they offer for sale. Consumers desire to purchase the product at the price-ceiling level, which creates a shortage in the short run; many consumers will be unable to obtain the good. As a result, those who are shut out of the market will turn to other means to acquire the good. The result is an illegal market for the good at a higher black-market price.

The black-market price is also set by supply and demand. Since prices above $2.00 are illegal, sellers are unwilling to produce more than Q_S. Once the price ceiling is in place, sellers cannot legally charge prices above the ceiling, so the incentive to produce along the original supply curve vanishes. Since a shortage still exists, an illegal market will form to resolve the shortage. The black market price will be above the price ceiling since there are people willing to pay a higher price to acquire gasoline. However, the price ceiling has created two unintended consequences: a smaller quantity of legally supplied gas (Q_S is less than Q_E), and a higher price for those who are forced to purchase it on the black market.

Incentives

There is one other thing to consider here. Remember that the market price maximizes the total surplus. At a lower price, consumer surplus rises but producer surplus falls. The question is whether the consumers are made sufficiently better off to compensate for producers' losses. When a price control prevents the market price from being established, the result is a reduction in the total number of legal transactions taking place. In other words, fewer trades are made. While buyers want to buy Q_D there is only Q_S available. Since Q_S is less than the equilibrium quantity (Q_E) the amount of legal trades is Q_S. Even though the buyers who can get the good pay less, there are fewer transactions, so the total surplus falls below what it was when the market set the price. The consumers' gains are too small to offset the producers' losses. Thus, price controls reduce market efficiency.

ECONOMICS IN THE MEDIA

Price Ceilings

Moscow on the Hudson

Soviet-era food-rationing coupon

This 1984 film starring Robin Williams chronicles the differences between living in the United States and the former Soviet Union. In Moscow, we see hundreds of people waiting in line to receive essentials like bread, milk, and shoes. In the Soviet Union, production was controlled and prices were not allowed to equalize supply and demand. As a result, shortages were common. Waiting in line served as a rationing mechanism in the absence of price adjustments.

This film is memorable because of the reactions that Robin Williams's character has once he immigrates to the United States. In one inspired scene, he walks into a supermarket to buy coffee. He asks the manager where the coffee aisle is located, and when he sees that the aisle isn't crowded, he asks the manager where the coffee line is located. The manager responds that there is no coffee line, so Williams walks down the coffee aisle slowly, naming each variety. We see his joy at being able to buy coffee without waiting and at having so many options to choose from. This scene effectively showcases the differences between the market system of the United States and the controlled economy of the former Soviet Union.

Soviet-era bread line

PRACTICE WHAT YOU KNOW

Price Ceilings: Concert Tickets

Question: **Suppose that fans of Katy Perry persuade Congress to impose a price ceiling of $25 for every Katy Perry concert ticket. Would this policy affect the number of people who attend her concerts? (Hint: think about concertgoers not only in the United States but also in other countries.)**

Answer: The price ceiling prevents supply and demand from reaching the equilibrium price. As a result, at $25 there is a shortage of tickets. Since Katy Perry controls when and where she tours, she

Will you be able to hear her roar more overseas?

(CONTINUED)

(CONTINUED)

will choose to tour less in the United States and more in countries that do not regulate the ticket prices she can charge. This will make it more difficult for her U.S. fans to see her perform live, so the answer to the question is yes: the policy will influence the number of people who attend Katy Perry concerts (fewer in the United States, and more abroad).

What Effects Do Price Ceilings Have on Economic Activity?

We have seen the logical repercussions of a hypothetical price ceiling on gasoline and the incentives it creates. Now let's use supply-and-demand analysis to examine a real-world price ceiling: price gouging laws.

Price Gouging

Price gouging laws place a temporary ceiling on the prices that sellers can charge during times of national emergency until markets function normally again. Over 30 states in the United States have laws against price gouging. Like all price controls, price gouging laws have unintended consequences. This became very apparent in the United States in 2012.

Price gouging laws place a temporary ceiling on the prices that sellers can charge during times of emergency until markets function normally again.

In 2012, the East Coast of the United States was hit with a late-season tropical storm that wreaked significant damage. Particularly hard hit were New York and New Jersey. Superstorm Sandy leveled houses, decimated shorelines, and left over 200 people dead. A few days after the storm passed, anti-gouging laws were put into effect in both states. These laws make it illegal to charge an "excessive" price immediately following a natural disaster. The laws are designed to prevent the victims of natural disasters from being exploited in a time of need. But do they work?

After the storm, individuals in New York and New Jersey made hundreds of calls claiming to be the victims of price gouging. Gas stations, hardware stores, and hotels were among the alleged perpetrators. A gas-station chain north of New York City was fined $50,000 for hiking gas prices. A hotel in Brooklyn, New York, was fined over $40,000 and forced to pay restitution to customers after raising its rates from $177 a night to over $400 a night. Interestingly, it wasn't the raising of the rates that was illegal. Hotels in New York and New Jersey raised their rates just as much for the 2014 Super Bowl, which was played in northern New Jersey close to New York City. What was illegal was the *timing* of the price increase. All told, businesses paid over a million dollars in fines for price gouging after Superstorm Sandy.

Large generator: $900 after Superstorm Sandy.

Prices act to ration scarce resources. When the demand for gasoline, hotel rooms, generators, or other necessities is high, the price rises to ensure that the available units are distributed to those who value them the most. More important, the ability to charge a higher price provides sellers with an

Incentives

incentive to make more units available. If there is limited ability for the price to change when demand increases, there will be a shortage. Therefore, price gouging legislation means that devastated communities must rely exclusively on the goodwill of others and the slow-moving machinery of government relief efforts. This closes off a third avenue, entrepreneurial activity, as a means to alleviate poor conditions. If you could divert gasoline deliveries from your station in Ohio to New Jersey and sell it at a profit, there would be more gasoline moving from where it wasn't as necessary to where it was greatly needed. The extra costs associated with getting the gas to New Jersey need to be covered, and this can be accomplished with the higher price. However, gouging laws prevent the increase in price. So with companies unable to pursue a profit motive, gas stays in Ohio.

Figure 4.7 shows how price gouging laws work and the shortage they create. If the demand for gasoline increases immediately after a disaster (D_{after}), the market price rises from \$4.00 to \$7.00. But since \$7.00 is considered excessive, sales at that price are made illegal. This creates a binding price ceiling for as long as a state of emergency is in effect. Whenever a price ceiling is binding, the result is a shortage. You can see the shortage in Figure 4.7 in the difference between quantity demanded and quantity supplied at the price ceiling mandated by the anti-gouging law ($P_{max\ under\ gouging\ law}$). In this case, the normal ability of supply and demand to ration the available gasoline is short-circuited. Since more people demand gas after the disaster than before it, those who don't get to the station soon enough are out of luck. When the emergency is lifted and the market returns to normal, the temporary shortage created by legislation against price gouging is eliminated.

FIGURE 4.7

Price Gouging

When a natural disaster strikes, price gouging laws go into effect. A prohibition on price gouging shifts the demand curve for gasoline to the right (from D_{before} to D_{after}) and causes the new equilibrium price (E_{after}) to rise above the legal limit. The result is a shortage. When the emergency is lifted, the market demand returns to normal, and the temporary shortage created by price gouging legislation is eliminated.

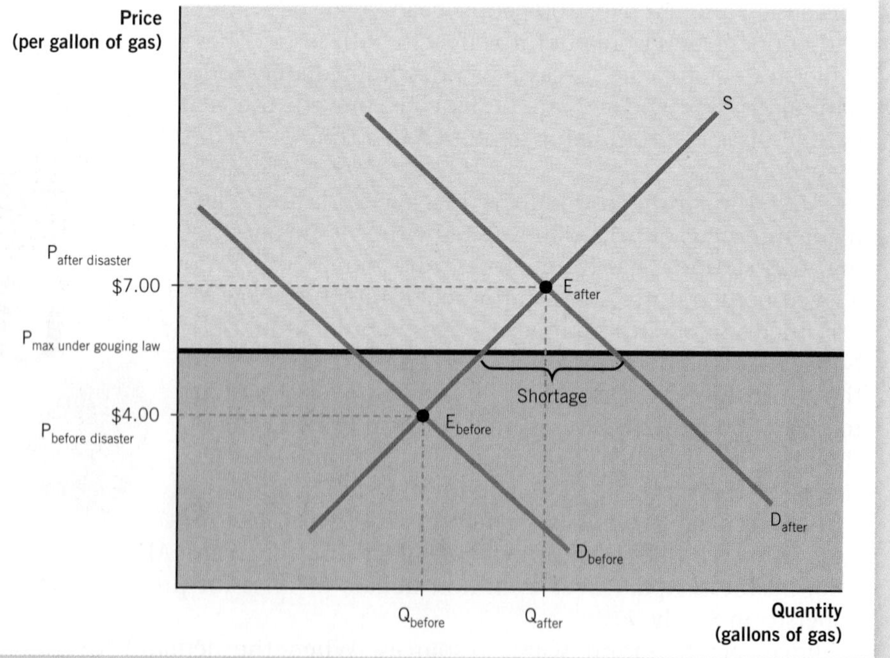

PRACTICE WHAT YOU KNOW

Price Ceilings: Student Rental Apartments

Here is a question that often confuses students.

Question: Imagine that a city council decides that the market price for student rental apartments is too high and passes a law that establishes a rental price ceiling of $600 per month. The result of the price ceiling is a shortage. Which of the following caused the shortage of apartments?

a. Both suppliers and demanders. Landlords will cut the supply of apartments, and the demand from renters will increase.

b. A spike in demand from many students who want to rent cheap apartments

c. The drop in supply caused by apartment owners pulling their units off the rental market and converting them into condos for sale

d. The price ceiling set by the city council

Answer: Many students think that markets are to blame when shortages (or surpluses) exist. The first reaction is to find the culpable party—either the supplier, the demander, or both.

Answer (a) is a typical response. But be careful. Supply and demand have not changed—they are exactly the same as they were before the price ceiling was implemented. What *has* changed is the quantity of apartments supplied at $600 per month. This change in quantity would be represented by a movement along the existing supply curve. The same is true for renters. The quantity demanded at $600 per month is much larger than it was when the price was not controlled. Once again, there will be a movement along the demand curve.

The same logic applies to answers (b) and (c). Answer (b) argues that there is a spike in student demand caused by the lower price. But price cannot cause a shift in the demand curve; it can only cause a movement along a curve. Likewise, (c) claims that apartment owners supply fewer units for rent. Landlords cannot charge more than $600 per unit, so they convert some apartments into private residences and offer them for sale in order to make more profit. Since fewer apartments are available at $600 per month, this situation would be represented by a movement along the apartment supply curve.

This brings us to (d). There is only one change in market conditions: the city council passed a new price-ceiling law. A binding price ceiling disrupts the market's ability to reach equilibrium. Therefore, we can say that the change in the price as a result of the price ceiling caused the shortage.

When Do Price Floors Matter?

Price floors create legally established minimum prices for goods or services. Like price ceilings, price floors create many unintended effects that policymakers rarely acknowledge. However, unlike price ceilings, price floors result from the political pressure of suppliers to keep prices high.

Most consumers prefer lower prices when they shop, so the idea of a law that keeps prices high may sound bad to you. However, if you are selling a product or service, you might think that legislation to keep prices high is a very good idea. For instance, many states establish minimum prices for milk. In Pennsylvania, milk costs $4.00 a gallon. In neighboring Ohio, the price is less than $3.00 a gallon. Guess which state has the price floor? If you said "Pennsylvania," you would be correct. The minimum wage law is another example of a price floor. In this section, we will follow the same progression that we did with price ceilings. We begin with a simple thought experiment. Once we understand how price floors work, we will use supply and demand analysis to examine the short- and long-term implications for economic activity.

Understanding Price Floors

Suppose that a politician suggests we should encourage dairy farmers to produce more milk so that supplies will be plentiful and everyone will get enough calcium. To accomplish these goals, a price floor of $6.00 per gallon—about twice the price of a typical gallon of fat-free milk—is enacted to make production more attractive to producers. What repercussions should we expect?

First, more milk will be available for sale. We know this because the higher price will cause dairies to increase the quantity that they supply. At the same time, because consumers must pay more, the quantity demanded will fall. The result will be a surplus of milk. Since every gallon of milk that is produced but not sold hurts the dairies' bottom line, sellers will want to lower their prices enough to get as many sales as possible before the milk goes bad. But the price floor will not allow the market to respond, and sellers will be stuck with milk that goes to waste.

If you're doing a handstand, you need the floor for support. A binding price floor keeps prices from falling.

What happens next? Since the surplus cannot be resolved through lower prices, the government will try to help equalize supply and demand through other means. This can be accomplished in one of two ways: by restricting the supply of the good or by stimulating additional demand. Both solutions are problematic. If production is restricted, dairy farmers won't be able to generate a profitable amount of milk. Likewise, stimulating additional demand isn't as simple as it sounds. In many cases, the increased demand comes from the government. Governments often purchase surplus agricultural production—most notably corn, soybeans, cotton, and rice. Once the government buys the surplus production, it often sells the surplus below cost to developing countries to avoid wasting the crop. This strategy has the unintended consequence of making it cheaper for consumers in these developing nations to buy excess agricultural output from developed nations like the United States than to have local farmers grow the crop. International treaties ban the practice of dumping surplus production, but it continues under the guise of humanitarian aid.

TABLE 4.4

A Price Floor on Milk

Question	Answer / Explanation	Result	
/ill the quantity of milk for ale change?	Consumers will purchase less since the price is higher (the law of demand), but producers will manufacture more (the law of supply). The net result will be a surplus of milk.		There will be a surplus of milk.
Would producers sell below the price floor?	Yes. A surplus of milk would give sellers a strong incentive to undercut the price floor in order to avoid having to discard leftover milk.		Illegal discounts will help to reduce the milk surplus.
Will dairy farmers be better off?	Not if they have trouble selling what they produce.		There might be a lot of spoiled milk.

Table 4.4 summarizes the result of our price-floor thought experiment using milk.

The Effect of Price Floors

We have seen that price floors create unintended consequences. Now we will use the supply and demand model to analyze how price floors affect the market.

Remember the purpose of a price floor. Someone has deemed the market price of some good or service to be too low. If the market price of milk is $2.00 a gallon and a policymaker thinks this price is too low, he certainly wouldn't advocate for a $1.00 price floor because the objective is to force the price higher, not lower. Therefore, a *binding* price floor, one that effectively raises the price, must be set above the equilibrium. The problem for the market is that this binding constraint prevents supply and demand from clearing the market. (A *nonbinding* price floor is set below the market equilibrium and therefore has no effect.)

A binding price floor causes the quantity supplied to exceed the quantity demanded. Figure 4.8 illustrates a binding price floor in the short run. Continuing our example of milk prices, at $6.00 per gallon the price floor is above the equilibrium price of $3.00. Market forces always attempt to restore the equilibrium between supply and demand at point E. So we know that there is downward pressure on the price. At a price floor of $6.00, we see that $Q_S > Q_D$. The difference between the quantity supplied and the quantity demanded results in a surplus. Since the price mechanism is no longer effective, sellers

Got milk? Maybe not, if there's a price floor.

Incentives

Full shelves signal a market at equilibrium.

find themselves holding unwanted inventories of milk. To eliminate the surplus, which will spoil unless it is sold, a black market may develop with prices substantially below the legislated price. At a price ($P_{black\ market}$) of \$2.00 per gallon, the black market eliminates the surplus that the price floor caused. However, the price floor has created two unintended consequences: a smaller quantity demanded for milk ($Q_D < Q_E$) and a black market to eliminate the glut.

It isn't just the glut that is the problem here. Once again, because the market price does not prevail, the total consumer and producer surplus is not maximized. At a higher price, producer surplus rises, but consumer surplus falls. If the gains to the producers outweigh the losses to the consumers, then the market is more efficient, but that will not happen here. The higher price reduces the amount buyers are willing and able to purchase from the equilibrium quantity (Q_E) to Q_D. Q_D is now the amount bought and sold in the market. Even though sellers would like to sell Q_S, buyers will not buy that amount at the price imposed by the price floor. As a result, fewer trades are made than at the equilibrium price, and market efficiency is diminished.

FIGURE 4.8

A Binding Price Floor in the Short Run

#5

A binding price floor creates a surplus. This price floor has two unintended consequences: a smaller quantity demanded than the equilibrium quantity ($Q_D < Q_E$) and a lower black-market price to eliminate the glut of the product.

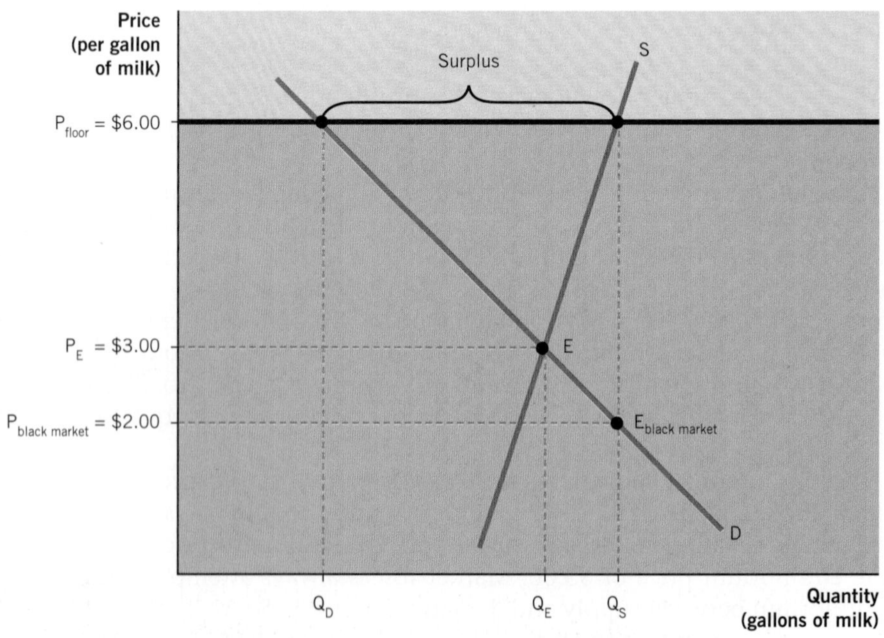

PRACTICE WHAT YOU KNOW

Price Floors: Fair-Trade Coffee

Fair-trade coffee is sold through organizations that purchase directly from growers. The coffee is usually sold for a higher price than standard coffee. The goal is to promote more humane working conditions for the coffee pickers and growers. Fair-trade coffee has become more popular but still accounts for a small portion of all coffee sales, in large part because it is substantially more expensive to produce.

Would fair-trade coffee producers benefit from a price floor?

Question: Suppose that a one-pound bag of standard coffee costs $8 and that a one-pound bag of fair-trade coffee costs $12. Congress decides to impose a price floor of $10 per pound on all coffee. Will this policy cause more or fewer people to buy fair-trade coffee?

Answer: Fair-trade producers typically sell their product at a higher price than mass-produced coffee brands. Therefore, a $10 price floor is binding for inexpensive brands like Folgers but non-binding for premium coffees, which include fair-trade sellers. The price floor will reduce the price disparity between fair-trade coffee and mass-produced coffee.

To see how this works, consider a fair-trade coffee producer who charges $12 per pound and a mass-produced brand that sells for $8 per pound. A price floor of $10 reduces the difference between the price of fair-trade coffee and the inexpensive coffee brands, which now must sell for $10 instead of $8. The price floor lowers the consumer's opportunity cost of choosing fair-trade coffee. Therefore, some consumers of the inexpensive brands will opt for fair-trade instead. As a result, fair-trade producers will benefit indirectly from the price floor. Thus, the answer to the question is that *more* people will buy fair-trade coffee as a result of this price-floor policy.

Opportunity cost

What Effects Do Price Floors Have on Economic Activity?

We have seen the logical repercussions of a price floor on milk and the incentives it creates. Now let's use supply and demand analysis to examine the most famous of price controls: minimum wage laws.

The Minimum Wage

The **minimum wage** is the lowest hourly wage rate that firms may legally pay their workers. Minimum wage workers can be skilled or unskilled, experienced or inexperienced. The common thread for minimum-wage workers is that they cannot easily move to a different, higher-paying, position. A minimum wage

The **minimum wage** is the lowest hourly wage rate that firms may legally pay their workers.

FIGURE 4.9

Price Floors and a Binding Minimum Wage Market

A binding minimum wage is a price floor above the current equilibrium wage, W_E. At \$10.10 per hour, the number of workers willing to supply their labor (Q_S) is greater than the demand for workers (Q_D). The result is a surplus of workers (which we recognize as unemployment).

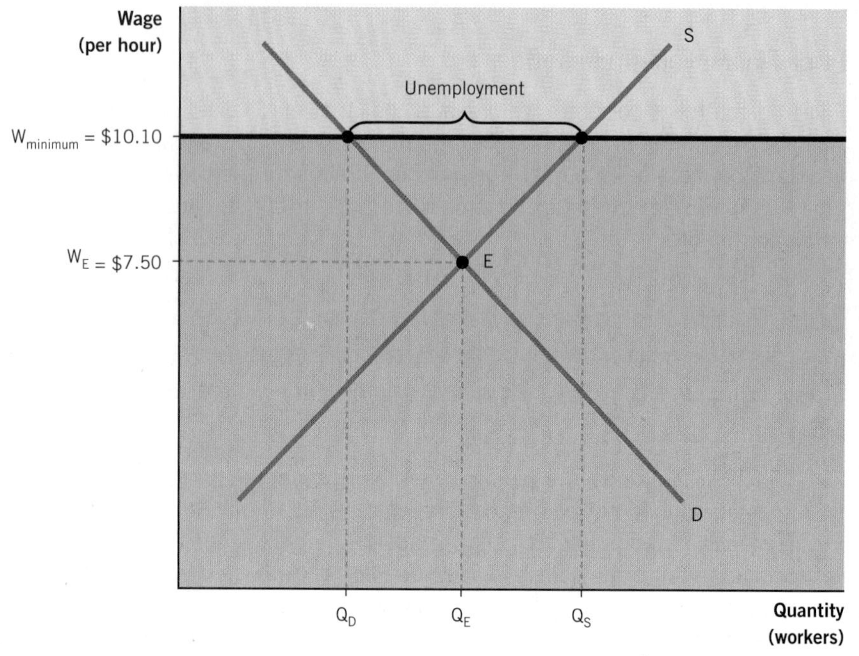

functions as a price floor. Figure 4.9 shows the effect of a binding minimum wage. Note that the wage, or the cost of labor, on the *y* axis (\$10.10 per hour) is the price that must be paid. However, the market equilibrium wage (\$7.50), or W_E, is below the minimum wage. The minimum wage prevents the market from reaching W_E at E (the equilibrium point) because only the wages in the green-shaded area are legal. Since the demand for labor depends on how much it costs, the minimum wage raises the cost of hiring workers. Therefore, a higher minimum wage will lower the quantity of labor demanded. At the same time, firms will look for ways to replace the now more expensive workers with other inputs such as capital, shorter working hours, or maybe relocation to countries with no minimum wage.

Over time, workers will adjust to the higher minimum wage. Some workers who might have decided to go to school full-time or remain retired, or who simply want some extra income, will enter the labor market because the minimum wage is now higher. This increases the quantity of labor supplied. The irony is that the minimum wage, just like any other price floor, has created two unintended consequences: a smaller quantity demanded for workers by employers (Q_D is significantly less than Q_E), and a larger quantity supplied of workers (Q_S is larger than Q_E) looking for those previously existing jobs. As a result, a binding minimum wage results in unemployment because $Q_S > Q_D$.

ECONOMICS IN THE MEDIA

The Minimum Wage

30 Days

The (2005) pilot episode of this reality series focused on the minimum wage. Morgan Spurlock and his fiancée spend 30 days in a poor neighborhood of Columbus, Ohio. The couple attempts to survive by earning minimum wage (at that time, $5.15 an hour) in order to make ends meet. In addition, they are required to start off with only one week's minimum wage (about $300) in reserve. Also, they cannot use credit cards to pay their bills. They experience firsthand the struggles that many minimum wage households face when living paycheck to paycheck. *30 Days* makes it painfully clear how difficult it is for anyone to live on the minimum wage for a month, let alone for years.

A quote from Morgan Spurlock sums up what the episode tries to convey: "We don't see the people that surround us. We don't see the people who are struggling to get by that are right next to us. And I have seen how hard the struggle is. I have been here. And I only did it for a month, and there's people who do this their whole lives."

Could you make ends meet earning the minimum wage?

After watching this episode of *30 Days*, it's hard not to think that raising the minimum wage is a good idea. Unfortunately, the economic reality is that raising the minimum wage does not guarantee that minimum wage earners will make more and also be able keep their jobs.

ECONOMICS IN THE REAL WORLD

Wage Laws Squeeze South Africa's Poor

Consider this story that appeared in the *New York Times* in 2010.*

NEWCASTLE, South Africa—The sheriff arrived at the factory here to shut it down, part of a national enforcement drive against clothing manufacturers who violate the minimum wage. But women working on the factory floor—the supposed beneficiaries of the crackdown—clambered atop cutting tables and ironing boards to raise anguished cries against it. Thoko Zwane, 43, who has worked in factories since she was 15, lost her job in Newcastle when a Chinese-run factory closed in 2004. More than a third of South Africans are jobless. "Why? Why?" shouted Nokuthula Masango, 25, after the authorities carted away bolts of gaily colored fabric. She made just $36 a week, $21 less than the minimum wage, but needed the meager pay to help support a large extended family that includes her five unemployed siblings and their children.

*Celia W. Dugger, "Wage Laws Squeeze South Africa's Poor," *New York Times*, September 27, 2010.

Trade-offs

The women's spontaneous protest is just one sign of how acute South Africa's long-running unemployment crisis has become. With their own economy saddled with very high unemployment rates, the women feared being out of work more than getting stuck in poorly paid jobs.

South Africans wait in line for unemployment benefits.

In the years since the end of apartheid, the South African economy has grown, but not nearly fast enough to end an intractable unemployment crisis. For over a decade, the jobless rate has been among the highest in the world, fueling crime, inequality, and social unrest. The global economic downturn has made the problem much worse, wiping out more than a million jobs. Over a third of South Africa's workforce is now idle. And 20 years after Nelson Mandela led the country to black majority rule, more than half of blacks ages 15 to 34 are without work—triple the level for whites. ✳

PRACTICE WHAT YOU KNOW

In today's Internet age, four degrees of separation are all that stand between you and the rest of the world.

Price Ceilings and Price Floors: Would a Price Control on Internet Access Be Effective?

A recent study found the following demand and supply schedule for high-speed Internet access:

Price of Internet (per month)	Connections demanded (millions of units)	Connections supplied (millions of units)
$60	10.0	62.5
$50	20.0	55.0
$40	30.0	47.5
$30	40.0	40.0
$20	50.0	32.5
$10	60.0	25.0

Question: What are the equilibrium price and equilibrium quantity of Internet service?

Answer: First, look at the table to see where supply and demand are equal. At a price of $30, consumers purchase 40 million units and producers supply 40 million units. Therefore, the equilibrium price is $30 and the equilibrium quantity is 40 million. At any price above $30, the quantity supplied exceeds

(CONTINUED)

(CONTINUED)

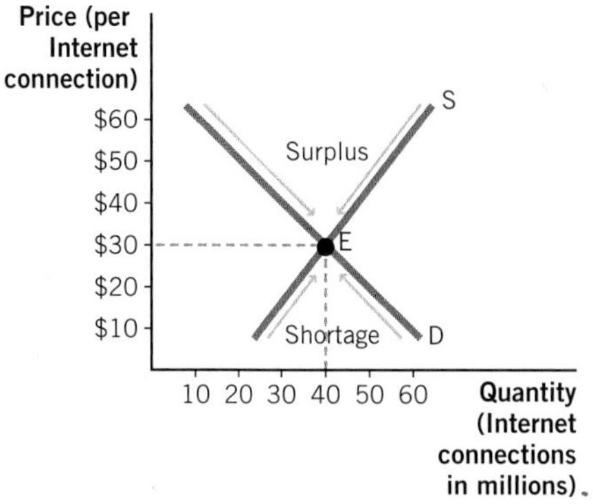

the quantity demanded, so there is a surplus. The surplus gives sellers an incentive to cut the price until it reaches the equilibrium point, E. At any price below $30, the quantity demanded exceeds the quantity supplied, so there is a shortage. The shortage gives sellers an incentive to raise the price until it reaches the equilibrium point, E.

Question: Suppose that providers convince the government that maintaining high-speed access to the Internet is an important element of technology infrastructure. As a result, Congress approves a price floor at $10 above the equilibrium price to help companies provide Internet service. How many people are able to connect to the Internet?

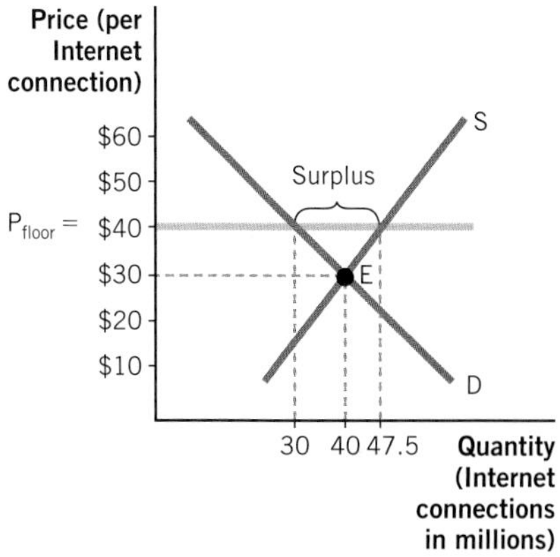

Answer: Adding $10 to the market price of $30 gives us a price floor of $40. At $40, consumers demand 30 million connections. Producers provide 47.5 million connections. This is a surplus of 17.5 million units (shown on the graph). A price floor means that producers cannot cut the price below that point to increase the quantity that consumers demand. As a result, only 30 million units are sold. So only 30 million people connect to the Internet.

Question: When teachers realize that fewer people are purchasing Internet access, they demand that the price floor be repealed and a price ceiling be put in its place. Congress acts immediately to remedy the problem, and a new price ceiling is set at $10 below the market price. Now how many people are able to connect to the Internet?

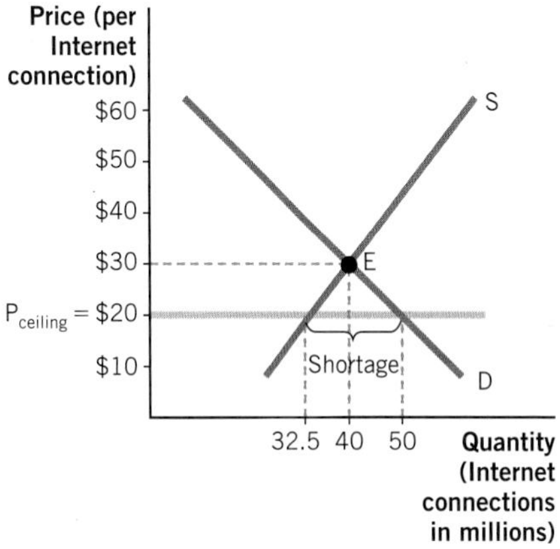

Answer: Subtracting $10 from the market price of $30 gives us a price ceiling of $20. At $20 per connection, consumers demand 50 million connections. However, producers provide only 32.5 million connections. This is a shortage of 17.5 million units (shown on the graph). A price ceiling means that producers cannot raise the price, which will cause a decrease in the quantity supplied. As a result, only 32.5 million units are sold, so only 32.5 million people connect to the Internet.

Question: Which provides the greatest access to the Internet: free markets, price floors, or price ceilings?

Answer: With no government intervention, 40 million connections are sold. When a price floor is established, there are 30 million connections. Under the price ceiling, 32.5 million connections are sold. Despite legislative efforts to satisfy both producers and consumers of Internet service, the best solution is to allow free markets to regulate access to the service.

Conclusion

Trade-offs

Does the minimum wage help everyone earn a living wage? We learned that it is possible to set the minimum wage high enough to guarantee that each worker will earn a living wage. However, the trade-off in setting the minimum wage substantially higher is that it becomes binding and many workers will no longer have jobs. In other words, setting the minimum wage high enough to earn a living wage won't raise every worker out of poverty because many of those workers will no longer be employed.

Undisturbed markets achieve efficiency. When the market sets a price, the largest combined consumer and producer surplus will result. Once policymakers start to intrude into the market, efficiency is endangered. Policies such as the minimum wage, price gouging laws, and other types of price controls are created to help promote equity, but altering the market produces unintended consequences. For this reason, attempts to control prices should be viewed cautiously. When the price signal is suppressed through a binding price floor or a binding price ceiling, the market's ability to maintain order is diminished, efficiency is forfeited, surpluses and shortages develop, and obtaining goods and services becomes difficult. However, as we saw in this chapter, there is a trade-off between efficiency and equity.

The role of markets in society has many layers, and we've only just begun our analysis. In the next chapter, we will begin to consider how firms function within the market system.

ANSWERING THE BIG QUESTIONS

What are consumer surplus and producer surplus?

* Consumer surplus is the difference between the willingness to pay for a good and the price that is paid to get it. Producer surplus is the difference between the willingness to sell a good and the price that the seller receives.
* Total surplus is the sum of consumer and producer surplus that exists in a market.

When is a market efficient?

* Markets maximize consumer and producer surplus, provide goods and services to buyers who value them most, and reward sellers who can produce goods and services at the lowest cost. As a result, markets create the largest amount of total surplus possible.
* Whenever an allocation of resources maximizes total surplus, the result is said to be efficient. However, economists are also interested in the distribution of the surplus. Equity refers to the fairness of the distribution of the benefits among the members of the society.

When do price ceilings matter?

- A price ceiling is a legally imposed maximum price. When the price is set below the equilibrium price, the quantity demanded will exceed the quantity supplied. The result will be a shortage. Price ceilings matter when they are set below the equilibrium price.

What effects do price ceilings have on economic activity?

- Price ceilings create two unintended consequences: a smaller quantity supplied of the good (Q_S) and a higher price for consumers who turn to the black market.
- Price controls reduce the amount of legal trade that takes place, causing the total surplus to fall.

When do price floors matter?

- A price floor is a legally imposed minimum price. The minimum wage is an example of a price floor. If the minimum wage is set above the equilibrium wage, a surplus of labor will develop. Thus, price floors matter when they are set above the equilibrium price.

What effects do price floors have on economic activity?

- Price floors lead to many unintended consequences, including surpluses, ($Q_S > Q_D$), the creation of black markets, and artificial attempts to bring the market back into balance.

ECONOMICS FOR LIFE

Price Gouging: Disaster Preparedness

Disasters, whether natural or human-made, usually strike quickly and without warning. You and your family may have little or no time to decide what to do. That's why it is important to plan for the possibility of disaster and not wait until it happens. Failing to plan is planning to fail. In this feature, we consider a few simple things you can do now to lessen the impact of a disaster on your personal and financial well-being.

During a disaster, shortages of essential goods and services become widespread. In the 30 states where price gouging laws are on the books, they prevent merchants from charging unusually high prices. If you live in one of these states, cash alone can't save you. You will have to survive on your own for a time before help arrives and communication channels are restored.

Taking measures to prepare for a disaster reduces the likelihood of injury, loss of life, and property damage far more than anything you can do after a disaster strikes. An essential part of disaster planning should include financial planning. Let's begin with the basics. Get adequate insurance to protect your family's health, lives, and property; plan for the possibility of job loss or disability by building a cash reserve; and safeguard your financial and legal records. It is also important to set aside extra money in a long-term emergency fund. Nearly all financial experts advise saving enough money to cover your expenses for six months. Most households never come close to reaching this goal, but don't let that stop you from trying.

Preparing a simple disaster supply kit is also a must. Keep enough water, nonperishable food, sanitation supplies, batteries, medications, and cash on hand for three days. Often, the power is out after a disaster, so you cannot count on ATMs or banks to be open. These measures will help you to weather the immediate impact of a disaster.

Finally, many documents are difficult to replace. Consider investing in a home safe or safe deposit box to ensure that your important records survive. Place your passports, Social Security cards, copies of drivers' licenses, mortgage and property deeds, car titles, wills, insurance records, and birth and marriage certificates out of harm's way.

Will you be ready if disaster strikes?

CONCEPTS YOU SHOULD KNOW

black market (p. 107)
consumer surplus (p. 97)
efficiency (p. 105)
equity (p. 105)
minimum wage (p. 117)
price ceiling (p. 106)
price control (p. 106)
price floor (p. 106)
price gouging laws (p. 111)
producer surplus (p. 99)
total surplus (p. 102)
willingness to pay (p. 97)
willingness to sell (p. 99)

QUESTIONS FOR REVIEW

1. Explain how consumer surplus is derived from the difference between the willingness to pay and the market-equilibrium price.
2. Explain how producer surplus is derived from the difference between the willingness to sell and the market-equilibrium price.
3. Does a binding price ceiling cause a shortage or a surplus? Provide an example to support your answer.
4. Does a non-binding price floor cause a shortage or a surplus? Provide an example to support your answer.
5. Are price gouging laws an example of a price floor or a price ceiling?
6. Why do most economists oppose attempts to control prices? Why does the government attempt to control prices anyway, in a number of markets?

STUDY PROBLEMS (*✱ solved at the end of the section*)

1. A college student enjoys eating pizza. Her willingness to pay for each slice is shown in the following table:

Number of pizza slices	Willingness to pay (per slice)
1	$6
2	$5
3	$4
4	$3
5	$2
6	$1
7	$0

   a. If pizza slices cost $3 each, how many slices will she buy? How much consumer surplus will she enjoy?
   b. If the price of slices falls to $2, how much consumer surplus will she enjoy?

2. Andrew paid $30 to buy a potato cannon, a cylinder that shoots potatoes hundreds of feet. He was willing to pay $45. When Andrew's friend Nick learns that Andrew bought a potato cannon, he asks Andrew if he will sell it for $60, and Andrew agrees. Nick is thrilled, since he would have paid Andrew up to $80 for the cannon. Andrew is also delighted. Determine the consumer surplus from the original purchase and the additional surplus generated by the resale of the cannon.

3. A new medical study indicates that eating blueberries helps prevent cancer. If the demand for blueberries increases, what will happen to the size of the consumer and producer surplus? Illustrate your answer in a fully labeled graph. Make sure to appropriately show the shift in demand, and label the new and old areas of consumer and producer surplus.

4. In the song "Minimum Wage," the punk band Fenix TX comments on the inadequacy of the minimum wage to make ends meet. Using the poverty thresholds provided by

the U.S. Census Bureau,* determine whether the federal minimum wage of $7.25 an hour provides enough income for a single full-time worker to escape poverty.

✱ 5. Imagine that the community you live in decides to enact a price control of $700 per month on every one-bedroom apartment. Using the following table, determine the market price and equilibrium quantity without the price control. How many one-bedroom apartments will be rented after the price-control law is passed?

Monthly rent	Quantity demanded	Quantity supplied
$600	700	240
$700	550	320
$800	400	400
$900	250	480
$1,000	100	560

6. Suppose that a group of die-hard sports fans is upset about the high price of tickets to many games. As a result of their lobbying efforts, a new law caps the maximum ticket price to any sporting event at $50. Will more people be able to attend the games? Explain your answer. Will certain teams and events be affected more than others? Provide examples.

7. Many local governments use parking meters on crowded downtown streets. However, the parking spaces along the street are typically hard to find because the metered price is often set below the market price. Explain what happens when local governments set the meter price too low. Why do you think the price is set below the market-clearing price?

8. Imagine that local suburban leaders decide to enact a minimum wage. Will the community lose more jobs if the nearby city votes to increase the minimum wage to the same rate? Discuss your answer.

*See: www.census.gov/hhes/www/poverty/data/threshld/index.html.

✱ 9. Examine the following graph, showing the market for low-skill laborers.

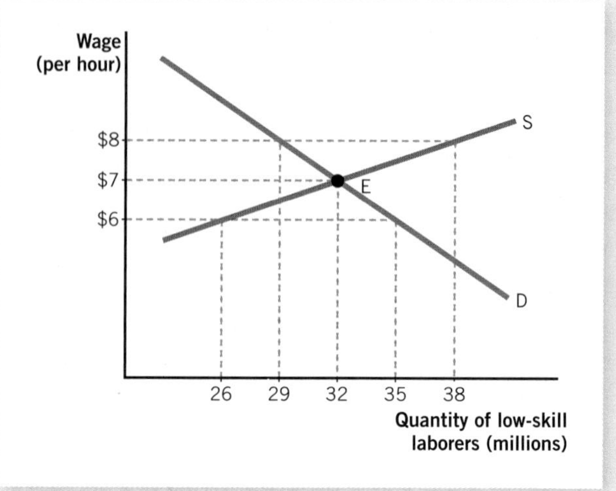

How many low-skill laborers will be unemployed when the minimum wage is $8 an hour? How many low-skill workers will be unemployed when the minimum wage is $6 an hour?

10. Demand and supply curves can be represented with equations. Suppose that the demand for low-skill labor, Q_D, is represented by the following equation, where W is the wage rate:

$$Q_D = 53{,}000{,}000 - 3{,}000{,}000W$$

The supply of low-skill labor, Q_S, is represented by the equation

$$Q_S = -10{,}000{,}000 + 6{,}000{,}000\,W$$

a. Find the equilibrium wage. (**Hint:** Set $Q_D = Q_S$ and solve for the wage, W.)
b. Find the equilibrium quantity of labor. (**Hint:** Now plug the value you got in part (a) back into Q_D or Q_S. You can double-check your answer by plugging the answer from part (a) into both Q_D and Q_S to see that you get the same result.)
c. What happens if the minimum wage is $8? (**Hint:** Plug $W = 8$ into both Q_D and Q_S.) Does this cause a surplus or a shortage?
d. What happens if the minimum wage is $6? (**Hint:** Plug $W = 6$ into both Q_D and Q_S.) Does this cause a surplus or a shortage?

SOLVED PROBLEMS

5. The equilibrium price occurs where the quantity demanded is equal to the quantity supplied. This occurs when $Q_D = Q_S = 400$. When the quantity is 400, the monthly rent is \$800. Next the question asks how many one-bedroom apartments will be rented after a price-control law limits the rent to \$700 a month. When the rent is \$700, the quantity supplied is 320 apartments. It is also worth noting that the quantity demanded when the rent is \$700 is 550 units, so there is a shortage of $550 - 320 = 230$ apartments once the price-control law goes into effect.

9. How many low-skill laborers will be unemployed when the minimum wage is \$8 an hour? The quantity demanded is 29 million, and the quantity supplied is 38 million. This results in 38 million − 29 million = 9 million unemployed low-skill workers.

How many low-skill workers will be unemployed when the minimum wage is \$6 an hour? Since \$6 an hour is below the market-equilibrium wage of \$7, it has no effect. In other words, a \$6 minimum wage is non-binding, and therefore no unemployment is caused.

PROFIT
LOSS

PART

II

MICROECONOMICS

CHAPTER 5

Costs and Production

How Do Businesses Work?

MIS CONCEPTION

The more you sell, the more profit you make.

Walmart is the largest retailer in the world. The company generated revenue of nearly $485 billion in 2014. But it wasn't the world's most profitable company. In fact, it didn't even make the list of the top-ten most profitable. The Industrial and Commercial Bank of China (ICBC) was the most profitable company in 2014 with a $42.7 billion profit on total revenue of $89.4 billion. However, the bank's profitability is closely linked to Chinese government policy. Apple was the second most profitable company at $37 billion on total revenue of $170.9 billion. Walmart's profit was "only" $16.4 billion. What happened to Walmart?

There is a significant difference between *revenue* and *profit*. Many people have the misconception that the only thing that matters is how much money a company brings in. Certainly, revenue—the money a company earns by selling the product or service that it makes or provides—is indeed important. But just as important is what it costs a company to produce the product(s) that it sells. Walmart sells a lot of items, and it makes a lot of money. Still, Walmart has many costs to consider. To acquire all of the goods it sells, Walmart pays a substantial amount to companies that produce those goods. For instance, EA Sports doesn't give its video games to Walmart for free. It sells them to Walmart, which then hopes to sell them to video game players for a little bit more than it paid EA Sports. Walmart may receive the $40 consumers pay for a video game, but in terms of profits it has to deduct the cost of buying the game from EA Sports.

A Walmart distribution center speeds goods to its stores.

If you add up all the sales for all of the millions of items that Walmart sold in 2014, you get $485 billion. But to determine the company's profit you need to subtract all of Walmart's costs from its sales. If a company's costs are greater than its revenues, then no matter how much it sells, it isn't profitable. ICBC and Apple don't sell the volume of items that Walmart does, but they're able to keep revenues above costs better than Walmart, so they are more profitable.

BIG QUESTIONS

- **What are the roles of profits?**
- **How are profits and losses calculated?**
- **How much should a firm produce?**

What Are the Roles of Profits?

Profits play three very important roles in the economy. First, they provide financial incentives. Second, profits make sure that resources are being directed to the businesses that are providing things customers value most. Third, profits determine which companies stay in business and which ones do not. It is essentially survival of the fittest. If you operate a well-run company providing valuable products, you will survive. If not, your business will fail.

Output is the production the firm creates.

Inputs are the things a firm needs to make its output.

Factors of production are the inputs (labor, land, capital, and entrepreneurship) used in producing goods and services.

To earn a profit, a firm must produce goods or services that consumers are willing to pay for. These goods and services are known as its **output**. By selling its output, the firm generates revenue. It must also control its costs. To do so, the firm must use resources efficiently. Those resources, or **inputs**, are the things a firm needs to make its output. There are four categories of inputs, known as the **factors of production**: labor, land, capital, and entrepreneurship.

- Labor generally consists of workers and the skills those workers bring to a job.
- Land consists of the geographic location and natural resources used in production.
- Capital consists of all the man-made resources that workers use to create the final product. This category includes machinery, tools, and other man-made goods.

- **Entrepreneurs** are the people who conceive and start a business. Entrepreneurship is a form of labor.

An **entrepreneur** is a person who conceives and starts a business.

Let's consider McDonald's as an example. The labor input includes managers, cashiers, cooks, and janitorial staff. The land input includes the land on which the McDonald's restaurant sits. The capital input includes the building itself, the pavement for the parking lot, the equipment used to make fast food, the signs, and all the hamburger patties, buns, fries, ketchup, and other foodstuffs. The entrepreneur is the person who decides to buy a McDonald's franchise and open the restaurant.

Financial Incentive

Incentives

Entrepreneurs are willing to risk their own money and reputation to follow an idea to completion and get it to market. They are instrumental in the market economy because they take the risks to get a business started.

Why do people start businesses? Some people think they have a better idea for doing something and want to try it out. Many people like the idea of being their own boss. Some aspiring business owners see a need going unfulfilled, while others want to provide a service to help humanity. Regardless of the reason, businesses begin because someone wants to make money (as in the case of for-profit businesses) or do something for others (as in the case of non-profit businesses). Starting a business takes a lot of work and a fair amount of risk. Obviously, this isn't for everyone.

Once the business is under way, there's a lot to do to make sure that it stays in business: employees have to be paid, inputs need to be acquired, customers must be courted, and the company website must be maintained. All these things need to be done before the entrepreneur pays herself. After paying all the bills, the owner can keep the rest of the money that the company brings in. This is the entrepreneur's chief financial incentive. The first role that profits play in an economy, then, is as a financial incentive to start and maintain a business.

Entrepreneurs don't necessarily have to sell a new or improved product. Sometimes, they just organize things better than others do. For example, Ray Kroc earned billions of dollars as the president of McDonald's. But Kroc didn't start the company. Rather, the McDonald brothers of San Bernardino, California, first opened the hamburger stands. Kroc believed that the brothers' production processes could be used on a large scale. He coordinated with the McDonald brothers and eventually bought them out, becoming the sole owner of McDonald's. Ray Kroc didn't invent the hamburger; he invented a way to make hamburgers of consistent taste and quality in a way that the average family could afford.

In addition to making hamburgers, the early McDonald's restaurants made a profit—often, a very large profit. Profits enabled McDonald's to expand its operations to the point where the company now has over 34,000 restaurants in 116 countries. Those profits also made the Kroc family extremely wealthy. Even though Kroc was a very driven individual, it's doubtful that McDonald's would have expanded to the extent that it has without the potential for the entrepreneurs involved in its creation to make money. However, profits do more than just make people rich. They also allocate resources.

Allocating Resources

Profits allocate the scarce resources that companies need to produce the goods that consumers are willing to pay for. Consider gold, which is used in a surprising number of products. Gold is an excellent conductor of electricity, helping to speed information from one location to another. Gold is therefore found in most electronic devices, including cell phones, GPS systems, and personal computers. It's also used in arthritis treatments, in windows to filter out UV rays, and even in our mouths as gold fillings or crowns (replacement teeth). However, gold is a very limited resource. While it has many uses and many industries would like to use more of it, there is only so much gold to go around.

So who gets this limited amount of gold? The answer in a market economy is "whoever is willing to pay for it." When firms make profits, they are making a product that consumers value. These profits enable the firm to acquire the inputs it needs to continue production. If there's a large demand for a product, the firm can charge higher prices, which will help cover its costs. For example, Nanostellar, a Silicon Valley materials-design company, uses gold in catalytic converters to reduce toxic emissions from cars. This use of gold is very beneficial to automakers because it's cheaper than catalytic converters using platinum, a more expensive metal. Thus, automakers are willing to buy many converters from Nanostellar, and Nanostellar makes a profit. The automakers can then use the profits to buy more gold.

Would you pay $25,000 for this dessert?

Now consider Serendipity 3, a New York City restaurant that used gold in some of its desserts. The gold was added to the chocolate sauce of a $1,000 ice cream sundae and as an ingredient in a $25,000 "Frozen Haute Chocolate." For this dessert, gold was mixed with the world's most expensive chocolate and topped with whipped cream, which was then sprinkled with more gold. Apparently, however, there wasn't much of an appetite for gold desserts. In part due to bad management and warnings from the New York City health department, Serendipity 3 closed down. Serendipity 3's lack of profitability freed up its inputs, including the gold, to be used in other ways.

Will the Company Stay in Business?

Profits determine winners and losers. To stay in business, a company needs a stream of income in order to pay its operating expenses. Workers rarely work for free, and the electric company won't keep the lights on just because the owner is a nice guy. Profits signal that a company is doing something right: it is efficiently providing a product that the public values. As much as people like to bash Walmart, the fact that the company is profitable indicates that it's providing things the general public values. A company that isn't profitable won't stay in business because it won't be able to pay for the costs of operation.

How does a company know if it is profitable? The company examines the two primary components of profits: revenues and costs.

How Are Profits and Losses Calculated?

Ray Kroc was able to take a simple idea—the hamburger stand—and turn it into a societal institution. His entrepreneurial skills made McDonald's a worldwide household name. However, before he made his first billion, or million, or even thousand in profit, Kroc needed to cover the costs of his operation. Let's take a closer look at the way profits are calculated.

Calculating Profit and Loss

To determine the potential profits of a business, the first step is to look at how much it will cost to run it. Consider a McDonald's restaurant. While you're probably familiar with the McDonald's menu, you may not know how an individual franchise operates. For one thing, the manager at a McDonald's restaurant must decide how many workers to hire and how many to assign to each shift. Other managerial decisions involve the equipment needed and what supplies to have on hand each day—everything from hamburger patties to paper napkins. In fact, behind each purchase a consumer makes at McDonald's there is a complicated symphony of delivery trucks, workers, and managers, all of which need to be paid for.

Profits and **losses** are determined by calculating the difference between expenses and revenues. If the difference is positive, you have a profit. If the difference is negative, you have a loss.

Total revenue is the amount a firm receives from the sale of the goods and services it produces.

Total cost is the amount a firm spends in order to produce the goods and services it sells.

The simplest way to determine **profit** or **loss** is to calculate the difference between expenses and revenues. If revenues are greater than costs, the firm has a profit. Losses occur whenever total revenue is less than total cost. The **total revenue** of a business is the amount the firm receives from the sale of the goods and services it produces. For McDonald's, the total revenue is determined on the basis of the number of items sold and their prices. **Total cost** is the amount that a firm spends in order to produce the goods and services it sells. Total cost is determined by adding the costs of all the resources used in producing the goods for sale. We can express this relationship as an equation:

$$\text{Profit (or loss)} = \text{total revenue} - \text{total cost} \qquad \text{(Equation 5.1)}$$

To calculate total revenue, let's look at the dollar amount that the business earns over a specific period. For instance, suppose that in a given day McDonald's sells 1,000 hamburgers for \$1.00 each, 500 orders of large fries for \$2.00 each, and 100 shakes for \$2.50 each. This is all that the restaurant sells on this particular day. The total revenue is the sum of all of these values, (1,000 × \$1.00 for hamburgers, 500 × \$2.00 for fries, and 100 × \$2.50 for shakes) or \$2,250. *But revenue is not the same thing as profit!* The profit is \$2,250 (total revenue) minus the total cost.

Calculating revenue is pretty straightforward. Calculating costs, however, is a little more complicated; we don't simply tally the cost of making each hamburger, order of large fries, and shake. Total cost has two parts—one that is visible and one that is largely invisible. In the next section, we will see that determining total costs is part art and part science.

Explicit Costs and Implicit Costs

Explicit costs are tangible out-of-pocket expenses.

Implicit costs are the opportunity costs of doing business.

Economists break costs into two components: explicit costs and implicit costs. **Explicit costs** are tangible out-of-pocket expenses. To calculate explicit costs, we add every expense incurred to run the business. For example, in the case of a McDonald's franchise, the weekly supply of hamburger patties is one explicit cost: the owner receives a bill from the meat supplier and has to pay it. **Implicit costs** are the opportunity costs of doing business.

Let's consider an example. Purchasing a McDonald's franchise costs about $1 million; this is an explicit cost. However, there's also a high opportunity cost—the next-best possibility for investing a million dollars. That money could have earned interest in a bank, been used to open a different business, or been invested in the stock market. Each alternative is an implicit cost.

Implicit costs are hard to calculate and easy to miss. Specifically, it's difficult to determine how much an entrepreneur could have earned from an alternative activity. Is the opportunity cost the 2% interest she might have earned by placing the money in a bank, the 10% she might have earned in the stock market, or the 15% she might have gained by investing in a different business? We can be sure that there is an opportunity cost for spending $1 million on the franchise, but we can never know exactly how much it is.

Opportunity cost

In addition to the opportunity cost of capital, implicit costs include the opportunity cost of the owner's labor. Often, business owners don't pay themselves a direct salary. However, since they could have been working somewhere else, it's reasonable to consider the fair value of the owner's time—income the owner could have earned by working elsewhere—as part of the business's costs. To fully account for all the costs of doing business, we must calculate the explicit costs, determine the implicit costs, and add them together:

(Equation 5.2)

$$\text{Total cost} = \text{explicit costs} + \text{implicit costs}$$

A simple way of thinking about the distinction between explicit costs and implicit costs is to consider someone who wants to build a bookcase. Suppose that John purchases $30 in materials and takes half a day off from work, where he normally earns $12 an hour. After four hours, he completes the bookcase. His explicit costs are $30, but his total cost is much higher because he also gave up four hours of work at $12 an hour. Therefore, his implicit cost is $48. When we add the explicit cost ($30) and the implicit cost ($48), we get John's total cost ($78).

Table 5.1 shows examples of a firm's implicit and explicit costs.

Economic Profit

Economic profit is calculated by subtracting both the explicit and the implicit costs of business from total revenue.

Considering both implicit and explicit costs helps us determine a firm's economic profit. **Economic profit** is calculated by subtracting both the explicit and the implicit costs of business from total revenue. Economic profit gives a more complete assessment of how a firm is doing.

(Equation 5.3)

$$\textbf{Economic profit} = \text{total revenues} - (\text{explicit costs} + \text{implicit costs})$$

TABLE 5.1

Examples of a Firm's Explicit and Implicit Costs

Explicit costs	Implicit costs
The electricity bill	The labor of an owner who works for the company but does not draw a salary
Advertising on the Internet	The alternative use of the capital invested in the business
Employee wages	The use of the owner's car, computer, or other personal equipment to conduct company business

Including implicit costs makes the calculation of economic profit more difficult. But ignoring them can provide a misleading perception of a company's financial health. For instance, if a company with \$1 billion in assets reports an annual profit of \$10 million, we might think it is doing well. After all, wouldn't you be happy to make \$10 million in a year? However, that \$10 million is only 1% of the \$1 billion that the company holds in assets. In fact, a 1% return is far less than the typical return available in a number of other places, including the stock market, bonds, or a savings account at a financial institution.

If the return on \$1 billion in assets is low compared to what an investor can expect to make elsewhere, the firm with the perceived \$10 million profit actually has a negative economic profit. Had the firm invested the \$1 billion in a savings account, it could have earned 2% (the average return on a savings account) on \$1 billion—that is, \$20 million.

As you can see, economic profit is never misleading. If a business has an economic profit, its revenues are larger than the combination of its explicit and implicit costs. This, of course, raises a question: why don't businesses always figure out economic profits? The reason is one of practicality. It's very difficult to determine the specific value of implicit costs. Despite this difficulty, determining costs is a vital part of making decisions. As we're about to see, if you don't know what your costs are, you'll very likely make the wrong choices.

PRACTICE WHAT YOU KNOW

Calculating Summer Job Profits

How much economic profit do you make from painting?

Kyle is a college student who works during the summers to pay for tuition. Last summer he worked at a fast-food restaurant and earned \$2,500. This summer he's working as a painter and will earn \$4,000. To do the painting job, Kyle had to spend \$200 on supplies.

(CONTINUED)

(CONTINUED)

Question: What is Kyle's profit without considering implicit costs?

Answer: Profit without implicit costs = total revenues − explicit cost
= \$4,000 − \$200 = \$3,800

Question: If working at the fast-food restaurant was Kyle's next-best alternative, how much economic profit will he earn from painting?

Answer: To calculate economic profit, we need to subtract the explicit and implicit costs from the total revenue. Kyle's total revenue from painting will be \$4,000. His explicit costs are \$200 for supplies, and his implicit cost is \$2,500—the salary he would have earned in the fast-food restaurant. So:

Economic profit = total revenues − (explicit cost + implicit cost)
= \$4,000 − (\$200 + \$2,500) = \$1,300

Kyle's economic profit will be \$1,300.

Question: Suppose that Kyle can get an internship at an investment banking firm. The internship provides a stipend of \$3,000 and tangible work experience that will help him get a job after graduation. Should Kyle take the painting job or the internship?

Answer: The implicit costs have changed because Kyle now has to consider the \$3,000 stipend and the increased chance of securing a job after graduation versus what he can make painting houses. Calculation of economic profit from painting is now:

Economic profit = \$4,000 − (\$200 + \$3,000) = \$800

So, at this point, his economic profit from painting would be only \$800. But this number is incomplete. There is also the value of the internship experience. If Kyle wants to work in investment banking after graduation, then the decision is a no-brainer. He should take the internship—that is, unless some investment banks value painting houses more than work experience!

How Much Should a Firm Produce?

Margins are incremental changes.

Every business must decide how much to produce. In this section, we describe the factors that determine output, and we explain how firms use inputs to maximize their production. Since it is possible for a firm to produce too little or too much, we must also consider when a firm should stop production. These decisions focus on the margin. **Margins** are incremental changes, and they show up in every decision a business makes. For Apple, the question isn't whether it should make iPads—an all-or-nothing decision—but, rather, whether it should make *one* more. That's making a decision at the margin. Fortunately for your understanding of marginal decision-making, you have probably gone through the process we're about to describe many times in your life without even thinking about it.

Costs

We've already talked about two different types of costs, explicit and implicit. As we look at how businesses choose how much to produce, we're going to focus on the most important cost of all: marginal cost.

Marginal cost (MC) is the increase in cost that occurs from producing one additional unit of output. Why is the additional cost important? Think about the question this way: what if you ran a lawn-mowing service? You charge $50 to mow lawns of a given size. Is that a good price? If you want to stay in business, the only time that it's advisable to mow a lawn at all is if it costs you at most $50 to do so. If it costs you $100 to mow a lawn but you charge $50, you would be losing money on every job. You would be better off doing something different. While this comparison of cost to price is obvious, costs are not always the same for all levels of production. Typically, the cost of producing a product falls as you increase production of a good—at least, up to a point. After some point, the costs begin to rise as you produce more. Let's take a look at why that happens.

Marginal thinking

Marginal cost is the increase in cost that occurs from producing one additional unit of output.

The Importance of Specialization

If you wanted to open a lawn-care service, you would have a lot to consider. What if, in an effort to keep costs down, you decided that you wouldn't hire any workers and instead do all of the work yourself? While your labor costs would go down, you wouldn't be very productive because there isn't enough of you to go around. You would have to do all of the mowing, trimming, maintenance, and marketing. That might be too much work for one person.

Adding workers helps to distribute the workload and increase the number of customers you can serve. One employee can focus on using the zero-turn mower while another uses the push mower. Another can become proficient at trimming, while a fourth maintains your equipment. As each employee specializes in a task, more gets accomplished. **Specialization** involves breaking up a job into tasks and assigning those tasks to different individuals. This process is also called the division of labor. When specialization in production occurs, more gets accomplished and it gets done more quickly. As a result, the cost of producing output falls on average. This sounds like a winning strategy—increase the number of workers and produce more while costs fall. Unfortunately, this can't go on forever.

Specialization, also called the division of labor, involves breaking up a job into tasks and assigning those tasks to individuals.

The Production Function

To keep costs down in the production process, a firm needs to find the right mix of inputs. A **production function** describes the relationship between the inputs a firm uses and the output it creates. Understanding what a production function is can help managers make better decisions on how to combine their inputs.

The **production function** describes the relationship between the inputs a firm uses and the output it creates.

When only a few workers share capital resources, the resources that each worker needs are readily available. But what happens when your business gets very busy? You can hire more employees for a time, but the number of

Mowing lawns for fun and profit—but only if revenue exceeds costs.

mowers, trimmers, and other equipment is fixed in the short run, which means that it cannot be changed. Because the added employees have to spread the limited capital among themselves, beyond a certain point the additional labor will not continue to increase your company's productivity at the same rate as it did at first. You might recognize this situation if you've ever had to wait for a table at a restaurant. There may be plenty of wait staff, but not enough tables. The restaurant can't keep up with customers' orders because there aren't enough ovens, grills, fryers, and other equipment in the kitchen. As a result, you have to wait.

Returning to the example of your lawn-care business, why don't you just buy another lawn mower? The question you need to ask yourself is: *What happens when summer starts and the rain stops?* During the dog days of summer, lawns burn out and don't need to be cut. This would mean you have employees *and* machines sitting around. It's easy to lay off workers, but you can't normally return a lawn mower to the equipment store, especially after you've used it. Business managers must therefore be able to (1) decide how many workers to hire for each shift and (2) manage the inventory of capital.

Let's look more closely at your decision about how many workers to hire. On the left side of Figure 5.1, we see what happens when workers are added, one by one. When you add one worker, output goes from 0 lawns mowed to 5 lawns mowed. Going from one worker to two workers increases total output to 15 lawns. This means that a second worker has increased the number of lawns mowed from 5 to 15, or an increase of 10. This increase in output is the **marginal product**, which is the change in output associated with one additional unit of an input. In this case, the change in output (10 additional lawns mowed) divided by the increase in input (1 worker) gives us a marginal product of 10 ÷ 1, or 10. Since the table in Figure 5.1 adds one worker at a time, the marginal product is just the increase in output shown in the third column.

Marginal thinking

Marginal product is the change in output associated with one additional unit of an input.

Here we're looking at margins from the perspective of how much a new worker adds to total output. Remember that we use the term "margin" in the context of a change from the total. As we look at the data in our table, we see that total output increases as we add workers, but it doesn't increase at the same pace, nor does it increase forever. Looking down the three columns, we see that after the first three workers, the rate of increase in the marginal product slows down. But the total output continues to expand, and it keeps growing through 8 workers. This occurs because the gains from specialization are slowly declining. By the ninth worker (going from 8 to 9), we see a negative marginal product. Once all of the equipment is manned, there isn't much for an extra worker to do. Eventually, extra workers will get in the way or distract other workers from completing their tasks.

FIGURE 5.1

The Production Function and Marginal Product

(a) Total output rises rapidly in the green-shaded zone from 0 to 3 workers, rises less rapidly in the yellow zone between 3 and 8 workers, and falls in the red zone after 8 workers. (b) The marginal product of labor rises in the green zone from 0 to 3 workers, falls in the yellow zone between 3 and 8 workers but remains positive, and becomes negative after 8 workers. Notice that the marginal product becomes negative after total output reaches its maximum at 8 workers. As long as marginal product is positive, total output rises. Once marginal product becomes negative, total output falls.

Number of workers	Total output (number of lawns mowed)	Marginal product of labor
0	0	
		5
1	5	
		10
2	15	
		15
3	30	
		12
4	42	
		10
5	52	
		8
6	60	
		5
7	65	
		2
8	67	
		–4
9	63	
		–8
10	55	

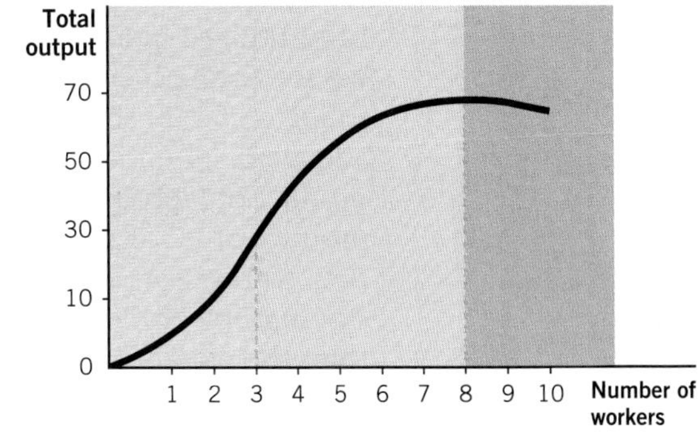

(a) Change in Total Output

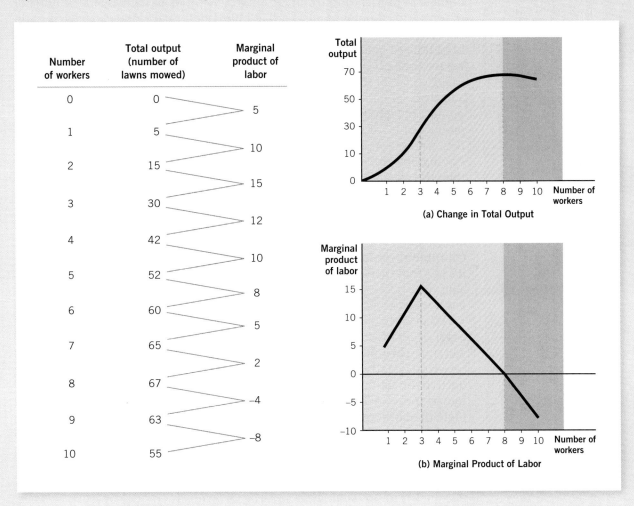

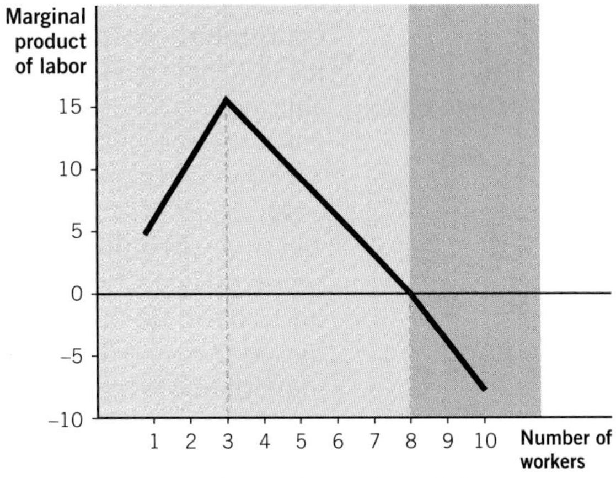

(b) Marginal Product of Labor

Diminishing Marginal Product

Let's now focus our attention on the contributions of each worker. Consider that each worker's marginal productivity either adds to or subtracts from the firm's overall output. Marginal product increases from 5 lawns mowed per day with the first worker to 15 lawns mowed per day with the third worker.

From the first worker to the third, each additional worker leads to increased specialization and teamwork. This explains the rapid rise—from 0 to 30 lawns mowed—in the total output. By the fourth worker, marginal product begins to decline. Looking back to the table in Figure 5.1, you can see that the fourth worker increases output by 12 lawns—3 fewer than the third worker. Successive increases in inputs are associated with a slower rise in output, a phenomenon known as **diminishing marginal product**.

Diminishing marginal product occurs when successive increases in inputs are associated with a slower rise in output.

Why does the rate of output slow down? Recall that in our example the number of mowers and trimmers is fixed. Without an increase in the number of tools and equipment, at a certain point additional workers have less to do or can even interfere with other workers' productivity. When all inputs are fully utilized, additional workers cause marginal product to decline, which we see through the data included with Figure 5.1. The production function in Figure 5.1(a) shows the change in total output (on the vertical axis) as we add workers (along the horizontal axis). Figure 5.1(b) shows the marginal product of labor plotted out. The curve shows what happens to the marginal product of labor (the additional output each worker contributes) as we add new workers. As we add workers 1, 2, and 3, the marginal product curve is sloping upward, indicating that each worker is adding more to total output than the worker before him, as shown by the area shaded in green. Once we add the fourth worker, the line begins to slope downward, indicating that the additional output contributed by this worker, while still positive, is less than it was for the first three workers. Output is growing, but not as quickly—this area is shaded in yellow. Once we get to the ninth worker, however, he is not contributing positively to output. He may be a fine person and a good worker; it's just that there are too many other workers for the space and capital available, so Worker 9's participation causes output to be less than it was with fewer workers, as shown by the area shaded in red.

Marginal thinking

What does diminishing marginal product tell us about the firm's labor-input decision? It gives us some indication of how many workers a manager will hire. The minimum requirement for expanding the workforce is that the new worker adds positively to output. If a new worker causes marginal productivity to become negative, it would be nearly impossible to justify hiring her. In the scenario depicted in Figure 5.1, no rational manager would hire more than 8 workers.

A common mistake when considering diminishing marginal product is to assume that a firm should stop production as soon as marginal product starts to fall. This isn't true. "Diminishing" does not mean "negative." There are many times when marginal product is declining but still high. In our example, diminishing marginal product begins with the fourth worker. However, that fourth worker still helps mow 12 extra lawns. If you can earn more by serving 12 additional customers than you pay the fourth worker, you should hire that worker and your company's profits will rise. But that could be a big "if." To understand whether that person should be hired, we need to go back to the marginal cost.

Decisions at the Margin: The Profit-Maximizing Rule

Every firm, whether just starting out or already well established and profitable, can benefit by assessing how much to produce and how to produce it

PRACTICE WHAT YOU KNOW

Diminishing Returns: Snow Cone Production

It's a hot day, and customers are lined up for snow cones at your small stand. The following table shows your firm's short-run production function for snow cones.

Number of workers	Total output of snow cones per hour
0	0
1	20
2	50
3	75
4	90
5	100
6	105
7	100
8	90

How many workers are too many?

Question: When does diminishing marginal product begin?

Answer: You have to be careful when calculating this answer. Total output is maximized when you have six workers, but diminishing marginal return begins before you hire that many workers. Look at the following table, which includes a third column showing marginal product.

Number of workers	Total output of snow cones per hour	Marginal product
0	0	
		20
1	20	
		30
2	50	
		25
3	75	
		15
4	90	
		10
5	100	
		5
6	105	
		−5
7	100	
		−10
8	90	

The marginal product is highest when you hire the second worker. After that, each subsequent worker you hire has a lower marginal product. Therefore, the answer to the question is that diminishing marginal product begins after the second worker.

more efficiently. As we just discussed, making production decisions involves looking at the contributions of each additional worker. We're going to continue focusing on labor, but this process would also apply to whether or not to buy another backhoe, expand a factory, or purchase a new plot of land. The focus of these decisions should be on the additional costs and benefits from these inputs.

As we've seen, inputs combine to produce output. But not every worker adds the same amount of output to the firm's overall production. Similarly, when it comes to costs, not every completed unit of output adds the same amount of cost to the total. Remember, we're focusing our attention on the additional cost of production. To determine whether it makes sense to produce one more unit, we need to compare the additional cost to the additional benefit of producing it. For firms, that additional benefit presents itself in terms of revenue. Sticking with the theme of making decisions at the margin, we call this revenue the **marginal revenue (MR)**, which is the additional revenue generated by the production and sale of one more unit of output.

Marginal revenue is the additional revenue generated by the production and sale of one more unit of output.

Marginal revenue is very closely associated with the price of a product, and consequently with the demand curve. Let's continue to examine the lawn-mowing business, which tends to be a competitive industry where the price for the job doesn't change. The price charged for mowing the first lawn is $50, the same as for the 100th lawn. By mowing one more lawn, your company adds $50 to its total revenue. Remember that total revenue is the price of the product times the number of things sold. If the price never changes, then the marginal revenue—the change in total revenue by selling one more unit—is the same as the price.

So should you try to mow 25 lawns a day? That would generate more revenue than mowing 10. But with that thinking, why not try to mow 100? After all, 100 lawns would generate even more revenue. At this point, you may be thinking, "Wait a minute. Revenues aren't the same as profits!" and you would be correct. A firm likes to make money, but it also has to pay the costs of operation. We need to compare the revenues *and the costs* to determine profits. To determine how many lawns your company should mow, you need to focus on the *marginal* revenue and the *marginal* cost.

Mowing more lawns generates both more revenue and more costs. So how much work should you do? As long as the marginal revenue is greater than the marginal cost, you will be increasing your profits. Does it make sense to find one more customer and cut the grass for $50 if it costs you $10 to do so? Sure it does! The additional revenue over the additional cost is profit. Does it make sense to mow another lawn if it costs $20 to provide this service? You bet it does! The profit isn't as large for this unit, but it still exists. What if the cost of mowing the next lawn is $49.99? Do it! You're still earning profit. In fact, if it costs $50 to mow the next lawn, you might as well do so. All costs are covered, and everyone is getting paid. But what happens when the additional cost rises above the $50 price?

If the marginal cost is $50.01, or $55 or $100, mowing another lawn doesn't make sense. Now the added costs of operation are greater than the additional revenue generated. This means you're losing money for the additional lawn mowed. Does this mean you should close up shop and lay off all the workers? Of course not. It just means that you should cut back on output. Marginal decision-making of this type is not an all-or-nothing proposal. Making decisions at the margin involves fine-tuning. Decision-makers are comparing added costs to added revenue to see if doing a little more of something is profitable.

The **profit-maximizing rule** states that profit maximization occurs when the firm chooses the quantity of output that causes marginal revenue to equal marginal cost, or MR = MC. Output should rise, and profits will too, as long as the marginal revenue exceeds the marginal cost. If marginal cost is greater than marginal revenue, profits fall. To keep that from happening, the business needs to produce less. Let's look at some numbers involving your lawn-mowing business to illustrate this point.

The **profit-maximizing rule** states that profit maximization occurs when the firm chooses the quantity that causes marginal revenue to equal marginal cost, or MR = MC.

Profit Maximization: A Tabular Example

Table 5.2 shows how much profit you'll make if you mow up to 10 lawns at a price of $50 each. Total profit (column 4) is determined by taking the total revenue (column 2) and subtracting the total cost (column 3). Your total profit starts out at −$71 because even if you have no customers you still have to pay for your equipment. (These costs are known as *fixed costs*.) To recover these costs, you need to generate revenue by cutting grass. As you mow more lawns, the losses (the negative numbers) shown in column 4 gradually contract; you begin to earn a profit by the time you mow your third lawn.

Total profit reaches a maximum of $79 in a range of 5 to 6 lawns mowed. From looking at Table 5.2, you might suppose that you can make a production decision based on the data in the Total Profit column. However, firms don't work this way. The total profit (or loss) is typically determined after the fact. For example, you may have to alter employees' hours, increase gasoline purchases at certain times of the year, pay to repair the mowers, or buy a new

TABLE 5.2

Calculating Profit for Your Lawn-Mowing Business

(1)	(2)	(3)	(4)	(5)		(6)	(7)
Quantity (Q = lawns cut)	Total revenue	Total cost	Total profit	Marginal revenue		Marginal cost	Change (Δ) in total profit
Abbreviation:	TR	TC		MR		MC	
Formula:			TR−TC	ΔTR		ΔTC	MR−MC
0	$0	$71	−$71				
1	50	107	−57	$50		$36	14
2	100	129	−29	50		22	28
3	150	143	7	50		14	36
4	200	150	50	50		7	43
5	250	171	**79**	50		21	29
6	300	221	**79**	**50**	=	**50**	0
7	350	307	43	50		86	−36
8	400	421	−21	50		114	−64
9	450	586	−136	50		165	−115
10	500	800	−300	50		214	−164

Note: Δ is the Greek letter delta; it means "change in."

trailer when the old one breaks down. Your accountant will keep track of all these costs to determine your profit, but all of this takes time. An accurate understanding of your profit may have to wait until the end of the summer or even the end of the year, in order to fully account for all the irregular expenses associated with running the business. This means that the information found in the Total Profit column isn't available until long after the business decisions have been made. So in day-to-day operations, the firm needs another way to make production decisions.

Marginal thinking

Although a firm can't wait for the yearly profit statement to make production decisions, by examining the marginal impact, shown in column 7, a firm can make good day-to-day operational decisions. This information helps you decide whether to take on new customers. The key to determining your profit comes from understanding the relationship between marginal revenue (column 5) and marginal cost (column 6). The marginal revenue is the change (Δ, the Greek letter delta) in total revenue when the firm produces additional units. So, looking down column 5, we see that for every lawn you mow, you earn \$50 in extra revenue. The marginal cost (column 6) is the change (Δ) in total cost when the firm produces additional units. Column 7 calculates the difference between the marginal revenue (column 5) and the marginal cost (column 6).

For instance, if you're mowing 2 lawns, you may decide to ramp up production and mow one more. At 3 lawns, total profit increases by \$36 and you go from losing money to making money. In other words, you are now profitable. Adding a new customer and expanding from 3 to 4 lawns increases revenue by an additional \$50 (total revenue goes from \$150 to \$200) and profit increases by \$43 (from \$7 to \$50). Increasing production again from 4 to 5 lawns raises profit by \$29. However, when you expand from 5 to 6 lawns, you discover that there is no additional profit, and at 7 lawns your profit starts to decrease. By the eighth lawn, you're losing money.

Why do you lose money at the eighth lawn? At this point, your additional costs for mowing one more lawn are greater than the additional revenue. Since marginal revenue is constant, your marginal costs must have risen. This happens for a number of reasons. Driving to the new job causes your gas bill to rise. Maybe you needed to hire a new employee to do the job. Perhaps you also needed to buy a new, expensive mower to take on that eighth lawn. If you continued to increase production, the losses would grow because your costs would grow. This would cause you to scale back your output to a more profitable level.

Looking at column 7, we see that where total profit equals \$79, the change in profit, MR − MC, is equal to \$0. (See the numbers in red in columns 4 and 7.) The profit-maximizing rule may seem counterintuitive, since at MR = MC (where marginal revenue is equal to the extra cost of production) there is no additional profit. However, according to the MR = MC rule, production should stop at the point at which profit opportunities no longer exist. Suppose that you choose a point at which MR > MC. At that point, producing additional units adds more to revenue than to costs, so production should continue. However, if MR < MC, the cost of producing additional units is more than the additional revenue those units bring in. At that point, production is not profitable. The point at which MR = MC is the exact level of production at which no further profitable opportunities exist and losses

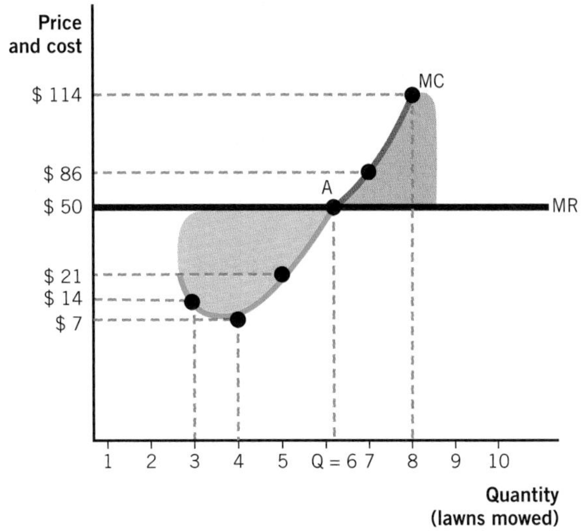

FIGURE 5.2

The Profit-Maximizing Rule

Using the profit-maximizing rule, you can locate the output where marginal revenue equals marginal cost, or MR = MC, to determine the ideal output level. If you produce an output (Q) to the left of the profit-maximizing point (point A), shown in green, MR exceeds MC and you can increase profits by increasing output. If you produce an output to the right of this point, shown in red, MR is less than MC. You can increase profits by decreasing output.

have not yet occurred. This is the optimal point at which to stop production. Thus, to exhaust all profit opportunities you should mow 6 lawns.

Profit Maximization: A Graph

The profit-maximizing rule can be illustrated in graphical form. Look at Figure 5.2. As with most graphs used in economics, we're looking for the points at which curves cross. When that happens, something interesting is going on. In this graph, the profit-maximizing price and quantity occur where the marginal revenue curve crosses the marginal cost curve, at point A. Dropping down to the Quantity axis shows us the profit-maximizing output of 6 lawns.

Marginal Thinking in Everyday Life

Marginal thinking works for businesses, and it works for everyday decisions too. In all cases, you're comparing the costs and benefits of a decision to see if doing a little more of something makes you better off. You can use marginal thinking, and you probably have, anytime you have to decide whether to do a little more of something. For instance, after eating one donut you ask yourself: *Should I have another?* Intuitively, you compare the additional cost (in terms of the price of the donut, the calories, and what it makes your stomach feel like) to the benefits in terms of how good that next donut will taste. If you deem the benefits to be greater than the costs, you proceed to eat a second donut. When faced with the decision to eat a third, fourth, or

What are the costs and benefits of eating one more hot dog?

fifth donut, you ask the same question and think along the same lines. Most people stop before reaching the fifth donut because eating too many donuts will make them feel sick, and that is part of the marginal benefit and cost comparison. Marginal thinking applies in nearly every choice you make: *Should you study one more hour, drive one more mile per hour faster, have one more soda?* You aren't deciding on whether or not to do something, but whether to do a little more of something.

Costs in the Long Run

One thing we haven't addressed in this discussion of cost is what happens over time. Firms have more control over their costs in the long run. Instead, we've been focusing on the **short run**, the period of time in which consumers and producers can partially adjust their behavior. In the **long run**, however, consumers and producers can fully adjust to market conditions. For a firm, the long run means the period in which it can change any aspect of its production process. A long-run time horizon allows a business to choose a scale of operation that best suits its needs. **Scale** refers to the size of the production process. A bigger store might help increase profits, but a new store doesn't spring up overnight. Given enough time (the long run), a new store can be built.

The **short run** is the period of time in which consumers and producers can partially adjust their behavior.

The **long run** is the period of time that allows consumers and producers to fully adjust to market conditions.

Scale refers to the size of the production process.

Let's look at another example. If a local health insurer experiences an increase in the number of customers in the short run, the manager can only hire more workers or expand the help-line hours to accommodate the greater number of insured individuals. These changes can take effect relatively quickly. Economists typically refer to the costs associated with **variable inputs** (that is, easily changeable inputs) as **variable costs**. While it might be helpful to change the computer system to handle higher case loads, in the short run that isn't possible. The inputs that cannot be changed in the short run are called **fixed inputs**, and the costs tied to them are called **fixed costs**. However, in the long run the manager can make any changes she wants, including an improved database management system, larger office space, or a more comprehensive wellness plan for customers. By increasing the size of the operation, essentially adding more and better inputs in the long run, the company eliminates the problem of diminishing marginal product. All employees have all the tools they need to be productive.

Variable inputs are inputs that can be easily changed, thereby altering output levels.

Variable costs are costs associated with variable inputs. These costs vary directly with the amount of output a firm produces.

Fixed inputs are inputs that cannot be changed in the short run.

Fixed costs are costs that do not vary with a firm's output in the short run.

In the long run, all costs are variable because everything can be changed: the number of employees, the size and location of operations, agreements with suppliers, and so on. As a result, in the long run, firms have more flexibility than in the short run. This flexibility allows them to find the most cost-effective means of production. In some cases, it allows them to be more profitable, but that won't always be the case. When firms are profitable in a particular industry, potential competitors sit up and take notice. Perhaps they'll want to enter that industry. If they enter the industry and are successful, other companies' profits may fall. In the next chapter, we will look at the results of market structure and how competition, or the lack thereof, affects output and prices.

PRACTICE WHAT YOU KNOW

Marginal Cost: The True Cost of Admission to Universal Studios

You and your family visit Orlando for a week. While there, you decide to go to Universal Studios. When you arrive, you notice that each family member can buy a day pass for $80 or a two-day pass for $90. Your parents are concerned about spending too much, so they decide to calculate the average cost of a two-day pass to see if it's a good value. The average cost is $90 ÷ 2, or $45 per day. The math is correct, but something you learned in economics tells you that they aren't thinking about this decision in the correct way.

Question: What concept can you apply to make the decision more clear?

Answer: Tell your parents about *marginal cost*. The first day costs $80, but the marginal cost of going back to the park on the second day is only the extra cost per person, or $90 − $80, which equals $10. Your parents still might not want to spend the extra money, but spending only an extra $10 for the second day makes the two-day ticket an extraordinary value. Someone who doesn't appreciate economics might think the second day costs an extra $45 because that's the average cost. But the average cost is misleading. Looking at marginal cost is the best way to weigh these two options.

However, a two-day ticket is a value only if it costs less than your other options. Don't forget, you're on vacation—and another day at Universal Studios is a day you can't do something else. While the marginal cost is $10 in monetary terms, there is also the opportunity cost of missing a day on the beach, going to Disney World (a substitute for Universal Studios), or just taking a nap.

Is one day enough to do it all?

ECONOMICS IN THE MEDIA

Reducing Production Costs

Modern Times

The 1936 comedy *Modern Times* is regarded as one of the top 100 English-language films of all time. The movie features Charlie Chaplin in his final silent-film role. Chaplin, who was a master of slapstick comedy, plays a tramp who finds work on an assembly line in a large factory. The company bosses are ruthless taskmasters. For the production process to remain in sync and maximum efficiency to occur, each assembly line worker must complete a small task and pass the product down the line. This is an example of specialization.

As the movie progresses, the bosses introduce a novel product called the Billows Feeding Machine. The idea is simple: if the lunch break were shorter, the workers' downtime would be minimized and production increased. Here is the exact transcript from the film:

> May I take the pleasure of introducing Mr. J. Widdecombe Billows, the inventor of the Billows Feeding Machine, a practical device which automatically feeds your men while at work. Don't stop for lunch: be ahead of your competitor. The Billows Feeding Machine will eliminate the lunch hour, increase your production, and decrease your overhead. Allow us to point out some of the features of this wonderful machine: its beautiful, aerodynamic, streamlined body; its smoothness of action, made silent by our electro-porous metal ball bearings. Let us acquaint you with our automaton soup plate—its compressed-air blower, no breath necessary, no energy required to cool the soup. Notice the revolving plate with the automatic food pusher. Observe our counter-shaft, double-knee-action corn feeder, with its synchro-mesh transmission, which enables you to shift from high to low gear by the mere tip of the tongue. Then there is the hydro-compressed, sterilized mouth wiper: its factors of control insure against spots on the shirt front. These are but a few of the delightful features of the Billows Feeding Machine. Let us demonstrate with one of your workers, for actions speak louder than words. Remember, if you wish to keep ahead of your competitor, you cannot afford to ignore the importance of the Billows Feeding Machine.

Would a feeding machine for workers lower long-run costs?

The company bosses are eager to test the feeding machine, but things go terribly wrong—in a hilarious way—when they select Chaplin as the human guinea pig. Because the machine doesn't work as promised, the company decides that the feeding machine isn't a practical idea.

Although no firm in the real world is likely to try something like the feeding machine, firms do constantly seek efficiency gains. Of course, not all ideas are practical. For instance, the assembly line depicted in *Modern Times* is efficient, but it wouldn't make sense for a company to use this process unless it sells a large volume of bolts. This situation is analogous to production in the automobile industry. Large manufacturers like Toyota and Ford use assembly lines to reduce production costs, while a small specialty shop that produces only a handful of vehicles a year builds each car by hand. These specialty cars are therefore much more expensive since the costs of production are much higher.

ECONOMICS IN THE MEDIA

Costs in the Short Run

The Office

The popular TV series *The Office* had an amusing episode devoted to the discussion of costs. The character Michael Scott establishes his own paper company to compete with both Staples and his former company, Dunder Mifflin. He then outcompetes his rivals by keeping his costs low.

In one inspired scene, we see the Michael Scott Paper Company operating out of a single room and using an old church van to deliver paper. The minimalist aspects of the business allow the company to keep costs low and prices low. In addition, Michael Scott keeps labor costs to a minimum by hiring only essential employees and not paying any benefits, such as health insurance. But this is a problem, since Michael Scott doesn't fully account for the cost of the paper he's selling. In fact, his prices are so low that they're below the costs of production! His advantage over his competitors is his low prices. But his low prices are actually driving him out of business.

Michael Scott doesn't understand the difference between revenue and profit.

Conclusion

Do firms that sell more have larger profits? Not always. Profitability is based on two things, revenues and costs. There are always bills to pay in the production process, and you can't count your revenues as profits until you pay for your inputs.

Marginal cost plays the most crucial role in a firm's cost structure. Good output decisions are based on the additional costs of producing one more unit. This is why economists place so much emphasis on marginal cost. Going forward, a solid grasp of marginal analysis will help you understand many of the most important concepts in microeconomics.

Marginal thinking

You now understand a good deal about a firm's decision-making process. It involves a constant comparison of costs and benefits. However, to provide a complete picture of how firms operate, we still need to examine how markets are structured. Firms are not all created equal, and neither are markets. While all firms want to be profitable, there are inherent problems in achieving that goal depending on the type of market in which a firm works. We'll look at different market structures in the next chapter.

ANSWERING THE BIG QUESTIONS

What are the roles of profits?

* Profits provide the financial incentive for entrepreneurs to enter a business. Without the prospect of financial gain, very few people would take the risk of starting a business.
* Profits also direct (allocate) resources to businesses that are producing things consumers want. If you don't make a profit, it's difficult to afford the inputs necessary to continue production.
* Profits determine which companies stay in business and which ones do not. A company that isn't making profits isn't covering its costs and will have to shut down.

How are profits and losses calculated?

* Profits and losses are determined by calculating the difference between expenses and revenue.
* Economists break cost into two components: explicit costs, which are easy to calculate, and implicit costs, which are hard to calculate. Economic profit accounts for both explicit costs and implicit costs. If a business has an economic profit, its revenues are larger than the combination of its explicit and implicit costs.

How much should a firm produce?

* A firm should produce an output that is consistent with the largest possible economic profit.
* In any short-run production process, diminishing marginal product will occur at the point at which additional units of a variable input do not generate as much output as before. Diminishing marginal output occurs because each firm has separate fixed and variable inputs.
* To maximize profits, firms need to produce at the point where marginal revenue (MR) equals marginal cost (MC). This profit-maximization rule tells the firm to continue to produce as long as the additional revenue from selling one more unit of a good exceeds the additional cost of producing it.

ECONOMICS FOR LIFE

How Much Does It Cost to Raise a Child?

Raising a child is one of life's most rewarding experiences, but it can be very expensive. According to the U.S. Department of Agriculture, the cost for a middle-income, two-parent family to raise a child from birth to age 18 is more than $250,000—and that doesn't include college. To determine this number, the government considers all related costs, such as food, clothing, medical care, and entertainment. In addition, the government apportions a share of the costs of the family home and vehicles to each child in the household. To put the cost of raising a child in perspective, the median home value in 2014 was $178,500. Talk about opportunity cost!

Opportunity cost

What if a family has more than one child? You wouldn't necessarily multiply the cost by two or three. For example, some things can be shared: the children might share a bedroom and wear hand-me-downs. Also, the family can purchase food in bulk. As a result, families that have three or more children can manage to spend an average of 22% less on each child.

The cost of raising children also forces families to make trade-offs. In many households, both parents must work or work longer hours. When one parent steps out of the workforce, the household loses a paycheck. While this may save in expenses associated with working (for example, certain clothes, transportation, and childcare), there are also hidden costs. For example, the lack of workplace continuity lowers the stay-at-home parent's future earning power.

Raising a child is an expensive proposition in both the short run and the long run. But don't let this discourage you; it is also one of the most rewarding investments you will ever make.

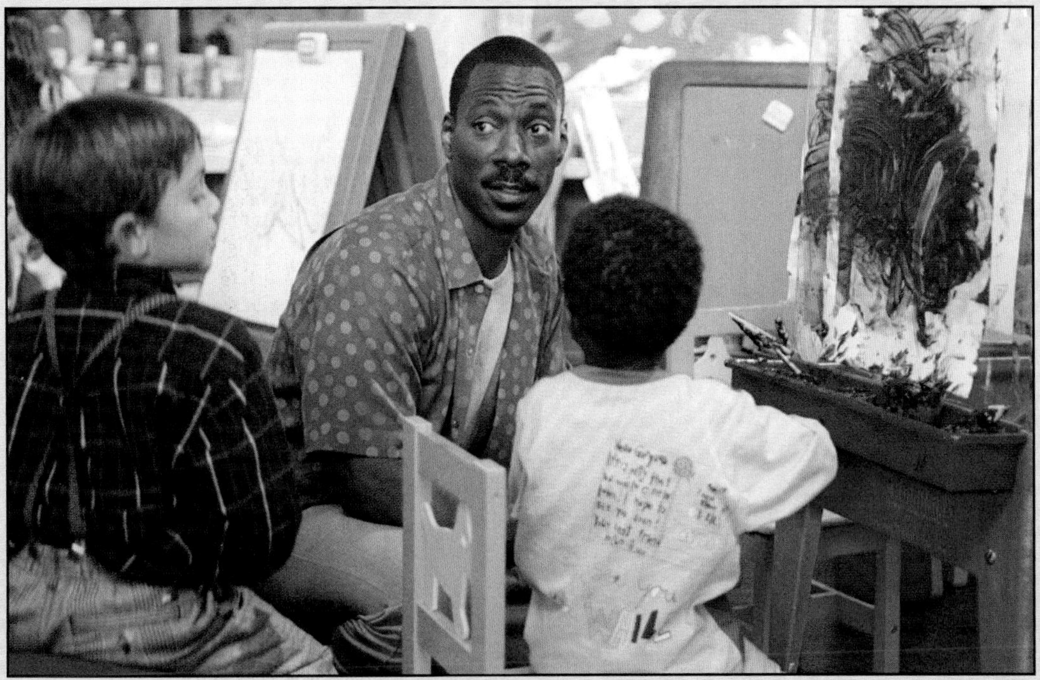

Daddy Day Care? Childcare expenses add up.

CONCEPTS YOU SHOULD KNOW

diminishing marginal product (p. 142)
economic profit (p. 136)
entrepreneur (p. 133)
explicit costs (p. 136)
factors of production (p. 132)
fixed costs (p. 148)
fixed inputs (p. 148)
implicit costs (p. 136)
inputs (p. 132)
long run (p. 148)
losses (p. 135)
marginal cost (MC) (p. 139)
marginal product (p. 140)
marginal revenue (MR) (p. 144)
margins (p. 138)
output (p. 132)
production function (p. 139)
profit-maximizing rule (p. 145)
profits (p. 135)
scale (p. 148)
short run (p. 148)
specialization (p. 139)
total cost (p. 135)
total revenue (p. 135)
variable costs (p. 148)
variable inputs (p. 148)

QUESTIONS FOR REVIEW

1. How do profits and losses act as signals that guide producers to use resources to make what society wants most?
2. What is the equation used to calculate a firm's profit (or loss)?
3. Which two types of costs does economic profit take into account?
4. What role does diminishing marginal product play in determining the ideal mix of labor and capital a firm should use?
5. Describe what happens to the total product of a firm when marginal product is increasing, decreasing, and negative.

STUDY PROBLEMS (✱ *solved at the end of the section*)

1. Go to www.lemonadegame.com. This free online game places you in the role of a lemonade seller. Nothing could be simpler, right? Not so fast! You still need to control costs and ensure you have the right ingredients on hand to be able to sell. You'll need to manage your supply of lemons, sugar, ice, and cups. You'll also have to set a price and decide how many lemons and how much sugar and ice to put in each glass of lemonade you produce. This is not a trivial process, so play the game. Your challenge is to make $20 in profit over the first five days. (Your business starts with $20, so you need to have $40 in your account by the end of day 5 to meet the challenge. Are you up to it?)

2. The following table shows a short-run production function for laptop computers. Use the data to determine where diminishing product begins.

Number of workers	Total output of laptop computers
0	0
1	40
2	100
3	150
4	180
5	200
6	205
7	200
8	190

3. A pizzeria has the cost structure described below. Calculate the marginal costs.

Output (pizzas per day)	Total cost of output
0	$25
10	75
20	115
30	150
40	175
50	190
60	205
70	225
80	250

4. True or false?
   a. Diminishing marginal product is a long-run constraint that prevents lower costs.
   b. Total cost divided by output is equal to marginal cost.

5. Many amusement parks offer two-day passes at dramatically discounted prices. If a one-day pass costs $40 but the two-day pass costs $50, what is the average cost for the two-day pass? What is the marginal cost of the two-day pass?

✱ 6. Suppose that you own a yard-care business. You have your own mower, flatbed truck, and other equipment. You are also the primary employee. Why might you have trouble calculating your economic profit?

7. A local snow cone business sells snow cones in one size for $3 each. It has the following cost and output structure per hour:

Output (cones per hour)	Total cost (per hour)
0	$60
10	$90
20	$110
30	$120
40	$125
50	$135
60	$150
70	$175
80	$225

a. Calculate the total revenue for the business at each rate of output.
b. Calculate the total profit for the business at each rate of output.
c. Calculate the profit-maximizing rate of output using the MR = MC rule. (**Hint**: to do this, you should first compute the marginal revenue and marginal cost from the table.)

8. In the following table, fill in the blanks. Assume the market is perfectly competitive. After you have completed the entire table, determine the profit-maximizing output.

Output	Price	Total revenue	Marginal revenue	Total cost	Marginal cost	Total profit
1	$20	___	___	$40	___	−$20
2	___	___	___	$50	___	___
3	___	___	___	$60	___	___
4	___	___	___	$65	$5	___
5	___	___	___	$85	___	___
6	___	$120	___	$120	___	___

9. Do you agree or disagree with the following statement? *A profit-maximizing firm should select the output level at which the difference between the marginal revenue and marginal cost is the greatest.* Explain your answer.

*10. Suppose you are the owner of a firm producing jellybeans. Your production costs are shown in the table below. Initially, you produce 100 boxes of jellybeans per time period. Then a new customer calls and places an order for an additional box of jellybeans, requiring you to increase your output to 101 boxes. She offers you $1.50 for the additional box. Should you produce it? Why or why not?

JELLYBEAN PRODUCTION

Boxes	Average cost per box
100	$1.00
101	$1.01
102	$1.02
103	$1.03

SOLVED PROBLEMS

6. When calculating your costs for the mower, truck, and other expenses, you're computing your explicit costs. However, you don't know your economic profit because you haven't determined your implicit costs. Because you are the primary employee, you also have to add in the opportunity cost of the time you invest in the business. You may not know exactly what you might have earned doing something else, but you can be sure it exists—this is your implicit cost. This is why you may have trouble computing your profits. You might discover that what you thought you made was less than you could have made by doing something else. If that is the case, your economic profit may actually be negative.

10. This problem requires marginal thinking. We know the profit-maximizing rule, MR = MC. Here all we need to do is compare the additional costs, or MC, against the additional revenue, or MR, to see if the deal is a good idea. We know that MR = \$1.50, because that's what the customer is offering to pay for another box of jellybeans. Now we need to calculate the marginal cost of producing the additional box.

JELLYBEAN PRODUCTION

Boxes	Average cost per box	Total cost	Marginal cost
100	\$1.00	\$100.00	—
101	\$1.01	\$102.01	\$2.01
102	\$1.02	\$104.04	\$2.03
103	\$1.03	\$106.09	\$2.05

First, we compute the total cost. To do this, we multiply the number of boxes, listed in the first column, by the average cost per box, shown in the second column. The results are shown in the Total Cost column.

Next we find the marginal cost. Recall that the marginal cost (MC) is the amount that it costs to produce one more unit. So we subtract the total cost of producing 101 boxes from the total cost of producing 100. For 101 boxes, MC = \$102.01 – \$100.00, or \$2.01. Since MR – MC is \$1.50 – \$2.01, producing the 101st box would create a loss of \$0.51. Therefore, at a price of \$1.50, your firm should not produce the 101st box.

CHAPTER

6 Market Structures

MISCONCEPTION

Firms set the prices they charge without any concern for the consumer.

Many people believe that firms set the prices for their products with little concern for the consumer. However, this is incorrect. The misconception occurs because many people think that the firm is central to the functioning of the market. However, market forces are much stronger than individual firms.

In this chapter, we more closely examine the way markets work. We focus on how the number of competitors in a market affects how much is produced and the price that a firm can charge for its product or service. In some markets, there are a lot of firms; in others, not very many. Sometimes, it's easy for new firms to join a market; at other times, entry is difficult because there are significant impediments for start-up firms. We also focus on whether the firm can distinguish its products from those of its competitors. These two conditions, the ease of entry and the ability to differentiate products, are the two primary conditions that define market structure. The term **market structure** refers to how the firms in a particular market relate to one another.

Market structure refers to the way the firms in a particular market relate to one another.

Understanding the differences between market structures will help us see how market forces limit firms' ability to set the price that they can charge. We begin with the market structure that most benefits consumers: competition. We then move on to the market structure that most benefits the producer: monopoly. In reality, most markets fall somewhere between these two extremes, but understanding the characteristics of each extreme gives us insight into what outcome will best serve society as a whole.

Individual vendors in flower markets face stiff competition.

BIG QUESTIONS

* How do competitive markets work?
* How are monopolies created?
* How much do monopolies charge, and how much do they produce?
* What are the problems with monopoly?
* What are monopolistic competition and oligopoly?

How Do Competitive Markets Work?

An **industry** is a group of firms that sell similar products or services.

Market power refers to the control that any individual firm has over the price that it can charge.

In a **competitive market**, firms have little to no market power.

A **price taker** has no control over the price set by the market.

Firms are typically clustered into industries. An **industry** is a group of firms that sell similar products or services. Within an industry, each firm faces similar conditions in its pursuit of profits. Sometimes, a firm has to be very aware of the actions of the other firms in its industry. At other times, a firm might be the only participant in an industry. As we begin our discussion of market structures, keep in mind that the market structure dictates the firm's **market power**, or how much control it has over the price that it can charge.

The first type of market structure that we will explore is a competitive market. In a **competitive market**, firms have little to no market power. Competitive markets are the best for consumers because prices are lower than in any other market structure.

Competitive markets exist when there are so many buyers and sellers that each one has only a small impact on the market price and output. Additionally, each seller is providing a good that is nearly identical. In Chapter 3 we used the example of the Pike Place Market, where each of the many fish vendors sells a similar product. Because each fish vendor is small relative to the whole market, no single firm can influence the market price. It doesn't matter where you buy salmon because the price is the same or very similar at every fish stall. When buyers are willing to purchase a product anywhere, sellers have no control over the price they charge. If one vendor tried to raise her prices, her customers would simply go a few stalls down to buy the same product for less money. As a result, firms that produce goods in competitive markets are price takers. A **price taker** has no control over the price set by the market. It "takes"—that is, accepts—the price determined from the overall supply and demand conditions that regulate the market.

Competitive markets have another feature in common as well: new competitors can easily enter the market. If you want to open a laundromat, all you have to do is rent store space and acquire some washers and dryers. There are no licensing or regulatory obstacles in your way. Likewise, there is very little to stop competitors from leaving the market. If you decide to close your laundromat, you can lock the doors, return any equipment you rented, and

TABLE 6.1

Characteristics of Competitive Firms

- Many sellers
- Similar products
- Firms are price takers
- Free entry and exit into and out of the market by firms

move on to something else. When barriers to entry into a marketplace are low, new firms are free to compete with existing businesses; this situation ensures the existence of competitive markets and low prices. Table 6.1 summarizes the characteristics of competitive firms.

Real-life examples of competitive markets usually fall short of perfection. Examples that are almost perfectly competitive, shown in Table 6.2, include the stock market, farmers' markets, online ticket auctions, and currency trading.

PRACTICE WHAT YOU KNOW

Price Takers: Mall Food Courts

Your instructor asks you to find an example of a competitive market nearby. A friend suggests that you visit the food court at a nearby mall.

Question: Do the restaurants in a food court meet the definition of a price taker, thereby signaling a competitive market?

Are the restaurants in a food court price takers?

Answer: Most food courts contain a lot of competition. Customers can choose among burgers, sandwiches, salads, pizza, and much more. Everywhere you turn, there's another place to eat and the prices at each place are comparable. Is this enough to make each restaurant a price taker? Not quite, since each restaurant has some market power because it serves different food. This enables the more popular places to charge somewhat more.

While the restaurants in the court are not price takers, the drinks (both fountain drinks and bottled water) that they sell are essentially the same. Any customer who is interested only in getting something to drink has a highly competitive market to choose from.

TABLE 6.2

Almost Perfect Markets

Example	How it works	Reality check
Stock market 	Millions of shares of stocks are traded every day on various stock exchanges, and generally the buyers and sellers have access to real-time information about prices. Since most of the traders represent only a small share of the market, they have little ability to influence the market price.	Because of the volume of shares that they control, large institutional investors, like Pacific Investment Management Company (PIMCO), manage billions of dollars in funds. As a result, they are big enough to influence the market price.
Farmers' markets 	In farmers' markets, sellers are able to set up at little or no cost. Many buyers are also present. The gathering of numerous buyers and sellers of similar products causes the market price for similar products to converge toward a single price.	Many produce markets do not have enough sellers to achieve a perfectly competitive result. Without more vendors, individual sellers can often set their prices higher.
Online ticket auctions 	The resale market for tickets to major sporting events and concerts involves many buyers and sellers. The prices for seats in identical sections end up converging quickly toward a narrow range.	Some ticket companies and fans get special privileges that enable them to buy and sell blocks of tickets before others can enter the market.
Currency trading 	Hundreds of thousands of traders around the globe engage in currency buying and selling on any given day. Since all traders have very good real-time information, currency trades in different parts of the world converge toward the same price.	Currency markets are subject to intervention on the part of governments that might want to strategically alter the prevailing price of their currency.

ECONOMICS IN THE REAL WORLD

Aalsmeer Flower Auction

The world's largest flower auction takes place in Aalsmeer, a small town in the Netherlands. Each week, producers sell over 100 million flowers there. In fact, over one-third of all the flowers sold in the world pass through Aalsmeer. Since the Aalsmeer market serves thousands of buyers and sellers, it is one of the best examples of a competitive market you will ever find. The supply comes from approximately 6,000 growers worldwide. More than 2,000 buyers attend the auction to purchase flowers.

The Aalsmeer flower market is almost perfectly competitive.

At Aalsmeer, individual buyers and sellers are small compared to the overall size of the market. In addition, the flowers offered by one seller are almost indistinguishable from those offered by the other sellers. As a result, individual buyers and sellers have no control over the price set by the market. ✱

In the next section, we will examine the profits that competitive firms make. After all, profits motivate firms to produce a product, so knowing how a business can make the most profit is central to understanding how competitive markets work.

The Profit-Maximizing Rule in Competitive Markets

If you are a price taker, you can't raise your prices to increase your revenue. Because there are so many other firms selling essentially the same thing, if you try to increase your prices your customers will simply go buy from someone else. So what is left for you to do? As a seller in this market, the only thing you have to decide is how much to produce in order to maximize profits at the given market price.

To examine the choices every firm has to make, throughout this section we refer to Mr. Plow (from the Economics in the Media box on p.164). Keep in mind that although the *Simpsons* episode centers on the rivalry between Homer and Barney—just two suppliers—they are part of a market with a huge number of suppliers. We'll look at the price Mr. Plow charges and how many driveways he clears, and then we'll compare his revenues to his costs in order to determine whether he is maximizing his profit.

The profit-maximizing rule we learned in Chapter 5 will provide a guide for Mr. Plow as he tries to deal with the competitive market. Table 6.3 provides the cost and revenue information for Mr. Plow. Revenue is based

ECONOMICS IN THE MEDIA

Competitive Markets

The Simpsons: Mr. Plow

In this episode, Homer buys a snowplow and goes into the snow-removal business. After a few false starts, his business, Mr. Plow, becomes a huge success. Every snowy morning, he looks out the window and comments about "white gold."

However, Homer's joy, profits, and notoriety are short-lived. Soon his friend Barney buys a bigger plow and joins the ranks of the "plow people." Barney's *entry* into the business shows how easy it is for competitors to enter the market. Then Homer, who has begun to get lazy and rest on his success, wakes up late one snowy morning to find all the driveways in the neighborhood already plowed. A nasty battle over customers ensues.

The episode illustrates each of the factors that go into making a competitive market. Businesses providing snow removal all offer the *same* service. Since there are many buyers (homeowners) and many businesses (the "plow people"), the market is competitive.

When firms can easily enter the market, any higher-than-usual profits that a firm enjoys in the short run will eventually dissipate due to increased competition. As a result, we can say that this *Simpsons* episode illustrates an industry that is not just competitive; it is perfectly competitive.

Homer's great idea is about to melt away.

TABLE 6.3

Calculating Profit for Mr. Plow

(1)	(2)	(3)	(4)	(5)	(6)	(7)	(8)
Quantity (Q = driveways cleared)	Total revenue	Total cost	Average total cost	Total profit	Marginal revenue	Marginal cost	Change (Δ) in total profit
Abbreviation:	TR	TC	ATC		MR	MC	
Formula:	P × Q		TC/Q	TR−TC	ΔTR	ΔTC	MR−MC
0	$0	$25		−$25			
1	10	34	34	−24	$10	$9	$1
2	20	41	20.5	−21	10	7	3
3	30	46	15.33	−16	10	5	5
4	40	49	12.25	−9	10	3	7
5	50	51	10.2	−1	10	2	8
6	60	54	9	6	10	3	7
7	70	60	8.57	10	10	6	4
8	80	70	8.75	10	**10** =	**10**	0
9	90	95	10.56	−5	10	25	**−15**
10	100	145	14.5	−45	10	50	**−40**

Note: Δ is the Greek letter delta; it means "change in."

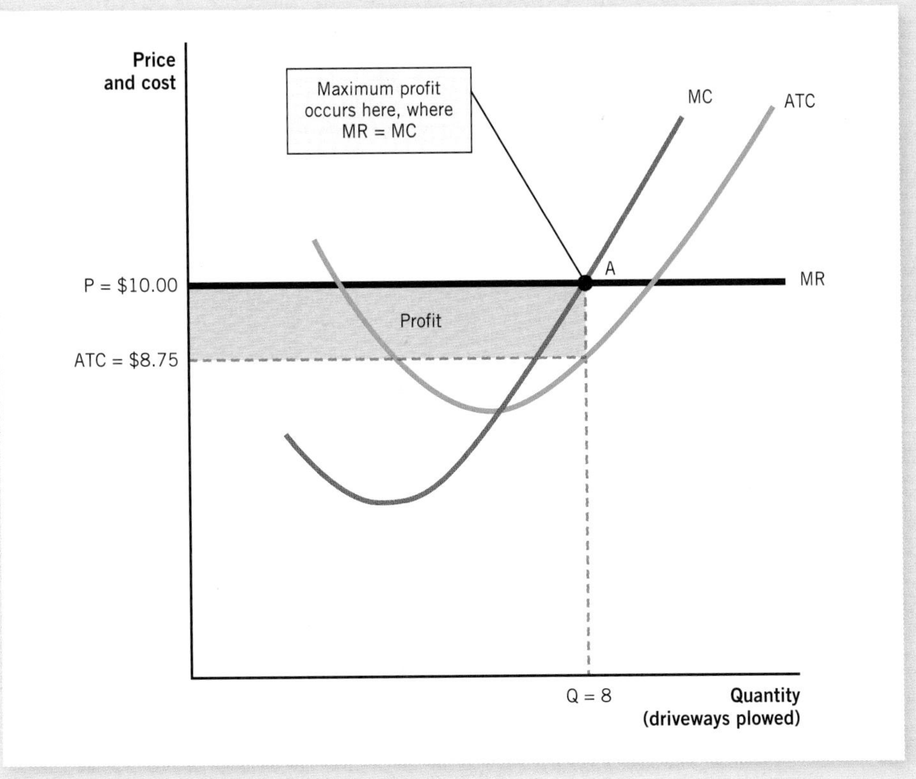

FIGURE 6.1

Profit Maximization

Mr. Plow uses the profit-maximizing rule to locate the point at which marginal revenue equals marginal cost, or MR = MC. This determines the ideal output level, Q. The firm takes the price from the market; this price is shown as the horizontal MR curve where price = $10. Since the price charged is higher than the average total cost (ATC) curve along the dashed line at quantity Q, the firm makes the profit shown in the green rectangle.

directly on the price charged for the service. The highest price that Mr. Plow can charge for clearing a driveway is found at the intersection of the market demand and supply curves. This price is $10, and it's the price that every other plow person charges. The profit-maximizing rule tells us to find the profit-maximizing output at the point where MR = MC. This point occurs at an output of 8 driveways. Figure 6.1 shows this data in graphical form. Note that average total cost (ATC) is included in the graph. **Average total cost** is the total cost of producing a particular amount of output divided by the amount of output.

Average total cost (ATC) is the total cost of producing a particular amount of output divided by the amount of output.

$$ATC = TC/Q \quad \text{(Equation 6.1)}$$

The ATC curve allows us to show Mr. Plow's profits in the graph. If the price the firm can charge is greater than the ATC, the firm will be making a profit. This profit is shown by the green-shaded box in Figure 6.1.

Competing the Profits Away

Incentives

Easy entry and exit characterize competitive markets. Existing firms and entrepreneurs decide whether to enter and exit a market based on incentives. When existing firms are enjoying profits, there is an incentive for them to produce more and also for entrepreneurs to enter the market. An increase in the number of firms leads to an increase in the quantity of the good supplied in the entire market. Likewise, when existing firms are experiencing losses, there is an incentive for them to exit the market; then the total amount of a good available to the market decreases. Entry and exit have the combined effect of regulating the amount of profit a firm can hope to make in the long run. As long as profits exist, firms will enter the market, increasing supply.

PRACTICE WHAT YOU KNOW

The Profit-Maximizing Rule: Show Me the Money!

Here is a question that often confuses students.

Question: At what point does a firm maximize profits?

a. where the increase in profit per unit is greatest

b. where total revenue is maximized

c. where total revenue equals total cost

d. where marginal revenue equals marginal cost

What is the rule for making the most profit?

Answer: Each answer sounds plausible, so the key is to think about each one in a concrete way. To help do that, we'll refer back to the Mr. Plow data in Table 6.3.

a. Incorrect. Making a large profit per unit sounds great. However, if the firm stops production when the increase in profit is the greatest—\$8 in column 8—it will fail to realize the additional profits—\$7 and \$4 in column 8—that come from continuing to produce until MR = MC.

b. Incorrect. Recall that total revenue is only half of the profit function, Profit = TR − TC. No matter how much revenue a business brings in, if total costs are more than revenue, the firm will experience a loss. Therefore, the firm wishes to maximize profits, not revenue. For example, looking at column 2, we see that at 10 driveways Mr. Plow earns total revenues of \$100. But column 3 tells us that the total cost of plowing 10 driveways is \$145. With a total profit of −\$45, this level of output would not be a good idea.

c. Incorrect. If total revenue and total cost are equal, the firm makes no profits.

d. Correct. Answers (a), (b), and (c) all sound plausible. But a firm maximizes profits where MR = MC. At this point, all profitable opportunities are exhausted. If Mr. Plow clears 7 or 8 driveways, his profit is \$10. If he clears 9 driveways, his profits fall from \$10 to −\$5 since the marginal cost of clearing that ninth driveway, \$25, is greater than the marginal revenue he earns of \$10.

As we have seen, when supply rises, the market price will drop. When losses exist, the number of firms in the market will decline. Supply will fall and the price will rise. As we discussed in Chapter 5, profits and losses act as signals for firms to enter or leave an industry. **Signals** convey information about the profitability of various markets.

Signals convey information about the profitability of various markets.

Since Mr. Plow is making a profit shortly after he begins his business, other would-be plowers see that there's money to be made in this market. As a result, Homer's friend Barney jumps into the plow business with a new firm called The Plow King. This entry into the market shifts the market supply curve to the right. However, the presence of more suppliers drives the equilibrium price lower and changes Mr. Plow's output from that found in Table 6.3. In Figure 6.2, we see this change in the market for driveway plowing. Panel (a) shows the decline in price and the increase in overall market quantity.

As the new firm enters the market, price is forced down just a little bit. You may think, "Wait a minute! I thought individual firms can't affect the market price." What's going on here? An individual firm is a price taker. This means that it has to accept the *market price*. It cannot simply say that it is going to

FIGURE 6.2

Adjustment of Price and Firm Output with Entry by New Competitors

When existing firms are making profits in a market, new firms enter the market seeking to capture some of those profits for themselves. The market supply curve shifts to the right, as shown by the movement from S_1 to S_2 in panel (a). As a result, the price falls from P_1 to P_2. For the firm shown in panel (b), marginal revenue falls from MR_1 to MR_2. The new profit-maximizing point occurs where $MR_2 = MC$. Here the firm produces at the minimum of its average total cost (ATC) curve.

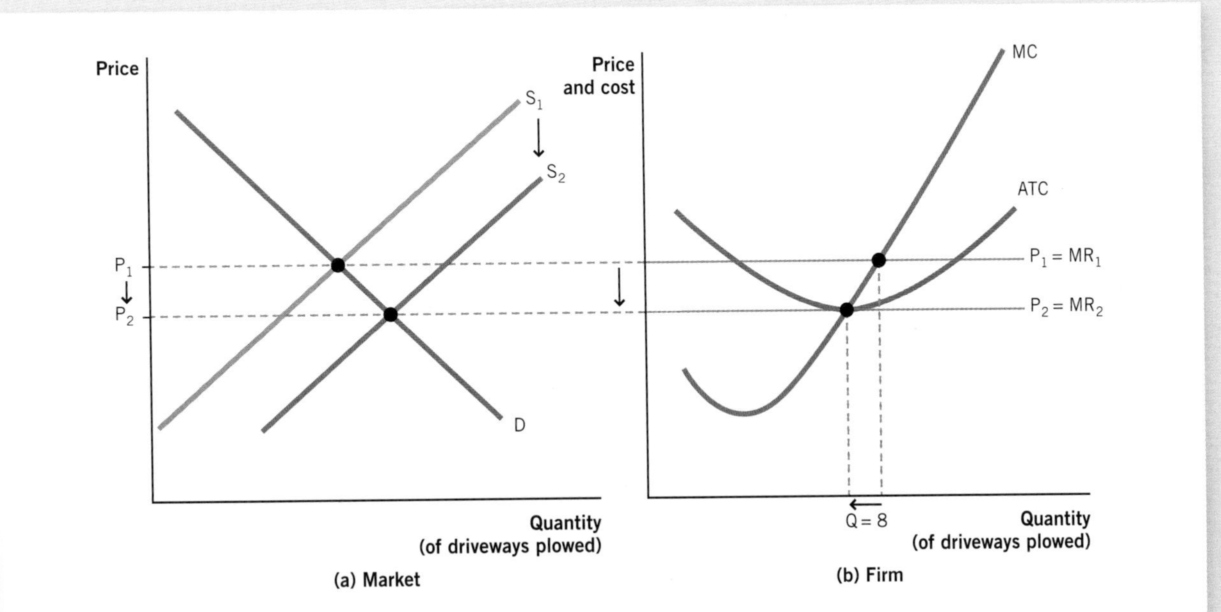

charge a higher price without losing sales because there are many other sellers providing the same product. However, when market conditions change—for example, when firms enter or leave the market—the overall market supply changes and so does the price. Therefore, when the market price changes, it's not due to a decision by the firm. Rather, it's a change in the market supply that alters the equilibrium market price. Remaining firms must now take this new market price.

Panel (b) of Figure 6.2 shows the impact on Mr. Plow's business specifically. This new market price changes the output decision for the existing firms. In a competitive market, the price a firm charges equals the marginal revenue. Why? For price takers, each unit is sold for the same price no matter how many units are sold. Your business is not significant enough in the grand scheme of the market to alter the price. Thus, the additional driveway plowed earns the same price as the last one. When the market price falls, marginal revenue also falls. And when marginal revenue falls, so do profits.

Regardless of the price, the profit-maximizing output for the firm occurs where MR = MC. However, something unique happens in a competitive market. As long as profits are being made, the market attracts entry. This higher number of firms continues to push the price and marginal revenue down. The question is: *How low will prices go?*

Firms enter the industry as long as price is greater than average total cost (ATC), and firms exit the industry once price falls below ATC. The market settles where price equals ATC. Therefore, entry and exit will stop when all firms precisely cover their costs. This happens when price (P) equals ATC.

If you look carefully at the graph in Figure 6.2, you'll notice that after the new firm enters the market, price falls. At the new price, P_2 = ATC at the lowest point of the ATC curve. Why is this point significant? Remember that markets are interested in efficiency, or producing a certain amount of output in the lowest-cost way. Competitive markets lead to this efficient outcome. Entry will occur and force firms to produce in the lowest-cost way. If they don't, prices won't cover the firms' cost of production and they'll have to exit the market.

Let's take this analysis to its logical conclusion. Price equals marginal revenue in a competitive industry, and the profit-maximizing output will occur where MR = MC. Because MR = P and P = ATC, then MR = MC = P = ATC in a competitive industry. At the point where Mr. Plow earns zero profit (breaks even), we have found the profit-maximizing output.

A Reminder about Economic Profit

The results you just read about may seem rather strange. If the most a firm can make is zero profit, you may think that competition is not a very desirable environment for businesses. Why would any ambitious entrepreneur start a business in a competitive market? If a firm cannot expect to make an economic profit in the long run, why bother?

When we say there are zero profits, we don't mean the entrepreneur makes nothing. In fact, those entrepreneurs who stay in business make at least as much as they would have made in alternative employment. Firms enter a

Entry and Exit

ECONOMICS IN THE MEDIA

I Love Lucy

I Love Lucy was the most-watched television comedy of the 1950s. The show featured two couples who are best friends, the Ricardos and the Mertzes, who get themselves in the most unlikely situations.

One particular episode finds Ricky Ricardo disillusioned with show business. After some conversation, Ricky and Fred Mertz decide to go into business together and start a diner. Fred and Ethel Mertz have the experience to run the diner, and Ricky plans to use his name and star power to help get the word out about the restaurant, which they name A Little Bit of Cuba.

If you've seen any of the *I Love Lucy* series, you already know that the business venture is destined to fail. Sure enough, the Mertzes get tired of doing all the hard work—cooking for and serving the customers—while Ricky and Lucy Ricardo meet and greet the guests. Things quickly deteriorate, and the two couples decide to part ways. The only problem is that they are both part owners, and neither can afford to buy out the other. So they decide to split the diner in half right down the middle!

The result is absurd and hilarious. On one side, guests go to A Little Bit of Cuba. On the other side, the Mertzes set up Big Hunk of America. Since both restaurants use the same facilities and sell the same food, the only way they can differentiate themselves is by lowering their prices. This leads to a hamburger price war to attract customers:

Ethel: "Three!"
Lucy: "Two!"
Ethel: "One-cent hamburgers."
Fred: "Ethel, are you out of your mind?" *[Even in the 1950s, a penny wasn't enough to cover the marginal cost of making a hamburger.]*
Ethel: "Well, I thought this could get 'em."
Fred: "One-cent hamburgers?"

After the exchange, Lucy whispers in a customer's ear and gives him a dollar. He then proceeds to Big Hunk of America and says, "I'd like 100 hamburgers!"

Fred Mertz replies, "We're all out of hamburgers."

How do the falling prices described here affect the ability of the firms in this market to make a profit?

The exchange is a useful way of visualizing how perfectly competitive markets work. Competition forces the price down, but the process of entry and exit takes time and is messy. The Ricardos and Mertzes can't make a living selling one-cent hamburgers—one cent is below their marginal cost—so one of the couples will end up exiting. At that point, the remaining couple would be able to charge more. If they end up making a profit, that profit will encourage entrepreneurs to enter the industry. As the supply of hamburgers expands, the price that can be charged will be driven back down. Since we live in an economically dynamic world, prices are always moving toward the long-run equilibrium.

market when they expect to be reasonably compensated for their investment. And they leave a market when the investment does not yield a satisfactory result. Economic profit is determined by deducting the explicit and implicit costs from revenue. Therefore, firms are willing to stay in competitive markets when they are breaking even because they're being reasonably compensated for the explicit expenses they have incurred and also for the implicit expenses—like the opportunity costs of other business ventures—that they would expect to make elsewhere.

Opportunity cost

For example, let's look at Mr. Plow's finances. If Mr. Plow asks his accountant how much the business earned during the year, the accountant adds up all of Mr. Plow's explicit costs and subtracts them from his revenues. The accountant reports back that Mr. Plow earned $25,000 in total revenue and had $10,000 in total explicit costs. By subtracting costs from revenues, he determines there was a $15,000 profit. Now $15,000 in profit would sound good to a lot of firms, so we would expect many new entrants in the plowing business. But not so fast! We haven't accounted for the implicit costs—the money Mr. Plow could have earned by working another job instead of plowing (say, $10,000) and the $50,000 he invested in the plow that could have yielded a return (say, $5,000) elsewhere. Mr. Plow's explicit and implicit costs are shown in Table 6.4. If we account for the implicit costs, we find the economic profit equals $0. (Total revenue of $25,000 – $10,000 explicit costs – $15,000 implicit costs.) Zero profit sounds unappealing, but it isn't. It means that Mr. Plow covered his forgone salary and also his next-best investment alternative. If you couldn't make any more money doing something else with your time or your investments, you might as well stay in the same place. So Mr. Plow is content to keep on plowing, while others outside the industry don't see any profit from entering the industry.

If all the owners' earnings end up being the same, why would anyone start a business? Even with zero economic profits, people have reasons to start or stay in business, even in a competitive industry. Many entrepreneurs receive value from being their own boss. Being in charge is a benefit that many people find particularly alluring. Other benefits include taking on the

TABLE 6.4

Mr. Plow's Economic Profit and the Entry or Exit Decision

Explicit costs per year	
Payment on the loan on his snow plow	$7,000
Gasoline	2,000
Miscellaneous equipment (shovels, salt)	1,000
Implicit costs	
Forgone salary	$10,000
The forgone income that the $50,000 invested in the snow plow could have earned if invested elsewhere	5,000
Total cost	$25,000

challenge of running a company, choosing whom to work with, and the pride of starting a business. Not all benefits from starting or running a business are monetary.

Economists view competition as the standard against which all other market structures should be measured. Why? Competition provides more output and lower prices than any other market structure, and while it is a difficult situation for producers, this result is very good for consumers. Competition also tends to lead to more rapid innovation as firms try to discover a way to get a leg up on other firms. The other extreme, the market structure that economists like the least, is monopoly. As we will see, this disdain for monopolies isn't due to the perceived wickedness of the monopolist but, rather, from what monopolies do to market efficiency.

How Are Monopolies Created?

A **monopoly** is an entity having the exclusive right or control over the selling of a product. A monopolist's power over the market stems from selling a well-defined product for which there are no good substitutes. Two conditions enable a single seller to become a monopolist. First, the firm must have something unique to sell. Second, it must have a way to prevent potential competitors from entering the market. Obviously, these two criteria set the monopolist in stark contrast to the firms in a competitive market. As you can imagine, a company that meets these two conditions has the ability to set whatever price it wants. However, as we will see later, that doesn't mean setting the price as high as possible.

A **monopoly** is an entity having the exclusive right or control over the selling of a product.

Monopolies occur in many places and for different reasons. We'll soon take a look at some ways a monopoly might arise, but it's important to recognize that regardless of how a company becomes a monopoly, the result is the limiting of competition. A lack of competition has consequences for the market. Without competition, the monopolist has market power that allows it to set prices rather than take them. Since entry into the market is difficult, prices will not fall. This situation allows monopolists to enjoy positive economic profits for as long as they can keep competitors away.

So what prevents competitors from arising to frustrate the monopolist? A monopoly operates in a market with high **barriers to entry**, which are restrictions that make it difficult for new firms to enter a market. As a result, monopolists have neither competition nor any threat of competition. There are two types of barriers: natural barriers and government-created barriers. Let's look at each.

Barriers to entry are restrictions that make it difficult for new firms to enter a market.

Natural Barriers

Some barriers exist naturally within the market. These include control of resources, problems in raising capital, and economies of scale.

Control of Resources

The best way to limit competition is to control a resource that is essential in the production process. If you control a scarce resource, other competitors

PRACTICE WHAT YOU KNOW

Monopoly: Can You Spot the Monopolist?

Here are three questions to test your understanding of the conditions necessary for market power to arise.

Question: Is LeBron James (an NBA superstar) a monopolist?

Answer: LeBron is a uniquely talented basketball player. Because of his physical gifts, he can do things that other players can't. But that doesn't mean there are no substitutes for him around the league. So no, LeBron is not a monopolist. But he does have market power. However, his market power is limited because new players are always entering the league and trying to establish themselves as the best.

Question: Is a sole, small-town hairdresser a monopolist?

Answer: For all practical purposes, yes. He or she sells a unique service. Because the nearest competitor is in the next town, the local hairdresser enjoys significant market power. At the same time, the town's size limits potential competitors from entering the market, since the small community may not be able to support two hairdressers.

Monopoly profits!

Question: Is Amazon a monopolist?

Answer: Amazon is the nation's largest bookseller, with sales that dwarf those of its nearest retail rival, Barnes & Noble. But Amazon's market share doesn't make it a monopolist. Amazon is a lot like Walmart: it relies on low prices to fend off its rivals. However, if Amazon forced Barnes & Noble out of business and subsequently charged higher prices, it would certainly be acting like a monopolist.

won't be able to find enough of it to compete. For example, in the late 1800s the De Beers Corporation began buying up diamond mines in South Africa. By 1902, De Beers controlled approximately 90% of rough diamond production and distribution worldwide. Ernest Oppenheimer took over De Beers and used the company's power to dictate the price of diamonds around the globe by determining how many diamonds would come on the market each year. When the discovery of diamonds in Russia threatened to derail the monopoly, De Beers essentially bought all the diamonds coming from the mines in Siberia.

Problems in Raising Capital

Monopolies are usually very big companies that have grown over an extended period. Even if an entrepreneur has a wonderful business plan, it's unlikely that a bank or a venture capital company would lend it enough money to start a business that could compete effectively with a well-established monopoly.

FIGURE 6.3

Comparing the Demand Curves of Perfectly Competitive Firms and Monopolists

(a) Firms in a competitive market have a horizontal demand curve. (b) Since the monopolist is the sole provider of the good or service, the demand for its product constitutes the industry—or market—demand curve, which is downward sloping. So while the competitive firm has no control over the price it charges, the monopolist gets to search for the profit-maximizing price and output.

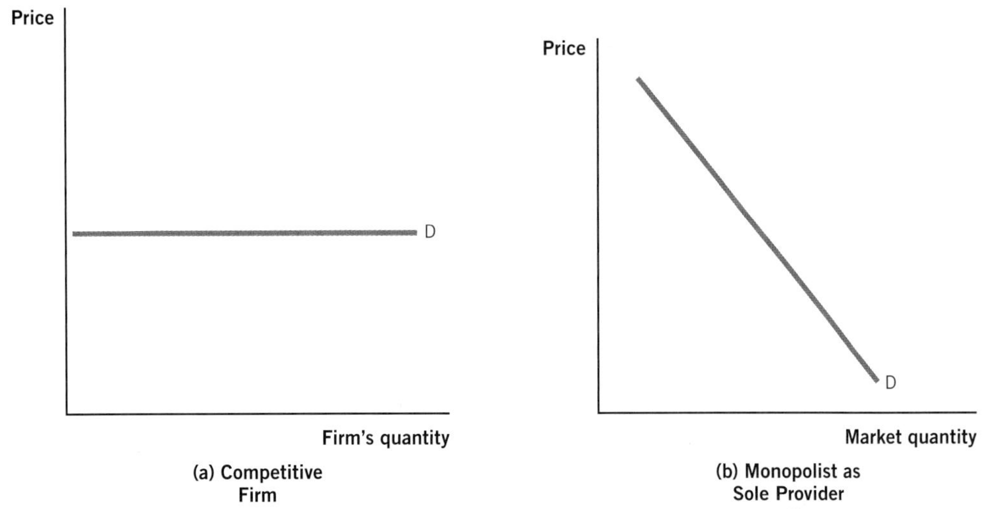

Table 6.6 shows the marginal revenue for a cable-TV company that serves a small community. Notice the inverse relationship between output (quantity of customers) and price in columns 1 and 2: as the price goes down, the quantity of customers goes up. Total revenue is calculated by multiplying output by price (TR = Q × P). At first, total revenue rises as the price falls. Once the price becomes too low ($40), total revenue begins to fall. As a result, the total revenue in column 3 rises to $250 (at 5 customers) before it falls off. The final column, representing marginal revenue, shows the change (Δ) in total revenue. In the competitive market P = MR, but for the monopolist MR is below price. For two customers the price is $80, but marginal revenue—moving from 1 to 2 customers—is $70. As the price drops, the gap between price and marginal revenue gets larger.

The change in total revenue reflects the trade-off that a monopolist encounters in trying to attract additional customers. To gain additional sales, the firm must lower its price. But the lower price is available to all customers. The impact of the lower price on total revenue therefore depends on how many new customers buy the good because of the lower price.

TABLE 6.6

Calculating the Monopolist's Marginal Revenue

(1) Quantity of customers (Q)	(2) Price of service (P)	(3) Total revenue (TR)	(4) Marginal revenue (MR)
Formula:		(Q) × (P)	Δ (TR)
0	$100	$0.00	
1	$90	90	$90
2	$80	160	70
3	$70	210	50
4	$60	240	30
5	$50	250	10
6	$40	240	−10
7	$30	210	−30
8	$20	160	−50
9	$10	90	−70
10	$0	0	−90

Deciding How Much to Produce

Deciding how much to produce returns us to the key objective of any firm: to make a profit. Finding where marginal revenue equals marginal cost will maximize that profit. However, there is one big difference: a monopolist does not charge a price equal to marginal revenue.

Figure 6.4 illustrates the profit-maximizing decision-making process for a monopolist. We will use a two-step process to determine the monopolist's profit:

1. Locate the point at which the firm will maximize its profits: MR = MC.
2. Set the price. From the point at which MR = MC, determine the profit-maximizing output, Q. From Q, move up along the dashed line until it intersects with the demand curve (D). From that point, move horizontally until you come to the *y* axis. The *y*-axis in this graph is measured in dollars, so it represents prices, costs, and revenues. This tells us the price (P) the monopolist should charge.

A common mistake when looking for the monopoly price is to find the point where MR = MC and from there go across to the y-axis. The problem with this method lies in the fact that the MR and MC curves do not provide information about prices. Rather, that information is found on the demand curve. The MR = MC rule locates the quantity, not the price. Since the demand curve plots quantity *and price* data, you need to be on the demand curve to find the price that corresponds to this profit-maximizing quantity. Otherwise, the monopolist will be charging a price that will not maximize profits.

So, using this two-step process, we can determine the monopolist's profit. Locate the average total cost of making Q units along the dashed line. From that point, move horizontally until you come to the y-axis and the point marked ATC. This tells you the average cost of making Q units. The difference between the price and the cost multiplied by Q tells us the profit (or loss) the firm makes.

Since the price (P) is higher than the average total cost (ATC) at Q, the firm makes the profit shown in the green-shaded rectangle. For example, if a small-town veterinarian charges $50 for a routine examination and incurs a cost of $35 for every exam, she earns $15 every time she sees a pet. If she provides 1,000 examinations a year, her profit is $15 × 1,000, or $15,000.

We can see another distinction between competitive markets and monopoly in Figure 6.4. Recall that firms in competitive industries are forced to produce efficiently. Efficiency occurs when the price equals the minimum ATC. At that point, competitive firms produce their profit-maximizing output at minimum cost. But monopolies don't face the same pressures as competitive firms. The profit-maximizing output for the monopoly occurs

FIGURE 6.4

The Monopolist's Profit Maximization

The firm uses the profit-maximizing rule to locate the point at which MR = MC. This determines the ideal output level, Q. Since the price (which is determined by the demand curve) is higher than the average total cost curve (ATC) along the dashed line at quantity Q, the firm makes the profit shown in the green-shaded area.

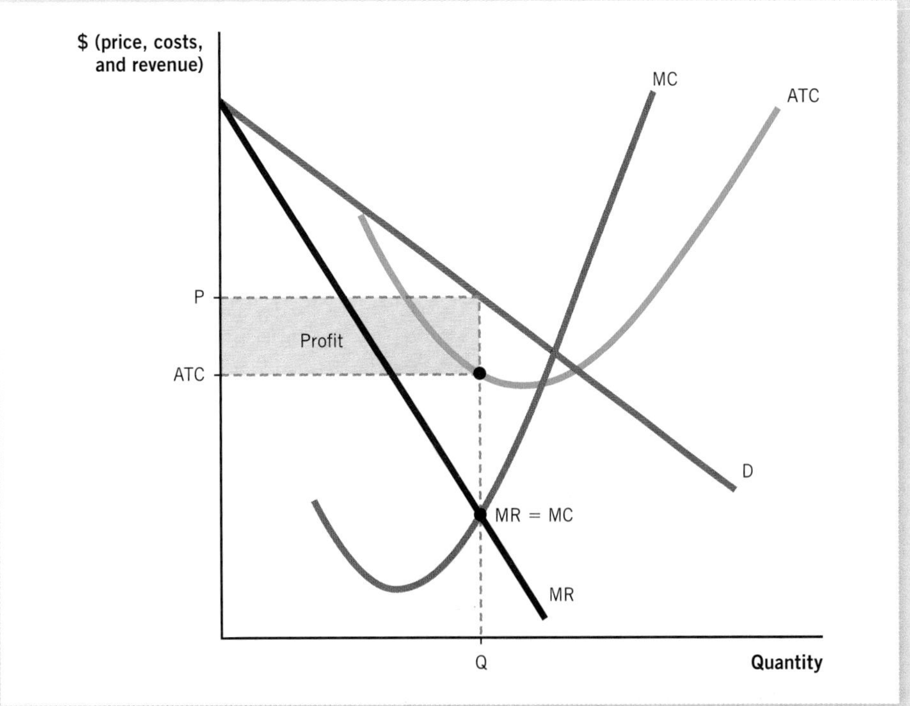

PRACTICE WHAT YOU KNOW

Monopoly Profits: How Much Do Monopolists Make?

Question: A monopolist always earns ____ economic profit.

a. a positive

b. zero

c. a negative

d. We cannot be sure about the profit a monopolist makes.

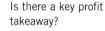

Is there a key profit takeaway?

Answers:

a. Incorrect. A monopolist is a price maker with considerable market power. This usually, but not always, leads to a positive economic profit.

b. Incorrect. Zero economic profit exists in competitive markets in the long run. Since a monopolist by definition does not operate in competitive markets, it is protected from additional competition that would drive its profit to zero.

c. Incorrect. Negative profit? There is absolutely no reason to think that would happen. Monopolists sell a unique product without close substitutes in a market that is insulated from competitive pressures.

d. Correct. Since a monopolist benefits from barriers that limit the entry of firms into the industry, we would expect an economic profit. However, a profit is not guaranteed. Monopolies do not control the demand for the product they sell. Consequently, in the short run the monopolist may experience either a profit (if demand is high) or a loss (if demand is low).

at a level that doesn't correspond to the minimum ATC. Since there's no pressure because firms aren't entering the market, there's less reason for the monopoly to focus on its production costs. Thus, its production processes tend to be inefficient relative to those of competitive firms.

Let's look at what we know thus far about competitive markets and monopolies. Table 6.7 summarizes the differences.

TABLE 6.7

The Major Differences between a Monopoly and a Competitive Market

Competitive Market	Monopoly
Many firms	One firm
Few barriers to entry	High barriers to entry
Has no market power (is a price taker)	Has significant market power (is a price maker)
Over time cannot earn economic profits	May earn economic profits over time
Produces an efficient level of output (since P equals the minimum ATC)	Produces less than the efficient level of output (since P is greater than the minimum ATC)

What Are the Problems with Monopoly?

Monopolies can adversely affect society by restricting output and charging higher prices than sellers in competitive markets do. These activities cause monopolies to operate inefficiently, provide less choice, promote an unhealthy form of competition known as *rent seeking*, and make economic profits that fail to guide resources to their highest-valued use. We use the term **market failure** when markets produce a result that is inefficient from society's point of view. The monopoly outcome is certainly inefficient and is therefore an example of market failure. But what does that mean? Let's take a more detailed look at the implications of this market failure.

Market failure occurs when markets produce a result that is inefficient from society's point of view.

Inefficient Output and Price

From an efficiency standpoint, the monopolist charges too much and produces too little. This result is evident in Figure 6.5, which shows what happens when a competitive market (denoted by the subscript C) ends up being controlled by a monopoly (denoted by the subscript M).

FIGURE 6.5

When a Competitive Industry Becomes a Monopoly

(a) In a competitive industry, the intersection of supply and demand determines the price (P_C) and quantity (Q_C).
(b) When a monopoly controls an entire industry, the supply curve becomes the monopolist's marginal cost (MC) curve. The monopolist uses MR = MC to determine its quantity (Q_M). The monopoly price (P_M) is found on the demand curve. As a result, the monopolist charges a higher price and produces a smaller output than when an entire industry is populated with competitive firms.

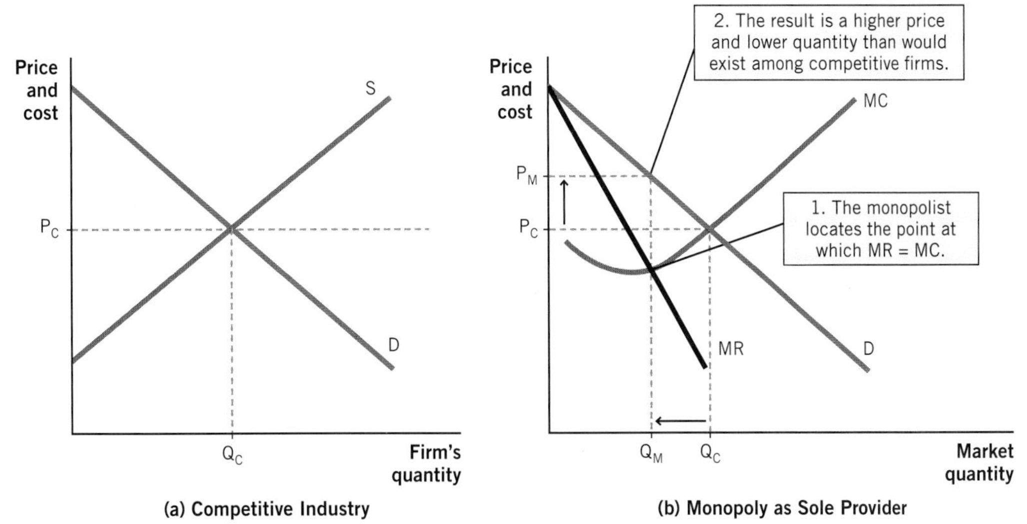

First, imagine a competitive fishing industry in which each boat catches a small portion of the fish, as shown in panel (a). Each firm is a price taker that must charge the market price. In contrast, panel (b) depicts pricing and output decisions for a monopoly fishing company when it confronts the same cost structure as presented in panel (a). When a single firm controls the entire fishing ground, it is the sole supplier; to set its price, it considers the downward-sloping demand and marginal revenue curves that serve the entire market. Therefore, it sets marginal revenue equal to marginal cost. This yields a smaller output ($Q_M < Q_C$) than the competitive industry and a higher price ($P_M > P_C$).

Trade creates value

This smaller output level results in a loss from the normal gains from trade that would happen in a competitive market. In Chapter 4, we discussed how competitive markets maximize the combined consumer and producer surpluses when equilibrium prevails. If we compare the monopoly result to the competitive result, we see that $Q_M < Q_C$, revealing that there are fewer trades taking place. In other words, there are people who want what the monopolist is selling and could afford it at the competitive price, but since the monopoly price is higher they choose not to buy. This means that there is consumer and producer surplus that could be generated by a competitive market that is *not* generated when a monopoly controls the market. A profit-maximizing monopolist will limit output to Q_M, thereby reducing the total surplus relative to the competitive situation. This reduction in total surplus is called a **deadweight loss** and is shown as the yellow triangular area in Figure 6.6.

Deadweight loss is the decrease in economic activity caused by market distortions. It occurs when there are fewer trades than would optimally occur, resulting in a reduction of the combined consumer and producer surplus.

FIGURE 6.6

The Deadweight Loss of Monopoly

Since the profit-maximizing monopolist produces an output of Q_M, an amount that is less than Q_C, the result is the deadweight loss shown in the yellow triangle. The blue rectangle is the consumer surplus that becomes producer surplus for the monopolist.

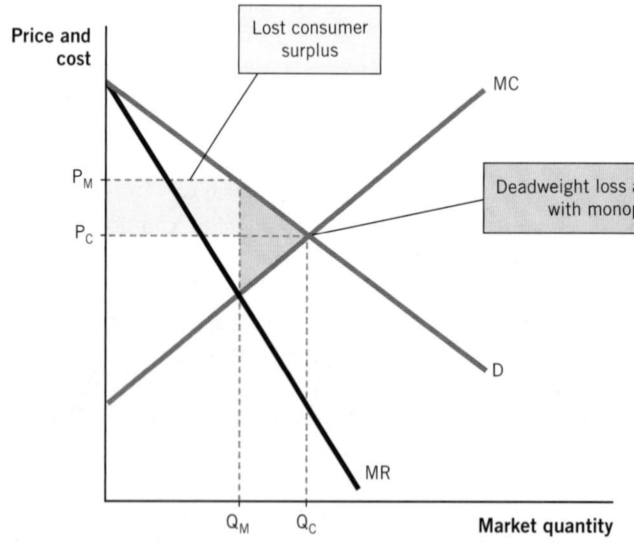

ECONOMICS IN THE MEDIA

The Problems of Monopoly

One-Man Band

This Pixar short animation from 2005 tells the story of two street musicians competing for the gold coin of a young peasant girl who wants to make a wish in the town square's fountain.

When the short opens, there is only one street musician in the plaza. He performs a little bit and almost coaxes the girl to place her coin in his tip basket. Just as she is about to give it to him, another street musician starts playing. Since there is no longer a single performer, a spirited rivalry develops between the two very eager musicians vying to win the little girl's attention and money.

A little competition goes a long way to reduce monopoly.

This clever story illustrates monopoly and competition in a number of compelling ways. The first street musician plays only halfheartedly in the beginning, when he doesn't face any competition. Indeed, lack of choice is one of the major criticisms of monopoly. But then the second musician's arrival changes the dynamic, inspiring a spirited competition for the gold coin. The "one-man band" isn't really a monopolist, however; he's providing a service that has many good substitutes, and he lacks the ability to keep imitators from entering the market.

Fewer Choices for Consumers

Another problem associated with monopoly is the lack of choice. Have you ever wondered why cable-TV companies offer their services in bundles? You can buy basic, digital, and premium packages, but you cannot buy just the cable channels you want. Why? Because cable companies function like monopolies, and monopolies limit consumer choice. Since the monopolist sells a good with few close substitutes, it can leverage its market power to offer product features that benefit itself at the expense of consumer choice. With a monopolist, consumers have only one choice: if they don't like the design, features, price, or any other aspect of the product provided, they have few other options. For example, in many communities there is only one cable-TV provider. In a hypothetical, competitive market, we would expect each company to provide more options to satisfy consumer preferences. For instance, in a competitive market you should be able to find a firm willing to sell only ESPN and the Weather Channel. In a monopoly situation, though, the cable company forces you to choose between buying more cable than you really want and going without cable altogether. Because the cable company has a good deal of market power, it can restrict your options and force you to buy more in order to get what you want. This is a profitable strategy for the company but a bad outcome for consumers.

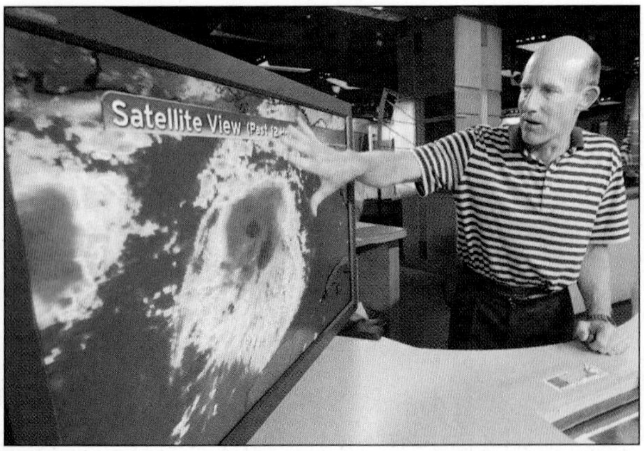

Would you rather watch the Weather Channel . . .

. . . or SportsCenter?

Rent Seeking

Rent seeking occurs when resources are used to secure monopoly rights through the political process.

The attempt to gain market power encourages rent seeking. **Rent seeking** occurs when resources are used to secure monopoly rights through the political process. Consider the U.S. steel industry, which has been in decline for many years and has lost market share to steel firms in China, Japan, and Europe. If a U.S. steel company is losing money because of foreign competition, it can address the situation in one of two ways. First, it can modernize by building new facilities and using the latest equipment and techniques. (In other words, it can become competitive with the overseas competition.) Or, second, it can lobby the government to limit foreign competition. In 2002, the U.S. government imposed tariffs (import taxes) of up to 30% on imported steel. Here is the danger: when lobbying is less expensive than building a new factory, the company will choose to lobby! If politicians give in and the lobbying succeeds, society is adversely affected because the gains from trade are smaller.

A former steel plant in Bethlehem, Pennsylvania.

ECONOMICS IN THE REAL WORLD

New York City Taxis

In 1932, during the depths of the Great Depression, New York City decided to license taxicabs. The goal was to standardize fares, operating procedures, and safety requirements. At that time, a taxicab license, or medallion, was available at no cost. Today, if you find one on the resale market, it costs over $850,000. The medallions are worth so much because the owners often make six-figure incomes from leasing and operating taxis in New York City.

The city did not intend to create an artificial monopoly, but it did. From 1932 until the 1990s, the number of medallions, which represents the supply of taxis, was fixed at approximately 12,000. During the same 60-year period, population growth and an increase in tourism caused the demand for taxi services to rise steeply. The number of medallions would have had to quadruple to keep up with demand.

In recent years, the city of New York has offered three auctions to introduce more medallions into the market. These auctions have netted the city over $100 million in revenue and have raised the number of medallions to slightly more than 13,000. Each of the current medallion holders owns a small part of an artificially created government monopoly. Collectively, the holders of medallions own a monopoly on taxi services worth 13,000 × $850,000 or about $11 billion. Yet demand for the medallions continues to far outpace the supply, and the market price has steadily climbed to an astonishing level.

Medallion owners in New York City are protected from competition.

However, owning and operating a taxi has all the makings of an industry with low barriers to entry. The only reason that medallions are worth so much is that there is an artificially created barrier to entry, which protects medallion holders from competition. A new threat to this monopoly has arisen with ride-sharing services like Uber and Lyft. The reaction by cab companies has been to petition cities to regulate these new firms and force drivers to take the same tests as cabbies, only use certain kinds of cars, and even limit the kinds of machines used to take payments.

Allowing Uber and Lyft to restore a competitive market for taxis in New York City would make each current medallion holder worse off by reducing the existing barriers to entry into the industry. This would cause the medallion owners' profits to fall. In fact, prices for taxi medallions have recently fallen from a high of over $1 million. Therefore, it's not surprising that medallion owners seek to keep the number of medallions as low as possible and to keep competition out of their market. ✳

What Are Monopolistic Competition and Oligopoly?

Competition and monopoly lie at the extremes of a spectrum. In reality, very few firms perfectly fit either category. If you were to draw a line between competition and monopoly as shown in Figure 6.7, you would find two other

FIGURE 6.7

Continuum of Market Structure

Competition — Monopolistic Competition —— Oligopoly — Monopoly market structures that exist between the extremes. As you can see, *monopolistic competition* falls closer to competition along the spectrum, while *oligopoly* lies closer to monopoly. Both of these market structures contain elements of competition and monopoly.

Monopolistic Competition

Monopolistic competition is characterized by free entry, many different firms, and product differentiation.

Product differentiation is the process that firms use to make a product more attractive to potential customers.

Some consumers prefer the fries at McDonald's, while others may crave a salad at Panera Bread or the Colonel's special blend of spices at KFC. Each fast-food establishment has a unique set of menu items. As a result, the different products in fast-food restaurants give each seller a small degree of market power. Having market power allows a firm to set a price for its products. This combination of market power and competition is typical of the market structure known as **monopolistic competition**, which is characterized by free entry, many different firms, and product differentiation. **Product differentiation** is the process firms use to make a product more attractive to potential customers. Firms use product differentiation to contrast their product's unique qualities with competing products. The differences can be minor and can involve subtle changes in packaging, quality, availability, and promotion.

To distinguish themselves from one another, monopolistically competitive firms will advertise. Consider the behavior of companies in the take-out and pizza-delivery industry, which is monopolistically competitive. Television commercials by national chains such as Domino's, Pizza Hut, Papa John's, and Little Caesars are widespread, as are flyers and advertisements for local pizza places. Since each pizza is slightly different, each firm's advertising seeks to increase the demand for its product. When advertising is effective, the gains from advertising go directly to the firm spending the money. This success generates a strong incentive for the company to continue advertising to gain new customers or to keep customers from switching to other products. Since each firm in the industry feels the same way, advertising becomes the norm among monopolistically competitive firms.

In competitive markets, firms are all selling the same product, so advertising doesn't make much sense. If one firm spends money on advertisements, those ads could easily benefit other firms selling the same good. In this case, the only effect of advertising is to raise the costs of the firm that pays for it. Advertising is not likely to increase revenues at all.

Advertising is unusual in markets characterized by monopolies as well. Since the monopoly has no competitors, advertising is strictly a cost that provides no added benefit. Your local water authority doesn't advertise because there are no alternatives. The U.S. Postal Service advertises only its package delivery service, for which there is competition from UPS and FedEx. The USPS doesn't advertise its first-class mail service because no other firms are allowed in that market.

So monopolistic competition is a lot like a competitive market. There are many firms and free entry and exit into and out of the market. But, like a monopoly, each firm has a little bit of market power. For this reason, each firm is a price maker that sets prices above marginal cost.

Oligopoly

Monopolistic competition is more like competition, but oligopoly is more like monopoly. Let's examine what sets this market structure apart from the others. An **oligopoly** exists when a small number of firms sell a product in a market with significant barriers to entry. An oligopolist is like a monopolistic competitor in that it sometimes (but not always) sells a differentiated product. But, like monopolists, oligopolists enjoy significant barriers to entry.

Oligopoly exists when a small number of firms sell a product in a market with high barriers to entry.

Firms in monopolistically competitive markets usually have a limited amount of market power. As a result, buyers often find low prices and wide availability of products. In contrast, an oligopoly sells in a market with significant barriers to entry and fewer rivals. Thus, the oligopolist has more market power than a firm operating under monopolistic competition. However, since an oligopolistic market has more than one seller, no single oligopoly firm has as much market power as a monopoly.

Big oil companies like Exxon, Royal Dutch Shell, and British Petroleum are oligopolies. There are significant barriers to entry in the market for oil exploration, and these firms have significant market power. However, since there's more than one firm in this industry, it certainly isn't a monopoly.

In an oligopolistic industry, firms' decisions have a direct impact on their competitors. The pricing and output decisions of firms are interdependent. In competitive markets, no firm is large enough to affect the market price. If one farmer increases his production of beets, the result will not be a collapse in world beet prices. In monopoly there is only one firm, so whatever it produces is the output for the entire market. Monopolistically competitive firms have some market power but are still a relatively small part of the market. For example, even though Subway has increased its output substantially over the last ten years, the company still hasn't captured a significant portion of the fast-food market. When an oligopolist changes output, however, the result could have a large impact on the prices they and their competitors can charge. We can analyze the decisions of oligopoly firms using a tool called game theory, which we will discuss in Chapter 7.

These different market structures give us some indication of how much influence a firm has on price. Table 6.8 lists the differences and similarities among the four market structures we have examined in this chapter. As you can see, firms are influenced by the market in which they operate.

TABLE 6.8

Summary of Market Structures

Competitive market	Monopolistic competition	Oligopoly	Monopoly
Many sellers	Many sellers	A few sellers	One seller
Similar products	Differentiated product	Typically differentiated product	Unique product without close substitutes
Free entry and exit	Easy entry and exit	Barriers to entry	Significant barriers to entry

ECONOMICS FOR LIFE

Playing Monopoly Like an Economist

In Monopoly, you profit only by taking from other players. The assets of the game's world are fixed in number. The best player drives others into bankruptcy and is declared the winner only after gaining control of the entire board.

Here is some advice on how to play the game like an economist.

- Remember that a monopoly is built on trade. You're unlikely to acquire a monopoly by landing on the color-groups you need. Instead, you have to trade properties in order to acquire the ones you need. Since every player knows this, acquiring the last property to complete a color-group is nearly impossible. Your competitors will never willingly hand you a monopoly unless they get something of great value in return.
- Don't wait to trade until it's obvious what you need. Instead, try to acquire as many properties as you can in order to gain trading leverage as the game unfolds. Always pick up available properties if no other player owns one of the same color-group; purchase properties that will give you two or three of the same group; or purchase a property if it blocks someone else from completing a set.
- Think about probability. Mathematicians have determined that Illinois Avenue is the property most likely to be landed on and that B&O is the best railroad to own. Know the odds, and you can weigh the risks and rewards of trade better than your opponents can. This is just like doing market research before you buy. Being informed matters in Monopoly and in business.
- When you get a monopoly, develop it quickly. Build as many houses as you can. That's sound advice in the board game and in life. Market power is fleeting—you must capitalize on your advantages as soon as possible.
- Finally, if you gain the upper hand and have a chance to bankrupt a player from the game, do it. Luck plays a key role in Monopoly as it does in life. Although it may sound harsh, eliminating a competitor moves you one step closer to winning the game.

The decisions you make while playing Monopoly are all about cost-benefit analysis. You have limited resources and only so many opportunities to use them to your advantage. The skilled player understands how to weigh the values of tradable properties, considers the risk-return proposition of every decision, manages money effectively, and eliminates competitors when given a chance.

Apply some basic economic principles, and you can win big.

Conclusion

Market structure impacts a firm's ability to earn and keep earning profits. Two primary conditions dictate the type of market in which a firm operates: (1) whether the firm is selling a unique good or service, and (2) how significant the barriers to entry are (that is, how easily firms can enter and exit the market).

In this chapter, we examined four market structures. The first, competition, provides the best outcomes for society. The second, monopoly, has many shortcomings. While competitive markets generally yield welfare-enhancing outcomes for society, monopolies often do the opposite.

Competitive markets and monopoly are market structures at opposite extremes of a spectrum. Indeed, we rarely encounter the conditions necessary for either a pure monopoly or a perfectly competitive market. Most economic activity takes place between these two alternatives. Monopolistic competition and oligopoly have some characteristics of both competition and monopoly.

The behavior of firms within these market structures has led economists to reconsider the expected outcomes of markets. In particular, contrary to what we would think, oligopolistic firms sometimes make decisions that actually lead to lower profits. To investigate this unexpected outcome, we need to expand the way we analyze human behavior beyond robotic decision-making. The cutting edge of microeconomics currently lies in behavioral economics, a cross between economics and psychology, and it is to that subject we turn in Chapter 7.

ANSWERING THE BIG QUESTIONS

How do competitive markets work?

* The firms in competitive markets sell similar products. Firms are free to enter and exit the market whenever they wish.
* A price taker has no control over the price it receives in the market.
* In competitive markets, the price and quantity produced are determined by market forces. The profit-maximizing rule is MR = MC = price = ATC. Competitive firms produce at the lowest point on their ATC curve.

How are monopolies created?

* Monopoly is a market structure characterized by a single seller that produces a well-defined product with few good substitutes.
* Monopolies operate in a market with high barriers to entry, their chief source of market power.
* A monopoly is created when a single firm controls the entire market. The monopolist's profit-maximizing rule is MR = MC.

How much do monopolies charge, and how much do they produce?

* Monopolies charge a higher price than firms in a competitive market. For a monopoly, the profit-maximizing price is found by identifying the point on the demand curve consistent with the profit-maximizing output.
* The profit-maximizing output is found by moving down to the quantity axis from the point where MR = MC. This output level is less than what would prevail in a competitive market.

What are the problems with monopoly?

* The most significant problem created by a monopoly is the reduction in the number of trades from the competitive market. This creates a deadweight loss that indicates a lower total market surplus. The dead weight loss results in more inefficient outcome than markets tend to produce.
* Monopolists produce lower output and charge higher prices than firms in competitive markets.
* Monopolies are also prone to rent seeking. This behavior is inefficient because firms use resources to protect their monopoly position rather than to develop more efficient business practices.

What are monopolistic competition and oligopoly?

* There are many sellers in competitive and monopolistically competitive market structures, few sellers in oligopoly, and only one seller in a monopoly.
* Barriers to entry are low in competitive and monopolistically competitive markets, and much higher for oligopoly and monopoly.
* Firms in competitive markets sell identical products. In monopolistic competition and oligopoly, there is some degree of product differentiation. In monopoly, there is a unique good without close substitutes.

CONCEPTS YOU SHOULD KNOW

average total cost (ATC) (p. 165)
barriers to entry (p. 171)
competitive market (p. 160)
deadweight loss (p. 182)
economies of scale (p. 173)
industry (p. 160)
market failure (p. 181)
market power (p. 160)
market structure (p. 158)
monopolistic competition (p. 186)
monopoly (p. 171)
natural monopoly (p. 173)
oligopoly (p. 187)
price maker (p. 176)
price taker (p. 160)
product differentiation (p. 186)
rent seeking (p. 184)
signals (p. 167)

QUESTIONS FOR REVIEW

1. What are the necessary conditions for a perfectly competitive market to exist?
2. Why do competitive firms earn zero economic profit in the long run?
3. Describe the two-step process used to identify the profit-maximizing level of output for a monopolist.
4. Describe the difference between a monopoly and a natural monopoly.
5. What are barriers to entry, and why are they crucial to the creation of potential long-run monopoly profits? Give an example of a barrier that can lead to monopoly.
6. Explain why a monopoly is a price maker but a perfectly competitive firm is a price taker.
7. How is monopolistic competition like competitive markets? How is monopolistic competition like monopoly?
8. What is an oligopoly? Provide an example of an oligopolistic industry not found in the chapter.

STUDY PROBLEMS (*✱ solved at the end of the section*)

1. Using the definition of a price taker as your guide, for the following industries explain why the outcome does not meet the definition.
   a. the pizza-delivery business
   b. the home-improvement business
   c. cell-phone companies
   d. breakfast cereals
2. Dave's Song and Dance Extravaganza is entering the competitive market of dinner theater in Columbus, Ohio. How does Dave's entry into this market affect the market price? What happens to the number of shows that existing theaters will produce? Assuming they were profitable before Dave's entry, what happens to the existing theaters' profits? Use two graphs, one for the market and one for the existing firms, to illustrate your answer.
3. In the figure on the right, identify the price the monopolist will charge and the output the monopolist will produce. How do these two decisions on the part of the monopolist compare to the efficient price and output?

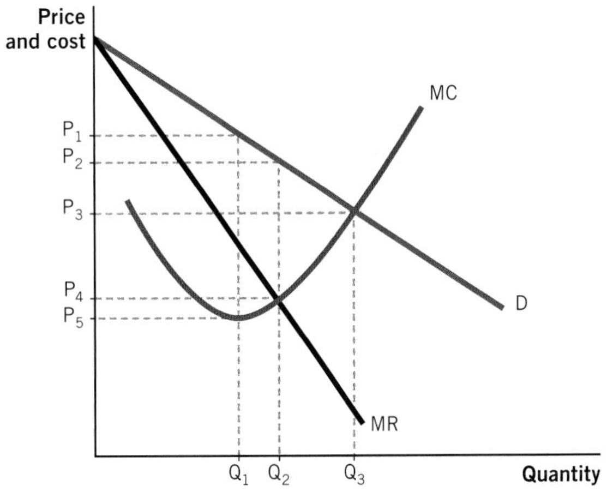

4. Which of the following could be considered a monopoly?
   a. your local water company
   b. Boeing, a manufacturer of airplanes
   c. Brad Pitt
   d. Walmart
   e. the only gas station along a 100-mile stretch of road

5. The year is 2278, and the starship *Enterprise* is running low on dilithium crystals, which are used to regulate the matter-antimatter reactions that propel the ship across the universe. Without the crystals, space-time travel is not possible. If there is only one known source of dilithium crystals, are the necessary conditions met to establish a monopoly? If the crystals are government-owned or -regulated, what price should the government set for them?

* 6. If demand falls, what is likely to happen to a monopolist's price, output, and economic profit?

7. Suppose that a monopolist's marginal cost curve shifts upward. What is likely to happen to the price the monopolist charges, the quantity it produces, and the profit it makes? Use a graph to illustrate your answer.

8. Which of the following could be considered a monopolistic competitor?
   a. local corn farmers
   b. the Tennessee Valley Authority, a large electricity producer
   c. pizza delivery
   d. grocery stores
   e. Kate Spade, a fashion designer

* 9. Consider two different companies. The first manufactures cardboard, and the second sells books. Which firm is more likely to advertise?

10. Which of the following markets are oligopolistic?
   a. passenger airlines
   b. cereal
   c. fast food
   d. wheat
   e. golf equipment
   f. the college bookstore on your campus

SOLVED PROBLEMS

6. There is a two-part answer here. The first graph shows the monopolist making a profit:

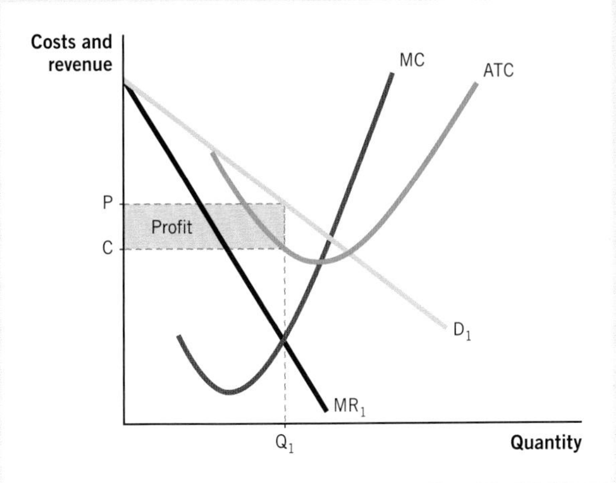

Now we show what happens if demand falls:

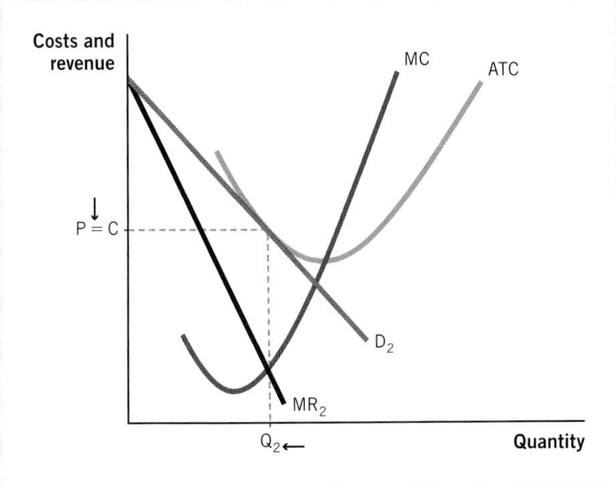

Lower demand causes the price to fall, the output to decline, and the profit to disappear. Note: When the demand curve falls, the marginal revenue curve falls as well.

9. The cardboard firm manufactures a product that is a component used mostly by other firms that need to package final products for sale. As a result, any efforts at advertising will only raise costs without increasing the demand for cardboard. This contrasts with the bookseller, who advertises to attract consumers to the store. More traffic means more purchases of books and other items sold in the store. The bookstore has some market power. In this case, it pays to advertise. A cardboard manufacturing firm sells exactly the same product as other cardboard producers, so it has no monopoly power, and any advertising expenses will only make its cost higher than its rivals'.

CHAPTER

7 Behavioral Economics and Game Theory

MISCONCEPTION

People always make rational decisions.

In this textbook, we have proceeded as if every person were *Homo economicus*, or a rationally self-interested decision-maker. *Homo economicus* is acutely aware of opportunities in the environment and strives to maximize the benefits received from each course of action while minimizing the costs. What does *Homo economicus* look like? If you are a fan of *Star Trek: The Next Generation*, you'll recall Data, the android with perfect logic. Data wasn't capable of human emotion and didn't face the complications that it creates in making decisions.

We don't want to leave you with the misconception that we're all like this! As human beings, we love, laugh, and cry. Sometimes, we seek revenge; other times, forgiveness. We can be impulsive and short-sighted, and we can fail to see the benefits of pursuing long-run gains. Each of these behaviors is real, although they don't fit squarely within our economic models. Human decision-making is far more complex than the standard economic model of behavior implies. In this chapter, we step back and consider why people don't always make rational decisions. To fold the broadest possible set of human behavior into economic analysis, we must turn to the field of *behavioral economics*, which enables us to capture a wider range of human motivations than the rational-agent model alone affords.

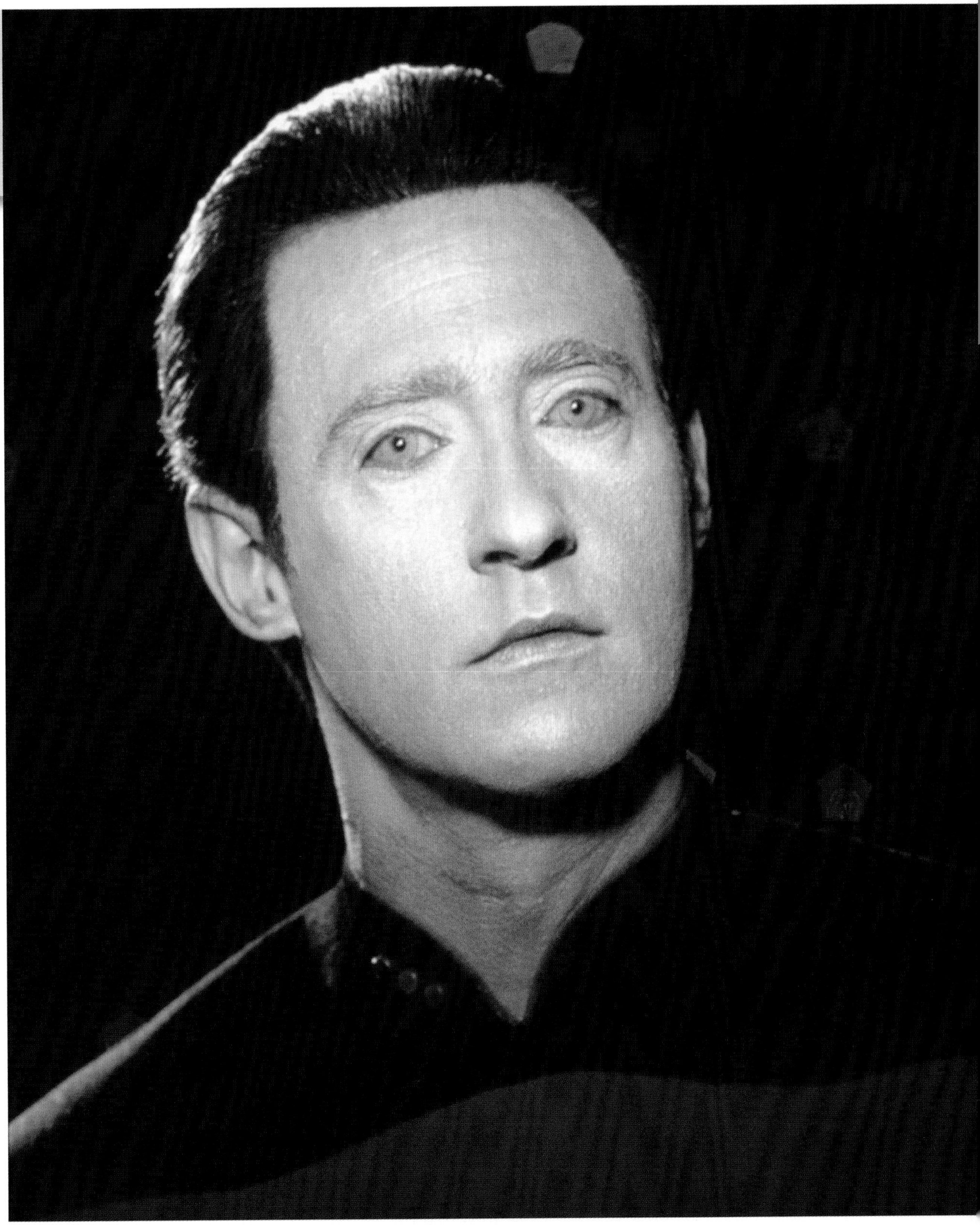

Data, the android in *Star Trek: The Next Generation*, exemplifies fully rational behavior.

BIG QUESTIONS

- How can economists explain irrational behavior?
- What is the role of risk in decision-making?
- How does game theory explain strategic behavior?

Behavioral economics is the field of economics that draws on insights from experimental psychology to explore how people make economic decisions.

Bounded rationality proposes that although decision-makers want a good outcome, either they are not capable of performing the problem-solving that traditional theory assumes, or they are not inclined to do so. Also called *limited reasoning*.

How Can Economists Explain Irrational Behavior?

Psychology, like economics, endeavors to understand the choices that people make. One key difference is that psychologists do not assume that people always behave in a fully rational way. As a result, psychologists have a much broader toolbox at their disposal to describe human behavior. **Behavioral economics** is the field of economics that draws on insights from experimental psychology to explore how people make economic decisions.

Until relatively recently, economists have ignored many human behaviors that don't fit their models. For example, because traditional economic theory assumes that people make optimal decisions like robots, economic theorists didn't try to explain why people might make an impulse purchase. Behavioral economists, however, understand that many behaviors contradict standard assumptions about rationality. They employ the idea of **bounded rationality**, which proposes that although decision-makers want a good outcome, either they aren't capable of performing the problem-solving that traditional theory assumes, or they aren't inclined to do so.

Will you say "yes" to the dress?

Bounded rationality, or limited reasoning, can be explained in three ways. First, the information that the individual uses to make the decision may be limited or incomplete. Second, the human brain has a limited capacity to process information. Third, there is often a limited amount of time in which to make a decision. These limitations prevent the decision-maker from reaching the results predicted under perfect rationality.

For example, suppose you're about to get married and find yourself at Kleinfeld Bridal with your bridesmaids. You enter the store to begin your search for the perfect wedding dress. You find a dress that you like, but it's a higher price than you were planning to spend. Do you make the purchase or not? The decision to buy depends on whether you believe that the value is high enough to justify the expense. But there's a problem: you have a limited amount of information. In a fully rational world, you would check out alternatives in other stores and on the Internet and then make the decision to purchase the dress only after you're satisfied that it's the best possible choice. Full rationality also assumes that your brain is able to recall the features of every dress. However, a dress you tried on at one location often blurs into another dress you tried on elsewhere. Wedding dresses are selected under a binding deadline. This means that you, the bride, must reach a decision quickly. Collectively, these three reasons often prevent brides from achieving the result that economists' rational models predict. In reality, you walk into a store, see something you love, and make the purchase using partial information. Whenever people end up making decisions without perfect information, the decisions reflect bounded rationality.

We will continue our discussion of behavioral economics by examining various behaviors that do not fit assumptions about fully rational behavior. These include (1) inconsistencies in decision-making and (2) judgments about fairness when making decisions. The goal in this section is to help you recognize and understand some of the behaviors that lead to contradictions between what economic models predict and what people actually do.

Inconsistencies in Decision-Making

If people were entirely rational, they would always be consistent. So the way a question is asked should not alter our responses, but research has shown that it does. Likewise, rational decision-making requires the ability to take the long-run trade-offs into account: if the returns are large enough, people should be willing to sacrifice current enjoyment for future benefits. Yet many of us make shortsighted decisions. In this section, we examine a variety of decision-making mistakes, including framing effects, priming effects, status quo bias, and intertemporal decision-making.

Framing and Priming Effects

Economic models do not entirely account for the behavior of real people. One common mistake that people make involves the **framing effect**, which occurs when an answer is influenced by the way a question is asked or a decision is influenced by the way alternatives are presented. Consider an employer-sponsored retirement plan. Companies can either (1) ask employees if they want to join or (2) use an automatic enrollment system that requires employees to opt out if they don't wish to participate. Studies have shown that workers who are asked if they want to join tend to participate at a much lower rate than those who are automatically enrolled and must opt out. Surely, a rational economic decision-maker would determine whether to participate by evaluating the plan itself, not by responding to the way the employer presents the option to participate. However, people are rarely that rational.

Framing effects occur when people change their answer (or action) depending on how the question is asked or how the alternatives are presented.

Another decision-making pitfall, known as the **priming effect**, occurs when the order of questions influences the answers. For example, consider two groups of college students. The first group is asked *How happy are you?* followed by *How many dates have you had in the last year?* The second group is asked *How many dates have you had in the last year?* followed by *How happy are you?* The questions are the same, but they're presented in reverse order. In the second group, students who had gone out on more dates reported being

Priming effects occur when the ordering of the questions influences the answers.

much happier than similar students in the first group! In other words, because they were reminded of the number of dates first, those who had more dates believed they were happier.

Status quo bias exists when people want to maintain their current choices.

Loss aversion occurs when individuals place more weight on avoiding losses than on attempting to realize gains.

Status Quo Bias

When people want to maintain their current choices, they may exhibit the **status quo bias.** This bias leads decision-makers to try to protect what they have, even when an objective evaluation of their circumstances suggests that a change would be beneficial. In behavioral economics, the status quo bias is often accompanied by **loss aversion**, which occurs when a person places more value on avoiding losses than on attempting to realize gains.

Opportunity cost

Loss aversion causes people to behave conservatively. The cost of this behavior is the missed opportunities that could potentially enhance welfare. For example, a loss-averse individual would maintain a savings account with a low interest rate instead of actively shopping for better rates elsewhere. This person would lose the potential benefits from higher returns on savings.

Are you on Team Dollar Bill or Team Dollar Coin?

Status quo bias also explains why new products and ideas have trouble gaining traction: many potential customers prefer to leave things the way they are, even if something new might make more sense. Consider the $1 coin. It is far more durable than the $1 bill. If people used the coin, the government would save about $5 billion in production costs over the next 30 years. That sounds like a slam-dunk policy change, but it isn't. Americans like their dollar bills and rarely use the $1 coin in circulation even though they repeatedly use nickels, dimes, and quarters to make change, to feed parking meters, and to buy from vending machines. Introducing more of the $1 coin and eliminating the $1 bill would be rational, but the status quo bias has prevented the change from happening.

ECONOMICS IN THE REAL WORLD

Are You an Organ Donor?

More than 25,000 organ transplants take place every year in the United States, with the vast majority coming from deceased donors. Demand greatly exceeds supply. Over 100,000 people are currently on organ-donation waiting lists. Most Americans are aware of the need, and 90% of all Americans say they support donation. But only 30% know the essential steps to take to be a donor.

There are two main donor systems: the opt-in system and the opt-out system. In an opt-in system, individuals must give explicit consent to be a donor. In an opt-out system, anyone who has not explicitly refused is considered a donor.

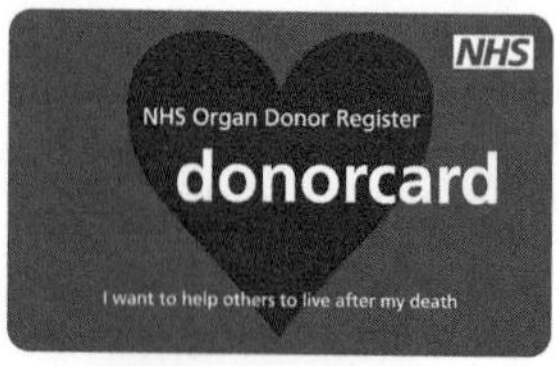

In the United Kingdom, organ donors must opt in.

In the United States, donors are required to opt in. Since opting in generally produces fewer donors than opting out, many states have sought to raise donation awareness by allowing consent to be noted on the individual's driver's license.

In Europe, many countries have opt-out systems, where consent is presumed. The difference is crucial. After all, in places with opt-in systems, many people who would be willing to donate organs never actually take the time to complete the necessary steps to opt in. In countries like France and Poland, where people must opt out, over 90% of citizens do not explicitly opt out, which means they give consent. This strategy yields organ donation rates that are significantly higher than those of opt-in programs.

According to traditional economic analysis, opting in or opting out shouldn't matter—the results should be the same. The fact that we find strong evidence to the contrary is a compelling illustration of the framing effect. ✷

Intertemporal Decision-Making

Intertemporal decisions occur across time. **Intertemporal decision-making**—that is, planning to do something over a period of time—requires the ability to value the present and the future consistently. For instance, many people, despite their best intentions, don't end up saving enough for retirement. The temptation to spend money today ends up overwhelming the willpower to save for tomorrow. In a perfectly rational world, a person wouldn't need outside assistance to save enough for retirement. In the real world, however, workers depend on 401(k) plans and other work-sponsored retirement programs to deduct funds from their paycheck so that they don't spend that portion of their income on other things.

Intertemporal decision-making involves planning to do something over a period of time; this decision-making process requires valuing the present and the future consistently.

The ability to resist temptation is illustrated by a classic research experiment conducted at a preschool at Stanford University in 1972. One at a time, individual children were led into a room devoid of distractions and were offered a marshmallow. The researchers explained to each child that he or she could eat the marshmallow right away or wait for 15 minutes and be rewarded with a second marshmallow. Very few of the 600 children in the study ate the marshmallow immediately. Most tried to fight the temptation. Of those who tried to wait, approximately one-third held out long enough to earn the second marshmallow. That finding is interesting by itself, but what happened next is truly amazing. Many of the parents of the children in the original study noticed that the children who had delayed gratification seemed to perform better as they progressed through school. Researchers have tracked the participants over the course of 40 years and found that the delayed-gratification group had higher SAT scores, more savings, and larger retirement accounts.

Can you resist eating one marshmallow now, in order to get a second one later?

Judgments about Fairness

The pursuit of fairness is another common behavior that is important in economic decisions but that standard economic theory cannot explain. For example, fairness is one of the key drivers in determining the tax-rate structure for income taxes. Proponents of fairness believe in *progressive taxation,* whereby the rich pay a higher tax rate on their income than those in lower income brackets. Likewise, some people object to the high pay of chief executive officers because they believe there should be an upper limit to what constitutes fair compensation.

While fairness is not normally modeled in economics, behavioral economists have developed experiments to determine the role of fairness in personal decisions. The **ultimatum game** is an economic experiment in which two players decide how to divide a sum of money. The game shows how

The **ultimatum game** is an economic experiment in which two players decide how to divide a sum of money.

fairness enters into the rational decision-making process. In the game, Player 1 is given a sum of money and is asked to propose a way of splitting it with Player 2. Player 2 can either accept or reject the proposal. If Player 2 accepts, the sum is split according to the proposal. However, if Player 2 rejects the proposal, neither player gets anything. The game is played only once, so the first player doesn't have to worry about reciprocity.

Consider an ultimatum game that asks Player 1 to share $1,000 with Player 2. Player 1 must decide how fair to make the proposal. The decision tree in Figure 7.1 highlights four possible outcomes to two very different proposals—what the figure shows as a fair proposal and an unfair proposal.

Traditional economic theory presumes that both players are fully rational and wish to maximize their income. Player 1 should therefore maximize his gains by offering the minimum, $1, to Player 2. The reasoning is that Player 2 values $1 more than nothing and so will accept the proposal, leaving Player 1 with $999. But real people aren't always economic maximizers because they generally believe that fairness matters. Most of the time, Player 2 would find such an unfair division infuriating and reject it.

Player 1 knows that Player 2 will definitely accept an offer of $500; this division of the money is exactly equal and, therefore, fair. Thus, the probability of a 50/50 split being accepted is 100%. In contrast, the probability of Player 2 accepting an offer of $1 is close to 0%. Offering increasing amounts from $1 to $500 will continue to raise the probability of an acceptance until it reaches 100% at $500.

Player 2's role is simpler: her only decision is whether to accept or reject the proposal. Player 2 desires a fair distribution but has no direct control over the division. To punish Player 1 for being unfair, Player 2 must reject the proposal altogether. The trade-off of penalizing Player 1 for unfairness is a complete loss of any prize. So while Player 2 may not like any given proposal, rejecting it would cause a personal loss. Player 2 might therefore accept a number of unfair proposals because she would rather get something than

FIGURE 7.1

The Decision Tree for the Ultimatum Game

The decision tree for the ultimatum game has four branches. If Player 1 makes a fair proposal, Player 2 will accept the distribution and both players will earn $500. However, if Player 1 makes an unfair proposal, Player 2 may reject the distribution even though this decision means receiving nothing.

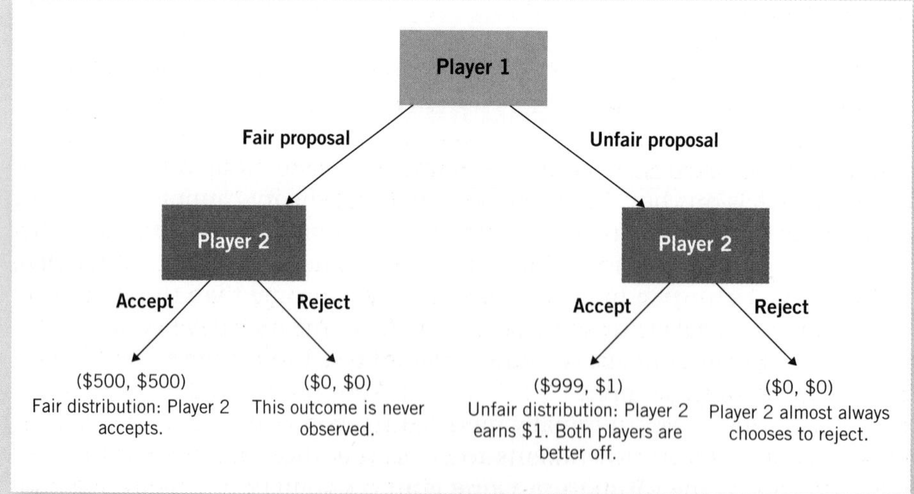

nothing. Research shows that offers are rejected about 20% of the time. This may be surprising, considering that the average offer is a 60–40 split.

Each of the ideas that we've presented in this section, including inconsistency in decision-making and judgments about fairness, represents a departure from the traditional economic model of rational maximization. In the next section, we focus on risk-taking. As you will soon learn, not everyone evaluates risk in the same way. This fact has led economists to reconsider their models of human behavior.

What Is the Role of Risk in Decision-Making?

In this section, we examine the role that risk plays in decision-making. The standard economic model of consumer choice assumes that people are consistent in their risk-taking preferences. However, people's risk tolerances actually vary widely and are subject to change. Thus, risk-taking behavior is not nearly as simple or predictable as economists once believed. We can gain insights by examining a phenomenon known as a *preference reversal.*

Preference Reversals

As you know, trying to predict human behavior isn't easy. Maurice Allais, the recipient of the 1988 Nobel Prize in Economics, noticed that people's tolerance for risk appeared to change in different situations. This observation did not agree with the standard economic model, which assumes that an individual's risk tolerance is constant and places the individual into one of three distinct groups.

Imagine that you're on a game show and could either win the monetary prize behind one of three doors or take a sure thing. Behind door number 1 is \$1. Behind door number 2 is \$100. Behind door number 3 is \$1,000. There is an equal chance that you would win any of these amounts since you get to choose which door.

To analyze the behavior of the game-show participants, economists calculate **expected value**, which is the predicted value of an event. Expected value is computed by multiplying each possible outcome by its respective probability and summing all of these amounts. Therefore, in this example, the expected value would be $1/3(\$1) + 1/3(\$100) + 1/3(\$1{,}000) = \$367$.

Risk-averse people prefer a sure thing over a gamble with a higher expected value. So if offered \$50, they would accept this offer rather than risk picking the door with the \$1 behind it, even though there's also the possibility of choosing a door with \$100 or \$1,000. **Risk-neutral people** choose the highest expected value regardless of the risk. These people would reject the guaranteed payoff up to \$367. **Risk takers** prefer gambles with lower expected values, and potentially higher winnings, over a sure thing. They would always elect to pick a door rather than take the sure thing unless they were offered the full \$1,000—and even then they might want to pick a door for the thrill of it.

Expected value is the predicted value of an event. It is calculated by multiplying each possible outcome by its respective probability and then summing all of these amounts.

Risk-averse people prefer a sure thing over a gamble with a higher expected value.

Risk-neutral people choose the highest expected value regardless of the risk.

Risk takers prefer gambles with lower expected values, and potentially higher winnings, over a sure thing.

TABLE 7.1

The Allais Paradox

Choose gamble A or B

Gamble A	Gamble B
No gamble—receive $1 million in cash 100% of the time.	A lottery ticket that pays $5 million 10% of the time, $1 million 89% of the time, and nothing 1% of the time.

Choose gamble C or D

Gamble C	Gamble D
A lottery ticket that pays $5 million 10% of the time and nothing 90% of the time.	A lottery ticket that pays $1 million 11% of the time and nothing 89% of the time.

Allais developed a means of assessing risk behavior by presenting the set of choices (known as the Allais paradox) depicted in Table 7.1. Individuals were asked to choose their preferred options between gambles A and B and then again between gambles C and D.

Economic science predicts that people will choose consistently according to their risk preference. As a result, economists understood that risk-averse individuals would choose the pair A and D. Likewise, the pair B and C makes sense if the participants wish to maximize the expected value of the gambles. Let's see why.

1. *Risk-Averse People:* People who select gamble A over gamble B take the sure thing. If they're asked to choose between C and D, we would expect them to try to maximize their chances of winning something by selecting D, since it has the higher probability of winning.
2. *Risk-Neutral People:* Gamble B has a higher expected value than gamble A. We know that gamble A always pays $1 million since it occurs 100% of the time. Calculating gamble B's expected value is more complicated. Recall that the expected value is computed by multiplying each outcome by its respective probability and then summing the outcomes. For gamble B, this means that the expected value is ($5 million $\times$ 0.10) + ($1 million $\times$ 0.89) + ($0 $\times$ 0.01), which equals $1.39 million. So a risk-neutral player will select gamble B. Likewise, gamble C has a higher expected value than gamble D. Gamble C has an expected value of ($5 million $\times$ 0.10), or $0.5 million. Gamble D's expected value is ($1 million $\times$ 0.11), or $0.11 million. Therefore, risk-neutral players who think at the margin will choose gambles B and C in order to maximize their potential winnings from the game.

Marginal thinking

While we would expect people to be consistent in their choices, Allais found that approximately 30% of his research population selected gambles A and C, which are contrasting pairs. Gamble A is the sure thing; however, gamble C, which has the higher expected value, carries more risk. This scenario illustrates a preference reversal. A **preference reversal** occurs when risk tolerance is not consistent. Allais argued that a person's risk tolerance depends on his or her financial circumstances. Someone who chooses gamble A over gamble B prefers the certainty of a large financial prize—the guarantee

A **preference reversal** occurs when risk tolerance is not consistent.

of $1 million over the uncertainty of the larger prize. Choosing gamble A could be seen as similar to purchasing insurance: you pay a fee, known as a premium, in order to protect your winnings. In this case, you forfeit the chance to win $5 million. In contrast, gambles C and D offer small chances of success, and therefore the choice is more like playing the lottery.

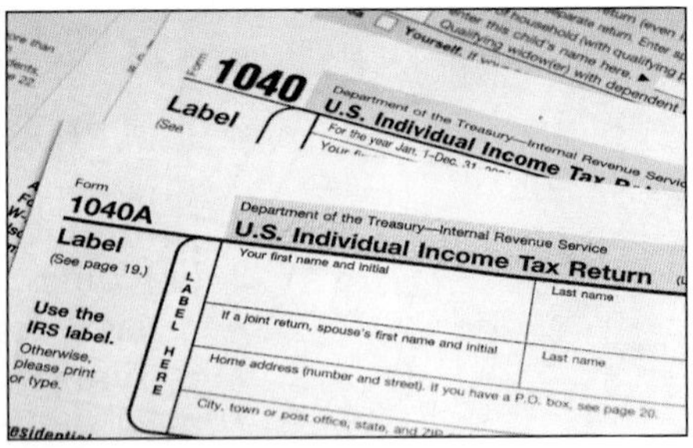

Withholding too much in the previous year and then paying your accountant to file for a rapid refund is a good example of a preference reversal.

It turns out that preference reversals are more common than economists once believed. For example, approximately 80% of all income tax filers expect to get a refund because they overpaid in the previous year. This behavior is odd, since there is an opportunity cost of waiting to get money back from the government when it didn't need to be paid in the first place. Employees could have asked their employers to withhold less and enjoyed their money sooner. In most circumstances, people have strongly **positive time preferences**: they prefer to have what they want sooner rather than later. So what do these taxpayers do when they learn the amount of their refund? In many cases, they pay their tax preparers an additional fee to have their refunds sent to their bank accounts electronically so they can receive the money sooner! Traditional economic analysis is unable to explain this behavior; but armed with Allais's insights, we now see this behavior as a preference reversal.

Positive time preferences indicate that people prefer to have what they want sooner rather than later.

PRACTICE WHAT YOU KNOW

Risk Aversion: Risk-Taking Behavior

Question: In the following situations, are the choices evidence of risk aversion or risk-taking?

1. You have a choice between selecting heads or tails. If your guess is correct, you earn $2,000. But you earn nothing if your guess is incorrect. Alternatively, you can simply take $750 without the gamble. You decide to take the $750.

Answer: The expected value of a 50/50 outcome worth $2,000 is $1,000. Therefore, the decision to take the sure thing, which is $250 less, is evidence of risk aversion.

2. You have a choice between (a) predicting the roll of a six-sided die, with a $3,000 prize for a correct answer, or (b) taking a sure $750. You decide to roll the die.

Answer: The expected value of the roll of the die is $1/6 \times \$3{,}000$, or $500. Therefore, the $750 sure thing has an expected value that is $250 more. By rolling the die, you are taking the option with the lower expected value and also more risk. This indicates that you are a risk taker.

How do you handle risky decisions?

How Does Game Theory Explain Strategic Behavior?

Until now we've used models like the demand-and-supply model to explain outcomes in the market. These models have a lot to tell us about how people behave, assuming they behave rationally. However, if behavioral economics is trying to explain behavior that appears not to be rational, then economists need different tools to conduct their analysis. One of these tools is called game theory.

Game theory is a branch of mathematics that economists use to analyze the strategic behavior of decision-makers.

Game theory is a branch of mathematics that economists use to analyze the strategic behavior of decision-makers. The techniques of game theory can help us determine what level of cooperation is most likely to occur between players who are trying to achieve a particular objective. Just like a board game, an economic game consists of a set of players and a set of strategies available to those players. What is a little different is that before the game is played, we can predict the payoffs, or the rewards, to each player depending on the combined strategies they adopt. The game is usually represented by a payoff matrix that shows the players, strategies, and payoffs. It is presumed that both players act simultaneously and without knowing the actions of the other.

In this section, we will learn about the prisoner's dilemma, an example from game theory that helps us understand how specific strategies often frame short-run decisions even though those strategies may not yield the highest payoffs. We will use the idea of the *dominant strategy* to explain why oligopolists often choose to advertise even when doing so doesn't yield the highest profit level. (For a review of oligopoly, see Chapter 6.) Finally, we will come full circle and argue that a dominant strategy in a game may be overcome in the long run through repeated interactions.

Strategic Behavior and the Dominant Strategy

In many decisions we make, the outcome hinges on the interaction of our choices with the choices of others. Oligopolies are different from other kinds of market structure in that the success of the firms is interdependent. This situation is analogous to a sporting event where the success of one team depends in part on the plays the other team runs. We can examine this interdependence by exploring a classic problem in game theory known as the *prisoner's dilemma*. The dilemma takes its name from a famous scenario devised by pioneer game theorist Al Tucker soon after World War II.

Incentives

The scenario goes like this: two prisoners are being interrogated separately about a crime they both participated in, and each is offered a plea bargain to cooperate with the authorities by testifying against the other. If both suspects refuse to cooperate with the authorities, neither can be convicted of a more serious crime, though they will have to spend some time in jail. But the police have offered full immunity if one cooperates and the other doesn't. This means that each suspect has an incentive to betray the other. The rub is

that if they both confess, they will spend more time in jail than if they had both stayed quiet. When decision-makers face incentives that make it difficult to achieve mutually beneficial outcomes, we say they are in a **prisoner's dilemma**. This situation makes the payoff for cooperating with the authorities more attractive than the result of keeping quiet. We can understand why this occurs by looking at Figure 7.2, a payoff matrix that shows the possible outcomes in a prisoner's dilemma situation. Starting in the upper-left-hand corner of the white box, we see that if both suspects testify against each other, they each get 10 years in jail. If one suspect testifies while his partner remains quiet—the upper-right and lower-left boxes—he goes free and his partner gets 25 years in jail. If both keep quiet—the result in the lower-right-hand corner—they each get off with one year in jail. This result is better than the outcome in which both prisoners testify.

The **prisoner's dilemma** occurs when decision-makers face incentives that make it difficult to achieve mutually beneficial outcomes.

Since each suspect is interrogated separately, the decision about what to tell the police cannot be made cooperatively; thus, each prisoner faces a dilemma. The interrogation process makes it a non-cooperative "game" and changes the incentives that each party faces.

Under these circumstances, what will our suspects choose? Let's examine the choices made by two criminals: Walter White and Jesse Pinkman. We'll begin with the outcomes for Walter. Suppose that he testifies. If Jesse also testifies, Walter will get 10 years in jail (the upper-left box). If Jesse keeps quiet, Walter will go free (the lower-left box). Now suppose that Walter decides

FIGURE 7.2

		Walter White: Testify	Walter White: Keep quiet
Jesse Pinkman	Testify	10 years in jail / 10 years in jail	25 years in jail / goes free
	Keep quiet	goes free / 25 years in jail	1 year in jail / 1 year in jail

The Prisoner's Dilemma

The two suspects know that if they both keep quiet, they'll spend only one year in jail. The prisoner's dilemma occurs because the decision to testify results in no jail time for the one who testifies if the other doesn't testify. However, this outcome means that both are likely to testify and get 10 years.

to keep quiet. If Jesse testifies, Walter can expect 25 years in jail (the upper-right box). If Jesse keeps quiet, Walter will get 1 year in jail (the lower-right box). No matter what choice Jesse makes, Walter is always better off choosing to testify. If his partner testifies and he testifies, he gets 10 years in jail as opposed to 25 if he keeps quiet. If his partner keeps quiet and he testifies, Walter goes free as opposed to spending a year in jail if he also keeps quiet. A similar analysis applies to the outcomes for Jesse.

A **dominant strategy** exists when a player will always prefer one strategy, regardless of what his or her opponent chooses.

When a player always prefers one strategy, regardless of what his opponent chooses, that player has a **dominant strategy**. We can see a dominant strategy at work in the case of our two suspects. They know that if they both keep quiet, they'll spend one year in jail. The dilemma occurs because both suspects are more likely to testify and get 10 years in jail. This choice is obvious for two reasons. First, neither suspect can monitor the actions of the other after they are separated. Second, once each suspect understands that his partner will save jail time if he testifies, he realizes that the incentives are not in favor of keeping quiet.

A **Nash equilibrium** occurs when decision-makers cannot, on their own, change their strategy and make themselves better off.

When both criminals follow their dominant strategies, the result is a special situation called a Nash equilibrium. A **Nash equilibrium** occurs when decision-makers cannot, on their own, change their strategy and make themselves better off. If each suspect reasons that the other will testify, the best response is also to testify. But from this point, if Walter changes his mind and keeps quiet, he ends up in jail for 25 years while Jesse walks free. Similarly, if Jesse clams up, he ends up serving a long sentence while Walter walks. Thus, once we get to the decisions in the upper-left box, neither prisoner can make a different choice without harming himself. Each suspect may wish that he and his partner could coordinate their actions and agree to keep quiet. However, without the possibility of coordination, neither has an incentive to withhold testimony. So they both think strategically and decide to testify.

Incentives

ECONOMICS IN THE REAL WORLD

Cheating in Professional Sports

Why did Lance Armstrong dope? Because everyone else was doing it.

The prisoner's dilemma can help us understand the rash of drug use in professional sports. Cycling and baseball have had serious problems with performance enhancing drugs (PEDs) recently. Knowing the harmful effects of steroids and other drugs, players still use them. Why? It's the prisoner's dilemma. If you don't cheat (by using PEDs) and others do, you're more likely to lose. Even if everyone agrees not to take drugs, are you willing to trust your competitors not to cheat?

Look at the matrix below. Here we're looking at two cyclists, Lance and Miguel. They both want to win and believe that they can win, but only if the playing field is level. If neither athlete takes the drugs, each has a 50/50 chance to win any given race. If they take PEDs, they increase their chance of winning considerably, from 50 percent to 80 percent, but only if the other cyclist doesn't take PEDs. The desire to win is so strong that each would want to take the drugs. Why? If his competitor is taking them, he needs to do the same to balance his chances of winning. The dominant strategy is to take the drugs.

		Miguel: PEDs	Miguel: No PEDs
Lance	PEDs	50 (Miguel) / 50 (Lance)	20 (Miguel) / 80 (Lance)
	No PEDs	80 (Miguel) / 20 (Lance)	50 (Miguel) / 50 (Lance)

This example illustrates how rationality can be suspended when ambition gets in the way. Because of the long-run health risks of consuming these drugs, we would expect that no one would take them. But the intense drive to win inherent in professional athletes can make them act in a manner inconsistent with what rationality predicts. ✳

Duopoly and the Prisoner's Dilemma

The prisoner's dilemma example suggests that cooperation can be difficult to achieve. This conclusion applies not just to criminals but to firms as well. In an oligopoly market structure, there is a tendency to collude—that is, for firms to work together to achieve mutually beneficial outcomes at the expense of the consumer. To get a better sense of the incentives that oligopolists face when trying to collude, we'll use game theory to evaluate the outcome in a duopoly example.

Let's assume we have two firms (a *duopoly*) in the cellphone market. The two companies, AT-Phone and Horizon, are likely to produce more output than they would if they were maximizing profits. Let's see why.

Figure 7.3 puts the output information for these firms into a payoff matrix and highlights the revenue that AT-Phone and Horizon could earn at various production levels. Looking at the bottom two boxes, we see that at high production Horizon can bring in either $30,000 or $24,000 in revenue, depending on what AT-Phone does. At a low production level, Horizon could earn either $27,000 or $22,500. Now look at the right-hand column, and you'll see that AT-Phone can earn either $30,000 or $24,000, depending on what Horizon does. At a low production level, it could earn either $27,000 or $22,500. Thus, the high production level is the dominant strategy for each firm. The two companies always have an incentive to serve more customers because this strategy yields the most revenue regardless of what the other firm chooses. A high level of production leads to a Nash equilibrium; both firms make $24,000. However, if the companies operate as a *cartel* (that is, they decide on their output level jointly to maximize profits), they can lower their production and both can earn $27,000. However, unless they can find some way to

Incentives

FIGURE 7.3

The Prisoner's Dilemma in Duopoly

Each company has a dominant strategy to serve more customers because it makes the most revenue even if its competitor also expands production. A high level of production leads to a Nash equilibrium at which both firms make $24,000. By colluding, AT-Phone and Horizon could agree to a low level of production and increase their revenue to $27,000 each, but the likelihood of cheating makes this an unstable equilibrium.

		AT-Phone	
		Low production: 300 customers	High production: 400 customers
Horizon	Low production: 300 customers	$27,000 revenue (AT-Phone) $27,000 revenue (Horizon)	$30,000 revenue (AT-Phone) $22,500 revenue (Horizon)
	High production: 400 customers	$22,500 revenue (AT-Phone) $30,000 revenue (Horizon)	$24,000 revenue (AT-Phone) $24,000 revenue (Horizon)

ECONOMICS IN THE MEDIA

Prisoner's Dilemma

Murder by Numbers

There is an especially compelling example of the prisoner's dilemma at work in *Murder by Numbers* (2002). In this scene, the district attorney's office decides to interrogate two murder suspects. Without a confession, they don't have enough evidence and the two murderers are likely to go free. Each is confronted with the prisoner's dilemma by being placed in a separate room and threatened with the death penalty. In order to get the confession, the detective tells one of the suspects, "Just think of it as a game. Whoever talks first is the winner." The detective goes on to tell one of the suspects that his partner in the other room is "rolling over" (even though the partner is not actually talking) and that the partner will get a lighter sentence because he is cooperating. This places added pressure on the suspect.

Would you rat on your partner in crime?

enforce the low-production level of output, one of the parties is likely to cheat because it can increase its revenue at the expense of its competition. This will raise the output of the combined firms above the profit-maximizing level.

To avoid cheating among its members, a cartel needs a way to enforce the preferred behavior. Gangs and mobsters have an unwritten code: they understand that some violent end will befall them or their family if they turn informant. The enforcement is carried out by the organization for which they work. In the business world, government regulations are intended to prevent cheating through **collusion**, but the threat of punishment must be large enough to scare firms. In U.S. antitrust cases, firms that are found guilty of collusion have to pay triple damages to the aggrieved party.

Collusion is an agreement among rival firms that specifies the price each firm charges and the quantity it produces.

Advertising and Game Theory

Oligopolists sell differentiated products. As a result, we should expect that firms in this kind of market structure would advertise to attract customers. However, because one firm's actions affect the performance of the other firms, advertising can create a contest among firms looking to increase sales. This contest may lead to skyrocketing advertising budgets and little, or no, net gain of customers. Therefore, oligopolists have an incentive to scale back their advertising, but only if their rivals also agree to scale back. Like all cooperative action among competitors, this is easier said than done.

Incentives

Figure 7.4 highlights the advertising choices of Coca-Cola and PepsiCo, two fierce rivals in the soft-drink industry. Together, Coca-Cola and PepsiCo

		Coca-Cola: Advertises	Coca-Cola: Does not advertise
PepsiCo	Advertises	$100 million profit (Coca-Cola) $100 million profit (PepsiCo)	$75 million profit (Coca-Cola) $150 million profit (PepsiCo)
PepsiCo	Does not advertise	$150 million profit (Coca-Cola) $75 million profit (PepsiCo)	$125 million profit (Coca-Cola) $125 million profit (PepsiCo)

FIGURE 7.4

The Prisoner's Dilemma and Advertising

The two companies each have a dominant strategy to advertise. We can see this by observing that Coca-Cola and PepsiCo each make $25 million more profit by choosing to advertise, given the other company's strategy. As a result, they both end up in the upper-left box, earning $100 million profit when they could have each made $125 million profit in the lower-right box if they had agreed not to advertise.

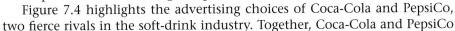

PRACTICE WHAT YOU KNOW

Dominant Strategy: To Advertise or Not—That Is the Question!

Question: University Subs and Savory Sandwiches are the only two sandwich shops in a small college town. If neither runs a special 2-for-1 promotion, both are able to keep their prices high and earn $10,000 a month. However, when both run promotions, their profits fall to $1,000. Finally, if one runs a promotion and the other does not, the shop that runs the promotion earns a profit of $15,000 and the other loses $5,000. What is the dominant strategy for University Subs? Is there a Nash equilibrium in this example?

How much should a firm charge for this sandwich?

		University Subs	
		Runs a 2-for-1 promotion	Keeps price high
Savory Sandwiches	**Runs a 2-for-1 promotion**	Makes $1,000 Makes $1,000	Loses $5,000 Makes $15,000
	Keeps price high	Makes $15,000 Loses $5,000	Makes $10,000 Makes $10,000

Answer: If University Subs runs the 2-for-1 promotion, it will make either $1,000 or $15,000, depending on its rival's actions. If University Subs keeps the price high, it will make either −$5,000 or $10,000, depending on what Savory Sandwiches does. So the dominant strategy will be to run the special, since it guarantees a profit of at least $1,000. Savory Sandwiches has the same dominant strategy and the same payoffs. Therefore, both companies will run the promotion and each will make $1,000. Neither firm has a reason to switch to the high-price strategy since it would lose $5,000 if the other company runs the 2-for-1 promotion. A Nash equilibrium occurs when both companies run the promotion.

account for 75% of the soft-drink market, with Coca-Cola being the slightly larger of the two firms. Both companies are known for their advertising campaigns, which cost hundreds of millions of dollars. To determine if they gain anything by spending so much on advertising, let's look at the dominant strategy. In the absence of cooperation, each firm will choose to advertise, because the payoffs under advertising ($100 million or $150 million) exceed those of not advertising ($75 million or $125 million). When each firm chooses to advertise, it generates a profit of $100 million. This is a second-best outcome compared to the $125 million profit each could earn if neither firm advertises. (Remember, profits are total revenues minus total costs. By not advertising, the firms increase their profits by not incurring the cost of the advertising.) The dilemma is that each firm needs to advertise to market its product and retain its customer base, but most advertising expenditures end up canceling each other out and costing the companies millions of dollars.

ECONOMICS IN THE REAL WORLD

The Cold War

The Cold War created a prisoner's dilemma for the United States and the Soviet Union.

The idea that companies benefit from spending less on advertising has an analog in warfare. Countries benefit from a "peace dividend" whenever war ends. There is no better example than the Cold War between the Soviet Union and the United States that began in the 1950s. By the time the Cold War ended in the late 1980s, both countries had amassed thousands of nuclear warheads in an effort to deter aggression.

This buildup put enormous economic pressure on each country to keep up with the other. During the height of the Cold War, each country found itself in a prisoner's dilemma in which spending more in an arms race was the dominant strategy. When the Soviet Union ultimately dissolved, the United States was able to spend less money on deterrence. In the post–Cold War world of the 1990s, the U.S. military budget fell from 6.5 to 3.5% of gross domestic product (GDP) as the nation reaped a peace dividend. Of course, the prisoner's dilemma cannot account for all military spending: following the terrorist attacks of 2001, U.S. military spending increased again to nearly 5% of GDP by 2004. ✷

Escaping the Prisoner's Dilemma in the Long Run

We have seen how game theory can be a useful tool for understanding strategic decision-making in non-cooperative environments. When you examine the prisoner's dilemma or the Nash equilibrium, the solution represents an outcome for a short-term, one-shot game. However, many interactions are long-term in nature, a situation that the dominant strategy does not consider.

Game theorist Robert Axelrod decided to examine the choices that participants make in a long-run setting. He ran a sophisticated computer simulation in which he invited scholars to submit strategies for securing points in a prisoner's dilemma tournament over many rounds. All the submissions were collected and paired, and the results were scored. After each simulation, Axelrod eliminated the weakest strategy and re-ran the tournament with the remaining strategies. This evolutionary approach continued until the best strategy remained. Among all strategies, including those that were solely cooperative or non-cooperative, tit-for-tat dominated. **Tit-for-tat** is a long-run strategy that promotes cooperation among participants by mimicking the opponent's most recent decision with repayment in kind. As the name implies, a tit-for-tat strategy is one in which you do whatever your opponent does. If your opponent breaks the agreement, you break the agreement too. If the opponent behaves properly, then you behave properly too.

Tit-for-tat is a long-run strategy that promotes cooperation among participants by mimicking the opponent's most recent decision with repayment in kind.

Since the joint payoffs for cooperation are high in a prisoner's dilemma, tit-for-tat begins by cooperating. In subsequent rounds, the tit-for-tat strategy mimics whatever the other player did in the previous round. The genius behind tit-for-tat is that it changes the incentives and encourages cooperation. Turning back to our example in Figure 7.4, suppose that Coca-Cola and PepsiCo want to save on advertising expenses. The companies expect to have repeated interactions, so they both know from past experience that any effort to start a new advertising campaign will be immediately countered by the other firm. Since the companies react to each other's moves in kind, any effort to exploit the dominant strategy of advertising will ultimately fail. This dynamic can alter the incentives that the firms face in the long run and lead to mutually beneficial behavior.

Incentives

Tit-for-tat makes it less desirable to advertise by eliminating the long-run benefits. Advertising is still a dominant strategy in the short run because the payoffs with advertising ($100 million or $150 million) exceed those of not advertising ($75 million or $125 million). In the short run, the firm that advertises could earn $25 million extra, but in every subsequent round—if the rival responds in kind—the firm should expect profits of $100 million because its rival will also be advertising. As a result, there is a large long-run opportunity cost for not cooperating. If one firm stops advertising and the other follows suit, they'll each find themselves making $125 million in the long run. Why hasn't this happened in the real world? Because Coca-Cola and PepsiCo don't trust each other enough to earn the dividend that comes from an advertising truce.

Opportunity cost

ECONOMICS IN THE MEDIA

Prisoner's Dilemma

The Dark Knight

In the movie *The Dark Knight* (2008), the Joker (played by the late Heath Ledger) always seems to be one step ahead of the law. The strategic interactions between the police and the conniving villain are an illustration of game theory in action.

Near the end of the movie, the Joker rigs two full passenger ferries to explode at midnight and tells the passengers that if they try to escape, the bomb will detonate earlier. To complicate matters, one of the ferries is carrying civilian passengers, including a number of children, while the other ferry is transporting prisoners. Each ferry can save itself by hitting a detonator button attached to the other ferry.

The Joker's plan sets up a prisoner's dilemma between the two boats and an ethical experiment. Are the lives of those on the civilian boat worth more than those of the prisoners? The Joker's intention is to have one of the ferries blow up the other and thereby create chaos in Gotham City.

In the payoff matrix, the dominant strategy is to detonate the other boat. Failing to detonate the other boat results in death—either one ferry blows up at midnight, or the other boat detonates it first.

In this scenario, the only chance of survival is if one ferry detonates the other ferry first. As the scene unfolds and the tension builds, the passengers on both boats realize their plight and wrestle with the consequences of their decisions. Gradually, everyone becomes aware that the dominant strategy is to detonate the other boat. What is interesting is how the civilians and prisoners react to this information.

What actually happens? Passengers on each boat decide that they would rather be detonated than willingly participate in the Joker's experiment. Watching the scene as a game theorist will give you a new appreciation for the film.

		Prisoner ferry	
		Detonate other boat	**Do not detonate other boat**
Civilian ferry	**Detonate other boat**	Cannot simultaneously happen (prisoner) Cannot simultaneously happen (civilian)	Die (prisoner) Survive (civilian)
	Do not detonate other boat	Survive (prisoner) Die (civilian)	Die (prisoner) Die (civilian)

The prisoner's dilemma nicely captures why cooperation is so difficult in the short run. But most interactions in life occur over the long run. For example, scam artists and sketchy companies take advantage of short-run opportunities that cannot last because relationships in the long run—with businesses and with people—involve mutual trust. In long-run relationships, cooperation is the default because you know that the other side is invested in the relationship. Under these circumstances, the tit-for-tat strategy works well.

A Caution about Game Theory

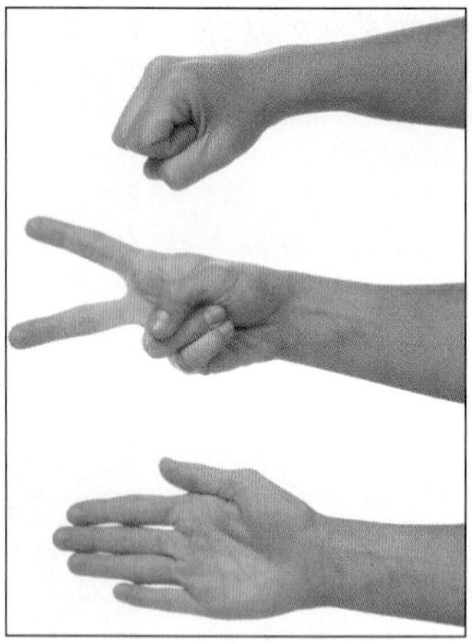

Rock, Paper, Scissors is a game without a dominant strategy.

Game theory is a decision-making tool, but not all games have dominant strategies that make player decisions easy to predict. Perhaps the best example is the game Rock, Paper, Scissors. This simple game has no dominant strategy: paper beats rock (because the paper will cover the rock) and rock beats scissors (because the rock will break the scissors), but scissors beats paper (because the scissors will cut the paper). The preferred choice is strictly a function of what the other player selects. Many situations in life, and business, are more like Rock, Paper, Scissors than the prisoner's dilemma. Winning at business in the long run often occurs because you are one step ahead of the competition, not because you deploy a strategy that attempts to take advantage of a short-run opportunity.

Consider two friends who enjoy playing racquetball together. Both players are of equal ability, so each point comes down to whether the players guess correctly about the direction the other player will hit the ball. Take a look at Figure 7.5. The success of Sheldon and Penny depends on how well each one guesses where the other will hit the ball.

In this competition, neither Penny nor Sheldon has a dominant strategy that guarantees success. Sometimes, Sheldon wins when hitting to the right; at other times, he loses the point. Sometimes, Penny wins when she guesses to the left; at other times, she loses. Each player guesses correctly only half the time. Since we cannot say what each player will do from one point to another, there is no Nash equilibrium. Any of the four outcomes are equally likely on successive points, and there is no way to predict how the next point will be played. In other words, we cannot expect every game to include a prisoner's dilemma and produce a Nash equilibrium. Game theory, like real life, has many different possible outcomes.

Conclusion

Behavioral economics helps to dispel the misconception that people always make rational decisions. Indeed, behavioral economics challenges the traditional economics model and invites a deeper understanding of human

		Penny: Guesses to the left	Penny: Guesses to the right
Sheldon	Hits to the left	Penny wins the point; Sheldon loses the point	Penny loses the point; Sheldon wins the point
Sheldon	Hits to the right	Penny loses the point; Sheldon wins the point	Penny wins the point; Sheldon loses the point

FIGURE 7.5

No Dominant Strategy Exists

Neither Penny nor Sheldon has a dominant strategy that guarantees winning the point. Any of the four outcomes are equally likely on successive points, and there is no way to predict how the next point will be played. As a result, there is no Nash equilibrium here.

behavior. Armed with the insights from behavioral economics, we can answer questions that span a wider range of behaviors. We have seen this in the examples in this chapter, which include the "opt in" or "opt out" debate, the economics of risk-taking, question-framing, and priming, intertemporal decision-making, and the status quo bias. These ideas do not fit squarely into traditional economic analysis. We've also examined the classic game theory model of the prisoner's dilemma. Understanding that the choices people make are interrelated with the decisions made by others helps us to explain behaviors that lead to suboptimal outcomes.

In the next chapter, we will start to apply some of what we've learned thus far to a market that will become a big part of your life in the near future: the labor market. Firms need to acquire resources to make things, but employees aren't always happy with the decisions that firms make in terms of wages and how many people to hire. Understanding the thought process that firms go through when making hiring decisions will help you as you head out into the job market.

ECONOMICS FOR LIFE

Bounded Rationality: How to Guard Yourself against Crime

Suppose that a recent crime wave has hit your community and you're concerned about your family's security. Determined to make your house safe, you consider many options: an alarm system, bars on your windows, deadbolts for your doors, better lighting around your house, and a guard dog. Which of these solutions will protect you from a criminal at the lowest cost? All of them provide a measure of protection—but there's another solution that provides deterrence at an extremely low cost.

The level of security you need depends, in part, on how rational you expect the robber to be. A fully rational burglar would stake out a place, test for an alarm system before breaking in, and choose a home that is an easy target. In other words, the robber would gather full information. But what if the burglar is not fully rational?

Since criminals look for the easiest target to rob, they'll find a house that's easy to break into without detection. If you trim away the shrubs and install floodlights, criminals will realize that they can be seen approaching your home. A few hundred dollars spent on better lighting will dramatically lower your chances of being robbed. However, if you believe in bounded rationality, there's an even better answer: a criminal may not know what's inside your house, so a couple of prominently displayed "Beware of dog!" signs would discourage the robber for less than $10! In other words, the would-be thief has incomplete information and only a limited amount of time to select a target. A quick scan of your house would identify the "Beware of dog!" signs and cause him to move on.

Beware of dog!

This is an example of bounded rationality since only limited, and in this case unreliable, information is all that is easily available regarding possible alternatives and their consequences. Knowing that burglars face this constraint can be a key to keeping them away.

ANSWERING THE BIG QUESTIONS

How can economists explain irrational behavior?

- Economists use a number of concepts from behavioral economics to explain how people make choices that display irrational behavior. These concepts include bounded rationality, framing and priming effects, the status quo bias, intertemporal decision-making, and judgments about fairness.
- Folding the behavioral approach into the standard model makes economists' predictions about human behavior much more robust.

What is the role of risk in decision-making?

- Risk influences decision-making since people can be either risk averse, risk neutral, or risk takers.
- In the traditional economic model, risk tolerances are assumed to be constant. People who are risk takers by nature would take risks in any circumstance. Likewise, people who do not like to take chances avoid risk.
- Maurice Allais proved that many people have inconsistent risk preferences, or what are known as preference reversals. Preference reversals are often connected to positive time preferences, which show that people prefer to have what they want sooner rather than later.

How does game theory explain strategic behavior?

- Game theory helps to determine when cooperation among oligopolists is most likely to occur. In many cases, cooperation fails to occur because decision-makers have dominant strategies that lead them to be uncooperative. A dominant strategy can cause firms to compete by advertising when they could potentially earn more profit by not advertising.
- A dominant strategy ignores the possible long-run benefits of cooperation and focuses solely on the short-run gains. Whenever repeated interaction occurs, decision-makers fare better under tit-for-tat, an approach that maximizes long-run profit.

CONCEPTS YOU SHOULD KNOW

behavioral economics (p. 196)
bounded rationality (p. 196)
collusion (p. 209)
dominant strategy (p. 206)
expected value (p. 201)
framing effect (p. 197)
game theory (p. 204)
intertemporal decision-making (p. 199)
loss aversion (p. 198)
Nash equilibrium (p. 206)
positive time preferences (p. 203)
preference reversal (p. 202)
priming effect (p. 197)
prisoner's dilemma (p. 205)
risk-averse people (p. 201)
risk-neutral people (p. 201)
risk takers (p. 201)
status quo bias (p. 198)
tit-for-tat (p. 212)
ultimatum game (p. 199)

QUESTIONS FOR REVIEW

1. What is bounded rationality? How is this concept relevant to economic modeling?
2. Explain the framing effect that may result from asking the following question: *Wouldn't you agree that people who have more money tend to be happier?*
3. How does the status quo bias reduce the potential benefits that consumers might enjoy as the result of a change?
4. Economists use the ultimatum game to test judgments of fairness. What result does economic theory predict?
5. How is game theory relevant to oligopoly? Does it help to explain monopoly? Give reasons for your response.
6. What is a Nash equilibrium? How does it differ from a dominant strategy?

STUDY PROBLEMS (*✷ solved at the end of the section*)

✷ 1. You have a choice between taking two jobs. The first job pays $50,000 annually. The second job has a base pay of $40,000 with a 30% chance that you will receive an annual bonus of $25,000. You decide to take the $40,000 job. On the basis of this decision, can we tell if you are risk averse or a risk taker? Explain your response.

2. Suppose that Danny Ocean decides to play roulette, one of the most popular casino games. Roulette is attractive to gamblers because the house's advantage is small (less than 5%). If Danny Ocean plays roulette and wins big, is Danny risk averse or a risk taker? Explain.

✷ 3. Suppose that a university wishes to maximize the response rate for teaching evaluations. The administration develops an easy-to-use online evaluation system that each student can complete at the end of the semester. However, very few students bother to complete the survey. The Registrar's Office suggests that the online teaching evaluations be linked to course scheduling. When students access the course scheduling system, they are redirected to the teaching evaluations. Under this plan, each student could opt out and go directly to the course scheduling system. Do you think this plan will work to raise the response rate on teaching evaluations? What would traditional economic theory predict? What would behavioral economics predict?

4. In your economics course, you have to do a two-student project. Assume that you and your partner are both interested in maximizing your grade, but you are both very busy and get more happiness if you can get a good grade with less work. Use the figure below to answer the following questions.
   a. What is your dominant strategy? Explain.
   b. What is your partner's dominant strategy? Explain.
   c. What is the Nash equilibrium in this situation? Explain.
   d. If you and your partner are required to work together on a number of projects throughout the semester, how might this requirement change the outcome you predicted in parts (a), (b), and (c)?

You \ Your partner	Work hard	Work less hard
Work hard	Grade = A, but you had to work 10 hours. Happiness = 7/10. Grade = A, but you had to work 10 hours. Happiness = 7/10.	Grade = A, and you only worked 5 hours. Happiness = 9/10. Grade = A, but you had to work 15 hours. Happiness = 4/10.
Work less hard	Grade = A, but you had to work 15 hours. Happiness = 4/10. Grade = A, and you only worked 5 hours. Happiness = 9/10.	Grade = B, but you only worked 5 hours. Happiness = 6/10. Grade = B, but you only worked 5 hours. Happiness = 6/10.

* 5. Trade agreements encourage countries to curtail tariffs (taxes on imports) so that goods may flow across international boundaries without restrictions. Using the following payoff matrix, determine the best policies for China and the United States.
   a. What is the dominant strategy for the United States?
   b. What is the dominant strategy for China?
   c. What is the Nash equilibrium for these two countries?
   d. Suppose that the United States and China enter into a trade agreement that simultaneously lowers trade barriers. Is this a good idea? Explain your response.

		China: Low tariffs	China: High tariffs
United States	Low tariffs	China gains $50 billion; U.S. gains $50 billion	China gains $100 billion; U.S. gains $10 billion
	High tariffs	China gains $10 billion; U.S. gains $100 billion	China gains $25 billion; U.S. gains $25 billion

6. A small town has only one pizza place, The Pizza Factory. A small competitor, Perfect Pies, is thinking about entering the market. The profits of these two firms depend on whether Perfect Pies enters the market and whether The Pizza Factory—as a price leader—decides to set a high or a low price. Use the payoff matrix to answer the questions that follow.
   a. What is the dominant strategy of The Pizza Factory?
   b. What is the dominant strategy of Perfect Pies?
   c. What is the Nash equilibrium in this situation?
   d. The combined profit for both firms is highest when The Pizza Factory sets a high price and Perfect Pies stays out. If Perfect Pies enters the market, what is the effect on the profits of The Pizza Factory? Would The Pizza Factory be willing to pay Perfect Pies not to enter the market? Explain.

		Perfect Pies: Enter	Perfect Pies: Stay out
The Pizza Factory	High price	Perfect Pies makes $10,000; The Pizza Factory makes $20,000	Perfect Pies makes $0; The Pizza Factory makes $50,000
	Low price	Perfect Pies loses $10,000; The Pizza Factory makes $10,000	Perfect Pies makes $0; The Pizza Factory makes $25,000

SOLVED PROBLEMS

1. The first job pays $50,000 annually, so it has an expected value of $50,000. The second job has a base pay of $40,000 with a 30% chance that you will receive an annual bonus of $25,000. To determine the expected value of the second job, the calculation looks like this: $40,000 + (0.3 × $25,000) = $40,000 + $7,500 = $47,500. Since you decided to take the job with lower expected value and potentially higher earnings, we can tell you are a risk taker.

3. Since students who access the course scheduling system are redirected to the teaching evaluations, they are forced to opt out if they don't wish to evaluate their instructors. As a result, behavioral economists would predict that the new system will raise the teaching evaluation response rate. Traditional economic theory predicts that the response rate won't change simply based on whether or not students opt in or opt out.

5.a. The dominant strategy for the United States is to impose high tariffs, because it always earns more from that strategy than if it faces low tariffs no matter what policy China pursues.

b. The dominant strategy for China is to impose high tariffs, because it always earns more from that strategy than if it faces low tariffs no matter what policy the United States pursues.

c. The Nash equilibrium for both countries is to levy high tariffs. Each country will earn $25 billion.

d. China and the United States would each benefit from cooperatively lowering trade barriers. In that case, each country would earn $50 billion.

CHAPTER

8 Labor Markets and Earnings

MISCONCEPTION

It's unfair that some jobs pay so much more than others.

Many people believe that the structure of compensation in the working world is unfair. After all, why should someone who does backbreaking work digging holes for fence posts make so much less than someone who sits behind a desk on Wall Street? Why do such large differences in income exist? The market for labor is like most other markets, and it's important to remember that markets are valued for efficiency, not equity. As a result, the prices that prevail in the labor market—what we typically call wages—are determined by many of the same things that determine prices in other markets. You may be an outstanding babysitter or short-order cook, but these jobs are unskilled. Therefore, there's a large supply of workers available to do these jobs, and many other workers can easily replace you. As a result, neither occupation will ever earn much more than the minimum wage. In contrast, even an average neurosurgeon gets paid very well, since few individuals have the skill and training to perform neurosurgery. In addition, society values neurosurgeons more than babysitters because the neurosurgeons are literally saving lives.

How, then, can you earn a sizable income? It's not enough to be good at something; that "something" needs to be an occupation that society values highly. What matters are your skills, what you produce, and the supply of workers in your chosen profession. Hard work is one way to get to the income level you desire, but it's only a part of the equation.

In this chapter, we explore the market for labor. We begin by applying what we've learned about supply and demand to the market for workers. This will help us gain a better understanding of how wages are set.

Why do neurosurgeons earn more than short-order cooks?

Using the tools of supply and demand, we can then begin to identify what happens to wages as the labor market changes. Next we turn our attention to other determinants of wages and examine why some people are willing to take less money for some jobs. Finally, we look at some of the reasons people make different wages. It isn't as clear as stories in the news want you to think.

BIG QUESTIONS

- **Where does the demand for labor come from?**
- **Where does the supply of labor come from?**
- **How does the labor market achieve equilibrium?**
- **Why do some workers make more than others?**
- **What additional factors determine wages?**

Where Does the Demand for Labor Come From?

Why can't I make more money? This is a question many workers ask themselves. No matter how hard they work, no matter how many hours they put in or how devoted they are to their jobs, their boss just doesn't seem to understand how important they are to the company's success. Your boss might be shortsighted in relation to your value to the company, but the real reasons that you can't make more money usually have to do with the market.

Labor is a part of the production process. Firms combine labor with land and capital to produce their output. Of course, land and capital don't talk much and therefore can't complain about what they get paid. People, however, talk a lot. As a society, we care about helping people, so we want them to earn enough to provide adequately for their needs. That said, labor is a cost of doing business. In fact, it's the largest cost of doing business. In some industries, particularly the service sector, wages and benefits together account for up to 70% of a firm's costs. Since a firm must carefully consider its costs, even if your boss wanted to pay you more, it's very possible that the firm can't afford to.

A **wage** is the payment made to labor, including benefits.

As we progress through our investigation of what affects an individual's income, we'll use the term **wage** to identify the payment made to labor. Typically, this includes not just monetary compensation but also non-monetary compensation, such as health insurance, vacation time, and contributions to a retirement plan. To simplify our analysis, we'll categorize all of the benefits you receive from a job as your wage. Keep in mind, though, that one reason your take-home pay might be smaller than you want is that your employer is typically giving you much more than just a paycheck.

So how does the labor market work? Let's begin by understanding why a business would want to hire someone.

A lack of customers is an ominous sign for restaurant workers.

Derived Demand

Businesses need workers; without workers, they can't make anything. Imagine that Sophia wants to open a Mexican restaurant named Agaves. Sophia will need a dining room staff, cooks, dishwashers, and managers to coordinate everyone else; these are the labor inputs. She'll also need a physical location; this is the land input. Finally, she'll need a building in which to operate, along with ovens and other kitchen equipment, seating and tableware, and a cash register; these are the capital inputs.

Of course, Sophia's restaurant won't need any inputs if there is no demand for the food she plans to sell. Presumably, Sophia did some market research to determine if there was a demand for a Mexican restaurant. Finding evidence that there would be some interest in her establishment, she got things rolling. As a result, she found that as the owner of the business she had a

PRACTICE WHAT YOU KNOW

Derived Demand: Tip Income

Your friend waits tables 60 hours a week at a small restaurant. He's discouraged because he works hard but can't seem to make enough money to cover his bills. He complains that the restaurant doesn't have enough business and that's why he has to work so many hours just to make ends meet.

Question: As an economist, what advice would you give him?

Answer: Since labor is a derived demand, he should apply for a job at a more popular restaurant. Working at a place with more customers will help him earn more tip income.

Want more tip income? Follow the crowd.

Derived demand is the demand for an input used in the production process.

demand for inputs. The demand for each of the factors of production that go into her restaurant (land, labor, and capital) is a **derived demand** because the factors are inputs that the firm uses to supply a good in another market—in this case, the market for Mexican cuisine—that the public wants. Because there is a demand for the food her restaurant will make and serve, there is now a demand for labor (and land and capital).

Derived demand exists anytime there's a demand for something that will help a firm make something else. Apple doesn't buy glass, batteries, plastic, and labor because it is interested in these things on their own. Rather, it buys these inputs so that it can produce iPads. The reason Apple wants to produce iPads is to sell them and make money. Apple's demand for inputs thus comes from the consumer demand for iPads. While companies demand inputs of all kinds, our focus in the remainder of this chapter will be on labor.

As we begin our investigation of why some jobs pay more than others, it is important to understand one significant difference between the labor market and the market for things people buy. We're used to seeing markets in which households demand goods and services, while firms produce them. In the labor market, those roles are reversed. The buyer of labor is the firm. This means that those who are producing things drive the demand side of the market. The supply in the market comes from households—more specifically, you.

The Marginal Product of Labor

As a student, you're probably hoping that one day your education will translate into tangible skills that employers will seek. As you choose a major, you might be thinking about potential earnings in different occupations. You have presumably noticed that there's a lot of variability in the salary and wages paid for various jobs. The question is: *Why?* For instance, economists generally earn more than elementary school teachers but less than engineers. Workers on night shifts earn more than those who do the same job during the day. And professional athletes and actors make much more for jobs that aren't as essential as the work performed by janitors, construction workers, and nurses. In one respect, the explanation is surprisingly obvious: demand helps to regulate the labor market in much the same way that it helps to determine the prices of goods and services sold in the marketplace.

Why do economists generally earn more than elementary school teachers?

To understand why some people get paid more than others, we will explore the output of each worker, called the marginal product of labor. In fact, the value that each worker creates for a firm is highly correlated with the demand for labor. To gain a concrete appreciation for how labor demand is determined, let's look at the restaurant business—a market that is highly competitive. In Chapter 5, we saw that a firm determines how many workers to hire by comparing the output of labor with the wages the firm must pay. We will apply this analysis to the labor market in the restaurant business. The format of Table 8.1 should look familiar to you; it highlights the key determinants of the labor hiring process.

TABLE 8.1

Deciding How Many Laborers to Hire

(1) Labor (number of workers)	(2) Output (daily meals produced)	(3) Marginal product of labor	(4) Value of the marginal product of labor (VMP)	(5) Wage (daily)	(6) Marginal profit
Formula:		Output	Price × marginal product of labor		Value of the marginal product of labor − wage
0	0				
1	50	50	$500	$100	$400
2	90	40	400	100	300
3	120	30	300	100	200
4	140	20	200	100	100
5	150	10	100	100	0
6	150	0	0	100	−100

Let's work our way through the table. Column 1 lists the number of laborers, and column 2 reports the daily numbers of meals that can be produced with differing numbers of workers. Column 3 shows the **marginal product of labor**, or the change (Δ) in output associated with adding one additional worker. For instance, when the firm moves from three employees to four, output expands from 120 meals to 140 meals. The increase of 20 meals is the marginal product of labor for the fourth worker. Note that the values in column 3 decline as additional workers are added. Recall from Chapter 5 that each successive worker adds less value. We call this phenomenon diminishing marginal product.

The **marginal product of labor** is the change in output associated with adding one additional worker.

It is useful to know the marginal product of labor because this tells us how much each additional worker adds to the firm's output. Combining this information about worker productivity with the price the firm charges gives us a tool that we can use to explain how many workers the firm will hire. Suppose that Agaves charges $10 for each meal. Multiplying the marginal product of labor in column 3 by the price ($10 per meal), we determine the value of the marginal product in column 4. The **value of the marginal product (VMP)** is the marginal product of an input multiplied by the price of the output it produces. Sophia compares the gain in column 4 with the cost of achieving that gain—the wage that must be paid—in column 5. This comparison reduces the hiring decision to a simple cost-benefit analysis in which the wage (column 5) is subtracted from the value of the marginal product (column 4) to determine the marginal profit (column 6) of each worker.

Marginal thinking

The **value of the marginal product (VMP)** is the marginal product of an input multiplied by the price of the output it produces: VMP = marginal product of labor × price.

You can see from the green numbers in column 6 that the marginal profit is positive for the first four workers. Therefore, Sophia is better off hiring four workers. In other words, the workers earn more for the firm than they cost to employ. After that, the marginal profit is zero for the fifth worker, shown in black. Sophia would be indifferent (neutral) about hiring the fifth worker

ECONOMICS IN THE MEDIA

Value of the Marginal Product of Labor

Moneyball

Moneyball, a film based on Michael Lewis's 2003 book of the same name, details the struggles of the Oakland Athletics (the A's), a major league baseball team. The franchise attempts to overcome some seemingly impossible obstacles with the help of its general manager, Billy Beane, by applying innovative statistical analysis known as Sabermetrics—a method of applying advanced statistical analysis to baseball data.

Traditional baseball scouts utilize experience, intuition, and subjective criteria to evaluate potential players. However, Beane, formerly a heavily recruited high school player who failed to have a successful professional career, knows firsthand that this method of scouting doesn't guarantee success. The Oakland A's lack the financial ability to pay as much as other teams. While trying to negotiate a trade with the Cleveland Indians, Beane meets Peter Brand, a young Yale economist who has new ideas about applying statistical analysis to baseball in order to build a better team. Brand explains that evaluating a player's marginal product would be a better tool for recruitment.

In the key scene in the movie, Brand briefly explains his methodology for evaluating players and how the A's can build a championship team:

> It's about getting things down to one number. Using the stats the way we read them, we'll find value in players that no one else can see. People are overlooked for a variety of biased reasons and perceived flaws: age, appearance, and personality. Bill James and mathematics cut straight through that. Billy, of the 20,000 notable players for us to consider, I believe that there is a championship team of 25 people that we can afford, because everyone else in baseball undervalues them.

The A's go on to have a remarkable season by picking up "outcasts" that no other team wanted.

Can a young economist's algorithm save the Oakland A's?

Thanks to Kim Holder of the University of West Georgia.

since the marginal cost of hiring that employee is equal to the marginal benefit. The marginal profit is negative for the sixth worker, as shown in red. Therefore, Sophia should definitely not hire the sixth worker.

This analysis works for any firm. As long as the value of the marginal product is higher than the market wage, shown here as $100 a day, the firm will hire more workers. For example, when the firm hires the first worker, the VMP is $500. This amount easily exceeds the market wage of hiring an extra worker and creates a marginal profit of $400. As the value of the marginal product declines, there will be a point at which hiring additional workers will cause profits to fall. This occurs because labor is subject to diminishing marginal product. Eventually, the value created by hiring additional labor falls below the market wage.

PRACTICE WHAT YOU KNOW

Value of the Marginal Product of Labor: Flower Barrettes

Question: Penny can make five flower barrettes each hour. She works eight hours each day. Penny is paid $75.00 a day. The firm can sell the barrettes for $1.99 each. What is Penny's VMP of labor? What is the barrette firm's marginal profit from hiring her?

Answer: In eight hours, Penny can make 40 barrettes. Since each barrette sells for $1.99, her value of the marginal product of labor, or VMP_{labor}, is $40 \times \$1.99$, or $79.60. Since her VMP_{labor} is greater than the daily wage she receives, the marginal profit from hiring her is $\$79.60 - \$75$, or $4.60.

How many flower barrettes could you make in an hour?

Changes in the Demand for Labor

We know that customers desire good food and that restaurants like Agaves hire workers to satisfy their customers. Figure 8.1 illustrates the relationship between wages for workers and the number of workers that Agaves wants to hire. Notice that the demand curve for labor is downward-sloping; this tells us that at high wages Agaves will use fewer workers and that at lower wages it

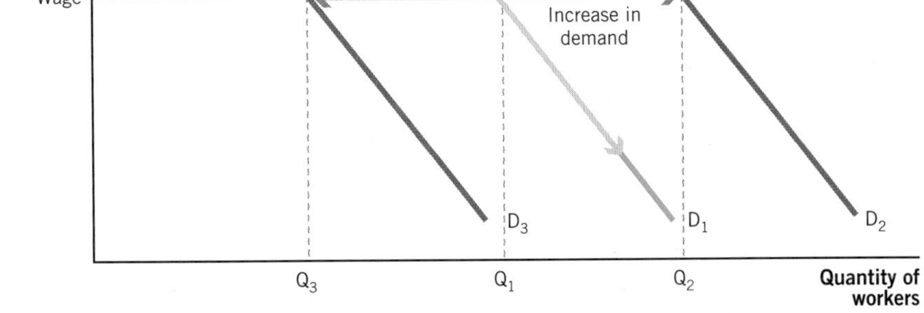

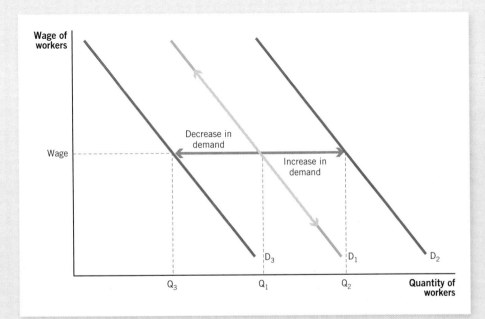

FIGURE 8.1

The Labor Demand Curve

When the wages of workers change, the quantity of workers demanded, shown by the gold arrow moving along the demand curve, also changes. Changes that shift the entire labor demand curve, shown by the gray horizontal arrow, include changes in demand for the product that the firm produces, in innovation labor productivity.

will hire more workers. This is the law of demand applied to the labor market, and it's illustrated with the gold arrow that moves along the original demand curve (D_1). Recall from Chapter 3 that the gold arrow indicates a change in the quantity demanded. In addition, the demand for workers depends on, or is derived from, the number of customers who visit the restaurant and place orders. So changes in the restaurant business as a whole can influence the number of workers that the restaurant hires. For example, if the number of customers increases, the demand for workers will increase, or shift to the right to D_2. Likewise, if the number of customers decreases, the demand for workers will decrease, or shift to the left to D_3.

Two primary factors shift labor demand: (1) a change in demand for the product that the firm produces and (2) a change in the cost of producing that product.

Changes in Demand for the Product the Firm Produces

A restaurant's demand for workers is derived from the firm's desire to sell meals. Because the firm is primarily interested in making a profit, it hires workers only when the value of the marginal product of labor is higher than the cost of hiring labor. Consider Agaves. If a rival Mexican restaurant closes down, many of its customers will likely switch to Agaves. Then Agaves will need to prepare more meals. Since the demand for the Agaves meals will rise, the entire demand curve for cooks, table clearers, and waitstaff also will rise. Figure 8.1 shows this increased demand as a rightward shift from D_1 to D_2.

Changes in Cost of Producing the Product

A change in the cost of production can sometimes be beneficial to the firm, such as when a new technology makes production less expensive. It can also be harmful to the firm, such as when an increase in the cost of a needed raw material makes production more expensive.

In terms of a beneficial change for the firm, technology can act as a substitute for workers. For example, microwave ovens enable restaurants to prepare the same number of meals with fewer workers. The same is true with the growing trend of using conveyor belts and automated systems to help prepare meals or even serve them. Therefore, changes in technology can lower a firm's demand for workers.

A machine at McDonald's helps to fill the drink orders.

In the short run, substituting technology for workers may seem like a bad outcome for the workers and for society in general. However, in the long run that isn't typically the case. Consider how technological advances affect the demand for lumberjacks in the forestry business. As timber companies invest in new harvesting technology, they can replace traditional logging jobs, which are dangerous and inefficient, with equipment that's safer and more efficient. By deploying the new technology, the lumber companies can cut down trees faster and more safely, and the workers are freed up to work in other parts of the economy. In the short run, that means fewer timber jobs; those workers must find employment elsewhere. Admittedly, this adjustment is painful for the workers involved, and they often have difficulty finding jobs that pay as well as the job that they lost. However, the new equipment requires trained, highly skilled operators who can fell more trees in a shorter period than traditional lumberjacks can. As a result, harvester operators have a higher marginal product of labor and can command higher wages.

One John Deere 1270D harvester can replace ten lumberjacks.

For every harvester operator employed at a higher wage, there are perhaps ten traditional lumberjacks displaced and in need of other jobs. But consider what happens after the short-run job losses. Overall production rises because while one new worker harvests trees, the ten former workers are forced to move into related fields or do something entirely different. It might take some of these displaced workers many years to find new work, but when they eventually do, society benefits in the long run. What once required ten workers to produce now takes only one, and the ten former workers are able to complete other jobs and grow the economy in different ways.

To summarize: if labor becomes more productive, the demand curve for labor shifts to the right, driving up both wages and employment. This is what occurs with the demand for harvester operators. There is the potential for substitution as well, causing the demand for traditional labor to fall. This is what has happened to traditional lumberjack jobs, leading to a decrease in those workers' wages.

Where Does the Supply of Labor Come From?

In this section, we examine the connection between the wage rate and the number of workers who are willing to supply their services to employers. Additional factors that influence the labor supply include other employment opportunities, the changing composition of the workforce, migration, and immigration; we explore these factors as well.

The Labor-Leisure Trade-off

In our society today, most individuals must work to meet their basic needs. However, once those needs are met, a worker might be inclined to use his or her extra time in leisure. Would higher wages induce an employee to give up leisure and, instead, work more hours? The answer is both yes and no.

The **labor-leisure trade-off** illustrates the opportunity costs people entail when choosing between working and not working.

While it's certainly true that many workers enjoy their jobs, this doesn't mean they would work for nothing. Many people experience satisfaction in their work, but most of us have other interests, obligations, and goals. As a result, the supply of labor depends both on the wage that is offered and on how individuals want to use their time. This situation is known as the **labor-leisure trade-off**.

If you were promised $100 an hour for as many hours as you wanted to work, you would likely increase the number of hours you spent on the job. This is the law of supply working in the labor market. As price goes up, you increase the quantity supplied. But there are certainly limits to how much time you would spend on the job. At some point you would want to sleep, take a shower, go to a movie, or just spend time on the couch. And there are only so many hours in the day that you can work. Thus, how many hours you can spend working is limited. Even if you were paid $500 an hour, you couldn't work 24 hours a day 7 days a week without succumbing to exhaustion.

Opportunity cost

By choosing to sleep and not work, you forgo some earnings. This means that not working entails a cost: when you decide not to work, you give up your wage. Thus, your wage is the opportunity cost of not working. Most people are quite happy to make this trade-off. Others are forced to. For example, truckers typically get paid by the mile driven. If they aren't driving, they aren't making money. However, if they spend too much time behind the wheel, they become dangerous to other drivers as fatigue sets in. Thus, there are laws limiting how long truck drivers can be on duty. While you may want to work more, in some cases you're better off forgoing the income and taking a break. Therefore, as we look at the supply side of the labor market, it's important to remember that there are natural limits on how much labor anyone can supply.

Changes in the Supply of Labor

If we hold the wage rate constant, a number of additional factors determine the supply of labor. Turning to Figure 8.2, the gold arrow along S_1 shows that the quantity of workers increases when the wage rate rises. But what will cause a shift in the supply curve? Three primary factors affect the supply curve: other employment opportunities, the changing composition of the workforce, and changes in the number of workers as a result of migration and immigration.

Other Employment Opportunities

The supply of workers for any given job depends on the employment opportunities and prevailing wage in related labor markets. Let's consider the supply of labor at Agaves. Notice that the supply curve for labor in Figure 8.2 is upward-sloping; this tells us that if Agaves offers higher wages, more workers, such as table clearers, would be willing to work there. We illustrate this situation with the gold arrow that moves along the original supply curve (S_1).

The supply of table clearers also depends on a number of non-wage factors. Since table clearers are generally young and largely unskilled, the number of laborers willing to work is influenced by the prevailing wages in similar jobs.

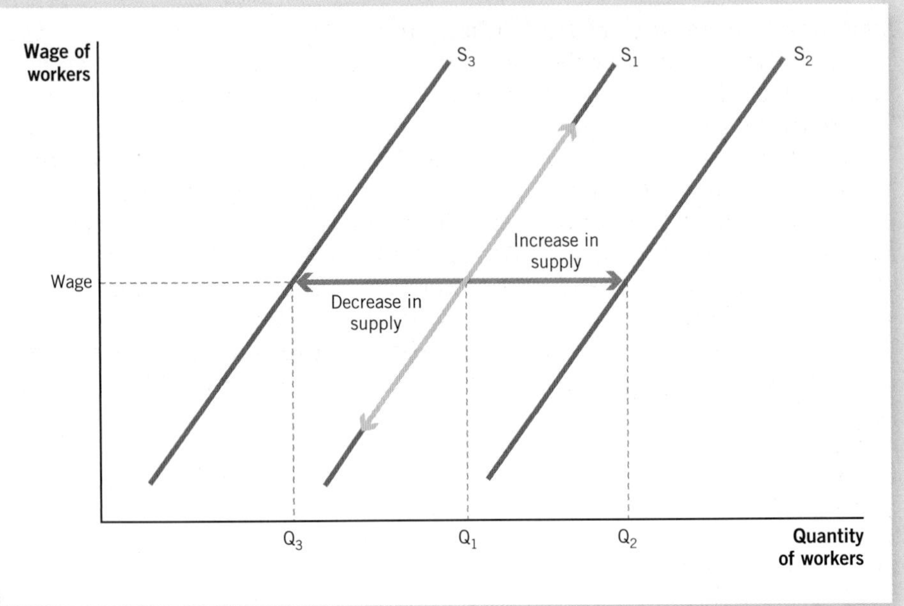

FIGURE 8.2

The Labor Supply Curve

A change in the quantity supplied occurs when wages change. This causes a movement along the supply curve S_1, shown by the gold arrow. Changes in the supply of labor, shown by the gray horizontal arrow, can occur due to immigration, migration, demographic shifts in the workforce, and other employment opportunities.

For instance, if the wages of baggers at local grocery stores decrease, some of those baggers would try to get jobs as table clearers at Agaves. This will increase the supply of table clearers and cause a rightward shift from S_1 to S_2. If the wages of baggers were to rise, the supply of table clearers would decrease, or shift to the left from S_1 to S_3. These shifts reflect the fact that when jobs that require comparable skills have different wage rates, the number of workers willing to supply labor for the lower-wage job will shrink and the number willing to supply labor for the better-paid job will grow.

The Changing Composition of the Workforce

Over the last 30 years, the labor-force participation rate has increased significantly in most developed countries. This has occurred in large part due to the increase in women in the workforce. Overall, there are many more women in the workforce today than there were a generation ago, and the supply of workers in many occupations has expanded significantly as a result. As the supply of workers increases, the supply curve shifts to the right.

Effects of Immigration and Migration

Demographic factors, including immigration and migration, also play a crucial role in the supply of labor. For example, immigration—both legal and illegal—increases the available supply of workers by a significant amount each year.

In 2013, over 800,000 people from foreign countries entered the United States through legal channels and gained permission to seek employment. Today, there are over 40 million legal immigrants in the United States. In

PRACTICE WHAT YOU KNOW

Changes in Labor Demand

Labor is always subject to changes in demand.

Question: A company builds a new facility that doubles its workspace and equipment. How is labor affected?

Answer: The company has probably experienced additional demand for the product it sells. Therefore, it needs additional employees to staff the facility, causing a rightward shift in the demand curve. When the demand for labor rises, wages increase and so does the number of people employed.

Question: A company decides to outsource 100 jobs from a facility in Indiana to Indonesia. How is labor affected in the short run?

Answer: This situation leads to two changes. First, a decrease in demand for labor in Indiana results in lower wages there and fewer workers hired. Second, an increase in demand for labor in Indonesia results in higher wages there and more workers hired.

addition, illegal immigrants account for an estimated 20 million workers in the United States, many of whom enter the country to work as hotel maids, janitors, and fruit pickers. Every time a state passes a tough immigration law, businesses in food and beverage, agriculture, and construction protest because they need inexpensive labor to remain competitive. Many states have wrestled with the issue, but policies that address illegal immigration remain controversial and the solutions are difficult. The states need the cheap labor but don't want to pay additional costs such as medical care or schooling for the illegal immigrants' children.

Migration patterns also affect the labor supply. Although the U.S. population grows at an annual rate of approximately 3%, there are significant regional differences. Indeed, large population influxes lead to marked regional changes in the demand for labor and the supply of people looking for work. According to the U.S. Census Bureau, between 2010 and 2012 eight of the ten fastest-growing states were in the South or the West. The exceptions were North and South Dakota. The Dakotas were gaining population as people relocated there to work in the growing oil and gas industry. North Dakota added more than 5% to its population over this time. States where population growth was much slower, less than ½%, include Maine, West Virginia, and New Hampshire. Meanwhile, Illinois, Michigan, and Rhode Island actually lost population due in part to very poor economies in those states during the same period.

ECONOMICS IN THE MEDIA

Immigration

A Day without a Mexican

This offbeat film from 2004 asks a simple question: *What would happen to California's economy if all the Mexicans in the state suddenly disappeared?* The answer: *The state economy would come to a halt.*

Indeed, the loss of the Mexican labor force would have a dramatic impact on California's labor market. For example, the film makes fun of affluent Californians who must do without low-cost workers to take care of their yards and homes. It also showcases a farm owner whose produce is ready to be picked without any migrant workers to do the job.

In addition, the film adeptly points out that migrants from Mexico add a tremendous amount of value to the local economy through their purchases as well as their labor. One inspired scene depicts a television commercial for a "disappearance sale" put on by a local business after it realizes that most of its regular customers are gone.

A Day without a Mexican illustrates both sides of the labor relationship at work. Because demand and supply are inseparably linked, the disappearance of all of the Mexican workers creates numerous voids that require serious adjustments for the economy.

What would happen to an economy if one-third of the workers suddenly disappeared?

How Does the Labor Market Achieve Equilibrium?

Now that we have considered the forces that govern demand and supply in the labor market, we are ready to see how the equilibrium wage is established. This analysis will enable us to examine the labor market in greater detail and identify what causes shortages and surpluses of labor and why outsourcing occurs. The goal of this section is to provide a rich set of examples that help you become comfortable using demand and supply curves to understand how the labor market operates.

We can think about wages as the price at which workers are willing to "rent" their time to employers. Turning to Figure 8.3, we see that at wages above equilibrium (W_{high}) the supply of workers willing to rent their time exceeds the demand for that time. The result is a surplus of available workers. The surplus, in turn, places downward pressure on wages. As wages drop,

FIGURE 8.3

Equilibrium in the Labor Market

At high wages (W_{high}), a surplus of workers exists. The surplus drives the wage rate down until the supply of workers and the demand for workers reach the equilibrium. At low wages (W_{low}), a shortage occurs. The shortage forces the wage rate up until the equilibrium wage is reached and the shortage disappears.

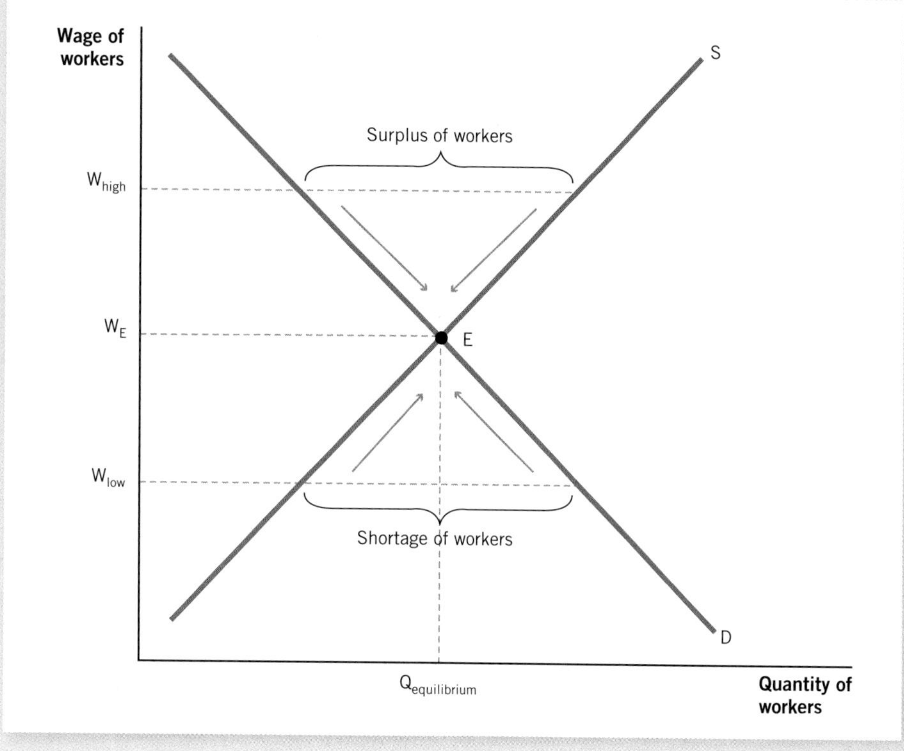

fewer workers are willing to rent their time to employers. When wages drop to the equilibrium wage (W_E), the surplus of workers is eliminated; at that point, the number of workers willing to work in that profession at that wage is exactly equal to the number of job openings that exist at that wage.

A similar process guides the labor market toward equilibrium from low wages. At wages below the equilibrium (W_{low}), the demand for labor exceeds the available supply. The shortage forces firms to offer higher wages in order to attract workers. As a result, wages rise until the shortage is eliminated at the equilibrium wage.

ECONOMICS IN THE REAL WORLD

Where Are the Nurses?

The United States is experiencing a shortage of nurses. A stressful job with long hours, nursing requires years of training. As baby boomers age, the demand for nursing care is expected to rise. At the same time, the existing pool of nurses is rapidly aging and nearing retirement. By some estimates, the shortage of nurses in the United States will approach one million by 2020. This makes nursing the #1 job in the country in terms of growth prospects, according to the Bureau of Labor Statistics.

However, economists are confident that the shortage of nurses will disappear long before 2020. After all, a shortage creates upward pressure on wages. In this case, rising wages also signal that nursing services are in high demand and that wages will continue to rise. This will lead to a surge in nursing school applications and will also cause some practicing nurses to postpone retirement.

Since the training process takes two or more years to complete, the labor market for nurses won't return to equilibrium immediately. The nursing shortage will persist for a few years until the quantity of nurses supplied to the market increases. During that time, many of the tasks that nurses traditionally carry out—such as taking patients' vital signs—will likely be shifted to nursing assistants or technicians.

Economics tells us that the combination of more newly trained nurses entering the market and the transfer of certain nursing services to assistants and technicians will eventually cause the nursing shortage to disappear. Remember that when a market is out of balance, forces are acting on it to restore it to equilibrium. ✳

Entering an occupation with a shortage of workers will result in higher pay.

Change and Equilibrium in the Labor Market

Now that we've seen how labor markets find an equilibrium point, let's see what happens when the demand or supply changes. Figure 8.4 presents two graphs: panel (a) shows a shift in labor demand, and panel (b) shows a shift in labor supply. In both cases, the equilibrium wage and the equilibrium quantity of workers employed adjust accordingly.

Let's start with a shift in labor demand, shown in panel (a). Imagine that the demand for medical care increases due to an aging population and that, as a result, the demand for nurses (as we noted in the Economics in the Real World feature) increases. The demand curve shifts from D_1 to D_2. (Recall that the demand for nurses is *derived* from the demand for nursing care.) This creates a shortage of workers equal to $Q_3 - Q_1$ at the existing wage. The shortage places upward pressure on wages, which increase from W_1 to W_2 by moving along the supply curve. As wages rise, nursing becomes more attractive as a profession; additional people choose to enter the field, and existing nurses decide to work longer hours or postpone retirement. Thus, the number of nurses employed rises from Q_1 to Q_2. Eventually, the wage settles at E_2 and the number of nurses employed reaches Q_2.

Turning to panel (b), we see what happens when the supply of nurses increases. As additional nurses are certified, the overall supply shifts from S_1 to S_2. This creates a surplus of workers equal to $Q_3 - Q_1$ at the existing wage, which places downward pressure on wages. As a result, the wage rate falls from W_1 to W_2. Eventually, the market wage settles at E_2, the new equilibrium point, and the number of nurses employed reaches Q_2.

Now that we have a general idea about how the parts of the labor market fit together, let's take on some of the thornier issues in labor. We'll start with a subject that receives a lot of attention in the media: outsourcing.

FIGURE 8.4

Shifting the Labor Market Equilibrium

In panel (a), the demand for nurses increases. This creates a shortage of workers equal to $Q_3 - Q_1$ at the existing wage, which leads to a higher equilibrium wage (E_2) and quantity of nurses employed (Q_2) than before. In panel (b), the supply of nurses increases. This leads to a surplus of workers equal to $Q_3 - Q_1$ at the existing wage and causes the equilibrium wage to fall (E_2) and the number of nurses employed to rise (Q_2).

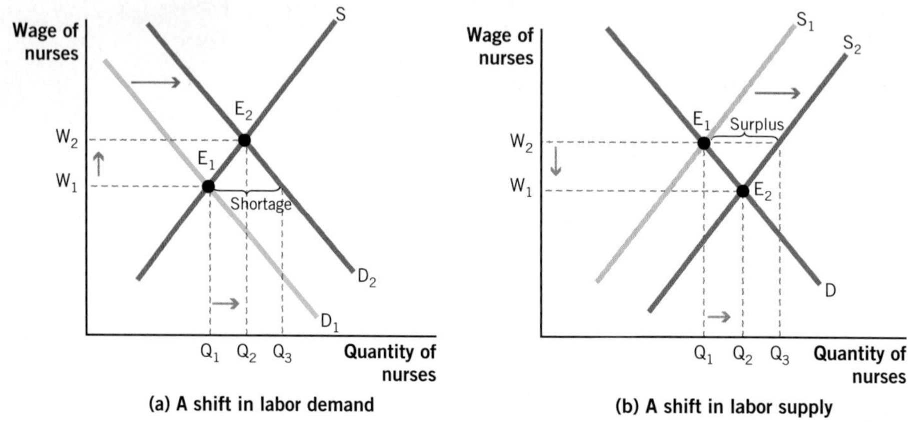

Outsourcing

Outsourcing of labor occurs when a firm shifts jobs to an outside company, usually overseas, where the cost of labor is lower.

The **outsourcing of labor** occurs when a firm shifts jobs to an outside company, usually but not always overseas, where the cost of labor is lower. In the publishing industry, for example, page make-up (also known as composition) is often done overseas to take advantage of lower labor costs. This outsourcing has been facilitated by the Internet, which eliminates the shipping delays and costs that used to constitute a large part of the business. Today, a qualified worker can lay out book pages anywhere in the world.

Sometimes, outsourcing occurs when firms relocate within the country to take advantage of cheaper labor or lower-cost resources. For example, when Seattle-based Boeing wanted to expand its operation, it decided to build an entirely new production facility in South Carolina, where wages were substantially lower than those in Seattle.

While we usually hear stories of U.S. companies outsourcing to other parts of the world, sometimes companies headquartered in other countries outsource their jobs to the United States. For example, the German auto manufacturer Mercedes-Benz currently builds many of its cars in Alabama. If you were an assembly-line worker in Germany who had spent a lifetime making cars for Mercedes, you would likely be upset if your job was outsourced to the United States. You would feel just like the American technician who loses a job to someone in India or the software writer who is replaced by a worker in China. Outsourcing always produces a job winner and a job loser. In the case

Outsourcing

ECONOMICS IN THE MEDIA

Outsourced

In this film from 2006, an American novelty products salesman from Seattle heads to India to train his replacement after his entire department is outsourced.

Some of the funniest scenes in this charming movie occur in the call center. The Indian workers speak fluent English but lack familiarity with American customs and sensibilities, so they often seem very awkward. In one memorable phone call, an American caller becomes irate when he learns that the product he's ordering wasn't made in the United States. He gives the voice on the other end of the line an earful about the loss of jobs in America. However, the call center supervisor devises a clever tactic to convince the disgruntled customer to buy the product despite his objections. She tells him that a manufacturer in the United States offers the same product for $20 more. He pauses and after some thought decides that he would rather buy the cheaper, foreign-made product.

Because *Outsourced* humanizes the foreign workers who benefit from outsourced domestic jobs, we learn to appreciate how outsourcing affects consumers, producers, domestic workers, and foreign laborers.

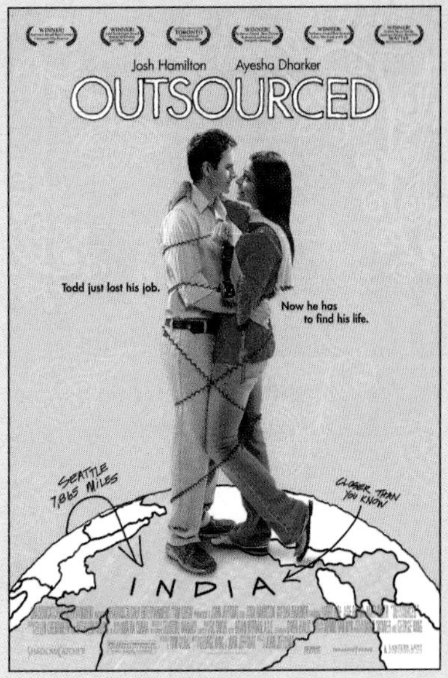

Outsourcing can connect different cultures in positive ways.

of foreign outsourcing to the United States, employment in the United States rises. In fact, the Mercedes-Benz plant in Alabama employs more than 3,000 workers. Those jobs were transferred to the United States because the company felt that it would be more profitable to hire American workers and make vehicles in the United States rather than constructing them in Germany and shipping them across the Atlantic Ocean.

When companies outsource, their pool of potential workers expands, causing the labor supply to increase. But whether a labor expansion is driven by outsourcing or by an increase in the domestic supply of workers, those who are already employed in that particular industry find that they earn less—and sometimes they become unemployed and don't earn anything at all.

ECONOMICS IN THE REAL WORLD

Pregnancy Becomes the Latest Job to Be Outsourced to India

When we think of outsourced jobs, we generally think of call centers, not childbirth. But a growing number of infertile couples have outsourced pregnancy to surrogate mothers in India. The process involves surrogate mothers being impregnated with eggs that have been fertilized in vitro with sperm taken from couples who are unable to carry a pregnancy to term on their own. Commercial surrogacy—"wombs for rent"—is a growing industry in India. While no reliable numbers track such pregnancies nationwide, doctors work with surrogates in virtually every major city in India.

Kaival Hospital in Anand, India, matches infertile couples with local women, such as these surrogate mothers.

In India, surrogate mothers earn roughly $5,000 for a nine-month commitment. This amount is the equivalent of what could take ten or more years to earn in many low-skill jobs there. Couples typically pay approximately $10,000 for all of the costs associated with the pregnancy, which is a mere fraction of what it would cost in the United States or Europe.

Commercial surrogacy has been legal in India since 2002, as it is in many other countries, including the United States. However, the difference is that India is the leader in making it a viable industry rather than a highly personal and private fertility treatment. ✳

Why Do Some Workers Make More than Others?

While most workers generally spend 35 to 40 hours a week at work, the amount they earn varies dramatically. Table 8.2 presents a number of simple questions that illustrate why some workers make more than others.

The table shows how demand and supply determine wages in a variety of settings. Workers with a high-value marginal product of labor invariably earn more than those with lower-value marginal product of labor. It is important to note that working an "essential" job does not guarantee a high income. Instead, the highest incomes are reserved for jobs that have high demand and a low supply of workers. In other words, our preconceived notions of fairness take a backseat to the underlying market forces that govern pay.

What Additional Factors Determine Wages?

We've seen that labor markets play a significant role in what people get paid. However, numerous additional factors contribute to earnings differences. Various non-monetary factors cause some occupations to pay higher or lower wages than supply and demand would seem to dictate. For example, some jobs have characteristics that make them more or less desirable. In this section, we examine non-monetary differences in wages, including compensating differentials, education and human capital, location and lifestyle, and labor unions.

Incentives

TABLE 8.2

Why Some Workers Make More than Others

Question	Answer
Why do economists generally earn more than elementary school teachers?	Supply is the key. There are fewer qualified economists than certified elementary school teachers. Therefore, the equilibrium wage in economics is higher than it is in elementary education. It's also important to note that demand factors may be part of the explanation. The value of economists' marginal product of labor is generally higher than that of most elementary school teachers since many economists work in industry.
Why do people who work the night shift earn more than those who do the same job during the day?	Again, supply is the key. Fewer people are willing to work at night, so the wage necessary to attract labor to perform the job must be higher. (That is, night shift workers earn what is called a compensating differential, which we discuss later in this chapter.)
Why do professional athletes and actors make so much when what they do is not essential?	Now demand takes over. The paying public is willing, even eager, to spend a large amount of income on entertainment. Thus, demand for entertainment is high. On the supply end of the equation, the number of individuals who capture the imagination of the paying public is small, and they are therefore paid handsomely to do so. The value of the marginal product that they create is incredibly high, which means that they can earn huge incomes.
Why do janitors, construction workers, and nurses—whose jobs are essential—have salaries that are a tiny fraction of celebrities' salaries?	Demand again. The value of the marginal product of labor created in these essential jobs is low, so their employers are unable to pay high wages. There are also so many more people who can perform these jobs (relative to those who fit the bill in entertainment) that wages stay low.

Compensating Differentials

Some jobs are more unpleasant, risky, stressful, inconvenient, or monotonous than others. If the characteristics of a job make it unattractive, firms must offer more to lure workers. For instance, roofing, logging, and deep-sea fishing are some of the most dangerous occupations in the world. Workers who do these jobs must be compensated with higher wages to offset the higher risk of injury. A **compensating differential** is the difference in wages offered to offset the desirability or undesirability of a job. If a job's characteristics make it unattractive, the compensating wage differential must be positive.

Likewise, some jobs are simply more fun, exciting, prestigious, or stimulating than others. In these cases, the compensating differential is negative and the workers are paid lower wages. Many employees of pro sports teams (other than the players) and radio DJs earn low pay. Video game testing is so desirable that most people who do it aren't paid at all.

Are you being paid enough to risk a fall?

A **compensating differential** is the difference in wages offered to offset the desirability or undesirability of a job.

Education and Human Capital

Another element in how much people get paid involves the worker's background. Many complex jobs require substantial education, training, and industry experience. Qualifying to receive the specialized education required for certain occupations—for example, getting into medical school—is often very difficult. Only a limited number of students are able to pursue these degrees. In addition, such specialized education is expensive, in terms of both tuition and the opportunity cost of forgone income.

Opportunity cost

The skills that workers acquire on the job and through education are collectively known as **human capital.** Unlike other forms of capital, investments

Human capital is the set of skills that workers acquire on the job and through education.

ECONOMICS IN THE MEDIA

Compensating Differentials

"Big Money"

Some jobs pay a significant compensating differential. In the song "Big Money," Garth Brooks tells the story of his brother Tommy, who was a lineman for the power company ("rest his soul"). When Garth asks why he climbs the high power poles, Tommy tells him that it pays big money (if you're willing to take a chance). Unfortunately for Tommy, he falls to his death and can't spend the money now. In the next verse, Garth sings about his uncle Charlie, who was a demolition hound. Charlie's work entails blowing things up. He also says that he takes the risk of working with dynamite because of the big money (but he sure can't spend it now). Garth ends the song not mourning his dead kin, but rather serenading his listeners about the big money—the compensating differentials—that Tommy and Charlie left him in their last wills and testaments.

in human capital belong to the employee. In other words, if you leave a job, you take your human capital with you. Human capital is unique to each person, as it includes the accumulation of all of that person's experience, education, knowledge, and skills. As a result, workers who have high human capital can shop their skills among competing firms. Engineers, doctors, and members of other professions that require extensive education and training can command high wages in part because the human capital needed to do those jobs is high. In contrast, low-skill workers such as ushers, baggers, and sales associates earn less because the human capital required to do those jobs is quite low; it's easy to find replacements.

Table 8.3 shows the relationship between education and pay. Clearly, attaining more education leads to higher earnings. Workers who earn advanced

TABLE 8.3

The Relationship between Education and Pay

Education level	Median annual earnings in 2014 (persons age 25 and over)
Advanced (master's or doctoral) degree	$72,072
Bachelor's degree	57,252
Some college or associate degree	39,572
High school degree (includes GED)	35,776
Less than high school diploma	25,376

Source: Bureau of Labor Statistics, Current Population Survey, January 2015.

degrees have higher marginal products of labor because their extra schooling has presumably given them extra skills for the job. These workers' higher marginal product helps to create greater demand for their skills. Furthermore, the time required to complete more advanced degrees limits the supply of workers with a high marginal product. Taken together, the firm's demand for workers with a high marginal product and the limited supply of such workers causes earnings to rise. Higher wages represent a compensating differential that rewards additional education.

ECONOMICS IN THE REAL WORLD

Does Education *Really* Pay?

An alternative perspective on the value of education argues that the returns to increased education are not the product of what a student learns, but rather a signal to prospective employers. According to this perspective, the degree itself (specifically, the classes taken to earn that degree) is not evidence of a skill set that makes a worker more productive. Rather, earning a degree and attending a prominent university are signals of a potential employee's quality. That is, prospective employers assume that a student who gets into college must be intelligent and willing to work hard. Students who have done well in college send another signal: they are able to learn quickly and perform well under stress.

It's possible to test the importance of signaling by looking at the returns to earning a college degree, controlling for institutional quality. At many elite institutions, the four-year price tag has reached extraordinary levels. For example, to attend Sarah Lawrence College in Yonkers, New York, the most expensive institution in the country, it cost $65,480 in 2014–2015. Over four years, that adds up to over a quarter of a million dollars! What type of return do graduates of such highly selective institutions make on their sizable investments? And are those returns the result of a rigorous education or a function of the institution's reputation? The answer is difficult to determine because the students who attend more selective institutions would be more likely to have higher earnings potential regardless of where they attend college. These students enter college as high achievers, a trait that carries forward into the workplace no matter where they attend school.

Economists Stacy Dale and Alan Krueger used data to examine the financial outcomes for over 6,000 students who were accepted or rejected by a comparable set of colleges. They found that 20 years after graduation, students who had been accepted at more selective colleges but who decided to attend a less selective college earned the same amount as their counterparts from more selective colleges. This finding indicates that actually attending a prestigious school is less important for future career success than the qualities that enable students to get accepted at a prestigious school.

Does an advanced degree mean you learned more or were simply smarter anyway?

Although Table 8.3 shows that additional education increases one's pay, the reason is not simply an increase in human capital. There is also a signal that employers can interpret about other, less observable qualities. For instance, Harvard graduates presumably learn a great deal in their time at school, but they were also highly motivated and likely to be successful even before they went to college. Part of the increase in income attributable to completing college is a function of a set of other traits that the student already possessed independent of the school or the degree. ✷

Location and Lifestyle

How much more would you pay to live near here?

For most people, sipping margaritas in Key West, Florida, sounds more appealing than living in Eureka, Nevada, along the most isolated stretch of road in the continental United States. Likewise, being able to see a show, visit a museum, or go to a Yankees game in New York City constitutes a different lifestyle from what you'd experience in Dodge City, Kansas. People find some places more desirable than others. So how does location affect wages? Where the climate is more pleasant, other things being equal, people are willing to accept lower wages because the non-monetary benefits of enjoying the weather act as a compensating differential. Similarly, jobs in metropolitan areas—where the cost of living is significantly higher than in most other places—pay higher wages as a compensating differential. The higher wages help employees afford a quality of life similar to what they would enjoy if they worked in less expensive areas.

Choice of lifestyle is also a major factor in determining wage differences. Some workers are not particularly concerned with maximizing their income; instead, they care more about working for a cause. This is true for many employees of nonprofits or religious organizations, or even for people who take care of loved ones. Others follow a dream of being a musician, writer, or actor. And still others are guided by a passion such as skiing or surfing. Indeed, many workers view their pay as less important than doing something they're passionate about. For these workers, lower pay functions as a compensating differential.

Labor Unions

A **union** is a group of workers that bargains collectively for better wages and benefits.

A **strike** is a work stoppage designed to aid a union's bargaining position.

A **union** is a group of workers that bargains collectively for better wages and benefits. Unions are able to secure increased wages by creating significant market power over the labor supply that is available to a firm. A union's ability to achieve higher wages depends on a credible threat of a work stoppage, known as a **strike.** In effect, unions manage to raise wages because they represent labor, and labor is a key input in the production process. Since firms cannot do without labor, an effective union can use the threat of a strike to negotiate higher wages for its workers.

Some unions are prohibited by law from going on strike. These include unions that represent transit workers, public school teachers, law enforcement officers, and workers in other essential services. If workers in one of these industries reach an impasse in wage and benefit negotiations, the union is required to submit to the decision of an impartial third party, a process known as binding arbitration. The television show *Judge Judy* is an example of binding arbitration in action: two parties with a small-claims grievance agree in advance to accept the verdict of Judith Sheindlin, a noted family court judge.

Because unions raise wages for firms, most people think that businesses would rather their workers not join a union. While this is typically true, businesses do gain something from the unionization of their workers. In large firms, negotiations with employees over wages can be time-consuming and costly. Since unions bargain wages for all employees, this reduces the negotiation costs. Instead of dealing with all workers individually, firms come to wage agreements for all employees collectively by bargaining with the union.

The effect of unions in the United States has changed since the early days of unionization in the late 1800s. Early studies of the union wage premium found wages to be as much as 30% higher for workers who were unionized. At the height of unionization approximately 60 years ago, one in three jobs was a unionized position. Today, only about one in eight workers is a union member. In a 2014 study, Paul Gabriel and Susanne Schmitz found the wage premium to be around 22%. The demise of many unions has coincided with the transition of the U.S. economy from a manufacturing base to a greater emphasis on the service sector, which is less centralized.

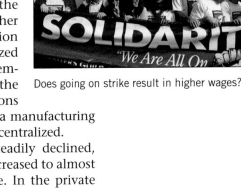

Does going on strike result in higher wages?

While union membership in the private sector has steadily declined, union membership in the public (government) sector has increased to almost 40%. This asymmetry is explained by competitive pressure. In the private sector, higher union labor costs prompt firms to substitute more capital and use more technology in the production process. Higher union labor costs also spur firms to relocate production to places with large pools of non-union labor. These competitive pressures limit unions' success at organizing and maintaining membership, as well as the wage premium they can secure. However, competition in the government sector is largely absent. Federal, state, and local governments can pay employees according to union scale without having to worry about cost containment. As a result, unions are common among public school teachers, police, firefighters, and sanitation workers.

We have seen that wages are influenced by factors that include compensating differentials, human capital, location and lifestyle, and union membership. Table 8.4 summarizes these determinants of income differences.

TABLE 8.4

The Key Non-monetary Determinants of Wage Differences

Determinant	Impact on wages	
Compensating differentials	Some workers are eager to have jobs that are more fun, exciting, prestigious, or stimulating than others. As a result, they are willing to accept lower wages. Conversely, jobs that are unpleasant or risky require higher wages.	
Education and human capital	Many jobs require substantial education, training, and experience. As a result, workers who acquire additional amounts of human capital can command higher wages.	
Location and lifestyle	When the location is desirable, the compensating wage will be lower. Similarly, when employment is for a highly valued cause, wages are less important. In both situations, the compensating wage will be lower.	
Labor unions	Since firms cannot do without labor, unions can threaten a strike to negotiate higher wages.	

ECONOMICS FOR LIFE

What Impacts How Much You Get Paid?

Now that we've covered the concepts of labor supply and demand, and examined some additional determinants of wages, let's return to the question of how you can increase your earning potential. The old adage that you can make more by working harder isn't necessarily true—although other things being equal, if you work harder than the person in the cubicle next to you, you're likely to earn more. More to the point, though, how do you get out of the cubicle?

The first thing to consider is your major. Not all majors earn the same, nor should they. If you're majoring in education, you have a lot more competition for existing jobs than someone who majors in petroleum engineering. Education majors start with an average salary of $40,000, while those in the much more specialized petroleum engineering major start at $98,000. That's a huge difference! But as a result of what we've covered in this chapter, we now know why. The pay differential is based on demand, supply, human capital, and working conditions. Based on this starting wage for petroleum engineers, we can deduce that there is a shortage of qualified people to fill a large number of openings. In education, there are many, many good candidates, which keeps wages down. Additionally, having the summers off compared to working 50 or more hours a week, year round, will create a distinct difference in the pay between these two occupations. The higher wages for petroleum engineers acts as an incentive for people to enter that field.

Another thing to consider is how productive you can be in a particular major. Hourly earnings for lawyers can exceed $400, while a nurse working at an end-of-life facility earns closer to $20 per hour. You might think that the nurse's job is much more valuable to society than the lawyer's job, yet the lawyer might earn 20 times more per hour. We've said that there is a nursing shortage, and no one ever says there are too few lawyers, so what is causing this disparity in wages? Consider the marginal revenue product of each. A high-priced lawyer can measure his or her worth by how much a client can make during a negotiation. A successful deal could be worth millions of dollars. Thus, what lawyers are able to produce in terms of monetary compensation for their clients is very large. In contrast, the nurse at the end-of-life facility is providing medical care for a dying patient. While this is a noble job, there isn't a market-determined dollar value attached to what he or she does; and in the end, no matter how good the care is, the patient will die. There isn't a way to increase the nurse's marginal revenue product, so the nurse's wages will remain far below the lawyer's. It may not seem right or fair, but basing how much we pay someone on market determinations sometimes leads to such outcomes.

All of this discussion gives us two things to think about. First, if you want to earn more, you need to work in an industry where the demand for workers is high but the supply of workers with the necessary human capital is low. Second, you need to be able to measure your marginal revenue product, and it needs to be high. You may want to make a positive change in the world, so you decide to pursue a career in public service, but you need to understand that wages won't be high even though you're doing something valuable. There are too many others who would be satisfied in such a job. Also, measuring marginal revenue product in the public sector (government jobs) is very difficult.

Finally, let's consider one of the more pressing questions when it comes to wages. Why do CEOs get paid so much more than their employees? Putting into practice what we've learned, we can conclude a couple of things. First, CEOs have an enormous amount of human capital. They are experts in their fields and have considerable experience managing companies. This is actually an exceptionally rare talent. The supply of people able to coordinate the operations of large companies is very low. However, the demand for these skills is very high. Supply and demand alone can explain a large part of a CEO's salary. Add to the mix the fact that the CEO's decisions have an enormous impact on the company's profitability, and you could conclude that a good

CEO can have a very large marginal revenue product. Also, CEOs can easily work 16 to 20 hours a day, seven days a week. The compensating differential has to be large to pay someone who essentially has no life outside of work. Moreover, the pressure on CEOs is enormous. If they don't produce or if even one decision goes awry, they can cost their company, and their shareholders, millions of dollars. One wrong decision can result in a CEO losing his or her job. The result might be a more conservative approach to the job. However, the high wage also acts as an incentive to take risks. If the risk doesn't work out, the CEO can fall back on what he or she has earned and saved, but if it does work out and the company becomes more profitable, the salary acts as compensation for the results generated by the CEO's leadership. In short, as compensation for all of the stresses and demands placed on them, CEOs receive pay far above the average worker.

So how do you make more money? Work hard, but do so in an industry where demand for workers is growing and supply is limited. Produce something that is of value to consumers so that there is always a need for your services. If the price of what you sell increases, your marginal revenue product will rise and you will earn more. Finally, invest in human capital to increase your value to potential employers. Table 8.5 shows average earnings for majors. There is variation within each major, of course, but this table gives you an idea of what you can expect to earn based on your choice of major. That being said, remember that money isn't everything.

TABLE 8.5

Average Salaries by Major

Major category	2014 average salary
Engineering	$62,719
Computer Science	$61,741
Business	$53,901
Health Science	$51,541
Communications	$43,924
Math and Sciences	$43,414
Education	$40,863
Humanities and Social Sciences	$38,365

Source: National Association of Colleges and Employers, Salary Survey.

Conclusion

We began this chapter with the misconception that it's unfair that different jobs pay different wages. Some stories in the media make it seem like firms are somehow repressing wages on certain segments of the labor force. While we all make different wages, it's a rare circumstance where that wage differential is based purely on unfairness.

Throughout this chapter, we have learned that the compensation for labor depends on the interaction between demand and supply. Labor demand is derived from the demand for the final product a firm produces, and labor supply depends on the other opportunities and compensation levels that exist in the market. As a result, the equilibrium prices and outputs in the markets for labor reflect, in large part, the opposing tensions between the separate forces of demand and supply.

One thing we didn't talk about in this chapter is the role that government plays in setting wages. In Chapter 4, we discussed minimum wage legislation. In markets governed by the minimum wage, there is a wage floor that limits how little a firm can pay its workers. There are also regulations governing when a firm must provide health insurance to its employees.

These regulations increase the costs of employing labor and will likely result in fewer people being hired, or at least fewer people working enough hours to qualify for employer-sponsored health insurance. In the next chapter, we take a closer look at how government intervenes in the economy. From the perspective of economists, government activities in the market need to be analyzed and planned carefully to avoid as many unintended consequences as possible.

ANSWERING THE BIG QUESTIONS

Where does the demand for labor come from?

* The demand for each factor of production is a derived demand that stems from a firm's desire to supply a good in another market. The demand for labor by firms is derived from the demand consumers have for what the firms produce.
* Labor demand is contingent on the value of the marginal product that is produced. Firms find hiring another worker to be beneficial only if the value of the marginal product exceeds the new worker's wage.
* Changes in the demand for labor can be created by changes in the demand for the product the firm produces and by changes in cost.

Where does the supply of labor come from?

* The supply of labor is affected by the wage rate that is offered. Each person must decide how much labor to supply based on his or her goals and other opportunities. This trade-off is at the heart of the labor-leisure decision.
* Three factors can shift the labor supply curve: other employment opportunities, the changing composition of the workforce, and the effect of migration and immigration.

How does the labor market achieve equilibrium?

* Labor markets reconcile the forces of demand and supply into a wage signal that conveys information to both sides of the market.
* At wages above the equilibrium, the supply of workers exceeds the demand for labor. The result is a surplus of available workers that places downward pressure on wages until they reach the equilibrium wage, at which point the surplus is eliminated.
* At wages below the equilibrium, the demand for labor exceeds the available supply of workers and a shortage develops. The shortage forces firms to offer higher wages in order to attract workers. Wages rise until they reach the equilibrium wage, at which point the shortage is eliminated.

Why do some workers make more than others?

* Many factors affect how much you get paid. While working hard at a job is a good start, it is certainly not the only thing that contributes to your paycheck. There must be a demand for what you are producing. The greater the demand, the more workers in that industry will get paid.
* Just as important is how much you contribute to the company you work for. The higher the value of your marginal product, the more you will likely be paid.

What additional factors determine wages?

* The amount of human capital you possess can also affect your wage. A college degree signals that you have developed additional human capital. It provides employers with information regarding your work ethic and your ability to learn and process new information.
* Other factors affect your wage as well. Compensating differentials are paid based on job characteristics. Some jobs are unpleasant; as a result, firms pay their workers more to do those jobs. Other jobs have non-monetary benefits, such as a desirable location or lifestyle. As a result, these jobs pay less. Members of labor unions tend to earn a wage premium.

CONCEPTS YOU SHOULD KNOW

compensating differential (p. 241)
derived demand (p. 226)
human capital (p. 241)
labor-leisure trade-off (p. 232)
marginal product of labor (p. 227)
outsourcing of labor (p. 238)
strike (p. 244)
union (p. 244)
value of the marginal product (VMP) (p. 227)
wage (p. 224)

QUESTIONS FOR REVIEW

1. Why is the demand for factor inputs, such as labor, a derived demand?
2. What rule does a firm use when deciding to hire an additional worker?
3. What are the two labor-demand shifters? What are the three labor-supply shifters?
4. If wages are below the equilibrium level, what would cause them to rise?
5. If workers become more productive, what would happen to the demand for labor, the wages of labor, and the number of workers employed?
6. List three desirable jobs that are likely to pay lower wages due to compensating differentials. Also list three undesirable jobs that are likely to pay higher wages due to compensating differentials. (Provide different examples from those found in the chapter.)
7. Why do garbage collectors make more than furniture movers?
8. What are union wages? Why are some employers willing to pay them?

STUDY PROBLEMS (*✱ solved at the end of the section*)

1. Maria is a hostess at a local restaurant. When she earned $8 per hour, she worked 35 hours per week. When her wage increased to $10 per hour, she decided to work 40 hours. However, when her wage increased again to $12 per hour, she decided to cut back to 37 hours per week. Draw Maria's supply curve. How would you explain her actions to someone who is unfamiliar with economics?
2. Would a burrito restaurant hire an additional worker for $10.00 an hour if that worker could produce an extra 30 burritos an hour and each burrito could add $0.60 in revenues?
✱ 3. Pam's Pretzels production is shown in the following table. It costs Pam's Pretzels $80 per day per worker. Each pretzel sells for $3.

Quantity of labor	Quantity of pretzels
0	0
1	100
2	180
3	240
4	280
5	310
6	330
7	340
8	320

a. Compute the marginal product and the value of the marginal product that each worker creates.
b. How many workers should Pam's Pretzels hire?

4. A million-dollar lottery winner decides to quit working. How can you explain this behavior using economics?

5. Illustrate each of the following changes by using a separate labor supply-and-demand diagram. Diagram the new equilibrium point, and note how the wage and quantity of workers employed changes.
   a. There is a sudden migration out of an area.
   b. Laborers are willing to work more hours.
   c. Fewer workers are willing to work the night shift.
   d. The demand for California wines suddenly increases.

* 6. A football team is trying to decide which of two running backs (A or B) to sign to a one-year contract.

Predicted statistics	Player A	Player B
Touchdowns	7	10
Yards gained	1,200	1,000
Fumbles	4	5

The team has done a statistical analysis to determine the value of each touchdown, yard gained, and fumble lost to the team's revenue. Each touchdown is worth an extra $250,000, each yard gained is worth $1,500, and each fumble costs $75,000. Player A costs $3.0 million, and Player B costs $2.5 million. Based on the predicted statistics in the table above, which player should the team sign?

7. Farmers in Utopia experience perfect weather throughout the entire growing season, and as a result their crop is double its normal size. How will this bumper crop affect the following factors?
   a. the price of the crop
   b. the marginal product of workers helping to harvest the crop
   c. the demand for the workers who help harvest the crop

8. Internships are considered a vital stepping-stone to full-time employment after college, but not all internship positions are paid. Why do some students take unpaid internships when they could be working summer jobs and earning an income? Include a discussion of human capital in your answer.

SOLVED PROBLEMS

3.a.

Quantity of labor	Quantity of pretzels	Marginal product	Value of the marginal product
0	0	0	$0
1	100	100	300
2	180	80	240
3	240	60	180
4	280	40	120
5	310	30	90
6	330	20	60
7	340	10	30
8	320	−20	−60

b. The VMP of the fifth worker is $90 and each worker costs $80, so Pam should hire five workers. Hiring the sixth worker would cause her to lose $20.

6.

Predicted statistics	Player A	VMP of Player A	Player B	VMP of Player B
Touchdowns	7	$1,750,000	10	$2,500,000
Yards gained	1,200	1,800,000	1,000	1,500,000
Fumbles	4	−300,000	5	−375,000
Total value		3,250,000		3,625,000

Player A has a value of $3.25 million and a cost of $3.0 million, so he is worth $0.25 million. Player B has a value of $3.625 million and a cost of $2.5 million, so he is worth $1.125 million. The team should sign Player B.

CHAPTER 9 Government in the Economy

MISCONCEPTION

Government should make us as safe as possible.

Nearly everyone agrees that one of government's main roles is to defend its citizens and their property. But in the face of increasing risks from terrorists, computer hackers, and concerns about climate change, to what extent should we expect to be protected? Politicians frequently claim that they will take the necessary steps to ensure the safety of all citizens. The same citizens often breathe a sigh of relief when they hear this promise. But do we really want to be protected from all threats?

If we want to be connected to the world and maintain some amount of freedom, then "as safe as possible" is not realistic. How do we figure out what the "right" level of protection is, and how do we get there? The answer is to examine the tension between costs and benefits, and to look carefully at the consequences of government action, or inaction, in the economy.

In the preceding chapters, we've seen that markets provide many benefits and that they work because participants pursue their own self-interests. But sometimes markets fail to ensure an efficient outcome. When a market fails, a government can provide order to promote efficiency. However, government solutions are like private decisions in that there are opportunity costs involved with adopting them. For example, an easy way to stop hackers from stealing credit-card information is simply to "unplug" the Internet. Government could do this for you, and you would be safe from hackers. But most people would find this action to be too extreme.

Opportunity cost

What is the most efficient way to deal with pollution?

Many people believe that the government can stimulate the economy and promote economic activity. Here, too, questions arise: *What exactly should the government do? How much is too much? How little is too little? How should the government deal with pollution? How much police protection should it provide? What are the likely consequences of government policies and actions?* These questions are the focus of this chapter.

BIG QUESTIONS

- **What are the roles of government in the economy?**
- **What are property rights and private property?**
- **What are private goods and public goods?**
- **What are the challenges of providing non-excludable goods?**
- **What are externalities, and how do they affect markets?**

What Are the Roles of Government in the Economy?

In the year 1776, the Declaration of Independence was not at the top of the best-seller list. In fact, at the time, most of the world gave little thought to the burgeoning American Revolution. Instead, people were engrossed in an economics book written by a Scotsman named Adam Smith. *An Inquiry into the Causes and Consequences of the Wealth of Nations* (known today simply as *The Wealth of Nations*) was one of the first efforts to explain why some countries are rich and others are poor. Smith's analysis of the division of labor (also called specialization) is the same one we discussed in Chapter 5. In fact, a lot of what we currently study in economics derives from *The Wealth of Nations* in one way or another.

In the final section of his book, Smith provides some direction for the basic responsibilities of government in a well-functioning economy. He begins by stating: "The first duty of the sovereign, that of protecting the society from the violence and invasion of other independent societies, can be performed only by means of a military force." This merely means that a government should provide an army to protect a country from invasion.

The second role of government, as Smith sees it, is similar to the first. In particular, citizens need protection from one another. Smith states that the second duty of government is "that of protecting, as far as possible, every member of the society from the injustice or oppression of every other member of it, or the duty of establishing an exact administration of justice." In other words, it is the government's responsibility to provide a police force and a judicial system to enforce the laws.

The last job of government relates to the provision of certain services. Smith notes that government should be about "erecting and maintaining those public institutions and those public works, which, though they may be in the highest degree advantageous to a great society, are, however, of such a nature that the profit could never repay the expence [*sic*] to any individual or small number of individuals, and which it therefore cannot be expected that any individual or small number of individuals should erect or maintain." Smith clarifies what he means, saying that these public works should be limited to those "facilitating the commerce of the society, and those for promoting the instruction of the people." In short, the government should provide goods and services that facilitate economic activity and promote the education of people because private firms cannot undertake these activities profitably.

While we have become accustomed to government providing certain amenities, the questions must be asked: *Why is it better for government to provide them than a private firm? What's wrong with a private police force or a private army?* Certainly, there are private schools and even privately run toll roads.

To answer these questions, we have to look more closely at what exactly government is doing. First, by protecting the country from foreign invasion, and by protecting citizens from the harmful actions of others, government is defending *property rights*. These rights are instrumental for a well-functioning economy. If people couldn't pay for a private police force to protect their property, it would likely be stolen or misused. Having an impartial arbiter and defender of right and wrong ensures that all people, regardless of status or income, can have their property protected.

Second, there are some things that economies need in order to function well but that private firms cannot make a profit providing. And there are some things called public goods that offer substantial benefits for society and from which we wouldn't want to exclude the people who cannot afford to pay for them. Public goods include things like national defense.

To understand the implications of government involvement on individuals and in the market, let's take a closer look at property rights and public goods.

What Are Property Rights and Private Property?

Market economies rely on the basic tenet that individuals own property. When property rights are unclear, markets can fail. **Market failure** occurs when the equilibrium price or quantity determined by the interaction of demand and supply is not in line with what society views as optimal. Society would like less pollution, but because no one owns air or water, there is no way to easily protect them. The result is that we have too much pollution, which is an example of a market failure.

Market failure occurs when the equilibrium price or quantity determined by the interaction of supply and demand is not in line with what society views as optimal.

Property Rights

Property rights give the owner the ability to exercise control over a resource.

A proper government can help promote an optimal level of economic activity by ensuring that property rights are protected. **Property rights** give owners the ability to exercise control over a resource, providing them with incentives to use their property in ways that make them happy. For some, property rights mean building a house. For others, property rights might mean leaving a parcel of land undeveloped. Whatever you do with your property, as the owner you can benefit financially from its improvement or sale. Similarly, if you misuse the property, you bear the financial losses. With a strong system of property rights in place, resources tend to be used in a way that increases the well-being of society at large. When property rights are not clearly defined, resources can be mistreated or misused. For instance, since no one owns the air, manufacturing firms often emit pollutants into it.

When property rights are poorly established or not enforced effectively, the wrong incentives come into play. Private owners have an incentive to keep their property in good repair because they bear the costs of fixing what they own when it no longer works properly. For instance, if you own a personal computer, you'll probably protect your investment by treating it with care and dealing with any problems immediately. However, if you access a public computer terminal in a campus lab or library and find that it's not working properly, you'll most likely ignore the problem and simply look for another computer. The difference between solving the problem and ignoring it is crucial to understanding why property rights matter.

ECONOMICS IN THE REAL WORLD

Berry Bikes: No Incentive for Care

Bike-sharing programs are sweeping the nation's college campuses. Bike-sharing companies like Zagster and the Collegiate Bicycle Company have worked with schools to place bikes at strategic locations on campus. Students use some sort of identification such as a swipe card to unlock the bike, which can be returned at any other campus station. The swipe card records information about the user and charges him or her accordingly. The companies can send email or text messages to users reminding them about returning a bike or giving them information about charges. If the bike is damaged, the rider who was in control of the bike when it was damaged can be easily identified.

Bike-sharing programs require riders to take responsibility for the bike they are using.

Being able to track damage to the shared property is extremely important. One of the first attempts at bike-sharing happened at Berry College in Mt. Berry, Georgia. In the spring term of 1998, the student government association (SGA) placed bikes around the campus that students could use free of charge. No record was kept of who the users were. Despite the hope that students' sense of honor would prevail, the results were exactly what an understanding of property rights would predict. The Berry Bikes were basically common property, so students had no incentive to care for them. Since the bikes were "owned" by everyone, they were really owned by no one, so nobody took care of them. The president of the SGA pled with students to treat the bikes as if they were their own, but to no avail. By the end of the semester, 4 of the 20 bikes were lost or stolen and 11 were in a state of total disrepair. Over the summer break, the bikes were restored to working order for the fall term. Unfortunately, the abuse continued. A month into the fall term, the SGA suspended the Berry Bikes program. ✳

Source: E. Frank Stephenson and Daniel L. Alban, "The Berry Bikes: A Lesson in Private Property," *The Freeman*, October 1, 1999.

Private Property

Private property provides an exclusive right of ownership that allows for the use, and especially the exchange, of property. Private property creates incentives to maintain, protect, and conserve property and to trade with others. Let's consider these four incentives in the context of automobile ownership.

Private property provides an exclusive right of ownership that allows for the use, and especially the exchange, of property.

1. *The incentive to maintain property.* Car owners have an incentive to maintain their vehicles. Routine maintenance, replacement of worn parts, and repairs keep the vehicle safe and reliable. In addition, a well-maintained car can be sold for more than one in poor condition.
2. *The incentive to protect property.* Owners have an incentive to protect their vehicles from theft or damage. They do this by using alarm systems, locking the doors, and parking in well-lit areas.
3. *The incentive to conserve property.* Car owners also have an incentive to extend the usable life of their automobiles by limiting the number of miles they put on their cars each year.
4. *The incentive to trade with others.* Car owners have an incentive to trade with others because they may profit from the transaction. Suppose someone offers to buy your car for \$5,000, and you think it's worth only \$3,000. Because you own the car, you can do whatever you want with it. If you decline to sell, you will incur an opportunity cost: you'll be giving up \$5,000 to keep something you value at \$3,000. There's no law requiring you to sell your vehicle, so you *could* keep the car—but you probably won't. Why? Because private property rights give you an incentive to trade for something better in the market.

Incentives

Opportunity cost

Because of the vital nature of private ownership in a market economy, government has a role to play in protecting people's property from the actions of others, whether those who would steal property are foreign or domestic. If you couldn't take action against those who stole your property, you would have no incentive to take care of it. If someone liked your newly washed and waxed car, he or she could just take it. You would likely seek the assistance of the police to get your car back. But if there were no police, what would you do? You might go after the thief yourself, but doing so could be dangerous.

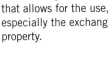

The safer option is to not wash your car. A dirty car is less likely to attract attention. This simple example illustrates why without a strong defense of property rights people have less incentive to take care of their property.

Intellectual property is non-physical property such as an idea, invention, or creative work that is a result of someone's intellect.

Another dire problem arises for society when *intellectual* property rights are not defended. **Intellectual property** is non-physical property such as an idea, invention, or creative work that is a result of someone's intellect. If someone's ideas can be taken or used without compensation, people will have little incentive to develop those ideas or bring them to market. The protection of property rights through patents and copyrights allows inventors to benefit financially from their work. If those protections were lifted, life-saving drugs, software, new music, and new books (to mention just a few things) would probably not be created.

Pizza is a private good.

What Are Private Goods and Public Goods?

As we just saw, property rights are quite important for the development of new products. However, not all goods can be easily put into private hands. When government is involved in providing a particular good or service, such as education or parks, we usually refer to these products as *public goods*. Let's take a look at the attributes that distinguish private goods from public goods.

Excludable goods are goods that the consumer must purchase before using.

Rival goods are goods that cannot be enjoyed by more than one person at a time.

Private goods have two characteristics: they are both excludable and rival in consumption.

Private Goods

To understand the difference between private and public goods, you need to know whether a good is excludable, rival, or both. An **excludable good** is one that the consumer is required to purchase before being able to use it. A **rival good** is one that cannot be enjoyed by more than one person at a time.

Most goods are privately owned—that is, they are **private goods**. For instance, when you find the perfect pair of jeans at the mall, the store can prohibit you from taking them if you don't pay for them; they are excludable. Similarly, putting on those jeans prohibits other people from using them at the same time; they are rival. Since the seller of the jeans gets to charge a price and the consumer gets to acquire a rival good, the stage is set for mutual gains from trade.

Trade creates value

Public Goods

Markets have no difficulty producing private goods, like jeans. To enjoy (consume) them, you must first purchase them. But when was the last time you paid to see a fireworks display? Hundreds of thousands of people view many of the nation's best displays of fireworks, but only a small percentage of those people pay admission to get a preferred seat. Fireworks displays are a **public good** because (1) they can be jointly consumed by more than one person, and (2) it's difficult to exclude non-payers. Since consumers cannot easily be

Public goods can be jointly consumed by more than one person, and non-payers are difficult to exclude.

PRACTICE WHAT YOU KNOW

Public Goods: Are Parks Public Goods?

Many goods have the characteristics of a public good, but few goods meet the exact definition.

Question: Are parks public goods?

Answer: We tend to think of public parks as meeting the necessary requirements to be a public good. But not so fast! Have you been to any of America's top national parks on a peak summer weekend? Parks are subject to congestion, which makes them rival. In addition, most national and state parks require an admission fee—translation: they are excludable. Therefore, public parks do not meet the exact definition of a public good.

Not surprisingly, there are many good examples of private parks that maintain, protect, and conserve the environment alongside their public counterparts. For instance, Natural Bridge is a privately owned and operated park in Virginia that preserves a rare natural arch over a small stream. The East Coast is dotted with private parks that predate the establishment of the national park system. Like their public counterparts, private parks are not public goods.

Natural Bridge in Virginia

forced to pay to observe fireworks, they may desire more of the good than is typically supplied. This situation leads a market economy to underproduce fireworks displays and many other public goods.

Public goods are often underproduced because people can get them without paying for them. Consider Joshua Bell, one of the most famous violinists in the world. The day after giving a concert in Boston, where patrons paid $100 a ticket, he decided to reprise the performance in a Washington, D.C., subway station and just ask for donations.[1] Any passer-by could listen to the music—it didn't need to be purchased to be enjoyed. In other words, it was *non-excludable* and *non-rival* in consumption. But because it's impossible for a street musician to force bystanders to pay, it's difficult for the musician—even one as great as Joshua Bell—to make a living performing for donations only. Suppose he draws a large crowd, and the music creates $500 worth of enjoyment among the audience. At the end of the performance, he receives a loud round of applause and then motions to the donation basket. A number of

World-renowned violinist Joshua Bell performs incognito in the Washington, D.C., Metro.

1. This really happened! The *Washington Post* and Bell conducted an experiment to test the public's reaction to performances of "genius" in unexpected settings. Our discussion here places the event in a hypothetical context. For the real-life result, see Gene Weingarten, "Pearls before Breakfast," *Washington Post*, April 8, 2007.

people come up and donate, but when he counts up the contributions he finds only $30—the actual amount he earned while playing in the subway station.

A **free-rider problem** occurs whenever someone receives a benefit without having to pay for it.

Why did Joshua Bell receive $30, when he created many times that amount in value? This phenomenon, known as a **free-rider problem**, occurs whenever people receive a benefit without having to pay for it. A street musician provides a public good and must rely on the generosity of the audience to contribute. If very few people contribute, many potential musicians won't find it worthwhile to perform. We tend to see very few street performances by talented people because free-riding lowers their returns. This means that street performances are undersupplied.

ECONOMICS IN THE REAL WORLD

Group Work

Perhaps you've been in a class where an assignment involves working in a group. Such assignments are valuable opportunities to experience something that businesses look for in potential employees: the ability to work as part of a team to accomplish a task. However, group work in class or in the workplace creates an environment for the free-rider problem. Many times, one of the group members doesn't put in the time or effort to complete the project. He realizes that he'll get the benefit of the group grade without incurring the full cost. You may think this is lazy or inconsiderate behavior, and it is, but it's nonetheless quite rational. The question for the free-rider is whether his actions will marginally impact the group's grade. Does the cost of completing part of the project justify what's likely to be only a small change in the grade earned by every member of the group? If his work raises the group's grade from a C to a C+, he may find that it's too costly to participate. To avoid this problem, instructors will often ask the group to grade each member's contribution to the group's overall output. The hope is that this system will incentivize the free-rider to pull his weight. ✷

Street performances are just one example of a public good. National defense, lighthouses, streetlights, clean air, and open-source software such as Mozilla Firefox are other examples. Let's examine national defense because it is a particularly clear example of a public good that is subject to a free-rider problem. All citizens value security, but consider the difficulty of trying to organize and provide adequate national defense through private contributions alone. How could you coordinate a missile defense system or get enough people to pay for an aircraft carrier and the personnel to operate it?

Concerned about security? Only the government is capable of providing adequate national defense.

Also think about the strategic problems for a country if someone didn't pay his or her share for national defense. In the United States, the Amish don't pay taxes. Would it make sense for the Secretary of Defense to declare that any foreign enemy can attack the

Amish with impunity because the Amish haven't contributed their fair share to national defense? As long as they stay away from places like Cleveland and Pittsburgh, attackers can take out eastern Ohio and all the Amish farms in that area. Even if you know nothing about military strategy, you probably can tell that this is a very bad idea. It gives your enemy a foothold in your country. Thus, despite the failure to pay for it, the Amish can still use national defense.

The Amish are a special example of free-riders. If the rest of society were to gain a tax exemption from paying for national defense, the nation would be underprotected. Many people wouldn't voluntarily contribute their fair share of the expense. For this reason, defense expenditures are paid for by the government and funded by tax revenues. This almost eliminates the free-rider problem in the context of national defense, unless you don't pay taxes.

You likely now understand why Adam Smith saw defense, as well as a system of domestic law enforcement, as the purview of government. The provision of roads and public education, however, may be a little less clear. Is either of these really a public good? Ask yourself: *Can you exclude people from using either?* In the case of education, the answer is absolutely yes. Schools regularly expel and suspend students, preventing them from entering school grounds. It can be difficult to prevent people from using highways, but with a toll system it is possible. In that case, the highway is more like a private good.

What about being non-rival in consumption? Does your learning experience diminish when there are too many students crammed into a classroom? What would happen if you added 10 more people to your economics class? What about 100 more? Would you have a desk? What about the number of distractions as people talk, text, and doodle? Similarly, highways have limited capacity. In highly populated cities, rush-hour traffic highlights the fact that roads are rival in consumption. If someone else uses the road, your enjoyment of the road is reduced. So why are governments building and providing things that aren't really public goods? The answer is that there are benefits that accrue to society from having an educated working class and a road system to transport goods, even if at times those things are overused. We'll look at those benefits shortly, but let's first wrap up our discussion by talking about the challenges of providing non-excludable goods.

What Are the Challenges of Providing Non-excludable Goods?

To better understand how governments work, let's look at some of the special challenges that arise in providing non-excludable goods.

Common resources are resources that have no legal owner.

Common Resources and the Tragedy of the Commons

The **tragedy of the commons** occurs when a good that is rival in consumption but non-excludable becomes depleted.

Common resources, which are resources that have no legal owner, often give rise to the **tragedy of the commons**, a situation that occurs when a good that is rival in consumption but non-excludable becomes depleted. The term "tragedy of the commons" refers to a phenomenon that the ecologist Garrett Hardin wrote about in the magazine *Science* in 1968. Hardin described the hypothetical use of a common pasture shared by local herders in pastoral communities. Herders know that intensively grazed land will be depleted and that this is very likely to happen to common land. Knowing that the pasture will be depleted creates a strong incentive for individual herders to bring their animals to the pasture as much as possible while it is still green, since every other herder will be doing the same thing. Each herder has the same incentive to overgraze, which quickly makes the pasture unusable. The overgrazing occurs as a result of poorly designed incentives and the absence of clearly defined private-property rights.

Incentives

Even though the concept of common ownership sounds ideal, it can be a recipe for resource depletion and economic disaster. Common ownership is obviously not private ownership. With a system of private-property rights, an owner can seek damages in the court system if his or her property is damaged or destroyed. The same cannot be said for common property. Since no one clearly owns the property, any party can use the resource as he or she sees fit. This common ownership creates incentives to use the resource now rather than later and to neglect it. In short, common property leads to abuse and depletion of the resource.

Private-property rights give owners an incentive to maintain, protect, and conserve their property and to transfer it if someone else values it more than they do. How are those incentives different under a system of common ownership? Let's examine a real-world example of the tragedy of the commons: the collapse of cod populations off the coast of Newfoundland,

ECONOMICS IN THE MEDIA

Tragedy of the Commons

South Park *and Water Parks*

If you've ever been to a water park or community pool, you know that the staff checks the pH of the water regularly to make sure it's clean. However, in a 2009 episode of *South Park* everyone is peeing in Pi Pi's water park. The resulting pee concentration ends up being so high that it triggers a disaster-movie-style cataclysm, unleashing a flood of pee that destroys the place.

Why did this happen? Because each person looked at all the water and thought it wouldn't matter if he or she peed in it. But when *everyone* thought the same way, the water quality was affected. This led to the tragedy of the commons, in which the overall water quality became degraded. Pee-ew.

Thankfully, the real world is cleaner than South Park.

Canada, in the 1990s. Over the course of three years, cod hauls fell from over 200,000 tons annually to close to zero. Why did the fishing community allow this to happen? The answer: incentives. Let's consider the incentives associated with common property in the context of the cod industry.

Common resources, such as cod, encourage overuse (in this case, overfishing).

1. *The incentive to neglect.* No one owns the ocean. As a result, fishing grounds in international waters cannot be protected. Even fishing grounds within territorial waters are problematic since fish do not adhere to political borders. Moreover, the fishing grounds in the North Atlantic cannot be maintained in the same way that one can, say, check the oil in an automobile. The grounds are too large, and the size of the cod population depends on variations in seawater temperature, salinity, and availability of algae and other smaller fish to eat. The idea that individuals or communities could "maintain" a population of cod in this wild environment is highly impractical.
2. *The incentive to overuse.* Each fishing-boat crew would like to maintain a sustainable population of cod to ensure future harvests. However, conservation on the part of one boat is irrelevant since other boats would catch whatever it leaves behind. Since cod are a rival and finite resource, boats have an incentive to harvest as much as they can before another vessel does. With common resources, no one has the authority to define how much of a resource can be used. Maintaining a level of economic activity that would ensure long-term viability of the fish population would require the coordination of thousands of vested interests, each of whom could gain by free-riding. For instance, if a socially responsible boat crew (or country) limits its catch in order to protect the species from depletion, this action doesn't guarantee that rivals will follow suit. Instead, rivals stand to benefit by overfishing what remains.

Since cod are a common resource, the incentives we discussed under a system of private ownership don't apply. With common property, resources are neglected and overused.

Solutions to the Tragedy of the Commons

Preventing the tragedy of the commons requires planning and coordination. Unfortunately, in our cod example, officials didn't recognize the problem with Atlantic cod until it was too late to prevent the collapse. Cod populations dropped to 1 percent of their former sizes. The collapse of the cod and many other species led to the loss of 40,000 jobs and over $300 million in income annually, crippling the economies of the communities in the affected region.

The lesson of the Atlantic cod is a powerful reminder that efforts to avoid the tragedy of the commons must begin before a problem develops. For example, king crab populations off the coast of Alaska have fared much

PRACTICE WHAT YOU KNOW

Common Resources: President Obama's Inauguration

Approximately two million people filled the National Mall for President Obama's 2009 inauguration. After the celebration concluded, the Mall was strewn with litter and trash.

Inaugural trash

Question: What economic concept explains why the National Mall was trashed after the inauguration?

Answer: Attendees brought snacks to eat and newspapers to read while they waited for the inauguration ceremony to begin. So a lot of trash was generated. Would you throw trash on your own lawn? Of course not. But otherwise conscientious individuals often don't demonstrate the same concern for public property. As a public space, the National Mall is subject to the tragedy of the commons. The grass is often trampled, and trash is very common even on normal days. No one person can effectively keep the park green and clean, so overuse and littering occur. When two million people filled the space for President Obama's inauguration, the tragedy of the commons became much more apparent.

better than cod thanks to proactive management. To prevent the collapse of the king crab population, the state of Alaska and the federal government enforce several regulations. First, the length of the fishing season is limited so that the king crab populations have time to recover. Second, regulations limit how much fishing boats can catch. Third, to promote sustainable populations, only adult males are harvested. It is illegal to harvest females and young crabs, since these are necessary for repopulation. Without government enforcement of these regulations, the tragedy of the commons would result because no one owns the ocean and therefore there's no way to prevent fishermen from using it.

What is the best way to curb global warming?

Can the misuse of a common resource be foreseen and prevented? If predictions of rapid global warming are correct, our analysis points to a number of solutions to minimize the tragedy of the commons. One approach would be to tax or heavily regulate the polluting behavior. This negative incentive would discourage businesses and individuals from producing emissions by raising the costs of doing so. However, the indirect incentive might be that jobs are lost as firms that can't bear these new costs decide to close.

A **cap and trade** policy creates an incentive for firms to pollute less by establishing markets for tradable emissions permits.

Another approach to emissions reduction, known as cap and trade, has received much attention lately. A **cap and trade** policy creates an incentive for firms to pollute less by establishing markets for tradable emission permits. Under cap and trade, the government sets a *cap*, or limit, on the amount of CO_2 (carbon dioxide) that can be emitted. Businesses and individuals are then issued permits to emit a certain amount of carbon dioxide each year.

Permit owners may *trade* permits. In other words, companies that produce fewer emissions can sell the permits they don't use. By establishing what amounts to the right to pollute the air, cap and trade causes firms to treat polluting activity as a cost and thereby seek out methods that lower emissions. Global warming is a complex process, but a cap and trade policy is one tangible step that minimizes free-riding, creates incentives for action, and promotes a socially efficient outcome.

Cap and trade is a good idea in theory. However, there are negative consequences as well. For example, cap and trade presumes that nations can agree on and enforce emissions limits, but such agreements have proven difficult to negotiate. Without an international consensus, nations that adopt cap and trade policies will experience higher production costs, while nations that ignore them—and free-ride in the process—will benefit. As an indicator of what cap and trade is likely to cost U.S. consumers, consider what other countries are already experiencing. Britain's Treasury, for example, estimates that the average family will pay roughly £25 ($43) a year in higher electric bills for carbon-cutting programs. With any policy, there are always trade-offs to consider.

ECONOMICS IN THE REAL WORLD

Deforestation in Haiti

Nothing symbolizes the vicious cycle of poverty in Haiti more than the process of deforestation. Haiti was once a lush tropical nation covered with pines and broad-leaf trees. Today, only about 3% of the country has tree cover. Several factors have contributed to this environmental catastrophe: shortsighted logging and agricultural practices, demand for charcoal, rapid population growth, and increased competition for land. Widespread deforestation caused soil erosion, which in turn caused the fertile topsoil layer to wash away. As a result, land that was once lush and productive became desert-like. This degradation of the environment has contributed to the widespread poverty in Haiti.

Haiti is an extreme example of the tragedy of the commons. Its tragedy is especially striking because Haiti shares the island of Hispaniola with the Dominican Republic. The starkest difference between the two countries is the contrast between the lush tropical landscape of the Dominican Republic and the eroded, deforested Haitian land. In Haiti, the land was a semi-public resource that was overused and abused and therefore subject to the tragedy of the commons. In the Dominican Republic, property rights preserved the environment. What does this mean for Haiti? The nation would not be as poor today if it had relied more on private property rights. ✳

Haiti, on the left in this aerial photo, is deforested. The Dominican Republic, on the right, has maintained its environment.

What Are Externalities, and How Do They Affect Markets?

As we have seen, a lack of property rights can prevent desirable outcomes from occurring. Sometimes, however, society as a whole is harmed by the normal functioning of a market. When mutually beneficial trades undertaken by participants in markets affect people who aren't part of the transaction, government might need to step into the market and change the outcome.

Externalities are the costs or benefits of a market activity that affect a third party.

Externalities, or the costs and benefits of a market activity that affect a third party, often lead to undesirable consequences. For example, in April 2010 an offshore oil rig in the Gulf of Mexico operated by British Petroleum (BP) exploded, causing millions of barrels of oil to spill into the water. Even though both BP and its customers benefit from the production of oil, others along the Gulf Coast had their lives severely disrupted. Industries dependent on high environmental quality, like tourism and fishing, were hit particularly hard by the spill.

Internal costs are the costs of a market activity paid by an individual participant.

For a market to work as efficiently as possible, two things must happen. First, each participant must be able to evaluate the **internal costs** of participation—the costs that only the individual participant pays. For example, when we choose to drive somewhere, we typically consider our personal costs—the time it will take to reach our destination, the amount we will pay for gasoline and tolls, and what we will pay for routine vehicle maintenance. Second, for a market to work efficiently, the external costs must also be paid. **External costs** are costs imposed on people who are not participants in that market. In the case of driving, the congestion and pollution that our cars create are external costs. Economists define **social costs** as the total internal costs and external costs of a market activity.

External costs are the costs of a market activity paid by people who are not participants.

Social costs are the internal costs plus the external costs of a market activity.

In this section, we discuss some of the mechanisms that encourage consumers and producers to consider the externalities that result from their actions.

Types of Externalities

An externality exists whenever a private cost (or benefit) diverges from a social cost (or benefit). For example, manufacturers who make vehicles and consumers who purchase them benefit from the transaction, but the making and using of those vehicles leads to externalities—including air pollution and traffic congestion—that adversely affect others.

Negative Externalities

In a **negative externality**, a third party is adversely affected.

If a third party is adversely affected by the economic activities of others, there is a **negative externality**. Negative externalities present a challenge to society because it is difficult to make consumers and producers take responsibility for the full costs of their actions. For example, a negative externality occurs when the volume of vehicles on the roads causes air pollution. Drivers typically don't consider this external cost of reaching their destination. Likewise, manufacturers would generally prefer to ignore the pollution they create, because addressing the problem would raise their costs without providing them with

PRACTICE WHAT YOU KNOW

Externalities: Fracking

How would a natural gas well affect your local area?

In 2003, energy companies began using a process known as hydraulic fracturing, or fracking, to extract underground reserves of natural gas in certain states, including Pennsylvania, Texas, West Virginia, and Wyoming. Fracking involves injecting water, chemicals, and sand into rock formations more than a mile deep. This process taps the natural gas that is trapped in those rocks, allowing it to escape up the well. The gas comes to the surface along with much of the water and chemical mixture, which now must be disposed of. Unfortunately, the chemicals in the mix make the water toxic. Consequently, as fracking activities have expanded to more areas, controversy has grown about the potential environmental effects of the process.

Question: What negative externalities might fracking generate?

Answer: People who live near wells worry about the amount of pollutants in the water mixture and the potential for them to leach into drinking water supplies. Additionally, the drilling of a well is a noisy process. Drilling occurs 24 hours a day for a period of a few weeks. This noise pollution affects anyone who lives close by. Another issue is that the gas has to be transported away from the well in trucks. Additional truck traffic can potentially damage local roads.

Question: What positive externalities might fracking generate?

Answer: Fracking has brought tremendous economic growth to the areas where it is occurring. The resulting jobs have employed many people, providing them with a good income. Local hotels and restaurants have seen an increase in business as temporary employees move from one area to another. As permanent employees take over well operation, housing prices climb as a result of increasing demand. Rising house prices benefit local homeowners.

significant direct benefits. Even noisy neighbors disregard the burden their actions place on others, otherwise they might keep the volume down.

In general, society would benefit if all consumers and producers considered both the internal and the external costs of their actions. If you took into account the pollution your car emitted while you travel to the grocery store, knowing the true cost of your driving would likely change your behavior. You would probably plan more carefully to reduce the number of times you have to travel during the week. Since most people don't consider the external costs that they generate, governments design policies that create incentives for firms and people to limit the amount of pollution they emit.

An effort by the city government of Washington, D.C., shows the potential power of incentives to alter behavior that generates negative externalities.

Incentives

In 2010, the District instituted a five-cent tax on every plastic bag a consumer picks up at a store. While five cents may not sound like much of a disincentive, shoppers responded by switching to cloth bags or reusing plastic ones. In Washington, D.C., the estimated number of plastic bags used every month fell from 22.5 million in 2009 to just 3 million in 2010, significantly reducing the amount of plastic waste entering landfills in the process.

Positive Externalities

In a **positive externality**, a third party is positively affected.

Not all externalities are negative. **Positive externalities** exist when a third party is positively affected. For instance, education creates a large positive externality for society beyond the direct benefits to individual students, teachers, and support staff. For example, a more knowledgeable workforce benefits employers who are looking for qualified employees and is more efficient and productive than an uneducated workforce. Because local businesses experience a positive externality from a well-educated local community, they have a stake in the educational process.

Many of the most successful businesses associated with Stanford have made large donations to the university.

A good example of the synergy between local business and higher education is Silicon Valley in California, which is home to many high-tech companies and Stanford University. As early as the late nineteenth century, Stanford's leaders felt that the university's mission should include fostering the development of self-sufficient local industry. After World War II, Stanford encouraged faculty and graduates to start their own companies. This encouragement led to the creation of Hewlett-Packard, Varian Associates, Bell Labs, and Xerox. A generation later, this nexus of high-tech firms gave birth to leading software and Internet firms like 3Com, Adobe, Facebook, and—more indirectly—Cisco, Apple, and Google.

Recognizing the benefits that they received, many of the most successful businesses associated with Stanford have donated large sums to the university. For instance, the Hewlett Foundation gave $400 million to Stanford's endowment for the humanities and sciences and for undergraduate education—an act of generosity that highlights the positive externality that Stanford University had on Hewlett-Packard. Thus, the Hewlett Foundation provided funding to encourage more of the activity that generated the positive externality.

So how does government go about dealing with externalities? Let's take a look.

Correcting for Negative Externalities

When externalities exist, there is either too much of something (in the case of a negative externality) or too little (in the case of a positive externality). To illustrate externalities, let's use supply and demand analysis to compare the

market outcome to the social optimum. The **social optimum** is the price and quantity combination that would exist if there were no externalities.

When oil refineries are permitted to pollute the environment without additional costs imposed, they are likely to overproduce.

Let's begin with supply and compare the difference between what market forces produce and what is best for society in the case of an oil refinery. A refinery converts crude oil into gasoline. This complex process generates many negative externalities, including the release of pollutants into the air and the dumping of waste byproducts.

Figure 9.1 illustrates the contrast between the market equilibrium and the social optimum in the case of an oil refinery. These costs are indicated on the graph by the supply curve $S_{internal}$, which represents how much the oil refiner will produce if it doesn't have to pay for the negative consequences of its activity. In this situation, the market equilibrium, E_M, accounts only for the internal costs of production.

The **social optimum** is the price and quantity combination that would exist if there were no externalities.

When a negative externality occurs, the government may be able to restore the social optimum by requiring externality-causing market participants to pay for the cost of their actions. In the case of the oil refinery, there

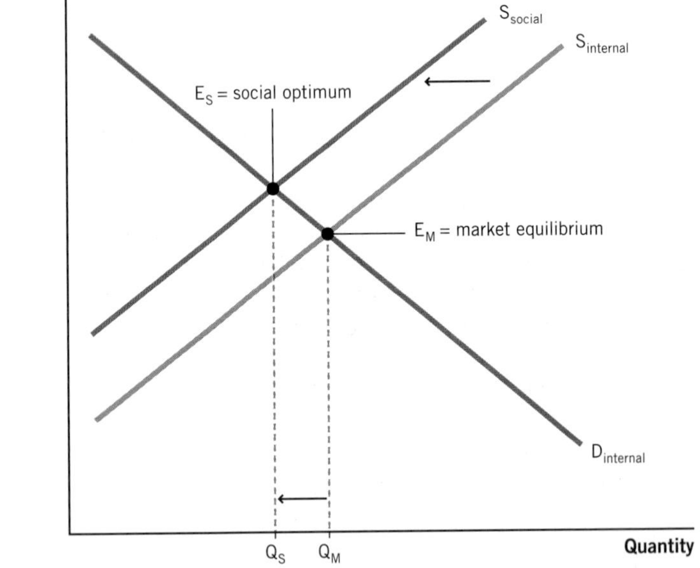

FIGURE 9.1

Negative Externalities and Social Optimum

When a firm is required to internalize the external costs of production, the supply curve shifts to the left, pollution is reduced, and output falls to the socially optimal level, Q_S.

TABLE 9.1

Private and Social Decision-Making

Personal decision	Social optimum	The problem	The solution
Based on internal costs	Social costs = internal costs plus external costs	To get consumers and producers to take responsibility for the externalities they create	Encourage consumers and producers to *internalize* externalities.

Incentives

are three potential solutions. First, the government can require the refiner to install pollution abatement equipment or to change production techniques to reduce emissions and waste byproducts. Second, the government can levy a tax as a disincentive to produce. Finally, the government can require the firm to pay for any environmental damage it causes. Each solution forces the firm to **internalize** the externality, meaning that the firm must take into account the external costs (or benefits) to society that occur as a result of its actions.

An externality is **internalized** when a firm takes into account the external costs (or benefits) to society that occur as a result of its actions.

Having to pay the costs of imposing pollution on others reduces the amount of the pollution-causing activity. By accounting for the external costs along with the internal costs, the firm finds production to be more expensive. The supply curve shifts to the left to S_{social} since each corrective measure requires the refiner to spend money to correct the externality. The result is a social optimum at a lower quantity, Q_S, than at the market equilibrium quantity demanded, Q_M. The trade-off is clear. We can reduce negative externalities by requiring producers to internalize the externality. However, doing so does not occur without cost. Since the supply curve shifts to the left, the quantity produced will be lower. In the real world, there is always a cost.

Table 9.1 outlines the basic decision-making process that guides private and social decisions. Private decision-makers consider only their internal costs, but society as a whole experiences both internal and external costs. To align the incentives of private decision-makers with the interests of society, we must find mechanisms that encourage the internalization of externalities.

ECONOMICS IN THE REAL WORLD

Congestion Charges

In 2003, London instituted a congestion charge. Motorists entering the charge zone, an area of roadways in central London, must pay a flat rate of £10 (approximately $16) between 7 a.m. and 6 p.m. Monday through Friday. A computerized scanner automatically bills the driver, so there's no wait at a toll booth. When the charge was first enacted, it had an immediate effect: the number of vehicles entering the zone fell by a third, the number of riders on public transportation increased by 15%, and bicycle use rose by 30%.

Why impose a congestion charge? The major goal is to prevent traffic-related delays in densely populated areas. Time is valuable, and when you add up all the hours that people spend stuck in traffic, it's a major loss for the economy! Heavy traffic in cities also exposes lots of people to extra pollu-

tion, with costs to health and quality of life. The congestion charge puts a price on these negative externalities and helps to restore the socially optimal level of road usage.

In 2007, Stockholm established a congestion-charge system with a new wrinkle—dynamic pricing. The pricing changes between 6:30 a.m. and 6:30 p.m. During the peak morning and evening commutes, motorists are charged 60 Swedish krona (approximately $7.25). At other times, the price ratchets down to 15 or even 10 krona. This pricing scheme encourages motorists to enter the city at non-peak times. ✷

Motorists must pay a flat-rate congestion charge to enter London's central business area on weekdays.

Correcting for Positive Externalities

Positive externalities have benefits for people who are not directly involved in an activity. As with negative externalities, economists use supply and demand analysis to compare the efficiency of the market with the social optimum. This time, we will focus on the demand curve. Consider a child who gets vaccinated against measles when she's very young. When the vaccine is administered, the recipient is immunized. This creates an internal benefit. But there is also an external benefit: because the child likely won't come down with the measles, fewer other people will catch the measles and become contagious, which helps to protect even those who don't get immunized. Therefore, we can say that vaccines convey a positive externality to the rest of society.

Incentives

Why do positive externalities exist in the market? Using our example of a measles shot, there is an incentive for people in high-risk groups to get vaccinated for the sake of their own health. In Figure 9.2, we capture this internal benefit in the demand curve labeled $D_{internal}$. However, the market equilibrium, E_M, only accounts for the internal benefits of individuals deciding whether to get vaccinated. To maximize the health benefits for everyone, public health officials need to find a way to encourage people to consider the external benefit of their vaccination, too. One way is to issue school vaccination laws, which require that all children entering school provide proof of vaccination against a variety of diseases. The requirement creates a direct incentive for vaccination and produces positive benefits for all members of society by internalizing the externality. The overall effect is that more people get vaccinated early in life, helping to push the market toward the socially optimal number of vaccinations.

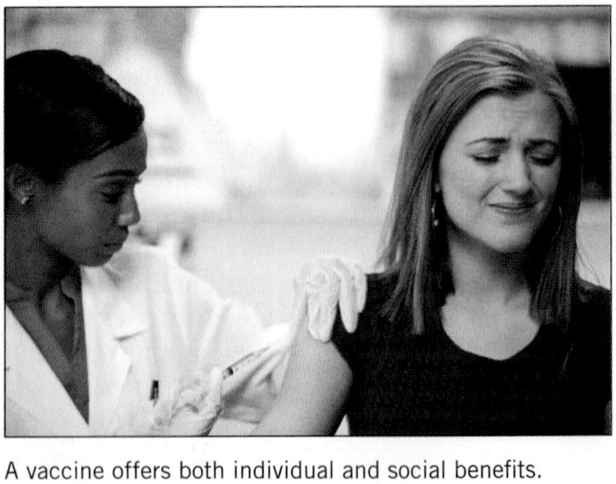

A vaccine offers both individual and social benefits.

Government can also promote the social optimum by encouraging economic activity that helps third parties. For example, it can offer a subsidy, or price break, to encourage more people to get vaccinated. The subsidy acts as a consumption incentive. In fact, governments routinely provide free or reduced-cost vaccines. The subsidy enables consumers to spend less money, which increases their willingness to get the vaccine, shifting the demand curve in Figure 9.2 from $D_{internal}$ to D_{social}. The social demand curve

FIGURE 9.2

Positive Externalities and Social Optimum

The vaccine subsidy encourages consumers to internalize the externality. As a result, consumption moves from the market equilibrium, Q_M, to a social optimum at a higher quantity, Q_S, and vaccinations increase.

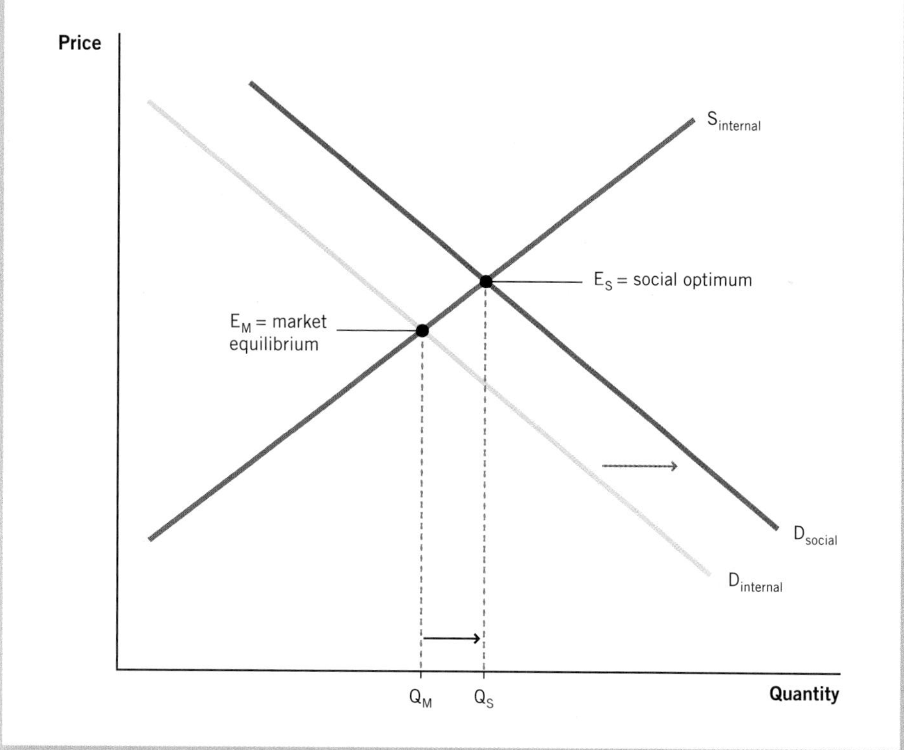

reflects the sum of the internal and social benefits of getting the vaccination. In other words, the subsidy encourages consumers to internalize the externality. As a result, the output moves from the market equilibrium quantity demanded, Q_M, to a social optimum at a higher quantity, Q_S.

Table 9.2 summarizes the key characteristics of positive and negative externalities and presents additional examples of each type.

Government Failure: A Caveat about Government Oversight

Firms with a profit motive have an incentive to minimize the costs of production, since lower costs translate directly into higher profits. Consequently, if the managers of a firm do a poor job, they will be fired. However, the same cannot be said about government managers or bureaucrats. Government employees are rarely let go, regardless of their performance. As a result, government oversight and management of an activity is problematic because there are fewer incentives to keep costs in check. Without the correct incentives in place, we would expect cost inefficiencies to develop.

Incentives

Public policy can mitigate the power of monopolies and help to deal with the commons problem and externalities, but positive outcomes are not guaranteed. When promoting government involvement in the economy, advocates frequently cite the need to eliminate inefficiencies in the market.

TABLE 9.2

A Summary of Externalities

	Negative externalities		Positive externalities	
Definition		Costs borne by third parties		Benefits received by third parties
Examples		Oil refining creates air pollution.	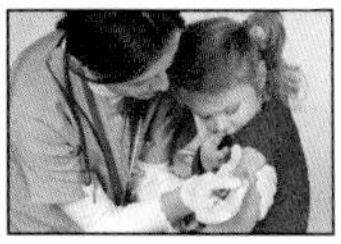	Flu shots prevent the spread of disease.
		Traffic congestion causes all motorists to spend more time on the road waiting.		Education creates a more productive workforce and enables citizens to make more informed decisions for the betterment of society.
		Airports create noise pollution.		Restored historic buildings enable people to enjoy beautiful architectural details.
Corrective measures		Taxes or regulation Cap and trade		Subsidies or government provision

However, this is not always the relevant comparison to make. Rather, we need to ask how the inefficiency of market failures compares with the inefficiencies associated with government involvement in the market. Sometimes, governments step in to fix problems and end up making them worse. This result is called **government failure**. When the costs of government involvement are greater than the efficiency gains that can be realized, the best solution to a market problem might be to do nothing.

Government failure occurs when government intervention makes a problem worse.

Conclusion

Although it's tempting to believe that government should protect people no matter what the cost, this is a misconception. It's possible to be too safe, eliminating the benefits from things like the Internet or airline travel. Providing perfect security would force businesses to shut down, curtailing people's ability to communicate and travel. A truly safe society would leave most people without the conveniences they have come to rely on. Therefore, the goal for protection is to increase it up to the point where the additional benefits equal the additional costs. As with all things, there are trade-offs.

Trade-offs

In this chapter, we considered two areas where government can intercede to address market failure: public goods and externalities. When public goods and externalities exist, the market does not provide the socially optimal amount of the good or service. Public goods present a challenge for the market. Free-riding leads to the underproduction of goods that are non-rival and non-excludable. Since not enough is produced privately, one solution is to

ECONOMICS FOR LIFE

Buying Used Is Good for Your Wallet and for the Environment

Many people waste their hard-earned money buying new. We could do our pocketbooks, and the environment, a favor by opting to buy used instead. Some customers are willing to pay a premium for that "new" feeling—but if you avoid that price markup, you'll save money *and* extend the usable life of a product. Here are a few ideas.

1. **Jewelry.** Would you buy something that immediately depreciates (loses value) by 70%? When you buy at a retail store, you'll rarely get even a third of it back if you need to sell. If you're comfortable with the risk, search Craigslist or a local pawn shop instead—just be sure to get an appraisal before buying.
2. **Sports equipment.** Let the enthusiasts buy the latest equipment. When they tire of it and switch to the newest golf clubs or buy a new kayak, you can swoop in and enjoy big savings.
3. **Video game consoles and games.** You can buy used and pay half price or less; the catch is that you'll have to wait. But the good news is that you'll never find out that your expensive new system isn't as exciting as advertised. Waiting means better information *and* lower prices. That's how you find a good deal.
4. **Automobiles.** The average new car can lose as much as 20% of its value during the first year after purchase. For a $30,000 car, that means $6,000 in depreciation. Let someone else take that hit while you buy a used vehicle instead.
5. **Tools and yard equipment.** Think twice before heading to the hardware store. Many tools such as hammers and shovels are designed to last—they might not look shiny-new, but used tools work just as well as new ones.

Every time you buy used, you extend the usable life of a product, which helps to maximize the value that society gets from its resources. Buying used also illustrates the benefit of private property: recall that owners have incentives to (1) maintain, (2) protect, and (3) conserve the products they own so that they can (4) maximize the value when they sell them.

Buying used can save you thousands.

eliminate free-riding by making involvement compulsory through taxation or regulation. A second problem occurs whenever goods are non-excludable, as is the case with common-resource goods such as the oceans. This condition gives rise to the tragedy of the commons and can lead to the overuse of valuable resources.

Likewise, government can encourage businesses to internalize externalities. It can do so through taxes and regulations that force producers to account for the negative externalities that they create. Similarly, subsidies can spur the production of activities that generate positive externalities. However, these actions do have costs. Raising taxes and regulating behavior can cause business activity to decline. Just like making you as safe as possible might curtail your freedoms, making the environment as clean as possible could reduce your job opportunities.

Regardless of what you think the role of government should be, there is still the issue of paying for these activities. We've already alluded to the financial considerations for government as it intervenes in the economy. Whether providing public goods or subsidizing activities that provide positive externalities, government needs to pay for what it does.

ANSWERING THE BIG QUESTIONS

What are the roles of government in the economy?

* According to Adam Smith, government must do three things to help an economy function. It should (1) protect the citizens and their property from foreign invasion, (2) protect citizens and their property from domestic theft, and (3) provide certain public goods like education and roads.

What are property rights and private property?

* Property rights give the owner the ability to exercise control over a resource.
* Private property provides an exclusive right of ownership that allows for the use and exchange of property. Private property provides incentives to maintain, protect, and conserve property and to trade with others.

What are private goods and public goods?

* Private goods have two characteristics: they are excludable and rival in consumption. Excludable goods are those that the consumer must purchase before using. Rival goods are those that cannot be enjoyed by more than one person at a time.
* A public good has two characteristics: it is non-excludable and non-rival in consumption. Public goods give rise to the free-rider problem and result in the underproduction of the good in the market.

What are the challenges of providing non-excludable goods?

* Under a system of common property, the incentive structure causes neglect and overuse, a situation called the tragedy of the commons. Governments can prevent the tragedy of the commons by recognizing problems and then taking steps (such as licenses, quotas, and cap and trade policies) to prevent overuse or abuse.

What are externalities, and how do they affect markets?

* An externality exists whenever an internal cost (or benefit) diverges from a social cost (or benefit). Third parties can experience negative or positive externalities from a market activity.
* When a negative externality exists, government can restore the social optimum by discouraging economic activity that harms third parties. When a positive externality exists, government can restore the social optimum by encouraging economic activity that benefits third parties.
* An externality is internalized when decision-makers must pay for the externality created by their participation in the market.

CONCEPTS YOU SHOULD KNOW

cap and trade (p. 264)
common resources (p. 261)
excludable goods (p. 258)
external costs (p. 266)
externalities (p. 266)
free-rider problem (p. 260)
government failure (p. 273)
intellectual property (p. 258)
internal costs (p. 266)
internalize (p. 270)
market failure (p. 255)
negative externality (p. 266)
positive externality (p. 268)
private goods (p. 258)
private property (p. 257)
property rights (p. 256)
public goods (p. 258)
rival goods (p. 258)
social costs (p. 266)
social optimum (p. 269)
tragedy of the commons (p. 261)

QUESTIONS FOR REVIEW

1. Does the market overproduce or underproduce when third parties enjoy positive externalities? Show your answer on a supply and demand graph.
2. Give two examples of positive externalities and two examples of negative externalities. Provide examples that are not in the textbook.
3. Describe some of the ways that externalities can be internalized.
4. Which two characteristics define a public good? Provide an example of a public good that was not discussed in the chapter.
5. What is the tragedy of the commons? Give an example that is not in the textbook.
6. What are the four incentives of private property? How do they differ from the incentives found in common property?
7. What is a cap and trade policy? How might such a policy help to decrease a negative externality?
8. What are the basic roles of government?

STUDY PROBLEMS (** solved at the end of the section*)

1. Many cities have noise ordinances that impose especially harsh fines and penalties for early-morning and late-evening disturbances. Explain why these ordinances exist and what they are intended to accomplish.
2. Indicate whether the following activities create a positive or a negative externality:
   a. Late-night road construction begins on a new bridge. As a consequence, traffic is rerouted past your house while the construction takes place.
   b. An excavating company pollutes a local stream with acid rock.
   c. A homeowner whose property backs up on a city park enjoys the sound of kids playing soccer.
   d. A student uses her cell phone discreetly during class.
   e. You and your friends volunteer to plant wildflowers along the local highway.
3. Can you think of a reason why making cars safer would create negative externalities? Explain.
4. Which of the following activities give rise to the free-rider problem? Explain.
   a. recycling programs
   b. biking
   c. studying for an exam
   d. riding a bus

* 5. The students at a crowded university have trouble waking up before 10 a.m., and most work jobs after 3 p.m. As a result, there is a great deal of demand for classes between 10 a.m. and 3 p.m., and classes before and after those hours are rarely full. To make matters worse, the university has a limited amount of classroom space and faculty. This means that not every student can take classes during the most desirable times. Building new classrooms and hiring more faculty are not options. The

administration asks for your advice about the best way to solve the problem of demand during the peak class hours. What advice would you give?

* **6.** Two companies, Toxic Waste Management and Sludge Industries, both pollute a nearby lake. Each firm dumps 1,000 gallons of goo into the lake every day. As a consequence, the lake has lost its clarity and the fish are dying. Local residents want to see the lake restored. But Toxic Waste's production process depends heavily on being able to dump the goo into the lake. It would cost Toxic Waste $10 per gallon to clean up the goo it generates. Sludge can clean up its goo at a cost of $2 per gallon.

   a. If the local government cuts the legal goo emissions in half for each firm, what are the costs to each firm to comply with the law? What is the total cost to both firms in meeting the goo-emissions standard?

   b. Another way of cutting goo emissions in half is to assign each firm tradable pollution permits that allow 500 gallons of goo to be dumped into the lake every day. Under this approach, will each firm still dump 500 gallons of goo? Why or why not?

7. Most colleges and universities have instituted quiet hours in dorms. How might you explain the adoption of such rules in terms of externalities? Illustrate this with a demand and supply graph.

8. In most areas, developers are required to submit environmental impact studies before work can begin on new construction projects. Suppose that a commercial developer wants to build a new shopping center on an environmentally protected piece of property that is home to a rare three-eyed toad. The shopping complex, if approved by the local planning commission, will cover 10 acres. The planning commission wants the construction to go forward since that means additional jobs for the local community, but it also wants to be environmentally responsible. One member of the commission suggests that the developer relocate the toads. She describes the relocation process as follows: "The developer builds the shopping mall and agrees to create 10 acres of artificial toad habitat elsewhere." Will this proposed solution make the builder internalize the externality? Explain.

SOLVED PROBLEMS

5. A flat-fee congestion charge is a good start, since this would reduce the quantity demanded between 10 a.m. and 3 p.m., but such a fee is a blunt instrument. Making the congestion charge dynamic (or varying the price by the hour) will encourage students to move outside the window with the most popular class times in order to pay less. For instance, classes between 11 a.m. and 2 p.m. could have the highest fee. Classes between 10 and 11 a.m. and between 2 and 3 p.m. would be slightly discounted. Classes between 9 and 10 a.m. and between 3 and 4 p.m. would be cheaper still, and those earlier than 9 a.m. and after 4 p.m. would be the cheapest. By altering the price of different class times, the university would be able to offer classes at less popular times and fill them up regularly, thus efficiently using its existing resources.

6. a. If the local government cuts the legal goo emissions in half for each firm, Toxic Waste will cut its goo by 500 gallons at a cost of $10 per gallon, for a total cost of $5,000. Sludge Industries will cut its goo by 500 gallons; at $2 per gallon, the cost is $1,000. The total cost to both firms in meeting the goo-emissions standard is $5,000 + $1,000 = $6,000.

   b. It costs Toxic Waste $10 per gallon to clean up its goo. It is therefore more efficient for Toxic to buy all 500 permits from Sludge—which enables Toxic to dump an additional 500 gallons in the lake and saves the company $5,000. At the same time, Sludge could not dump any goo in the lake. Since it costs Sludge $2 per gallon to clean up its goo, it will have to pay $1,000. Since Toxic is saving more than it costs Sludge to clean up the goo, the two sides have an incentive to trade the permits.

PART

III

MACROECONOMICS

CHAPTER

10 What Is Macroeconomics?

MISCONCEPTION

When a major macroeconomic problem occurs, economists always know how to fix it.

When problems arise in the economy, most people expect government leaders to seek the advice of economic experts and then act on that advice. Economists do understand more about the economy than the average person, but that doesn't mean that they know how to fix every problem. In fact, economists sometimes provide conflicting advice to policymakers. President Harry Truman famously quipped, "Give me a one-handed economist! All my economists say, 'on one hand . . . on the other.'" Truman wanted someone who would give him a straight, easy answer. Unfortunately, in macroeconomics answers can be elusive.

Microeconomics provides us with the tools we need to understand individual behavior. Economists have so much experience dealing with decision-making by individuals, households, and businesses that they can predict people's and firms' reactions to changed circumstances with a fair degree of accuracy. But when it comes to understanding the economy as a whole—the *macroeconomy*—there are too many component parts, and it can be impossible to predict all of the results from one change in circumstance. Policies that are designed to fix one problem can have unintended consequences for other parts of the economy. In addition, the ups and downs of economies are subject to unpredictable events such as wars, terrorist attacks, oil-supply disruptions, and extreme weather. These events can upset even the most vibrant of economies. The problems can then be exacerbated by bad or shortsighted policies, even though the same policies might have been useful during previous economic downturns.

The U.S. economy produces almost one-fourth of all goods and services in the world.

No need to despair, though. Policymakers can and do make effective decisions, but they need a solid understanding of the macroeconomic fundamentals in order to do so.

BIG QUESTIONS

- **How is macroeconomics different from microeconomics?**
- **What are the three major topics in macroeconomics?**

How Is Macroeconomics Different from Microeconomics?

As we discussed briefly in Chapter 1, there are two primary divisions of economics: microeconomics and macroeconomics. In the first two parts of this book we dealt with *microeconomics*, the use of economic tools for understanding the behavior and choices of individuals and firms. *Macroeconomics* is different because it attempts to aggregate (combine) all of the individual decisions that are made by billions of people and firms. The normal unit of analysis in macroeconomics is the nation.

In microeconomics, we study what people buy, what jobs they take, and how they distribute their income between purchases and savings; we also examine the decisions of firms and how they compete with other firms. In macroeconomics, we consider what happens when the *national* output of goods and services rises and falls, when overall *national* employment levels rise and fall, and when the *overall* price level goes up and down.

A pink slip for one person is a microeconomic issue . . .

. . . but widespread unemployment is a macroeconomic issue.

TABLE 10.1

Comparing the Perspectives of Microeconomics and Macroeconomics

Topic	Microeconomics	Macroeconomics
Income	The income of a person or the revenue of a firm	The income of an entire nation or a national economy
Output	The production of a single worker, firm, or industry	The production of an entire economy
Employment	The job status and decisions of an individual or firm	The job status of a national population, particularly the number of people who are unemployed
Prices	The price of a single good	The combined prices of all goods in an economy

Here's a more specific example. In microeconomics, we studied the markets for salmon (an example from Chapter 3). We analyzed the behavior of people who consume salmon and the firms that sell salmon—demanders and suppliers. Then we brought these two parts of the market together to see how the equilibrium price depends on the behavior of demanders *and* suppliers.

Macroeconomics is the study of the broader economy. It looks at the big picture created by all markets in the economy—the markets for salmon, coffee, computers, cars, haircuts, and health care, just to name a few. In macroeconomics, we examine *total* output in an economy rather than just a single firm or industry. We look at *total* employment across the economy rather than employment at a single firm. We consider *all* prices in the economy rather than the price of just one product, such as salmon. To illustrate these differences, Table 10.1 compares a selection of topics from the different perspectives of microeconomics and macroeconomics.

What Are the Three Major Topics in Macroeconomics?

President Truman signs the Employment Act of 1946.

When studying macroeconomics, it is important to understand that almost everything is viewed through the prism of the Great Depression of the 1930s, an event that happened nearly a century ago. This was such a volatile time in the world that economists and policymakers still evoke memories of it when discussing new initiatives. The Great Depression created a rift in the way economists approach the macro economy. We explain more about these divisions in the appendix to this chapter. The Great Depression was so scarring, in fact, that immediately after World War II ended, the U.S. government passed a transformative piece of legislation designed to prevent another great depression. In 1946, President Truman signed the Employment Act. The opening paragraph of the Act expressly states:

> The Congress hereby declares that it is the continuing policy and responsibility of the federal government to use all practicable means consistent with its needs and obligations and other essential considerations of national policy with the assistance and cooperation of industry, agriculture, labor, and state and local governments, to coordinate and utilize all its plans, functions, and resources for the purpose of creating and maintaining, in a manner calculated to foster and promote free and competitive enterprise and the general welfare, conditions under which there will be afforded useful employment for those able, willing, and seeking work, and to promote maximum employment, production, and purchasing power.

Economic stability occurs when those who wish to work have jobs in an environment where the economy experiences growth and stable prices.

This paragraph means that a key goal of the U.S. government is to pursue **economic stability** through policies that promote employment for those who wish to work, thereby fostering economic growth in an environment where prices are stable. The passing of the Employment Act didn't mean that economic ups and downs wouldn't occur. It meant that for the first time the federal government would try to manage those ups and downs. After the signing of the Employment Act, it became the norm for the U.S. government to actively use policy to manage three major macroeconomic variables: employment, output, and inflation. To understand macroeconomics, you need to start with an understanding of these variables.

Employment

Employment focuses on how many people have jobs. The main measure of employment, though, is the unemployment rate.

People voluntarily leave a job for many reasons—for example, to have children, to return to school, or to take another job. Others lose a job that they wish to keep. For example, an employee might be let go for poor performance or because the company is downsizing. When macroeconomists consider unemployment, they explicitly look at workers who seek employment but are unable to secure it. **Unemployment** occurs when a worker who is not currently employed is searching for a job without success.

Unemployment occurs when a worker who is not currently employed is searching for a job without success.

The **unemployment rate (u)** is the percentage of the labor force that is unemployed.

Economists use the unemployment rate to monitor the level of unemployment in an economy. The **unemployment rate (u)** is the percentage of the labor force that is unemployed. Figure 10.1 plots the U.S. unemployment rate from 1960 to 2014. This graphic is one way of quickly measuring national economic frustration. As the unemployment rate climbs, people are more likely to be disappointed in their pursuit of a job.

Economists distinguish three types of unemployment: *structural, frictional,* and *cyclical*. You can think of each type as deriving from a different source. As it turns out, structural and frictional unemployment occur even when the economy is healthy and growing. For this reason, they are often referred to as *natural unemployment*. We consider them first.

Structural Unemployment

Unemployment is difficult on households, and resources are wasted when idle workers sit on the sidelines. However, a dynamic, growing economy is an economy that adapts and changes. No one would consider it an improvement

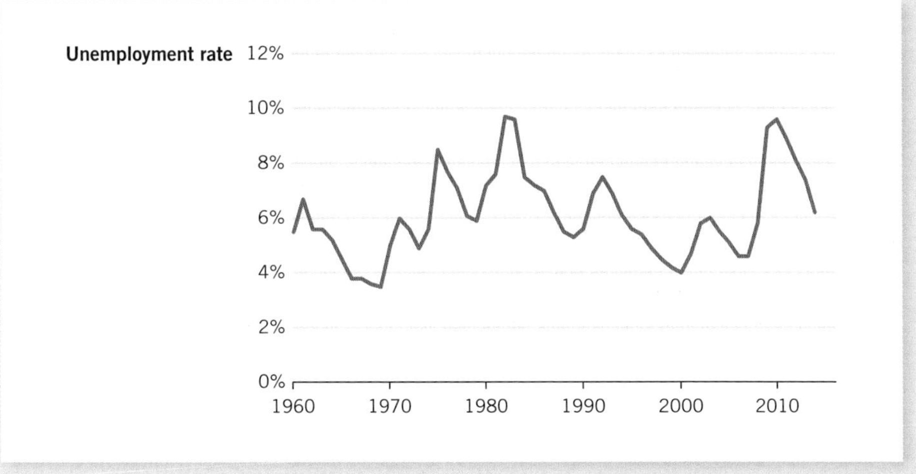

FIGURE 10.1

U.S. Unemployment Rate, 1960–2014

The unemployment rate is an important indicator of the economy's health. Since 1960, the average unemployment rate in the United States has been about 6%.

Source: U.S. Bureau of Labor Statistics.

if we returned to the economy of early America, where 90% of Americans toiled in manual farm work and earned wages that just barely provided the basic necessities of life. The transformation to a modern economy has brought new jobs but also has required completely different skills. Some jobs have become obsolete, which has led inevitably to a certain amount of unemployment, even if just temporarily. Dynamic, growing economies are evolving economies. If we want an economy that adapts to changes in consumer demands and technology, we must accept some unemployment, at least temporarily, as a byproduct of growth. This dilemma, when the introduction of new products and technologies leads to the end of other industries and jobs, is called **creative destruction.**

Creative destruction occurs when the introduction of new products and technologies leads to the end of other industries and jobs.

Consider that in the past we produced no refrigerators, smartphones, or polio vaccines. Subsequent inventions of new products and technologies

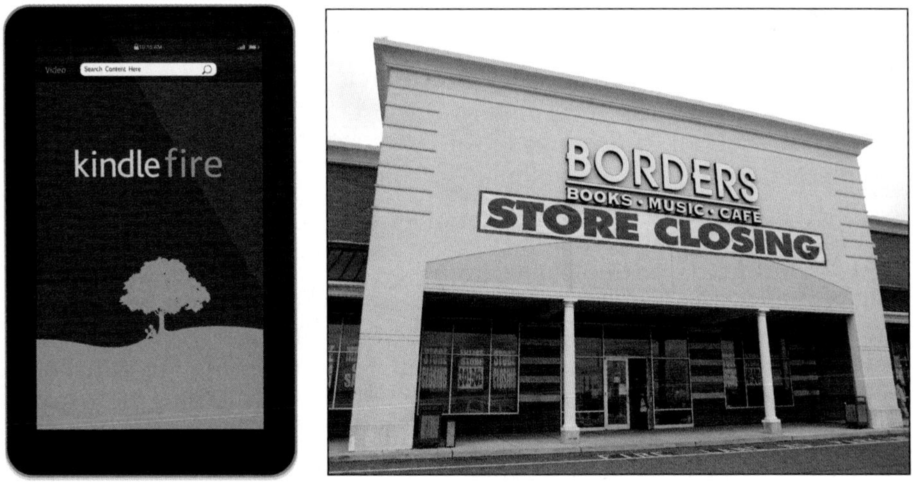

Creative destruction in the retail book market means that when new products and jobs are created, other jobs are destroyed.

enabled us to produce more and better output with fewer resources. But we also produced less of some other things—such as wagon wheels, cassette tapes, and typewriters. These changes left some workers unemployed.

The newspaper industry is a good example of an industry that has changed dramatically over the centuries. Since the founding of the United States, newspapers have been easily available and cheap sources of news. Some papers would put out multiple versions during the day, a morning and an evening edition, to provide readers with the most current news as quickly as possible. Additionally, big cities had multiple daily papers along with biweekly and weekly options. Chicago had 11 daily papers and 22 weekly papers in 1860. Papers catered to specific constituencies such as ethnic groups and political parties. Today, there are just four major daily papers and three major weeklies in Chicago. Despite that city's much greater population today, the newspaper industry is in significant trouble not only in Chicago but all over the country as well. The *Chicago Tribune*, perhaps the most popular paper in the Windy City, has been cutting jobs in recent years because of declining sales. As more people turn to the Internet for their news, the newspaper industry is falling into obscurity.

As the newspaper industry contracts, workers are losing their jobs. For example, New Orleans no longer has a daily paper. When the *Times-Picayune* became primarily an online newspaper (with three printed editions per week), the company laid off over 200 employees, including almost half of its reporters. At that point, the laid-off *Times-Picayune* employees found themselves the victims of **structural unemployment**: they lost their jobs as a result of changes in the industrial make-up (structure) of the economy.

Structural unemployment is unemployment caused by changes in the industrial makeup (structure) of the economy.

The steel industry provides another example. Steel helped to revolutionize life in the late nineteenth and early twentieth centuries. It is an essential component of automobiles, appliances, bridges, buildings, and even road construction. However, while steel has been around for centuries, the number of workers needed to manufacture it has steadily dwindled. As recently as 1980, almost 500,000 people in the United States were employed making steel. That number fell to 225,000 in 2000 and declined again to about 150,000 in 2010. Where did all the jobs go? Some went overseas, but advanced engineering made it possible for firms to replace workers with automated equipment. As a result, steel production has become much safer and more efficient. The trade-off—jobs in exchange for safety and efficiency—is reflected in the employment numbers for the industry.

From these examples, we can begin to understand why unemployment can occur even in a healthy economy. For instance, in 2006—a typical year prior to the economic slowdown of the late 2000s—2 million new jobs were created. Yet there were approximately 5 million *job separations*, meaning people who either quit or were laid off, every month. In a dynamic economy, job turnover is normal.

While structural unemployment can't be eliminated, it can be reduced. Workers must often retrain, relocate, or change their expectations in some way before they can work elsewhere. Lumberjacks may need to become computer repair specialists, or autoworkers may need to relocate from Michigan to Kentucky. Government can also enact policies to alleviate the pain of structural unemployment—for example, by establishing job-training programs and relocation subsidies.

ECONOMICS IN THE REAL WORLD

Americans Don't Appear to Want Farm Work

In September 2010, Garance Burke of the Associated Press wrote an article about the frustration of U.S. farmers trying to find Americans to harvest fruit and vegetables. Even though the unemployment rate at the time was very high, Americans didn't apply for available farm jobs. Burke notes that the few Americans who do take such jobs usually don't stay in the fields for long. The AP analysis showed that from January to June 2010, California farmers advertised 1,160 farm-worker jobs available to U.S. citizens and legal residents; only 36 were hired. One farmer named Steve Fortin noted problems with American workers: "A few years ago when domestic workers were referred here, we saw absentee problems, and we had people asking for time off after they had just started. Some were actually planting the plants upside down."

Comedian Stephen Colbert partnered with the United Farm Workers (UFW) union in a "Take Our Jobs" campaign, aimed at getting farm jobs filled with American workers. Colbert even spent a day picking beans in a field, concluding that farm work is "really, really hard."

Ironically, during the 2007–2009 economic downturn, many migrant farm jobs were available for unemployed Americans, who refused to apply for them. This lack of interest contrasts with events during the Great Depression more than 80 years earlier, when displaced farmers from the Great Plains states flooded California looking for work. So when some people today claim that immigrants are taking jobs away from American citizens, we can say that in the heart of California—the nation's biggest farming state—this is certainly not true. ✳

Why don't Americans want a career picking grapes?

Frictional Unemployment

Even when jobs are available and qualified employees live nearby, it takes time for workers and employers to find one another and agree to terms. **Frictional unemployment** is caused by delays in matching available jobs and workers. Frictional unemployment is another type of natural unemployment. No matter how healthy the economy may be, there is always some frictional unemployment.

Frictional unemployment is unemployment caused by delays in matching available jobs and workers.

Consider how a successful new product launch at McDonald's affects Burger King. Suppose that McDonald's introduces a new product called the Quad Stack, which is really just four Quarter Pounders stacked on top of one another. Also suppose that customers can't get enough of the new burger, and that because of the spike in new business, McDonald's needs to hire more employees. At the same time, Burger King loses customers to McDonald's and decides to lay off some of its workers. Of course, the laid-off Burger King workers will take some time searching for new jobs, and McDonald's will take time deciding how many new workers it needs and which applicants to hire. Because some workers are unemployed during this transition, frictional unemployment results.

Frictional unemployment occurs even in the healthiest economy. Because we live in a world of imperfect information, there are incentives for employees to keep searching for the perfect job or for employers to search longer for the best employees. For example, as you approach graduation from college, you'll probably take some time to search for a job and to determine which offer to accept; you won't be interested in just any job. Similarly, employers rarely hire the first applicant they see, though it may be costly to leave a position vacant. Even if there's a perfect job available for every worker, it will still take time to match workers and jobs. These time lags create friction in the labor market, and the result is temporary, frictional unemployment.

Unemployment, Government Policies, and Incentives

Even though it's natural, frictional unemployment can be exacerbated if incentives aren't designed properly. Let's look at how government policies can cause frictional unemployment. These policies include unemployment compensation and government regulations related to the hiring and firing of employees.

Unemployment insurance is a government program that reduces the hardship of joblessness by guaranteeing that unemployed workers receive a percentage of their former income while they are unemployed. Also called federal jobless benefits.

Unemployment insurance, also known as *federal jobless benefits*, is a government program that reduces the hardship of joblessness by guaranteeing that unemployed workers receive a percentage of their former income while they're unemployed. Governments provide unemployment insurance to workers for many reasons. The benefit cushions the economic consequences of being laid off, and it provides workers time to search for new employment. In addition, unemployment insurance can help contain macroeconomic problems before they spread to other industries. Consider what happens if the auto industry is struggling and workers are laid off: the unemployed autoworkers won't be able to pay for goods and services that they previously purchased, and the reduction in their overall spending will hurt other industries. For example, if unemployed workers can't pay their mortgages, lenders will suffer and the downturn will spread to the financial industry. Viewed in this way, unemployment insurance serves to reduce the severity of the overall economic contraction.

However, unemployment insurance also creates unintended consequences. For one thing, receiving the cushion of unemployment benefits makes some people feel less inclined to search for and take a job. These workers spend more time unemployed when they have insurance; without unemployment insurance, they're much more motivated to seek immediate employment. For example, in late 2007 the U.S. economy entered into a downturn now called the Great Recession, which ended in mid-2009. But several years after the recession was declared over, the level of unemployment has remained high. Why? One reason might be the frictional unemployment that occurred because of special policies put in place during the recession. In November 2009, the U.S. government extended unemployment insurance to 99 weeks—that is, nearly 2 years, the highest level in history. While it certainly seems appropriate to help the jobless during recessions, this policy likely created an incentive to search longer for a new job, which, in turn, contributed to frictional unemployment.

Incentives

Government regulations on hiring and firing also contribute to frictional unemployment. Regulations on hiring include restrictions on who can and must be interviewed, paperwork that employers must complete for new hires, and additional tax documents that must be filed for employees. Regulations on firing include mandatory severance pay, written justification, and government fines. While these labor-market regulations may be instituted to help workers by giving them greater job security, they have unintended consequences. When it's difficult to hire employees, firms take longer to do so, which increases frictional unemployment. When it's difficult to fire employees, firms take greater care in hiring them. Again, the longer search time increases frictional unemployment.

ECONOMICS IN THE REAL WORLD

Employment, Italian Style

The intention of labor market restrictions may be to help workers, but too often workers themselves bear the costs, as fewer jobs are created. Consider the labor market regulations in Italy, as reported in the *Wall Street Journal*. The key point of the article relates to the inability to draw the Italian economy out of stagnation in 2012. The authors point to hiring regulations as one significant problem impeding employment:

Italian firms like Fiat would likely hire many more employees if hiring regulations weren't so stringent.

> Imagine you're an ambitious Italian entrepreneur, trying to make a go of a new business. You know you will have to pay at least two-thirds of your employees' social security costs. You also know you're going to run into problems once you hire your 16th employee, since that will trigger provisions making it either impossible or very expensive to dismiss a staffer.
>
> But there's so much more. Once you hire employee 11, you must submit an annual self-assessment to the national authorities outlining every possible health and safety hazard to which your employees might be subject. These include stress that is work-related or caused by age, gender and racial differences. You must also note all precautionary and individual measures to prevent risks, procedures to carry them out, the names of employees in charge of safety, as well as the physician whose presence is required for the assessment.
>
> Now say you decide to scale up. Beware again: Once you hire your 16th employee, national unions can set up shop. As your company grows, so does the number of required employee representatives, each of whom is entitled to eight hours of paid leave monthly to fulfill union or works-council duties. Management must consult these worker reps on everything from gender equality to the introduction of new technology.
>
> Hire No. 16 also means that your next recruit must qualify as disabled. By the time your firm hires its 51st worker, 7% of the payroll must be handicapped in some way, or else your company owes fees in-kind. During hard times, your company may apply for exemptions from these quotas—though as with everything in Italy, it's a toss-up whether it's worth it after the necessary paperwork.

> Once you hire your 101st employee, you must submit a report every two years on the gender dynamics within the company. This must include a tabulation of the men and women employed in each production unit, their functions and level within the company, details of compensation and benefits, and dates and reasons for recruitments, promotions and transfers, as well as the estimated revenue impact.*

From one view, regulations like these can be seen as helpful to employees. After all, we all want greater job benefits and protections. But such highly complex regulations clearly reduce an employer's incentives for hiring. The result is greater frictional unemployment. ✷

Cyclical Unemployment

Cyclical unemployment is unemployment caused by economic downturns.

The third type of unemployment, **cyclical unemployment**, occurs during economic downturns. This type of unemployment generates the greatest concern among economists and policymakers. It is the most serious type of unemployment because it means that jobs are not available for many people who want to work. And while both structural and frictional unemployment are consistent with a growing, evolving economy, the root cause of cyclical unemployment is an unhealthy economy. Unlike structural unemployment and frictional unemployment, cyclical unemployment is not considered a natural type of unemployment.

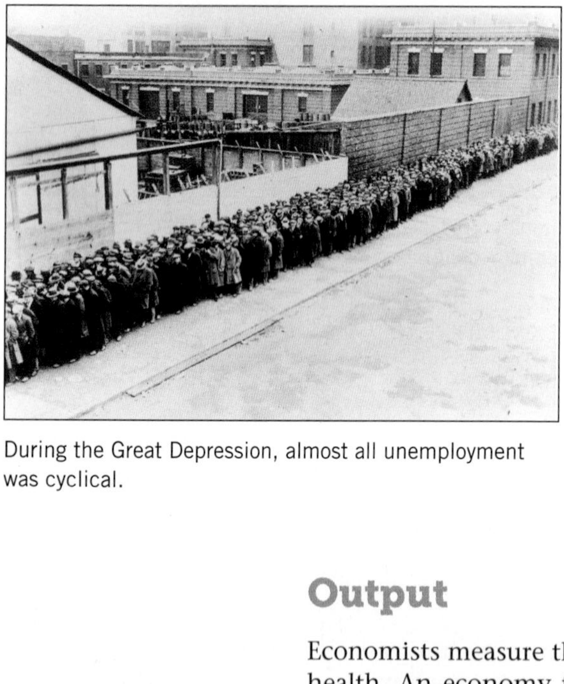

During the Great Depression, almost all unemployment was cyclical.

Although all three types of unemployment are temporary and disappear when workers are matched with jobs, the duration of cyclical unemployment is open-ended. No one knows how long a general macroeconomic downturn might last. Fortunately, recent recessions (downturns) in the United States have been fairly short. The Great Recession of 2007–2009 was unusually long, lasting for 18 months. This recession led to more cyclical unemployment than at any time in the previous 30 years.

Output

Economists measure the total output of an economy as a gauge of its overall health. An economy that produces a large amount of valuable output is a healthy economy. If output falls for a certain period, there's something wrong in the economy. The same is true for individuals. If you have a fever for a few days, your output goes down—you study less, you don't go to the gym, and you might call in sick for work. We care about measuring our nation's economic output because it gives us a good sense of the overall health of the economy, much like a thermometer that measures your body temperature can give you a general indication of your overall health. In this section, we introduce and explain how nations measure their economy's output.

* "Employment, Italian Style," *Wall Street Journal*, June 25, 2012.

PRACTICE WHAT YOU KNOW

Three Types of Unemployment: Which Type Is It?

Question: In each of the following situations, is the unemployment that occurs a result of cyclical, frictional, or structural changes? Explain your responses.

How long will you search for work?

a. Workers in a high-end restaurant are laid off when the establishment experiences a decline in demand during a recession (an economic downturn).

b. A group of automobile workers lose their jobs as a result of a permanent reduction in the demand for automobiles.

c. It takes a new college graduate three months to find his first job.

Answers:

a. *Cyclical changes.* Short-run fluctuations in the demand for workers are often the result of the ebb and flow of the economy. When the economy picks up, the laid-off workers can expect to be rehired.

b. *Structural changes.* These workers cannot expect their old jobs to return. Therefore, they must engage in retraining in order to re-enter the labor force.

c. *Frictional changes.* The recent college graduate has skills that the economy values, but finding an employer still takes time. This short-term job search process is a perfectly natural part of finding a job.

Production Equals Income

Nations and individuals that produce large amounts of highly valued output are relatively wealthy. Nations and individuals that don't produce much highly valued output are relatively poor. This is no coincidence. National output and national income are very closely linked—so closely, in fact, that they're essentially interchangeable.

Adding up the dollar sales is a way of measuring both production and income.

Let's say you open a coffee shop in your college town. You buy or rent the supplies and equipment you need to produce coffee—everything from coffee beans and espresso machines to electricity. You hire the workers you need to keep the business running. Using these resources, you produce output such as cappuccinos, espressos, and draft coffee. On the first day, you sell 600 different coffee drinks at an average price of $4 each, for a total of $2,400. This dollar figure is a measure of your firm's production, or *output*, on that day, and it's also a measure of the income you received. You use the income to pay for your resources and to pay yourself. If you sell even more coffee products on the second day, the income generated increases. If you sell less, the income goes down.

Gross domestic product (GDP) is the market value of all final goods and services produced within a country during a specific period.

The same holds true for nations. **Gross domestic product (GDP)** is the market value of all final goods and services produced within a nation during a specific time period. GDP is the primary measure used to gauge a nation's output. But it also measures a nation's income.

GDP is the sum of the value of all the output from coffee shops, doctor's offices, software firms, fast-food restaurants, and all the other firms that produce goods and services within a nation's borders. The sale of this output becomes income to the firms' owners and the resource suppliers. This dual function of GDP is part of the reason we focus on GDP as a barometer of the economy. When GDP goes up, national output and income are both higher. When GDP falls, the economy is producing less than before, and total national income is falling.

Two Additional Uses of GDP Data

GDP can be used as a measure of other things, not just output. Let's take a look at the uses we have for this piece of data.

Measuring Living Standards. Imagine two very different nations. In the first nation, people work long hours in physically taxing labor, yet their pay enables them to purchase only life's barest necessities—meager amounts of food, clothing, and shelter. In this nation, very few individuals can afford a high school education or health care from a trained physician. In the second nation, virtually no one starves, people tend to work in an air-conditioned environment, almost everyone graduates from high school, and many receive college degrees. The first nation experiences life similar to that in the United States two centuries ago; the second describes life in the United States today. Everyone would agree that living standards are higher in the United States today because most people can afford more of what they generally desire: goods, services, and leisure.

We can see these differences in living standards in GDP data. Indeed, GDP in the modern United States is much higher than it was in nineteenth-century America, meaning that (1) output and income today exceed that of 200 years ago, and (2) living standards are also higher. While not perfect, GDP offers us a way of measuring living standards across both time and place.

Let's look at the nations with highest GDP in the world. Table 10.2 lists the world's largest economies by GDP in 2013. Column 3 shows GDP for the top 15 economies, giving a picture of these nations' overall output and income. Total world GDP in 2013 was nearly $75 trillion, which means that the United States alone produced over 22% of all final goods and services in the world. The Chinese economy continues to increase its GDP rapidly and has moved up the list considerably over the last 20 years, but it is now stuck at number two. Despite the huge gains, China's GDP is still only 55% that of the United States.

Per capita GDP is gross domestic product (GDP) per person.

Although total GDP is important, it's not the best indicator of living standards for a typical person. Table 10.2 reveals that India and Canada had nearly the same amount of overall GDP in 2013. Yet the population of India was about 35 times the population of Canada. When we want to gauge living standards for an average person, we compute **per capita GDP**, or GDP per

TABLE 10.2

World's Largest Economies by GDP, 2013

(1) Rank	(2) Country	(3) 2013 GDP (billions of dollars)	(4) Per capita GDP (dollars)
1	United States	$16,800	$53,143
2	China	9,240	6,807
3	Japan	4,902	38,492
4	Germany	3,635	45,085
5	France	2,735	41,421
6	United Kingdom	2,522	39,351
7	Brazil	2,245	11,208
8	Russian Federation	2,097	14,612
9	Italy	2,071	34,619
10	India	1,877	1,499
11	Canada	1,825	50,910
12	Australia	1,561	67,468
13	Spain	1,358	29,118
14	South Korea	1,305	25,977
15	Mexico	1,261	10,307

Source: World Bank. All data are in 2013 U.S. dollars.

person (column 4 of Table 10.2). That is, we divide the country's total GDP by its population. When using this measure, the average Canadian appears to be much better off than the average Indian. GDP per person shows that there was almost $51,000 worth of GDP for every person in Canada in 2013, while there was less than $1,500 worth of GDP for every person in India in 2013. This observation raises an important point about macroeconomic data: the data you report can tell a very different story about an economy's health.

Measuring Economic Growth. We also use GDP data to measure *economic growth.* You can think of economic growth as changes in living standards over time. When economies grow, living standards rise. This result is evident in GDP data.

Figure 10.2 shows the change in per capita real GDP in the United States from 1960 to 2014. The overall positive slope of the curve indicates that living standards rose over the last 54 years in the United States, even though growth wasn't positive in every year. The data shows that income for the average person in 2014 was nearly three times what it was in 1960. So the typical person can now afford about three times as much education, food, vacations, air conditioning, houses, and cars as the average person in 1960.

You might notice that in this section we've added the word "real" to our discussion of GDP. Figure 10.2 plots *real* per capita GDP. Because we're now looking at data over time, we have to adjust the GDP data for changes in prices that occur over time. **Real GDP** is GDP adjusted for changes in prices.

Real GDP is gross domestic product (GDP) adjusted for changes in prices.

FIGURE 10.2

U.S. Per Capita Real GDP, 1960–2014

The positive slope in this graph indicates increased living standards in the United States since 1960. It shows that the average person earns significantly more income today, even after adjusting for price increases. Over this period, real GDP per person increased by an average of 2% per year.

Source: U.S. Bureau of Economic Analysis; U.S. Census Bureau.

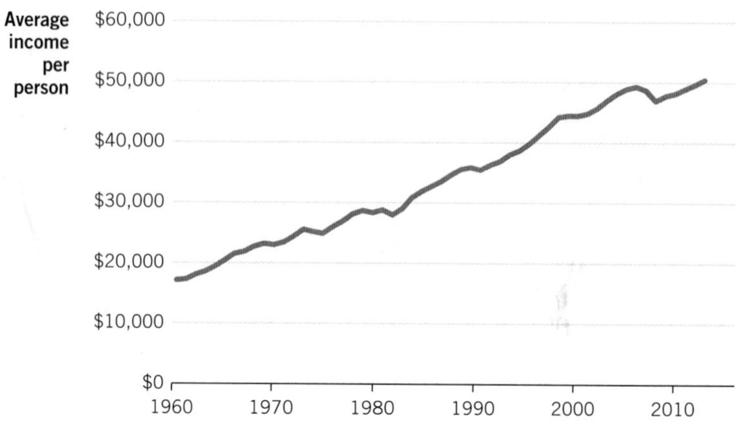

This is a very important distinction. Anytime we evaluate GDP figures over time, we must use real GDP. Otherwise, we aren't comparing data on an equal footing.

Let's look at some data for the United States. Table 10.3 shows two sets of GDP figures. Column 1 shows GDP from a particular year and reflects *nominal data*—that is, data not adjusted for price changes. Column 2 shows GDP adjusted for changes in price (what we call being adjusted for inflation).

TABLE 10.3

Adjusted and Non-adjusted U.S. GDP (Billions of Dollars)

Year	(1) Non-adjusted GDP	(2) Real GDP
1970	$1,076	$4,722
1975	$1,689	$5,385
1980	$2,862	$6,450
1985	$4,347	$7,594
1990	$5,980	$8,955
1995	$7,664	$10,175
2000	$10,285	$12,560
2005	$13,094	$14,234
2010	$14,964	$14,783

Real data is in 2009 U.S. dollars. This means that we use 2009 prices for all years, thereby removing the impact of price changes from year to year. You can use the prices from any year for comparison purposes. The Bureau of Economic Analysis, the source of this data, currently uses 2009.
Source: Bureau of Economic Analysis.

PRACTICE WHAT YOU KNOW

Three Uses of GDP Data: GDP as an Economic Barometer

What does GDP data tell us about Haiti?

Question: In each case described below, which of the three uses of GDP data was applied?

a. In 2011, many analysts claimed that India's economy began slowing as GDP growth declined from 8.4% in 2010 to 6.9% in mid-2011.

b. Nicaragua and Haiti are the poorest nations in the Western Hemisphere, with annual 2013 per capita GDP of only $1,367 and $473, respectively.

c. Italy's economy has slowed considerably over the past two decades, as evidenced by an average growth of real GDP of only 0.66% per year from 1993 to 2013.

Answers:

a. This case reflects a use of GDP data to measure national output.

b. This statement uses data to show living standards. The figures indicate that average Nicaraguans and Haitians have to live on very small amounts of income each year.

c. This observation considers growth rates over 20 years, which means that GDP data were applied to look at long-run economic growth.

Notice the difference. Both columns are growing through time, but the non-adjusted data begins at a much lower level because it specifies the GDP of that particular year *as reported in that year*. In contrast, all the data in column 2 are adjusted to remove the impact of price changes. Two issues are apparent in the non-adjusted column: output is rising *and* prices are rising, which skews our evaluation of the economy when we want to compare one year to another. As prices increase over time, the non-adjusted GDP increases more quickly because it rises as output increases *and* as prices increase. If we don't adjust GDP for these price changes, we can't tell whether output is increasing or if what appears to be an increase in output is just an increase in prices.

Economic growth is measured as the percentage change in real per capita GDP from one period to another. Notice that this measure starts with GDP data but then adjusts for both population growth and price increases. Given this definition, you should view Figure 10.2 as a picture of economic growth in the United States.

Economic growth is measured as the percentage change in real per capita gross domestic product (GDP) from one period to another.

Despite what you see in the U.S. real GDP data, you shouldn't presume that economic growth is automatic or even typical. Figure 10.3 shows the experience of six other nations with six distinct experiences. The per capita real GDP in Chile, Mexico, and Turkey rose significantly over the period,

FIGURE 10.3

Per Capita Real GDP in Six Nations, 1960–2013

Growth in real per capita GDP in six nations shows that growth is not guaranteed. The levels for Chile, Mexico, and Turkey more than doubled since 1960. And while India began to grow more recently, Kenya has grown very slowly and despite early growth, Nicaragua has hardly moved from its 1960 level.

Source: The World Bank: World Development Indicators.

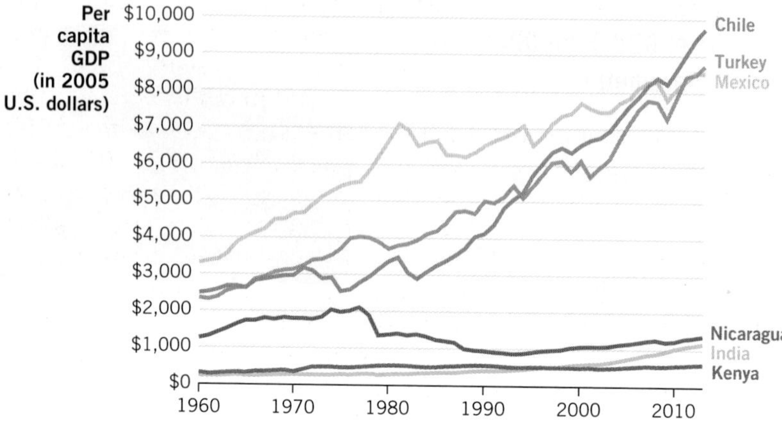

more than doubling since 1960. India's remained very low for many years and then recently began to grow. Sadly, the data for Nicaragua and Kenya indicate that citizens in these nations are hardly any better off now than they were in 1960.

Economic growth and its causes constitute a primary area of interest for macroeconomists. In Chapter 13, we will consider the factors that lead to growth like that which the United States, Poland, Turkey, and Mexico (and, more recently, India) have enjoyed. We will also consider why economies like those of Nicaragua and Kenya struggle to grow. Because real per capita GDP measures living standards, these issues are critical to real people's lives around the globe.

Inflation

Inflation is the growth in the overall level of prices in an economy.

The prices of goods and services almost always rise over time. **Inflation** is the growth in the overall level of prices in an economy.

There are two ways to view inflation. First, inflation occurs when there is a sustained increase in the general price level. At the macroeconomic level, we are concerned with all goods and services produced. As a result, we can no longer simply focus on the price of one good. Rather, we need to consider the prices of *all* things bought and sold. The fact that the price of gasoline goes up doesn't mean there is inflation. It could be that the price of video games falls to offset the rise in gas prices. Inflation happens only when prices *as a whole* increase. If inflation is occurring, the price of gas, video games, cereal, cellphone plans, and almost everything else would be increasing.

Purchasing power refers to how much your money can buy.

The second way to think about inflation is to focus on **purchasing power**, or how much your money can buy. If the dollars in your pocket can buy a lot, purchasing power is high. Your purchasing power increases when prices are lower. Purchasing power falls when prices rise. Thus, when inflation rises, your purchasing power falls.

Inflation affects consumers negatively because their incomes don't change as often as prices do. While prices can rise or fall every day, you aren't likely to get a raise that often to keep up with price changes. Let's look at an example.

Imagine that you go to sleep with $10 in your wallet. When you wake up, you find you now have $20. You stop at a donut shop to celebrate your sudden riches and notice that a donut now costs $1.50 instead of 75 cents. Curious . . . that's double the price it was yesterday! A cup of coffee also seems to be more expensive. Instead of $1.00 it now costs $2.00. In fact, everywhere you go, you find that prices have exactly doubled, matching the doubling of the money in your wallet. What we have here is a case of inflation. Prices have all risen. However, since the money you have to spend has also gone up, you haven't lost any purchasing power. If the money you have to spend were to instantly change to match the increase in prices, inflation wouldn't be much of a problem. However, now consider what happens when you stop to buy donuts and coffee, but you still have only $10 in your wallet and prices everywhere have doubled. The purchasing power of your money has fallen (in fact, it has been cut in half) because you cannot buy as much at the higher prices.

The Cause of Inflation

The printing press: the cause of inflation.

Inflation poses a problem. If purchasing power declines as prices rise, individuals have a more difficult time satisfying their needs and wants with their current income. Since inflation presents this serious macroeconomic cost, you might assume that there's significant debate about the causes of inflation. But the answer is much simpler. Economist Milton Friedman famously said, "Inflation is always and everywhere a monetary phenomenon, in the sense that it cannot occur without a more rapid increase in the quantity of money than in output." What he meant is that inflation is consistently caused by increases in a nation's money supply relative to the quantity of real goods and services in the economy.

Figure 10.4 shows average inflation rates and money-supply growth rates across 157 nations for the years 1991–2011. For practically all nations, the relationship appears to be almost one-to-one. The blue line is a hypothetical one-to-one line. This line represents the hypothetical situation in which a nation's average inflation rate is exactly equal to the average growth rate of the money supply. It is difficult to distinguish all 160 nations, because almost all of the data points (149 out of 160) are right on this one-to-one line, with inflation rates of less than 100%. The United States, for example, has an average annual inflation rate of 5.7% and a money-supply growth rate of 5.5%. In contrast, the few nations with even higher average inflation rates are easy to pick out. For example, in this sample the average inflation rates in Brazil were 323% per year (this is not a typo!), and that inflation stemmed from monetary growth rates of about 331%.

The intuition is straightforward: when the money supply in an economy grows *relative to the quantity of goods and services,* then it takes more money to buy any particular good or service. Money then becomes less valuable relative to goods and services—and this relationship constitutes inflation. The principle holds true regardless of the type of money used. For example, when

FIGURE 10.4

Inflation and Money Growth Rates in 157 Countries, 1991–2011

The relationship between inflation rates and money growth rates is virtually one-to-one for many countries over long periods. This connection applies to nations with low inflation rates and to nations with high inflation rates.

Source: World Bank.

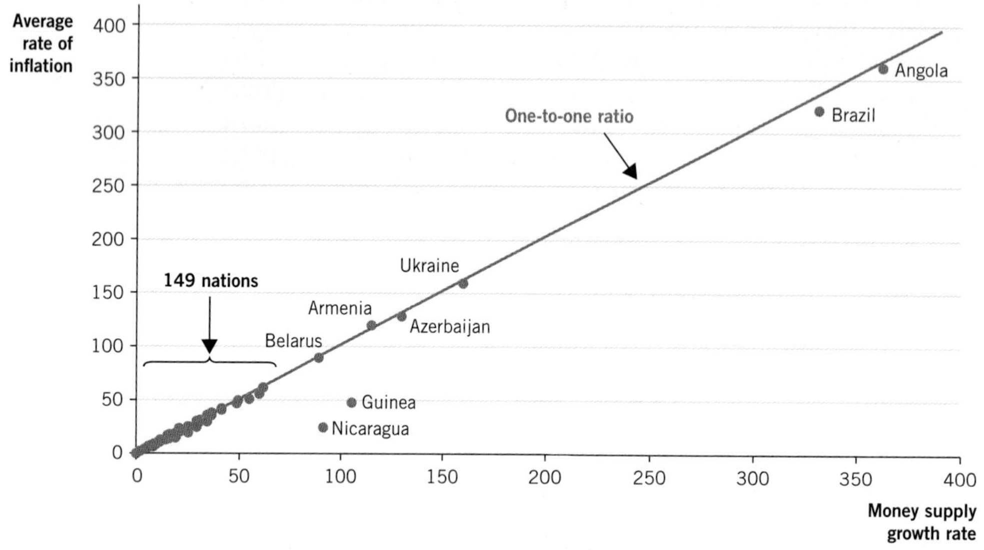

Spanish conquistadors brought gold back to Europe from Latin America in the sixteenth century, the supply of money (gold) in Europe increased, and the result was inflation.

How do employment, growth, and inflation interact in terms of economic stability? We want people to be employed. If there aren't enough jobs to go around, we aren't using our resources very well and our economy is less productive than it could be. When we aren't productive, economic growth will slow down. GDP per person may even stagnate, and quality of life will decrease. A government policy to help growth also usually helps employment, and policies to promote employment often stimulate growth. The problem is inflation. We want inflation to be low so that prices aren't rising too quickly and so that purchasing power stays strong. However, when economies grow too quickly, they can experience inflation. When employment increases, people have more money. They want to spend it, but if there aren't enough things to spend money on, prices get bid up. The result is inflation and a decrease in purchasing power.

Conclusion

Employment, economic growth, and inflation are the key macroeconomic measures that most economists and policymakers watch. We want people to be working and the economy to be expanding. Keeping prices under control (that is, managing inflation) helps to maintain the purchasing power of money. However, when dealing with the macroeconomy, there's one simple fact that stymies the goal of macroeconomic stabilization: with so many things going on, it is impossible to fully coordinate the economy.

This chapter has introduced the basics of macroeconomics. While there are other components of the macroeconomy to consider, for now we will keep our attention on the three major macro variables of unemployment, growth, and inflation. To understand these better, in the next chapter we will examine how these statistics are calculated and how economists use them to explain the current state of economic health.

ANSWERING THE BIG QUESTIONS

How is macroeconomics different from microeconomics?

- Microeconomics is the study of individuals and firms, but macroeconomics considers the entire economy.
- Many of the topics in both areas of study are the same; these include income, employment, and output. But the macro perspective is much broader than the micro perspective.

What are the three major topics in macroeconomics?

- Three key topics, or variables, in macroeconomics are employment, economic growth, and inflation.
- Unemployment may be structural, frictional, or cyclical.
- Economists use gross domestic product (GDP) to measure output, but GDP also helps to measure standard of living and economic growth.
- Inflation is the growth in the overall level of prices in an economy, and it leads to reduced purchasing power. Inflation is tied to growth in the money supply.

ECONOMICS FOR LIFE

Understanding the Great Depression in Today's Context

You lived through the Great Recession, the major economic downturn of 2007–2009. Perhaps it affected you personally. Certainly, many people experienced hardships as a result of the economic downturn. However, very few of us were forced to move into shanties on the street as a result of the downturn.

But the Great Depression was different. Living through it scarred an entire generation of Americans. Perhaps your grandparents or great-grandparents were part of this generation. Now might be a good time to talk to them and ask how their life changed during the 1930s.

Many American families lost their homes and jobs during the Depression. The best remaining alternative for many in some parts of the country was sharecropping, or living on a farm and harvesting the crops on behalf of the owners. For other families, the best available living arrangement was in shantytowns outside of major cities. These shantytowns became known as Hoovervilles, named after President Hoover. Although homelessness and unemployment are still issues for some people in the United States, the extent of the problems is far smaller today—and was far smaller during the Great Recession—than it was during the Great Depression.

We can use a familiar consumer item to illustrate the difference between the two economic contractions. During the Great Recession years of 2007–2009, the number of Starbucks locations in the United States grew from 10,684 to 11,128.* Thus, a chain of coffee shops that sell basic drinks for about $4 each actually expanded during the Great Recession. Yes, the coffee is very good, but that could never have happened during the Great Depression.

Now think again about how the Great Recession affected you or someone you know. How much more extreme might those effects have been during the Great Depression?

*"Starbucks Company Statistics," Statistic Brain, September 2012, statisticbrain.com.

Unemployed workers gather together in New York City, December 1937. They have a Christmas tree near their shanty.

Stores like this one would not have survived the Great Depression.

CONCEPTS YOU SHOULD KNOW

creative destruction (p. 285)
cyclical unemployment (p. 290)
economic growth (p. 295)
economic stability (p. 284)
frictional unemployment (p. 287)
gross domestic product (GDP) (p. 292)
inflation (p. 296)
per capita GDP (p. 292)
purchasing power (p. 296)
real GDP (p. 293)
structural unemployment (p. 286)
unemployment (p. 284)
unemployment insurance (p. 288)
unemployment rate (u) (p. 284)

QUESTIONS FOR REVIEW

1. Explain the relationship between output and income for both an individual and an entire economy.
2. A friend of yours is reading a financial blog and comes to you for some advice about GDP. She wants to know what "real" GDP is. How would you explain the concept to her?
3. Until the late 1960s, most economists assumed that less unemployment was always preferable to more unemployment. Define and explain the two types of unemployment that are consistent with a dynamic, growing economy.
4. What type of unemployment is affected when online job search engines reduce the time necessary for job searches? Does this outcome affect the natural rate of unemployment? If so, how?
5. How do economists use GDP to measure various aspects of the economy?
6. What is the cause of inflation? What does inflation do to the purchasing power of money?

STUDY PROBLEMS (* *solved at the end of the section*)

1. In his song "Allentown," Billy Joel sings about the demise of the steel and coal industry in Pennsylvania. Why do you think the loss of manufacturing jobs was so difficult on the workers in areas like Allentown and other parts of the Midwest where manufacturing was once the largest employer? What type of unemployment is the song about?
2. Visit www.bls.gov and search through the tables on unemployment to answer the following questions:
   a. What is the current national unemployment rate for the United States?
   b. What is the current unemployment rate among people most like you? (Consider your age, sex, and ethnicity.)
3. * You have a friend who is interested in European history. In her reading, she comes across a statistic showing that the German inflation rate after World War I was 29,500%. Explain what this rapid rate of inflation meant for prices in Germany and the value of the German currency.
4. A friend who knows of your interest in economics comes up to you after reading the latest GDP data and excitedly exclaims, "Did you see that nominal GDP rose from $17 trillion to $17.5 trillion?" What should you tell your friend about this news?

✱ 5. Of the topics in the following list, which are macro and which are micro?
   a. Caterpillar International expands its line of earth-mover equipment.
   b. The local fruit market closes for the winter and lays off its entire staff.
   c. The inflation rate in Japan falls below zero.
   d. Gross domestic product for the small country of Belize was unexpectedly high.
   e. The closing of one of two Mexican restaurants creates a monopoly for the remaining store.
   f. Frictional unemployment in Canada edged up last year, but structural unemployment fell.

SOLVED PROBLEMS

3. A rate of inflation this high means that prices would have risen very, very quickly. In this case, prices were doubling every 3.7 days! Of course, with prices going up this fast, the value of the German currency was falling precipitously. There are photos of people using their money to wallpaper their homes during this time period because when inflation gets this high, money becomes utterly worthless.

5.a. Because this example involves the production decisions for a single company, it is a micro topic.
   b. Unemployment is a significant macroeconomic topic. But this example involves a single business. It is therefore a micro topic.
   c. When we're discussing a national statistic like the inflation rate, we're talking about a macro topic. (And yes, an inflation rate below zero is indeed possible. Inflation less than zero is *deflation*.)
   d. Regardless of the size of the country, when talking about GDP we're dealing with macro data.
   e. We are dealing with a particular firm in a particular industry (food service): this is a micro topic. Additionally, a business with monopoly power is a very micro topic.
   f. Discussing the types of unemployment prevalent in a country means we're talking about a macro topic.

Schools of Thought in Macroeconomics

APPENDIX

10A

A **school of thought** is a cohesive way of thinking about a subject. For example, there are many schools of thought in psychology; behaviorism, functionalism, psychoanalysis, and cognitivism are different ways that psychologists help people understand themselves better. Political science also has various schools of thought, including communism, Marxism, democracy, and libertarianism. Here we will examine two economic schools of thought about the economy as a whole: classical economics and Keynesian economics. Other economic schools of thought focus on particular aspects of the macroeconomy, such as the role of money (monetarist school) or how the incentives facing political decision-makers affect their choices (public-choice school).

A **school of thought** is a cohesive way of thinking about a subject.

Classical Economics

Classical economics is a school of thought that stresses the importance of aggregate supply and generally believes that the economy can adjust back to full employment equilibrium on its own.

The classical school of economics is based on the writings of a group of economists, most notably Adam Smith, David Ricardo, and John Stuart Mill. From the mid-eighteenth century to the mid-1920s, the precepts of the classical school as they related to macroeconomics can be boiled down to four main points. Foremost among these is the idea that markets effectively distribute goods and services. Interference in the markets is a recipe for disaster because, as we have seen in earlier chapters, fewer people would be served and social welfare would fall.

The second point is closely related to the first. Because markets will rapidly restore order when the economy contracts, the government does not need to use its power to tax or spend to help the economy. The term **laissez faire** means "allow to do" in French. Basically, laissez faire implies that business should be allowed to do what it does without government interference. In fact, beyond a few specific tasks, government should not be involved in the macroeconomy. Under the principle of laissez faire, using tax policy or spending to stimulate growth is unthinkable, or at least highly inadvisable.

Laissez faire means "allow to do" in French. The term implies that governments should allow firms to conduct their business without interference.

The third major principle of the classical school focuses on what government *should* do. If policy affecting the economy is passed, it should be designed to encourage businesses to do more business. Thus, government policy should be targeted toward the supply side of the markets. Classical economists believe that stimulating business leads to more workers being hired, which then increases output economy-wide.

Finally, the classical school believes that money is useful for facilitating trade, but the use of money as a policy tool has no lasting effects and therefore should not be used to stimulate economic growth. This belief is connected to the idea that printing money causes inflation. Eventually, everyone will experience wage growth, and any gains from trying to increase spending by increasing the money supply will dissipate. Essentially, the classical school says that even if prices do rise, eventually incomes will rise as well and everything will be as it was. At an individual level, you might have more in your wallet, but price increases offset the increase in your income.

Let's now look at how the Great Depression changed economists' view of the world from one based on the classical understanding of the economy to one dominated by Keynesian (pronounced KANES-ee-an) economics.

Prior to the stock market crash of 1929 that initiated the Great Depression in the United States, economists typically assumed that markets would adjust rather quickly to restore order in the wake of an economic slowdown. While the pain of a recession in the short run was acute for some people, these unpleasant periods usually lasted less than a year and were followed by robust growth. There was no national economic policy, nor was there much inclination to extend the role of government into the markets. Unlike previous downturns, though, things didn't improve as 1929 moved into 1930 and 1931 and 1932. In the light of new theories from British economist John Maynard Keynes, the belief that the government had no role to play began to erode. Keynesian economics differed from the prevailing classical approach in significant ways. This new approach moved government from the role of disinterested bystander to the star of the show.

Keynesian Economics

Keynesian economics is a school of thought that stresses the importance of aggregate demand and generally believes that the economy needs help in moving back to full employment equilibrium.

John Maynard Keynes studied economics at Cambridge University in England. He learned the classical version of economics because there weren't other points of view at the time, but he wasn't in full agreement with the precepts of classical economics. Keynesian economics has evolved somewhat since Keynes died in 1946; however, the basics of this perspective are essentially intact. Comparing them to the classical principles, you will see a set of opposites.

Keynes had a much dimmer view of the market than the classical theorists did. He believed that markets do not reach equilibrium quickly. In fact, he believed that wages and prices could be very slow to adjust to market conditions. The result could be markets producing too much or too little output relative to what was best for society. Because markets are slow to react, Keynes envisioned a much more expansive role for government in the economy. In particular, he believed that government should be much more involved in spending to stimulate economic activity. Remember, Keynes's ideas took root during the Great Depression, when unemployment rates were rising and economic output was falling. People weren't getting back to work, so households couldn't spend. Keynes suggested that the government should spend money, even if it had to borrow to do so, a policy known as **deficit spending**. Keynes thought that the consequences of not balancing the budget would pale in comparison to not helping people. Put another way, the opportunity cost of not spending was an increase in unemployment. We'll talk more about government budgets, debts, and deficits in Chapter 17, but for now it's enough to remember that non-wartime deficit spending became the norm as a result of Keynes's ideas.

Deficit spending means borrowing money in order to spend it.

Opportunity cost

Unlike the classical school, which directed policy toward the supply side of the economy, Keynes was much more interested in the demand side. His main point was that economic output begins with households wanting things. If

The Big Disagreements in Macroeconomics

ECONOMICS IN THE MEDIA

"Fear the Boom and the Bust"

This highly original rap video imagines how two giants of economics, F. A. Hayek and John Maynard Keynes, would defend their ideas to the current generation. F. A. Hayek represents the classical economists. Here is one of the best lines:

> We've been going back and forth for a century
> **[KEYNES]** I want to steer markets,
> **[HAYEK]** I want them set free
> There's a boom and bust cycle and good reason to fear it

It's Keynes versus Hayek!

F. A. Hayek was the twentieth century's most significant defender of free markets. In 1943, he wrote *The Road to Serfdom*, a book that cautions against central planning. Hayek characterizes markets as having the ability to organize spontaneously, to the benefit of an economy. *The Road to Serfdom* appeared in print just a few years after John Maynard Keynes published his *General Theory* in 1936. How could these two giants of economics see the world so differently?

Hayek, who received the 1974 Nobel Prize in Economics, lived long enough to observe that economics had come full circle. His Nobel acceptance speech was titled "The Pretense of Knowledge." In the talk, he criticized the economics profession for being too quick to adopt Keynesian ideas. Keynes had argued that the economy moves slowly to long-run equilibrium. Hayek countered that efforts to stimulate demand presume that economists know what they are doing; he argued that just because we can build elaborate macroeconomic models doesn't mean that the models can anticipate every change in the economy. Hayek pointed to the high inflation rates and high unemployment rates of the 1970s as evidence that the Keynesian model was incomplete. Accordingly, he concluded, it would be best to put our faith in the one thing that all economists generally agree on: that eventually the economy will naturally return to full employment output levels.

"Fear the Boom and the Bust" presents the views of Hayek and Keynes to make you think. While there are many references in the rap that you might not "get" just yet, watch it anyway (and tell your friends to watch it). The subject it treats is an important, ongoing debate, and one of the goals of your study of economics is to acquire the information you need to decide for yourself what approach is best for the economy.

they don't have an income, they cannot buy things and firms will shut down. Thus, for production to increase, demand has to increase. If households don't have incomes, then the government should either provide jobs for them or spend the money itself.

Finally, Keynes rejected the idea that monetary policy—that is, central bank policy that affects the money supply—doesn't affect the health of the market. From the Keynesian perspective, increasing the availability of money stimulates demand. The impact of additional demand, even if only in the short run, was important enough to justify some inflation. If income and prices eventually double, there would be at least some short-term gain to consumers during the time they have more money in their wallets (but before prices increase). The result: consumers buy more, and economic activity increases.

TABLE 10A.1

Comparing Classical and Keynesian Economics

	Classical school	Keynesian school
View of markets	When economic conditions change, markets will adjust quickly.	Markets are slow to adjust. Markets cannot keep up with the pace of economic activity and may need supervision.
Role of government	A laissez-faire approach to the market allows businesses to operate without much government interference.	Government's role is much more extensive. Government should be involved in the macroeconomy, especially when times are bad. Deficit spending is acceptable and even encouraged.
Market focus	Supply side. Businesses hire workers, so policy should encourage business activity so that households have income. Then households can go and spend it.	Demand side. Businesses need customers. If customers don't have incomes, they can't buy and businesses won't produce. If necessary, government can be the buyer.
Role of money in policy	Printing of money will only cause prices to rise. Eventually, incomes will catch up and there will be no difference in how much people can afford. Other than higher prices, nothing changes.	Printing of money can stimulate demand in the short run. If there is more money available, people can spend and economic growth will follow.

Table 10A.1 compares the four major differences between the classical and Keynesian schools of thought. Clearly, these two schools find themselves far apart on some important issues. Economic schools of thought typically develop in response to a problem, but no school has all of the answers all of the time. As a result, economic disagreements continue.

PRACTICE WHAT YOU KNOW

The Big Debates: Guess Which View

Question: Below are three statements. Which type of economist, Keynesian or classical, would likely support each statement? Explain your answers.

a. "If you want to help the economy, you should increase your spending."

b. "Government policy should focus on counteracting short-run fluctuations in the economy."

c. "Government policy should not intervene in the economy because the economy can correct itself."

Which type of economist would recommend this shopping trip?

Answer:

a. *Keynesian.* The Keynesian approach focuses on spending as the fundamental factor in the economy.

b. *Keynesian.* The Keynesian approach emphasizes inherent instability in the macroeconomy and the resulting need for government action to counteract any ups or downs in the economy.

c. *Classical.* The classical approach emphasizes price flexibility, which means that the economy can correct itself.

CONCEPTS YOU SHOULD KNOW

classical economics (p. 303)
deficit spending (p. 304)
Keynesian economics (p. 304)
laissez faire (p. 303)
school of thought (p. 303)

CHAPTER 11

Measuring the Macroeconomy, Unemployment, and Inflation

MISCONCEPTION

Measuring the macroeconomy is an exact science.

Economists like to think of themselves as scientists. They construct elaborate models to test theories, and they use the models to develop national policies. These policies will affect the lives of millions or perhaps billions of people. However, model-building and policy recommendations are only as good as the data that economists use. Macro-level data often presents a number of challenges.

The three major macroeconomic variables that we discussed in the previous chapter—unemployment, output, and inflation—are all based on data collected over time. Each of these measures provides a snapshot of an economy's health, but each has potentially serious shortcomings. What is and is not included in the data will affect the measure. For example, in the case of output, measurements tend to vastly undercount production. Unemployment is typically undercounted as well. Inflation might be either overstated or understated.

If we know these problems exist, why do we rely on this data? More important, why don't we fix it? The simple answer is that the data used is the best that we have. As you will see, collecting data at the macro level is a complicated process. Fortunately, despite their shortcomings, the macroeconomic measures that we use often provide a close approximation of the actual situation.

One of the most difficult things in macroeconomics is trying to measure economic activity.

BIG QUESTIONS

- **How is GDP computed?**
- **What are some shortcomings of GDP data?**
- **What can we learn from unemployment data?**
- **How is inflation measured?**
- **What problems does inflation bring?**

How Is GDP Computed?

As we learned in Chapter 10, output is measured by calculating gross domestic product (GDP). Recall that GDP is *the market value of all final goods and services produced within a country during a specific period.* In this section, we break down the components of GDP in order to give you a deeper understanding of what is counted in GDP and what is not.

Counting Market Values

Nations produce a wide variety of goods and services, which are measured in various units. Computation of GDP literally requires the addition of apples and oranges, as well as every other final good and service produced in a nation. How can we add everything from cars to corn to haircuts to gasoline to prescription drugs in a way that makes sense? Certainly, we can't just add quantities. For example, in 2013 the United States produced about 11 million motor vehicles and about 13.9 billion bushels of corn. Looking only at quantities, one might conclude that because the nation produced about 1,260 bushels of corn for every car, corn production is much more important to the U.S. economy than cars are. But of course this is wrong, because a bushel of corn isn't worth nearly as much as a car.

When you visit the grocery store, you often purchase both goods (groceries) and services (clerking and bagging).

To add corn and cars and the other goods and services that make up GDP, economists use market values. That is, they include not only the quantity data but also the price of the good or service. Figure 11.1 offers an example with fairly realistic data. If corn pro-

FIGURE 11.1

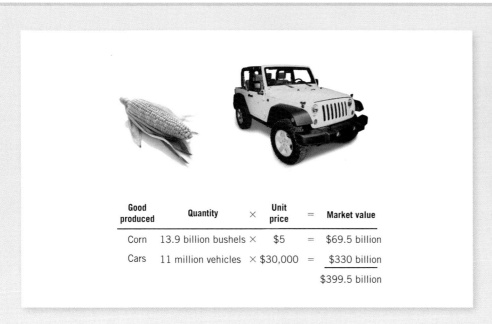

Good produced	Quantity	×	Unit price	=	Market value
Corn	13.9 billion bushels	×	$5	=	$69.5 billion
Cars	11 million vehicles	×	$30,000	=	$330 billion
					$399.5 billion

Using Market Values to Compute GDP

GDP reflects market values added together for many types of goods. In this simple example, the contribution to GDP from corn production is $69.5 billion and the contribution from car production is $330 billion.

duction is 13.9 billion bushels and these bushels sell for $5 each, the contribution of corn to GDP is 13.9 billion × $5 = $69.5 billion. If car production is 11 million vehicles and each car sells for $30,000, the contribution of cars to GDP is $330 billion. If corn and cars were the only goods produced in a given year, GDP would be $69.5 billion + $330 billion = $399.5 billion.

Including Final Goods and Services

The composition of U.S. GDP has evolved over time. In the past, the dominant industries in the United States were manufactured goods such as tractors, steel, and blenders. Today, in contrast, a majority of U.S. GDP comes from services. **Services** are outputs that provide benefits without the production of a tangible product. Consider a service like a visit to your doctor for a physical. The doctor examines you and offers some medical advice, but you leave with no tangible output. Other services include entertainment, financial, transportation, education, and technology services.

A **service** is an output that provides benefits without the production of a tangible product.

Figure 11.2 shows services as a percentage of U.S. GDP since 1960. As you can see, the share of services grew from 50% in 1960 to about 70% in 2010.

Note that the definition of GDP refers to *final* goods and services. But not all spending on goods and services is included in GDP. To see why, consider all the spending involved in building a single good—say, a cell phone. Table 11.1 outlines some intermediate steps required to produce a cell phone that sells for $199. In the process of producing this phone, the manufacturer uses many intermediate goods. **Intermediate goods** are goods that firms repackage or bundle with other goods for sale at a later stage in the production process. For example, the cell phone's outer case and keyboard are intermediate goods because the phone manufacturer combines them with other

An **intermediate good** is a good that firms repackage or bundle with other goods for sale at a later stage in the production process.

FIGURE 11.2

Services as a Share of U.S. GDP, 1960–2010

A century ago, the U.S. economy produced mostly manufactured goods; but this trend has shifted in recent decades, and now services account for most U.S. output.

Source: U.S. Bureau of Economic Analysis.

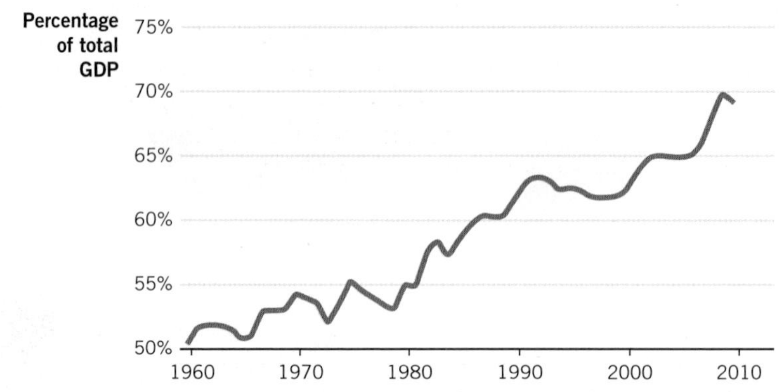

A **final good** is a good sold to final users.

This Intel processor is an intermediate good, buried inside your computer.

intermediate goods, such as the operating system, to produce the cell phone, which is the final good. **Final goods** are goods that are sold to final users. The sale of the cell phone is included as part of GDP, but the value of the intermediate goods is not.

What happens if we count the value added during each intermediate step in making a cell phone? We start with the outer case and keyboard, which costs $5 to produce. Once the case and keyboard have been purchased, the internal component hardware, which costs $10, must be installed, bringing the value of the phone to $15. The operating system software, which costs $15, is then installed, raising the value to $30. Next, a service provider purchases the phone and connects it to a network; this costs another $49, raising the phone's value to $79. Finally, the phone is sold to the consumer for a retail price of $199 reflecting a $120 production cost for transacting the retail sale. The final value in this string of events, the retail price, is the true value that the cell phone creates in the economy. If we counted the value of each

TABLE 11.1

Intermediate Steps in Cellphone Production

Steps	Cost of each production step (in dollars)	Cumulative value of completed steps (in dollars)
1. Assemble outer case and keyboard	$5	$5
2. Prepare internal component hardware	10	15
3. Install operating system software	15	30
4. Connect to network	49	79
5. Transact retail sale	120	199
Total	$199	$338

intermediate step, we would arrive at a total of $338, which would overstate the phone's value in the economy because it sells for only $199.

We cannot get an accurate measure of GDP by summing all the sales made throughout the economy during the year, because so many of those sales reflect intermediate steps in the production process. In our example of the cell phone, the operating system (OS) is part of the phone, and its value is included as part of the phone in the final sale. If we counted the sale of the OS to the phone manufacturer and then again as a part of the phone itself, we would be double-counting and thus overstating GDP.

Within a Country

The word "domestic" in the phrase "gross domestic product" is important. GDP includes only goods and services produced domestically, or within the physical borders of a nation. The output of foreign-owned firms that is produced inside the United States is included in U.S. GDP, but the output of U.S. firms that is produced overseas is included in the GDP of the overseas nation. For example, Nike is a U.S. firm that produces shoes in Thailand. Thus, all the Nike shoes produced in Thailand count as GDP for Thailand.

Nike shoes produced in Thailand count as GDP for Thailand.

Including Only Production from a Particular Period

GDP only counts goods and services that are produced during a given period. Goods or services produced in earlier years don't count in a current year's GDP. For instance, when a new car is produced, it adds to GDP in the year it is sold. However, a used car that is resold doesn't count in current GDP since it was already counted in GDP for the year when it was produced and sold the first time. GDP measures production. If we counted a used car (or any other used good or service) when it was resold, we would be counting that car as part of GDP twice—double-counting—even though it was produced only once.

Looking at GDP as Different Types of Expenditures

In this section, we look more closely at different categories of goods and services included in GDP. The U.S. Bureau of Economic Analysis (BEA) is the U.S. government agency that tallies GDP data in a process known as *national income accounting*.* The BEA breaks GDP into four major categories:

*The web site for the U.S. Bureau of Economic Analysis is www.bea.gov. Here you will find data covering GDP and all of the component parts of GDP.

consumption (C), investment (I), government purchases (G), and net exports (NX). These four categories represent four groups of actors purchasing goods and services in an economy. Households consume, businesses invest, governments spend, and foreigners buy things produced domestically by other countries. Using this framework, it is possible to express GDP as the following equation:

(Equation 11.1)
$$GDP = C + I + G + NX$$

Table 11.2 details the composition of U.S. GDP in 2014. For that year, total GDP was over $17,400 billion (or $17.4 trillion). To get a sense of what that amount represents, imagine creating a path of 17.4 trillion one-dollar bills. That would be enough to cover every U.S. highway, street, and county road more than twice! U.S. GDP is more than triple the GDP of every other nation except China.

Looking at Table 11.2, you can see that consumption is by far the largest component of GDP, followed by government purchases and then by investment. Note that the value of net exports is negative. This negative value occurs because the United States imports more goods than it exports. Let's take a closer look at each of these four components of GDP.

Consumption (C) is the purchase of final goods and services by households, excluding new housing.

Non-durable consumption goods are goods that are consumed over a short period.

Durable consumption goods are goods that are consumed over a long period.

Investment (I) is private spending on tools, plant, and equipment used to produce future output, along with purchases of newly built houses.

TABLE 11.2

Composition of U.S. GDP, 2014

Category	Individual expenditures (billions of dollars)	Total expenditures per category (billions of dollars)	Percentage of GDP
Consumption (C)		**$11,930.3**	68.5%
Durable goods	$1,302.5		
Non-durable goods	2,666.2		
Services	7,961.7		
Investment (I)		**2,851.6**	16.4%
Fixed investment	2,769.6		
Change in business inventories	82.0		
Government purchases (G)		**3,175.2**	18.2%
Federal	1,219.2		
State and local	1,956.1		
Net exports (NX)		**–538.2**	-3.1%
Exports	2,337		
Imports	–2,875.2		
Total GDP		**$17,418.9**	100.0%

Source: U.S. Bureau of Economic Analysis. Some totals may not add up due to rounding.

Consumption (C)

Consumption (C) is the purchase of final goods and services by households, with the exception of new housing. Most people spend a large majority of their income on consumption goods and services. Consumption goods include everything from groceries to your cellphone plan. You can see in Table 11.2 that services are a very big portion of consumption spending. They include things such as haircuts, doctor's visits, and help from a real-estate agent.

Consumption goods can be divided into two categories: non-durable and durable. **Non-durable consumption goods** are consumed over a short period, and **durable consumption goods** are consumed over a long period. This distinction is important when the economy swings back and forth between good times and bad times. Sales of durable goods—for example, automobiles, appliances, and computers—are subject to significant cyclical fluctuations that correlate with the health of the economy. Since durable goods are generally designed to last for many years, consumers tend to purchase more of these when the economy is strong. When the economy is weak, consumers put off purchases of durables and make those that they already have last longer—for example, by working with an old computer for another year rather than replacing it with a new model right away. However, non-durables don't last very long, so consumers must often purchase them regardless of economic conditions.

Ice cream cones count as non-durable consumption goods.

Refrigerators count as durable consumption goods.

Investment (I)

When you hear the word "investment," you likely think of savings or stocks and bonds. But in economics, **investment (I)** refers to private spending on the tools, physical plant, and equipment used to produce future output. Investment can be something as simple as the purchase of a shovel, a tractor, or a personal computer to help a small business produce goods and services for its customers. But investment also includes more complex endeavors such as the construction of large factories. For example, when Horizon Wind builds a new wind farm in Ohio, it is making an investment. When Walmart builds a new warehouse, that expense is an investment. And when a family purchases a newly built house, that expense also counts as an investment. This way of accounting for house purchases may seem odd, since most of us think of a home purchase as something that is consumed; but in the national income accounts, such a purchase counts as an investment. Once again, though, we only count the house the first time it is sold. Every other time the home is re-sold, it doesn't add to GDP. That would be re-counting.

Investment also includes all purchases by businesses that add to their inventories. For example, in preparation for Christmas, an electronics retailer will order more TVs, cameras, and computers. GDP rises when business inventories increase. GDP is calculated this way because we want to measure output in the period when it is produced. Investment in inventory is just one more way that firms spend today to increase output in the future.

When firms buy tools to aid in production, they are making an investment.

Government Spending (G)

Government spending (G) includes spending by all levels of government on final goods and services.

National, state, and local governments purchase many goods and services. These purchases are included in GDP as **government spending (G)**, which includes spending by all levels of government on final goods and services. For example, every government employee receives a salary, which is considered a part of GDP. Similarly, governments spend money by purchasing buildings, equipment, and supplies from private-sector firms. Governments also make expenditures on public-works projects, including national defense, highway construction, schools, and post offices.

Transfer payments are payments made by the government to groups or individuals when no good or service is received in return.

However, one form of government outlay does not count in GDP. **Transfer payments** that the government makes to households, such as welfare payments or unemployment insurance, are not direct purchases of new goods and services. These transfer payments merely move income from one group to another. For instance, Social Security payments made to your grandparents are movements of money from those who are working to those who are retired. This isn't production; it's just moving money around. Since GDP measures productive activities, the money given to Social Security recipients, as well as money spent for welfare recipients, Medicare, and food stamps, is not included in GDP.

Exports are goods and services produced domestically but purchased and used abroad.

Net Exports (NX)

Imports are goods and services produced abroad but purchased and used domestically.

Net exports (NX) are exports minus imports of final goods and services.

Because we use spending to measure GDP, it's important that we include spending only on goods *produced in the country*. Therefore, spending by people in other countries who buy things made in the United States is counted in GDP. We include **exports** as we calculate GDP because they're produced in the United States but bought by people in other countries. However, people in the United States buy many things made in other countries. These **imports** are produced elsewhere but are used domestically within the United States. Because our goal is to measure domestic production accurately, GDP includes only **net exports (NX)**, which are exports minus imports of final goods and services. We can write the calculation of net exports in equation form as:

(Equation 11.2)
$$\text{net exports (NX)} = \text{exports} - \text{imports}$$

When spending on imports is larger than spending on exports, net exports are negative. Net exports are typically negative for the United States.

Notice that imports enter the GDP calculations as a negative value:

(Equation 11.3)
$$\text{GDP} = \text{C} + \text{I} + \text{G} + (\text{exports} - \text{imports})$$

From this equation, it would be easy to conclude that imports are harmful to an economy because they seem to reduce GDP. However, adding the different components together (C, I, G, and NX) in the process of national income accounting really is just that—accounting. More imports coming in means more goods and services for people in this nation. Other things being equal, imports do not make us worse off.

As we've said, GDP reflects market values, and these values include both price and quantity information. Market values enable us to add together many types of goods. At the same time, market values rely on prices, which can rise when inflation occurs. What if the prices of both cars and corn rise but the quantities produced remain unchanged? In that case, the GDP figure will rise even though the production level stays the same. This is why we need to compute real GDP by adjusting for inflation. Recall from Chapter 10 that *real GDP* is GDP adjusted for changes in prices.

Real GDP: Adjusting GDP for Price Changes

According to the U.S. Bureau of Economic Analysis, in 2004 the nation's economy produced a GDP of $12.3 trillion. Just over a decade later, in 2014, it produced over $17.4 trillion. That's a 41.9% increase in just ten years. Is that really possible? Think about this question in long-run historical terms. Is it possible that the nation's economy grew to $12.3 trillion over more than two centuries, but then just ten years later grew to over $17.4 trillion despite the economic downturn of 2007–2009? If we look more closely, we'll see that much of the recent increase in GDP is actually due to inflation.

The raw GDP data, based on market values, is computed on the basis of the prices of goods and services current at the time the GDP data is produced. Economists refer to these prices as the *current prices*. The GDP calculated from current prices is called **nominal GDP.** Figure 11.3 compares U.S. nominal and real GDP from 2004 to 2014. Notice that nominal GDP rises much faster than real GDP does. While nominal GDP rose by 41.9%, real GDP increased by 17.1%. The difference between these percentages reflects inflation.

Nominal GDP is GDP measured in current prices and not adjusted for inflation.

In short: to compute real GDP, we need to adjust for inflation. We can do so more easily if we look at growth rates of GDP over time.

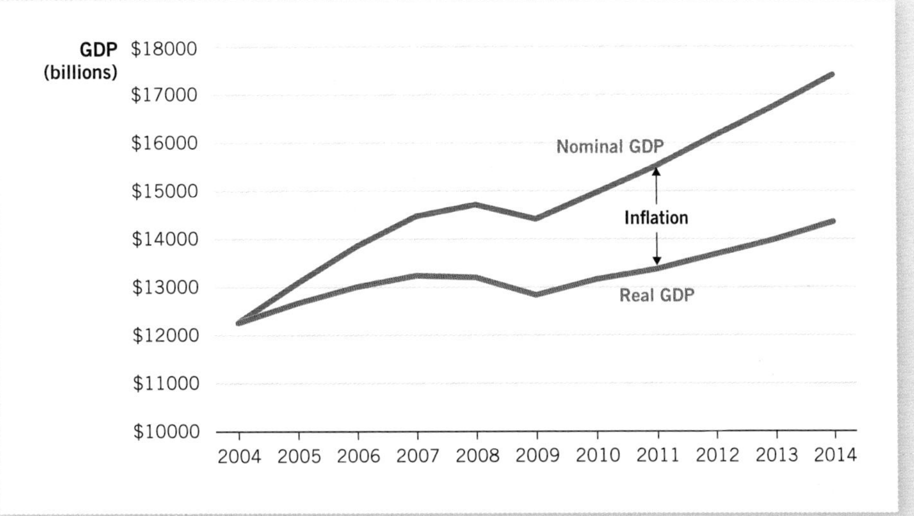

FIGURE 11.3

U.S. Nominal and Real GDP, 2004–2014 (2009 Dollars)

Nominal GDP typically rises faster than real GDP because it rises with growth in both real production and prices (inflation). From 2004 to 2014, nominal GDP in the United States rose by 41.9%, but nearly 25% of that increase was due to inflation. The increase in real GDP during the same period was 17.1%.

Source: U.S. Bureau of Economic Analysis.

Growth Rates

For many macroeconomic applications, it's useful to calculate growth rates. For example, let's say you read that the GDP in Mexico in 2010 was about $1 trillion. You might consider this information to be troubling for the future of the Mexican economy, since $1 trillion is very small compared to U.S. GDP. But maybe you also read that Mexico's GDP grew by 18% in 2010 (it did!). In that case, you'll probably get a different, and more positive, impression. In general, growth rates convey additional, often more illuminating, information than simple GDP data.

Growth rates are calculated as percentage changes in a variable. For example, the growth of U.S. nominal GDP in 2013 is computed as:

(Equation 11.4)

$$\text{nominal GDP growth in 2013} = \frac{GDP_{2013} - GDP_{2012}}{GDP_{2012}} \times 100$$

Unless noted otherwise, the data comes from the end of the period. Therefore, Equation 11.4 tells us the percentage change in U.S. GDP from the end of 2012 to the end of 2013, or over the course of 2013. Using actual data, this growth rate is:

$$\begin{aligned}\text{nominal GDP growth in 2013} &= \text{\% change in nominal GDP}\\ &= \frac{16{,}768.1 - 16{,}163.2}{16{,}163.2} \times 100 = 3.7\%\end{aligned}$$

To adjust nominal GDP for inflation, we also need to know how fast prices were increasing in 2013. Inflation in the U.S. economy in 2013 was 1.6%. That is, overall prices rose by 1.6%.

The growth rate of real GDP is approximately equal to the difference between the percentage change in nominal GDP and the percentage change in inflation:

(Equation 11.5)

$$\begin{aligned}\text{\% change in real GDP} &\approx \text{\% change in nominal GDP}\\ &\quad - \text{\% change in inflation}\end{aligned}$$

This equation gives us a simple way of dissecting the growth of GDP into its respective parts. We know that nominal GDP grew by 3.7% in 2013 and that the price level grew by 1.6%. Thus, real GDP grew by 3.7% – 1.6% ≈ 2.1%.

PRACTICE WHAT YOU KNOW

Computing Real and Nominal GDP Growth: GDP Growth in Mexico

The table on the next page presents GDP data for Mexico. Use the data to answer the questions that follow.

(CONTINUED)

(CONTINUED)

Question: What was the rate of growth of real GDP in Mexico in 2012?

By how much is Mexico's economy growing?

Answer: Using Equation 11.5, we know:

$$\% \text{ change in real GDP} = \% \text{ change in nominal GDP} - \% \text{ change in inflation}$$

For 2012, we have:

$$\% \text{ change in real GDP} = 1.4 - 3.0 = -1.6$$

This means that 2012 was a pretty rough year for the Mexican economy.

Question: Now how would you compute real GDP growth in Mexico in 2013?

Answer: Using the 2013 data in the same equation, we get:

$$\% \text{ change in real GDP} = 6.3 - 2.0 = 4.3$$

This means that 2013 was a much better economic year for Mexico.

Year	Nominal GDP growth rate	Price-level growth rate (change in inflation)
2012	1.4	3.0
2013	6.3	2.0

Source: World Bank.

What Are Some Shortcomings of GDP Data?

We now have a picture of GDP, but as the misconception at the beginning of the chapter noted, there are some challenges with relying on GDP data as a measure of a nation's well-being. In this section, we highlight four shortcomings that limit the effectiveness of GDP as a measure of the health of an economy. At the end of this section, we consider why economists continue to rely on GDP.

Not counted in GDP: washing your own car.

Non-Market Goods

Many goods and services are produced but not sold. Those goods and services aren't counted in GDP data even though they create value for society. For instance, washing your own dishes, raking leaves in your yard, or just changing a light bulb are services, but they aren't counted in GDP. When the non-market segment of an economy is large, there can be a dramatic undercounting of the annual output being produced. For example, Haiti's GDP is very low. In 2013, its GDP was $8.5 billion. This is one-third the output of Vermont. However, Haiti's recorded GDP doesn't mean that there was less production. In Haiti, if you don't work, you may not have enough food to survive. Many households live off the land and produce goods for their own consumption. This output doesn't get counted in GDP. As a result, Haiti's GDP is understated.

The **underground economy** (shadow economy) encompasses transactions that are not reported to the government and therefore are not taxed.

Underground Economy

The **underground economy** (also known as the shadow economy) encompasses transactions that are not reported to the government and therefore are not taxed. Usually, these transactions are settled in cash. Some of these

ECONOMICS IN THE MEDIA

The Underground Economy

Traffic

Traffic, a crime film from 2000, looks at America's war on drugs through the lives of the people involved in it. The characters offer a fascinating range: from the nation's drug czar, to his cocaine-using daughter, to the cops who fight the war on both sides of the U.S./Mexican border, to the drug dealers who profit from trafficking the drugs.

In one scene, two agents from the Drug Enforcement Agency are interrogating a suspected drug trafficker. The suspect explains that the cocaine flow from Mexico into the United States cannot be stopped because there's too much demand in the United States and because Mexican dealers are willing to "throw supply at the problem." That is, the Mexican drug lords recognize that some of their shipments will be seized but that enough will get through to reach their customers in the United States to make the risks worthwhile.

One of the ironies about measuring GDP is that even though the drug trades aren't part of GDP—because those illegal market transactions aren't formally recorded—the people involved in fighting the war on drugs, as well as the sales of drug paraphernalia, are included in GDP.

How does more illegal drug traffic lead to higher GDP?

The movie also traces the life of a successful businessman who has made millions selling drugs. We see his estate, luxury cars, trophy wife, and all the accoutrements of success. His purchases are counted in GDP because it measures the sales of final goods and services even though they were bought using money obtained through illegal sales. Thus, while GDP cannot measure the economic activity in the underground economy, it can indirectly capture some of those transactions when the gains from selling drugs are used to purchase legal products.

transactions are legal, such as when contractors build additions to homes, landscapers mow lawns, or teenagers babysit for their neighbors. But the underground economy also includes transactions like illegal exchanges of drugs. Transactions in the underground economy aren't directly measurable because the income isn't reported. Therefore, these activities are not included in official measures of GDP.

How big is the underground economy? No one is sure. Economist Friedrich Schneider has estimated that for wealthy developed economies it is roughly 15% of GDP and that in transitioning economies the percentage rises to between 21% and 30% of GDP. However, in the world's most underdeveloped economies, like those of Nigeria or Armenia, the underground economy can be as much as 40% of GDP.

The United States is widely believed to have one of the smallest shadow economies in the world, with less than 10% of GDP unaccounted for in the official measurement. Why is the underground economy so small in the United States? The simple answer is that in the United States, and in many other developed economies, most citizens can earn more by legitimately participating in the economy than by engaging in illegal activities.

Quality of the Environment

Since GDP only measures the final amount of goods and services produced in a given period, it cannot distinguish how those goods and services are produced. Imagine two economies, both with the same real GDP per capita. One economy relies on clean energy for its production, and the other has lax environmental standards. Citizens in both countries enjoy the same *measured* standard of living, but their well-being isn't the same. The lax environmental standards in the second economy lead to air and water pollution, as well as health problems for its citizens. Since there is more to quality of life than the goods and services we buy, using GDP to infer that both places are equally desirable would be inaccurate. The truth of this statement is obvious in China. While GDP per person is increasing in that nation, on many days in Beijing the sun is blotted out by air pollution so thick that people have to wear masks.

Not counted in GDP: a clean environment.

Leisure Time

Since GDP only counts market activity, it fails to capture how long laborers work to produce goods and services. For most developed nations, according to the Organization for Economic Cooperation and Development (OECD), the average workweek is slightly over 35 hours. However, there are wide variations in how hard laborers work. At the high end, laborers in South Korea average 46 hours per week. In contrast, laborers in the Netherlands average fewer than 28 hours per week. This means that comparisons of GDP across countries don't account for the extra time available to workers in countries with substantially fewer hours worked. For example, in the United States

Not counted in GDP: extra time to relax.

the average workweek is 36 hours. A comparison with Japan, which also averages 36 hours per workweek, would be valid; but a comparison of GDP in the United States with that of Sweden (31-hour workweek) or Greece (41-hour workweek) would be misleading.

Why don't economists correct some of the deficiencies of GDP by adjusting for these flaws in their calculations? If they did, GDP might be a better gauge of well-being. For instance, in addition to the production of goods and services, economists might use other measures to determine whether a country is a good place to live: life expectancy, educational levels, access to health care, crime rates, and a host of other statistics.

One problem with including these additional factors in GDP is that they are also difficult to measure; the combined statistic that we would generate would be even more challenging to understand. Therefore, we limit GDP to measuring economic production, knowing that it isn't a perfect measure of well-being. In addition, GDP is actually correlated with many of the variables we care about; a country with a higher GDP per capita can focus on economic values beyond the basic necessities. Indeed, higher levels of GDP are highly correlated with a better environment, higher-quality and better access to health care, more education, more leisure time, and lower crime rates.

PRACTICE WHAT YOU KNOW

Some nations have more stay-at-home parents than others. How does this fact affect GDP comparisons?

Shortcomings of GDP Data: Use Caution in Interpreting GDP as an Economic Barometer

In many parts of the world, a significant amount of effort goes into non-market production in the household, such as stay-at-home parenting. For example, Zimbabwe has a very high rate of non-market household production. In contrast, Canada has a low rate of non-market household production.

Question: How does the difference in non-market household production affect a comparison of GDP between Zimbabwe and Canada?

Answer: The GDP statistics for Zimbabwe are biased downward more than the statistics for Canada, since a larger portion of Zimbabwe's actual production goes unreported. While Zimbabwe is indeed a poorer nation than Canada, official statistics exaggerate the difference slightly, making Zimbabwe seem poorer than it is.

What Can We Learn from Unemployment Data?

Who exactly counts as "unemployed"? For example, many college students don't have jobs, but that doesn't mean they're officially unemployed. In fact, just because you don't have a job doesn't mean you're unemployed. So how is unemployment calculated? Before we take a look at that question, let's examine the natural rate of unemployment.

The Natural Rate of Unemployment (u*)

In Chapter 10, we saw that there are three types of unemployment: structural, frictional, and cyclical. Figure 11.4 illustrates the relationship among these types of unemployment during both **recessions**, which are short-term economic downturns that typically last about 6 to 18 months, and healthy macroeconomic conditions. Notice that structural and frictional unemployment are always present. However, during healthy economic periods, cyclical unemployment falls toward zero.

A **recession** is a short-term economic downturn that typically lasts about 6 to 18 months.

When we acknowledge a certain level of normal or natural unemployment, we must also recognize a natural rate of unemployment. The **natural rate of unemployment (u*)** is the typical unemployment rate that occurs when the economy is growing normally. Because frictional and structural unemployment are always present, zero unemployment isn't possible. Economists never know the exact numerical value of the natural rate because people don't put themselves into an unemployment category. Currently, however, most economists feel that the natural rate of unemployment in the United States is between 4% and 6%.

The **natural rate of unemployment (u*)** is the typical unemployment rate that occurs when the economy is growing normally.

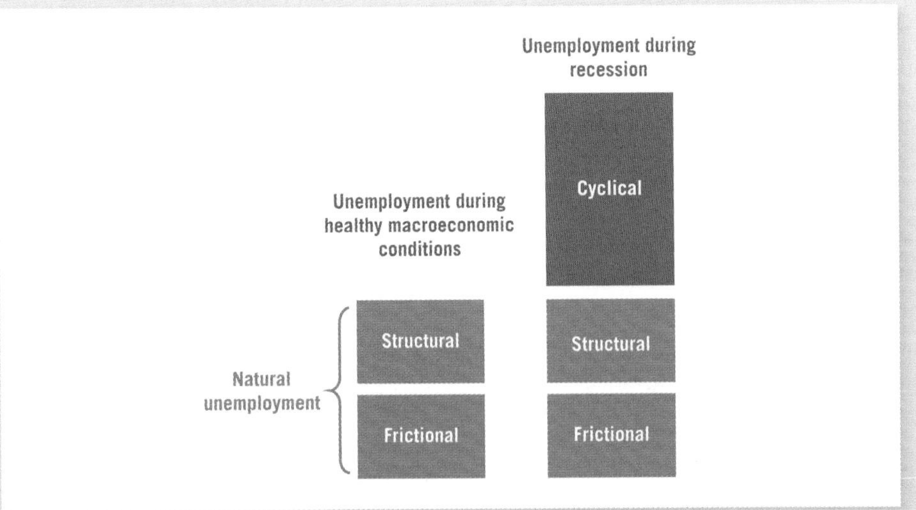

FIGURE 11.4

Three Types of Unemployment

During healthy macroeconomic conditions, both structural and frictional unemployment are present. During recessions, cyclical unemployment also appears.

The Unemployment Rate (u)

The **unemployment rate (u)** is the percentage of the labor force that is unemployed.

The most commonly discussed number when examining the employment picture in a country is the unemployment rate. The **unemployment rate (u)** is defined as the percentage of the labor force that is unemployed. This statistic is computed by the U.S. Bureau of Labor Statistics.* We measure this rate as follows:

(Equation 11.6)

$$\text{unemployment rate} = \text{u} = \frac{\text{number of unemployed persons}}{\text{labor force}} \times 100$$

The **labor force** includes people who are already employed or actively seeking work.

Let's look at this definition more closely. To be officially unemployed, a person has to be in the labor force. A member of the **labor force** is someone who is already employed or actively seeking work. If a jobless person hasn't sought a job in four weeks, that person isn't counted in the unemployment statistics. This is an important point. If you don't have a job but you stop looking for work, for any reason, then you aren't officially counted as unemployed! Other individuals not included in the official definition of the labor force (the relevant population for counting the labor force) include retirees, stay-at-home parents, people who are in jail, military personnel, children under age 16, and many full-time students.

Table 11.3 provides data for different labor market categories. Starting with the relevant U.S. population—those people who are civilian (not in the military), non-institutionalized (not in jail, mental facilities, or homes for the aged), and over the age of 16 (250,663,000)—we find that less than two-thirds of it is counted in the labor force (157,073,000). Of this, in June 2015,

TABLE 11.3

Unemployment in the United States, June 2015

To compute the unemployment rate, we divide the relevant adult population between those who are in the labor force and those who are not. To be counted in the labor force, a person must either have a job or be actively seeking work. The unemployment rate is the percentage of the labor force that is unemployed.

Relevant population (civilian, non-institutionalized population, over the age of 16): 250,663,000

Not in the labor force: 93,626,000

Labor force: 157,037,000

Employed: 148,739,000

Unemployed: 8,299,000

Source: U.S. Bureau of Labor Statistics.

*The U.S. Bureau of Labor Statistics web site is www.bls.gov. You can find the monthly unemployment rate, inflation statistics, and other more specific information on the labor force here.

fully 8,299,000 were unemployed. Plugging these numbers into Equation 11.6 yields:

$$u = \frac{8{,}299{,}000}{157{,}073{,}000} \times 100 = 5.3\%$$

This is a relatively high unemployment rate.

Shortcomings of the Unemployment Rate

The unemployment rate, released monthly, is a timely and consistent indicator of the health of the macroeconomy. However, it has three shortcomings as an economic indicator. Let's look at each in turn.

Discouraged and Underemployed Workers. The first shortcoming of the unemployment rate is related to exclusions. People who are unemployed for a long time may just stop looking for work—not because they don't want a job, but because they get discouraged. When they stop looking for work, they fall out of the labor force and no longer count as unemployed. In other words, they are excluded from the statistics. **Discouraged workers** are defined as those who are not working, have looked for a job in the past 12 months and are willing to work, but have not sought employment in the past 4 weeks.

Discouraged workers are those who are not working, have looked for a job in the past 12 months and are willing to work, but have not sought employment in the past 4 weeks.

Another group not properly accounted for are **underemployed workers**, defined as workers who have part-time jobs but who would prefer to work full-time. These workers are not counted as unemployed. In fact, the official unemployment rate includes only workers who have no job and who are actively seeking work. This definition excludes both discouraged and underemployed workers, groups that increase during economic downturns. Figure 11.5 shows the official U.S. unemployment rate for the period 1994–2014 versus an alternative measure that includes discouraged and underemployed workers. Not only does the alternative measure show a much higher rate than the unemployment rate, but the difference expands significantly during and after recessions (the blue-shaded regions).

Underemployed workers are those who have part-time jobs but who would prefer to work full-time.

The Length of Unemployment. The second shortcoming of the official measurement of unemployment is that it doesn't answer another important set of questions about who is unemployed or how long they've been out of work. Are people unemployed for short spells, or is the duration of their joblessness long-term? If most unemployment is short-term, we might not be as concerned with a higher unemployment rate, since it indicates that the unemployment is a temporary situation rather than a long-term problem for workers. To help fill in this part of the unemployment picture, the Bureau of Labor Statistics keeps an alternative measure of unemployment that tracks the length of time workers have been unemployed.

Table 11.4 shows the duration of unemployment in the United States in 2007 and 2013. The year 2007 came at the end of a long expansionary period in the U.S. economy. At that time, more than two-thirds of total unemployment was short-term (14 weeks or less), and just 17.6% of those unemployed were out of work for longer than 27 weeks. In contrast, consider

FIGURE 11.5

A Broader Measure of U.S. Labor Market Problems, 1994–2014

The orange line includes workers who are officially unemployed, discouraged workers who have given up the job search, and workers who are underemployed (working part-time when they would rather work full-time). The gap between this broader measure and the official unemployment rate, shown by the blue line, grows when the economy enters a recession. The most recent gap is particularly evident beginning in 2008.

Source: U.S. Bureau of Labor Statistics.

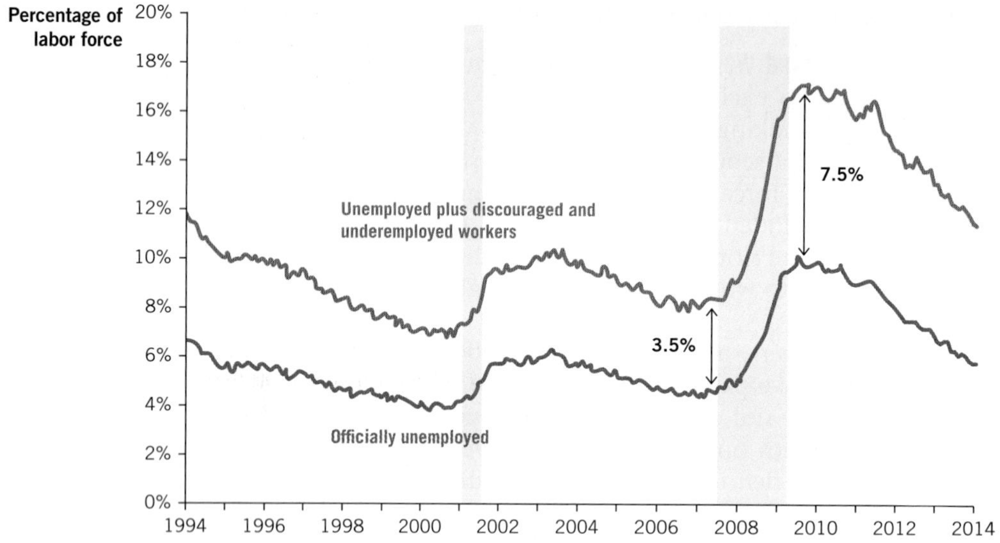

TABLE 11.4

Duration of Unemployment in the United States, 2007 and 2013

	Percentage of total unemployed	
Duration	**2007**	**2013**
Short-term	67.4%	46.6%
Less than 5 weeks	35.9	22.5
5 to 14 weeks	31.5	24.1
Long-term	32.6	53.4
15 to 26 weeks	15.0	15.8
27 weeks and over	17.6	37.6

Source: U.S. Bureau of Labor Statistics.

2013, after the U.S. economy experienced a significant recession. There we see a big increase in the percentage of those unemployed for the very long term—27 weeks or more—which was more than 37% of total unemployment in 2013.

Who Is Unemployed? A final issue to consider is exactly who is unemployed. Consider the unemployment rate for two different months. If the unemployment rate is 6.2% in April and 6.2% in May, you might think that those people unemployed in April are still unemployed in May. After all, the unemployment rate hasn't changed. But the unemployment rate is a national statistic. It tells you what percentage of the overall labor force is actively seeking work, but it doesn't tell you who those people are. It's possible that the 6.2% unemployment in May constitutes an entirely different group of people from the 6.2% of people who were unemployed in April. Jobs are lost in one part of the country and gained somewhere else. Thus, it would be a mistake to think that the same people are unemployed month after month. While this is certainly true for the long-term unemployed, those who make up the short-term unemployed are usually different from month to month.

Other Labor Market Indicators

Macroeconomists use several other indicators to get a more complete picture of the labor market. These include the labor-force participation rate and statistics on gender and race.

Labor-Force Participation

The size of the labor force is an important macroeconomic statistic. To see why, consider two hypothetical island economies called 2K and 2K14. Each island has a population of one million people, and the islands are identical in every way except in the size of their labor forces. On the first island, 2K, the labor force is 670,000. On the second island, 2K14, the labor force is just 627,000. Island 2K has 43,000 more workers to produce goods and services for a population that's exactly the same size as that of island 2K14. The **labor-force participation rate** is the portion of the relevant population that is in the labor force:

The **labor-force participation rate** is the percentage of the relevant population that is in the labor force.

$$\text{labor force participation rate} = (\text{labor force} \div \text{relevant population}) \times 100 \qquad \text{(Equation 11.7)}$$

On 2K, the labor-force participation rate is 67%; but on 2K14, the labor-force participation rate is just 62.7%.

By now, you may have guessed that these are the labor-force participation rates for the U.S. economy in the years 2000 and 2014. Figure 11.6 shows the evolution of the labor-force participation rate in the United States from 1990 to 2014. You can see that it peaks at 67.3% in 2000 but then falls to 62.7% by the end of 2014. Other things being equal, this means that in 2014 there were fewer people working relative to the overall population in the United States than in any of the previous years shown in the graph, including the year 2000.

The changing demographics of the U.S. population are likely to reduce the labor-force participation rate even further over the coming decades.

FIGURE 11.6

U.S. Labor-Force Participation Rate, 1990–2014

The labor-force participation rate in the United States peaked at 67.3% in 2000, but it has subsequently fallen below 63%.

Source: U.S. Bureau of Labor Statistics.

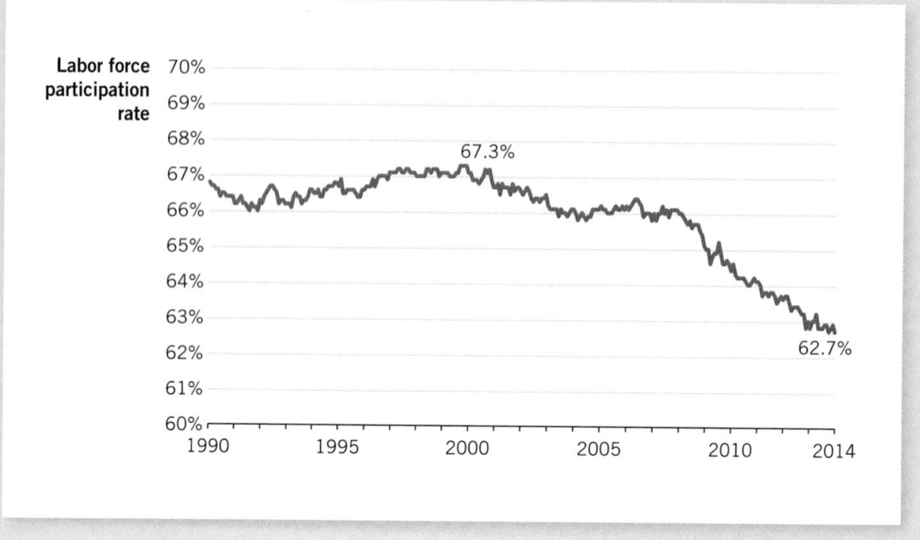

The term "baby boom" refers to the period after the end of World War II when U.S. birthrates temporarily rose dramatically. The U.S. Census Bureau pegs this period at 1946–1964. So there is now a bubble in the U.S. population known as the baby boomers. (This group most likely includes your parents.) But now, as the oldest baby boomers begin to retire, the labor-force participation rate will fall.

Gender and Race Statistics

As Figure 11.7 indicates, the composition of the U.S. labor force today is markedly different from that of two generations ago. Not only are more women working (from 32% in 1948 to almost 60% today), but male labor-force participation has fallen dramatically (from over 87% to under 70%). Men still remain more likely to participate in the labor force than women, but the participation gap has significantly narrowed. These changes are a function of shifting social attitudes.

Compared to two generations ago, men are more likely to stay at home today.

How do we explain the fact that fewer males are working? There are several reasons for the decline. Men are living longer, acquiring more education, and spending more time helping to raise families. Since men who are retired, in school, or staying at home to care for children aren't counted as part of the labor force, these shifts have lowered the labor-force participation rate for males.

Unemployment rates also vary widely across ages and races. Table 11.5 breaks down these statistics by age, race, and gender. Looking first at unemployment rates, in June 2015 the overall unemployment rate was 5.3%. But the rate by group ranges from a low of 4.2% for white males (over 20 years

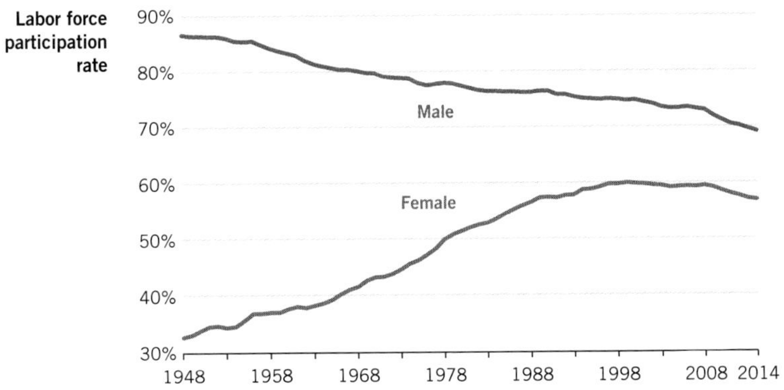

FIGURE 11.7

Trends in U.S. Labor-Force Participation, 1948–2014

Over the past 65 years, the composition of the U.S. labor force has shifted drastically. While more women have entered the labor force, the percentage of men in the labor force has dropped from almost 90% to just 70%.

Source: U.S. Bureau of Labor Statistics.

old) to a high of 39.2% for black teenage males. Notice also that labor-force participation rates are very low among teenagers, with white female teenagers at about 43.8% but black female teenagers at just 28.8%.

TABLE 11.5

U.S. Unemployment and Labor-Force Participation Rates by Age, Race, and Gender, June 2015

Group	Unemployment rate	Labor-force participation rate
Overall	5.3%	62.6%
Adults (age 20+)		
Black males	9.5	67.6
Black females	7.9	62.0
White males	4.2	72.1
White females	4.2	57.5
Teenagers (age 16–19)		
Black males	39.2	34.3
Black females	38.0	28.8
White males	20.8	43.8
White females	15.4	43.0

Source: U.S. Bureau of Labor Statistics.

PRACTICE WHAT YOU KNOW

This German worker is employed at a textile plant.

Unemployment and Labor-Force Participation Rates: Can You Compute the Rates?

The following data is from Germany in 2013:

Relevant population = 70,503,000
Labor force = 44,200,000
Employed = 42,276,000

Question: Using the data, how would you compute the number of unemployed workers, the unemployment rate, and the labor-force participation rate for Germany in 2013?

Answer: The unemployment rate is the total number of unemployed people as a percentage of the labor force. First, determine the number of unemployed people by taking the total labor force minus the number of employed:

$$\text{unemployed} = \text{labor force} - \text{employed} = 1{,}924{,}000$$

Use this to determine the unemployment rate, which is the number of unemployed people divided by the labor force:

$$\text{unemployed} \div \text{labor force} = 1{,}924{,}000 \div 44{,}200{,}000 = 4.3\%$$

Finally, the labor-force participation rate is the labor force as a percentage of the relevant population:

$$\begin{aligned}\text{labor-force participation rate} &= \text{labor force} \div \text{relevant population}\\ &= 44{,}200{,}000 \div 70{,}503{,}000\\ &= 62.7\%\end{aligned}$$

How Is Inflation Measured?

You might notice inflation on a routine shopping trip or especially when you see a reference to prices in an old book or movie. For example, in the 1960 movie *Psycho*, a hotel room for one night was priced at just $10. Recall that *inflation* is defined as the growth in the overall level of prices in an economy—so inflation occurs when prices rise throughout the economy. When overall prices rise, our budget is affected; we can buy less with our income. When overall prices fall, our income goes farther and we can buy more goods and services.

Hyperinflation is an extremely high rate of inflation that completely stymies economic activity.

Imagine an annual inflation rate of 100%. At this rate, prices would double every year. How would this inflation affect your life? Would it change what you buy? Would it change your savings plans? Would it change the salary you negotiate with your employer? Yes, it would change your life on a daily basis. Now imagine that prices double *every day*. This was the situation in Zimbabwe in 2008 when the inflation rate reached almost 80 billion percent per month! The Zimbabwe situation is an example of **hyperinflation**, an extremely high

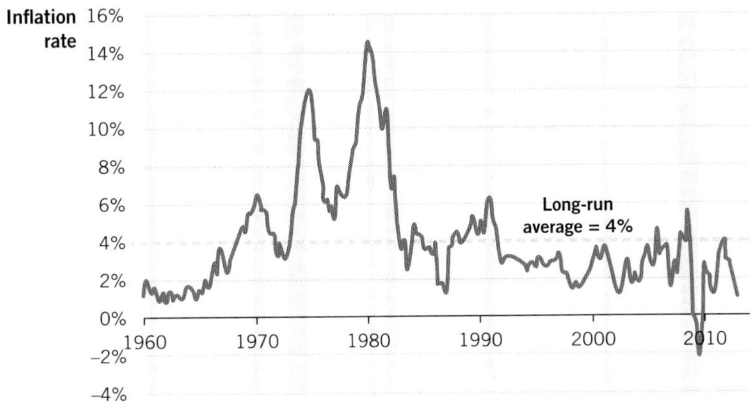

FIGURE 11.8

Inflation in the United States, 1960–2013

From 1960 to 2013, inflation rates in the United States averaged 4% each year. This number is high because of excessive inflation in the 1970s. The inflation rate peaked at nearly 15% in 1980. Since 2000, inflation rates have averaged 2.4%.

Source: U.S. Bureau of Labor Statistics.

rate of inflation that completely stymies economic activity. In Zimbabwe, for example, average citizens could barely afford necessities like bread and eggs.

Figure 11.8 shows inflation in the United States from 1960 to 2013. The long-run average over this period was 4%, meaning that prices as a whole rose 4% per year on average. In some years, the rate was much higher than 4%. At one point in 1980, the inflation rate was almost 15%. But since the early 1980s, inflation seems well controlled in the United States. Looking again at Figure 11.8, you might notice a brief spell of deflation in 2009. **Deflation** occurs when overall prices fall; it is negative inflation. Notice, too, that periods of recessions—the blue-shaded vertical bars in Figure 11.8—often (but not always) coincide with falling inflation rates. See, for example, 1982, 1991, and 2009.

Deflation occurs when overall prices fall.

Stagflation occurs when inflation rises during times of recession. (The term is a combination of the words "stagnation" and "inflation.") Stagflation occurred during the recession of the mid-1970s. This unexpected outcome caused economists to re-evaluate the deficit spending suggestions of Keynesian economists (for more on Keynesian economics, see Appendix 10A). The result was the supply-side revolution of the 1980s, when policy focused on promoting business activity. Whenever unusual macroeconomic events take place, new thinking about the macroeconomy often comes to the forefront.

Stagflation occurs when inflation rises during times of recession.

Measuring inflation accurately requires great care. First, prices don't all move together; some prices fall even when most others rise. Second, some prices affect consumers more than others. For example, a 10% increase in the cost of housing is significantly more painful than a 10% increase in the cost of hot dogs. Before we arrive at a useful measure of inflation, we have to agree on what prices to monitor and how much weight we'll give to each price. In the United States, the Bureau of Labor Statistics (BLS) measures and reports inflation data. In this section, we describe how the BLS estimates the overall price level. The **price level (P)** is a measure of the average prices of goods and services throughout an economy.

The **price level (P)** is a measure of the average prices of goods and services throughout an economy.

The Consumer Price Index (CPI)

Let's look at the most common price level used to compute inflation. The **consumer price index (CPI)** is a measure of the price level based on the consumption patterns of a typical consumer. When you read or hear about inflation in the media, the report almost certainly focuses on this measure. The CPI is essentially the price of a typical "basket" of goods purchased by a representative consumer in the United States. Think about this situation as if you were going to the planet's hugest Super Walmart. You get an enormous shopping cart and start buying things to include in the basket. But what exactly goes in the basket?

In addition to groceries, you would buy clothing, transportation, housing, medical care, education, and many other goods and services. The goal of the CPI is to include everything a typical consumer buys, thereby giving a realistic measure of a typical consumer's cost of living.

The CPI is based on prices from a typical "basket" of all consumer goods.

Figure 11.9 displays how the CPI was allocated among major spending categories in December 2014. Prices for very specific goods are included in each of these categories. For example, "Food and beverages" includes prices for everything from potato chips to oranges (both Valencia and navel) to flour (both white and all-purpose). These are the goods in the "basket" purchased by typical American consumers.

The **consumer price index (CPI)** is a measure of the price level based on the consumption patterns of a typical consumer.

Of course, none of us is exactly typical in our spending. College students allocate significantly more than 3.3% of their spending on education, senior citizens spend a lot more than average on medical care, a fashionista spends more than average on clothing, and those with lengthy commutes spend

FIGURE 11.9

The Pieces of the Consumer Price Index, December 2014

The weights assigned to the different categories of expenditures are based on the spending patterns of a typical American consumer. For example, 15.3% of a typical American's spending is on transportation; this includes car payments and fuel, among other expenses. (The sum of percentages does not equal exactly 100 due to rounding.)

Source: U.S. Bureau of Labor Statistics.

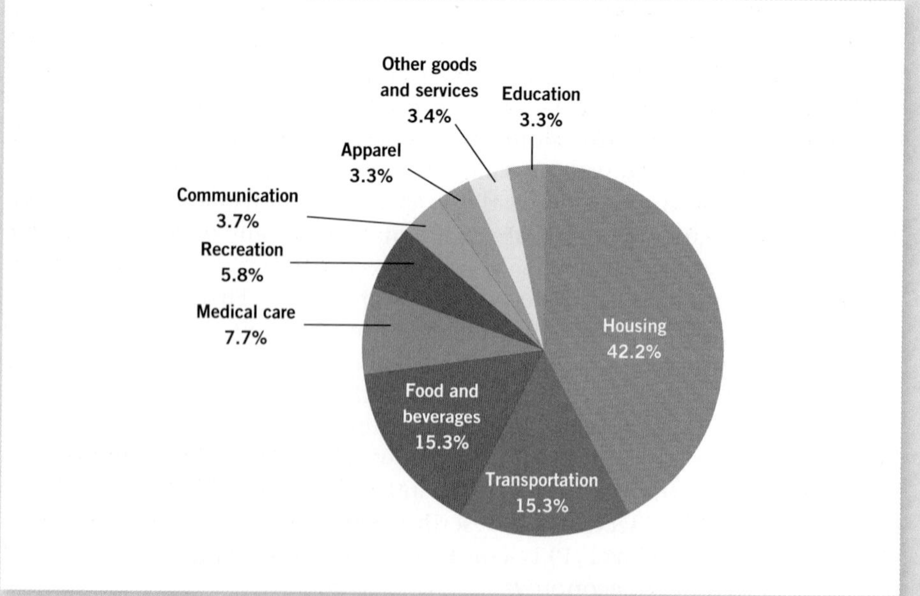

more than average on transportation. The CPI reflects the overall rise in prices for consumers *on average*.

Computing the CPI

Each month, the BLS conducts surveys by sending employees into stores in 38 different geographic locations to gather and input price information on over 8,000 goods. The BLS estimates prices on everything from apples in Chicago, Illinois, to electricity in Scranton, Pennsylvania, to gasoline in San Diego, California. In addition to inputting price information, the BLS surveyors estimate how each good and service affects a typical consumer's budget. Once they do this, they attach a weight to the price of each good in the consumer's "basket" so that the things people spend more money on are counted more heavily. For example, Figure 11.9 indicates that the typical consumer spends 15.3% of his or her budget on transportation. Therefore, transportation prices receive 15.3% of the total weight in the typical consumer's basket of goods. Once the BLS has compiled the prices and budget-allocation weights, it can construct the CPI.

ECONOMICS IN THE REAL WORLD

Sleuthing for Prices

Tracking the prices in the CPI requires a great deal of effort and precision. In September 2007, Nancy Luna of the *Orange County Register* followed one of the 350 employees of the Bureau of Labor Statistics who is charged with finding current prices of the goods included in the CPI. The BLS employee, Frank Dubich, traveled 800 miles per month tracking prices.

The items to be priced were very specific. For example, Dubich was asked to visit a grocery store to find the price of "an 18.5-ounce can of Progresso Rich & Hearty creamy chicken soup with wild rice," which turned out to be $1.98. Dubich also had to note that this was a sale price.

In another instance, Dubich was embarrassed to be seen pricing because the item was a prom dress. He noticed several clerks staring at him as he hunted for the price tag, so he quickly recorded the price and left.

In macroeconomics, we generally see one single number that indicates how much prices have changed. But it's important to remember that there are thousands of prices tracked each month by government workers like Frank Dubich. ✷

The government considers prom dresses to be a typical consumer item.

Measuring Inflation Rates

Once the CPI is computed, economists use it to measure the inflation rate. The inflation rate (i) is calculated as the percentage change in the price level (P). Using the CPI as the price level, the inflation rate from period 1 to period 2 is:

$$\text{inflation rate (i)} = \frac{CPI_2 - CPI_1}{CPI_1} \times 100 \qquad \text{(Equation 11.8)}$$

Note that this is a growth rate, computed just like the growth rate of GDP we computed earlier. Assume the CPI rises from 100 to 125 in one year. The inflation for that year would be 25%, computed as:

$$\text{inflation rate (i)} = \frac{125 - 100}{100} \times 100 = 25\%$$

The BLS releases CPI estimates every month; however, inflation rates are officially measured over the course of a year, showing how much the price level grows in a 12-month period. Over time, we see significant changes in the overall price level. The CPI was just 30 in 1961 and rose to 233 by 2013. This means that the typical basket of consumer goods rose in price nearly eightfold between 1961 and 2013.

ECONOMICS IN THE REAL WORLD

Prices Don't All Move Together

While it's clear that prices generally rise, not all prices go up. An increase in the CPI indicates that the price of the overall consumer basket rises. However, some individual prices stay the same or even fall. For example, consumer electronic prices almost always fall. When flat-panel plasma TVs were introduced in the late 1990s, a 40-inch model cost more than $7,000. Fifteen years later, 50-inch flat-panel TVs are available for less than $500. This drop in price is the result of technological advancements: as time passes, it often takes fewer resources to produce the same item or something better.

Computers are another example. In 1984, Apple introduced the Macintosh computer at a price of $2,495. The CPU for the Macintosh ran at 7.83 MHz, and the 9-inch monitor was black and white. Today, you can buy an Apple iMac for less than $1,800. This new Apple computer has a quad-core processor that runs at a total of 11,200 MHz, and the monitor is 27 inches (color, of course). The new computer is better by any measure, yet it costs less than the early model. These kinds of changes in quality make it difficult to measure the CPI over time. ✷

The 1984 Macintosh price was $2,495 . . .

. . . but this 2014 Apple iMac cost just $1,799.

The Accuracy of the CPI

Computing the CPI isn't simple. Yet for economists to understand what's happening in the macroeconomy, it's important that the CPI be accurate. For example, sometimes a rapid fall in inflation signals a recession, as it did in 1982 and 2008. Like real GDP and the unemployment rate, inflation is an indicator of national economic conditions.

How accurate is the CPI? If consumers always bought the same goods from the same suppliers, it would be extremely accurate, and economists would be able to compare the changes in price from one year to the next very easily. But this isn't a realistic scenario. Consumers buy different goods from different stores at different locations, and the quality of goods changes over time. Because the typical basket of consumer goods keeps changing, it's difficult to measure its price. The most common concern is that the CPI overstates true inflation. There are three reasons for this concern: (1) the substitution of different goods and services, (2) changes in quality, and (3) the availability of new goods, services, and locations.

Substitution

When the price of a good rises, consumers instinctively look to substitute less expensive alternatives. This substitution makes CPI calculations difficult because the typical consumer basket changes. If you go to the store looking for potato chips but find that pretzels are on sale, you're substituting away from a more expensive good if you buy the pretzels instead of the potato chips. This substitution alters the weights of all the goods in the typical consumption basket. If the CPI didn't acknowledge the substitution of less-expensive items, it would exaggerate the effects of the price increase, leading to upward bias (that is, an estimate of inflation that is too high). Since 1999, the BLS has attempted to deal with this problem by using a formula that accounts for both the price increase and the shift in goods consumption; however, keeping track of changing consumer behavior is very difficult.

Changes in Quality

Over time, the quality of goods generally increases. For example, the movies that you watch at home are probably on Blu-ray Discs. You can still get DVDs, but Blu-ray Discs are a higher quality and thus more expensive: the price of movies has risen from about $15 to about $25. This price increase might seem like inflation, since movie prices on disc have gone up. Yet consumers are getting "more" movie for their buck, because the quality has improved. If the CPI did not account for quality changes, it would have an upward bias, but the BLS also uses an adjustment method to try to account for quality changes.

New Products and Locations

In a dynamic, growing economy, new goods are introduced and new buying options become available. For example, tablet computers, iTunes downloads, and even cell phones weren't in the typical consumer's basket 20 years ago. In addition, Amazon.com and eBay weren't options for consumers to make purchases before the 1990s.

ECONOMICS IN THE MEDIA

Equating Dollar Values through Time

Austin Powers: International Man of Mystery

The Austin Powers series is a hilarious spoof of the James Bond films. In *International Man of Mystery,* we are introduced to British secret agent Austin Powers, who was cryofrozen at the end of the 1960s. Thirty years later, Austin Powers is thawed to help capture his nemesis, Dr. Evil, who was cryofrozen at the same time as Austin and has now stolen a nuclear weapon to hold the world hostage.

Being frozen for 30 years causes Dr. Evil to underestimate how much he should demand in ransom money: "Gentlemen, it's come to my attention that a breakaway Russian republic called Kreplachistan will be transferring a nuclear warhead to the United Nations in a few days. Here's the plan. We get the warhead, and we hold the world ransom . . . FOR ONE MILLION DOLLARS!"

There is an uncomfortable pause.

Dr. Evil's Number Two speaks up: "Don't you think we should ask for more than a million dollars? A million dollars isn't that much money these days. Virtucon alone makes over nine billion dollars a year."

Dr. Evil responds (pleasantly surprised): "Oh, really? ONE HUNDRED BILLION DOLLARS!"

"ONE HUNDRED BILLION DOLLARS!"

International Man of Mystery takes place in 1997, and Dr. Evil was frozen in 1967. How much did the price level rise over those 30 years? The CPI was 33.4 in 1967 and 160.5 in 1997. Dividing 160.5 by 33.4 yields a ratio of 4.8. So if Dr. Evil thought that $1 million was a lot of money in 1967, an equivalent amount in 1997 would be $4.8 million. Dr. Evil doesn't let that stop him from asking for more!

Traditionally, the BLS updated the CPI goods basket only after long time delays. This strategy biased the CPI in an upward direction for two reasons. First, the prices of new products typically drop in the first few years after their introduction. If the CPI basket doesn't include the latest prices, this price drop is lost. Second, new retail outlets such as Internet stores typically offer lower prices than traditional retail stores do. If the BLS continued to check prices only at traditional retail stores, it would overstate the price that consumers actually pay for goods and services.

What Problems Does Inflation Bring?

We intuitively understand that something is wrong when a country doesn't grow or when unemployment rates are high. But inflation is a problem too, and most people understand that if prices rise and their incomes don't, they are worse off as a result. But inflation also brings other problems that directly impact you. Let's look at the most important ones.

Uncertainty about Future Price Levels

Imagine you decide to open a new coffee shop in your college town. You want to produce espressos, café mochas, and cappuccinos. Of course, you hope to sell these for a profit. But before you can sell a single cup of coffee, you have to spend funds on your resources. You have to buy (that is, invest in) capital goods like an espresso bar, tables, chairs, and a cash register. You also have to hire workers and promise to pay them. All firms, large and small, face this situation. Before any revenue arrives from the sales of output, firms have to spend on resources. The same is true of the overall macroeconomy: to increase GDP in the future, firms must invest today. The funds required to make these investments are typically borrowed from others.

The timeline of production shown in Figure 11.10 illustrates how this process works. At the end, the firm sells its output. Recall that output is the production that a firm creates. The important point is that in a normal production process, funds must be spent today and then be repaid in the future—after the output sells. But for this sequence of events to occur, businesses must make promises to deliver payments in the future, including payments to workers and lenders. Thus, two types of long-term agreements form the foundation for production: wage and loan contracts. Both of these involve agreements for dollars to be delivered in future periods.

But inflation affects the real value of these future dollars. When inflation confuses workers and lenders, these essential long-term agreements seem risky and people are less likely to enter into them. Inflation can cripple loan markets because people don't know what future price levels will be. When firms cannot borrow money or hire long-term workers, future production is limited. Thus, inflation risk can lead to lower economic output (that is, lower GDP).

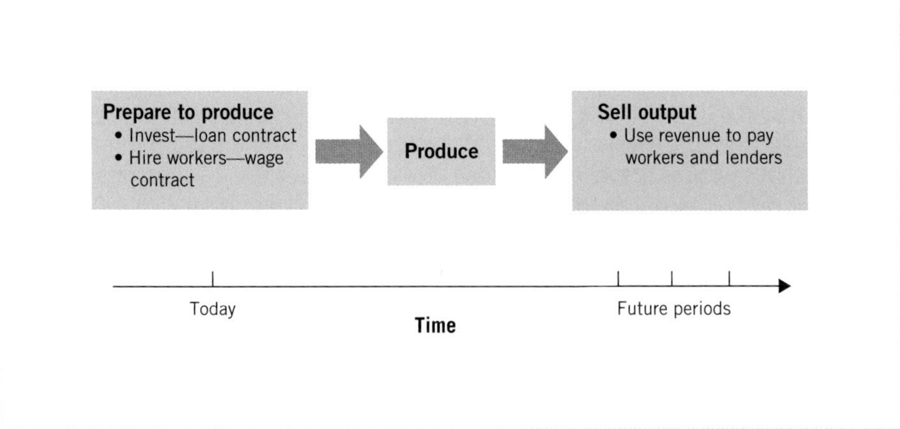

FIGURE 11.10

The Timeline of Production

The way output is typically produced begins with preparation, which includes purchases of equipment, labor, and other resources. Actual output and revenue from the sale of output come later. Thus, the firm can only begin production with promises of future payments to resource suppliers.

Wealth Redistribution

Inflation can also redistribute wealth between borrowers and lenders. If you borrow $20,000 to finance your college education, you're doing so with the promise to pay back more than what you borrowed because you'll be paying interest on the loan. Let's say you agree to a 5% interest rate. This means you will pay back $21,000. The catch is that you have time to repay the loan. Assume you have 10 years to pay it back. If inflation unexpectedly rises during those years, the inflation will devalue your future payment to the lender. As a result, you'll be better off because the money you're repaying has less purchasing power than what you borrowed, but the lender will be worse off. Thus, inflation redistributes wealth from lenders to borrowers.

If both you and the lender fully expect the inflation to occur, the lender will require more in return for the loan. In the United States, inflation has been low and steady since the mid-1980s. Therefore, surprises are rare. But nations with higher inflation rates also have a higher variability of inflation, which makes it difficult to predict the future. This is one more reason why high inflation increases the risk of making the loans that are an important source of funding for business ventures.

Impact on Savings

You may have heard the phrase "saving is a virtue." When you were younger, perhaps you saved money to buy a new bike or video game. Later in life, it's important that you save in order to put a down payment on a house and provide for your retirement. However, inflation can erode your savings.

PRACTICE WHAT YOU KNOW

Problems with Inflation: How Much Does the Bank Have to Pay You to Make Saving Worthwhile?

Suppose you're hoping to save money to buy your first house. You look around to find the best place to put your money and find that banks are paying interest rates of 1%. This means that they'll pay you 1% of whatever amount you have in your account at the end of each year just for keeping your money in the bank. Now 1% isn't a lot, and when you compare it to inflation, it may mean that saving is actually a bad idea. For example, if the inflation rate is 3% per year, then you need a 3% interest rate just to keep pace with inflation. Note that you can see inflation rates by visiting the Bureau of Labor Statistics web site (www.bls.gov). Once there, look up inflation rates based on the CPI.

Question: What happens to the purchasing power of your money if the interest rate you earn is 1% but inflation is 3%?

Answer: If the inflation rate is greater than the 1% interest rate, then keeping your money in the bank would actually cause a decline in your purchasing power since prices rise faster than the interest you earn.

FIGURE 11.11

Future Dollars Needed to Match Today's $1.00 in 40 Years

The rate of inflation determines how many dollars you will need in the future to maintain your current purchasing power. With the time frame of 40 years, a 1% inflation rate means that you will need $1.49 to buy what $1.00 would buy you today. If inflation were 5%, you would need $7.04 to buy what $1.00 would buy you today.

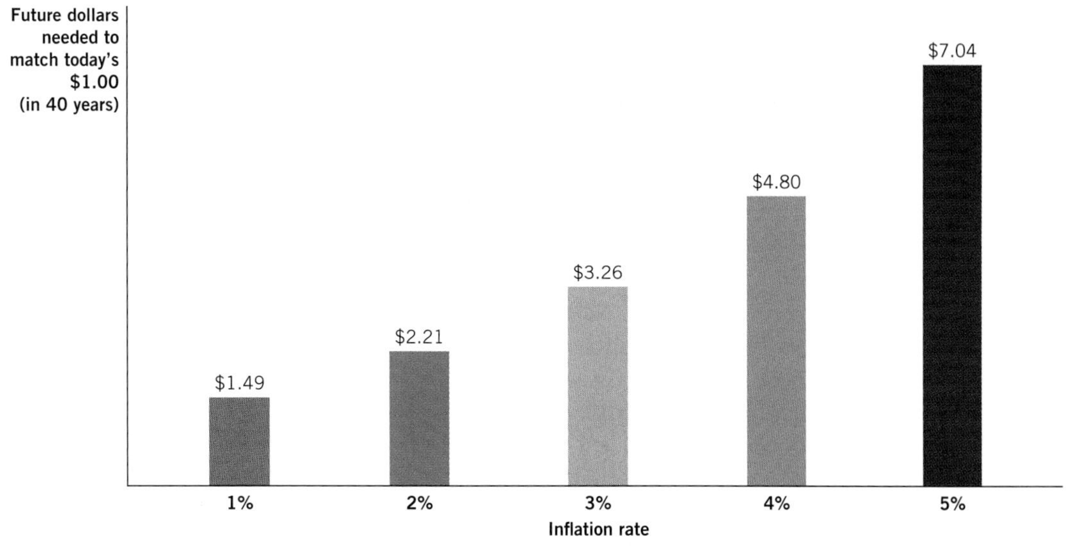

One way to think about the effect of inflation on future dollars is to ask what amount of future dollars it will take to match the real value of $1.00 today. Figure 11.11 answers this question based on a retirement date of 40 years in the future. The different inflation rates are specified at the bottom of the graph. If the inflation rate averages 4% over the next four decades, you'll need $4.80 in savings just to buy the same goods and services you can buy today for $1.00.

What does this mean for your overall retirement plans? Let's say that you decide you could live on $50,000 per year if you retired today. If the inflation rate is 4% between now and your actual future retirement date, though, you would need enough savings to supply yourself with $50,000 × $4.80, or $240,000 per year, just to keep pace with inflation.

Conclusion

This chapter began with the misconception that measuring the macroeconomy is a straightforward process. While we have ways of calculating the three primary data points of macroeconomics—unemployment, output, and inflation—

ECONOMICS FOR LIFE

Economic Statistics: Deciphering Data Reports

Economics is all around us, and economic topics are constantly reported in the media. In addition to monthly reports on unemployment and inflation, there are monthly releases and revisions of GDP data for the United States and other nations. These updates often get a lot of attention. Unfortunately, media reports are not as careful with their economics terminology as we would like. Because they aren't worded carefully, the reports can be misleading.

After learning about how economic measurements are computed, you might find new interest in the economic data reports that appear almost every month in the mainstream media. However, you must carefully evaluate the data they present. Now that you have perspective on economic statistics, you can determine for yourself whether economic news is positive or negative. For example, a *New York Times* article from July 2014 offers the following description of economic growth in the United States for the second quarter:

> The United States economy rebounded strongly in the second quarter of the year, shaking off the negative effects of an unusually harsh winter and stirring hopes that it might finally be establishing a solid enough footing to put the lingering effects of the recession squarely in the past.
>
> The Commerce Department . . . reported on Wednesday that the economy grew at a seasonally adjusted annual rate of 4 percent, surpassing expectations.

Good economists are very careful with language, because certain terms have very specific meanings. For example, we know (from Chapter 10) that "economic growth" always refers to changes in *per capita* real GDP, not simply GDP or real GDP. But economic reports in mainstream media outlets often blur this distinction. That is exactly the case with the report in the *New York Times* article excerpted above.

Economic reports in the media are often misleading.

Even though the author of the article uses the term "seasonally adjusted annual rate," additional research reveals that she's talking about real GDP growth, but not adjusting the data for population changes. This is a fairly common mistake, so you should watch out for it when you read economic growth reports. It turns out that the population growth rate in the United States was about 0.7% in 2013. Assuming the same rate for 2014, this means that the growth rate of per capita real GDP in the second quarter was closer to 3.3%.

Source: Dionne Searcey, "Economy Grew 4% for Quarter," *New York Times,* July 30, 2014.

each of them has its own challenges. Nevertheless, economists stick to the processes that they have been using for some time, making changes when new measurement techniques allow them to do so. The following chapters focus on how the major parts of the macroeconomy, along with policy, influence GDP, unemployment, and inflation. We'll begin by looking at a model that helps us understand the business cycle, or the ups and downs of the economy.

ANSWERING THE BIG QUESTIONS

How is GDP computed?

* Economists typically compute GDP by adding four types of expenditures in the economy: consumption (C), investment (I), government spending (G), and net exports (NX).
* For many applications, it is necessary to compute real GDP, which is nominal GDP adjusted for changes in prices.

What are some shortcomings of GDP data?

* GDP data does not include the production of non-market goods, the underground economy, production effects on the environment, or the value placed on leisure time.

What can we learn from unemployment data?

* The unemployment rate reflects the portion of the labor force that is not working and is unsuccessfully searching for a job.
* The natural rate of unemployment is the typical rate of unemployment that occurs when the economy is growing normally. Most economists feel that the natural rate of unemployment in the United States is between 4% and 6%.
* The labor-force participation rate reflects the portion of the population that is working or searching for work.
* Unemployment rates differ among groups based on age, race, and gender.

How is inflation measured?

* The inflation rate is calculated as the percentage change in the price level.
* Economists most commonly use the CPI to determine the general level of prices in the economy.
* Determining which prices to include in the CPI can be challenging for several reasons: consumers change what they buy over time, the quality of goods changes, and new products and sales locations are introduced.

What problems does inflation bring?

* Inflation causes uncertainty about future price levels and can lead to a redistribution of wealth.
* Inflation can also impact how much people save. Inflation erodes purchasing power over time, so you need to save more to meet savings targets.

CONCEPTS YOU SHOULD KNOW

consumer price index (CPI) (p. 332)
consumption (C) (p. 314)
deflation (p. 331)
discouraged workers (p. 325)
durable consumption goods (p. 314)
exports (p. 316)
final good (p. 312)
government spending (G) (p. 316)
hyperinflation (p. 330)
imports (p. 316)
intermediate good (p. 311)
investment (I) (p. 314)
labor force (p. 324)
labor-force participation rate (p. 327)
natural rate of unemployment (u*) (p. 323)
net exports (NX) (p. 316)
nominal GDP (p. 317)
non-durable consumption goods (p. 314)
price level (P) (p. 331)
recession (p. 323)
service (p. 311)
stagflation (p. 331)
transfer payments (p. 316)
underemployed workers (p. 325)
underground economy (p. 320)
unemployment rate (u) (p. 324)

QUESTIONS FOR REVIEW

1. What is the most important component (C, I, G, or NX) of GDP? Give an example of each component.
2. Is a larger GDP always better than a smaller GDP? Explain your answer with an example.
3. If Max receives an unemployment check, would we include that transfer payment from the government in this year's GDP? Why or why not?
4. Phil owns an old set of golf clubs that he purchased for $1,000 seven years ago. He decides to post them on Craigslist and quickly sells the clubs for $250. How does this sale affect GDP?
5. Real GDP for 2010 is less than nominal GDP for that year. But real GDP for 2000 is more than nominal GDP for that year. Why?
6. How does the most recent unemployment rate relate to the long-run average?
7. What groups does the Bureau of Labor Statistics count in the labor force? Explain why the official unemployment rate tends to underestimate the level of labor market problems.
8. Does the duration of unemployment matter? Explain your answer.
9. What are three issues regarding the accuracy of the CPI? Give an example of each issue.
10. If the prices of houses go up by 5% and the prices of concert tickets rise by 10%, which will have the larger impact on the CPI? Why?
11. What are some problems caused by inflation, other than a decrease in purchasing power? Briefly explain each one.

STUDY PROBLEMS (*✱ solved at the end of the section*)

1. In the following situations, explain what is counted in this year's GDP and what isn't:
   a. You bought a new PS4 at GameStop last year and resold it on eBay this year.
   b. You purchase a new copy of an *Investing for Dummies* book at Barnes & Noble.
   c. You purchase a historic home using the services of a real estate agent.
   d. You detail your car so that it is spotless inside and out.
   e. You purchase a new hard drive for your old laptop.

f. Your physical therapist receives $300 for physical therapy services but reports only $100 on her taxes.
g. Apple buys 1,000 motherboards for use in making new computers.
h. Toyota produces 10,000 new Camrys that remain unsold at the end of the year.

2. To which component of GDP expenditure (C, I, G, or NX) does each of the following belong?
   a. Swiss chocolates imported from Europe
   b. the salary of a new employee at the Department of Justice in Washington, D.C.
   c. a candle you buy at a local store
   d. a new house
   e. the sale of a U.S.-made Ford F-150 truck to a man in Mexico City
   f. a puppy purchased from a farmer on the side of the road
   g. a new watch that you bought from Amazon .com

3. A mechanic builds an engine and then sells it to a custom body shop for $7,000. The body shop installs the engine in a car and sells the car to a dealer for $20,000. The dealer then sells the finished vehicle for $35,000. A consumer drives off with the car. By how much does GDP increase? What is the value added at each step of the production process?

4. Many goods and services are illegally sold or legally sold but not reported to the government. How would increased efforts to count those goods and services affect the calculation of GDP?

5. Leisure time is not included in GDP, but what would happen if it were included? Would high-work countries like South Korea fare better or worse in international comparisons of well-being?

6. A country with a civilian population of 90,000 (all over age 16) has 70,000 employed and 10,000 unemployed persons. Of the unemployed, 5,000 are frictionally unemployed and another 3,000 are structurally unemployed. On the basis of this data, answer the following questions:
   a. What is the size of the labor force?
   b. What is the unemployment rate?
   c. What is the natural rate of unemployment for this country?
   d. Is this economy doing well or poorly? Explain.

7. Consider a country with 300 million residents, a labor force of 150 million, and 10 million unemployed. Answer the following questions:
   a. What is the labor-force participation rate?
   b. What is the unemployment rate?
   c. If 5 million of the unemployed become discouraged and stop looking for work, what is the new unemployment rate?
   d. Suppose instead that 30 million jobs are created, attracting 20 million new people into the labor force. What would be the new rates for labor-force participation and unemployment?

* 8. Consider the following hypothetical data from the peaceable nation of Adirolf, where there is no military, the entire population is over the age of 16, and no one is institutionalized for any reason. Then answer the questions.

Classification	Number of people
Total population	200 million
Employed	141 million
Full-time students	10 million
Homemakers	25 million
Retired persons	15 million
Seeking work but without a job	9 million

   a. What is the unemployment rate in Adirolf?
   b. What is the labor-force participation rate in Adirolf?

For questions c through f: assume that 15 million Adirolfian homemakers begin seeking jobs and that 10 million find jobs.

   c. Now what is the rate of unemployment in Adirolf?
   d. How does this change affect cyclical unemployment in Adirolf?
   e. What will happen to per capita GDP?

f. Is the economy of Adirolf better off after the homemakers enter the labor force? Explain your response.

✳ 9. In each of the following situations, determine whether or not the person would be considered unemployed.
   a. A 15-year-old offers to pet-sit, but no one hires her.
   b. A college graduate spends the summer after graduation touring Europe before starting a job search.
   c. A part-time teacher is able to work only two days a week, even though he would like a full-time job.
   d. An automobile worker becomes discouraged about the prospects for future employment and decides to quit looking for work.

✳ 10. If healthcare costs make up 10% of total expenditures and they rise by 15% while the other components in the consumer price index remain constant, by how much will the price index rise?

11. Wage agreements and loan contracts are two types of multi-period agreements that are important for economic growth. Suppose you sign a two-year job contract with Wells Fargo stipulating that you will receive an annual salary of $93,500 plus an additional 2% over that amount in the second year to account for expected inflation.
   a. If the inflation rate turns out to be 3% rather than 2%, who will be hurt? Why?
   b. If the inflation rate turns out to be 1% rather than 2%, who will be hurt? Why?

Suppose that you also take out a $1,000 loan at the Colonial Credit Union. The loan agreement stipulates that you must pay it back with 4% interest in one year, and again, the inflation rate is expected to be 2%.

   c. If the inflation rate turns out to be 3% rather than 2%, who will be hurt? Why?
   d. If the inflation rate turns out to be 3% rather than 2%, who will be helped? Why?

SOLVED PROBLEMS

8a. The unemployment rate in Adirolf is 6%. To calculate the unemployment rate, use:

unemployment rate = u = (number unemployed ÷ labor force) × 100

- The number of unemployed: 9 million
- Labor force can be calculated in two ways:
  - Employed plus unemployed: 141 million + 9 million = 150 million
- Total population minus those not in labor force (students, homemakers, retirees):

200 million − (10 million + 25 million + 15 million) = 150 million

Note: because the total population is composed only of non-institutionalized civilians over the age of 16, we can use this number (200 million) as the relevant population.

Unemployment rate = u = (number unemployed ÷ labor force) × 100 = (9 ÷ 150) × 100 = 6%

b. The labor-force participation rate in Adirolf is 75%. To calculate the labor-force participation rate, use:

labor force participation rate = (labor force ÷ population) × 100

- Labor force (calculated above): 150 million
- Population: 200 million

labor-force participation rate = (labor force ÷ population) × 100 = (150 ÷ 200) × 100 = 75%

c. Now the rate of unemployment in Adirolf is 8.5%. To calculate the new unemployment rate, use the same equation as above. However, the figures have changed with new entrants to the labor force:
- The new number of unemployed: 9 million + 5 million = 14 million
- The new number of employed: 150 million + 10 million = 160 million

- The new labor force can be calculated in three ways:
  Previous labor force plus new entrants:
  150 million + 15 million = 165 million
  Employed plus unemployed:
  151 million employed + 14 million unemployed = 165 million
  Total population minus those not in labor force (students, homemakers, retirees):

  200 million − (10 million + 10 million + 15 million) = 165 million

  unemployment rate = u
  = (number unemployed ÷ labor force) × 100
  = (14 ÷ 165) × 100 = 8.5%

Note: even though the number of employed increased, because the size of the labor force increased by a larger amount, the unemployment rate has increased.

d. The change does not affect cyclical unemployment, which is generally associated with economic downturns. Instead, the entrance of new workers into the labor force represents a change in the labor-force participation rate. In general, the entry of new workers to the labor force is associated with good economic times. Because most of the homemakers were able to find jobs, we can conclude that the economy of Adirolf is growing.

e. With an increase in the number of employed workers, total output in the economy will increase. However, the size of the population has not changed. Thus, per capita GDP will increase as a result of the change.

f. Adirolf has a stronger economy with more working homemakers. Even though the unemployment rate has increased as a result of many homemakers entering the labor force, the increase in unemployment isn't the result of economic downturn; rather, it's a sign of a growing economy. Adirolf has a stronger economy with higher GDP per capita and a greater labor-force participation rate as a result of this change.

9a. No. The relevant population used to measure unemployment and the labor force comprises individuals 16 years of age or older. This 15-year-old is not part of the relevant population, so she is not considered unemployed.

b. No. To be counted in the unemployment statistics, an individual must have made efforts to get a job in the past four weeks. This college graduate is not actively seeking work during the summer, so he is not counted as an unemployed individual.

c. No. This part-time teacher is underemployed because he would prefer a full-time position, but under the unemployment rate measurements he's considered to be employed.

d. No. The automobile worker is a discouraged worker if he has searched for work in the past year but stopped looking for work over four weeks ago. However, since he isn't actively looking for work now, he is no longer considered to be part of the labor force.

10. The CPI will rise by 1.5%. Suppose the CPI in the first year is 100. If healthcare costs are 10% of total expenditures, then they account for 10 of the 100 points, with the other 90 points falling in other categories. If healthcare costs rise by 15% in the second year, then those 10 points become 11.5 points. Since the prices of the other categories have not changed, the CPI now stands at 101.5, since 11.5 + 90 = 101.5.

Using our formula for calculating the inflation rate, the increase in healthcare costs has raised the overall price level by 1.5%: [(101.5 − 100) ÷ 100] × 100 = 1.5.

CHAPTER 12

Aggregate Demand and Aggregate Supply

MISCONCEPTION

Recessions are inevitable and occur every few years.

Many people believe that every few years the economy plunges into a recession and then, after a short period of slow growth, rebounds for a period of expansion. They consider this pattern inevitable, with recessions happening every six to eight years. The term "business cycle" is a popular way to describe the recession-expansion phenomenon because so many people are convinced that the recessions and expansions occur in a regular cycle.

But, in fact, recessions are rarer today than at any other time in U.S. history. While there have been 22 U.S. recessions since 1900, there have been just three since 1982. In addition, no two recessions are exactly alike in either cause or effect.

We begin this chapter by looking at a simple model that illustrates the normal fluctuations in an economy, which we call the business cycle. We then move on to a more detailed examination of how major macroeconomic variables (GDP growth, unemployment, and inflation) fit together in a formal aggregate model that combines the demand for all goods and services with the supply of all goods and services. This model provides a picture of the economy's short-run ups and downs and its long-run trends. It also helps us understand the causes of the business cycle.

Worldwide recession from 2007 to 2009 left many economic resources underutilized, like these homes in Spain.

BIG QUESTIONS

- **What is a business cycle, and why are business cycles so difficult to predict?**
- **What is aggregate demand?**
- **What is aggregate supply?**
- **How does the aggregate demand–aggregate supply model help us understand the economy?**

What Is a Business Cycle, and Why Are Business Cycles So Difficult to Predict?

A **recession** is a short-term economic downturn that typically lasts about 6 to 18 months.

The **Great Recession** was the U.S. recession lasting from December 2007 to June 2009.

We have seen that GDP data is used to measure living standards and economic growth. It is also used to determine whether an economy is expanding or contracting in the short run. In recent years, this use of GDP data has received a lot of media attention as a result of the Great Recession. A **recession** is a short-term economic downturn that typically lasts about 6 to 18 months. Even the mere threat of recession strikes fear into people's hearts, because income levels fall and many individuals lose their jobs or cannot find work during recessions. The U.S. recession that began in 2007 and lasted into 2009 has been dubbed the **Great Recession** because of its length and depth. It lasted for 19 months, and real GDP fell by almost 9% in the last three months of 2008. In addition, the recovery from the Great Recession has been very slow.

The **long run** is a period of time sufficient for all parts of the economy to adjust to economic conditions.

The **short run** is the period of time in which only some parts of the economy adjust.

As we explore macroeconomic changes, it's important to consider the time frame of our analysis. As we discussed in Chapter 5, firms evaluate decisions in both the short run and the long run. In the macroeconomy, this distinction is a little bit different. The **long run** in macroeconomics is a period of time sufficient for all parts of the economy to adjust to economic conditions. The long run doesn't arrive after a set period of time; it arrives when all prices have adjusted. However, in the **short run**, only some parts of the economy can adjust. The aggregate demand–aggregate supply model we examine in the second part of this chapter considers both time frames. Business cycles, however, illustrate changes only in the short run.

Business Cycles

A **business cycle** is a short-run fluctuation in economic activity.

Even if an economy is expanding in the long run, it is normal for it to experience temporary downturns. **Business cycles** are short-run fluctuations in economic activity. Figure 12.1 illustrates a theoretical business cycle in relation to a long-term trend in real GDP growth. The straight line represents the

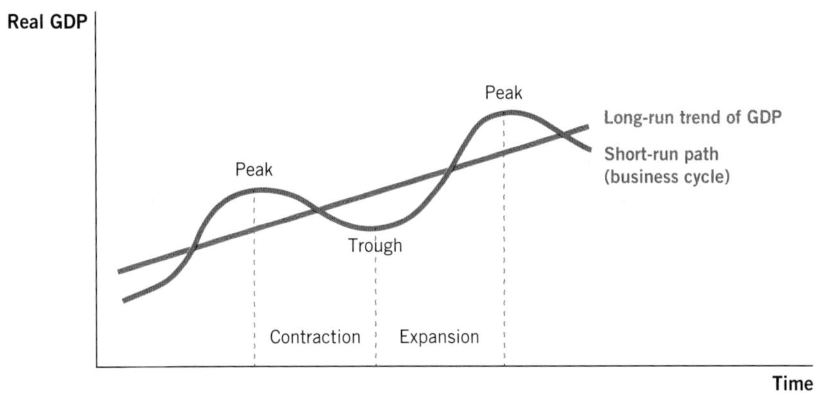

FIGURE 12.1

The Business Cycle

The long-run trend of GDP shows consistent growth. The business cycle reflects the fluctuations that an economy typically exhibits. When the economy is growing faster than the long-run trend, it is in the expansion period of the business cycle. But when growth is slower than the trend, the economy is in a contraction. In real life, the cycle is not nearly as smooth and easy to spot as we illustrate here.

long-run trend of real GDP. The slope of the trend line is the average long-run growth of real GDP. For the United States, this is about 2% per year. But real GDP doesn't typically grow at exactly 2% per year. Instead of tracking exactly along the trend line, the economy experiences fluctuations in output. The wavy line represents the actual path of real GDP over time. It climbs to *peaks* (high points) when GDP growth is higher than usual and falls to *troughs* (low points) when output growth is lower than usual.

The peaks and troughs divide the business cycle into two phases: expansions and contractions. An **economic expansion** occurs from the bottom of a trough to the next peak, when the economy is growing. After a certain period, the economy enters a recession, or an **economic contraction**—the period extending from the peak downward to the trough. During this phase, the economy is shrinking. During expansions, jobs are relatively easy to find and average income levels climb. During contractions, more people lose their jobs and income levels often fall.

An **economic expansion** is a phase of the business cycle during which the economy is growing.

An **economic contraction** is a phase of the business cycle during which the economy is shrinking.

Figure 12.1 makes it look like business cycles are uniform and predictable, but the reality is very different. Figure 12.2 plots U.S. real GDP over time, with contractionary periods—the recessions—shaded. You can easily spot the Great Recession, which began in December 2007 and lasted through June 2009.

GDP declines during recessionary periods and increases during expansions, but these phases don't occur in a consistent, predictable pattern. Therein lies the problem. If you know a tornado is coming, you'll try to get out of its path before it hits. Unfortunately, you don't always know where and when a tornado will strike. Additionally, sometimes forecasts for tornadoes are wrong and all you get is a stiff breeze. The same is true of business cycles. Specifically, there are three uncertainties surrounding the business cycle: duration, depth, and dispersion.

- *Duration* refers to how long a business cycle lasts. We measure the length of a business cycle from the peak to the next peak. No two business

FIGURE 12.2

U.S. Real GDP and Recessions, 1960–2014 (in 2009 U.S. dollars)

Over time, U.S. real GDP fluctuates. The shaded areas indicate periods of recession, when real GDP consistently declines. The Great Recession, which began in December 2007 and lasted through June 2009, was a particularly deep and lengthy modern recession.

Source: U.S. Bureau of Economic Analysis.

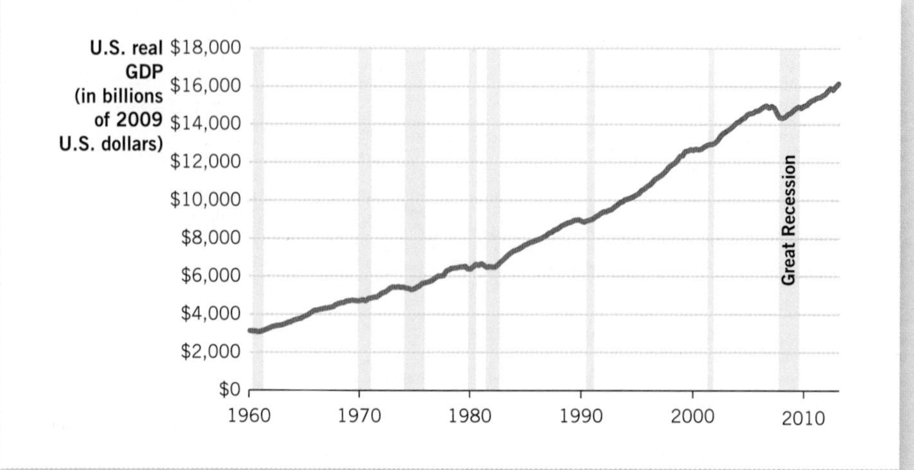

cycles last the same amount of time, which makes preparing for and dealing with them more difficult. Similarly, we don't know how long the phases of any given cycle will last. For example, the recovery after the recession ending in 1982 lasted almost eight years. The recovery after the 1980 recession lasted just a little over one year.

- The *depth* of a business cycle indicates its severity. How low the trough goes, and how high the peak might be, are unique to each cycle. No one knows beforehand whether the next recession will be like the Great Recession or whether it will be like the recession of 1991, which was so minor that most people didn't even know about it until after it was over.
- *Dispersion* refers to the segments of the economy that are affected by the recession. Firms in industries that sell necessities perform more consistently during the ups and downs of the business cycle. People need food, medicine, and gasoline whether the economy is good or bad, and they tend to hold their levels of consumption of these goods fairly constant regardless of the state of the economy. They might buy more generic products in particularly bad times, but they're still buying food. Other industries are more prone to harm from economic downturns. They also are the industries that do very well during recoveries. For example, companies that sell high-end electronics, designer clothing, and automobiles are more subject to the fluctuations in the business cycle. People will put off buying a new car or a pair of expensive Lucky Jeans when times are tight. When the economy is roaring along, though, people are more willing to purchase these products.

Because there is no pattern to the depth and duration of the phases of the business cycle, attempting to deal with them is particularly challenging. We have mentioned (in Chapter 10) that the objective of government policy is economic stability. With the business cycle in mind, we now have a way to examine that policy goal. Stabilization means preventing the highs of the business cycle from getting too high. Why? A recovery means economic growth and increased employment, but it's often accompanied by higher inflation. If things are roaring along too well, prices might be rising unacceptably quickly.

Stabilization also means preventing the lows from getting too low. A contraction (another term for recession) means that economic growth is negative, the economy is shrinking in terms of per capita GDP, and unemployment rates are getting higher. Usually, inflation is low, but that's of little comfort if you don't have a job.

Not knowing how long a recession might last makes advancing good policy quite difficult. To illustrate this, let's now take a look at what was going on during the Great Recession, in terms of both the actual events and the policy reaction.

The Great Recession

> By now, it's clear to everyone that we have inherited an economic crisis as deep and dire as any since the days of the Great Depression. Millions of jobs that Americans relied on just a year ago are gone; millions more of the nest eggs families worked so hard to build have vanished. People everywhere are worried about what tomorrow will bring.
>
> —President Obama, February 5, 2009

In the quote above, dated just two weeks after President Obama took office for his first term, he declared that the recession was as bad as any since the Great Depression. But while the Great Recession was certainly a rough patch for the U.S. economy, it wasn't nearly as severe as the Great Depression, which lasted for most of the 1930s.

In December 2007, the U.S. economy entered the downturn we now call the Great Recession. Some analysts named it the Great Recession because the downturn was longer and deeper than typical recessions (although not nearly as long or as deep as the Great Depression). In addition, the Great Recession was accompanied by significant problems in the financial markets—another similarity with the Great Depression. Finally, the name stuck when the effects of the recession refused to subside for several years after the recession was technically over. Let's look more closely at just how serious the contraction was.

The Depth and Duration of the Great Recession

The official duration of the Great Recession was 19 months (December 2007 to June 2009), making it the longest recession since World War II. But even this duration understates the full amount of time that it affected the U.S. economy. For several years after the recession was deemed to be over, unemployment remained high and real GDP grew slowly.

One way to grasp the depth and duration of the Great Recession is to compare it with the other recessions that have occurred since World War II. Figure 12.3 shows comparative data on real GDP and the unemployment rate. Panel (a) compares the pattern of real GDP during the Great Recession and an average pattern of the other recessions since World War II. To illustrate the two paths of GDP, we set them to 100 at the onset of the contraction. Notice that during a typical recession, real GDP falls slightly and then comes back to its original level after about a year and a half. In contrast, during the Great Recession output fell significantly and then recovered more slowly. In fact, it took nearly four years for real GDP to reach its pre-recession level in the third quarter of 2011.

FIGURE 12.3

Unemployment Rate and Real GDP, Great Recession versus All Other Post-WWII Recessions

(a) During the Great Recession, real GDP fell further and rebounded more slowly than it did during other postwar recessions. (b) The unemployment rate during the Great Recession rose to levels far higher than occurred in the other postwar recessions, and it remained high long after the rate typically falls.

Sources: Panel (a): U.S. Bureau of Economic Analysis; panel (b): U.S. Bureau of Labor Statistics.

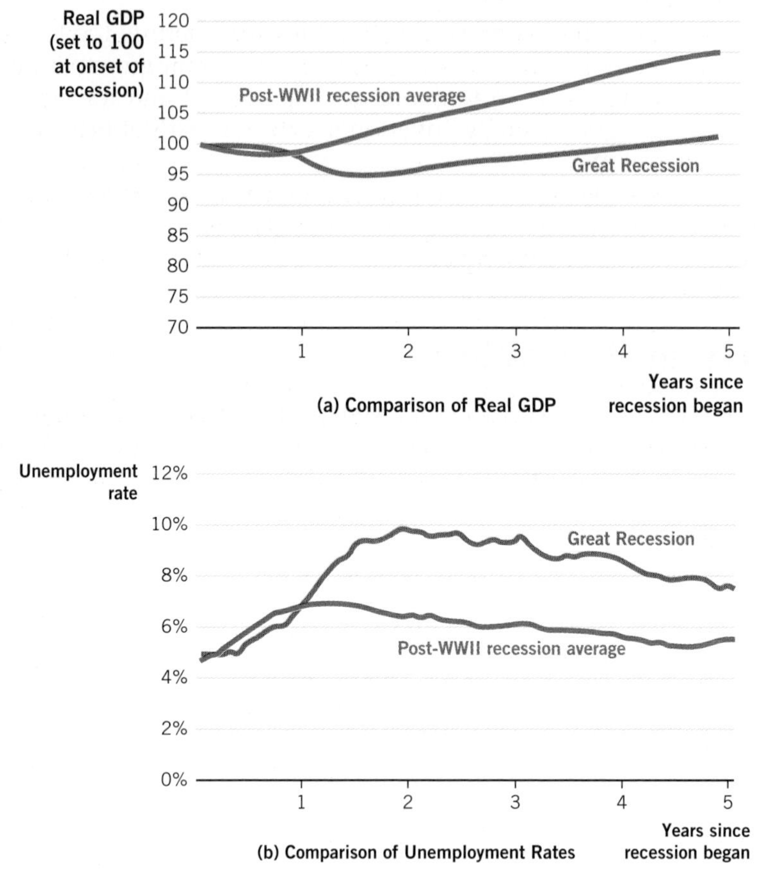

Panel (b) shows the monthly unemployment rate for the Great Recession as compared to an average unemployment rate across the other post–World War II recessions. For a typical recession, the unemployment rate climbed to around 7% and then declined after about 12 to 15 months. But for the Great Recession, the unemployment rate climbed to 10% in October 2009 (22 months after the recession began) and remained at or near 8% even five years after the recession began. Taken together, panels (a) and (b) indicate that the Great Recession was more severe than a typical recession.

Stabilization Policy, Lags, and the Great Recession

The idea of using policy to mitigate the business cycle originated with John Maynard Keynes, the British economist whose ideas rose to prominence during the Great Depression (see Chapter 10, Appendix 10.A). Keynes believed that government taxing and spending power could be used to offset the ups and downs of business cycles. This approach is called **countercyclical fiscal policy** because the government uses its taxing and spending powers to reduce the disruptions caused by the cycles. If the economy is bad, the government attempts to stimulate it by raising spending or cutting taxes. If the

A **countercyclical fiscal policy** is a government policy intended to reduce disruptions caused by business cycles.

economy is good, the government cuts spending and raises taxes to keep the economy from growing too quickly. While these policies sound reasonable, there are consequences to consider.

In the United States, economic policy must be approved by both Congress and the president. Whether or not these two branches of government get along, there are timing issues to consider. The first issue is that it takes time to realize there's a problem. This **recognition lag** is inherent in dealing with business cycles. You just don't know ahead of time when the economy will change directions. The second timing problem is that policymakers have to agree on a plan. This doesn't happen overnight. It can take days, weeks, or even months to hammer out an acceptable strategy. Economists don't always agree on a proper course of action, and politicians are equally slow to reach consensus. This time gap is known as an **implementation lag**. Finally, once the plan is finalized, it must be put into action. The time between passing legislation and observing its effectiveness constitutes an **impact lag.**

A **recognition lag** occurs when it takes time to recognize the existence of a problem in the economy.

An **implementation lag** occurs when it takes time to decide on a course of action and pass the legislation required to solve a problem in the economy.

An **impact lag** is the time between passing legislation and observing its effectiveness.

During the Great Recession, President Barack Obama signed into law a policy to stimulate the economy. The American Recovery and Reinvestment Act of 2009 was supposed to help reinvigorate the economy, which had been in recession since late 2007. While the recognition lag was fairly short during the Great Recession, the implementation lag was quite a bit longer. The stimulus legislation includes spending through 2019, meaning that the spending authorized by the law will take place over a ten-year period. This is an extraordinarily long implementation lag. The Great Recession officially ended in 2009. Thus, the vast majority of the policy designed to get the country out of recession was put into effect after the recession had ended! It was feared that the law could therefore stoke inflationary pressures in the coming years. The impact lag could be longer still. When a policy takes a long time to implement, judging its impact is very difficult. Is the economy improving because of the policy, or is it recovering on its own?

This is where the difficult balance must be struck. Most economists can make suggestions for how to fix things when they appear to be broken. Because every situation is different, though, these recommendations might work in some instances and not in others. As a result, we can do our best to monitor the economy and try to limit the fluctuation, but economists have yet to find a foolproof way of limiting the naturally occurring ups and downs of the business cycle.

Regardless of the various opinions on how policy should be used, policymakers rely on a specific model of the macroeconomy when deciding on policy. This model helps them predict the impact of policy changes on the major macro variables (GDP growth, unemployment, and inflation) in both the short run and over time. We now turn our attention to this *aggregate demand–aggregate supply model*, which is one of the more useful macroeconomic models.

ECONOMICS IN THE REAL WORLD

Comparing Recessions

While our focus has been on the Great Recession, and how it compares to the Great Depression of the 1930s, these are not really comparable events. It turns out that the contraction from July 1981 to November 1982 (let's call it the 1982 recession) is similar to the Great Recession.

FIGURE 12.4

	1982 Recession	Great Recession (2007 to 2009)
Length	16 months	19 months
Worst quarter	–6.4%	–8.9%
Total decline	2.64%	2.95%

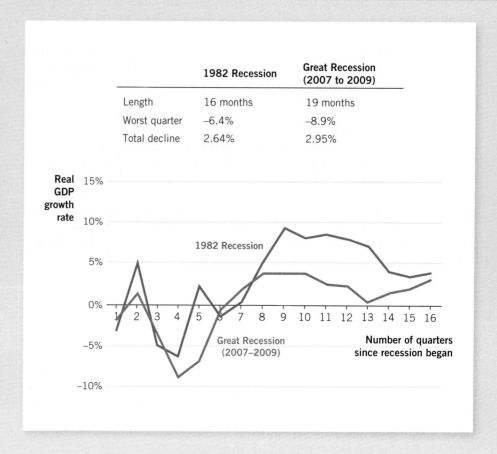

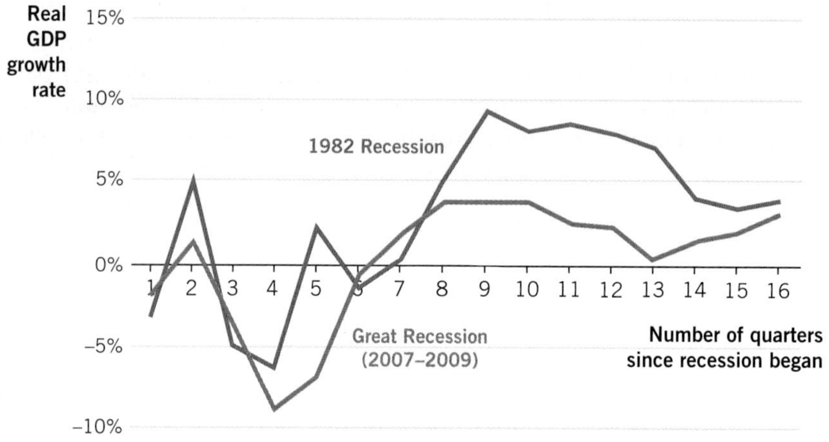

Real GDP Growth Rates for the United States during Two Recessions

The quarterly changes in real GDP for the United States were very similar over the course of the 1982 recession and the Great Recession of 2007–2009. However, real GDP rebounded to very high growth rates after the recession was over at the end of 1982. When the Great Recession ended in 2009, the growth rates were much lower and remained low for much longer.

Source: U.S. Bureau of Economic Analysis.

First, consider real GDP growth over the course of both recessions. Figure 12.4 compares quarterly GDP growth rates beginning near the official start of each recession. The two recessions were similar in duration: the 1982 recession lasted for 16 months, and the Great Recession lasted for 19 months. They were also similar in depth: the worst quarter during the 1982 recession witnessed −6.4% growth, while the Great Recession saw −8.9% growth in its worst quarter. However, the big difference between the two episodes is in the economic recovery after the recessions officially ended. In 1982 and 1983, the economy rebounded with growth rates of almost 10%. But following the Great Recession, in 2010 and 2011 real GDP growth rates were only 2% to 3%.

Now let's compare unemployment rates for the two recessions, as shown in Figure 12.5. The unemployment rate in the 1982 recession was consistently higher than the unemployment rate of the Great Recession during the actual recession period. But the real difference is in the slow recovery following the Great Recession. While during both recessions unemployment clearly remained above the natural rate of between 4% and 6% for some time, the unemployment rate in the 1982 recession began to fall soon after the official end of that downturn (see the vertical orange line). In the case of the Great Recession, unemployment remained above 9% for nearly 18 months after recession was declared to be over (noted by the vertical blue line).

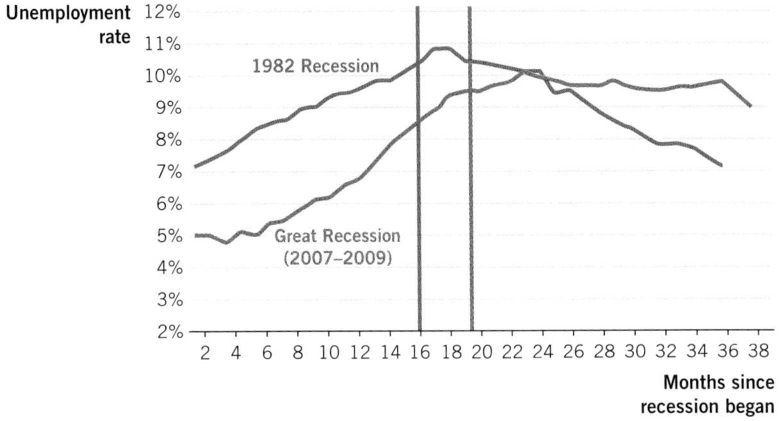

FIGURE 12.5

U.S. Unemployment Rates during Two Recessions

The 1982 recession and the Great Recession of 2007–2009 both led to unemployment rates above 10%. However, in each case the recovery, indicated by vertical lines, was very different. The most recent recession left unemployment lingering above 9% for several years.

Source: U.S. Bureau of Labor Statistics.

The unemployment data is consistent with the GDP data. Both sets of data show two recessions similar in depth and duration. But the 1982 recession was followed by a swift recovery, while the effects of the Great Recession lingered for several years afterward. How do these findings compare to the Great Depression from the 1930s? Consider this: during the Great Depression, real GDP fell by 30% over three years, and the unemployment rate, which actually topped 25% at one point, remained higher than 15% for almost an entire decade. Thankfully, we haven't seen conditions that bad at any time since. ✷

What Is Aggregate Demand?

The business cycle model from Figure 12.1 illustrates the movement of GDP over time, but it doesn't tell us much else. To get a more complete picture of the economy, we turn to a more comprehensive model: the *aggregate demand–aggregate supply model*.

The word "aggregate" means "total." At the core of the model are the concepts of demand and supply, which are already familiar to you. In earlier chapters, we looked at the demand and supply of a single good, like salmon. But now we look at the demand and supply of all final goods and services in an economy—the demand and supply of GDP. **Aggregate demand** is the total demand for final goods and services in an economy. **Aggregate supply** is the total supply of final goods and services in an economy.

Aggregate demand is the total demand for final goods and services in an economy.

Aggregate supply is the total supply of final goods and services in an economy.

We consider each side of the economy separately before bringing them together. The next section explains aggregate demand; after that, we look at aggregate supply.

Determining Aggregate Demand

We have an experiment for you to try. Ask five people the following question: *How can you personally help our economy?* We predict that most responses will focus on buying something or spending money somewhere. In our model of the economy, this is demand. Aggregate demand is the spending side of the economy. When people spend on goods and services, aggregate demand increases, and most people believe that this spending is what drives the economy. We'll see later that this is only partially true.

To determine aggregate demand, we sum up spending from different sources in the economy. These sources include private domestic consumers, who buy cars, food, clothing, education, and many other goods and services. Business firms are another major group; they buy resources needed to produce output. The government is a large purchaser of labor and other resources used to produce government services. Finally, foreign consumers buy many goods and services produced in the United States. These four major groups constitute the four pieces of aggregate demand: consumption (C), investment (I), government (G), and net exports (NX). The total of these four yields aggregate demand (AD) in a given period:

(Equation 12.1)
$$AD = C + I + G + NX$$

As we study aggregate demand, we'll consider factors that affect each of these sources. (You may recognize all of these factors as the components of GDP, as discussed in Chapter 11.)

Figure 12.6 shows a graph of the aggregate demand curve. On the horizontal axis, we plot quantities of all final goods and services, which constitute real GDP. On the vertical axis, we measure the overall **price level (P)** in the economy. This is not the price of any particular good or service, but rather a general level of prices for the whole economy. A rise in P indicates inflation in the economy.

The **price level (P)** is the general level of prices for the whole economy. It is a measure of the average prices of goods and services throughout the economy.

FIGURE 12.6

The Aggregate Demand Curve

The aggregate demand curve shows the inverse relationship between the quantity demanded of real GDP and the economy's price level (P).

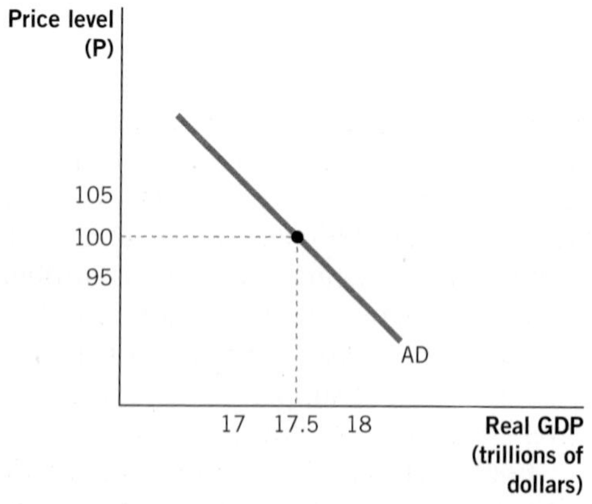

On the graph in Figure 12.6, we have labeled a particular point where the price level is 100 and the quantity of aggregate demand (real GDP) is $17.5 trillion, which was the size of the U.S. economy in 2014. The negative slope of the aggregate demand (AD) curve means that increases in the price level lead to decreases in the quantity of aggregate demand. Similarly, when the price level falls, the quantity of aggregate demand rises. The aggregate demand curve thus has the familiar downward slope.

It's important to remember as we investigate the aggregate model that the different components of GDP (consumption, investment, government spending, and net exports) are affected by changes in the price level. Consumption is the largest part of GDP, so when the price level changes, the changes in consumption typically have a much more significant impact on GDP than any of the other components of GDP do.

It's also important to distinguish between *shifts in* versus *movements along* the aggregate demand curve. Moving along the aggregate demand curve is a result of a change in the economy's price level. In contrast, shifts in the demand curve occur when people demand more goods and services at a given price level. These shifts can come from any of the components of aggregate demand: consumption, investment, government spending, and net exports. In the next section, we look at five factors that shift aggregate demand—in other words, these are things that cause the aggregate demand curve to move.

Shifts in Aggregate Demand

Aggregate demand shifts for a variety of reasons. In fact, anything that affects any of the four components of GDP can shift the aggregate demand curve. When people demand more goods and services at all price levels, aggregate demand shifts to the right, signifying an increase in aggregate demand. When people demand fewer goods and services at all price levels, aggregate demand shifts to the left, indicating a decrease in aggregate demand. In this section, we consider five common factors that shift aggregate demand: changes in real wealth, expected income, expected future prices, foreign income and wealth, and the value of the dollar.

Real Wealth

One determinant of people's spending habits is their current wealth. If your great-aunt died and left you $1 million, you'd probably start spending more right away. You'd go out to eat more often, upgrade your wardrobe, and maybe even shop for some bigger-ticket items. This observation also applies to entire nations. When national wealth increases, aggregate demand increases. If wealth falls, aggregate demand declines.

Median home prices fell from $248,000 to $222,000 between 2007 and 2010. That roughly 10% drop led to a significant decrease in many people's wealth, as well as a decline in aggregate demand.

For example, many people own stocks or mutual funds that are tied to the stock market. When the stock market fluctuates, the wealth of a large portion of the population is affected. When overall stock values rise, wealth increases, which increases aggregate demand. However, if the stock

ECONOMICS IN THE MEDIA

Changes in Wealth

Dumb and Dumber

In this comedy from 1994, two likeable but incredibly simpleminded friends, Harry and Lloyd, try to return a suitcase to its owner. For most of the movie, they have no idea that the suitcase they're trying to return is filled with a million dollars.

When they accidentally open the case while en route to Aspen, Colorado, the friends discover the cash and decide to spend the money freely by writing IOUs and placing them in the suitcase to be repaid later. The newfound money creates a change in Harry and Lloyd's wealth. The two friends immediately enjoy their unexpected wealth by staying at a lavish hotel, giving away $100 bills as tips for the staff, and even using money to wipe their noses when they can't find ordinary tissues to do the job.

What kind of tuxedo would you buy if you had a suitcase full of money?

In one sense, Harry and Lloyd are much like the rest of us. A change in our wealth affects our demand for goods and services. But Harry and Lloyd are dumb and dumber in that their spending is completely based on someone else's wealth.

market falls significantly, then wealth declines and aggregate demand decreases. Widespread changes in real-estate values also affect wealth. For many people, a house represents a large portion of their wealth. When real-estate values rise and fall, individual wealth follows, and this outcome affects aggregate demand.

Expected Income

Expected future income also affects aggregate demand. If people expect higher income in the future, they spend more today. For example, graduating college seniors often begin spending more as soon as they secure a job offer, even though the job and the corresponding income may not start until months later. But expectations aren't always accurate. We consume today based on what we anticipate for the future, even though the future is uncertain. Still, the entire economy can be affected by a change in consumers' general sentiment.

How much income does your future hold?

One measure of consumer expectations is the *consumer confidence* or *consumer sentiment index*. This index uses survey data to estimate how consumers feel about the economy's future direction. Confidence, or lack of confidence, in the economy's future changes consumer spending today. Consumer confidence can swing up and down with unpredictable events such as national elections or international turmoil. When these sentiments change, they shift aggregate demand.

Expected Prices

Expectations also matter when it comes to future prices. When people expect higher prices in the future, they're more likely to spend today, so current aggregate demand increases. Consider a nation with rampant inflation. When people in this nation get paid, they'll spend their income quickly to take advantage of today's lower prices. If, instead, people expect lower prices in the future, today's aggregate demand will decline.

Foreign Income and Wealth

When the income of people in foreign nations grows, their demand for U.S. goods increases. For the United States, this means that exports will increase, causing net exports to increase as well. Since net exports are a part of aggregate demand, when foreign citizens buy more U.S. goods and services the result is increased aggregate demand in the United States. In contrast, if a foreign nation goes into recession, its demand for U.S. goods and services falls. One recent positive example is the growth of large emerging economies and their demand for U.S. goods. As Brazil, China, and India have grown wealthier, their demand for U.S. goods and services has increased.

ECONOMICS IN THE REAL WORLD

General Motors Sales Up in China, but Down in Europe

General Motors, one of the world's largest car manufacturers, now sells over 250,000 vehicles per month in China. GM announced in November 2014 that it had already sold more than 3 million vehicles in China, well ahead of its 2013 numbers. Sales of the Cadillac line were particularly strong, rising 58% from 2013. This trend is contrary to the growth of the luxury car's performance in the United States, where 2014 sales were slightly down from 2013.

GM's Buick product line does exceptionally well in China. Buick now sells about four times as many cars in China as in the United States. This sales growth for GM is thanks in large part to the growing incomes of many Chinese citizens.

The bad news for GM comes from Europe. Increased sales in China have been offset by slowing sales in Europe, where many economies were recovering from recessions, but only mildly. By mid-2014, GM was continuing to see declining sales of its cars in Europe. ✳

In China, people say that they would rather drive a Buick.

Value of the Dollar

Exchange rates are another international factor that shifts aggregate demand. We cover these in more detail in Chapter 18. For now, think in terms of the value of the dollar in world markets. When the value of the dollar rises relative to the currency of other nations, Americans find that imports are less expensive. At the same time, it becomes more expensive for other nations to buy U.S. exports. These two factors combine to reduce net exports, so a stronger dollar leads to a decline in net exports, which reduces aggregate demand.

Figure 12.7 summarizes how the five factors that we have discussed shift aggregate demand. On the graph, initial aggregate demand is shown as AD_1. Aggregate demand shifts to the right (to AD_2) with *increases* in real wealth, expected income, expected future prices, and foreign income and wealth, or with *decreases* in the value of the U.S. dollar. In contrast, aggregate demand shifts to the left (to AD_3) with *decreases* in real wealth, expected income, expected future prices, and foreign income and wealth, or with *increases* in the value of the U.S. dollar.

Before we move on to aggregate supply, let's tie this in with our earlier discussion of the business cycle. Recessions, or slowdowns in economic activity, are normally associated with decreases in aggregate demand. Notice how a leftward shift in AD reduces output and raises unemployment. These are the conditions that typify recessions. It is important to keep this in mind going forward because policies that are designed to stimulate the economy usually focus on trying to increase AD.

FIGURE 12.7

Factors That Shift the Aggregate Demand Curve

The aggregate demand curve shifts to the right with *increases* in real wealth, expected income, expected future prices, and foreign income and wealth, or with a *decrease* in the value of the dollar. The aggregate demand curve shifts to the left with *decreases* in real wealth, expected income, expected future prices, and foreign income and wealth, or with an *increase* in the value of the dollar.

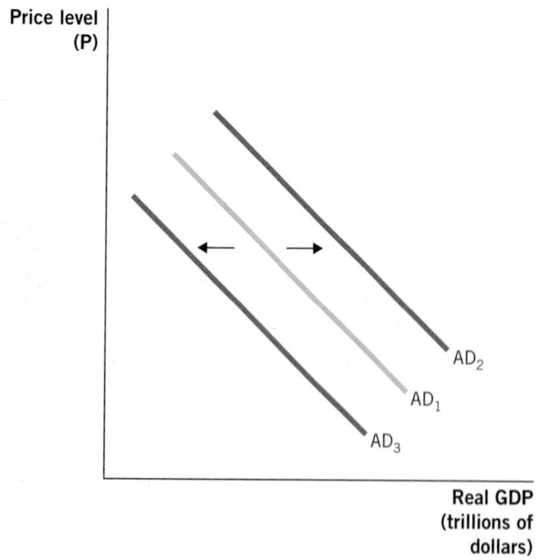

Shift factor	Increase in factor leads to:	Decrease in factor leads to:
Real wealth	Increase to AD_2	Decrease to AD_3
Expected income	Increase to AD_2	Decrease to AD_3
Expected price level	Increase to AD_2	Decrease to AD_3
Foreign income	Increase to AD_2	Decrease to AD_3
Value of the dollar	Decrease to AD_3	Increase to AD_2

PRACTICE WHAT YOU KNOW

Aggregate Demand: Shifts in Aggregate Demand versus Movements along the Aggregate Demand Curve

One of the challenges in applying the aggregate demand–aggregate supply model is distinguishing shifts in aggregate demand from movements along the aggregate demand curve. Here we present four scenarios.

Question: Does each scenario below cause a movement along the curve or a shift in the curve? Explain your response each time.

1. Consumers read positive economic news and then expect strong future economic growth.
2. Due to an increase in the price level in the United States, consumers substitute out of clothes made in the United States and into clothes made in Nicaragua.
3. Several European economies go into recession.
4. A decrease in the price level leads to greater purchasing power for consumers.

Answers:

1. This scenario involves an increase in expected future income, which increases aggregate demand and shifts the curve to the right.
2. This scenario begins with a change in the price level, so we know it will involve a movement along the curve. Here the price level rises, so it is a movement back along the curve, signaling a decrease in the quantity of aggregate demand.
3. Foreign recession leads to lower foreign income and wealth, an outcome that decreases the demand for goods and services made in the United States (U.S. exports). Less demand for U.S. products causes a decrease in aggregate demand in the United States. The aggregate demand curve shifts to the left.
4. Since this scenario involves a change in the price level, it will lead to a movement along the aggregate demand curve. In this case, the lower prices lead consumers to spend more, thereby increasing the quantity of aggregate demand.

Textile workers in Nicaragua depend on the export economy as a source of jobs.

What Is Aggregate Supply?

We have seen that aggregate demand embodies the spending desires of an economy. It tells us how many goods and services people want at different price levels. But peoples' wants and desires alone don't determine GDP. We must also consider the supply side of the economy, which tells us about the producers' willingness and ability to supply output.

To understand aggregate supply, we need to consider how changes in the overall price level (P) affect the firm's supply decisions. But the influence of the price level on aggregate supply depends on the time frame we're considering. Recall that the *long run* in macroeconomics is a period of time sufficient for all parts of the economy, including prices, to adjust. However, in the *short run*, only some prices can change.

The **full-employment output level (Y*)** is the output produced in the economy when unemployment is at the natural rate.

Because there is a short run and a long run, there are two versions of aggregate supply. Long-run aggregate supply reflects the economy's tendency to revert to the **full-employment output level (Y*)**, which is the output produced in the economy when unemployment (u) is at the natural rate (u*). (Recall from Chapter 11 that the natural unemployment rate is the typical unemployment rate that occurs when the economy is growing normally.) Short-run aggregate supply illustrates the fluctuation around the long-run trend that we saw in the business-cycle model.

Long-Run Aggregate Supply

As we will explore in more detail in Chapter 13, an economy's long-run economic growth depends on resources, technology, and institutions. In the short run there may be fluctuations in real GDP, but in the long run the economy moves toward the full-employment output level (Y*). Because all prices (including the prices of inputs) can adjust in the long run, firms can change their production processes and the way they use inputs to produce a sustainable level of output consistent with the full-employment output level. Therefore, no matter what the price level, the economy can produce only this level of output in the long run unless the conditions in the economy change.

Figure 12.8 plots the economy's long-run aggregate supply curve (LRAS). Notice that we plot this curve with the economy's price level (P) on the vertical axis and real GDP (Y) on the horizontal axis. Because prices don't affect the full-employment output level, the LRAS curve is a vertical line at Y*. If the price level is 100, the quantity of aggregate supply is equal to Y*. If the price level rises to 110 or falls to 90, output in the long run is still Y*.

Shifts in Long-Run Aggregate Supply

The long-run aggregate supply curve shifts when there is a long-run change in a nation's ability to produce output. The factors that shift long-run aggregate supply are the same factors that determine economic growth, as we discuss in Chapter 13: resources, technology, and institutions.

For example, new technology leads to increases in long-run aggregate supply. Consider what would happen if a firm develops a safe, effective, and

FIGURE 12.8

The Long-Run Aggregate Supply Curve

The LRAS curve is vertical at Y* because in the long run the price level does not affect the quantity of aggregate supply. Y* is the full-employment output level, where the unemployment rate (u) is equal to the natural rate of unemployment (u*).

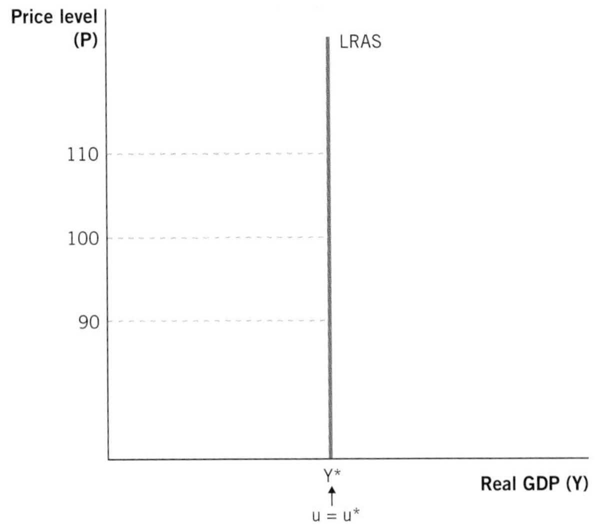

affordable way to transport people across long distances—let's call it a transporter. This technology enables people to travel more quickly and reduces congestion on the roads. It would therefore increase long-run aggregate supply because it would increase productivity in the economy: we would now produce more with our limited resources.

We can illustrate economic growth by using the long-run aggregate supply curve. As the economy grows over time, full-employment output increases and the LRAS curve shifts to the right.

Figure 12.9 illustrates shifts in long-run aggregate supply. Initially, the LRAS curve is vertical at Y*, which depends on a fixed level of resources, technology, and institutions. After the transporter technology is introduced, $LRAS_1$ shifts to the right (to $LRAS_2$) because now the economy's full-employment output is greater than before. Notice that both before and after the shift, the unemployment rate is at the natural rate (u*). The new technology does not reduce the unemployment rate, but workers in the economy are more productive. The new output rate, Y**, represents a new full-employment output rate.

But the $LRAS_1$ curve can also shift to the left (to $LRAS_3$). This shift would occur with a permanent decline in the economy's resources or with the adoption of inefficient institutions.

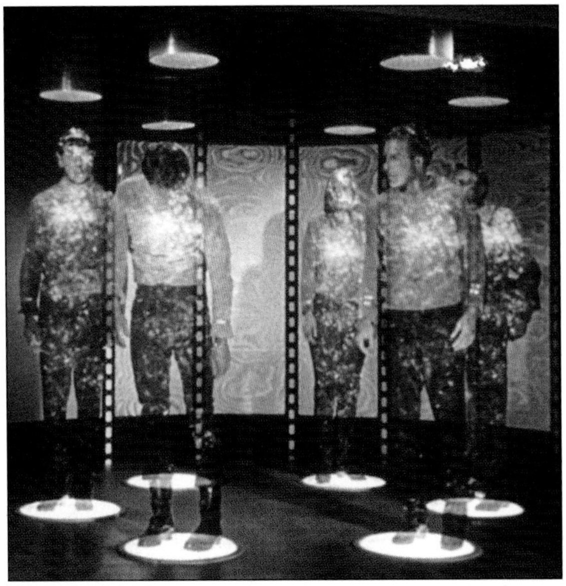

If a transporter could be developed, people would move around much more easily, traffic would subside, and the economy's LRAS curve would shift to the right.

FIGURE 12.9

Shifts in Long-Run Aggregate Supply

Shifts in the long-run aggregate supply curve occur when there is a change in an economy's resources, technology, or institutions. A technological advance moves an economy from $LRAS_1$ to $LRAS_2$. This is a picture of economic growth. When the LRAS curve shifts to the right, this movement also indicates a change in the economy's full-employment output level from Y^* to Y^{**}. The unemployment rate doesn't change, but workers are more productive. A shift to $LRAS_3$ indicates a decrease in an economy's resources or technology, or the adoption of inefficient institutions. One of these changes would decrease the full-employment output level from Y^* to Y^{***}.

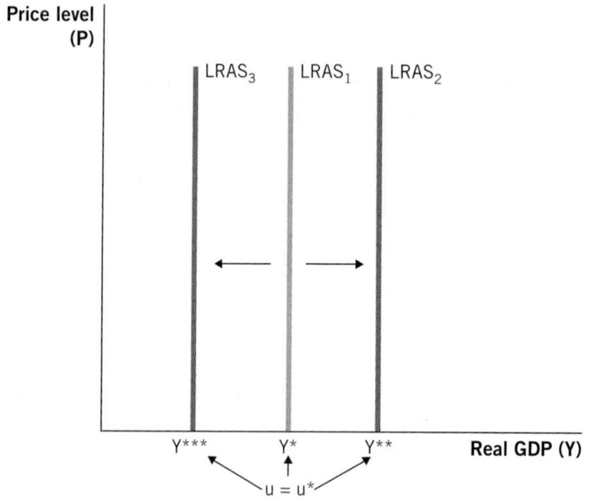

Short-Run Aggregate Supply

We just saw that the price level does not impact aggregate supply in the long run. However, in the short run there's a positive relationship between the price level and the quantity of aggregate supply. The primary reason for this relationship is inflexible input prices.

Let's look more closely at input prices. As an employer, you would pay workers a particular wage, and this wage is set for a period of time. In addition, interest rates for your loans are normally fixed. Economists say that these input prices are *sticky*, since they take time to change. In contrast, output prices tend to be more flexible. Whereas input prices are typically set in a written contract, output prices are generally easy to change. For example, coffee shop prices are often written on a chalkboard, which makes it pretty easy to change them from day to day.

The distinction between sticky input prices and flexible output prices is at the center of our discussion of aggregate supply because it affects the way firms react when prices do move. If you owned a coffee shop, you might negotiate one-year contracts with your workers. Your coffee-bean suppliers fix their prices for a certain period as well. If inflation begins to push up all prices in the macroeconomy, you pull out your chalkboard eraser and raise the price of lattes, espressos, and mochas; these are output prices, and they're very flexible. But your input prices are sticky (the coffee beans still cost the same, and you have to pay your employees the same amount)—at least for a while. Therefore, your costs remain the same. And here is the link to aggregate supply: because your costs don't rise but your revenues do, it makes sense for you to increase output. When you and other firms raise output, GDP rises.

These output prices are very flexible—they can be changed with the push of a button.

The dynamic between sticky input prices and flexible output prices explains the positive slope of the short-run aggregate supply curve. Figure 12.10 shows the short-run aggregate supply curve, labeled SRAS. When the price level rises from 100 to 110, firms produce more in the short run and real GDP rises from \$17.5 trillion to \$18 trillion. In this case, firms want to increase output because profit margins (the gap between prices they charge and input prices) are rising. When the price level falls to 90, firms produce less in the short run because flexible output prices fall but sticky input prices stay relatively high, thereby narrowing profit margins. As a result, real GDP decreases to \$17 trillion.

Any type of price stickiness leads to a positively sloped aggregate supply curve in the short run. But keep in mind that since all prices can change in the long run, the long-run aggregate supply curve is vertical at the full-employment output level.

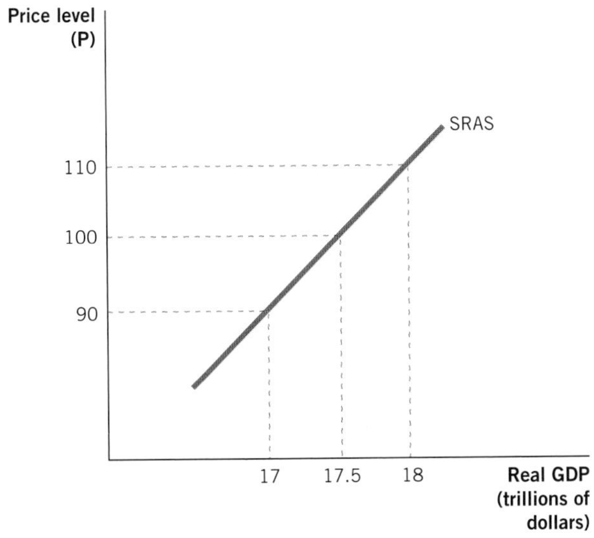

FIGURE 12.10

The Short-Run Aggregate Supply Curve

The positive slope of the short-run aggregate supply curve indicates that increases in the economy's price level lead to an increase in the quantity of aggregate supply in the short run. For example, if the price level rises from 100 to 110, the quantity of aggregate supply rises from \$17.5 trillion to \$18 trillion in the short run. The reason is that some prices are sticky in the short run.

ECONOMICS IN THE REAL WORLD

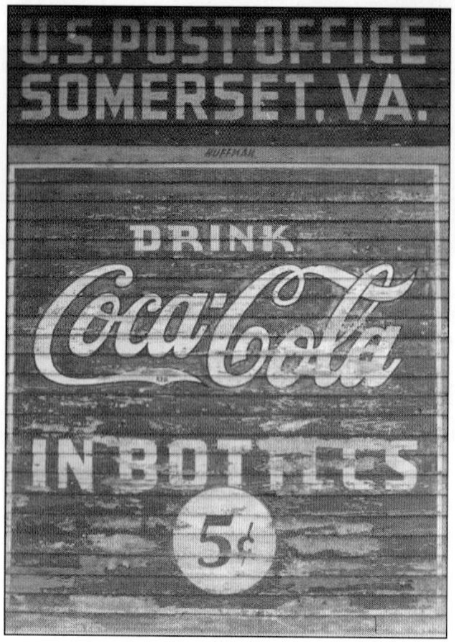

5-Cent Coca-Cola

In November 2012, National Public Radio ran a story on what might be the stickiest price of all time.* In 1886, people could buy a Coca-Cola for a nickel. Fully 70 years later, the price for a bottle of Coke was still a nickel. Think about all the changes that happened in the world between 1886 and 1956: two world wars, the Great Depression, flu epidemics, the invention of countless products—and perhaps most important, hundreds of competitors in the soft-drink market. So why, after all that time and despite all the events that had transpired, was Coke still only selling for 5 cents?

One of the reasons was a particularly bad decision on the part of Coca-Cola management. In 1899, Coke was sold only at soda fountains. The company's president was approached by two lawyers who wanted to start selling Coke in bottles. The president didn't think the idea would go very far, so he granted permission as long as the bottlers bought the syrup from Coke. His mistake? The term of the contract. The offer had no end date! The bottlers could buy the syrup at a fixed price forever. As a result, if sellers of Coke raised their prices, the company got nothing. The only way for Coca-Cola to make money was to sell more syrup, and to do this the company wanted to keep the price low. Therefore, it launched an advertising campaign announcing that everyone could get Coke for 5 cents. As a result, everyone expected the price to be 5 cents, and it stayed that way. The input price was fixed, and the output price remained fixed too. Eventually, the contract for syrup was renegotiated, but that didn't cause prices to rise. Why? Because there was another problem: vending machines.

The vending machines used by Coca-Cola only took nickels. Reconfiguring the machines to take dimes wasn't cost-effective, and the company didn't want to double the price of the popular soft drink. One thought was to petition the government to mint a 7.5-cent coin, the size of a nickel, to fit the Coke vending machines. This idea was pitched to President Dwight Eisenhower, who happened to be a hunting partner of the CEO of Coca-Cola. The plan was, of course, rejected.

So what killed the 5-cent Coke? It wasn't politics, but economics. During this period, prices for all other goods fluctuated, even if only seasonally; yet over these many decades, everywhere, even at U.S. military posts overseas during World War II, at all times of year the price of Coke was only 5 cents. It never changed! Adjusting for inflation over this period, Coke should have more than tripled in price, but it didn't. Inflation didn't catch up until after the Korean War, when 5-cent Coke simply became unsustainable. It is believed that the last 5-cent Coke was sold in 1959.✳

---

*David Kestenbaum, "Why Coke Cost a Nickel for 70 Years," *Planet Money*, NPR, November 15, 2012.

Shifts in Short-Run Aggregate Supply

A shift of the long-run aggregate supply curve signals a permanent change that affects the long run and the short run. Therefore, all long-run aggregate supply curve shifts also shift the short-run aggregate supply curve. In addition to the factors that shift long-run aggregate supply, we can single out three factors that shift only short-run aggregate supply: temporary supply shocks, changes in expected future prices, and errors in past price expectations.

Supply Shocks

In December 2013 and January 2014, frigid temperatures across much of the United States caused economic activity in some sectors to freeze up. Construction projects were put on hold, airlines cancelled thousands of flights, and producers had trouble filling orders. The so-called "polar vortex" had an unexpected negative impact on the economy, resulting in negative GDP growth in the first three months of 2014. Surprise events that change a firm's production costs are called **supply shocks.** Supply shocks can be negative or positive. Negative supply shocks lead to higher production costs; positive supply shocks reduce production costs. When supply shocks are temporary, they shift only the short-run aggregate supply curve.

A **supply shock** is a surprise event that changes a firm's production costs.

A price change in an important factor of production is another supply shock. For example, in the year between June 2007 and June 2008, oil prices increased from $59 a barrel to over $123 a barrel (in 2014 dollars). You may recall this period because gas prices rose from about $2 per gallon to more than $4 per gallon in the summer of 2008. Figure 12.11 plots the price of oil from 2004 to 2014. Oil is an important input to many production processes, so when its price doubles, a macroeconomic supply shock occurs. But notice how prices fell in late 2008/early 2009 and late 2014. This drop in oil prices acted as a positive supply shock. As you can see in Figure 12.11, the price of oil rises and falls somewhat erratically. For the price to "shock" the macroeconomy, the change needs to be unexpected—and fairly substantial.

Freezing temperatures kept trucks from operating during the polar vortex.

Expected Future Prices

If you're going to sign a long-term wage contract, you'll want to form some expectation about future prices. After all, the real value of your future income depends on prices in the future. Other things being equal, when workers and firms expect higher prices in the future, they negotiate higher wages. The result is higher labor costs, which reduce firms' profitability and make them less willing to produce at any price level. Therefore, higher expected future prices lead to a lower quantity of aggregate supply.

The process works in reverse if workers and firms expect a lower price level. Subsequent negotiations produce a labor agreement with lower wages,

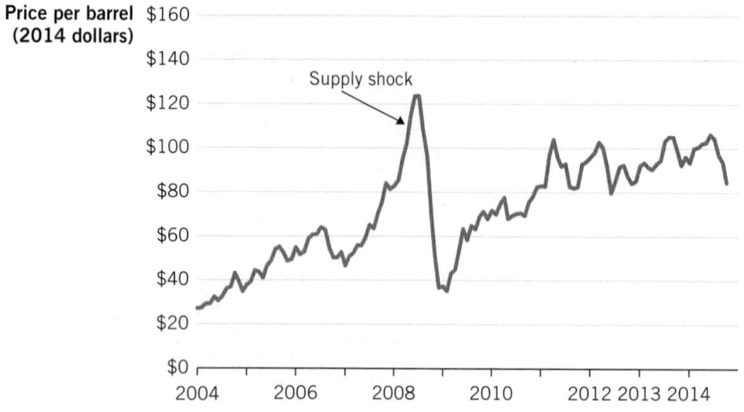

FIGURE 12.11

Price of Crude Oil

Increases and decreases in crude oil prices are examples of supply shocks, since production costs for firms throughout the economy rise or fall drastically.

Source: U.S. Energy Information Administration.

which reduces labor costs. When labor costs fall, additional production is more profitable at any price level, and the short-run aggregate supply curve shifts to the right.

Corrections of Past Errors in Price Expectations

We've seen that both workers and resource suppliers sign contracts on the basis of some expectation of future prices. But these expectations aren't always correct. When the expectations turn out to be wrong, workers will want to renegotiate or adjust their wages in later periods. This renegotiation affects costs, which in turn affects short-run aggregate supply. For example, let's say you sign a wage contract under the assumption that the inflation rate will be about 2% in the next year, but it turns out to be 5%. At the end of the year, you need to renegotiate with your employer. When workers renegotiate their wages upward, short-run aggregate supply decreases. If workers renegotiate their wages downward, short-run aggregate supply increases.

Figure 12.12 summarizes the three factors that shift short-run aggregate supply. The short-run aggregate supply curve increases, or shifts to the right (to $SRAS_2$), with the following changes: positive supply shocks, expectations of future prices being lower, and adjustments to lower price expectations. The short-run aggregate supply curve decreases, or shifts to the left (to $SRAS_3$), with the following changes: negative supply shocks, expectations of future prices being higher, and adjustments to higher price expectations.

This raises a dilemma for policymakers. We noted earlier that recessions are usually a result of diminished AD; but if SRAS falls, we also see a reduction in output and an increase in unemployment. This sounds like a recession, but it's an atypical recession. If AD falls, price levels fall; but if the SRAS falls, price levels rise. As we will see when we start talking about fiscal policy, if you don't know the cause of the recession—a shift in AD or a shift in SRAS—your policy could result in perpetuating economic problems.

FIGURE 12.12

Factors That Shift the Short-Run Aggregate Supply Curve

The short-run aggregate supply curve shifts to the right when there are positive supply shocks, prices are expected to be lower, and anticipated price levels turn out to be too high. The curve shifts to the left when there are negative supply shocks, prices are expected to be higher, and anticipated price levels turn out to be too low.

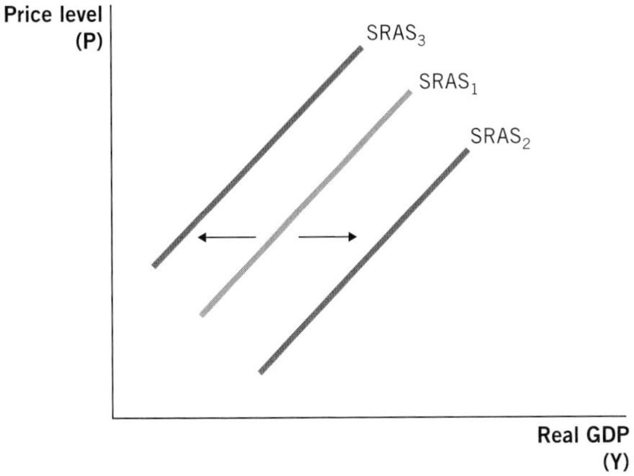

Shift factor	Positive change in factor leads to:	Negative change in factor leads to:
Supply shock	Increase to $SRAS_2$	Decrease to $SRAS_3$
Expected price level	Decrease to $SRAS_3$	Increase to $SRAS_2$
Corrections to past errors in expectations	Decrease to $SRAS_3$	Increase to $SRAS_2$

PRACTICE WHAT YOU KNOW

Long-Run Aggregate Supply and Short-Run Aggregate Supply: Which Curve Shifts?

In the real world, change is typical. In our aggregate demand–aggregate supply model, change means that the curves shift. Careful application of the model requires that you determine which curve shifts, and in which direction, when real-world events occur.

Question: In each of the scenarios listed below, is there a shift in the long-run aggregate supply curve, the short-run aggregate supply curve, both, or neither? Explain your answers.

1. New shale gas deposits are found in North Dakota.
2. Hot weather leads to lower crop yields in the Midwest.

This oil rig sits atop the Bakken shale formation in North Dakota, where vast new shale gas resources have been discovered.

(CONTINUED)

(CONTINUED)

3. The Organization of Petroleum Exporting Countries (OPEC) agrees to increase world oil output, leading to lower oil prices for six months.
4. U.S. consumers expect greater income in 2018.

Answers:

1. This scenario leads to an increase in both long-run aggregate supply and short-run aggregate supply. The shale-gas discovery represents new resources, which shifts the long-run aggregate supply curve to the right. In addition, every shift in the long-run aggregate supply curve affects the short-run aggregate supply curve.
2. The lower crop yields are not permanent, so only the short-run aggregate supply curve shifts to the left. After the bad weather passes, the short-run aggregate supply curve shifts back to the right.
3. This scenario causes a short-run aggregate supply curve shift, because it doesn't represent a permanent change in oil quantities.
4. Neither the short-run aggregate supply curve nor the long-run aggregate supply curve shift. A change in expected income shifts the aggregate demand curve.

How Does the Aggregate Demand–Aggregate Supply Model Help Us Understand the Economy?

In a market economy, output is determined by exchanges between buyers and sellers. As we'll see, this means that the economy will tend to move to the point at which aggregate demand is equal to aggregate supply. In this section, we bring aggregate demand and aggregate supply together and consider how changes in the economy affect real GDP, unemployment, and the price level.

Equilibrium in the Aggregate Demand–Aggregate Supply Model

Figure 12.13 plots the aggregate demand and the aggregate supply curves in the same graph. The point where they intersect, A, is the equilibrium point at which the opposing forces of supply and demand are balanced. At point A, the price level is P^*, the output level is Y^*, and unemployment is u^*. In the normal demand and supply model, adjustments in the *price of the good or service* naturally direct the particular market toward the equilibrium point. In contrast, in the aggregate demand–aggregate supply model, changes in the *price level* move the economy closer to equilibrium.

To understand why the economy tends toward equilibrium at price level P^*, consider other possible price levels. For example, if the price level is P_H, which is higher than P^*, aggregate supply will be greater than aggregate demand. In this case, producers are producing more than consumers desire at current prices. Therefore, prices naturally begin to fall to eliminate a potential

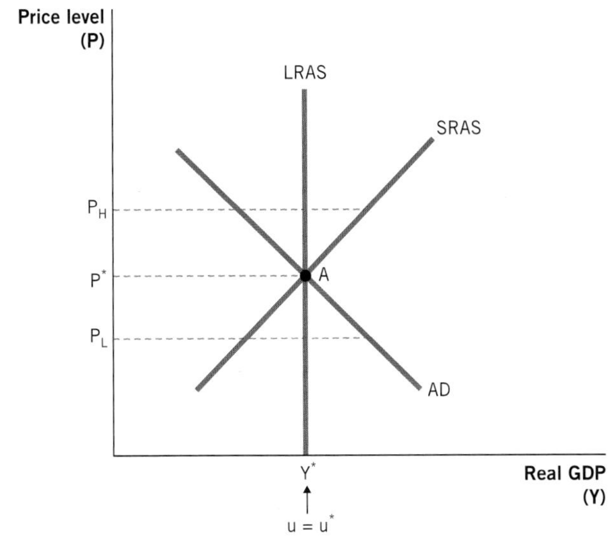

FIGURE 12.13

Equilibrium in the Aggregate Demand–Aggregate Supply Model

Forces in the economy naturally move it toward equilibrium at point A, where aggregate supply is equal to aggregate demand, $P = P^*$, $Y = Y^*$, and $u = u^*$. At P_H, aggregate supply exceeds aggregate demand, which puts downward pressure on prices and moves the economy toward equilibrium at P^*. At P_L, where aggregate demand exceeds aggregate supply, upward pressure on prices moves the economy toward equilibrium at P^*.

surplus of goods and services. As prices fall, the quantity of aggregate demand increases, the quantity of aggregate supply decreases, and the economy moves toward a new equilibrium at P^*.

In contrast, if the price level is P_L, which is lower than P^*, aggregate demand will exceed aggregate supply. At those prices, buyers desire more than producers are willing to supply. Because demand exceeds supply, prices rise and the price level moves toward P^*. The only price level at which the plans of suppliers and demanders match is P^*. Market forces automatically push the economy to the price level at which aggregate demand is equal to aggregate supply.

In the real world, things are always changing; everything from technology to weather to wealth and expectations can change. Now that we've built our model, we can use it to examine how changes in the real world affect the macroeconomy.

When we consider a change, we follow a sequence of five steps that lead us to the new equilibrium. Once we determine the new equilibrium, we can assess the impact of the change on real GDP, unemployment, and the price level. The five steps are as follows:

1. Begin with the model in long-run equilibrium.
2. Determine which curve(s) are affected by the change(s), and identify the direction(s) of the change(s).
3. Shift the curve(s) in the appropriate direction(s).
4. Determine the new short-run and/or long-run equilibrium points.
5. Compare the new equilibrium(s) with the starting point.

As we compare the new equilibrium to the original equilibrium, we're trying to determine the impact on our three primary macroeconomic variables:

growth, unemployment, and inflation. If Y increases, then we can say there is growth. Unemployment moves in the opposite direction from growth. As Y increases and the economy grows, presumably there will be more people working, so unemployment falls. If Y declines, less output is being produced. Fewer workers are hired, and unemployment rises. Inflation is indicated by the change in the price level. If the price level increases, there is inflation. If the price level falls, there is deflation.

Now let's consider shifts in the aggregate curves in order to predict changes in the macroeconomy. Our focus will be on the short-run, normal fluctuations in the economy that lead to recessions and recoveries. We focus on long-run shifts in Chapter 13 when we examine economic growth.

PRACTICE WHAT YOU KNOW

Using the Aggregate Demand–Aggregate Supply Model: Typhoon Haiyan and the Philippines

Typhoon Haiyan destroyed many capital goods in Philippine coastal towns.

In 2013, a devastating typhoon ripped across the central Philippines, killing nearly 6,000 people and disrupting the lives of millions. Coastal cities were leveled, and infrastructures such as roads and power lines were destroyed.

Question: How would you use the aggregate demand–aggregate supply model to illustrate the effect of this disaster on the Philippine economy?

Answer: Typhoon Haiyan was a natural disaster, so hopefully its effects will be temporary and will only impact the short-run aggregate supply. Keep in mind that if a disaster is severe enough to destroy resources, the long-run aggregate supply will also decline. As an extreme example, think about

(CONTINUED)

(CONTINUED)

the destruction of the ancient Roman city of Pompeii in AD 79 when Mt. Vesuvius erupted. Over 2,000 people were killed, and the city was buried for nearly 2,000 years. Since all of the city's inputs were completely destroyed, economic output would have fallen in the long run as well as the short run.

Let's consider the short-run effects of Typhoon Haiyan. The SRAS curve shifts to the left in panel (a). Output falls and employment is interrupted, causing u to fall below u^*. Some jobs are temporarily lost while things get cleaned up. Price levels rise. This is illustrated by the shift from the long-run equilibrium point A to the short-run equilibrium point b.

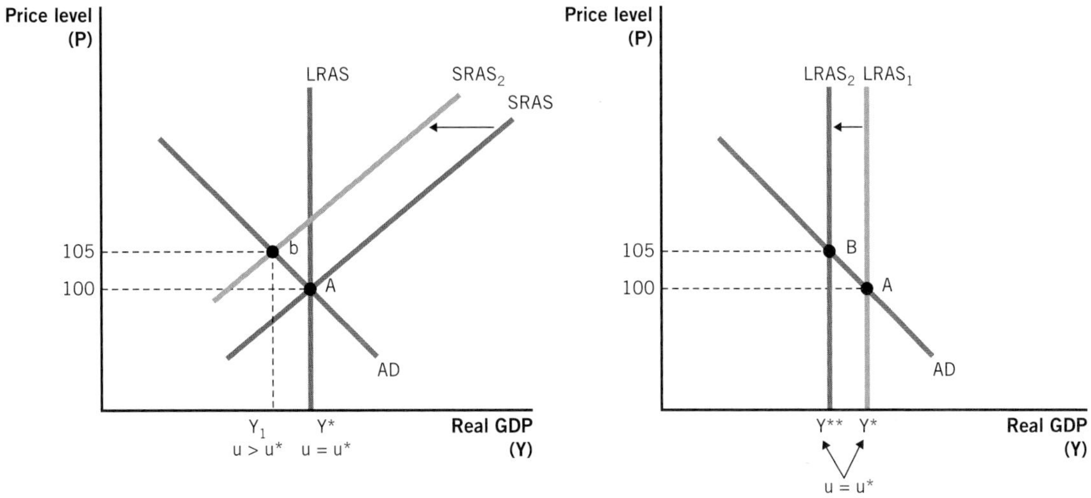

(a) Short-Run Effects

(b) Long-Run Effects

If there is a long-run impact on output, the result is different. In panel (b), the LRAS curve shifts to the left due to the destruction of resources, resulting in a new long-run equilibrium B. Notice that the unemployment rate (u) is equal to the natural rate (u^*) both before and after the shift. Jobs remain because there's plenty of work to do in the aftermath of a natural disaster. However, in the long run the Philippines has fewer resources after the typhoon than it had before, and this outcome limits the nation's economic growth.

Question: How does the Philippine disaster affect the U.S. economy?

Answer: Real foreign income falls in the Philippines, which leads to a decline in aggregate demand for U.S. goods and services.

Adjustments to Shifts in Short-Run Aggregate Supply

Consider what happens when an oil-pipeline break disrupts short-run supply. This is an example of a supply shock. Since oil is a resource that is used in many production processes, the disruption temporarily reduces the economy's ability to produce goods. We show this effect in Figure 12.14 by shifting the short-run aggregate supply curve to the left, from $SRAS_1$ to

FIGURE 12.14

How Short-Run Aggregate Supply Shifts Affect the Economy

A temporary negative supply shock shifts short-run aggregate supply from $SRAS_1$ to $SRAS_2$. In the short run, the economy moves to equilibrium at point b (denoted with a lowercase letter to distinguish it from long-run equilibrium). This equilibrium entails higher prices, lower real GDP, and higher unemployment. In the long run, the economy returns to equilibrium at point A.

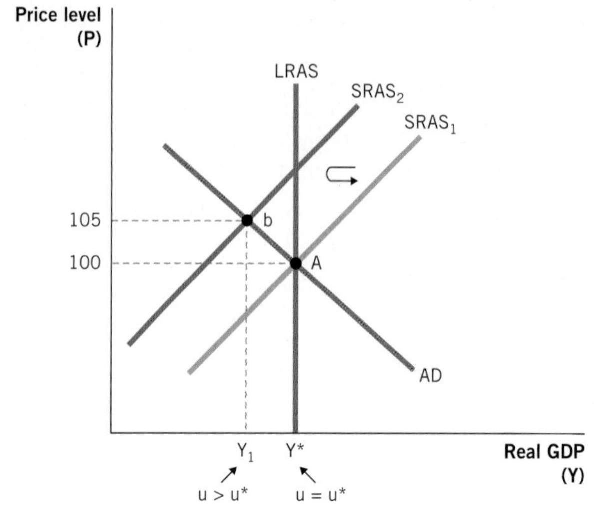

$SRAS_2$. The new equilibrium is at point b, with a higher price level (105) and a lower level of output (Y_1). Because this is a short-run equilibrium, we use the lowercase b. The lower output means increased unemployment in the short run ($u > u^*$). Notice that nothing happened to long-run aggregate supply—in the long run, the pipeline will be fixed and oil can be produced at output level Y^* again.

Since the disruption is temporary, eventually the short-run aggregate supply curve will shift back to the right until it reaches $SRAS_1$ again. Short-run disruptions in aggregate supply do not alter the long-run equilibrium in the economy; eventually the price level, output, and the unemployment rate return to their long-run equilibrium levels at point A. But in the short run, an economic downturn brings higher unemployment and lower real GDP.

ECONOMICS IN THE REAL WORLD

The Drought of 2014 Sends Prices Higher

According to an article in the *Wall Street Journal* in March 2014, prolonged droughts in Texas and California are partly responsible for rising food prices.* According to estimates by the U.S. Department of Agriculture, food prices were projected to rise by as much as 3.5% in 2014.

*Tony C. Dreibus, Leslie Josephs, and Julie Jargon, "Food Prices Surge as Drought Exacts a High Toll on Crops," *Wall Street Journal* online, March 18, 2014.

These higher prices for foods, particularly grains for livestock feeds, have an added impact on restaurants. As beef and chicken prices rise due to the higher cost of raising these animals, restaurants have to make decisions about how much of their costs they want to pass on to consumers. White Castle, a hamburger chain with headquarters in Columbus, Ohio, claimed that its beef costs increased by 12% in February 2014 alone.

The prolonged drought is a classic example of supply shock, and the result is exactly what the aggregate demand–aggregate supply model predicts: short-run aggregate supply shifts to the left, which leads to higher prices throughout the economy. ✳

These fields were supposed to be much greener in 2014.

Adjustments to Shifts in Aggregate Demand

Aggregate demand shifts for many reasons. Some shifts occur because of expectations rather than actual events, yet they still affect the macroeconomy. For example, let's say that consumer confidence rises unexpectedly: consumers wake up one morning with expectations of higher future income. This change causes increased aggregate demand because consumers start spending more. Can this kind of change have real effects on the economy? That is, will a change in consumer confidence affect unemployment and real GDP? Let's look at the model.

Figure 12.15 illustrates the changes in the economy from the increased consumer confidence. We start with long-run equilibrium at point A, where the price level is 100, real GDP is at full-employment output level Y^*, and unemployment is equal to the natural rate ($u = u^*$). Then, as a result of the change in consumer confidence, aggregate demand shifts from AD_1 to AD_2. The economy moves to short-run equilibrium at point b. The short-run equilibrium is associated with higher prices ($P = 105$) and higher real GDP (Y_1). In addition, the unemployment rate drops below u^*.

Our example presents a positive result—unemployment falls and real GDP rises. Now let's complete this example by following through to long-run equilibrium. Recall the difference between the long run and the short run: in the long run, all prices adjust. As all prices adjust, the short-run aggregate supply curve shifts to the left from $SRAS_1$ to $SRAS_2$, moving the economy to long-run equilibrium at point C. Why does the SRAS curve shift? Because everyone can eventually adjust their prices. Thinking about your coffee shop, in the long run you can renegotiate wages and all other long-term contracts. Thus, if there's a 10% increase in prices throughout the economy, both input and output prices rise by 10%. The price of a \$4 latte rises to \$4.40, and the barista wage of \$10 per hour rises to \$11 per hour. When input prices rise to

FIGURE 12.15

How Aggregate Demand Shifts Affect the Economy

An increase in aggregate demand moves the economy from the initial equilibrium at point A to a new short-run equilibrium at point b. The positive aggregate demand shift increases real GDP and decreases unemployment in the short run ($u < u^*$). In the short run, prices adjust—but only partially, because some prices are sticky. In the long run, when all prices adjust, the short-run aggregate supply curve shifts to $SRAS_2$ and the economy moves to long-run equilibrium at point C, where $Y = Y^*$ and $u = u^*$.

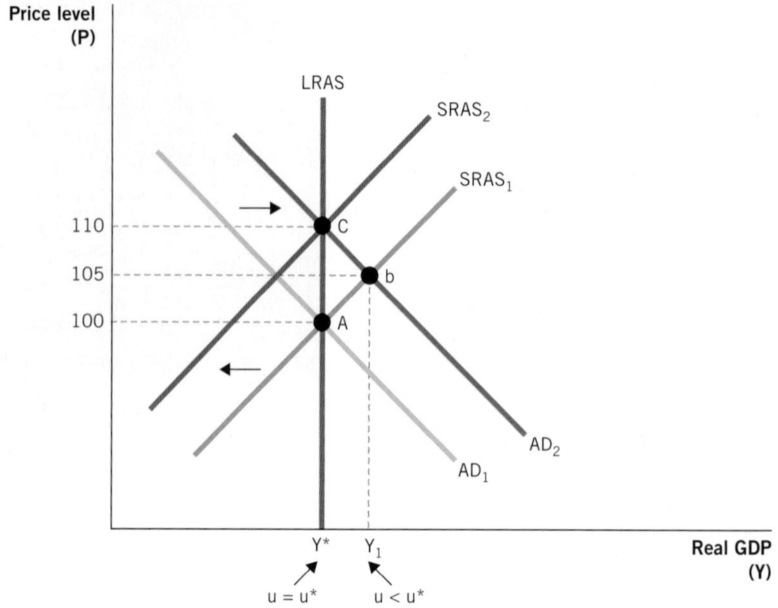

match output price changes, the short-run aggregate supply curve shifts to the left, to $SRAS_2$. In the long run, once all prices adjust, the price level does not affect the quantity of output supplied and output returns to Y^*, the full-employment level.

What are the consequences of this move to long-run equilibrium, and how does it compare to the short-run equilibrium? At point b, real GDP is up and unemployment is down. But not everyone is happy. Workers with sticky wages are now paying more for their final goods and services, but their wages didn't adjust upward in the short run. In fact, any sellers with sticky prices are hurt in the short run when other prices rise.

When we move to point C, notice that we are back to the original output level (Y^*) and natural unemployment level (u^*), but prices are higher ($P = 110$). The model is telling us that demand changes have no effects on output or employment in the long run because once the SRAS adjusts to the higher prices, we return to Y^*, where only the price level is affected.

Table 12.1 summarizes the economic effects of aggregate demand changes in both the short run and the long run. In order to achieve a positive long-run impact on the economy on output and unemployment, there has to be a change in the long-run aggregate supply curve. That happens when there is economic growth, the subject to which we now turn.

ECONOMICS FOR LIFE

Recession-Proof Your Job

Recessions are hard on almost everyone in an economy, but there are ways you can shield yourself from unemployment.

The first thing you need is a college degree. In October 2014, the U.S. national unemployment rate was 5.9% for the entire labor force, but just 3.1% for college graduates.

Unemployment can occur in the macroeconomy when wages are sticky, meaning that they don't respond to changes in the economy. This outcome applies to individuals too. If you do happen to lose your job, you may need to consider accepting a lower wage or even a change of career so as to obtain another job. The more flexible your wage range, the less likely you are to experience long-term unemployment.

Finally, if you lose your job, be sure to take advantage of all the modern job-search tools available today. There are millions of jobs available, even when unemployment rates are very high—you just need to know how to find those jobs. For example, the web site indeed.com turns up thousands of job vacancies for almost any job description. As of November 2014, searching for either "accountant" or "CPA" yielded nearly 39,000 results, a search for "civil engineer" yielded 13,732 results, and "marketing" yielded 289,884 results.

Don't let this happen to you!

TABLE 12.1

Summary of Results from Aggregate Demand Shifts

	Increase in aggregate demand		Decrease in aggregate demand	
	Short run	**Long run**	**Short run**	**Long run**
Real GDP (Y)	Y rises	Y returns to original level	Y falls	Y returns to original level
Unemployment (u)	u falls	u returns to original level	u rises	u returns to original level
Price level (P)	P rises	P rises even further	P falls	P falls even further

Conclusion

We began this chapter with the misconception that recessions are normal occurrences that happen every few years. In fact, they are anything but normal. They occur with unpredictable frequency and are caused by many different factors. Recessions in business cycles are often caused by changes in aggregate demand, but the same symptoms can also reflect short-run aggregate supply shifts.

This chapter introduced the aggregate demand–aggregate supply model, which helps us understand how changes in the real world affect the macroeconomy in both the short run and the long run. In the next chapter, we look more closely at economic growth, which is a long-run phenomenon.

ANSWERING THE BIG QUESTIONS

What is a business cycle, and why are business cycles so difficult to predict?

* Business cycles are short-run fluctuations in economic activity marked by peaks and troughs.
* No two business cycles have the same duration, depth, or dispersion, making them notoriously difficult to predict.

What is aggregate demand?

* Aggregate demand represents the spending side of the economy. It includes consumption (C), investment (I), government spending (G), and net exports (NX).
* The aggregate demand curve shifts when there are changes in real wealth, expected income, expected future prices, foreign income and wealth, and the value of the dollar.

What is aggregate supply?

* Aggregate supply represents the producing side of the economy.
* Long-run aggregate supply is relevant when all prices are flexible. This curve is vertical at full-employment output and is not influenced by the price level.
* The long-run aggregate supply curve shifts when there is a long-run change in a nation's ability to produce output. The factors that shift long-run aggregate supply include changes in resources, technology, and institutions.
* In the short run, when some prices are sticky, the short-run aggregate supply curve is relevant. This curve indicates a positive relationship between the price level and real output supplied.
* Anything that causes the long-run aggregate supply curve to shift also shifts the short-run aggregate supply curve. In addition, we can single out three factors that shift only short-run aggregate supply: temporary supply shocks, changes in expected future prices, and errors in past price expectations.

How does the aggregate demand–aggregate supply model help us understand the economy?

* We can use the aggregate demand–aggregate supply model to see how changes in aggregate demand or aggregate supply affect real GDP, unemployment, and the price level.

CONCEPTS YOU SHOULD KNOW

aggregate demand (p. 355)
aggregate supply (p. 355)
business cycle (p. 348)
countercyclical fiscal policy (p. 352)
economic contraction (p. 349)
economic expansion (p. 349)
full-employment output level (Y*) (p. 362)
Great Recession (p. 348)
impact lag (p. 353)
implementation lag (p. 353)
long run (p. 348)
price level (P) (p. 356)
recession (p. 348)
recognition lag (p. 353)
short run (p. 348)
supply shock (p. 367)

QUESTIONS FOR REVIEW

1. What are the four parts of a business cycle?
2. How do business cycles differ from each other?
3. What are at least three factors that shift the aggregate demand curve?
4. What are at least three factors that shift the short-run aggregate supply curve? What about the long-run aggregate supply curve?
5. Why is the long-run aggregate supply curve vertical?
6. How does strong economic growth in China affect aggregate demand in the United States?
7. Consider two economies, both in recession. In the first economy, all workers have long-term contracts that guarantee high wages for the next five years. In the second economy, all workers have annual contracts that are indexed to changes in the price level (that is, their wages change immediately if there is inflation or deflation). Which economy will return to full-employment output first? Explain your response.

STUDY PROBLEMS (*✱ solved at the end of the section*)

1. Sketch out a normal business cycle, labeling all the parts and the axes. How might a long implementation lag affect the economy's recovery?
2. Describe whether the following changes cause short-run aggregate supply to increase, decrease, or neither.
   a. The price level increases.
   b. Input prices decrease.
   c. Firms and workers expect the price level to fall.
   d. The price level decreases.
   e. New policies increase the cost of meeting government regulations.
   f. The number of workers in the labor force increases.
3. Describe whether the following changes cause long-run aggregate supply to increase, decrease, or neither.
   a. The price level increases.
   b. More machinery, tools, and other capital inputs become available.
   c. More natural resources become available.
   d. The price level decreases.
   e. Firms and workers expect the price level to rise.
   f. The number of workers in the labor force increases.

4. On the following graph, illustrate the short-run and long-run effects of an increase in aggregate demand. Describe what happens to the price level, output, and unemployment in both the short run and the long run.

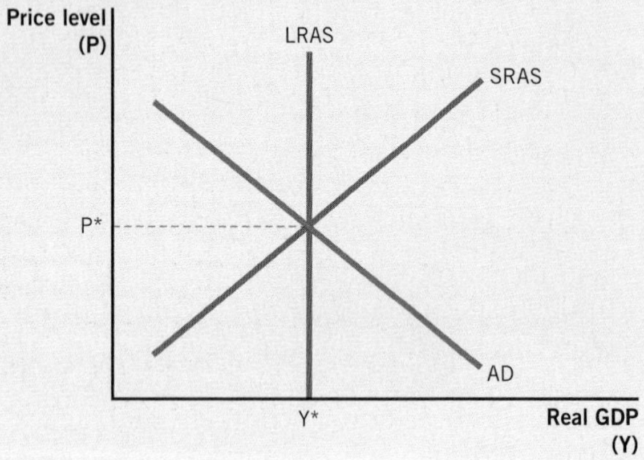

5. How does a lower price level in the United States affect the purchases of imported goods? Explain, using aggregate demand.

✱ 6. Describe whether the following changes cause aggregate demand to increase, decrease, or neither.
   a. The price level increases.
   b. Investment decreases.
   c. Imports decrease and exports increase.
   d. The price level decreases.
   e. Consumption increases.
   f. Government purchases decrease.

✱ 7. Suppose that a sudden decrease in aggregate demand moves the economy from its long-run equilibrium.
   a. Illustrate this change using the aggregate demand–aggregate supply model.
   b. What are the effects of this change in the short run and the long run?

8. In the summer of 2008, global oil prices spiked to extremely high levels before coming down again at the end of that year. This temporary event had global effects because oil is an important resource in the production of many goods and services. Focusing only on the U.S. economy, determine how this kind of event affects the price level, unemployment rate, and real GDP in both the short run and the long run. Assume the economy was in long-run equilibrium before this change, and consider only this stated change.

✱ 9. You work for Dr. Zhang, the autocratic dictator of Zhouland. After taking an economics course, you decide that devaluing your currency (Zhoullars) is the way to increase GDP. Following your advice, Dr. Zhang orders massive increases in the supply of Zhoullars, a move that reduces the value of Zhoullars in world markets. As a result, exports to the world are cheaper and imports into Zhouland are more expensive. Use the AD–AS model to determine the effects on real GDP, unemployment, and the price level in Zhouland in both the short run and the long run. Assume the economy was in long-run equilibrium before this change, and consider only this stated change.

SOLVED PROBLEMS

6.a. Neither. A change in the price level (P) leads to a movement along the AD curve. When the price level rises, the quantity of aggregate demand declines along the curve.
   b. Investment (I) is one component of aggregate demand, so a decrease in investment decreases aggregate demand.
   c. Net exports (NX) is a component of aggregate demand. An increase in exports and a decrease in imports imply that net exports rise, so aggregate demand increases.
   d. Aggregate demand neither increases nor decreases with a change in the price level (P). A change in the price level leads to movement along the AD curve. When the price level decreases, the quantity of aggregate demand increases along the curve.
   e. Consumption (C) is a component of aggregate demand, so an increase in consumption means an increase in aggregate demand.
   f. Government purchases (G) are a component of aggregate demand, so a decrease in

government purchases causes a decrease in aggregate demand.

7.a. Aggregate demand decreases from AD_1 to AD_2. In the short run, equilibrium will move from point A to point b.

b. In the short run, real GDP falls, the unemployment rate rises, and the price level falls. In the long run, equilibrium is restored at point C. Prices fully adjust to the lower levels, so the short-run aggregate supply curve shifts to the right. Real GDP goes back to the full-employment level as prices fully adjust, the unemployment rate returns to the natural rate, and the price level falls further.

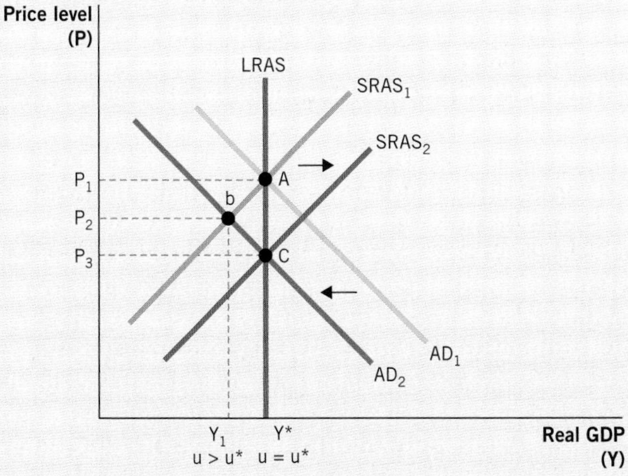

9. The reduction in the value of the Zhoullar means an increase, or positive shift, in the aggregate demand curve as net exports increase. This shift causes AD to increase from AD_1 to AD_2.

In the short run, there is greater real GDP (Y_1 is higher than Y^*), lower unemployment ($u < u^*$), and a higher price level (P_2 is higher than P_1). This short-run equilibrium is shown at point b in the figure.

The short-run aggregate supply shifts to the left as expectations of higher prices set in and the economy returns to the full-employment level of output. In the long run, the only change is an increase in the price level (from P_2 to P_3), as indicated by the new long-run equilibrium at point C in the figure. Note that this result is consistent with our discussion of the cause of inflation in Chapter 10: that is, the cause of inflation is monetary expansion. When Dr. Zhang commanded that the number of Zhoullars should increase, he also guaranteed that inflation would eventually arrive.

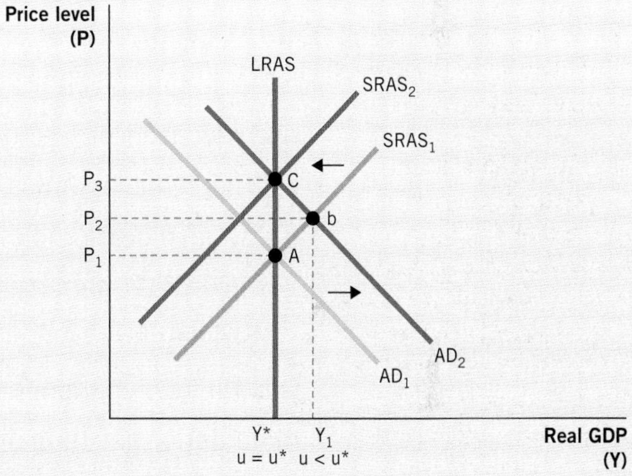

CHAPTER 13

Economic Growth and the Wealth of Nations

MISCONCEPTION

Natural resources are the key to economic prosperity.

Many people believe that natural resources such as trees, oil, and farmland are the primary sources of economic growth. They believe that nations like the United States and Australia are prosperous because they have vast natural resources that can be used to produce goods and services. A variation on this idea emphasizes geography—that nations with the best shipping locations and the mildest climates have more prosperous economies. But what about the two Koreas? North and South Korea have the same natural resources, yet the two economies are as different as night and day. In this chapter, we explore some of the things that cause differences in economic growth across nations.

Striving for economic growth is not only about accumulating more wealth. Yes, economic growth brings iPads and Jet Skis, but it's much more important than simply creating more wealth or producing more products. Economic growth means that more women and infants survive childbirth, more people have access to clean water and better sanitation, and people live healthier, longer, and more educated lives.

We begin this chapter by looking at the implications of economic growth for human welfare. We then consider the impact of an economy's resources and technology on economic growth. Finally, we discuss the key elements that an economy needs in order to grow.

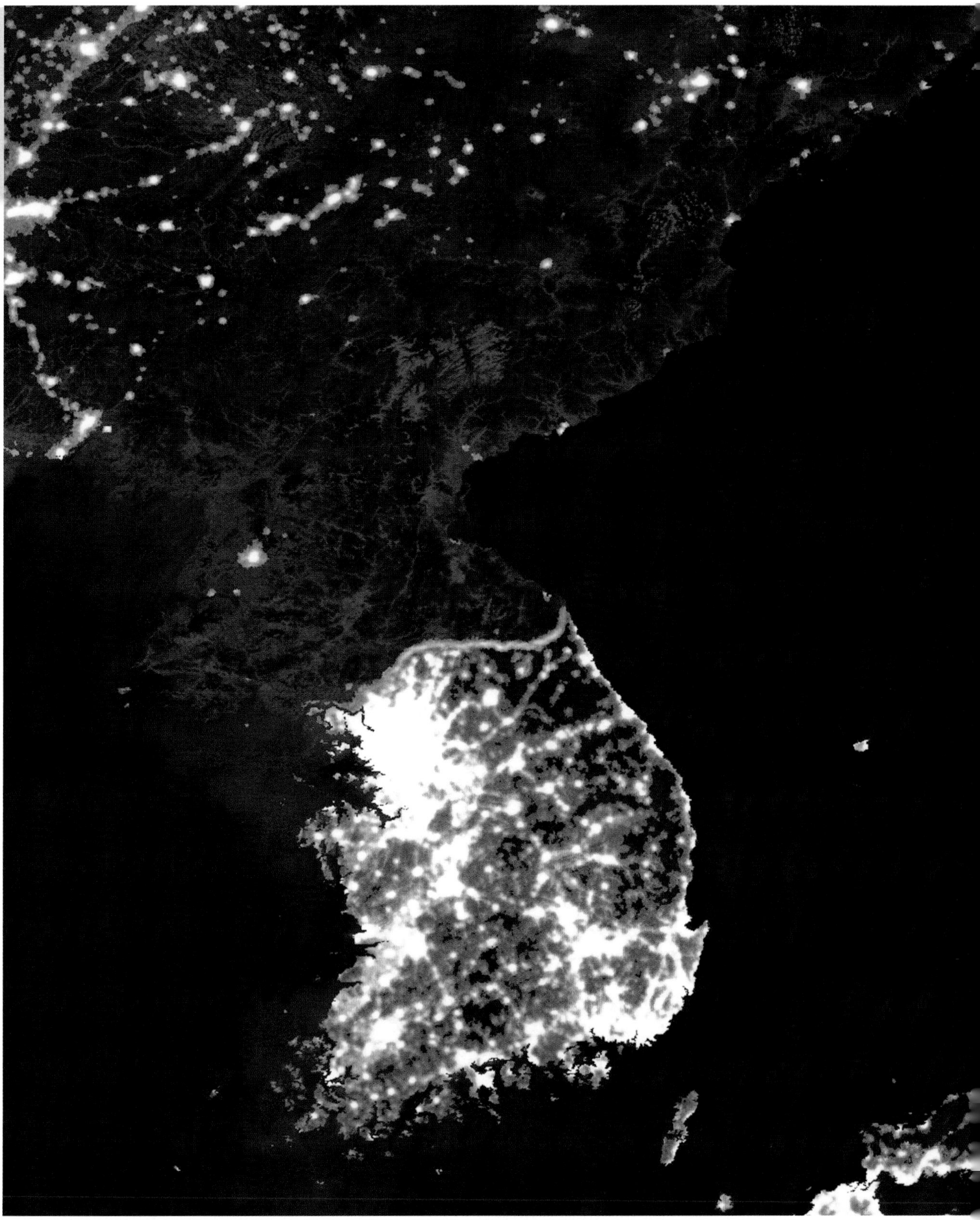

The two Koreas at night: South Korea bursting with light, and North Korea mired in economic darkness.

BIG QUESTIONS

* **Why does economic growth matter?**
* **How do resources and technology contribute to economic growth?**
* **What institutions foster economic growth?**

Why Does Economic Growth Matter?

In 1900, life expectancy in the United States was 47 years. Income—adjusted for inflation—was a little over $6,000 per person. Roughly 140 of every 1,000 children died before their first birthday. Only about one-third of American homes had running water. Most people lived less than a mile from their job, and almost nobody owned an automobile. While this is a description of life in the United States in 1900, it is also a description of life in many poor countries today. What happened in the United States since 1900? The answer is *economic growth*.

Economic growth doesn't impact only the rich. It impacts the lives of average people around the world in dramatic ways. To see how, let's begin by examining the historical data on economic growth. We then explore the way economists determine *growth rates*, which measure how quickly a country is growing. But be careful. Depending on how the numbers are reported, you might not be getting an accurate picture of the situation.

Some Ugly Facts

In Chapter 10, we talked about macroeconomic well-being as measured by real per capita GDP. We know that real per capita GDP measures the average level of real income in a nation. But for most people, life is not all about the pursuit of more income. The fact remains that economic growth alleviates human misery and lengthens lives. Wealthier nations attain higher living standards, which include better nutrition, educational opportunities, health care, freedom, and even sources of entertainment.

Let's look around the world and compare life in poor countries with life in rich countries. Table 13.1 presents human welfare indicators for a selection of rich and poor countries. Among the poor nations are Afghanistan, Bangladesh, Ethiopia, Haiti, Liberia, Nepal, North Korea, Tanzania, and Zimbabwe. The wealthy nations include Australia, Denmark, Germany, Israel, Japan, South Korea, and the United States, among others.

Consider the first group of life indicators, which are related to mortality. In poor countries, 56 out of every 1,000 babies die at birth or in the first year of their life, while in rich nations the number is only 4 out of every 1,000. This means that infants are nearly 15 times more likely to die in poor nations. Those that survive one year in poor nations are about 16 times more likely

TABLE 13.1

Human Welfare in Poor versus Rich Nations

Life indicators	Poor nations	Rich nations
GDP per capita (2005 US$)*	$664	$43,864
Infant mortality rate (per 1,000 live births)	56	4
Under-5 mortality rate (per 1,000)	82	5
Life expectancy at birth (years)	62	81
Physicians (per 1,000 people)	0.2	2.9
Births attended by skilled health staff (%)	49	100
Access to improved water source (% of population)	69	100
Access to improved sanitation (% of population)	37	100
Internet users (per 100 people)	7.1	81.2
Motor vehicles (per 1,000 people)	12	627
Mobile cellular subscriptions (per 100 people)	53	112
Literacy rate, adult male (%)	68	99
Literacy rate, adult female (%)	54	99
Ratio of female to male secondary enrollment (%)	89	99
Ratio of female to male post-secondary enrollment (%)	66	124

Source: World Bank. Poor nations are 34 poorest; rich nations are 31 high-income OECD nations.

*GDP data is from 2013 and is held constant using 2005 U.S. dollars. Other indicators are from 2010, 2012, and 2013.

to die before their fifth birthday, as indicated by the under-5 mortality rates. Overall, life expectancy in poor nations is 62 years, while in wealthy nations it is 81 years. Just being born in a wealthy nation adds almost a quarter-century to an individual's life.

The second group of indicators in Table 13.1 helps to explain the mortality data. Rich nations have access to about 15 times as many doctors per person: 2.9 physicians per 1,000 people versus 0.2 per 1,000. Clean water and sanitation are available to only a fraction of people in poor nations, while these are generally available to all in rich nations. Children in poor nations die every year because they can't get water as clean as the water that comes out of virtually any faucet in the United States. Lack of clean water leads to common ailments like tapeworms and diarrhea, which are life-threatening in poor nations. In fact, in 2010 the World Health Organization estimated that 3.6 million people die each year from waterborne diseases.

Clean water, even in a bag, saves lives.

The third group of indicators lists a selection of nonessential conveniences that people in rich nations often take for granted. Fully 81 people out of every 100 use the Internet in rich nations, but only 7 people per 100 are able to use it in poor nations. Rich nations have over 52 times more motor vehicles per 1,000 people and twice as many cellphone subscriptions.

The last group of indicators in Table 13.1 tells the sobering story about education. First, notice that literacy rates in poor countries are significantly lower than literacy rates in wealthy countries. But there is also a striking difference in literacy rates between men and women in poor nations. Women have less access to both secondary and post-secondary education than men in poor nations; equal access would imply an enrollment ratio of 100%. In rich countries, there are more women than men pursuing a college education! So, while educational opportunities are more rare for all people in poor nations, women fare even worse.

The data in Table 13.1 supports our contention that per capita GDP matters—not solely for the sake of more income per se, but also because it correlates with better human welfare conditions, which matter to everyone.

Learning from the Past

We can learn a lot about the roots of economic growth by looking at historical experiences. Until very recently, the common person's existence was devoted to *subsistence*, which involved simply trying to find enough shelter, clothing, and nourishment to survive. As we saw in the previous section, even today many people still live on the margins of subsistence. What can history tell us about how rich nations achieved economic development? The answer will help to identify what policies countries might pursue to encourage growth going forward.

We Were All Poor Once

When you look around the globe today, you see rich nations and poor nations. You can probably name many rich nations: the United States, Japan, and the western European nations, among others. You might also know the very poor nations: almost all nations in Africa, many of those in Latin America, and significant numbers in parts of Asia. But the world wasn't always this way. If we consider the longer history of humankind, only recently did the incomes of common people rise above subsistence level. The Europe of 1750, for instance, was not noticeably richer than Europe at the time of the birth of Jesus of Nazareth.

Consider the very long run. Angus Maddison, a noted economic historian, estimated GDP levels for many nations and for the whole world back to the year AD 1. Figure 13.1 plots Maddison's estimates of per capita GDP, in 2010 U.S. dollars. Clearly, something happened around 1800 that dramatically changed the path of average world living standards.

Maddison estimated that the average level of income in the world in 1350 was about $816. Given that the number is adjusted to 2010 prices, this would be comparable to you having an annual income of $816. If you had $816 to live on for an entire year, it's clear that your solitary focus would be on basic necessities like food, clothing, and shelter. Of course, there were global variations in income before 1700. For example, average income in western Europe in the year 1600 was about $1,400, while in Latin America it was less than $700. This means that western Europeans were twice as wealthy as Latin Americans in 1600. But average Europeans were still very poor. The experience for nearly every person was meeting their basic needs to survive.

FIGURE 13.1

Long-Run World Per Capita Real GDP (in 2010 U.S. dollars)

Historical accounts often focus on monarchs and other wealthy people. But for the average person, living standards across the globe didn't change considerably from the time of Jesus to the time of Thomas Jefferson. The data plotted here is per capita GDP in 2010 U.S. dollars, which is adjusted for prices across both time and place.

Source: Angus Maddison, *Statistics on World Population, GDP and Per Capita GDP, 1–2008 AD.* All figures converted to 2010 U.S. dollars.

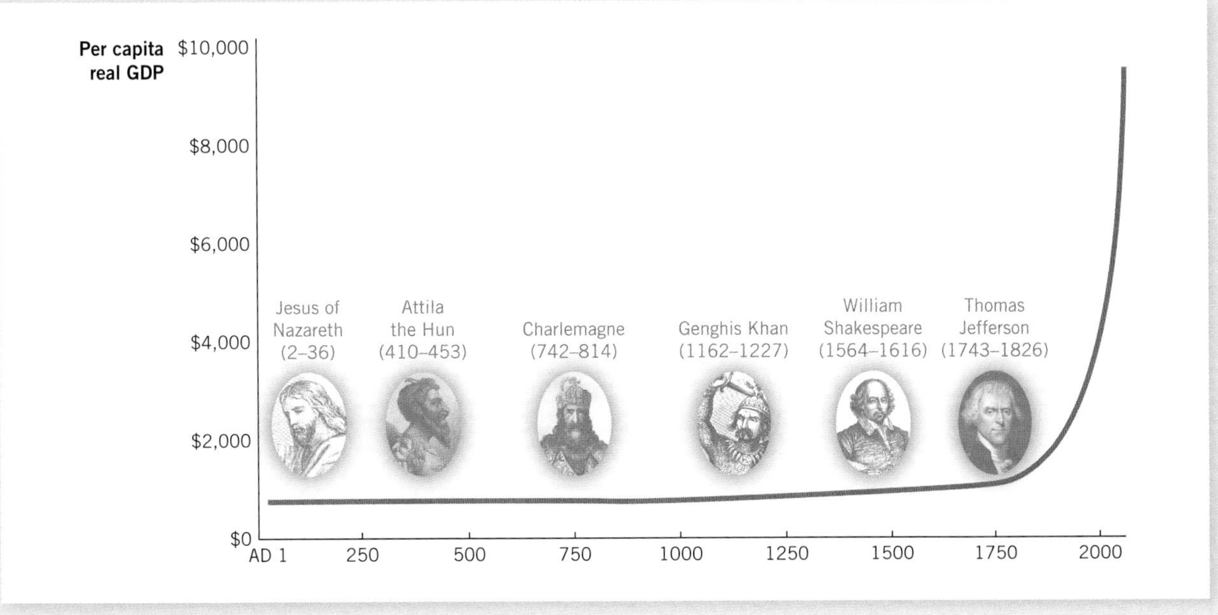

The Industrial Revolution of the 1800s, during which many economies moved away from agriculture and toward manufacturing, is at the very center of the big increase in world income growth. Beginning with the Industrial Revolution, the rate of technological progress became so rapid that it was able to outpace population growth. The foundations for the Industrial Revolution, which included private-property protection and several technological innovations, were laid in the preceding decades. We don't claim that the Industrial Revolution was idyllic for those who lived through it, but the legal and technological innovations of that era surely paved the way for the unprecedented gains in human welfare that most people have experienced since.

This data doesn't imply that life is always easy and predictably comfortable for everyone in the modern world. But the opportunities afforded to the average person alive today are very different from those afforded to the average person in past centuries. Table 13.2 lists a sampling of some of the major innovations that have taken place in the past 150 years. Try to imagine life without any of these, and you'll get a sense of the gains we've made since the Industrial Revolution.

TABLE 13.2

Important Inventions since the U.S. Civil War

Typewriter	1867	Nuclear reactor	1942
Sheep shears	1868	Microwave oven	1945
Telephone	1876	Cruise control	1945
Phonograph	1877	Computer	1946
Milking machine	1878	Xerography	1946
Two-stroke engine	1878	Videotape recorder	1952
Blowtorch	1880	Airbags	1952
Slide rule	1881	Satellites	1958
Arc welder	1886	Laser	1960
Diesel engine	1892	Floppy disk	1965
Electric motor (AC)	1892	Microprocessor	1971
X-ray machine	1895	Personal computer	1975
Electric drill	1895	Fiber optic cables	1977
Radio	1906	Fax machine	1981
Assembly line	1908	Camcorder	1982
Cash register	1919	Cell phone	1983
Dishwasher	1924	Compact disc	1983
Rocket	1926	GPS	1989
Television	1926	Laser eye surgery	1989
Antilock brakes	1929	Internet	1991
Radar	1934	MP3 player	2001
Tape recorder	1935	Mass-produced electric car	2003
Jet engine	1939	Blu-ray player	2006
Electron microscope	1939	Smartphone	2007
Electric clothes dryer	1940		

Source: Michael Cox and Richard Alm, *Myths of Rich and Poor* (New York: Basic Books, 1999), and miscellaneous other sources.

Some Got Rich, Others Stayed Poor

Although wealth has increased over the past two centuries, it is not evenly distributed around the globe. Figure 13.2 shows per capita real GDP (in 2010 U.S. dollars) for various world regions. In 1800, the income of the average U.S. citizen was just less than $2,000 (in 2010 dollars). Imagine trying to live on $3 per day in today's world—that is, $3 to buy all the food, clothing, shelter, education, transportation, and anything else you might need to purchase. That was life in the United States in 1800, and it's comparable to life in many nations today.

FIGURE 13.2

Per Capita Real GDP over 200 Years (in 2010 U.S. dollars)

Two hundred years ago, all regions and nations were poor. The modern differences in wealth that we see around the world today began to emerge before 1900. But the twentieth century saw unprecedented growth take hold in the United States and western Europe. Unfortunately, some parts of the globe today are no better off than the United States and western Europe were in 1800.

Source: Angus Maddison, *Statistics on World Population, GDP and Per Capita GDP, 1–2008 AD.* All figures converted to 2010 U.S. dollars.

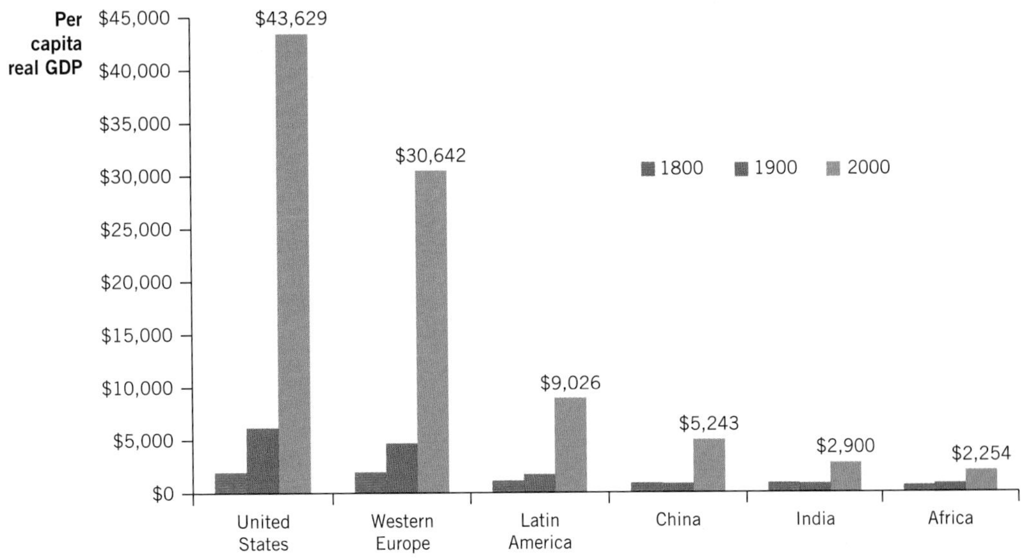

By 1900, some regions had broken the stranglehold of poverty. In 1900, per capita real GDP in western Europe was $4,701; in the United States, it was $6,153. Prior to 1900, general income levels this high had never been experienced. In China, India, and Africa, the averages were still less than $1,000 in 1900. The twentieth century proved to be even more prosperous for some, as the income gap widened between the United States and western Europe and the rest of the world. Unfortunately, per capita real income on the African continent today is still less than that of the United States in 1850, which was $2,768.

While many of the current disparities between nations began about 200 years ago, some nations have moved from poor to rich as recently as the past few decades. In 1950, for example, South Korea, with per capita real GDP of just $1,309, was poorer than Haiti, at $1,610. Today, South Korea is one of the wealthiest countries in the world, with a per capita income of more than $30,000, while Haiti has actually become poorer, with $706 in per capita income in 2013.

ECONOMICS IN THE MEDIA

Economic Growth Can Be Good for All

"I wanna be a billionaire"

In the song "Billionaire," Travie McCoy and Bruno Mars think about all of the things they could spend their money on if they were billionaires. They would be famous and could travel anywhere they wanted whenever they wanted. And they could give away a lot of money to help alleviate hunger and poverty. People in wealthier countries, not just billionaires, appear to share this dream of helping the poor.

The richest country in the world, the United States of America, also gives away the most money. Why? Because with economic growth comes the ability to share our excess. George Lucas has said he will give away the $4 billion he made when he sold the rights to *Star Wars* to Walt Disney. Bill Gates and Warren Buffett, among other billionaires, have signed a pledge to give away their fortunes rather than pass those riches on to their heirs. Overall, Americans donate over $300 billion a year, the vast majority of that giving comes from individuals. While it's difficult to determine how much of this money goes to international causes, out of a pot of $300 billion it is very likely that poor people around the world benefit from economic growth that occurs in the richest of countries.

Bruno Mars and Travie McCoy want to be billionaires for themselves and others.

Interestingly, one of the signs that poor countries are becoming better off is the percentage of their populations who donate to charities. According to the *Chronicle of Philanthropy*, the percentage of people in countries such as Thailand and the Republic of Indonesia giving to charities is at an all-time high. It's not a coincidence that these two countries are growing quickly.

ECONOMICS IN THE REAL WORLD

One Child Who Needs Economic Progress

This is a true story about a girl named Alice Toe, who is four years old. In her photo, you can see from her eyes that she is mischievous and has a sparkling personality. When this picture was taken, she was digging for crabs for the sole purpose of frightening a visiting American economist.

Alice lives in Monrovia, the capital of Liberia, an impoverished country in West Africa about the size of Virginia. She was three years old when she contracted tapeworms by drinking water from the neighborhood well. Unfortunately, her family couldn't afford to send her to a doctor. Her stomach became enlarged and her hair bleached—indicators of malnutrition caused by tapeworms. Filtered water, which costs about $3 per gallon in Liberia, is too expensive for most families and must be transported by foot.

Tapeworm infection is easily treated with a pill that costs less than 25 cents and lasts for six months. But Alice and her grandfather couldn't afford even this inexpensive treatment—that's how poor they were. Fortunately, an American missionary happened to meet Alice and made sure that she received the treatment she needed. Without help, she probably would have died.

Alice and her brother Reuben search for crabs in Monrovia, Liberia.

Alice's story is not unusual. Many thousands of children die each year from illnesses like tapeworm infection. Worldwide, 138 of every 1,000 children born in the poorest nations don't reach the age of five, although many could be saved with treatments that literally cost pennies. The good news is that economic growth can bring improvements in quality of life. For the sake of Alice Toe and other children like her, let's hope that economic progress will take root in Liberia. ✷

Measuring Economic Growth

Overall, people today are much wealthier than they were 200 years ago. However, this prosperity didn't occur overnight. Rather, income grew a little bit each year. There is a striking mathematical truth about growth: small differences in growth rates lead to large differences in wealth levels over time. In this section, we explain how growth rates are computed, and we consider the level of growth a nation needs for its population to experience significant improvements in living standards.

The Mathematics of Growth Rates

The big decrease in poverty began during the nineteenth century. Table 13.3 shows data on world economic growth in different periods. From 1800 to 1900, average world GDP growth was only 0.64%. From 1900 to 1950, world economic growth increased to about 1%. The difference between roughly 0% and 1% might seem trivial; it certainly doesn't seem like much if your exam grade goes from 85 to 86. But when economic growth increases by 1%, it makes a big difference. In this section, we show how growth is calculated.

TABLE 13.3

World Economic Growth for Different Historical Eras

Years	Growth rate
AD 1–1800	0.02%
1800–1900	0.64%
1900–1950	1.04%
1950–2000	2.12%

Source: Angus Maddison, *Statistics on World Population, GDP and Per Capita GDP, 1–2008 AD.*

We have seen that *economic growth* is the annual growth rate of per capita real GDP. It is our measure of how an average person's income changes over time, including an allowance for price changes. But the government reports overall GDP data in nominal

TABLE 13.4

Computing an Economic Growth Rate

U.S. GDP in 2013 (millions of $)	$16,768,100	
U.S. GDP in 2014 (millions of $)	$17,418,900	
Nominal GDP growth	3.9%	
− Price growth (inflation)	0.8%	
= Real GDP growth	3.1%	
− Population growth	0.7%	
= Real per capita GDP growth	2.4%	= Economic growth rate

Source: GDP data, U.S. Bureau of Economic Analysis; inflation data, U.S. Bureau of Labor Statistics; population data, U.S. Census Bureau.

terms. Therefore, to get an accurate growth rate, we need to account for both inflation and population growth. We can use the following equation to approximate economic growth, where $\%\Delta$ indicates the percentage change in a variable:

(Equation 13.1) $$\text{economic growth} \approx \%\Delta \text{ nominal GDP} - \%\Delta \text{ price level} - \%\Delta \text{ population}$$

Let's walk through the equation for the economic growth rate using actual U.S. data as shown in Table 13.4. Starting with nominal GDP data for 2013 and 2014, we compute nominal GDP growth as 3.9%. But part of the increase in nominal GDP is due to inflation. In 2014, the price level grew by 0.8%. We subtract this inflation from nominal GDP growth to get real GDP growth of 3.1%. This number applies to the entire nation, but population also increased by 0.7% in 2014. When we subtract population growth, we're left with 2.4% as the rate of real economic growth per capita for the United States in 2014. This growth rate is a little above normal: since 1950, average economic growth in the United States has been about 2.1%.

A word of caution about terminology is in order. There's a big difference between nominal GDP growth, real GDP growth, and real per capita GDP growth (economic growth rate). Looking at Table 13.4, you can see these terms highlighted in orange. But sloppy economic reporting sometimes confuses the terms. You may read something like "the U.S. economy grew by 3.1% in 2014." But the quoted statistic, 3.1%, often refers to real GDP growth and isn't calculated on a per capita basis. It would be an even bigger mistake to claim that U.S. economic growth in 2014 was 3.9%, a number that isn't adjusted for either population growth or inflation. Such confusing wording is a common mistake in reports on international economic growth statistics.

Another thing to consider when examining growth rates is your starting point. Would you want to live in a country with a growth rate of over 100% per year? This sounds like a country that's generating a lot of economic activity. What about a country with a growth rate of –62%? This sounds like a place that doesn't have many opportunities. In reality, these two countries are actually the same place, and the huge differences in growth rates

TABLE 13.5

Economic Growth Rate in Libya, 2004–2013

Year	Real GDP growth rate
2004	4.4%
2005	9.9%
2006	5.9%
2007	6.0%
2008	3.8%
2009	2.1%
2010	5.0%
2011	−62.1%
2012	104.5%
2013	−10.9%

Source: World Bank.

occurred only two years apart! Table 13.5 shows the growth rates for Libya from 2004 through 2013. Libya was growing fairly consistently from 2004 through 2010, but political upheaval and a civil war plunged the country into an economic black hole in 2011. The reason the growth rate in 2012 was so large was that GDP had dropped so far the year before. It's important to understand that a one-year snapshot of a nation's growth rate may not be telling the whole story.

Growth Rates and Income Levels

Before we consider policies that might aid economic growth, we need to look more closely at how growth rates affect income levels.

First, consider how significant it is when income doubles, or increases by 100%. If your income doubled today—other things being equal—you could afford twice as much of everything you're currently buying. Now imagine what would happen if income doubled for an entire country or even for all countries. In the United States, per capita real GDP more than doubled in the 40 years between 1970 and 2010. This means that the average person living in the United States in 2010 could afford twice as much food, clothing, transportation, education, and even government services as the average U.S. resident in 1970. That's quite a difference.

But increasing real income by 100% in a single year isn't realistic. Let's pick a number closer to reality—say, 2%. With a growth rate of 2%, how long would it take to double your income? For example, let's say you graduate from college and, given your expertise in economics, you get several job offers. One offer is for $50,000 per year with a guaranteed raise of 2% every year. How long will it take for your salary to reach $100,000?

The first answer that pops into your head might be 50 years (based on the idea that 2% growth for 50 years adds up to 100% growth). But this answer

TABLE 13.6

Compound Growth

	Income	2% increase in income	Income in next year
Year 1	$50,000.00	$1,000.00	$51,000.00
Year 2	$51,000.00	$1,020.00	$52,020.00
Year 3	$52,020.00	$1,040.40	$53,060.40
Year 4	$53,060.40	$1,061.21	$54,121.61
Year 5	$54,121.61	$1,082.43	$55,204.04
...			
Year 35	$100,000		

would be wrong because it ignores the fact that growth *compounds* over time. As your salary grows, 2% growth leads to larger and larger dollar increases. Because of this compounding effect, it actually would take only about 35 years to double your income at a 2% growth rate.

Table 13.6 illustrates the process of compounding over time by showing the increase from year to year. Income starts at $50,000 in year 1, and a 2% increase yields $1,000, so that one year of growth results in income of $51,000. Subsequent 2% growth in the second year yields $1,020 of new income (2% of $51,000), so after two years income is $52,020. Looking at year 3, the 2% increase yields $1,040.40. Each year, the dollar increase in income (the green column) gets larger, as 2% of a growing number continues to grow.

Thanks to compounding, it takes only 35 years for income to double at a growth rate of 2%. This scenario corresponds with the experience of the U.S. economy. Since 1970, per capita real GDP in the United States has more than doubled. Yet this jump occurred while U.S. economic growth rates averaged "only" about 2%. Think about that: during your parents' lifetime, average real income levels in the United States doubled.

The Rule of 70

In the example above, we saw that when income grows at 2% per year, a given income doubles in just 35 years. A simple rule known as the **rule of 70** determines the length of time necessary for a sum of money to double at a particular growth rate. According to the rule of 70:

The **rule of 70** states that if the annual growth rate of a variable is *x*%, the size of that variable doubles every 70 ÷ *x* years.

> If the annual growth rate of a variable is *x*%, the size of that variable doubles every 70 ÷ *x* years.

The rule of 70 is an approximation, but it works well with typical economic growth rates.

Table 13.7 illustrates the rule of 70 by showing how long it takes for each $1.00 of income to double in value, given different growth rates. At an annual growth rate of 1%, each dollar of income will double every 70 ÷ 1 =

TABLE 13.7

A Dollar of Income at Different Growth Rates

Annual growth rate	Years to double	Value after 70 years (approximate)
0%	Never	$1.00
1%	70	$2.00
2%	35	$4.00
3%	23.3	$8.00
4%	17.5	$16.00

70 years. If growth increases to 2%, then a dollar of income will double every $70 \div 2 = 35$ years. Consider the impact of a 4% growth rate. If this rate can be sustained, income doubles every $70 \div 4 = 17.5$ years. In 70 years, income doubles 4 times, ending up at 16 times its starting value! China has been recently growing at almost 10% per year, and indeed its per capita income has been doubling about every 7 years—a remarkable rate of growth.

The rule of 70 shows us that small and consistent growth rates, if sustained for a decade or two, can greatly improve living standards. Over the long course of history, growth rates were essentially zero and the general human condition was poverty. But over the past two centuries, we have seen small, consistent growth rates, and the standard of living for many has increased dramatically.

We can look at actual growth rates of various countries over a long period to see the impact on income levels. Table 13.8 presents growth rates of several countries over 54 years from 1960 to 2014. Let's start with Honduras and South Korea. In 1960, both nations had roughly the same income per person. But South Korea grew 7.6% annually, and Honduras grew at about 0.1% annually. As a result, the average income in South Korea in 2014 was over 11 times the average income in Honduras.

This entire Shanghai skyline was built in the past 20 years, testament to an astonishing rate of growth.

Also in Table 13.8, you see other nations that have grown very quickly. In 1960, Japan's per capita income was similar to Turkey's. Yet 5.6% growth led to an income of over $38,000 per person in Japan by 2014. Singapore, with 6.3% growth over the entire period, moved from a relatively poor country to one of the world's richest.

Focusing more closely on China, we see one of the most impressive growth stories of recent times. Only 20 years ago, it was among the world's poorer nations. In Table 13.8 we see that China's growth rate from 1960 to 2014 was 5.4%; however, growth in China has been more concentrated in the last 20 years. Since 1995, China has grown at nearly 10% a year. Even if its astonishing growth slows considerably, China will still move into the group of the wealthiest nations in the coming decades.

Clearly, economic growth experiences have varied widely across time and place. But relatively small and consistent growth rates are sufficient to move a nation out of poverty over the period of a few generations. And this movement out of poverty really matters for the people who live in these nations.

TABLE 13.8

Economic Growth, 1960–2014

	Average annual growth rate (%)		Real per capita GDP in 1960	Real per capita GDP in 2014
Less than 2% growth	−0.3	Zimbabwe	1,714	905
	0.1	Honduras	1,024	2,291
	1.5	Philippines	1,554	2,765
	1.5	Kenya	596	994
About 2% growth	1.8	Guatemala	1,539	3,478
	1.9	Nepal	325	694
	2.1	Belize	1,862	4,834
	2.1	United States	17,594	53,143
Between 2% and 4% growth	2.4	India	511	1,499
	2.5	South Africa	2,585	6,618
	3.3	United Kingdom	8,429	39,337
	3.8	Turkey	3,102	10,946
Greater than 4% growth	4.1	Mexico	2,061	10,307
	5.4	China	542	6,807
	5.6	Japan	2,925	38,492
	6.3	Singapore	2,613	55,182
	7.6	South Korea	950	25,977

Source: World Bank. All figures converted to 2013 U.S. dollars.

PRACTICE WHAT YOU KNOW

Computing Economic Growth: By How Much Is Brazil Growing?

GDP in Brazil has grown rapidly in recent years. But historically Brazil has struggled with inflation rates. The table below gives 2013 statistics for Brazil.

Nominal GDP growth rate	Price-level growth rate	Population growth rate
10.15%	5.91%	0.9%

How much does inflation affect Brazil's growth data?

Question: What was Brazil's rate of economic growth in 2013?

Answer: First, recall Equation 13.1:

$$\text{economic growth} \approx \%\Delta \text{ nominal GDP} - \%\Delta \text{ price level} - \%\Delta \text{ population}$$

Now, for Brazil, we have:

$$\text{economic growth} \approx 10.15\% - 5.91\% - 0.9\% = 3.34\%$$

Question: If Brazil continues to grow at 3.34% per year, how long will it take to double the level of per capita real GDP?

Answer: Use the rule of 70:

$$70 \div 3.34 = 20.96 \text{ years}$$

Clearly, the growth of GDP in Brazil in 2013 was significant, even after accounting for both inflation and population growth.

Data source: International Monetary Fund, World Economic Outlook, April 2014.

ECONOMICS IN THE REAL WORLD

How Does 2% Growth Affect Average People?

How different was life when your grandparents were your age?

We have seen that economic growth in the United States has averaged 2% per year over the past 50 years. What does this mean for a typical person's everyday life? In Table 13.9, we've assembled some basic data on economic aspects of life in the United States for an average person in 1960. This may be about the time your grandparents were your age.

Today, average real income is more than double the level of 1960. Americans live 12% longer, have access to almost twice as many doctors, live in houses that are twice as big, enjoy more education, and own more and better cars and household appliances. We work about 15% fewer hours and hold jobs that are

TABLE 13.9

The United States: 1960 versus 2010

General Characteristics	1960	2010
Life expectancy	69.7 years	78.3 years
Real income (2010 dollars)	$17,747	$47,772
Physicians per 10,000 people	14.8	27
Years of school completed	10.5 (median)	12 (average)
Portion of income spent on food	27%	8%
Average workweek	40.9 hours	34 hours
Workforce in agriculture or manufacturing	37%	19%
Home ownership	61.9%	67.4%

New Home		
Size	1,200 square ft	2,457 square ft
Bedrooms	2	3
Bathrooms	1	2.5
Central air conditioning?	no	yes

Best-Selling Car		
Model	Chevrolet Impala	Toyota Camry
Price (2010 dollars)	$19,753	$26,640
Miles per gallon	13–16	20–29
Horsepower	135	268
Air conditioning?	optional	standard
Automatic transmission?	optional	standard
Airbags?	no	standard
Power locks and windows?	no	standard

Phone		
Percentage of homes with a telephone	78.5%	97.6%

TV		
Size	23 inches	50 inches
Display	black & white	high-definition color
Price (2010 dollars)	$1,391	$700

Source: U.S. Census Bureau, *Statistical Abstract of the United States*, and U.S. Bureau of Labor Statistics.

physically less taxing. In 1960, there were no cell phones, and over 20% of households didn't have a telephone. Today, there are more telephones than there are people in the United States. In addition, many modern amenities weren't available in 1960. Can you imagine life without a personal computer and the Internet, DVDs, microwave ovens, and central air conditioning? Take a look at Table 13.9 to see a striking contrast. ✷

How Do Resources and Technology Contribute to Economic Growth?

At this point, you may wonder what can be done to provide the best opportunity for economic growth. We see economic growth in many, though certainly not all, nations. But even in those nations that have grown in the past, future growth is not assured. So now we turn to the major sources of economic growth.

Economists continue to debate the relative importance of the factors that lead to economic growth. However, there's a general consensus on the significance of three factors for economic growth: resources, technology, and institutions. In this section, we examine the first two of these. Institutions are a more recent addition to the list of what can facilitate economic growth. We explore this topic in the final section of the chapter.

Resources

Other things being equal, the more resources there are available to a nation, the more output that nation can produce. **Resources**, also known as factors of production, are the inputs used to produce goods and services. When new resources are discovered, or existing ones improved, countries can experience economic growth. Economists divide resources into three major categories: (1) natural resources, (2) physical capital, and (3) human capital.

Resources, also known as factors of production, are the inputs used to produce goods and services.

Natural Resources

Natural resources include physical land and the inputs that occur naturally in or on the land. Coal, iron ore, diamonds, and lumber are examples of natural resources. Less obvious examples are mountains, beaches, temperate weather patterns, and scenic views—resources that residents enjoy consuming and that sometimes lead to tourism as a major industry.

Natural resources are an important source of economic wealth for nations. For example, the United States has fertile farmland, forests, coal, iron ore, and oil. In fact, the United States is the world's largest oil and gas producer.

Geography—the physical location of a nation—is also a natural resource that can contribute to economic growth. Geographic location facilitates trade and affects other important variables such as disease control and weather. The world map in Figure 13.3 shows global GDP per square kilometer. As you can see, locations on coasts or along rivers have developed more rapidly than areas far inland. These are the locations that were more naturally suited to trade in the days before railroads, trucks, and airplanes.

Diamonds may be a girl's best friend, but are they essential for economic growth?

FIGURE 13.3

Global GDP Density

The world's wealthiest areas (shown in darkest colors on this map) are often those located near natural shipping lanes along coasts and rivers, where trade naturally flowed. This pattern is evidence that geography matters in economic development.

Source: John Luke Gallup, Jeffrey D. Sachs, and Andrew D. Mellinger, "Geography and Economic Development," Working Paper No. 1, Center for International Development at Harvard University, March 1999.

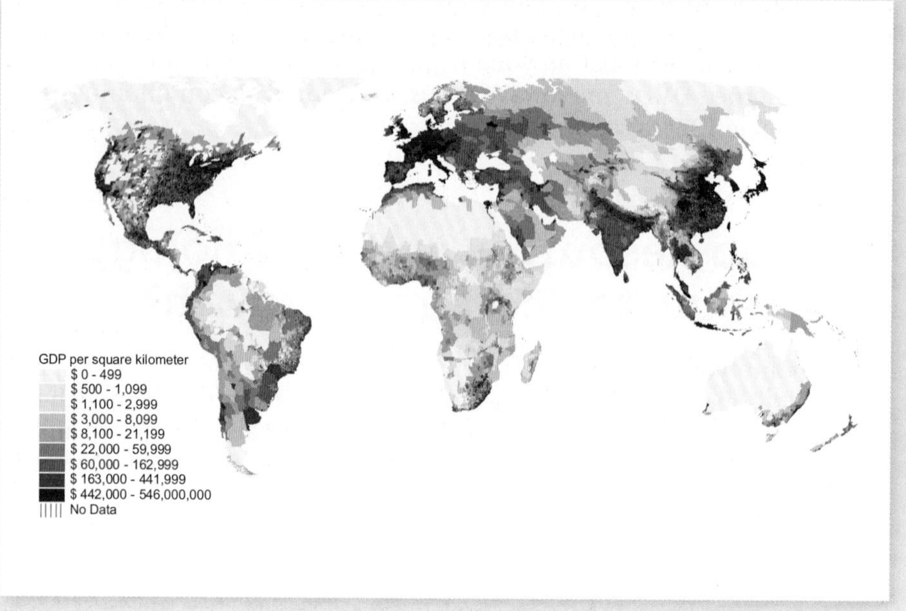

Natural resources clearly help to increase economic development, but they aren't enough to make a nation wealthy. After all, many poor nations are rich in natural resources. For example, Liberia has mahogany forests, iron-ore deposits, rubber-tree forests, diamonds, and a beautiful coastline along the Atlantic Ocean. Despite all these natural resources, Liberia is still poor. In contrast, think about Hong Kong, which is very small and densely populated with few natural resources. Yet the citizens of Hong Kong are among the wealthiest people in the world.

Capital comprises the tools and equipment used in the production of goods and services.

Physical Capital

The second category of resources is physical capital, or just capital. Recall that **capital** comprises the tools and equipment used in the production of goods and services. Examples of capital include factories, tractors, roads and bridges, computers, and shovels. The purpose of capital is to aid in the production of future output.

This cargo ship, bearing hundreds of individual shipping containers, is arriving in San Francisco with goods from Asia.

Consider the shipping container, a basic tool that has aided the movement of goods around the globe. The shipping container is a standard-size (20- or 40-foot-long) box used to move goods worldwide. In 1954, a typical cargo ship traveling from New York to Germany might have carried as many as 194,582 individual items. Transportation involved bags, barrels, cartons, and many other different means of packaging and storing goods. Loading and unloading the ship required armies of men working long hours for days on end. Not surprisingly, shipping goods from one country to another was expensive.

The standardized shipping container was first used in 1956. Suddenly, it was possible to move cargo around the globe without repacking every time the mode of transportation changed. Once a cargo ship enters the port, cranes lift the containers 200 feet in the air and unload about 40 large boxes each hour. Dozens of ships can be unloaded at a time, and computers run most of the operation. A container full of iPods can be loaded on the back of a truck in Shenzhen, China, transported to port, and loaded onto a ship that carries 3,000 containers. The ship can bring the iPods to the United States, where the containers are loaded onto a train and, later, a truck. This movement happens without anyone touching the contents. Clearly, the shipping container is a tool that has revolutionized world trade.

As the quantity of physical capital per worker rises, so does output per worker. Of course, workers are more productive with more and better tools. Look around the world: the productive nations have impressive roads, bridges, buildings, and factories. In poor nations, paved roads are non-existent or in disrepair, vehicles are of lower quality, and computers are a luxury. Even public electricity and sewage-treatment facilities are rare in many developing nations.

Because of the obvious correlation between tools and wealth, many of the early contributions to growth theory focused on the role of physical capital goods. As a result, much international aid went into the building of roads and factories, in the hope that prosperity would follow automatically. But today most people understand that capital alone is not sufficient to produce economic growth. Factories, dams, and other large capital projects bring wealth only when they mesh well with the rest of the economy. A steel factory is of little use in a region better suited for growing corn. Without a good rail network or proper roads, a steel factory cannot get the tools it needs and cannot easily send its products to markets. Dams that are not maintained fall into disrepair within years. The point is that simply building new capital in a nation doesn't ensure future sustained economic growth.

Human Capital

The output of a nation also depends on people. **Human capital** is the resource represented by the quantity, knowledge, and skills of the workers in an economy. It is possible to expand human capital by increasing the number of workers available, by educating the existing labor force, or both.

Human capital is the resource represented by the quantity, knowledge, and skills of the workers in an economy.

Labor itself is an important resource. You need people to produce output, but a larger population doesn't necessarily mean a larger GDP. For example, Pakistan has a population of over 170 million, the sixth highest population in the world, but its GDP places it 44th, behind much smaller countries like Belgium, Hong Kong, and Singapore. Economic growth requires increasing output *per capita*. If people enter the labor force and find jobs, GDP per capita can increase. For example, as we discussed in Chapter 8, women have entered the U.S. labor force in record numbers over the past 50 years. This change certainly contributed to increases in measured GDP and per capita GDP. When the primary output of adult women in the United States was non-market output such as homemaking services, it wasn't counted in the official GDP statistics. As more women join the official labor force, their output increases both GDP and per capita GDP.

Education enhances human capital, but is it the key ingredient to economic growth?

There is another important dimension of human capital: the knowledge and skills of the workers themselves. In this context, it's possible to increase human capital through education and training. Training includes everything from basic literacy to college education, and from software competencies to specific job training.

Not many people would doubt that a more educated labor force is more productive. And certainly, to boost per capita output, educating the labor force is more helpful than merely increasing the quantity of workers. But education alone isn't enough to ensure economic progress. For many years, for example, India struggled with economic growth, even while its workers were among the most educated in the world.

Technology

Technology is the knowledge that is available for use in production.

A **technological advancement** introduces new techniques or methods that enable firms to produce more valuable outputs per unit of input.

We all know that the world would be much poorer without computers, automobiles, electric light bulbs, and other goods that have resulted from productive ideas. **Technology** is the knowledge that is available for use in production. Though technology is often embodied in machines and productive techniques, it is really just knowledge. New technology enables us to produce more while using fewer of our limited resources. A **technological advancement** introduces new techniques or methods that enable firms to produce more valuable outputs per unit of input. We can either produce more with the same resources or use fewer resources to produce the same quantity.

For example, the assembly line was an important technological advance. Henry Ford adopted and improved the assembly line in 1913 at the Ford Motor Company in Michigan. In this new approach to the factory, workers focused on well-defined jobs such as screwing on individual parts. The conveyor belt moved the parts around the factory to workers' stations. The workers themselves, by staying put rather than moving around the production floor, experienced a lower rate of accidents and other mishaps.

Agriculture is a sector where technological advances are easy to spot. For example, we know that land resources are necessary to produce corn. But technological advances mean that over time it has become possible to grow and harvest more corn per acre of land. In fact, in the United States the corn yield per acre is now six times what it was in 1930. In 1930, the United States produced about 25 bushels of corn per acre, but now the yield is consistently over 150 bushels per acre. How is this possible? Through technology that has produced hybrid seeds, herbicides, fertilizers, and improved irrigation techniques.

Like capital, technology produces value only when it is combined with other inputs. For example, simply carrying plans for a shoe factory to Haiti wouldn't generate much economic value. The mere knowledge of how to produce shoes, while important, is only one piece of the growth puzzle. An economy must have the physical capital to produce shoes, must have the human capital to staff the factory and assembly line, and must create favorable conditions and incentives for potential investors. Economic growth occurs when all these conditions come together. This is one reason why it's incorrect to identify technological innovations as the sole cause of differences in wealth across nations.

Moreover, technological innovations don't occur randomly across the globe. Some places produce large clusters of such innovations. Consider that information technology largely comes from MIT (the Massachusetts Institute of Technology) and Silicon Valley, movie and television ideas generally come from Hollywood, and new fashion designs regularly come from Paris, Milan,

PRACTICE WHAT YOU KNOW

Resources: Growth Policy

Many policies have been advocated to help nations escape poverty, and the policies often focus on the importance of resources.

Question: For each policy listed below, which resource is the primary focus?

a. international loans for infrastructure like roads, bridges, and dams
b. mandated primary education
c. restrictions on the development of forested land
d. immigration policy
e. international aid for construction of a shoe factory

The Akosombo Dam in Ghana was built with international aid funds.

Answers:

a. Infrastructure is physical capital.
b. Education involves human capital.
c. These restrictions focus on maintaining a certain level of natural resources.
d. Immigration policy affects how many people are allowed into a country, but policy often also targets human capital. In many countries, immigration laws allow individuals with specialized skills to effectively move to the front of the immigration line.
e. The focus here is on physical capital.

Tokyo, and New York. Technological innovations tend to breed more innovations. This leads us to reword an earlier question: Why do some regions innovate (and grow) more than others? A large part of the answer lies in our next topic: institutions.

What Institutions Foster Economic Growth?

The study of economic growth has expanded beyond economic factors to the political and social conditions in a country. Variation in inputs alone has not explained the very different growth rates between nations. Consider Liberia and Taiwan. In 1950, residents of the African nation Liberia were wealthier than those on the island of Taiwan off the Chinese coast. Today, however, per capita GDP in Taiwan is more than 20 times that of Liberia. Yes, much of this wealth gap stems from obvious current differences in physical capital, human capital, and technology. But simply observing these differences doesn't explain why Taiwan experienced increases in capital and technology and Liberia didn't. Without a doubt, the biggest difference between Taiwan and Liberia since 1950 is the final growth factor we consider in this chapter: institutions.

An **institution** is a significant practice, relationship, or organization in a society. Institutions are the official and unofficial conditions that shape the environment in which decisions are made.

An **institution** is a significant practice, relationship, or organization in a society. Institutions are the official and unofficial conditions that shape the environment in which decisions are made. Discussions often focus on institutions such as the laws and regulations in a nation. But other institutions such as social mores and work habits are also important.

Institutions are not always tangible physical items that we can look at or hold. There might be a physical representative of an institution, such as the U.S. Constitution or the building where the Supreme Court meets, but the essence of an institution encompasses expectations and habitual practices. The rules and the mindset within the Supreme Court are what's important, not the building or the benches.

In this section, we consider the most significant institutions that affect production and income in a nation. These include private-property rights, political stability and the rule of law, open and competitive markets, efficient taxes, and stable money and prices. Many of these topics are examined in detail elsewhere in this book, so we cover them only briefly here.

Private-Property Rights

Private-property rights encompass the rights of individuals to own property, to use it in production, and to own the resulting output.

The single greatest incentive for voluntary production is ownership of what you produce. The existence of **private-property rights** means that individuals can own property—including houses, land, and other resources. When they use their property in production, they own the resulting output.

Think about the differences in private-property rights between Liberia and Taiwan. In Liberia, the system of land ownership isn't dependable. As a result, Liberians who wish to purchase land often must buy the land multiple times from different "owners," because there's no dependable record of true ownership. Taiwan, in contrast, has a well-defined system of law that protects property rights. Without private-property rights, people have very little incentive to improve the value of their assets.

One of the driving factors in the growth of the Chinese economy has been the government's relaxing of its laws against ownership of private property. These reforms stem from a risky experiment in the rural community of Xiaogang. In 1978, the heads of 21 families in Xiaogang signed an agreement that became the genesis of private-property rights in China. This remarkable document read:

> December 1978, Mr. Yan's Home. We divide the field (land) to every household. Every leader of the household should sign and stamp. If we are able to produce, every household should promise to finish any amount they are required to turn in to the government, no longer asking the government for food or money. If this fails, even if we go to jail or have our heads shaved, we will not regret. Everyone else (the common people who are not officers and signees of this agreement) also promise to raise our children until they are eighteen years old. First signer: Hong Chang Yan.*

The agreement stipulated that each family would continue to produce the government quota for their agricultural output. But they would begin keeping anything they produced above this quota. They also agreed to stop tak-

*Literal translation by Chuhan Wang.

PRACTICE WHAT YOU KNOW

Institutions: Can You Guess This Country?

Question: The following is a list of characteristics for a particular country. Can you name the country?

Hint: the nation's flag is one of those shown here.

1. This country has almost no natural resources.
2. It has no agriculture of its own.
3. It imports water.
4. It is located in the tropics.
5. It has four official languages.
6. It occupies 274 square miles.
7. It has one of the world's lowest unemployment rates.
8. It has a literacy rate of 96%.
9. It had a per capita GDP of $78,744 in 2013.
10. It has one of the densest populations per square mile on the planet.

Answer: Congratulations if you thought of Singapore! At first blush, it seems almost impossible that one of the most successful countries on the planet could have so little going for it.

Question: How could a country with so few natural resources survive, let alone flourish? How can an economy grow without any agriculture or enough fresh water?

Answer: What Singapore lacks in some areas it more than makes up for in others. Singapore has a lot of human capital from a highly educated and industrious labor force. It has been able to attract plenty of foreign financial funds by creating a stable and secure financial system that protects property rights and encourages free trade. Singapore also has a strategically situated deep-water port in Southeast Asia that benefits from proximity to the emerging economies of China and India.

ing food or money from the government. This agreement was dangerous in 1978—so dangerous that those who signed the document also stipulated that they would raise one another's children if any of the signees were put in jail.

The Xiogang agreement led to an agricultural boom that other communities copied. Seeing the success of this experiment in property rights, Deng Xiaoping and other Chinese leaders subsequently instituted market reforms in agriculture in the 1980s, and then in manufacturing in the 1990s. China's economy is growing rapidly today not because the Chinese found new resources or updated their technology. They are wealthier because they now recognize private-property rights in many different industries.

Political Stability and the Rule of Law

Bullet casings litter the street in Monrovia, Liberia, in 2003.

To understand the importance of political stability and the rule of law, consider again Liberia and Taiwan. Political unrest and armed conflict has been the norm in Liberia since 1980, when armed opposition members murdered the president. Government officials in Liberia typically assume office through the use of violence, and national leaders consistently use their power to eradicate their opponents. In contrast, Taiwan's political climate has been relatively stable since 1949. If you were an entrepreneur deciding where to build a factory, would you want to invest millions of dollars in a country with constant, violent unrest, or would you choose a peaceful country instead? Which nation would you predict is more likely to see new factories and technological innovation?

Political instability is a disincentive for investment. After all, investment makes sense only if there is a fairly certain payoff at the end. In an environment of political instability, there's no incentive to invest in either human or physical capital because there's no predictable future payoff.

Rule of law refers to consistent and trustworthy enforcement of a nation's laws.

Consistent and trustworthy enforcement of a nation's laws, sometimes called the **rule of law**, is crucial for economic growth. Corruption is one of the most common and dangerous impediments to economic growth. When government officials steal, elicit bribes, or hand out favors to friends, their behavior reduces incentives for private investment. If individuals cannot count on consistent returns to investment in human or physical capital, investment declines. And this decline reduces future growth.

The World Justice Project has collected data on the rule of law worldwide. Figure 13.4 shows the world's nations broken down into five groups, based on

FIGURE 13.4

The Rule of Law and Per Capita Income

Consistent and fair enforcement of a nation's laws pays off with economic growth. The nations with the least corruption have average per capita GDP of $38,350, but the most corrupt nations have average per capita GDP of just $4,785.

Source: World Justice Project, Annual Report 2011. GDP figures are adjusted using PPP (constant 2005 international $), 2005–2009.

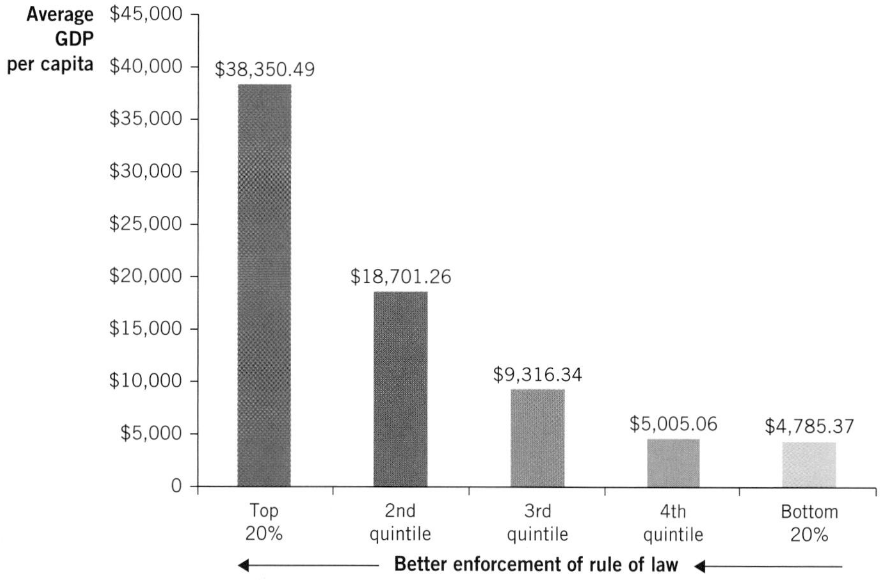

consistent enforcement of the rule of law. It's no surprise that nations scoring in the top group on this index are also those with the highest levels of per capita GDP. The most corrupt nations are also those with the lowest levels of income per person.

ECONOMICS IN THE REAL WORLD

What Can Parking Violations Teach Us about International Institutions?

Until 2002, diplomatic immunity protected United Nations diplomats in New York City from fines or arrest because of parking violations. This immunity gave economists Raymond Fisman and Edward Miguel* the idea for a unique natural experiment: they studied how officials responded to the lack of legal consequences for violating the law. Parking violations under these conditions are an example of corruption because they represent the abuse of power for private gain. Therefore, by comparing the level of parking violations of diplomats from different societies, the economists created a way to compare corruption norms among different cultures.

Would you get more parking tickets if you weren't compelled to pay for them?

Fisman and Miguel compared unpaid parking violations with existing survey-based measures on levels of corruption across nations. They found that diplomats from high-corruption nations accumulated significantly more unpaid parking violations in New York City than those from low-corruption nations. Among the worst offenders were diplomats from Kuwait, Egypt, Chad, Sudan, and Bulgaria. Among those with zero unpaid parking violations were Australia, Canada, Denmark, Japan, and Norway.

This finding suggests that cultural or social norms related to corruption are quite persistent: even when stationed thousands of miles away, diplomats behave as if they are at home. Norms related to corruption are apparently deeply ingrained.

In 2002, enforcement authorities acquired the right to confiscate the diplomatic license plates of violators. And guess what? Unpaid violations dropped by almost 98%. This outcome illustrates the power of incentives in influencing human behavior. ✻

Incentives

*Raymond Fisman and Edward Miguel, "Corruption, Norms and Legal Enforcement: Evidence from Diplomatic Parking Tickets," *Journal of Political Economy* 115, no. 6 (2007): 1020–1048.

Competitive and Open Markets

In this section, we take a quick look at three aspects of markets that are essential for economic growth: competitive markets, international trade, and the flow of funds across borders. We cover these market characteristics in detail elsewhere in this book.

Competitive Markets

In Chapter 6, we explored how competitive markets ensure that consumers can buy goods at the lowest possible prices. When markets aren't competitive, people who want to participate face barriers to entry. These barriers inhibit competition and innovation. Yet many nations monopolize key industries by preventing competition or by establishing government ownership of industries. This strategy limits economic growth.

International Trade

Trade creates value

Recall from Chapter 2 that trade creates value. International trade is very much like trade between individuals in the same country. In some cases, trade enables nations to consume goods and services that they wouldn't produce on their own. Specialization and trade make nations better off because each can produce goods for which it enjoys a comparative advantage. Output increases when nations (1) produce the goods and services for which they have the lowest opportunity cost, and then (2) trade for the other goods and services they wish to consume.

International trade barriers reduce the benefits available from specialization and trade. Chapter 18 is devoted to the study of international trade.

Flow of Funds across Borders

Savings play a role in economic growth. If firms and individuals are to invest in physical or human capital, someone has to save—because firms need to borrow consumers' savings in order to invest. Opportunities for investment expand if companies can access savings from around the globe. That is, if foreigners can funnel their savings into a nation's economy, that nation's firms can use these funds to expand their operations. However, many developing nations have restrictions on foreign ownership of land and physical plants within their borders. Restrictions on the flow of capital across borders handcuff domestic firms because they're forced to seek funds solely from domestic savers. The result can be lower rates of economic growth.

Efficient Taxes

On the one hand, taxes must be high enough to support effective government. Political stability, the rule of law, and private-property rights protection all require strong and consistent government. And taxes provide the revenue to pay for government services. On the other hand, if we tax activities that are fundamental to economic growth, there will be fewer of these activities. In market economies, output and income are strictly intertwined. If we tax income, we're taxing output, and that is GDP. In short: taxes are necessary, but they can also reduce incentives for production.

Before the U.S. federal government instituted an income tax, government services were largely funded by taxes on imports. But international trade is also an essential institution for economic growth. So taxes on imports also impede growth.

Efficient taxes are taxes sufficient to fund the activities of government while impeding production and consumption decisions as little as possible. It's not easy to determine the efficient level of taxes or even to determine what activities should be taxed. We deal with this topic more when we examine fiscal policy in Chapter 17.

Stable Money and Prices

High and variable inflation is a sure way to reduce incentives for investment and production. If prices change constantly, the result is confusion in the economy. When people are unsure about future price levels, they are

Helping Alleviate Global Poverty

ECONOMICS FOR LIFE

The information presented in this chapter reveals a picture of significant and persistent poverty across much of the globe. It's possible that this discussion and your classroom lectures have inspired you to learn more about global poverty or even to try to help those who are less fortunate around the globe. Toward those ends, we can give a little advice.

The surest way to learn about world economic reality is to travel to a developing nation. We suggest taking an alternative spring break or even studying abroad for an entire semester in a developing nation. These are costly ventures, but they will almost certainly change your perspective on life. If you get the chance to travel, be sure to speak directly to people on the streets and ask them to share their personal stories with you. Talk to small business owners, parents, and children. If possible, try to speak to people who have nothing to gain by sharing their story.

It is possible that you wish to give financially to help the less fortunate around the globe. There are many international aid charities, but unfortunately not all are truly helpful or even completely honest. We recommend visiting the Givewell Website (www.givewell.org), which researches charitable organizations from around the world and recommends a few that have proven to be honest and effective.

If you want to study more about growth economics, you should start with two books. The first book is by economist William Easterly, titled *The Elusive Quest for Growth: Economists' Adventures and Misadventures in the Tropics* (2001). In this book, Easterly weaves personal narrative and economic theory together in a unique way to help readers understand how economic theories regarding growth have evolved through the years. He both explains past failures and argues compellingly for future policy proposals. The second book, by economists Daron Acemoglu and James Robinson, is titled *Why Nations Fail: The Origins of Power, Prosperity, and Poverty* (2012). This book presents the best arguments for institutions as the primary source of economic growth. Even though this book is written by leading macroeconomists, it is enjoyable reading for mass audiences.

A University of Virginia student helps with eye surgeries in Tema, Ghana.

certainly more reluctant to sign contracts that deliver dollar payoffs in the future. For this reason, unpredictable inflation diminishes future growth. In the United States, the Federal Reserve Bank (the Fed) is charged with administering *monetary policy* (that is, policy that affects the money supply). The Fed's role is designed to reduce incentives for politically motivated monetary policy, which typically leads to highly variable inflation rates. We cover the Fed in greater detail in Chapter 15.

Conclusion

We began this chapter with the misconception that natural resources are the primary source of economic growth. While it doesn't hurt to have a strong supply of natural resources, they are certainly not sufficient for economic growth. Modern economics also points to growth as strongly influenced by the institutions that frame the environment within which business and personal decisions are made. One of those institutions is a stable financial system, the importance of which has become more obvious in the last few years as a result of upheaval in national and world financial markets. To get a better understanding of how the financial system works, we turn in the next chapter to the loanable funds market.

ANSWERING THE BIG QUESTIONS

Why does economic growth matter?

* Economic growth affects human welfare in meaningful ways.
* Historical data shows that sustained economic growth is a relatively modern phenomenon.
* Relatively small but consistent growth rates are the best path out of poverty.

How do resources and technology contribute to economic growth?

* Natural resources, physical capital, and human capital all contribute to economic growth.
* Technological advancements, which lead to the production of more output per unit of input, also foster economic growth.

What institutions foster economic growth?

* Private-property rights secure ownership of what an individual produces, creating incentives for increased output.
* Political stability and the rule of law enable people to make production decisions without worrying about a corrupt government.
* Competitive and open markets enable everyone to benefit from global productivity.
* Efficient taxes are high enough to support effective government, but low enough to provide positive incentives for production.
* Stable money and prices enable people to make long-term production decisions with minimal risk.

CONCEPTS YOU SHOULD KNOW

capital (p. 400)
human capital (p. 401)
institution (p. 404)
private-property rights (p. 404)
resources (p. 399)
rule of law (p. 406)
rule of 70 (p. 394)
technological advancement (p. 402)
technology (p. 402)

QUESTIONS FOR REVIEW

1. What are the three factors that influence economic growth?
2. What is human capital, and how is it different from the quantity of workers available for work? Name three ways to increase a nation's human capital. Is an increase in the size of the labor force also an increase in human capital? Explain your answer.
3. How is economic growth measured?
4. How would you describe the pattern of world economic growth over the past 2,000 years? Approximately when did economic growth really take off?
5. What are five human welfare conditions that are positively affected by economic growth?
6. Many historical accounts credit the economic success of the United States to its abundance of natural resources.
   a. What is missing from this argument?
   b. Name five poor nations that have significant natural resources.
7. The difference between 1% growth and 2% growth seems insignificant. Explain why it really matters.
8. What do economists mean by the term "institutions"? How are institutions related to economic growth?

STUDY PROBLEMS (** solved at the end of the section*)

* 1. Real per capita GDP in China in 1959 was about $350, but it doubled to about $700 by 1978, when Deng Xiaoping started market reforms.
   a. What was the average annual economic growth rate in China over the 20 years from 1959 to 1978?
   b. Chinese per capita real GDP doubled again in only seven years, reaching $1,400 by 1986. What was the average annual economic growth rate between 1979 and 1986?

* 2. The table below presents long-run macroeconomic data for two hypothetical nations, A and B.

	A	B
Nominal GDP growth	12%	5%
Inflation	10%	2%
Unemployment rate	12%	5%
Population growth	1.5%	1%

Assume that both nations start with real GDP of $1,000 per citizen. Fill in the blanks in the table below, assuming the data above applies for every year considered.

	A	B
Economic growth rate	______	______
Years required for real per capita GDP to double	______	______
Real per capita GDP 140 years later	______	______

3. Let's revisit the data from Table 13.3, showing the following world economic growth rates for specific historical eras:

Years	Growth rate
AD 1–1800	0.02%
1800–1900	0.64%
1900–1950	1.04%
1950–2000	2.12%

How many years will it take for average per capita real GDP to double at each of those growth rates?

4. Use the data in the table below to compute economic growth rates for the United States for the period 2008–2011. Note that all data is from the end of the year specified.

Date	Change in nominal GDP (billions of current $)	Change in the price level	Population growth
2008	−2.0	−0.4	0.9
2009	3.8	1.0	0.9
2010	3.7	3.2	0.8
2011	4.2	2.1	0.7

5. The rule of 70 applies in any growth-rate application. Let's say you have $1,000 in savings, and you have three alternatives for investing these funds:
   - a savings account earning 1% interest per year
   - a U.S. Treasury bond earning 3% interest per year
   - a stock market mutual fund earning 8% interest per year

   How long would it take to double your savings in each of the three accounts?

6. Assume that you plan to retire in 40 years and are evaluating the three different accounts in question 5 above. How much would your $1,000 be worth in 40 years under each of the three alternatives?

SOLVED PROBLEMS

1. a. The rule of 70 tells us that we can divide 70 by the rate of growth to get the number of years before a variable doubles. Therefore, if we know the number of years that a variable actually did take to double, we can rearrange the rule of 70 to determine the average growth rate, x:

$$70 \div x = 20$$
$$70 \div 20 = x$$
$$= 3.5$$

Therefore, China's economy grew by an average of 3.5% over the 20-year period from 1959 to 1978.

b. Now, with real per capital GDP doubling in just seven years, the rule of 70 implies:

$$70 \div 7 = 10$$

Therefore, China's economy grew by an average of 10% over the seven-year period from 1979 to 1986.

2. To determine economic growth rate, we use the approximations formula:

nominal GDP growth rate
− inflation
− population growth rate

economic growth rate

For nation A: 12% − 10% − 1.5% = 0.5%

For nation B: 5% − 2% − 1% = 2%

To determine the years required for real per capita GDP to double, we use the rule of 70:

For nation A: 70 ÷ 0.5 = 140

For nation B: 70 ÷ 2 = 35

To determine real per capita GDP 140 years later, use the rule of 70 results. Nation A's level doubles in exactly 140 years, at which time it will be two times the original level of $1,000, so $2,000. Nation B's level doubles after 35 years and then doubles again after 35 more years. So after 70 years, its level of real per capita GDP is four times the original level. It doubles again in 35 years, so after 105 years it is eight times the original level. Then it doubles again in 35 more years, so after 140 years its real per capita GDP is 16 times the original level, or $16,000.

	A	B
Economic growth rate	0.5%	2%
Years required for real per capita GDP to double	140	35
Real per capita GDP 140 years later	$2,000	$16,000

CHAPTER 14

Savings, Investment, and the Market for Loanable Funds

MISCONCEPTION

The government sets interest rates.

An *interest rate* is the price you pay to borrow money. There are many interest rates, including the rate you pay on student loans, credit cards, car loans, and mortgages, and the rate banks pay people who save. Just about anything you read or hear about interest rates in the popular media leaves you with the impression that the government sets interest rates. This isn't exactly true. For sure, the government can influence many rates. But almost all interest rates in the U.S. economy are determined privately—on the basis of the interaction between the market forces of supply and demand. In fact, you can understand why interest rates rise and fall by applying supply and demand analysis to the market for loans. That's what we do in this chapter. Along the way, we also consider the many factors that influence savers and borrowers.

In this chapter, we also discuss how investors, financial institutions, and markets affect the macroeconomy. Even though investment decisions are made by individuals (a microeconomic choice), the combined impacts of these decisions have macroeconomic consequences. When we're finished, you will understand why interest rates rise and fall, and you will also appreciate the role of the loanable funds market in the larger macroeconomy.

These traders play one of many important roles in the market for loanable funds.

BIG QUESTIONS

- What is the loanable funds market?
- What factors shift the supply of loanable funds?
- What factors shift the demand for loanable funds?
- How do we apply the loanable funds market model?

What Is the Loanable Funds Market?

The **loanable funds market** is the market where savers supply funds for loans to borrowers.

Firms and governments obtain funds, or *financing,* for their operations in financial markets. These funds come primarily from household savings across the economy. In economics, we analyze financial markets in the context of a loanable funds market. The **loanable funds market** is the market where savers supply funds for loans to investors. In fact, this is the real purpose of this market. Without the ability to get savings to investors, economies will have difficulty moving forward.

This market isn't in a single physical location. Rather, it includes places like stock exchanges, investment banks, mutual fund firms, and commercial banks. In this section, we explain the characteristics of the loanable funds market and the significant role it plays in the overall economy.

Figure 14.1 illustrates the role of the loanable funds market. Savings flow into the market and, through a variety of methods, become loans to investors. We could call it the market for savings, or even the market for loans. The term "loanable funds" captures both ideas.

FIGURE 14.1

The Purpose of the Loanable Funds Market

The market for loanable funds is where savers supply funds, making them available to investors. Households (private individuals and families) are the primary suppliers of loanable funds. Firms are the primary demanders, or investors, of loanable funds. When this market is functioning well, firms get the funds necessary for production and savers are paid for lending.

On the left side of the figure, the suppliers of funds—those who save—include households and foreign entities. Households are private individuals and families. Foreign entities include foreign governments, firms, and private citizens that choose to save in the United States. For most of the applications we discuss, we focus on households as the primary suppliers of loanable funds. If you have a checking or savings account at a bank, you are a supplier of loanable funds. You deposit funds into your bank account, but these funds don't just sit in a bank vault. Rather, banks loan out the majority of these funds. Household savings in retirement accounts, stocks, bonds, and mutual funds are other significant sources of loanable funds.

Notice that we say "savings" in stocks and bonds. Investment in the economic sense isn't something that people do when buying stocks, bonds, or mutual funds. When you're preparing for retirement or trying to earn a little extra income through the stock market (see Chapter 19), you, as an individual, are saving. Economists reserve the terms "investors" and "investment" for those who are growing businesses and attempting to expand output.

The demanders of loanable funds include firms and governments. In this chapter, we focus on firms as the primary demanders of loanable funds and refer to them as investors. To reinforce the significance of this market, think about why firms want loanable funds: without them, firms wouldn't have the resources to invest. That is, firms looking to produce output in the future must borrow funds in order to pay their expenses today and to grow their businesses.

Figure 14.2 shows the production timeline. At the end of the timeline is output, or GDP. When this output is sold, it produces revenue for the firms, and the revenue serves to pay bills. But *future* GDP depends on spending today for necessary resources. This spending comes before any revenue is gained from the sale of output. Therefore, firms must borrow in order to generate *future* GDP—that's how important the loanable funds market is to the entire economy. Without a well-functioning loanable funds market today, future GDP dries up.

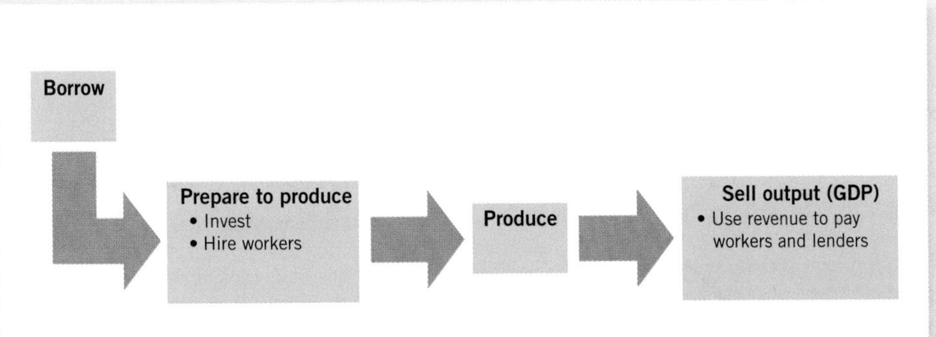

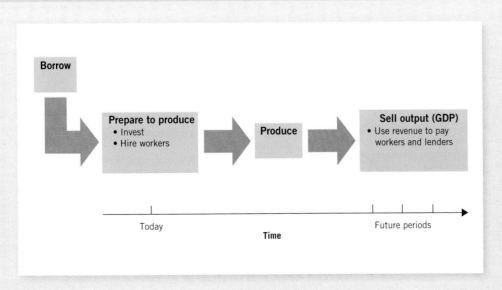

FIGURE 14.2

The Production Timeline

The production timeline illustrates that future GDP depends critically on the loanable funds market. At the end of the production timeline we see output, or GDP. But before a firm can produce output, it must purchase resources. Since these purchases occur before the revenue comes in, firms must borrow at the beginning of the timeline.

Before you can sell college apparel, you have to buy equipment and other supplies.

Imagine that you're an entrepreneur who decides to start a company that will produce and sell college apparel. If you succeed, you'll contribute to national GDP. But you don't really think of it this way; you simply hope that you've discovered a great business opportunity. Before you ever sell your first shirt, hat, or pair of sweatpants, you have to spend money on the resources you'll use in the production process. For example, if you plan on silk-screening your college logo onto hooded sweatshirts, you have to buy sweatshirts, paint, and a screen printing press. Here is where the loanable funds market comes into play: since you have no revenue yet, you need to borrow in order to make these investments.

Borrowing by businesses fuels investment, which leads to future output. But notice that *every dollar borrowed requires a dollar saved.* Without savings, we cannot sustain future production. If you want to invest in your business to buy the resources you need to produce college apparel, someone else has to save. Working backward, the chain of crucial relationships looks like this: output (GDP) requires investment; investment requires borrowing; borrowing requires savings. And all the links in this chain require a loanable funds market that efficiently channels funds from savers to investors.

We will study this crucial market from the perspective of prices, quantities, supply, and demand—like any other market. The good in this market is loanable funds. The demanders (or consumers) are investors; the suppliers are savers. Figure 14.3 presents a picture of supply (Savings, or S) and demand (Investment, or D) for loanable funds, along with a summary of the parts of the loanable funds market.

An **interest rate** is a price of loanable funds, quoted as a percentage of the original loan amount.

One advantage of this demand and supply approach is that it clarifies the role of interest rates. An **interest rate** is a price of loanable funds. It's like the

FIGURE 14.3

The Loanable Funds Market

Savings (S) is channeled into investment (D) in the loanable funds market. In this market, loanable funds are the goods that are bought and sold. The price is an interest rate. This price, like any other market-determined price, is reached through the interaction between supply and demand.

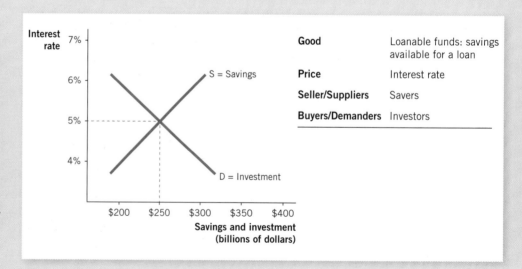

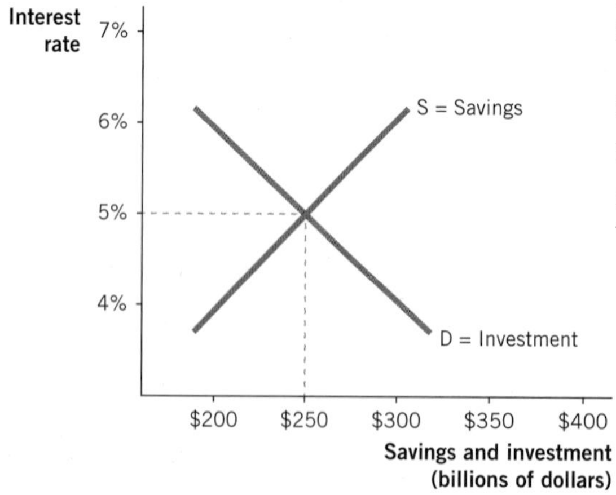

Good	Loanable funds: savings available for a loan
Price	Interest rate
Seller/Suppliers	Savers
Buyers/Demanders	Investors

price of toothpaste or computers or hoodies; it's simply quoted differently—as a percentage of the original loan amount. People who are thinking about planning for retirement or making a big purchase such as a house or a car worry about interest rate fluctuations but don't necessarily understand why interest rates rise and fall. If we acknowledge that an interest rate is just the price of loanable funds, we can use supply and demand to reveal the factors that make interest rates rise and fall.

We now turn to the two different views of interest rates: the view of the saver and the view of the investor.

Interest Rates as a Return for Saving

If you are a saver, the interest rate is the return you get for supplying funds to the market. For example, let's say your parents gave you some cash when you came to college this semester. After buying textbooks, groceries, and other supplies, you have $1,000 left, which you consider saving. You go to a bank near campus and inquire about opening a new account. In this transaction, the bank is the buyer, and it offers a certain price for the use of your savings. When it does offer a price, it's not in dollars. Instead, the bank quotes a price in interest rates, or as a percentage of how much you save. So if you're saving $1,000, the bank might tell you, "We'll pay you 2% if you save that money for a year." Since 2% of $1,000 is $20, this is equivalent to saying, "We'll pay you $20 if you save that money for a year."

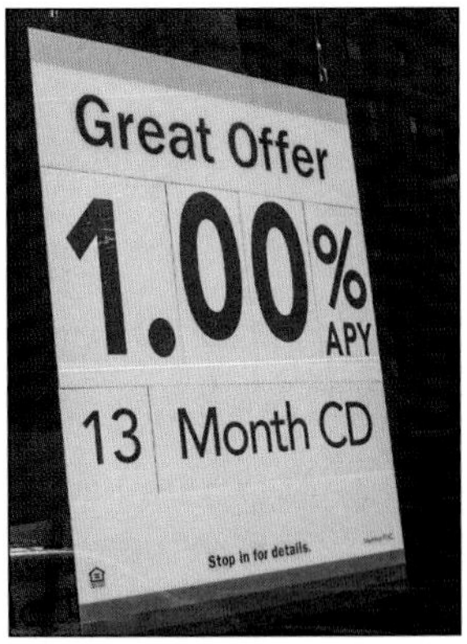

Banks are willing to pay you for your savings. The price they pay is the interest rate.

If you save $1,000 for one year with an interest rate of 2%, your total amount of savings is $1,020 next year, which is computed as:

$$\$1{,}000 + (2\% \text{ of } \$1{,}000) = \$1{,}000 + \$20 = \$1{,}020$$

For savers, the interest earned is the payoff for saving. Every dollar saved today returns more in the saver's account in the future. The higher the interest rate, the greater the payoff will be in the future. Table 14.1 illustrates how interest rates affect $1,000 worth of savings. An interest rate of 0.5% yields $1,005 one year later; an interest rate of 4% yields $1,040.

Think of the interest rate as the opportunity cost of consumption. Consider the $1,000 savings in Table 14.1. If you were to make a $1,000 purchase today instead of saving that money with 0.5% interest, you'd be giving up $5 to make the purchase. But at an interest rate of 4%, using the $1,000 for

TABLE 14.1

Higher Interest Rates and Greater Future Returns

Interest rate	Value of $1,000 after 1 year
0.5%	$1,005
1%	1,010
2%	1,020
4%	1,040

If you save $1,000 for one year at an interest rate of 2%, the value of your account will be $1,020 next year, computed as:

$$\begin{aligned} & \$1{,}000 + (2\% \text{ of } \$1{,}000) \\ = & \$1{,}000 + (0.02 \times \$1{,}000) \\ = & \$1{,}000 + \$20 \\ = & \$1{,}020 \end{aligned}$$

Opportunity cost

consumption today means giving up an additional $40 next year. Interest rates on savings accounts in the United States today are typically less than 2%, which means that the opportunity cost of consumption is pretty low. Now imagine an interest rate of 10% for a savings account. This was actually the situation in the United States in the 1980s. With an interest rate that high, even college students could find a way to save.

Incentives

As we have mentioned, savings constitutes the supply of loanable funds. The higher the interest rate, the greater is the incentive to save. This is the loanable funds version of the law of supply: as the interest rate rises, the quantity of savings rises. The reverse is true as well. When the interest rate falls, the quantity of savings falls. This positive relationship between interest rates and savings is reflected in the slope of the supply curve (S, or Savings), illustrated in Figure 14.4, panel (a). When the interest rate is 4%, the quantity of loanable funds supplied is $200 billion per year; at 5% the quantity supplied increases to $250 billion, and at 6% it increases to $300 billion.

FIGURE 14.4

Supply of and Demand for Loanable Funds

(a) Changes in the interest rate cause a movement along the supply curve for loanable funds. As the interest rate rises, individuals want to save more because the return for doing so increases. At lower interest rates, people save less because they earn less interest. This is the law of supply in action. As the interest rate rises, the quantity supplied rises. As the interest rate falls, the quantity supplied falls. (b) When the interest rate changes, there is also a movement along the demand curve for loanable funds. As the interest rate rises, firms want to borrow less because investment is now more expensive and achieving a rate of return high enough to justify projects is more difficult. When the interest rate is lower, more projects will earn a high enough rate of return to be justified; thus, firms want to borrow more. This is the law of demand in the loanable funds market. As the interest rate rises, the quantity demanded falls. As the interest rate falls, the quantity demanded rises.

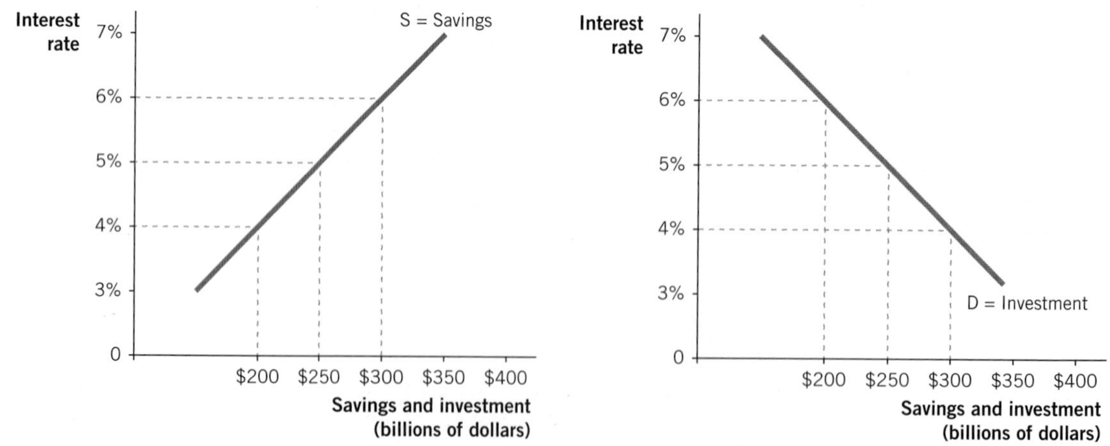

(a) Supply of Loanable Funds

(b) Demand for Loanable Funds

Interest Rates as a Cost of Borrowing

We now turn to the demand, or investor, side of the loanable funds market. For this, we shift to the firm's perspective and return to your plan to produce college apparel. Recall that you need to buy the sweatshirts, paint, and screen printing press to produce hoodies and other products with a college logo. Assume that you need \$100,000 to start your business. If you borrow \$100,000 for one year at an interest rate of 6%, you'll need to repay \$106,000 in one year. It makes sense to borrow this money only if you expect to earn more than 6%, or \$6,000, on this investment. If you expect to earn less than this, you are planning to lose money.

For investors, the interest rate is the cost of borrowing. Firms borrow only if they expect the return on their investment to be greater than the costs of the loan. For example, at an interest rate of 6% a firm would borrow only if it expected to make more than a 6% return with its use of the funds. Let's state this as a rule:

Profit-maximizing firms borrow to fund an investment if and only if the expected return on the investment is greater than the interest rate on the loan.

The lower the interest rate, the more likely a business will succeed in earning enough to exceed the interest it will owe at the end of the year. For example, if your firm can borrow at an interest rate of just 4%, you'll need to make a return greater than 4%. There are probably several investments available today that would pay more than a 6% return; but there are even more that would yield returns greater than 4%, and more still that would pay greater than 2%. If we apply our rule from above, we'll see a larger quantity of loans demanded as the interest rate drops. This is the law of demand applied to the market for loanable funds; it gives us the inverse relationship between the interest rate and quantity demanded for loans that is reflected in the slope of the demand curve for loanable funds.

The graph of the loanable funds market in Figure 14.4, panel (b), illustrates the demand curve (D, or Investment) for loanable funds across the entire U.S. economy. At an interest rate of 6%, the quantity of loans demanded by all business firms in the economy is \$200 billion. In other words, firms believe that only \$200 billion worth of investment will pay returns greater than 6%. At an interest rate of 5%, firms estimate that another \$50 billion worth of total loans will earn between 5% and 6%, and the quantity of loans demanded rises to \$250 billion. If the rate were to fall to 4%, the quantity demanded for loans would rise to \$300 billion. Lower interest rates lead to a greater quantity demanded for loanable funds.

How Inflation Affects Interest Rates

If you save \$1,000 for a year at an interest rate of 2%, your reward for saving is \$20. But inflation affects the real value of this reward. For example, imagine that the inflation rate is exactly 2% during the year you save. This inflation means that next year it will take \$1,020 to buy the same quantity of goods and services that you can buy this year for \$1,000. In this case, your interest rate of 2% and the inflation rate of 2% cancel each other out. The \$20 you

The **real interest rate** is the interest rate that is corrected for inflation.

The **nominal interest rate** is the stated interest rate before it is corrected for inflation.

The **Fisher equation** states that the real interest rate equals the nominal interest rate minus the inflation rate.

earned in interest just covers the general increase in prices. In other words, you break even, and that's no reward.

When making decisions about saving and borrowing, people care about the real interest rate, not the nominal interest rate. The **real interest rate** is the interest rate that is corrected for inflation; it is the rate of return in terms of real purchasing power. In contrast, the **nominal interest rate** is the interest rate before it is corrected for inflation; it is the stated interest rate. In our example, the interest rate of 2% is the nominal interest rate. But with 2% inflation, the real return on your savings disappears, and the real interest rate is zero—or 0%. In general, we can approximate the real interest rate by subtracting the inflation rate from the nominal interest rate in an equation known as the **Fisher equation**:

(Equation 14.1) $$\text{real interest rate} = \text{nominal interest rate} - \text{inflation rate}$$

For example, if the inflation rate this year is 1%, a nominal interest rate of 2% on your savings yields a 1% real interest rate. The Fisher equation is named after economist Irving Fisher, who formulated the relationship between inflation and interest rates.

Savers and investors care about the real rate of interest on a loan because this is the rate that describes how the real purchasing power of their funds changes over the course of the loan. A lender expects to earn a particular real rate of return to justify lending, rather than spending, money. Therefore, if inflation rises, nominal interest rates increase as well. This mechanism ensures that the funds being repaid are compensating the lender for any loss of purchasing power due to inflation. Stable inflation is important for economic growth. Fluctuating inflation rates destabilize the market for loanable funds because savers don't want to save if unexpectedly high inflation erodes the value of their savings. Similarly, lenders don't want to lend if they can't be sure what their real rate of return will be. Without saving, there will be no lending. Without lending, there is no investment. We see this problem in countries like Argentina, where inflation rates vary widely from year to year and investment is tepid at best.

We can rewrite the Fisher equation to see how inflation generally increases nominal interest rates:

(Equation 14.2) $$\text{nominal interest rate} = \text{real interest rate} + \text{inflation rate}$$

For a given real interest rate, the higher the rate of inflation, the higher the nominal interest rate will be. Table 14.2 shows how the nominal interest rate rises with inflation rates for a given real interest rate. If the real interest rate is 4% and there is no inflation, then the nominal interest rate is also 4%.

TABLE 14.2

How Inflation Affects Nominal Interest Rates

Inflation rate		Real interest rate		Nominal interest rate
0%	+	4%	=	4%
2%	+	4%	=	6%
4%	+	4%	=	8%

PRACTICE WHAT YOU KNOW

Interest Rates and Quantity Supplied and Demanded: U.S. Interest Rates Have Fallen

In 1981, many interest rates in the United States were 15%, but the inflation rate was 10%. In 2014, many interest rates were less than 1.5%, and the inflation rate was 2%.

Question: What were the real interest rates in 1981 and 2014?

Answer: Using Equation 14.1, we compute the real interest rate as:

$$\text{real interest rate} = \text{nominal interest rate} - \text{inflation rate}$$

For 1981, the real interest rate was: $15\% - 10\% = 5\%$

For 2014, the real interest rate was: $1.5\% - 2\% = -0.5\%$

Question: Other things being equal, how does the drop in interest rates between 1981 and 2014 affect the quantity of loanable funds supplied?

Answer: The quantity supplied decreases along the supply curve. Lower interest rates reduce the incentive to save. Remember, a change in interest rates only changes your position along the curve. The supply curve itself remains unchanged.

But if the inflation rate rises to 2%, the nominal interest rate increases to 6%. If the inflation rate rises further to 4%, then the nominal interest rate rises to 8%.

We can picture the Fisher equation by looking at real and nominal interest rates over time. Figure 14.5 plots real and nominal interest rates in the United

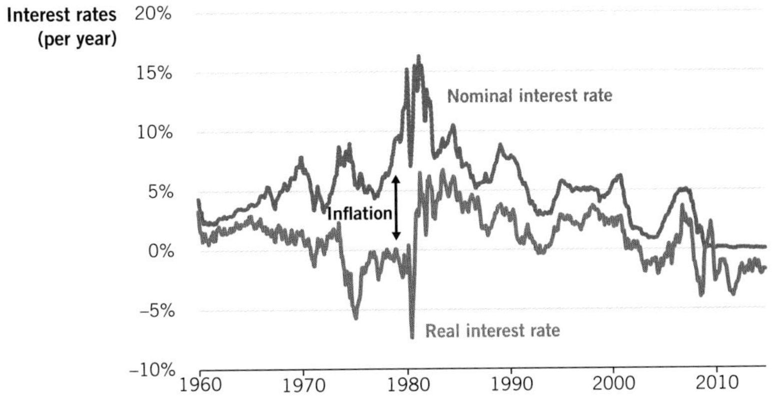

FIGURE 14.5

Real and Nominal Interest Rates, 1960–2014

The difference between real and nominal interest rates is the rate of inflation. The experience of the 1970s illustrates that nominal interest rates are historically high when inflation is also high.

Sources: Federal Reserve Bank of St. Louis FRED database; U.S. Bureau of Labor Statistics.

States from 1960 to 2014. The difference between them is the inflation rate. Notice that this gap was particularly high during the inflationary 1970s but that it narrowed considerably as inflation rates fell in the 1980s. After 2008, nominal interest rates in the United States were less than 1%. Given that inflation rates were around 2%, this implies negative real interest rates. In this case, your savings lose purchasing power, so why would you save?

Unless otherwise stated, in this text we use nominal interest rates. We do so for two reasons. First, nominal interest rates are the stated interest rates—the rates you read about and consider in actual financial transactions. Second, low and steady inflation means that the difference between real and nominal interest rates doesn't fluctuate much.

In the next two sections, we consider the factors that cause shifts in the supply of and demand for loanable funds.

What Factors Shift the Supply of Loanable Funds?

Recall that the supply of loanable funds comes from savings. If you have either a savings or a checking account, you're a participant in this market. To understand what happens when the supply of loanable funds changes, let's examine three factors that determine the level of the supply curve for loanable funds: income, time preferences, and consumption smoothing. When these factors change, the supply curve shifts.

As India grows from poor to rich, much of the funds that its citizens save find their way into the U.S. loanable funds market.

Income

Do you save now? Maybe a little, but most students find saving to be difficult. You know it's probably a good idea, but you don't know how you can save when your income is small or perhaps nonexistent. Once you graduate and get a job, you'll start thinking about saving because your income will be higher. At that time, you'll have the ability to save. Other things being equal, people prefer to have more savings. Thus, increases in income generally produce increases in savings. If income declines, people save less. These changes shift the loanable funds supply curve.

The relationship between income and savings is true across the globe. As incomes grow, nations save more. Over the past 20 years, the increase in foreign savings has often made its way into the U.S. loanable funds market. For example, a businessman in Mumbai, India, may find himself with extra savings. He'll probably put some into an Indian bank and some into Indian stocks and bonds. But there's a good chance he'll also channel some of his savings into the United States. Historically, U.S. financial markets have offered relatively greater returns than markets in other countries. In addition, the U.S. financial markets are often considered less risky than other global markets because of the size and relative robustness of the U.S. economy. Therefore, as global economies have grown, there has been an increase in savings in the United States.

The increase in foreign savings came at a good time for the United States because domestic savings began falling in the 1980s. Without the influx of foreign funds, U.S. firms would have had difficulty funding investment. Of course, there is no guarantee that foreign savings will continue to flow into the United States. But as long as some foreign funds still enter the U.S. financial markets, their presence will allow more opportunities for domestic firms to borrow for investment than if firms relied solely on domestic savers.

Time Preferences

Imagine that your parents promised you a cash reward for getting a good grade in economics. Does it matter if they pay immediately or wait until you graduate? Yes, it matters—you want the money as soon as you earn it. This is not unusual. People always prefer to receive funds sooner than later, and the same applies to goods and services. The term **time preferences** refers to the fact that people prefer to receive goods and services sooner rather than later. Because people have time preferences, someone must pay them to save. While time preferences are generally stable over time, if the rate of time preference in a society changes, the supply of loanable funds shifts.

The term **time preferences** refers to the fact that people prefer to receive goods and services sooner rather than later.

While we all prefer sooner to later, some people have greater time preferences than others. Think of those with the strongest time preferences as being the least patient: they *strongly* prefer now to later. Someone with weaker time preferences has more patience. Other things being equal, people with stronger time preferences save less than people with weaker time preferences.

There are other ways that time preferences can be observed. For example, people with very strong time preferences may not even go to college, since the returns to getting a college education aren't typically realized until years later. Time spent in college is time that could have been spent earning income. The fact that you are a college student demonstrates that you're more patient than some others who choose instead to work for more income now.

You'll be happy to know that there is a definite payoff to getting a college education. College graduates earn significantly more than high-school graduates. Figure 14.6 shows median annual salary in the United States by educational attainment. Some college dropouts—for example, Facebook founder Mark Zuckerberg—earn millions of dollars a year. But the figure's data shows that the median worker with a basic college degree earns about $15,000 more a year than those who don't graduate from college. Patience pays off!

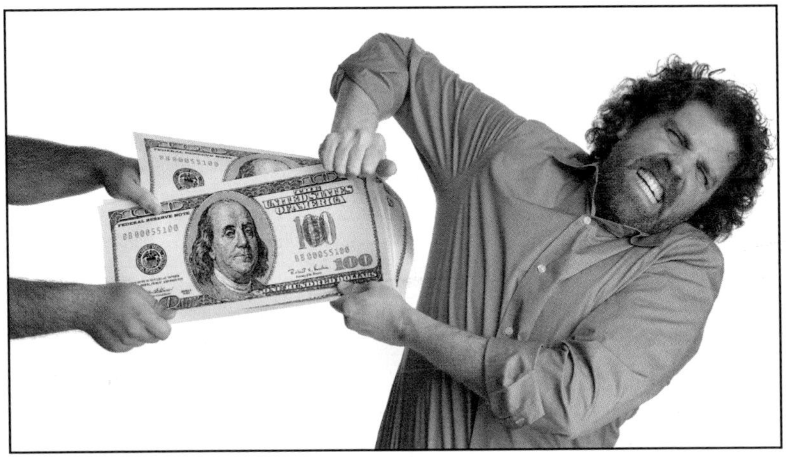

Do you care how long it takes for a friend to repay your loan?

FIGURE 14.6

Median Annual Salary and Educational Attainment

It takes patience, or relatively low time preferences, to stay in school. But annual earnings based on years of schooling show that education pays off for most graduates.

Source: U.S. Bureau of Labor Statistics.

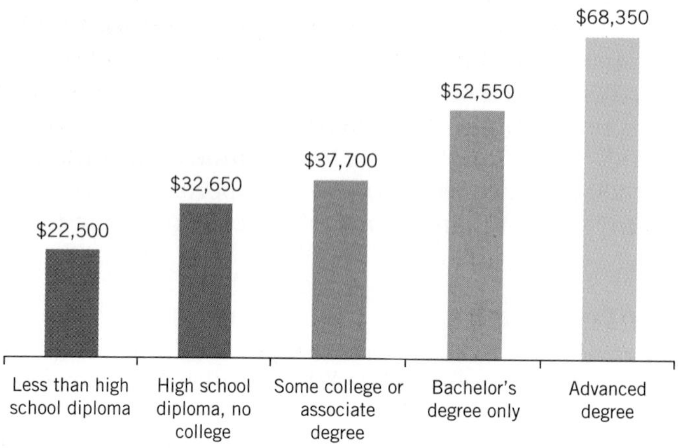

PRACTICE WHAT YOU KNOW

Time Preferences: HIV in Developing Nations

A man wears a T-shirt for AIDS awareness in Lagos, Nigeria. How does a pandemic affect the market for loanable funds?

The worldwide AIDS pandemic is an especially serious problem in developing nations, where infection rates can be extremely high. For example, in 2003, almost 40% of people age 15 to 49 in the nation of Botswana were living with HIV/AIDS, and life expectancy at birth was below 35 years. There are many terrible effects of a situation like this. For now, let's focus on how a pandemic affects people's time preferences.

Question: How does a drop in life expectancy affect time preferences and the supply of loanable funds?

Answer: With life expectancy plummeting to under 35 years, people are less likely to plan for the future. As time preferences increase, the supply of loanable funds goes down. Thus, when a nation is hit hard by a pandemic such as HIV/AIDS, one side effect is lower savings, which means a reduced supply of loanable funds—which in turn leads to lower economic output in the future.

Source: IndexMundi.com.

ECONOMICS IN THE REAL WORLD

One and Done

Jabari Parker used to attend Duke University. Duke is a prestigious school with a superb academic reputation. A degree from Duke goes a long way in finding a very good job. But Jabari quit Duke after one year. His problem was that attending Duke was actually keeping him from earning a tremendous amount of money. In case you haven't heard of him, Jabari Parker is an extraordinarily good basketball player. He was the second overall pick in the NBA draft by the Milwaukee Bucks and was guaranteed to earn $8.5 million in his rookie year. Thus, staying in college had a huge opportunity cost for Jabari. His time preference was very strong, even if a diploma from Duke is worth a lot. Strong time preferences motivate many of the so-called "one and dones" who quit college basketball after one year in order to join a professional basketball team. ✷

Strong time preferences lead some college athletes, including Jabari Parker, to drop out.

Consumption Smoothing

Over the course of a typical lifetime, income varies drastically. Early in life, income levels are relatively low, but income generally rises through midlife. As people near retirement, their income levels fall again. Figure 14.7 illustrates a typical economic life cycle. Income (the green line) is highest in the middle "prime earning years" and lower at both the beginning and end of an individual's work life.

But no one wants to *consume* according to this pattern over their lifetime; most people prefer to consume in a more consistent way throughout their life. Thus, when we're young, we often borrow and spend more than we're earning. We may borrow for college education or to buy our first home. Also, when we retire, our income levels fall, but we don't want our spending to fall just as much. So we generally smooth our consumption over the course of our lifetime. The blue line in Figure 14.7 represents a normal consumption pattern, which is smoother than the income pattern. This **consumption smoothing** is accomplished with the help of the loanable funds market.

Consumption smoothing occurs when people borrow and save in order to smooth consumption over their lifetime.

Early in life, we spend more than we earn. Therefore, we have to borrow. In Figure 14.7, borrowing is the red shaded area between income and consumption in early life. Midlife, or the prime earning years, is the time to repay

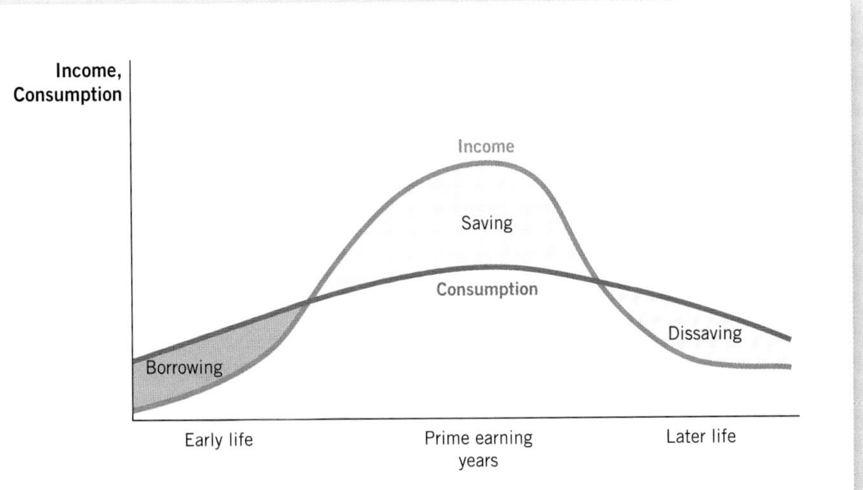

FIGURE 14.7

Savings over a Typical Life Cycle

For most people, income is relatively low in early life, rises in the prime earning years, and falls in later life. But people generally prefer to smooth their consumption over the course of their lifetime. This means that they borrow early in life for items like education and their first home; save during midlife when their income is highest; and finally, draw down savings when they retire.

loans and save for retirement. During this period of the life cycle, the income line exceeds the consumption line; this is the area shaded in green. Later in life, when people retire and their income falls, they tend to live on their savings. Economists call this dissaving. **Dissaving** occurs when people withdraw funds from their previously accumulated savings. Figure 14.7 shows dissavings as the shaded yellow area between income and consumption in later life.

Dissaving occurs when people withdraw funds from their previously accumulated savings.

We can use the concept of consumption smoothing to clarify a situation that is currently affecting the U.S. economy. If we have a steady flow of people moving into each life stage, the amount of savings in the economy is stable and there will be a steady supply in the market for loanable funds. But if a significant portion of the population leaves the prime earning years at the same time, overall savings will fall. As it turns out, this is the current situation in the United States because the baby boomers (people born between 1946 and 1964) are now retiring from the labor force. The oldest members of this group reached retirement age in 2011. Over the next 10 to 15 years, U.S. workers will enter retirement in record numbers. This means an exit from the prime earning years and, consequently, much less savings. We analyze this potential problem in greater detail in the last section of this chapter.

Figure 14.8 illustrates the effect on the supply of loanable funds when there are changes in income, time preferences, or consumption smoothing. The initial supply of loanable funds is represented by S_1. The supply of loanable funds increases to S_2 if there's a change that leads to an increase in savings at all levels of interest rates. For example, an increase in foreign income would increase the supply of savings. Similarly, if people's time preferences fell—if they became more patient—the supply of loanable funds would

FIGURE 14.8

Shifts in the Supply of Loanable Funds

The supply of loanable funds shifts to the right when there are increases in foreign income; decreases in time preferences; and more people in midlife, when savings is highest. The supply of loanable funds shifts to the left when there are decreases in foreign income; increases in time preferences; and fewer people in midlife, when savings is highest.

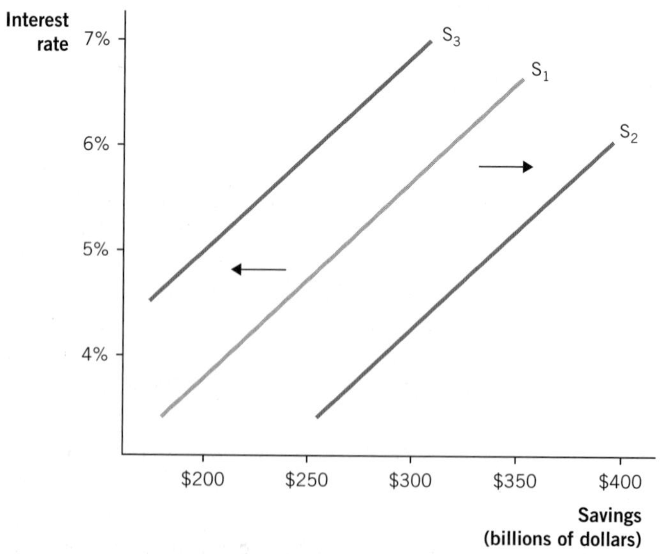

TABLE 14.3

Factors That Shift the Supply of Loanable Funds

Factor	Direction of effect	Explanation
Income	• *Increases* in income *increase* the supply of loanable funds. • *Decreases* in income *decrease* the supply of loanable funds.	Savings is more affordable when people have greater income.
Time preferences	• *Increases* in time preferences *decrease* the supply of loanable funds. • *Decreases* in time preferences *increase* the supply of loanable funds.	Lower time preferences indicate that people are more patient and more likely to save for the future.
Consumption smoothing	• If *more* people are in midlife and their prime earning years, savings is *higher*. • If *fewer* people are in midlife, savings is *lower*.	Income varies over the life cycle, but people generally like to smooth their consumption.

increase. Finally, if a relatively large portion of the population moved into midlife, when savings is highest, savings would also increase from S_1 to S_2.

At other times, however, the supply of loanable funds might decrease. For example, if income declines, people would save less across all interest rates. This is illustrated as a shift from S_1 to S_3 in Figure 14.8. Also, if time preferences increase, people would become more impatient, which would reduce the supply of loanable funds. Finally, if a relatively large population group moved out of their prime earning years and into retirement, the supply of loanable funds would decrease. This last example describes what's happening with baby boomers in the United States right now.

Table 14.3 summarizes our discussion of the factors that either increase or decrease the supply of loanable funds.

ECONOMICS IN THE REAL WORLD

Why Is the Savings Rate in the United States Falling?

Are Americans becoming increasingly short-sighted? Many people believe that Americans' time preferences are indeed climbing, because savings rates have fallen significantly over the past few decades. Figure 14.9 shows the savings rate in the United States since 1960. The **savings rate** is personal saving as a portion of disposable (after-tax) income. As you can see, the U.S. savings rate on the whole has fallen consistently for almost 30 years, beginning in the early 1970s. In 1971, the savings rate was almost 13.5%. The decline continued until about 2005, when the savings rate bottomed out at just 2.5%. We are now in a position to consider possible causes. In particular, is this decline due to changes in income, time preferences, or consumption smoothing?

The **savings rate** is personal saving as a portion of disposable (after-tax) income.

We can rule out a decline in income as a cause of the savings slump. In fact, the decline continued throughout the 1980s and 1990s, which were both decades of significant income growth. In addition, the savings rate increased during the Great Recession that began in late 2007. Second, we can rule out the idea that the savings rate declined as consumption smoothing occurred.

FIGURE 14.9

Savings Rate in the United States, 1960–2013

In the United States, the savings rate (savings as a portion of disposable income) has fallen significantly over the past three decades. In 1971, the savings rate was 13.3%; but it fell to just 2.5% in 2005.

Source: U.S. Bureau of Economic Analysis.

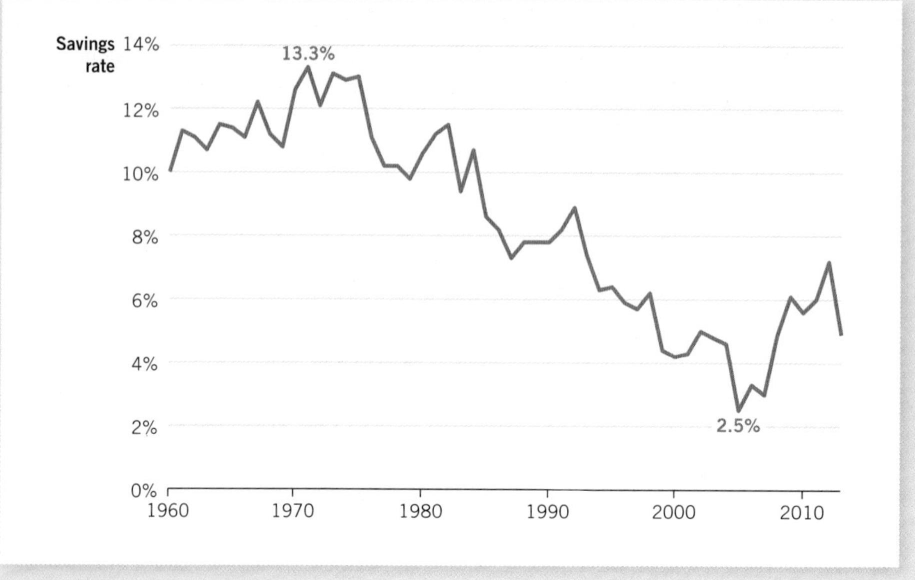

After all, during the period of savings decline, the baby boom population was a significant part of the labor force. Consumption smoothing would imply an increase in savings rates through the 1980s and 1990s, given that the Baby Boomers were working throughout this period.

Many people believe that savings have dropped because time preferences have risen. Perhaps you've heard older Americans talking about the impatience of today's younger workers. If today's working Americans are more focused on instant gratification, they save less. Are stronger time preferences really the cause of the savings decline? If so, why have time preferences become stronger? Economists don't have consistent answers to these questions.

Is your generation too short-sighted?

A closer look at the data indicates that there may be something else behind the decline in personal savings—it could just be a measurement issue. In reality, there are several alternative ways to save for the future, not all of which are counted in the official definition of "personal savings." For example, let's say you buy a house for $200,000 and the value of the house rises to $300,000 in just a few years. This means you now have gained $100,000 in personal wealth. The gain in the value of your house helps you prepare for the future just like increased savings would. But gains of this nature aren't counted as personal savings. In addition to real-estate gains, the gains from purchases of stocks and bonds are also not counted in personal savings.

Here is an alternative view of the recent trends. From 1980 to 2007, real-estate and stock-market values rose significantly. Recognizing these as alternative paths to future wealth, many people shifted their personal savings into these assets. The result is that personal savings rates, as officially measured, plummeted. Not convinced yet? Look what happened to personal savings rates in 2008 and 2009, as both real-estate and stock prices tumbled: personal savings rates climbed to almost 6%.

Are today's Americans less patient than earlier generations? Perhaps. But given the way personal savings rates are measured, it's difficult to determine a clear answer to this question. ✳

What Factors Shift the Demand for Loanable Funds?

To look at the demand side, we shift our perspective to those who borrow in the loanable funds market. As we've seen, the demand for loanable funds derives from the desire to invest or purchase capital goods that aid in future production. We know that the interest rate matters and that investors' desires are reflected in the slope of the demand curve. We now examine two factors that cause shifts in the demand for loanable funds: the productivity of capital and investor confidence.

Productivity of Capital

Consider a firm that is trying to decide whether to borrow for an investment. Perhaps your own firm is trying to decide whether to borrow to buy a new silk-screening machine, the SS-1000, for your college clothing business. This machine is capital, and its purchase counts as an investment. To determine whether you should take a loan, recall our rule: *a firm should borrow to fund an investment only if the expected return is greater than the interest rate on the loan.* Therefore, if the interest rate on the loan is 6%, you will borrow to buy the SS-1000 only if you expect to earn more than a 6% return from it.

Let's say that after crunching the numbers on expected costs and sales from the SS-1000, you estimate a return of just 4% from an investment in the SS-1000. You decide not to buy the new machine.

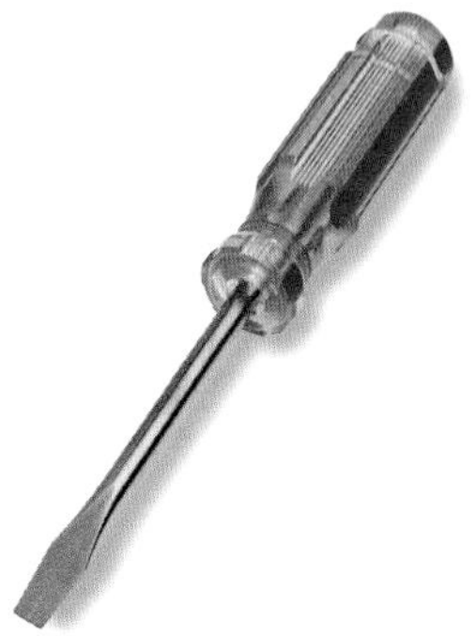

This manual screwdriver is capital . . .

But then something changes. That something is the availability of the brand-new SS-2000. The SS-2000 is an improved machine that prints T-shirts at double the rate of the SS-1000. Given this new machine, which is slightly more expensive, you calculate that your expected return will be 7%, so you decide to take the loan and buy the machine. Thus, your demand for loanable funds has increased as a direct result of the availability of the new machine.

What are the implications for the macroeconomy? Remember that firms borrow in order to pay for their investments. Therefore, the level of demand for loans depends on the productivity of capital, and changes in capital productivity shift the demand for loanable funds. If capital is more productive, the demand for loans increases; if capital is less productive, the demand for loans decreases.

. . . and this electric version of a screwdriver represents an increase in capital productivity.

Productivity can change for a number of reasons. Consider the impact of the Internet. A connection to the Internet provides quick access to data and networking capabilities that people only dreamed of 20 years ago. The Internet also increases the productivity of computers, which are a major capital expense. Over the past 20 years, an increase in expected returns associated

ECONOMICS IN THE MEDIA

How Does a Criminal Get a Loan?

Despicable Me

In the movie *Despicable Me* (2010), we find the aging villain Gru trying to compete with other, younger villains. His plan to steal the moon would get him back in the criminal headlines, but he doesn't have the finances to put his plan into action. Like any entrepreneur looking to get his business venture off the ground, Gru goes to the bank hoping to secure a loan. Being a villain, he goes to the Bank of Evil (Formerly Lehman Brothers) and presents his business plan. While impressed with his audacity, Mr. Perkins, the bank manager, insists on seeing more progress before extending the loan. Gru has financed other schemes through the bank that haven't panned out, and Mr. Perkins is understandably reluctant to lend Gru more money when the return on investment is so uncertain. Mr. Perkins also informs Gru that there are better risks in the market—villains with more recent successes who are also seeking funding. Therefore, Mr. Perkins demands to see the shrink ray, which Gru will use in his plot to steal the moon, as a form of collateral.

Gru: Evil villain, motivated entrepreneur, or both?

This animated version of the lending process isn't all that far off from what happens in the real world. Banks do want to lend to businesses, but they want to make sure a new business has a chance of success. Otherwise, the borrower will be less likely to repay the loans, and that is bad for the bank—even an evil bank.

with the Internet has made investment in computer equipment (capital) more attractive. This means that investment in capital yields greater returns, which in turn increases the demand for loans. When capital is more productive, firms are more likely to borrow to finance purchases of this type of capital.

Investor Confidence

Investor confidence is a measure of what firms expect for future economic activity.

The demand for loanable funds also depends on the beliefs or expectations of investors. If a firm believes its sales will increase in the future, it invests more today to produce future goods. If, instead, it believes its future sales will fall, it invests less today. **Investor confidence** is a measure of what firms expect for future economic activity. If confidence is high, they're more likely to borrow for investment at any interest rate. Economist John Maynard Keynes referred to an investor's drive to action as "animal spirits," meaning that investment demand may not even be based on rational decisions or real factors in the economy. Despite Keynes's derisive term, confidence is an important factor that contributes to the demand for loanable funds.

Figure 14.10 illustrates shifts in the demand for loanable funds. If capital productivity increases, demand for investment increases from D_1 to D_2—that

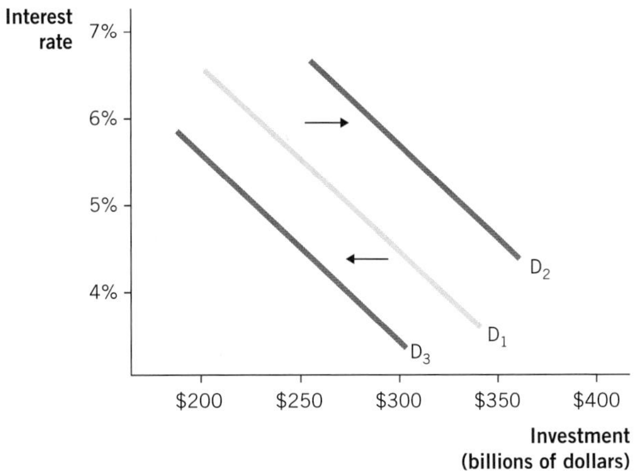

FIGURE 14.10

Shifts in the Demand for Loanable Funds

Increases in capital productivity and investor confidence lead to an increase in the demand for loanable funds at all interest rates, shifting demand from D_1 to D_2. Decreases in capital productivity and investor confidence decrease the demand for loanable funds from D_1 to D_3.

PRACTICE WHAT YOU KNOW

Demand for Loanable Funds: SpongeBob and Loanable Funds

Question: Which of the following changes would affect the demand for loanable funds, and how?

a. Research shows that watching the cartoon *SpongeBob SquarePants* can shorten a child's attention span. Now assume that an entire generation of children grows up watching this cartoon and becomes less patient, or their time preferences increase.

b. A technological advance leads to greater capital productivity.

c. The interest rate falls.

Do sponges increase your time preferences?

Answers:

a. This factor wouldn't affect the demand for loanable funds, but it would affect the supply of loanable funds. Less patience means that time preferences increase and the supply of loanable funds declines.

b. A technological advance increases the demand for loanable funds.

c. The falling interest rate would lead to a movement along the demand curve, rather than a shift in loanable funds.

is, demand is higher across all interest rates. Similarly, if investor confidence rises, demand for loanable funds increases from D_1 to D_2. In contrast, if capital productivity or investor confidence falls, the demand for loanable funds falls from D_1 to D_3.

How Do We Apply the Loanable Funds Market Model?

We're now ready to begin using the loanable funds market to study applications that we see in the real world. First, we consider the implications of equilibrium in this market. After that, we examine past and future views of the U.S. loanable funds market.

Equilibrium

Equilibrium in the loanable funds market occurs at the interest rate where the plans of savers match the plans of investors—that is, where quantity supplied equals quantity demanded. In Figure 14.11, equilibrium (point E) occurs at an interest rate of 5%, where savers are willing to save $250 billion and investors desire $250 billion in loans (in other words, they seek to invest $250 billion). At interest rates above 5%, the quantity of loanable funds supplied exceeds the quantity demanded. At these interest rates the return to savers is high, so more people save; but these higher interest rates mean fewer projects will earn a high enough rate of return to justify paying the higher interest

FIGURE 14.11

Equilibrium in the Market for Loanable Funds

Equilibrium in the loanable funds market occurs where supply (savings) equals demand (investment), at an interest rate of 5% and a quantity of $250 billion. Because investment is limited by savings, exactly $250 billion is saved and $250 billion is invested.

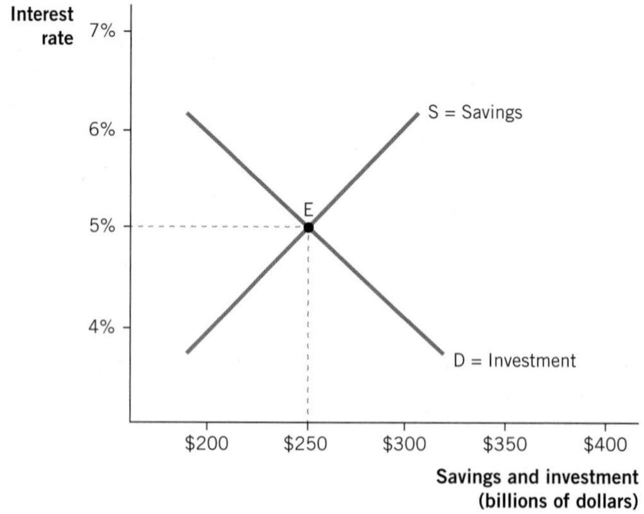

rate. This imbalance leads to downward pressure on the interest rate. At interest rates below 5%, the quantity demanded exceeds the quantity supplied. Now the opportunity cost of saving rises because the reward for doing so has fallen. People save less; however, more investment projects are financially supportable at the lower interest rates, so the quantity demanded goes up. This imbalance leads to upward pressure on interest rates.

Opportunity cost

The loanable funds market, like other markets, naturally tends to move toward equilibrium, where supply is equal to demand. This equilibrium condition reinforces a key relationship between savings and investment. Equilibrium occurs when:

$$\textit{Savings} = \textit{Investment}$$

In Figure 14.11, we can say that households and foreign entities have decided to save a combined total of \$250 billion at an interest rate of 5%. Subsequently, firms borrow this \$250 billion for investment. Thus, dollars that are saved make their way into the loanable funds market and are then channeled to firms for investment purposes.

Equilibrium also helps to clarify an important principle. Investment requires saving because:

Every dollar borrowed requires a dollar saved.

If an economy is to grow over time, someone has to invest in capital that helps to produce more in the future. But investment requires savings. Without savings, the economy cannot grow.

Equilibrium is a helpful starting point for understanding how the loanable funds market functions. But in the real world, financial market conditions change frequently. We can account for these changes in our model by using shifts in the supply and demand curves. Let's consider two examples: a decline in investor confidence and a decrease in the supply of loanable funds.

A Decline in Investor Confidence

When the overall economy slows, firms often reduce investment because they expect reduced sales in future periods; this move reflects a decline in investor confidence. This happened in the United States during the Great Recession that began at the end of 2007. Panel (a) of Figure 14.12 shows how a decline in investor confidence affects the loanable funds market. When investment demand declines (shown in the figure as the change between D_{2007} and D_{2008}), the loanable funds model predicts lower interest rates (a drop from R_1 to R_2) and a lower equilibrium level of investment (a drop from I_1 to I_2). Panel (b) of Figure 14.12 shows that investment fell during the recessions of 2001 and the Great Recession (the blue-shaded bars) in the years shown. During the Great Recession, real investment fell from \$2.2 trillion to just \$1.4 trillion—a 36% drop in less than two years.

A Decrease in the Supply of Loanable Funds

Let's now return to the potential effects of the baby boomers' retirement over the next 10 to 15 years. As we saw in the discussion of consumption smoothing, this will likely lead to a decrease in the supply of loanable funds

FIGURE 14.12

A Decline in Investment Demand

(a) When decision-makers at firms lose confidence in the future direction of the economy, investment demand declines and lower investment results. (b) In the United States, real investment declined during both recessions that occurred between 2000 and 2012.

Source: Panel (b): U.S. Bureau of Economic Analysis.

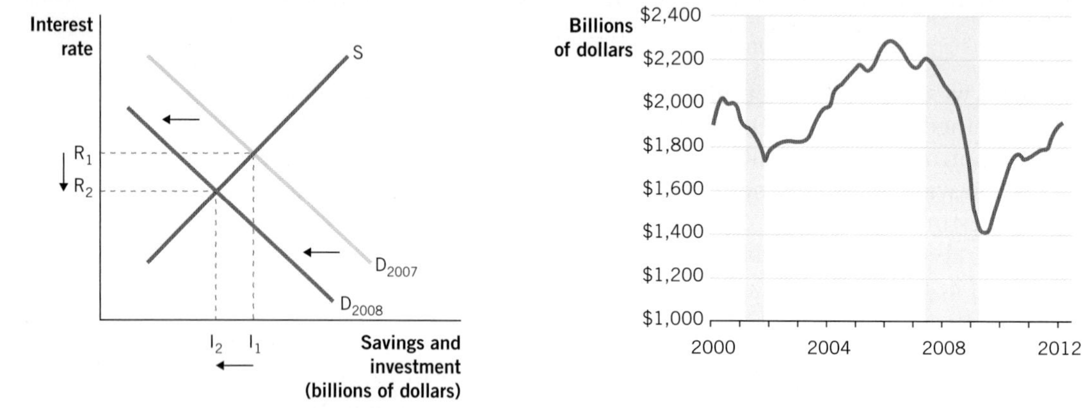

(a) Decline in Investment Demand

(b) Real U.S. Investment, 2000–2012

FIGURE 14.13

The Possible Future of the U.S. Loanable Funds Market

As baby boomers retire and draw down their savings, supply in the loanable funds market will decrease. Without increases in savings from other sources, we will see higher interest rates and lower levels of investment.

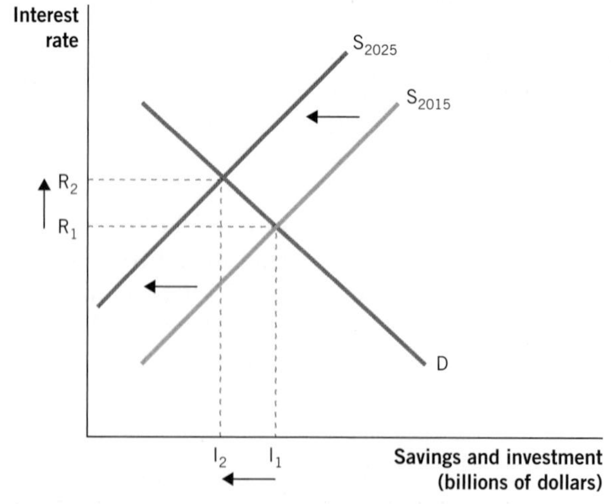

in the United States. Figure 14.13 illustrates this kind of change. The curve labeled S_{2015} represents the supply of loanable funds in 2015. But as the baby boomers retire, supply is expected to shift back to S_{2025} one decade later.

Other things being equal, this shift means higher interest rates (in the figure, an increase from R_1 to R_2), a lower level of investment (in the figure, a drop from I_1 to I_2), and lower GDP growth going forward. However, many other factors may change over the next few years to increase savings in the United States. For example, as other nations grow, foreigners may continue to increase their savings in the United States. Or perhaps U.S. savings rates will reverse course. These increases could offset the effects of the baby boomers' retirement and keep interest rates low for U.S. firms.

PRACTICE WHAT YOU KNOW

Working with the Loanable Funds Model: Foreign Savings in the United States

How does foreign economic growth affect the U.S. loanable funds market?

Recently, the economies of China and India have begun to grow very rapidly. This growth increases their citizens' incomes. In turn, Chinese and Indian citizens increase their savings in their country and also in the United States.

Question: When foreign savings enter the U.S. loanable funds market, which curve is affected—supply or demand? How is this curve affected?

Answer: The supply of loanable funds increases as savings increase.

Question: How would you graph the U.S. loanable funds market both before and after the increase in foreign savings?

Answer:

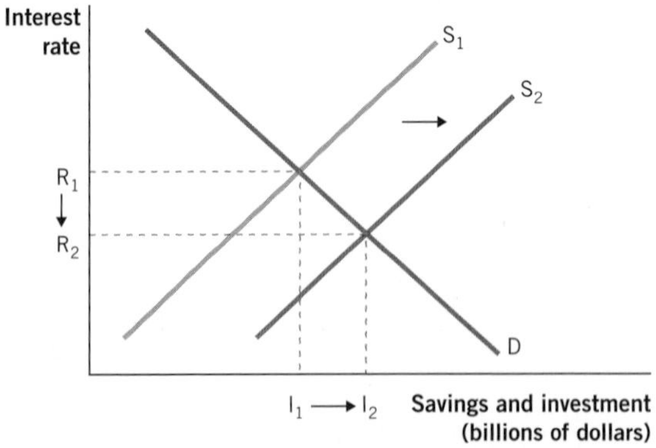

(CONTINUED)

(CONTINUED)

Before the increase in foreign savings, supply is designated as S_1 and demand as D. The intersection of these curves implies an interest rate of R_1 and a savings/investment amount of I_1. When new foreign savings enter the market, supply increases to S_2, which decreases the interest rate to R_2 and increases the savings/investment amount to I_2.

Question: How does the change in foreign savings affect both investment and future output in the United States?

Answer: When the interest rate falls, the quantity of investment increases. Firms can afford to borrow more to build and expand their businesses. This increase in investment means that future output, or GDP, will be higher in the United States.

Conclusion

In macroeconomics, few topics are more important than investment. And investment is the result of equilibrium in the market for loanable funds. Savers supply the funds that support loans; investors demand the loans in order to acquire the capital necessary to expand their operations. Equilibrium determines the quantity of investment and the interest rate in an economy.

What about the type of borrowing you engage in? School loans, car loans, and mortgages—not to mention the use of your credit card to make purchases—are all forms of borrowing, and interest rates are the prices involved in those activities as well. We will discuss these in the context of personal finance in Chapter 19. What we've been covering here involves the impact of investor borrowing on the macroeconomy.

We began this chapter with the misconception that interest rates are set by the government. While the government doesn't set interest rates per se, there's one entity related to the government that does have a significant impact on interest rates. In the next chapter, we begin looking at banking. The banking system in developed countries is governed by a central bank. In the United States, this central bank is called the Federal Reserve Bank, or more commonly the Fed. As we'll see, along with its job of controlling the money supply, the Fed can affect the interest rates we all pay. But interest rates are actually set in the market through the interaction of supply and demand.

Compound Interest: When Should You Start Saving for Retirement?

When you graduate from college, get a job, and start earning a steady income, you'll have several choices to make. Should you buy or lease a car? Should you buy or rent a home? Should you donate money or time to charity? Regardless of your decisions on issues such as these, you should always make room in your budget for savings.

We know that everyone has positive time preferences, so other things being equal, you probably would rather consume now than later. But other things aren't equal in this case. That is, a little less consumption now will lead to a lot more consumption later, even under assumptions of very reasonable interest rates. The return to savings is an exponential function: the longer you save, the greater your return to savings, even at a constant interest rate. The reason is based on compound interest, which implies that the interest you earn becomes savings—which also bears interest. Let's see how compounding works.

Consider two people who choose alternate paths. Dirk understands the power of compound interest and chooses to start saving $100 per month when he's 25 years old. Lee has stronger time preferences and decides to wait until age 45 to start saving $100 per month. If both Dirk and Lee work until they're 65 years old, Dirk saves for 40 years and Lee saves for 20.

You might guess that Dirk will end up with twice as much in his retirement account, since he saved twice as long. But you'd be wrong. It turns out that Lee's retirement savings will increase to $53,988. That's not too bad, considering he saved just $100 per month over 20 years, or 240 months—the interest payments certainly helped. But what about Dirk? His retirement savings will increase to $281,767! That's more than five times the size of Lee's, and Dirk saved only twice as much.

What did we assume to get these returns? We assumed a 7% interest rate, which is the long-run historical real rate of return on a diversified stock portfolio. But any interest rate would illustrate the key point here: compound interest increases the value of your savings exponentially. So even with very strong time preferences, it makes sense to start saving early.

Compound interest produces more interest income.

The graph illustrates the returns to saving $100 per month at an average annual return of 7% until retirement. The only difference is when you start saving. Notice that as you move along the horizontal axis, for each additional five years' worth of savings the amount by which total savings grows will increase.

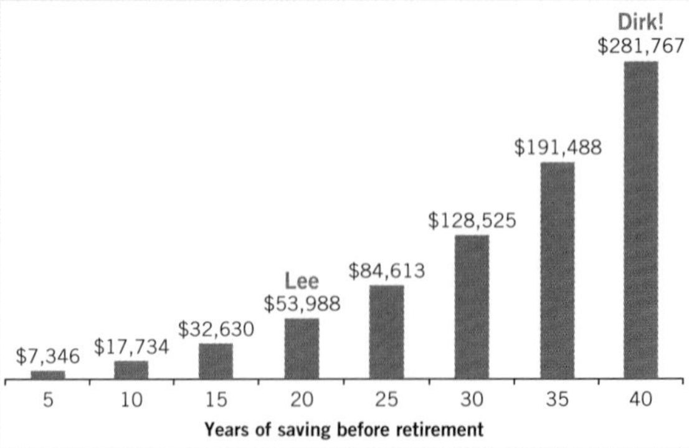

ANSWERING THE BIG QUESTIONS

What is the loanable funds market?

* The loanable funds market connects savers with investors.
* Savers are the suppliers of loanable funds, and they earn interest as a return for saving.
* Investors are the buyers of loanable funds, and they pay interest as the cost of investing.

What factors shift the supply of loanable funds?

* Changes in income shift the supply of loanable funds.
* Changes in time preferences also affect the supply of loanable funds.
* Consumption smoothing is another factor that shifts the loanable funds supply.

What factors shift the demand for loanable funds?

* Capital productivity is a key determinant of the demand for loanable funds.
* Investor confidence also affects the demand for loanable funds.

How do we apply the loanable funds market model?

* We can use the loanable funds market model to examine real-world changes in both supply and demand for loanable funds.
* The loanable funds model also clarifies the important implication that every dollar borrowed requires a dollar saved.

CONCEPTS YOU SHOULD KNOW

consumption smoothing (p. 427)
dissaving (p. 428)
Fisher equation (p. 422)
interest rate (p. 418)
investor confidence (p. 432)
loanable funds market (p. 416)
nominal interest rate (p. 422)
real interest rate (p. 422)
savings rate (p. 429)
time preferences (p. 425)

QUESTIONS FOR REVIEW

1. Explain the importance of the loanable funds market to basic GDP in a macroeconomy.
2. Other things being equal, what does a lower interest rate mean for investors? What does a lower interest rate mean for savers?
3. Consider two alternatives to prepare for retirement: (1) saving in a bank where your funds earn interest, and (2) buying fine art that rises in value over time. Each grows your retirement account over time.
   a. If the rates of return on fine art purchases fall, how would you expect the allocation of retirement funds to change across the macroeconomy?
   b. If the national savings rate is based only on the first option (saving in a bank), then what happens to the national savings rate when the allocation of retirement funds shifts as you describe in your response to part (a)?
4. List the factors that affect the supply side of the loanable funds market.
5. List the factors that affect the demand side of the loanable funds market.
6. Why does inflation have a positive effect on nominal interest rates?

STUDY PROBLEMS (*✱ solved at the end of the section*)

1. Assume that the residents of a nation become more patient (experience a reduction in their time preferences).
   a. What will happen to the interest rate in that nation? What will happen to the equilibrium level of investment in that nation? Explain your answers in a fully labeled graph.
   b. Over time, how will the lower time preferences affect the levels of capital and income growth in that nation?
2. Many interest rates in the United States recently fell. Which of the following factors could have been the cause?
   a. increase in the demand for loanable funds
   b. decrease in the demand for loanable funds
   c. increase in the supply of loanable funds
   d. decrease in the supply of loanable funds
3. Use the Fisher equation to fill in the blanks in the following table.

Inflation rate	Real interest rate	Nominal interest rate
____	2%	7%
____	0%	7%
2%	____	6%
9%	____	6%
2%	2%	____
10%	2%	____

✱ 4. Consider two hypothetical nations: Wahooland and Wildcat Island. Initially, these nations are identical in every way. In particular, they're the same with regard to population size and age, income, and time preferences.

They also have the same interest rates, saving, and investment.

a. Suddenly, in the year 2015, the interest rate in Wahooland rises. After some investigating, economists determine that nothing has happened to the supply of loanable funds. What are the possible reasons for this rise in interest rates in Wahooland?

b. Given your answer to part (a), what can you say about the level of investment in Wahooland relative to that in Wildcat Island in 2015? What can you say about future income levels in Wahooland versus Wildcat Island?

c. Often, we think of lower interest rates as always being preferable to higher interest rates. What has this question taught us about that idea?

* 5. Some people have proposed an increase in retirement age for Americans. Consider the effects of this proposed new policy.

a. Show how the change would affect supply and demand in the market for loanable funds.

b. How would this change affect the equilibrium interest rate and investment?

c. Over time, how would this change affect real GDP in the United States?

SOLVED PROBLEMS

4.a. If supply doesn't change, the rise in interest rates must be due to a change in demand. If rates went up, then demand must have increased. An increase in the demand for loanable funds occurs from one or both of the following: (1) an increase in the productivity of capital, or (2) an increase in investor confidence.

b. Investment will be higher in Wahooland than in Wildcat Island. Future GDP will be higher in Wahooland, which means that income will be higher.

c. Higher interest rates could be caused by very productive capital. Thus, an innovative nation that tends to have new productive ideas and then high capital productivity might also have higher interest rates. These interest rates can indicate very high returns to capital investment, which is certainly not bad for an economy.

5.a. The key is to examine how the policy change would affect savings through people's preferences for consumption smoothing. If Americans start working longer, they would delay the dissaving period in their life and increase their savings. So supply would increase (shift outward). Demand would not change.

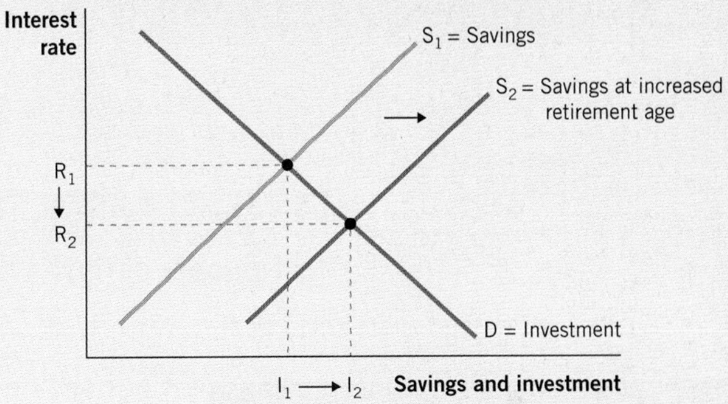

b. The equilibrium interest rate would fall from R_1 to R_2, and investment would increase from I_1 to I_2.

c. Real GDP would be greater, other things being equal, due to the increase in investment. Basically, the new savings would become investment in capital. Thus, in the future there would be more tools for production in the United States, and output would be higher.

CHAPTER 15

Money and the Federal Reserve

MISCONCEPTION

It's easy to control the amount of money in an economy.

Most people believe that controlling the amount of money in the economy is a simple task. After all, there's a fixed number of "green pieces of paper" floating around the economy, and only the government has the authority to print more. But the job is actually very difficult. In fact, banks and private individuals influence the money supply with their daily, private decisions. That's right: even *you* can make the money supply rise or fall.

We begin this chapter by looking closely at the definition of money. It turns out that anything can be used as money, but some things work better than others. Because banks also play an integral role in the money-supply process, we discuss how they operate and how their decisions affect the amount of money in the economy. We also look at the Federal Reserve System and examine how it oversees the amount of money in the economy. This background provides essential preparation for the discussion of monetary policy that comes in Chapter 16.

Money is more than just green paper!

BIG QUESTIONS

- **What is money?**
- **What is the Fed?**
- **How is the money supply measured?**
- **How do banks create money?**

What Is Money?

Currency is the paper bills and coins that are used to buy goods and services.

It may seem strange to ask: *What is money?* After all, we use money all the time. Even children know we use money to buy goods and services. When someone mentions money, we usually first think of the "green pieces of paper" we call currency. **Currency** is the paper bills and coins that are used to buy goods and services. (Actually, U.S. paper bills are made of textile fiber, not paper, but we'll follow standard usage and call them paper money.) However, people also make many purchases without using currency. Just think of the last time you bought something online. Did you pay with cash?

Interestingly, societies haven't always had paper money. In fact, societies haven't always been able to agree on what the official currency should be. Today, money itself is typically just paper. Sometimes it's little round bits of metal, but the metal your coins are made from isn't worth much on its own. So why do people want money? The answer is that they don't. They want the things money can buy. This means there's more to money than meets the eye. To appreciate the roles money plays in an economy, we need to know what makes something work well as money. We also need to understand why money has value. We will address these three topics—the functions of money, what works well as money, and the reason money has value—in the next section.

Three Functions of Money

Money has three functions: as a medium of exchange, as a unit of account, and as a store of value. Let's look at each function in turn.

A Medium of Exchange

People will do many things to get money. They'll sell their possessions; they'll work long hours at jobs that they hate; they'll beg, borrow, and steal. Sometimes, they will even kill to get it. But once they have it, so what? You can't eat money. You could conceivably stitch it together and make a shirt out of it, but it certainly wouldn't be very comfortable or keep you very warm. You could burn it to stay warm, but that defeats the purpose of getting money. Of course, what you do with money once you get it is to exchange it for something else that you really want: food, clothes, a new Xbox, or a tank of gas. The main function of money is as a common **medium of exchange**—that is, it is what people trade for goods and services.

A **medium of exchange** is what people trade for goods and services.

Nearly every society develops a medium of exchange. The alternative is barter. **Barter** involves individuals trading some good or service that they already have for something else that they want. The problem here is that barter requires a **double coincidence of wants**, in which each party in an exchange transaction happens to have what the other party desires. A double coincidence is pretty unusual, which is why a medium of exchange naturally evolves in a society.

Barter involves the trade of a good or service without a commonly accepted medium of exchange.

A **double coincidence of wants** occurs when each party in an exchange transaction happens to have what the other party desires.

Consider how you would get what you want without money. Let's say you're hungry. In order to get something to eat, you get a job at a Subway restaurant. At the end of the day, you get paid. You eagerly choose a foot-long meatball sub as payment for your day's work. Satisfied, you walk home, where you find that your landlord is demanding payment for your monthly rent. Having no money, you agree to pay him with a six-inch turkey sub every other day for the next month. Fortunately, the landlord likes Subway sandwiches. Unfortunately for you, when you get upstairs there's a message from the cable company. It needs to be paid as well. You call the company up and offer food from Subway, but the company doesn't want food; instead, it wants to be paid with gasoline. Its service trucks don't run on sandwiches. To pay your cable bill, you need to find someone who will trade sandwiches for gasoline so that you can trade gasoline for cable.

You probably see where this is going. A barter system is extremely inefficient. You spend most of your time looking for someone or a group of people to trade with. The double-coincidence-of-wants problem makes getting what you desire, and hence dealing with scarcity, a very cumbersome chore.

Without money, what would you trade for a candy bar?

Thus, societies develop a medium of exchange. Even in economies without government provision, a preferred medium of exchange usually emerges. For example, in colonial Virginia, before there was any government mandate regarding money, tobacco became the accepted medium of exchange. Economist Milton Friedman wrote this about tobacco's use: "It was the money that the colonists used to buy food, clothing, to pay taxes—even to pay for a bride."*

Commodity Money. Historically, the first medium of exchange in an economy has been a commodity that is actually traded for goods and services. **Commodity money** involves the use of an actual good in place of money. In this situation, the good itself has value apart from its function as money. Examples include gold, silver, and the tobacco of colonial Virginia. But commodities are often difficult to carry around when the holder needs to make purchases. Thus, money evolved into certificates that represented a fixed quantity of the commodity. These certificates became the medium of exchange but were still tied to the commodity, because they could be traded for the actual commodity if the holder demanded it.

Commodity money is the use of an actual good instead of paper money.

Commodity-backed money is money that can be exchanged for a commodity at a fixed rate. For example, until 1971, U.S. dollars were fixed in

Commodity-backed money is money that can be exchanged for a commodity at a fixed rate.

*Milton Friedman and Rose Friedman, *Free to Choose* (New York: Harcourt, 1979), p. 250.

The money pictured here looks much like our modern money, but the dollar bill is a commodity-backed silver certificate from 1957. At that time, it could be traded for a dollar's worth of silver. The quarter from 1964 is made of real silver.

value to specific quantities of silver and gold. When seen in a picture, a one-dollar U.S. silver certificate looks much like dollar bills in circulation today, but the print along the bottom of the note reads, "one dollar in silver payable to the bearer on demand." Until 1964, coins in the United States were commodity money. U.S. quarters from 1964 look like the same quarters we use today; but unlike today's quarters, they were made of real silver.

Fiat money is money that has no value except as the medium of exchange; there is no inherent or intrinsic value to the currency.

Fiat Money. While commodity money and commodity-backed money evolve privately in all economies, the type of money used in most modern economies depends on government. In particular, most modern economies use fiat money for their medium of exchange. **Fiat money** is money that has no value except as the medium of exchange; there is no inherent or intrinsic value to the currency. In the United States, the currency is just pieces of green paper. This paper has value because the government has mandated that we can use the currency to pay our debts. On U.S. dollar bills, you can read the statement "This note is legal tender for all debts, public and private."

There are advantages and disadvantages to fiat and commodity monies. On the one hand, commodity-backed money ties the value of the holder's money to something real. If the government is obligated to trade silver for every dollar in circulation, this obligation certainly limits the number of dollars it can print, which probably limits inflation levels. Fiat money offers no such constraint on the expansion of the money supply. Rapid monetary expansion and then inflation often occur without a commodity standard that ties the value of money to something real.

On the other hand, tying the value of a nation's currency to a commodity is dangerous when the market value of that commodity fluctuates. Imagine how a new discovery of gold affects prices in a nation with gold-backed currency. An increased supply of gold reduces gold prices, and therefore more gold is required in exchange for all other goods and services. This situation constitutes inflation: the price of everything in terms of the money (gold) rises. This is exactly what occurred in Europe as Spanish conquistadors brought back tons of gold from Central and South America between the mid-fifteenth and the mid-seventeenth centuries. Because a change in the value of a medium of exchange affects the prices of all goods and services in the macroeconomy, it can be risky to tie a currency to a commodity.

A Unit of Account

A **unit of account** is the measure in which prices are quoted.

Money also serves as a unit of account. A **unit of account** is the measure in which prices are quoted. Money enables you and someone you don't know to speak a common language. For example, when the cashier says that the mangoes you want to buy cost 99 cents each, she's communicating the value of mangoes in a way that you understand. Consider a world without an accepted unit of account. In that world, goods would be priced in multiple ways. Theoretically, you might go shopping and find goods priced in terms of any possible currency or even other goods. Imagine how difficult it would be to shop! Using money as a unit of account is so helpful that a standard unit of account generally evolves, even in small economies.

Expressing the value of something in terms of dollars and cents also enables people to make accurate comparisons between items. Thus, money also serves as a measuring stick and a recording device. Think of your checkbook for a moment. You don't record that you bought a couple of candy bars; instead, you write down that you spent $4. You tally the debits and credits to keep track of your account and to record transactions in a consistent manner.

Thank goodness each of these fruits is priced in a common unit of account.

A Store of Value

Money's third function is as a store of value. A **store of value** is a means for holding wealth. Traditionally, money has served as an important store of value. Think of bags of gold coins from the Middle Ages. In both fiction and nonfiction stories, forbidden treasures or pirate's treasures are generally represented by gold; this precious metal was the vehicle for storing wealth. But in modern economies we have other options for holding our wealth, many of which offer greater returns than keeping dollar bills in a sock drawer or stuffed under a mattress. We can easily put our dollars into bank accounts or investment accounts that earn interest. These options have caused money's role as a store of value to decline.

A **store of value** is a means for holding wealth.

What Works Well as Money?

A medium of exchange certainly helps make our lives easier, but not any old thing can serve as money. For something to be used as money, it must have certain characteristics.

1. *Portability*. Money should be easy to carry around. You can stuff some bills in your pocket without getting weighed down. For higher values of money, the government can print certificates with larger numbers on them. Thus, a $20 bill doesn't weigh more than a $1 bill. That's a nice feature of money.
2. *Durability*. You don't want to worry whether your money will hold up to rough treatment. Yes, we use paper as money, but it isn't tissue paper. Rocks would be more durable, but they aren't easily portable. The paper we use for currency can get wet without falling apart, and it won't tear until it gets really old (or you choose to tear it up). In fact, the paper used for U.S. currency is designed for extra durability.

3. *Recognizability*. Money should be easy to recognize. You may have seen currency from another country and thought it looked odd. You wouldn't accept it as payment because you wouldn't be able to use it to trade where you live. If someone gave you a 100-yen note from Japan it might be a nice souvenir, but you wouldn't try to spend it because the cashier at the store wouldn't recognize it as money. (And it wouldn't buy you much, anyway. Today, 100 yen is worth less than a dollar.)
4. *Easy divisibility*. Money needs to be broken down easily into smaller units. If you had only dollars and nothing else, smaller transactions either would be difficult to make or would get more expensive. A pack of gum would cost $1 because that would be the smallest unit of currency. Instead we have quarters, dimes, nickels, and pennies to make smaller transactions.

The money we use today fits all of these characteristics. U.S. currency is certainly portable, durable, recognizable, and easily divisible. U.S. currency isn't the only thing that works as money, though. Until 2004 in some prisons, the usual currency was cigarettes. Why? They have the characteristics we just discussed. They're portable and recognizable. They're easy to divide into cartons, packs, or individual cigarettes, enabling prisoners to purchase large or small items or services. The only shortcoming of cigarettes is that they aren't particularly durable. Don't put a cigarette through the wash or leave it out in the rain.

ECONOMICS IN THE REAL WORLD

The Evolution of Prison Money

In the past, cigarettes were often the preferred unit of account and medium of exchange in prisons. This commodity money was useful as currency in addition to its manufactured purpose. But in 2004 the U.S. government outlawed smoking in federal prisons, and this decision led to the development of a new medium of exchange.

In an October 2008 *Wall Street Journal* article, Justin Scheck reported on one federal facility where cans of mackerel had taken over as the accepted money. According to one prisoner, "It's the coin of the realm." This "bartering" is not legal in federal prisons. Prisoners can lose privileges if they're caught exchanging goods or services for mackerel. Nonetheless, mackerel remains the medium of exchange and the unit of account. For example, haircuts cost about two "macks." The cans of fish also serve as a reliable store of value. Some prisoners even rent lockers from others so they can store their mackerel money.

But even though mackerel is popular, it isn't the only commodity that serves as money in federal prisons. In some prisons, protein bars or cans of tuna serve this role. One reason why mackerel is preferred to other alternatives is that each can costs about one dollar—so it's a simple substitute for U.S. currency, which inmates are not allowed to carry. ✳

The evolution of prison money.

Why Is Money Valuable?

If money grew on trees, it wouldn't be worth much.

Why is money valuable? After all, it's just paper. While you would be happy to accept a $100 bill for your birthday, if your friends stuffed an envelope with thousands of dollars of money from the board game Monopoly you wouldn't be as excited. But both are made of paper, so what makes one kind of money valuable and the other not? The easiest explanation is the fact that we *believe* that the U.S. currency has value and the Monopoly money doesn't. If one individual stopped believing that money has value, this individual decision would have no impact on the economy. But if everyone stopped accepting money because they no longer believed it had value, then there would be a problem. This scenario has actually happened in Russia. Teachers in the western part of Siberia are often paid in vodka because the local governments don't always have money (Russian rubles) to pay the workers. Rubles often aren't desired, anyway. Because of rampant inflation, people have lost faith in the currency. Essentially, the vodka can be traded for goods and services, but the rubles cannot. When people don't believe the currency has value, then it doesn't—even when the government declares that it is the nation's currency.

Another reason why money has value is that it is scarce. Have you ever wished that money grew on trees? This would be wonderful! All you would have to do is collect a bunch of money leaves, and then you could buy whatever you wanted. But not so fast! Unless you had the only money tree in the world, this money-tree idea has a huge downside. Think about what happens in the autumn. The leaves on trees turn color and fall off. Untold billions of leaves are raked and bagged around the country. If there were money trees, money would be as common as the leaves that many of us bag, compost, or burn. Money trees would make money so common that it would be essentially useless. Imagine taking a bag full of leaves to a movie theater to buy a ticket. You probably wouldn't be let in.

This final point about scarcity might seem silly. If you owned the only money tree, then the money that grew from it would maintain its scarcity; but if there were lots of money trees, the leaves would lose their value. To keep money from becoming too common, someone needs to control the supply of money. That job is left to the country's central bank. In the United States, the central bank is called the Federal Reserve—or, more commonly, the Fed.

What Is the Fed?

There's a good chance you've heard of the Fed even outside economics class. Janet Yellen, the chair of the Fed's Board of Governors, is perhaps the most recognized economist in the world. And while we've referred to the Fed periodically throughout this text, now it's time to examine it closely.

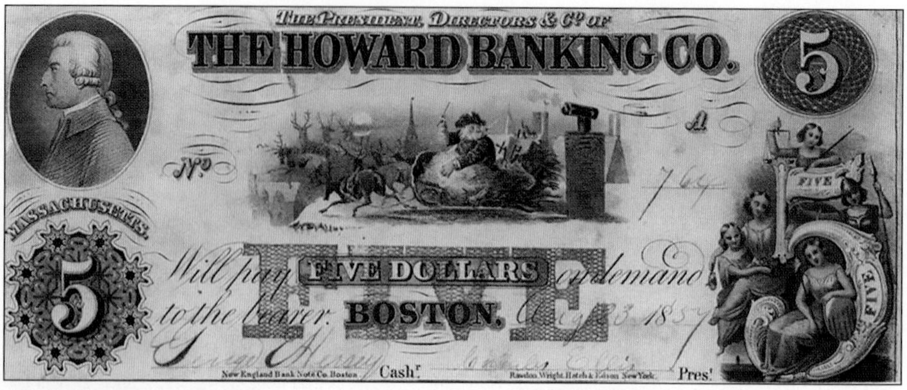

Is this real money? Yes it is, and yes—that's Santa Claus. Before the Fed existed, banks could issue their own money. Instead of putting a picture of the bank president (whom no one would recognize) on their bills, banks used images of famous people, and one of the most famous people of all time is Santa Claus!

The Origins of the Fed

In the early days of the United States, the economy advanced in fits and starts. As the country grew, exchange was often inhibited by a lack of currency. Individual states, counties, and even banks themselves would issue currency, usually backed by gold or silver, but there were times when there wasn't enough money to go around. The banking system was unregulated and inconsistent. Banks were repositories of savings and in some cases made loans; but for companies looking to expand, loans were often difficult to come by. The federal government attempted to establish a national banking system as far back as 1791. Alexander Hamilton, the first Secretary of the Treasury and the gentleman pictured on the $10 bill, organized the creation of this bank to help facilitate lending. However, citizens were concerned with the concentration of financial power in the hands of a small number of people, and the First Bank of the United States was not allowed to continue.

The lack of a centralized banking system created mass confusion in the United States. Currency availability fluctuated wildly, and the myriad of different currencies made conducting business difficult. Local banks' inability to meet the needs for loans in the growing nation, and their inability to move money where it was needed, led to a series of booms and busts as well as a general economic uncertainty. In 1907, a severe recession caused the closure of several prominent banks. Financier J. P. Morgan prevented an utter collapse of the banking system by buoying it with his own money. It was clear that something had to be done. Despite the continued misgivings of some who didn't trust the centralization of financial power, the Federal Reserve was born.

Janet Yellen was appointed chair of the Fed's Board of Governors in 2014.

The Fed's Many Jobs

The Fed was established in 1913 as the central bank of the United States. Before we get to what the Fed does, though, it will help to understand the different kinds of banks we'll be discussing. When we talk about banks, most people think about **commercial banks.** These are the places where people have their checking accounts and where they might go to get a loan. There are also **investment banks**, which most commonly help firms raise money to invest. The Fed is different from these types of banks. The Fed is the **central bank**, a term that means that the Fed is a "bank for banks." Individuals cannot open banking accounts at the Fed. The Fed's customers are the commercial banks where you save. Now let's take a look at what the Fed was chartered to do.

Commercial banks are the banks where most people have their checking and savings accounts and where most households would go to get a loan.

Investment banks are banks that most commonly help firms raise money to invest.

A **central bank** is the bank for the banks. A central bank's roles include controlling the money supply, providing loans to struggling banks, and regulating the banking system.

The Fed's primary responsibilities are threefold:

1. *Monetary policy*: The Fed controls the U.S. money supply and is charged with regulating it to offset macroeconomic fluctuations. This is the Fed's most important role.
2. *Central banking*: The Fed serves as a bank for banks, holding their deposits and extending loans to them. Given the macroeconomic danger of bank failure, the Fed serves an important role as a backup lender to private banks that have difficulty borrowing elsewhere.
3. *Bank regulation*: The Fed is one of the primary entities charged with ensuring the financial stability of banks. The Fed monitors banks' balance sheets with an eye toward limiting the riskiness of the assets the banks hold. One of the Fed's key responsibilities is making sure a commercial bank isn't lending more than it should.

In Chapter 16, we'll be focusing on how the Fed controls the money supply. For now, let's take a look at how the Fed attempts to count the money in the economy, and what makes that a little bit trickier than it sounds.

How Is the Money Supply Measured?

The Fed has many jobs, but they all center around its primary function: controlling the supply of money. In Chapter 10, we introduced the idea that the money supply in an economy affects the overall price level. In particular, a nation's inflation rate is dependent on the growth rate of its money supply. Because money has such profound macroeconomic influences, it is important to measure it accurately. But doing so isn't quite as simple as just adding up all the paper money and the coins in the economy.

To get a sense of the difficulties of measuring the money supply, think about all the different ways you make purchases. You might hold some currency for emergencies, to make a vending machine purchase, or to do laundry. On top of this, you might write a check to pay your rent, tuition, or utility bills. Moreover, you probably carry a debit card that lets you withdraw cash from your savings or checking accounts. To measure the quantity of money in an economy, we must somehow find the total value of all these alternatives that people use to buy goods and services. Clearly, currency alone is not enough—people buy things all the time without using it. Currency is money, but it constitutes only a small part of the total money supply.

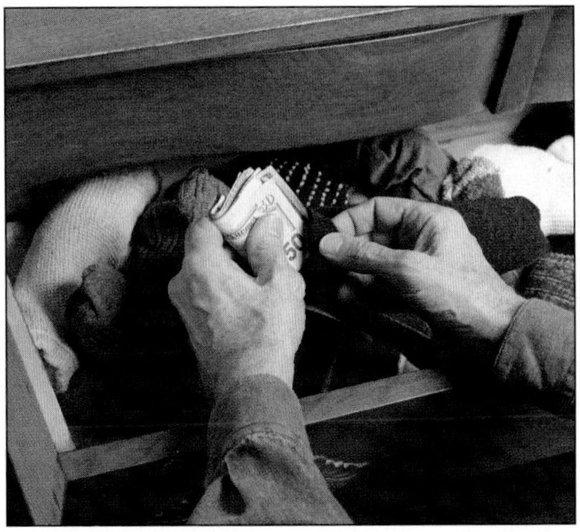

By keeping your money in a sock drawer, you make the Fed's job of counting the money supply easier.

Checkable deposits are deposits in bank accounts from which depositors may make withdrawals by writing checks or using debit cards.

M1 is the money-supply measure that is composed of currency and checkable deposits, plus traveler's checks.

Liquidity refers to how easily something can be spent.

M2 is the money-supply measure that includes everything in M1 plus savings deposits, money-market mutual funds, and small-denomination time deposits (CDs).

M1 and M2

As we broaden our definition of money beyond currency, we first acknowledge bank deposits for which checks can be written. **Checkable deposits** are deposits in bank accounts from which depositors may make withdrawals by writing checks or using debit cards. These deposits represent purchasing power that is very similar to currency, since personal checks and debit cards are used at many places. Adding checkable deposits to currency gives us a money-supply measure known as M1. **M1** is the money supply that is composed of currency (both paper and coins) and checkable deposits. M1 also includes traveler's checks, but these account for a very small portion of M1. The types of money that make up M1 are those that are the easiest to spend. The term **liquidity** refers to how easily something can be spent, and M1 comprises the most liquid forms of money.

A broader measure of the money supply, **M2**, includes everything in M1 plus savings deposits, money-market mutual funds, and small-denomination time deposits (certificates of deposit, or CDs). These additions to the money supply take a little more effort to spend. Think of your savings account. You can go to the bank, make a withdrawal, and then spend the cash. How much easier can it get? The catch is that you have to get to the bank and get your money out of your account. What if the bank is closed or the automated teller machine (ATM) isn't working? You'll have to wait to access your money. Even though you may not have to wait long, you still have to wait a little, which means that your savings are a little less liquid than cash. The key point to remember is that the money supply in an economy includes both currency and bank deposits:

$$\text{money supply (M)} = \text{currency} + \text{deposits} \quad \text{(Equation 15.1)}$$

FIGURE 15.1

Measures of the U.S. Money Supply, July 2014

M1 and M2 are the most common measures of the money supply. M1 includes currency and checkable deposits. M2 includes everything in M1 plus savings deposits, small-denomination time deposits (CDs), and money-market mutual funds.

Source: Federal Reserve, Money Stock Measures.

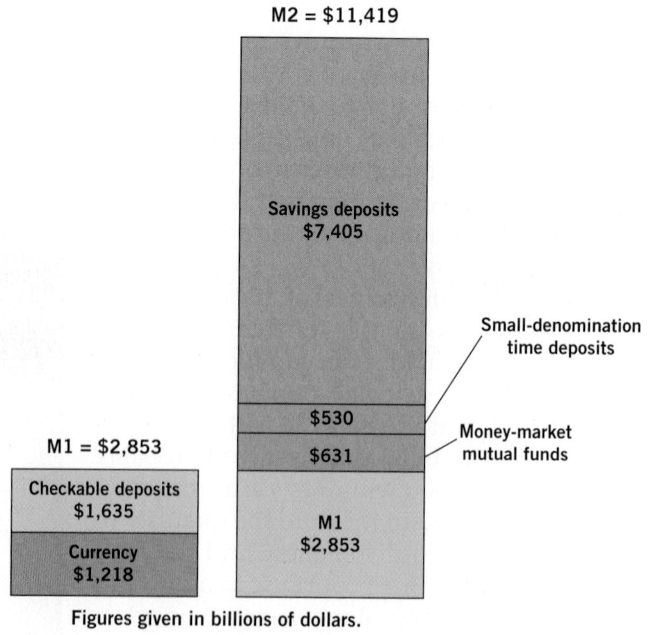

Equation 15.1 is an approximation of the general money supply. The Fed regularly publishes actual data for both M1 and M2. Figure 15.1 shows the components of M1 and M2 as of July 2014. Notice that currency in the United States is about $1.2 trillion. Adding checkable deposits of another $1.6 trillion yields M1 of about $2.9 trillion. But M2 was above $11 trillion in 2014, over $7 trillion of which was held in savings accounts.

Note that credit cards are not part of the money supply. Purchases made with credit cards involve a loan extended at the cash register. When the loan is made, a third party is paying for the purchase until the loan is repaid. Therefore, since credit-card purchases involve the use of borrowed funds, credit cards are not included as part of the money supply.

PRACTICE WHAT YOU KNOW

The Definition of Money

People on the street sometimes use the word "money" in ways that are inconsistent with the definition given in this chapter.

Is this M1 or M2? It is both.

Question: Is each of the following statements consistent with our definition of money? Explain your answer each time.

a. "He had a lot of money in his wallet."

b. "She made a lot of money last year."

c. "I use my Visa card for money."

d. "She has most of her money in the bank."

Answers:

a. This statement is *consistent* with our definition, since currency is part of the medium of exchange.

b. This statement is *inconsistent* with the definition. It refers to income, not to money.

c. This statement is *inconsistent*. Payment with a credit card requires a loan, so it's technically not counted in the money supply.

d. This statement is *consistent*, since bank deposits count as money because they represent part of the medium of exchange.

How Do Banks Create Money?

We now have a working definition of money: money includes both currency and deposits at banks. And while private individuals and firms in the economy are not permitted to print currency—this is called counterfeiting and

FIGURE 15.2

The Business of Banking: Financial Intermediation

The primary function of commercial banks is financial intermediation: they accept deposits and extend loans.

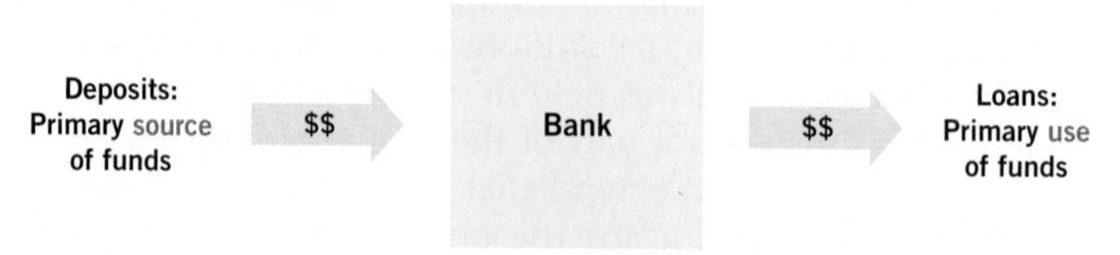

will land you in jail for a very long time—private actions absolutely influence the total money supply in the economy, because individuals and banks affect deposits. In this section, we explain how banks create money simply as a byproduct of their daily business activity. As a reminder, when we use the term "bank" or "banks," we're talking about commercial lending banks, the place where you have your checking account. These banks are different from the central bank.

We begin by looking closely at the daily activities of typical banks. After that, we can consider how they influence the money supply.

The Business of Banking

Banks serve two very important roles. First, they are critical participants in the market for loanable funds. As we saw in Chapter 14, they provide a way for savers to supply their funds to investors. Second, they play a role in the money-supply process.

Financial intermediaries act as go-betweens for savers and investors by taking in deposits and extending loans.

To understand how banks create money, let's look at the operations of a bank, illustrated in Figure 15.2. Banks are middlemen in the market for loans. Another way to describe this is that banks act as **financial intermediaries**. They act as a go-between for savers and investors by taking in deposits and extending loans. Deposits are the primary source of funds, and loans are the primary use of those funds. Banks can be profitable if they charge a higher interest rate on the loans they make to borrowers than the interest rate they pay to savers.

A **balance sheet** is an accounting statement that summarizes a firm's key financial information.

A **t-account** is a basic balance sheet where the assets on one side equal the liabilities on the other.

Assets are the items that a firm owns.

Liabilities are the financial obligations that a firm owes to others.

The Bank's Balance Sheet

Information about a bank's financial operations is available in the bank's balance sheet. A **balance sheet** is an accounting statement that summarizes a firm's key financial information. We will use a simplified version of the balance sheet called a t-account to illustrate how banks create money. A **t-account** is a very basic balance sheet on which the assets on one side equal the liabilities on the other.

Figure 15.3 shows a hypothetical balance sheet for University Bank. The left side of the balance sheet details the bank's **assets**, which are the items the firm owns. Assets indicate how the bank uses the funds it has raised from various sources. The right side of the balance sheet details the bank's liabilities. **Liabilities** are the financial obligations the firm owes to others.

FIGURE 15.3

Assets: Uses of funds (in millions)		Liabilities: Sources of funds (in millions)	
Loans	$650	Deposits	$800
Required reserves	$80		
Excess reserves	$70		
Total assets	$800	Total liabilities	$800

Balance Sheet for University Bank

A bank's balance sheet summarizes its key financial information. The bank's assets are recorded on the left side; assets show how the bank chooses to use its funds. The sources of the firm's funds (liabilities) are recorded on the right side. For the financial statement to be balanced, the two sides of the balance sheet must be equal.

As you can see, University Bank has extended $650 million in loans. Many of these loans went to firms to fund investment, but some also went to households to purchase homes, cars, and other consumer items. A second important asset held by banks is reserves. **Reserves** are the portion of bank deposits that are set aside and not lent out. Reserves include both currency in the bank's vault and funds that the bank holds in deposit at its own bank, the Federal Reserve. Because of the way the banking system works, there are actually two types of reserves.

Reserves are the portion of bank deposits that are set aside and not lent out.

Bank Reserves

Our modern system of banking is called fractional reserve banking. **Fractional reserve banking** occurs when banks hold only a fraction of their deposits on reserve. The alternative is 100% reserve banking. Banks in a 100% reserve system don't loan out deposits; these banks are essentially just safes, keeping deposits on hand until depositors decide to make a withdrawal.

Fractional reserve banking occurs when banks hold only a fraction of their deposits on reserve.

Figure 15.4 illustrates the process of fractional reserve banking. Deposits come into the banks, and the banks send out a portion of these funds in loans. In recent years, U.S. banks have typically loaned out almost 90% of their deposits, keeping barely over 10% on reserve. Banks loan out most of their deposits because reserves earn very little interest; every dollar kept on reserve costs the bank potential income. In 2014, bank reserves paid just 0.25% interest. If a business is willing to take out a loan at a 5% interest rate, the bank will make a larger profit by making the loan than by letting the money sit around collecting only 0.25% interest.

Banks hold reserves for two reasons. First, they must accommodate withdrawals by their depositors. You'd be pretty unhappy if you tried to make a withdrawal from your bank and it didn't have enough on reserve to honor your request. If word spread that a bank was having difficulty meeting its

FIGURE 15.4

Fractional Reserve Banking

In a fractional reserve banking system, banks lend out only a fraction of the deposits they take in. The remainder is set aside as reserves.

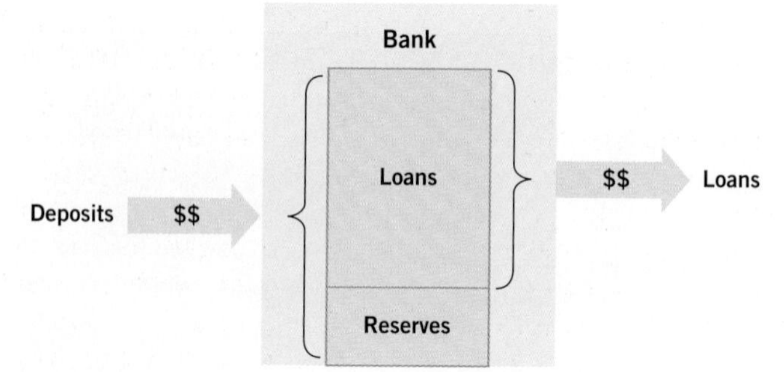

A **bank run** occurs when many depositors attempt to withdraw their funds at the same time.

The **required reserve ratio (rr)** is the portion of deposits that banks are required to keep on reserve.

depositors' withdrawal requests, that news would probably lead to a bank run. A **bank run** occurs when many depositors attempt to withdraw their funds at the same time.

Second, banks are legally bound to hold a fraction of their deposits on reserve. The **required reserve ratio (rr)** is the portion of deposits that banks are required to keep on reserve. For a given bank, the dollar amount of required reserves is determined by multiplying the required reserve ratio by the bank's total amount of deposits:

(Equation 15.2)

$$\text{required reserves} = \text{rr} \times \text{deposits}$$

Currently, the required reserve ratio is 10% (rr = 0.10). This means that your bank can legally lend out up to 90 cents of every dollar you deposit.

Opportunity cost

Consider University Bank, whose balance sheet we saw in Figure 15.3. The bank currently has $800 million in deposits. University Bank pays some interest on the deposits and offers services, such as checking, to its depositors. University Bank can't afford to keep the $800 million sitting in the vault—the opportunity cost is too high. If the bank is going to stay in business, it needs to loan out at least part of the $800 million. With a reserve requirement of 10%, required reserves in this case are $80 million, so University Bank can legally loan up to $720 million. This is the first kind of reserves: required reserves. **Required reserves** are the portion of deposits that a bank must have readily available for withdrawal.

Required reserves are the portion of deposits that a bank must have readily available for withdrawal.

Excess reserves are any reserves held in excess of those required.

Banks rarely keep their level of reserves exactly at the required level. As a result, they also hold a second kind of reserves. Any reserves above the required level are called **excess reserves**:

(Equation 15.3)

$$\text{excess reserves} = \text{total reserves} - \text{required reserves}$$

The balance sheet of University Bank, presented in Figure 15.3, indicates that the bank currently holds total reserves of $150 million. The bank has $80 million in required reserves; therefore, it has $70 million in excess reserves. Given the opportunity cost of holding these excess reserves, University Bank will probably seek to loan out most of this balance in the future.

ECONOMICS IN THE REAL WORLD

Twenty-First-Century Bank Run

For a modern example of a bank run, consider England's Northern Rock Bank, which experienced a bank run in 2007—the first British bank run in over a century. Northern Rock (which is now owned by Virgin Money) earned revenue valued at over $10 billion per year. But extensive losses stemming from investments in mortgage markets led it to near collapse in 2007.

In September of that year, depositors began lining up outside Northern Rock locations because they feared they wouldn't get their deposits back. In February 2008, the British government took over Northern Rock because it was unable to repay its debts or find a buyer.

In the United States, over three hundred banks failed between 2008 and 2011 without experiencing a bank run. The difference is a reflection of the level of deposit insurance offered in the two nations. In England, depositors are insured for 100% of their deposits up to a value of $4,000, then for only 90% of their next $70,000. So British depositors get back a fraction of their deposits up to about $74,000. In contrast, Federal Deposit Insurance Corporation (FDIC) insurance in the United States offers 100% insurance on the first $250,000.

FDIC insurance has greatly decreased the frequency of bank runs. But it also has created a *moral hazard* situation. A **moral hazard** occurs when a party that is protected from risk behaves differently from the way it would behave if it were fully exposed to the risk. FDIC insurance means that neither banks nor their depositors have an incentive to monitor risk; no matter what happens, they're protected from the consequences of risky behavior.

A **moral hazard** occurs when a party that is protected from risk behaves differently from the way it would behave if it were fully exposed to the risk.

Consider two types of banks in this environment. Type A banks are conservative, take little risk, and earn relatively low returns on their loans. Type A banks make only very safe loans with very little **default risk** and, consequently, relatively low rates of return. Type A banks rarely fail, but they make relatively low profit and pay relatively low interest rates to their depositors. In contrast, Type B banks take huge risks, hoping to make extremely large returns on their loans. Type B loans carry greater default risk but also pay higher returns. Type B banks often fail, but the lucky ones—the ones that survive—earn very handsome profits and pay high interest rates on their customers' deposits.

Default risk is the risk that a borrower will not repay the full value of a debt on the maturity date.

Moral hazard draws individual depositors and bankers to Type B banking. There is a tremendous upside and no significant downside, since FDIC

Depositors queue outside a Northern Rock Bank location in September 2007.

ECONOMICS IN THE MEDIA

Moral Hazard

Wall Street: Money Never Sleeps

This 2010 film is a sequel to the original *Wall Street* movie from 1987. This film focuses on the historical events leading up to and during the financial crisis that began in 2007. One recurring theme in the movie is that some financial firms are "too big to fail." How can a firm be too big to fail?

If one bank fails, it is unable to repay its depositors and other creditors. This situation puts all the bank's creditors into similar financial difficulty. If the failing bank is large enough, its failure can set off a domino effect in which bank after bank after bank fails and the entire financial system collapses. If regulators deem a bank too big to fail, they will use government aid to keep the bank afloat.

However, this situation introduces a particularly strong case of moral hazard. After all, banks have incentives to take on risk so that they can earn high profits. If we eliminate the possibility of failure by providing government aid, there is almost no downside risk.

Gordon Gecko understands moral hazard.

In this movie, Gordon Gecko, played by Michael Douglas, defines moral hazard during a public lecture. His definition is this: "when they take your money and then are not responsible for what they do with it."

Gecko is right: when a financial institution isn't required to bear the costs of making poor decisions, it isn't responsible for mishandling its depositors' funds.

insurance protects depositors against losses. This is the environment in which our modern banks operate, which is why many analysts argue that reserve requirements and other regulations are necessary to help ensure stability in the financial industry. The case for these regulations is even stronger when we realize that recessions often start in the financial industry. ✷

How Banks Create Money

We have seen that banks function as financial intermediaries. They help get savings into the hands of investors. But as a byproduct of their everyday activity, banks also create new money. Modern U.S. banks don't print currency, but they do create new deposits, and deposits are a part of the money supply.

To see how banks create money, let's start with a hypothetical example that involves the Federal Reserve, which supplies the currency in the United States. (Note that the Treasury Department prints currency, but the Fed issues it.) Let's say that the Federal Reserve decides to increase the U.S. money supply. To do this, it takes a single $1,000 bill and drops it out of a helicopter. Perhaps you're the lucky person who finds this brand-new $1,000 bill. If you keep the $1,000 in your wallet, then the money supply increases by only this amount. But if you deposit the new money in a bank, then the bank can use it to create even more money.

Let's walk through how this process works. Consider what happens if you deposit the $1,000 into a savings or checking account at University Bank. When you deposit the $1,000, it's still part of the money supply, because both currency and bank deposits are counted in the money supply. You don't have the currency anymore, but in your wallet you have a debit card that enables you to access the $1,000 to make purchases. Therefore, the deposit still represents $1,000 worth of the medium of exchange.

But University Bank doesn't keep your $1,000 in reserve; it uses part of your deposit to extend a new loan that earns interest income for the bank. You still have the $1,000 in your account (as a deposit), but someone else receives money from the bank in the form of a loan. Thus, University Bank creates new money by loaning out part of your deposit. What's more, you helped the bank in the money-creation process because you put your funds into the bank in the first place.

This is just the first step in the money-creation process. We'll now explore this process in more detail, utilizing the bank's balance sheet. For this example, we need to make two assumptions to help understand the general picture:

Assumption 1: All currency is deposited in a bank.

Assumption 2: Banks hold no excess reserves.

Neither of these assumptions is completely realistic. But let's work through the example under these conditions, and later we can consider the effect of each assumption.

Consider first how your deposit changes the assets and liabilities of University Bank. The t-account below summarizes all initial changes to the balance sheet of University Bank when you deposit your new $1,000 (Assumption 1):

University Bank

Assets		Liabilities	
Reserves	$1000	Deposits	$1,000

With a required reserve ratio of 10% (rr = 0.10), University Bank loans out $900 of your deposit (Assumption 2 states that banks hold no excess reserves, so only 10% of deposits are held on reserve). Perhaps the bank loans this amount to a student named Alexis. At this point, the money supply has changed. You still have access to the original $1,000 in your checking account. But Alexis is walking out of University Bank with $900. Alexis may have $900 in cash or in the form of a check that she's going to deposit in her own checking account. Regardless, the money supply is now $1,900: your original $1,000 plus Alexis's $900.

Including your initial deposit and this $900 loan, the balance-sheet changes at University Bank are summarized in this t-account:

University Bank

Assets		Liabilities	
Required reserves	$100	Deposits	$1,000
Loans	$900		

Let's say that Alexis is going to use the \$900 to pay part of her college tuition. She gives her college the \$900, and the college then deposits this amount into its own bank, named Township Bank. But the money-multiplication process doesn't end here. Township Bank also keeps no excess reserves, so it loans out 90% of the \$900, which is \$810. This move creates \$810 more in money supply, so that total new money is now \$1,000 + \$900 + \$810 = \$2,710. The balance-sheet changes at Township Bank are then:

Township Bank

Assets		Liabilities	
Required reserves	\$90	Deposits	\$900
Loans	\$810		

You can now see that whenever banks make loans, they create new money. As long as dollars find their way back into the banking system, banks turn them into more loans—which means more money. Table 15.1 summarizes this process of money creation. If the lending process continues on until there's nothing left to lend, the initial \$1,000 bill ultimately leads to \$10,000 worth of money. When monetary funds are deposited into banks, banks can multiply these deposits; and when they do, they create money.

The **simple money multiplier** (m^m) is the rate at which banks multiply money when all currency is deposited into banks and they hold no excess reserves.

In the end, the impact of a deposit on the money supply is a large multiple of the initial increase in paper money. The exact multiple depends on the required reserve ratio (rr). The rate at which banks multiply money when all currency is deposited into banks and they hold no excess reserves is called the **simple money multiplier (m^m)**. The formula for the money multiplier is:

(Equation 15.4)

$$m^m = \frac{1}{rr}$$

In our example above, rr = 0.10, so the multiplier is 1 ÷ 0.10, which is 10. To determine how much money is created with the initial deposit, we multiply the money multiplier by the amount of the deposit. When the money multiplier is 10, a new \$1,000 bill issued by the Federal Reserve eventually leads to \$1,000 × 10 = \$10,000 in new money.

TABLE 15.1

Money Creation

Assumption 1: All currency is deposited in banks.

Assumption 2: Banks hold no excess reserves.

Required reserve ratio (*rr*) = 10%

Initial new money supply = \$1,000

Round	Deposit	Money Supply
1	\$1,000	\$1,000
2	\$900	\$1,900
3	\$810	\$2,710
4	\$729	\$3,429
.	.	.
.	.	.
.	.	.
Sum		\$10,000

PRACTICE WHAT YOU KNOW

Fractional Reserve Banking: The B-Money Bank

When banks extend loans, the money supply increases.

Use this balance sheet of the B-Money Bank to answer the questions below. Assume the required reserve ratio is 10%.

B-Money Bank

Assets		Liabilities	
Reserves	$50,000	Deposits	$200,000
Loans	$150,000		

Question: What are the required reserves of B-Money Bank?

Answer: B-Money is required to hold 10% of deposits, which in this case is $20,000.

Question: What is the maximum new loan that B-Money can extend?

Answer: B-Money is holding $50,000 in reserves, but it only has to hold $20,000. Therefore, it has $30,000 in excess reserves, so it can extend a total of that amount in new loans.

Question: How would you rewrite B-Money's t-account, assuming that this loan is made?

Answer: Deposits remain at $200,000, but when the bank increases its lending, both reserves and loans are changed. Reserves would decline by $30,000, and loans would increase by $30,000.

B-Money Bank

Assets		Liabilities	
Reserves	$20,000	Deposits	$200,000
Loans	$180,000		

Question: What would be the maximum impact on the money supply from the initial $200,000 deposit?

Answer: Using the simple money multiplier, we can see that the money supply could grow by as much as $2,000,000 from depositing the $200,000.

$$\$200{,}000 \times m^m = \$200{,}000 \times \frac{1}{0.10} = \$200{,}000 \times 10 = \$2{,}000{,}000$$

Of course, in the real world our two assumptions don't always hold. There is a more realistic money multiplier that relaxes the two assumptions. Consider how a more real-world money multiplier would compare to the simple money multiplier. First, if people hold on to some currency (relaxing Assumption 1), banks cannot multiply that currency, so the more realistic multiplier is smaller than the simple money multiplier. Second, if banks hold excess reserves (relaxing Assumption 2), these dollars aren't multiplied, and again the real multiplier is smaller than the simple version. So, in reality, money doesn't multiply at quite the rate represented by the simple money multiplier. Rather, the simple money multiplier represents the *maximum* size of the money multiplier.

ECONOMICS IN THE REAL WORLD

Bitcoin

The Internet has enabled people to interact on a worldwide scale. In most countries, all that's needed to conduct business across oceans is a connection to the Web. One of the problems with conducting any kind of transaction is how to pay for it. As we'll discuss in Chapter 18, people in different countries use different forms of currency. Americans want to be paid in dollars, but if you live in China you want to be paid in yuan. Therefore, international trade becomes complicated by the types of money that people use. One way to overcome this problem and facilitate trade over the Internet is to use a common currency, which might take the form of digital or crypto-currency.

There are many digital currencies vying to establish themselves as the "money of the Internet," but the most well known of these is bitcoin. Bitcoin first appeared in 2009 and was started by an unknown person or persons using the name Satoshi Nakamoto. Originally, people acquired bitcoins by "mining" them. No picks or explosives were required, however. This kind of mining was accomplished by solving complicated math problems. Correct solutions were rewarded with bitcoins. While you can still mine bitcoins, they are more easily available at exchanges. Just like you can buy foreign currency at a foreign currency exchange, you can use your dollars to buy bitcoins.

Unlike actual currency, however, bitcoins are intangible. You never actually take possession of a bitcoin because they're entirely digital. Nonetheless, more and more people and businesses are accepting bitcoins as payment. Companies like Amazon and eBay are logical candidates to accept the digital currency, but brick-and-mortar stores like Target, Whole Foods, and Home Depot also allow customers to pay in bitcoins. Even the Sacramento Kings of the National Basketball Association lets fans pay for their tickets using bitcoins.

A number of problems exist with bitcoins, however. To the people who use them, one of the benefits is anonymity. Because you can pay with bitcoins, no one needs to know who you are. Unlike a credit-card transaction, bitcoin transactions cannot be traced. However, this anonymity means that your bitcoins can be stolen and there's little you can do about it. One of the largest repositories of bitcoins, Mt. Gox, was hacked in early 2014, and over $460 million of bitcoins simply disappeared.

Additionally, bitcoins are not tied to any country, and no central bank controls their supply. Since no government is responsible for bitcoins, there is

FIGURE 15.5

The Value of the Bitcoin in U.S. Dollars from Its Inception in 2009

The dollar value of the bitcoin started off small when it wasn't accepted as money. Once people began to believe it had value by accepting it for purchases on a larger scale in 2013, the value began to rise. Fears about security, speculation, and government regulation have contributed to the wild ups and downs in the price of the bitcoin.

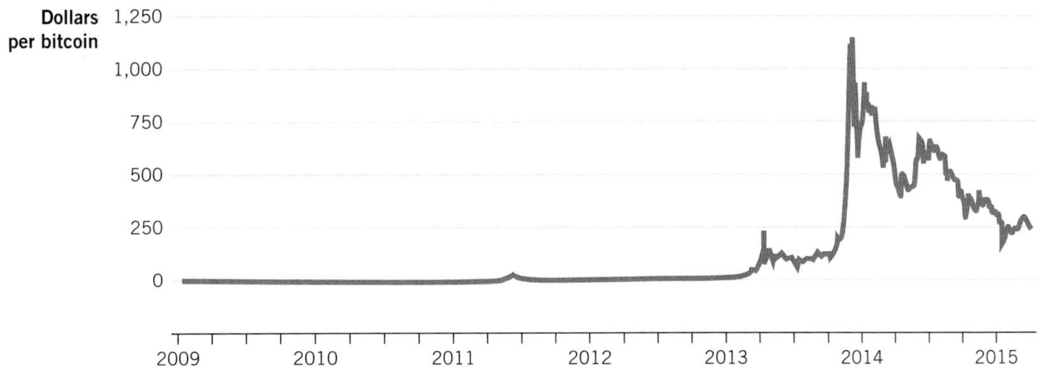

the potential for counterfeiting and excessive production, which would drive their value down. Another issue is that bitcoins are subject to wildly fluctuating valuations. This is shown in Figure 15.5. The incredible ups and downs of bitcoins' value began in 2013. As companies announced they would accept bitcoins, the currency's value grew. Rampant speculation (a fancy name for financial betting) has contributed to keeping the prices unstable. Since there aren't that many bitcoins in existence, it's fairly easy for a small group of people to manipulate their price. Discussions by governments over how to regulate the crypto-currency also add to the drama. Still, as long as businesses and individuals are willing to accept them as a medium of exchange, bitcoins are here to stay. ✷

Conclusion

We started this chapter with a common misconception about the money supply in an economy. Many people believe that it's pretty simple to regulate the economy's money supply. Even though currency in modern economies is issued exclusively by government, money also includes bank deposits. Banks cause the money supply to expand when they extend loans, and they cause the money supply to contract when they increase their level of reserves. In fact, even individuals' influence is significant: we all can cause the money supply to rise and fall when we change the amount of currency we hold outside the banking system. Taken together, these truths mean that the Fed's job of monitoring the money supply is very difficult. The Fed often attempts to expand or contract the money supply, but its efforts may be offset by the actions of commercial banks and individuals.

The material in this chapter sets the stage for a discussion of monetary policy and the way it affects the economy, which we undertake in Chapter 16.

ANSWERING THE BIG QUESTIONS

What is money?

* Money is primarily the medium of exchange in an economy; it's what people trade for goods and services. Money also serves as a unit of account and a store of value.
* Anything can be used as money, but not everything works well as money. Money should be portable, durable, recognizable, and easily divisible. Unless people accept the item as money, it cannot serve as a medium of exchange.

What is the Fed?

* The Fed is the central bank of the United States. It was created in 1913 in response to a series of financial crises brought on in large part due to an inconsistent money supply.
* The Fed's main job is to control the money supply. It keeps track of how much money is in the economy in order to help preserve its value. It also serves as a bank for banks and is charged with ensuring commercial banks' financial stability.

How is the money supply measured?

* Money includes more than just physical currency; it also includes bank deposits, since people often make purchases with checks or cards that withdraw from their bank accounts. M1 includes currency (paper money and coins) and checkable deposits, plus traveler's checks. M2 includes M1 plus savings deposits, CDs, and money-market mutual funds.

How do banks create money?

* Banks create money whenever they extend loans. A new loan represents new purchasing power, and the deposit that backs the loan is also considered money. Each time a bank receives a new deposit, it is able to create money through new loans.

CONCEPTS YOU SHOULD KNOW

assets (p. 456)
balance sheet (p. 456)
bank run (p. 458)
barter (p. 447)
central bank (p. 453)
checkable deposits (p. 454)
commercial bank (p. 453)
commodity money (p. 447)
commodity-backed money (p. 447)
currency (p. 446)
default risk (p. 459)
double coincidence of wants (p. 447)
excess reserves (p. 458)
fiat money (p. 448)
financial intermediaries (p. 456)
fractional reserve banking (p. 457)
investment bank (p. 453)
liabilities (p. 456)
liquidity (p. 454)
M1 (p. 454)
M2 (p. 454)
medium of exchange (p. 447)
moral hazard (p. 459)
required reserves (p. 458)
required reserve ratio (rr) (p. 458)
reserves (p. 457)
simple money multiplier (m^m) (p. 462)
store of value (p. 449)
t-account (p. 456)
unit of account (p. 448)

QUESTIONS FOR REVIEW

1. What is the difference between commodity money and fiat money?
2. What are the three functions of money? Which function is the most important?
3. What are the characteristics that something needs to possess in order to function as money?
4. What are the components of M1 and M2? List them.
5. Suppose you withdraw $100 from your checking account. What impact would this action alone have on the following?
   a. the money supply
   b. your bank's required reserves
   c. your bank's excess reserves
6. Why is the actual money multiplier usually less than the simple money multiplier?
7. Why can't a bank lend out all of its reserves?
8. How does a commercial bank increase the money supply?
9. What is the current required reserve ratio? What would happen to the money supply if the Fed decreased the ratio?

STUDY PROBLEMS (✱ *solved at the end of the section*)

1. Suppose that you take $150 in currency out of your pocket and deposit it in your checking account. Assuming a required reserve ratio of 10%, what is the largest amount by which the money supply can increase as a result of your action?
2. Consider the balance sheet for the Wahoo Bank as presented here.

Wahoo Bank Balance Sheet

Assets		Liabilities	
		Liabilities:	
Required reserves	$400	Checking deposits	$4,000
Excess reserves	$0		
Loans	$3,600		

Using a required reserve ratio of 10% and assuming that the bank keeps no excess reserves, write the changes to the bank's balance sheet for each of the following scenarios:

a. Bennett withdraws $200 from his checking account.

b. Roland deposits $500 into his checking account.

✱ 3. Using a required reserve ratio of 10%, which of the following scenarios produces a larger increase in the money supply? Explain.

a. Someone takes $100 from under his mattress and deposits it into a checking account. The bank immediately makes a loan with this money, leaving no excess reserves.

b. Someone deposits $1,000 cash into a checking account at a bank that does not lend it.

4. Using a required reserve ratio of 10% and assuming that banks keep no excess reserves, imagine that $300 is deposited into a checking account. By how much more does the money supply increase if the Fed lowers the required reserve ratio to 7%?

5. Determine if the following changes affect M1 and/or M2:

a. an increase in savings deposits

b. a decrease in credit-card balances

c. a decrease in the amount of currency in circulation

d. the conversion of a savings account into a checking account

✱ 6. What is the simple money multiplier if the required reserve ratio is 15%? If it is 12.5%?

SOLVED PROBLEMS

3. In scenario (a), the deposit is used to make a loan and therefore increases the money supply. With a 10% reserve ratio, \$90 is created. The money supply thus increases to \$190. Of course, there may be further lending, which would increase the money supply even more. A simple money multiplier of 10 (= 1/0.10) would lead to a potential \$1,000 increase in the money supply.

The \$1,000 deposit in scenario (b) doesn't increase the money supply at all. This deposit simply changes the form of money from cash to a checking account. Unless the bank makes a loan, no money is created.

6. When the required reserve ratio is 15% the money multiplier is: $m^m = \frac{1}{rr} = \frac{1}{0.15} = 6.67$.

When the required reserve ratio is 12.5% the money multiplier is: $m^m = \frac{1}{rr} = \frac{1}{0.125} = 8$.

CHAPTER

16 Monetary Policy

MISCONCEPTION

Central banks can steer economies out of every recession.

From 1982 to 2008—for 26 years—the U.S. economy hummed along with unprecedented success. Although there were two recessions during this period, neither was severe or lengthy. Economists and many other observers actually believed that the business cycle had been tamed once and for all. Much of the credit for this "great moderation" was given to Alan Greenspan, the chair of the Board of Governors of the Federal Reserve Board (the Fed). Analysts thought that his savvy handling of interest rates and money supply had been the key to the sustained economic growth, and that enlightened supervision of central banks was the path to future economic growth throughout the world.

Unfortunately, the upturn did not last. The Great Recession, which started in late 2007, plunged the world into one of the worst economic downturns since the Great Depression. Moreover, since 2008 the Fed's extraordinary, but only moderately successful, efforts to stimulate U.S. economic growth have shown just how little power a central bank has when the economy gets really bad.

In this chapter, we consider how changes in the money supply work their way through the economy. We build on earlier material, drawing heavily from the discussions of money, the loanable funds market, and the business-cycle model. We begin by looking at the short run, when monetary policy is most effective. We then consider why monetary policy cannot always turn an economy around.

The Federal Reserve plays a powerful role in the world economy, but it's not as powerful as some people think.

BIG QUESTIONS

* What are the tools of monetary policy?
* What is the effect of monetary policy in the short run?
* Why doesn't monetary policy always work?

What Are the Tools of Monetary Policy?

In the misconception that opened this chapter, we mentioned that many analysts gave the Fed credit for the economic expansion that began in the 1980s and lasted through the early 2000s. This statement raises a larger question: *What are the specific ways the Fed, or the central bank of any country, can promote economic growth?* The short answer is that they use **monetary policy** to alter the money supply.

Monetary policy involves adjusting the money supply to influence the macroeconomy.

When the Fed implements monetary policy, it has several tools at its disposal. In this section we discuss these policy tools, but our emphasis is on the key tool the Fed uses every day: open market operations.

Open Market Operations

If the Fed decided to increase the money supply, it could do so in a number of direct ways. Here is a list of three possible ways the Fed might directly increase the amount of money in the economy; see if you can guess which one the Fed would prefer:

1. Throw money out of the back of an armored truck.
2. Distribute $50,000 in new $100 bills to every private bank.
3. Use new money to buy something in the economy.

If you chose option 3, you are right on the money—so to speak. **Open market operations** involve the purchase or sale of things by a central bank.

Open market operations involve the purchase or sale of bonds by a central bank.

Essentially, the Fed could bring about its desired effects through buying any kind of goods or services such as real estate, fine art, coffee and bagels, or car detailing. It would be as if the Fed prints a batch of new currency and then goes shopping. When it's done shopping, it leaves behind all the new currency in the economy. Whatever it buys on its shopping spree becomes an asset on the Fed's balance sheet. That being said, there is one thing the Fed usually buys and sells: bonds.

A **bond** is an IOU that joins two parties in a contract that specifies the conditions for repayment of the loan.

A **bond** is a paper IOU that joins two parties in a contract. The buyer of the bond is lending money to the seller of the bond. The bond itself specifies the conditions for repayment of this loan. (We'll focus on government bonds as we look at monetary policy, but we'll also consider corporate bonds in Chapter 19.) After two parties form a bond, the actual paper can be traded to someone else in what is called a secondary market. People trade bonds for money in the bond market like they trade stocks or baseball cards. There is no more borrowing or lending when this happens; the only change involves who owns the bond. The Fed is a participant in this secondary market, albeit a very unique participant. If you buy or sell a bond, you use or receive money that's already in the economy. When the Fed buys and sells bonds, it alters the money supply of the entire country because it uses brand-new money to buy the bonds. When the Fed sells bonds, the money it receives is taken out of circulation, meaning that the money is no longer available for use. So when the Fed wants to increase the money supply, it buys bonds; when it wishes to decrease the money supply, it sells bonds.

The Fed buys and sells bonds for two reasons. First, the Fed's goal is to get money directly into the market for loanable funds. When the Fed buys or sells bonds in the secondary market, it typically buys and sells from banks because banks hold large amounts of bonds. The Fed could buy and sell directly to households, but it would have to conduct many more transactions to achieve the results it gets by trading with banks. By buying from and selling to banks, the Fed ensures that bank reserves are altered. If the Fed buys bonds, reserves increase. The banks can now make more loans and increase the money supply through the lending process, which we described in Chapter 15. If the Fed sells bonds, reserves decrease as banks use excess reserves to pay for the bonds, thereby reducing their ability to lend and decreasing the money supply.

Second, a typical day's worth of open market operations might entail as much as $20 billion worth of purchases from the Fed. If the Fed bought coffee and bagels, it would cause problems in that market. Imagine being the manager of a bagel shop in Washington, D.C., and having Janet Yellen (the current chair of the Fed's Board of Governors) walk in with a request for $20 billion worth of bagels. That would be an impossible request! But the market for U.S. government bonds is big enough to accommodate this level of purchases seamlessly. The daily volume in the U.S. Treasury market is over $500 billion, so the Fed can buy and sell without affecting the market's operations.

Figure 16.1 summarizes how open market operations work. In panel (a), we see that when the Fed purchases bonds it creates new money and trades this money with financial institutions for their U.S. government bonds. The result is more money in the economy. In panel (b), we see that when the Fed sells bonds to financial institutions it exchanges bonds for existing money, taking the money out of the economy. The result is less money in the economy.

The Fed undertakes open market operations every business day. As such, open market operations are the primary tool that the Fed uses to expand or contract the money supply in order to affect the macroeconomy.

Quantitative Easing

The end of 2008 marked the single worst quarter for the U.S. economy in over half a century. Real GDP declined by 8.9%, and the unemployment rate was ratcheting upward. In November 2008, hoping that more money would stimulate the economy, the Federal Reserve determined that it should take additional measures to increase the money supply. The method it chose is a new type of open market operations known as quantitative easing.

FIGURE 16.1

Open Market Operations

In open market purchases, the Fed buys government bonds from financial institutions. This action injects new money directly into financial markets. In open market sales, the Fed sells bonds back to financial institutions. This action takes money out of financial markets.

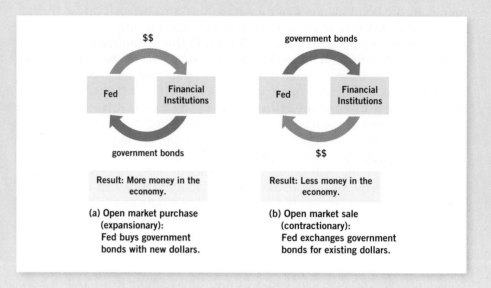

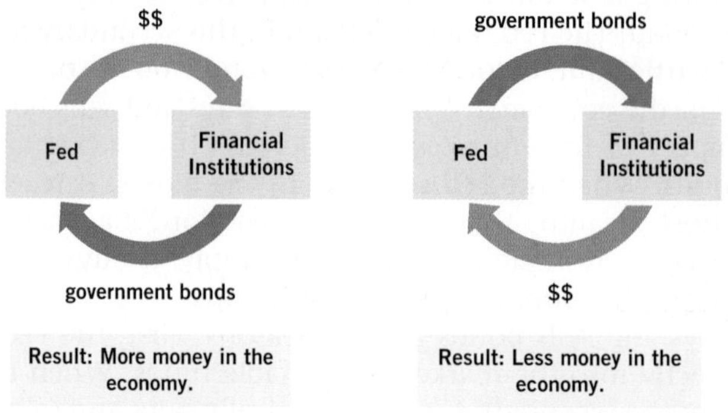

(a) Open market purchase (expansionary): Fed buys government bonds with new dollars.

(b) Open market sale (contractionary): Fed exchanges government bonds for existing dollars.

Quantitative easing is the targeted use of open market operations in which the central bank buys securities in specific markets.

Quantitative easing is the targeted use of open market operations in which the central bank buys securities in specific markets. With its quantitative easing in late 2008, the Fed expanded its purchases beyond short-term government bonds to include \$300 billion in long-term government bonds. It also purchased \$1.25 trillion in mortgage-backed securities, specifically targeting the housing market. Together with an additional \$175 billion in purchases of securities from government-sponsored enterprises, this amounted to almost \$2 trillion in new funds injected into the economy.

This move was bold and unprecedented in both size and scope. The first round of quantitative easing started in November 2008 and continued into the first quarter of 2010. At that point, the Fed was convinced that economic recovery was well under way. But conditions deteriorated over the second half of 2010 as the unemployment rate stayed around 9% and real GDP growth stalled.

Because of the lackluster U.S. economic performance in November 2010, the Fed decided to engage in a second round of quantitative easing, dubbed QE 2. This round involved purchasing an additional \$600 billion in long-term government bonds. Figure 16.2 illustrates the timeline for these quantitative easing programs along with the quarterly growth rates of real GDP. The Fed implemented these two rounds of quantitative easing when it was clear that traditional open market operations were not returning the economy to stable growth rates. As lackluster growth continued through 2012, the Fed announced an ongoing program to buy \$85 billion per month in mortgage-backed securities and longer-term government bonds. This program, with no termination date, became known as QE 3. The buying began to slow only in late 2013, and in late 2014 the Fed announced an end to the buying.

In summary, quantitative easing is a new variation of open market operations that was introduced during the slow recovery from the Great Recession. However, this new tool did not immediately return the U.S. economy to strong growth.

FIGURE 16.2

Quantitative Easing, 2007–2014

Beginning in 2008, the Federal Reserve began the unprecedented practice of quantitative easing (QE) to inject money into the economy. The QE initiatives were implemented when traditional monetary policy seemed to be failing to push the economy back to consistent growth.

Source: GDP data is from the U.S. Bureau of Economic Analysis. QE data is from the Federal Reserve. Data quoted in 2009 dollars.

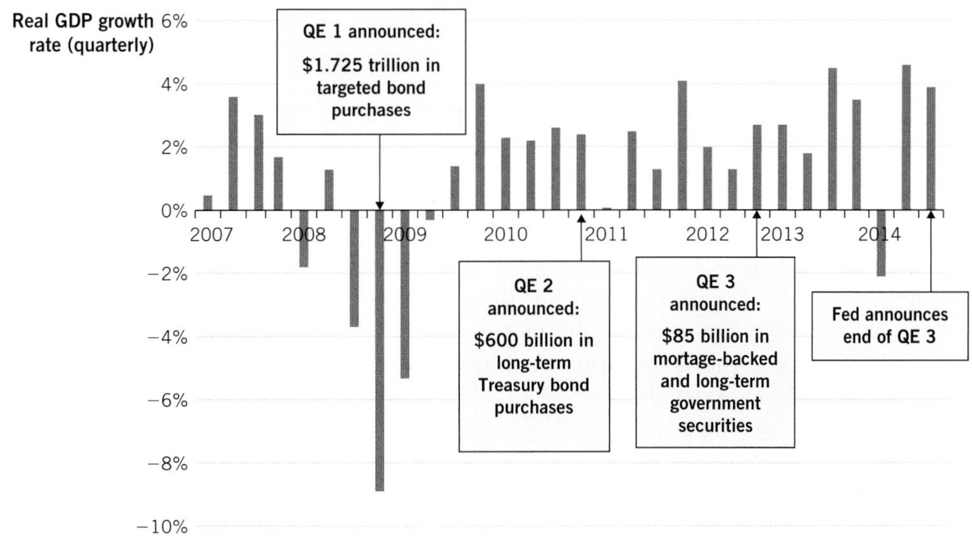

Reserve Requirements and Discount Rates

In the past, the Fed made use of two other tools in its administration of monetary policy: **reserve requirements** and the **discount rate**. Neither of these has been used recently for monetary policy, but they are available and historically important.

The **reserve requirement** is the amount of deposits that a bank must hold in reserve as determined by the central bank. This limits the amount of deposits a bank can lend.

The **discount rate** is the interest rate on discount loans made by the Federal Reserve to private banks.

Recall our two earlier observations (from Chapter 15) regarding reserve requirements:

1. The Fed sets the ratio of deposits that banks must hold on reserve. This ratio is the required reserve ratio (rr).
2. The simple money multiplier (m^{m}) depends on the required reserve ratio (rr), since $\text{m}^{\text{m}} = \frac{1}{\text{rr}}$.

Taken together, these observations imply that the Fed can change the money multiplier by changing the required reserve ratio. If the Fed lowers the required reserve ratio, the money multiplier increases; if the Fed raises the required reserve ratio, the money multiplier falls.

For example, consider what would happen if the Fed lowered the reserve ratio to 5% from its current level of 10%. The new simple money multiplier would be 1/.05 = 20. This action alone would double the simple money

TABLE 16.1

Required Reserves and the Simple Money Multiplier

rr	m^m	
0.05	20	Decrease in rr ⟶ Increase in m^m
0.10	**10**	
0.125	8	
0.20	5	Increase in rr ⟶ Decrease in m^m
0.25	4	

multiplier. Lowering the required reserve would mean that banks could loan out larger portions of their deposits, enabling them to create money by multiplying deposits to a greater extent than before.

If, instead, the Fed raised the reserve ratio to 20%, the simple money multiplier would fall to just 1/0.20 = 5. Table 16.1 shows different values of the simple money multiplier given different reserve requirements.

The reserve ratio is not as precise or predictable as open market operations are. Since small changes in the money multiplier can lead to large swings in the money supply, changing the reserve requirement can cause the money supply to change too much. In addition, changing the reserve requirements can have unpredictable outcomes because the overall effects depend on the actions of banks. It's possible that the Fed could lower the reserve requirement to 5% and banks wouldn't make new loans. It is also possible that firms and households wouldn't want to borrow. As a result of its unpredictable nature, the reserve requirement isn't used often to alter the money supply. It was last changed in 1992.

The Fed has also used the discount rate to administer monetary policy. Recall that the *discount rate* is the interest rate that the Fed charges commercial banks when they have to borrow from the Fed in its role as lender of last resort. In the past, the Fed would (1) increase the discount rate to discourage borrowing by banks and to decrease the money supply, or (2) decrease the

TABLE 16.2

Tools of the Fed and How They Affect the Money Supply

	Expansionary (increases money supply)	Contractionary (decreases money supply)
Open market operations	Buy bonds. Doing so puts funds directly in the loanable funds market, enabling banks to increase lending.	Sell bonds. Doing so removes bank reserves that could have been lent in the loanable funds market, preventing banks from lending.
Reserve requirements	Decrease the reserve ratio so that banks may lend more of their deposits. Doing so enables banks to increase lending.	Increase the reserve ratio so that banks cannot lend as many of their deposits. Doing so limits banks' lending behavior.
Discount rate	Decrease the rate, making it less expensive to borrow from the Fed, thus stimulating lending.	Increase the rate, making it more expensive to borrow from the Fed, thus discouraging lending.

discount rate to encourage borrowing by banks and to increase the money supply. The Fed used this tool actively until the Great Depression era of the 1930s. Currently, the Fed discourages discount borrowing unless banks are struggling. Changing the discount rate to affect bank borrowing is no longer viewed as a helpful tool for changing the money supply.

Table 16.2 summarizes the tools used by the Fed for expansionary or contractionary monetary policy. **Expansionary monetary policy** occurs when a central bank acts to increase the money supply in an effort to stimulate the economy. **Contractionary monetary policy** occurs when a central bank takes action that reduces the money supply in the economy.

An **expansionary monetary policy** entails a central bank acting to increase the money supply in an effort to stimulate the economy.

A **contractionary monetary policy** entails a central bank acting to decrease the money supply.

ECONOMICS IN THE REAL WORLD

Excess Reserves Climb in the Wake of the Great Recession

The simple money multiplier assumes that individuals and banks don't hoard cash: individuals deposit their funds into the banking system, and banks hold no excess reserves. However, these assumptions aren't always realistic.

Figure 16.3 shows the excess reserves held by banking institutions in the United States between 1990 and 2014. Until the fall of 2008, banks held virtually no excess reserves. But then excess reserves climbed to unprecedented levels, reaching almost $2,700 billion in August 2014.

The cause of this increase was twofold. First, in the wake of the financial turmoil of the Great Recession of 2007–2009, banks were probably more risk averse than before. Holding more reserves gave them a buffer against additional

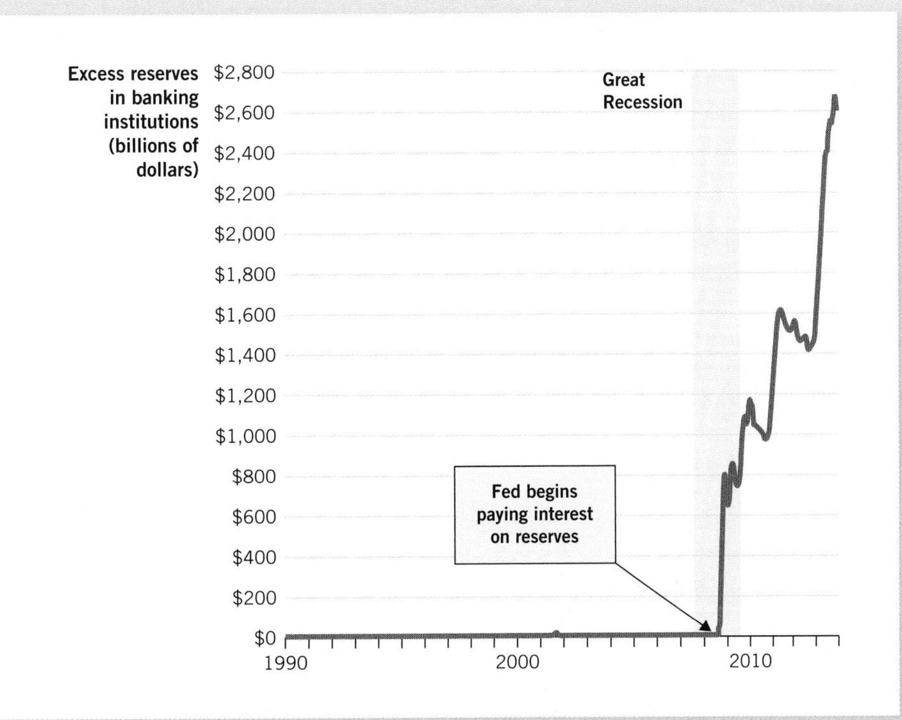

FIGURE 16.3

Excess Reserves, 1990–2014

Banks began holding significant excess reserves in 2008. One reason was the risky nature of loans during the Great Recession, but it's no coincidence that the excess reserves climbed immediately after the Fed began paying interest on reserves.

Source: Federal Reserve Bank of St. Louis, FRED database.

failures. But more important, the Federal Reserve began paying interest on reserves beginning in October 2008. This historic change in policy means that banks now have less incentive to loan out each dollar above the required reserve threshold. The Fed put this policy in place to reduce the opportunity cost of excess reserves.

Opportunity cost

The increase in excess reserves means that the money multiplier is much smaller than our earlier analysis implied. When banks hold more dollars in reserve, fewer are loaned out and multiplied throughout the economy. ✳

What Is the Effect of Monetary Policy in the Short Run?

Of the three primary tools the Fed can use to alter the money supply, it most often uses open market operations. Therefore, let's take a look at how these operations affect the economy. To gain some insight about the macroeconomic results of money-supply changes, let's return to an example we talked about in an earlier chapter: your hypothetical college apparel business. Suppose you already have one retail location where you sell apparel, and you're now considering opening a second. Before you can open a new store, you need to invest in several resources: a physical location, additional inventory, and some labor. You expect the new store to earn the revenue needed to pay for these resources eventually. But you need a loan to expand the business now, so you go to the bank. The bank is willing to grant you a loan, but the interest rate is higher than your expected return on the investment. So you regretfully decide not to open a new location.

But then the Fed decides to expand the money supply. It buys government bonds from banks, which increases the level of reserves in the banking system. As a result, interest rates fall at your local bank. You then take out a loan, open the second apparel shop, and hire a few employees.

In this example, monetary policy affects your actions, and your actions affect the macroeconomy. First, investment increases because you spend on equipment, inventory, and a physical location. Second, GDP increases because your investment is part of overall GDP. Finally, as a result of the increase in real GDP, unemployment falls as your output rises and you hire workers. These effects show what new money can do in the short run: it expands the amount of credit (loanable funds) available and paves the way for economic expansion.

Now let's trace the impact of this kind of monetary policy on the entire macroeconomy. In doing this, we draw heavily on what we've presented in preceding chapters. Below is a short list of concepts from previous chapters that we use in the discussion that follows. The chapters are identified so that you can review as necessary.

1. The Fed uses open market operations to implement monetary policy. Open market operations involve the purchase or sale of bonds.
2. Government bonds are one important part of the loanable funds market (Chapter 14).
3. The price in the loanable funds market is the interest rate. Lower interest rates increase the quantity of investment demand, just as lower prices increase the quantity demanded in any product market (Chapter 14).

4. Investment is one component of GDP, so changes in investment lead to corresponding changes in GDP (Chapter 11).
5. In the short run, increases in aggregate demand increase output and lower the unemployment rate. Decreases in aggregate demand decrease output and increase the unemployment rate (Chapter 12).

We have studied each of these concepts separately. Now it's time to put them together for a complete picture of how monetary policy works.

Expansionary Monetary Policy

As we have noted, the Fed most commonly expands the money supply (an expansionary monetary policy) through open market purchases: it buys bonds.

When the Fed buys bonds from financial institutions, new money moves directly into the loanable funds market. This action increases the funds that banks can use for new loans. Panel (a) of Figure 16.4 illustrates the short-run effects of expansionary monetary policy in the loanable funds market. First, notice that conducting open market operations means the new funds directly

FIGURE 16.4

Expansionary Monetary Policy in the Short Run

(a) When the central bank buys bonds, it injects new funds directly into the loanable funds market. This action increases the supply of loanable funds (S_1 shifts to S_2) and decreases the interest rate from 5% to 3%. The lower interest rate leads to an increase in the quantity of investment demand (D) from \$200 billion to \$210 billion, which increases GDP. (b) The increase in aggregate demand (AD) causes real GDP to rise from \$17.5 trillion to \$18 trillion and reduces unemployment in the short run. The general price level rises to 105 (inflation).

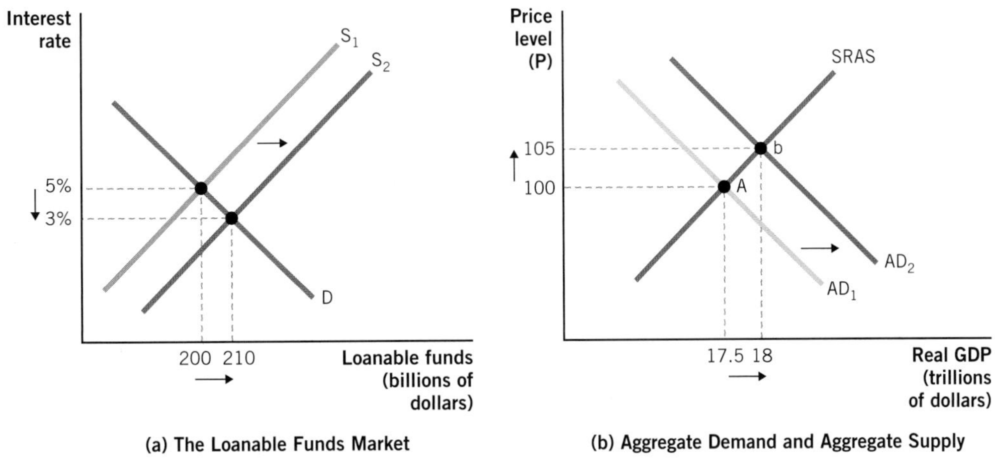

Results summary	GDP	Unemployment	Price level (P)
Short run	↑	↓	↑

enter into the loanable funds market. The supply of funds increases from S_1 to S_2.* This new supply reduces the interest rate from 5% to 3%. At the lower interest rate, firms take more loans for investment, and the quantity demanded of loanable funds increases from $200 billion to $210 billion.

Remember from Chapter 11 that GDP is made up of four components: C, I, G, and NX. Since investment is a component of GDP, an increase in the quantity of investment increases GDP. The increase in GDP leads to more jobs as output increases; therefore, it also leads to lower unemployment. However, as the money supply increases, the value of money falls and we observe inflation.

We can show this change in output and the price level using the aggregate demand and supply model we learned in Chapter 12. In panel (b) of Figure 16.4, the increase in the money supply shifts the AD curve to the right, from AD_1 to AD_2. The economy moves from equilibrium point A to a short-run equilibrium point at b. The result is a higher GDP (which we see as we move from $17.5 trillion to $18 trillion along the real GDP axis) and higher employment (which we don't specifically see in the graph) as more people are hired to produce the additional output. The price level (P) rises as well, from 100 to 105, meaning that the economy experiences inflation.

In summary, in the short run, expansionary monetary policy reduces unemployment and increases real GDP. In addition, the overall price level (P) rises somewhat. These results are summarized in the table at the bottom of Figure 16.4.

You may be asking: *Isn't inflation a bad thing?* If we increase the money supply, prices rise and purchasing power falls. Why would the Fed want this? The answer is that the Fed is weighing the costs of continued low GDP and high unemployment against the harm of higher prices. Usually, the Fed is willing to accept some inflation if it is offset by lower unemployment. This macroeconomic result is consistent with the way monetary policy affected your hypothetical college apparel firm. That being said, later in the chapter we'll see that not everyone is happy with this outcome. Inflation does indeed negatively impact portions of the population.

Real versus Nominal Effects

We have seen that changes in the money supply lead to real changes in the economy. This means that an increase in the money supply impacts real GDP and the unemployment rate—both real variables. You may be wondering if the process is really so simple. That is, if a central bank can stimulate real GDP and job creation by simply printing money, why would it ever stop? After all, fiat money is just paper. Unfortunately, as we have noted, the eventual outcome of printing money is inflation and the devaluation of money.

Think of it this way: let's say the Fed's preferred method of increasing the money supply is to hand all college students backpacks full of newly printed

---

*In our discussion of the loanable funds market, we said that the supply of loanable funds comes from savers. In the case of monetary policy, the Fed increases the funds that banks have available to loan when it buys the bonds held by banks. Thus, monetary policy can increase the supply of loanable funds without involving the contribution of savers.

bills. This may not seem like a bad idea, but let's focus on the macroeconomic effects. Eventually, the new money will devalue the entire money supply, since prices will rise. But since you get the money first, you get it before any prices have adjusted. So these new funds represent real purchasing power for you. This is why monetary policy can have immediate real short-run effects: initially, no prices have adjusted. But eventually stores will realize there is more money flowing through the markets. Prices will adjust to the increased money supply, and the effects of the new money wear off.

How would you like it if new money entered the economy through backpacks full of currency given to all college students?

Injecting new money into the economy eventually causes inflation, but inflation doesn't happen right away and prices don't rise uniformly. These outcomes reflect the idea of sticky prices we discussed in Chapter 12. During the time that prices are increasing, the value of money is constantly moving downward. Figure 16.5 illustrates the real purchasing power of money as time goes by. Panel (a) shows adjustments to the price level. When new money enters the economy (at time t_0), the price level begins to rise and then reaches its new level (at time t_{LR}). Panel (b) shows the value of money relative to these price-level adjustments. When the new money enters the economy, it has its highest value, as prices have not yet adjusted. As prices rise, the real purchasing power of all money in the economy falls. Eventually, all prices adjust, and then the real value of money reaches its new lower level. At this point, the real impacts of the monetary policy dissipate completely.

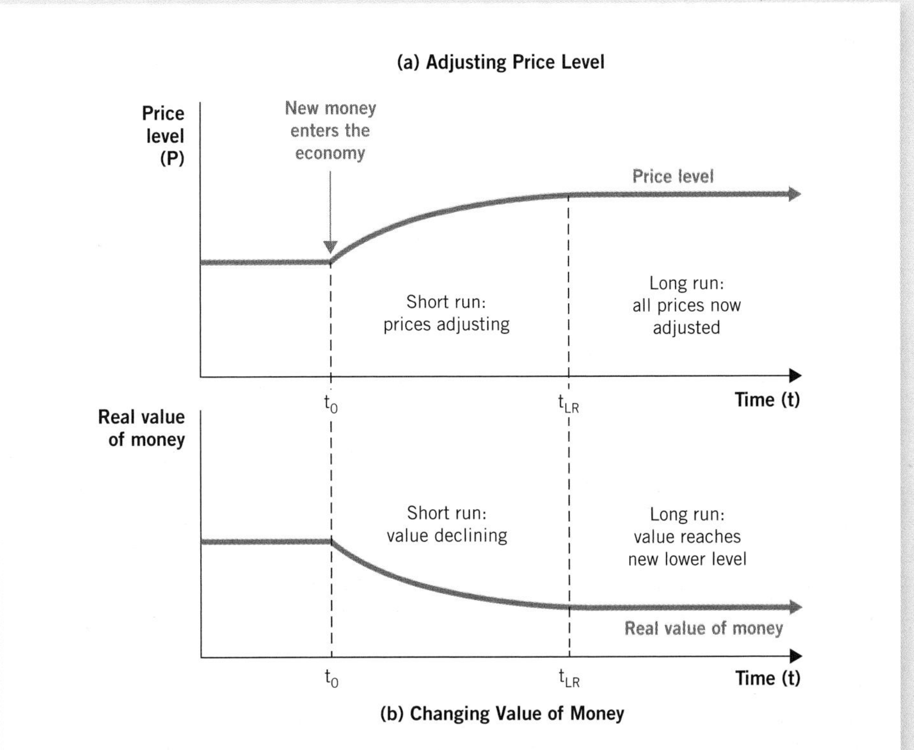

FIGURE 16.5

The Real Value of Money as Prices Adjust

(a) If the central bank increases the money supply at time t_0, the price level begins rising in the short run. In the long run, all prices adjust and the price level reaches its new higher level. (b) As the price level increases, the real value of money declines throughout the short run. In the long run, at t_{LR} the real value of money reaches a new lower level.

Unexpected Inflation Hurts Some People

Let's now consider how expansionary monetary policy affects different people across the economy. The basic macroeconomic results, summarized in Figure 16.4, seem very positive: real GDP goes up and the unemployment rate falls, even if there is some inflation. Consider the case in which you're living in an economy where these conditions exist. Everywhere you look, the news seems positive as the media, politicians, and firms focus on the expanding economy. But the expanding economy doesn't help everyone.

For example, consider workers who signed a two-year wage contract just before the inflation hit the economy. These workers now pay more for goods and services such as groceries, gasoline, education, and health care—yet their wages were set before the inflation occurred. Their incomes don't buy as many things as they did before; so in real terms, these workers have taken a pay cut.

In addition to workers, lenders (the suppliers of funds used for business expansion) are harmed when inflation is greater than anticipated. Imagine that you're a banker who extends a loan with an interest rate of 3%, but then the inflation rate turns out to be 5%. The Fisher equation, discussed in Chapter 14, implies that the loan's real interest rate is actually –2%. A negative interest rate means the money that is being repaid has less purchasing power than when it was lent. This is a losing proposition for the lender.

In sum: unexpected inflation, while potentially helpful to the overall economy, is also harmful to those whose prices take time to adjust, whether those prices are wages or interest rates.

Contractionary Monetary Policy

We have seen how the central bank—the Fed—uses expansionary monetary policy to stimulate the economy. However, sometimes policymakers want to slow down the economy. A central bank often undertakes contractionary monetary policy when the economy is expanding rapidly and the downsides of inflation begin to outweigh the upsides.

To trace the effects of contractionary policy, we once again begin in the loanable funds market. The central bank reduces the money supply via open market operations: it sells bonds in the loanable funds market. Selling the bonds takes funds out of the loanable funds market because the local commercial banks buy the bonds from the central bank (the Fed) with money they might otherwise lend out. The loanable funds market pictured in panel (a) of Figure 16.6 shows this reduction in supply from S_1 to S_2. The interest rate rises, and equilibrium investment falls from \$200 billion to \$190 billion.

Lower investment reduces GDP. Because there is less output, firms need fewer workers. The lower money supply also leads to downward pressure on the price level (P), but input prices don't change quickly, meaning that firms cannot adjust their workers' wages or the terms of their loans in the short run. Therefore, firms reduce output and lay off some workers.

This result is illustrated in panel (b) of Figure 16.6. Initially, the market is in equilibrium at point A. The decline in investment leads to a drop in

FIGURE 16.6

Contractionary Monetary Policy in the Short Run

(a) The central bank sells bonds, which pulls funds out of the loanable funds market. This action decreases the supply of loanable funds (S_1 shifts to S_2) and increases the interest rate from 5% to 6%. The higher interest rate leads to a decrease in investment from \$200 billion to \$190 billion, and this outcome decreases GDP. (b) The decrease in aggregate demand (from AD_1 to AD_2) as a result of lower investment causes real GDP to decline from \$17.5 trillion to \$17 trillion and increases unemployment in the short run. The general price level falls to 95 (a deflation).

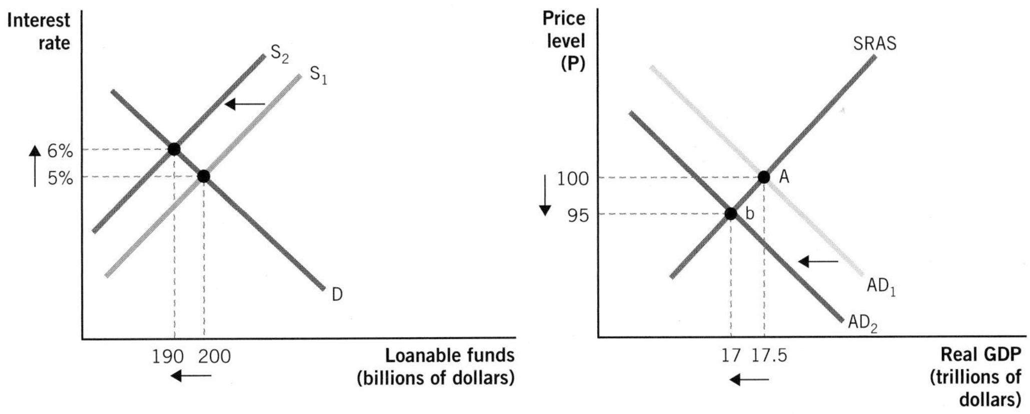

(a) The Loanable Funds Market

(b) Aggregate Demand and Aggregate Supply

Results summary	GDP	Unemployment	Price level (P)
Short run	↓	↑	↓

aggregate demand, shifting the curve leftward from AD_1 to AD_2. The new short-run equilibrium at point b reveals lower GDP (shown by a move from \$17.5 trillion to \$17 trillion on the real GDP axis), and consequently lower employment (not shown) because fewer workers are needed as output falls. The price level (P) also falls from 100 to 95, meaning there is deflation. These results are summarized in the table at the bottom of the figure.

ECONOMICS IN THE REAL WORLD

Monetary Policy's Contribution to the Great Depression

As if monetary policy isn't hard enough to implement and control, consider that the money supply is not completely controlled by a central bank. In Chapter 15, we explained how the actions of private individuals and banks can increase or decrease the money supply via the money multiplier. Banks increase the money supply when they lend out reserves, and they decrease

What happens when all these people want to withdraw their funds?

the money supply when they hold more reserves. In addition, individuals increase the money supply when they deposit funds into bank accounts and the banks multiply that money by making loans. When individuals withdraw their funds and hold on to more currency, they decrease the money supply because banks cannot multiply those funds.

Now imagine a scenario with massive bank failures. As more and more banks fail, people withdraw their funds all over the country. While it makes sense that individuals would want to withdraw their money, as people nationwide continue to remove money from banks, the supply of loanable funds declines significantly. These bank runs reduce lending and banks' ability to increase the money supply. The result is an economic contraction.

This type of monetary contraction is exactly what happened at the beginning of the Great Depression. From 1929 to 1933, over 9,000 banks failed in the United States. Because of these bank failures, people began holding their money outside the banking system. This action contributed to a significant contraction in the money supply. Figure 16.7 shows the money supply prior to and during the Great Depression. After peaking at $676 billion in 1931, the M2 money supply fell to just $564 billion in 1933. This drastic decline was one of the major causes of the Great Depression. Economists today agree that the Federal Reserve should have done more to offset the decline in the money supply at the onset of the Great Depression. This was perhaps one of the biggest policy errors in U.S. macroeconomic history. Former Fed chairman Ben Bernanke gained his reputation in part for his active monetary policy during the Great Recession of 2007–2009. He based the Fed's reaction to the economic slowdown on his study of the Fed's failures during the Great Depression. ✷

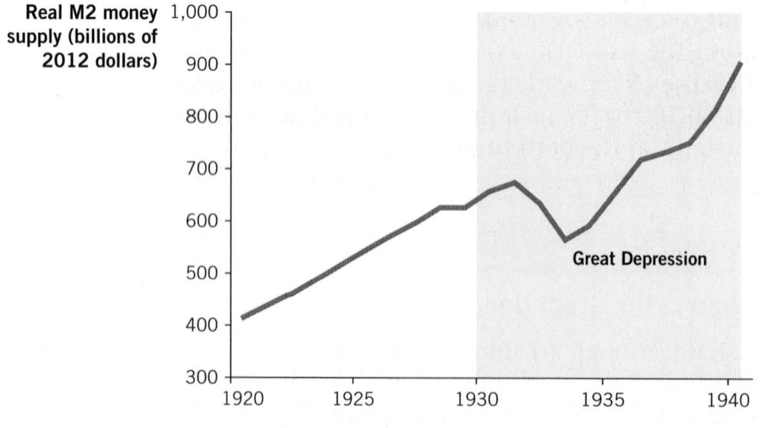

FIGURE 16.7

U.S. Money Supply before and during the Great Depression

The M2 money supply grew to $676 billion in 1931, but then it plummeted to $564 billion by 1933. The huge decline in the money supply was a major contributor to the Great Depression. (Values for real money supply are expressed in 2012 dollars.)

Source: Historical Statistics of the United States, Colonial Times to 1970.

PRACTICE WHAT YOU KNOW

Expansionary versus Contractionary Monetary Policy: Monetary Policy in the Short Run

The Federal Open Market Committee is the group that determines monetary policy.

Question: How does expansionary monetary policy affect real GDP, unemployment, and the price level in the economy?

Answer: Real GDP increases, the unemployment rate falls, and the price level rises.

Question: How does contractionary monetary policy affect real GDP, unemployment, and the price level in the economy?

Answer: Real GDP decreases, the unemployment rate rises, and the price level falls.

Question: What real-world circumstance might lead to contractionary monetary policy?

Answer: If the Federal Reserve thought that inflation was an imminent danger, it might implement contractionary monetary policy.

Why Doesn't Monetary Policy Always Work?

So far in this chapter, we have seen that monetary policy can have significant effects on the macroeconomy. Monetary policy can affect real GDP and unemployment. But recall our correction to the chapter-opening misconception: central banks *cannot* always steer an economy out of a recession. Monetary policy is limited in what it can do. In this section, we consider three limitations of monetary policy. First, we look at the diminished effects of monetary policy in the long run. Next we consider how expectations can dampen the effects of monetary policy. Finally, we see that sometimes people don't respond in a way that facilitates the Fed's policies.

Long-Run Adjustments

We have noted that some prices take longer to adjust than others. The long run is a period long enough for *all* prices to adjust, including wages and interest rates. Output prices can adjust relatively quickly. Think about the output prices at a coffee shop, which are often displayed on a chalkboard behind the cash register; they're easy to change in the short run. In contrast, input prices, such as workers' wages, are very slow to adjust. After all, these wages are often set by lengthy contracts that will be in force for several years. Eventually, though, these contracts expire. At that time, those wages will adjust to any inflation caused by monetary policy.

Both types of prices, output and input, affect the decisions made by firms across the economy, and therefore they affect output and unemployment. For example, consider your hypothetical small business producing and selling college apparel. Earlier in this chapter, you secured a loan to open a new retail location because the Fed increased the money supply, which expanded the supply of funds in the loanable funds market. When you initially received your loan, the costs for resources such as workers, equipment, inventory, and a physical plant were relatively low because prices for these inputs had not yet adjusted to the increase in the money supply. But in the long run, these resource prices will adjust. If everything works out well for you, the monetary expansion will lead to new demand for your product and you'll be able to keep your new store open. But it's also possible that after the prices of resources rise you may not be doing well enough to afford those resources. At that point, with your costs rising, you may have to reduce your output, lay off some workers, or perhaps even close your new store. In the long run, as prices adjust throughout the macroeconomy, the stimulating effects of expansionary monetary policy wear off.

One important implication of these long-run results is a lack of real economic effects from monetary policy; in the long run, all prices adjust. Therefore, in the long run, monetary policy does not affect real GDP or unemployment, which return to the levels they were prior to the change in monetary policy. The only predictable result of more money in the economy over the long run is inflation. Printing more money doesn't affect the economy's long-run productivity or its ability to produce; these outcomes are determined instead by resources, technology, and institutions.

Monetary neutrality is the idea that the money supply does not affect real economic variables like real GDP or employment.

The idea that the money supply does not affect real economic variables like real GDP or employment is known as **monetary neutrality**. Given that money is neutral in the long run, you might question the value of short-run monetary policy. In fact, many of the substantive debates in macroeconomics focus on the relative importance of the short run versus the long run. These debates are reminiscent of two topics we discussed earlier. First, an increase in the money supply causes inflation. Second, the role of monetary policy is one of the major differences between the classical and Keynesian schools of thought (see the Chapter 10 appendix). Keynesians believe it is best to focus on short-run effects, which are very real. After all, during recessions many people lose their jobs, which can be a very painful experience. When the money supply is expanded, firms can get loans at lower rates and then hire more workers. From the Keynesian perspective, central banks ought to take a very active role in the macroeconomy: increase the money supply during economic downturns, and contract the money supply during economic expansions, because monetary policy can potentially smooth out the business cycle.

Economists from the classical school discount the short-run expansionary effects of monetary policy and, instead, focus on the problems of inflation. In Chapter 11, we explored the negative effects of inflation. These include uncertainty about future price levels, wealth redistribution, and a devaluing of savings. These byproducts of inflation can stifle economic growth.

Both schools of thought have an important point to make. The immediate impact of policy is of great importance to people, especially if expansionary monetary policy might help the unemployed find a job. However, there is no such thing as a policy without some consequences. Over time, inflation will happen when expansionary monetary policy is used.

Adjustments in Expectations

Unexpected inflation harms workers and other resource suppliers who have fixed prices in the short run. Therefore, to avoid this fate, workers have an incentive to expect a certain level of inflation and to negotiate their contracts accordingly. For instance, many contracts have cost of living adjustment (COLA) clauses that force the employer to increase wages by the same percentage as inflation. The key incentive for anticipating the correct rate of inflation is straightforward: people are harmed when inflation is a surprise. But when inflation is expected, the real effects on the economy are limited.

Monetary policy has real effects only when some prices don't react immediately. But if inflation is expected, prices aren't sticky; they adjust because people plan on the inflation. To the extent that price increases are expected, the effect of monetary policy will be limited, even in the short run, because people have prepared for the price change.

Uncooperative People

In discussing the ways that the Fed conducts monetary policy, we mentioned that individuals have a role to play. Since money is created when loans are made, individuals need to borrow money if the Fed wants to expand the money supply. Similarly, banks need to be willing to make more loans. The Fed provides incentives to change household and bank behavior, but that doesn't mean that people and banks will do what the Fed wants them to do. The unexpectedly tepid response to monetary policy was one of the reasons the recovery from the Great Recession was so slow. Households were reluctant to borrow as unemployment rates remained high. Even those who had jobs were hesitant to incur more debt due to worry over maintaining their employment. Tighter lending restrictions as a result of new legislation meant that banks had their hands tied somewhat regarding how much lending they could do. Since fewer loans were being made, the Fed's efforts to expand the money supply didn't have the impact it had hoped for.

ECONOMICS IN THE REAL WORLD

Federal Reserve Press Conferences

On April 27, 2011, Ben Bernanke held the first press conference by a Fed chairman specifically to talk about the actions of the Fed's policymaking committee. This press conference was an unprecedented leap toward transparency. In the past, the Fed had always released carefully worded official statements that often used cryptic language to describe the Fed's outlook for the future.

Former Fed Chairman Bernanke's willingness to hold a news conference reflected his belief that central bankers should be more transparent.

In the spring of 2011, the economy was struggling to emerge from the 2008 recession; unemployment was still over 9%. In the midst of these problems, the Fed decided to lay all its cards on the table. Many observers saw this move as risky. Jacob Goldstein, writing for NPR's *Planet Money* the day before the press conference, explained why the press conference was so important:

> Because everything the head of the Federal Reserve says is a big deal. One off-hand comment can send global markets soaring or plunging. And because Fed chairmen, as a general rule, don't give press conferences. They release official statements that are very, very carefully worded. And they appear before Congress. Since the financial crisis, though, the Fed has come under increased scrutiny. The carefully worded statements and congressional appearances weren't carrying the day. So the leaders of the Fed have decided to send the chairman out for press conferences every few months ("to further enhance the clarity and timeliness of the Federal Reserve's monetary policy communication," in Fedspeak).

Bernanke's moves toward greater Fed openness reflected his belief that central bankers ought to be transparent. ✳

PRACTICE WHAT YOU KNOW

Monetary Policy Isn't Always Effective: Why Couldn't Monetary Policy Pull Us Out of the Great Recession?

The Great Recession officially lasted from December 2007 to June 2009. But the effects lingered on for several years thereafter, with slow growth of real GDP and high unemployment rates. These effects all occurred despite several

(CONTINUED)

(CONTINUED)

doses of expansionary monetary policy. Not only did the Fed push short-term interest rates to nearly 0%, but it also engaged in several rounds of quantitative easing, in which it purchased hundreds of billions of dollars' worth of long-term bonds.

Question: What are three possible reasons why monetary policy was not able to restore expansionary growth during and after the Great Recession?

Answer:

1. *Monetary policy is ineffective in the long run.* While we don't know the exact length of the short run, prices certainly had time to adjust by 2010 or 2011, yet the economy was still sluggish. Thus, one possibility is that prices adjusted, so the effects of monetary policy wore off. This answer alone is probably inadequate, given that the effects of monetary policy weren't evident even in the short run.
2. *Monetary policy was expected.* It seems unlikely that monetary policy is much of a surprise nowadays. The Federal Reserve releases official statements after each monetary policy meeting and generally announces the direction it will follow for the next several months.
3. *People didn't respond as the Fed had hoped.* Households didn't want to borrow, and banks were legally restricted in whom they could lend to. Without the cooperation of individuals and banks, the money supply didn't increase to the extent the Fed wanted, thus limiting the impact of monetary policy.

Conclusion

We started this chapter with the misconception that central banks can always steer economies out of recession. If this were true, the U.S. economy certainly would not have experienced the sustained downturn that began at the end of 2007. So what can a central bank do? In the short run, if monetary policy is a surprise, a central bank can stimulate the economy and perhaps lessen the effects of recession. But these results are mitigated when people anticipate monetary policy actions.

In the next chapter, we turn to another kind of policy with macroeconomic implications. In most countries, the legislative body and the chief executive (the Congress and the president, in the United States) have the authority to tax citizens and spend the proceeds. Taxes affect consumption and business spending, and government spending itself is part of GDP. This taxing and spending activity is called fiscal policy, and it is a tool used by the government to try to manage the economy.

ECONOMICS FOR LIFE

How to Protect Yourself from Inflation

In this chapter, we've talked about how inflation harms some people. We've also talked about how inflation doesn't harm people if they know it's coming—if it's expected.

If you're worried about inflation harming you, it's possible to protect yourself from its effects. In recent history, U.S. inflation has been low and steady. When this is the case, inflation doesn't really harm anyone because it's easy to predict. But if you live in a country such as Argentina, where inflation has often been a problem because it has been high and unpredictable, or if you're worried about future inflation in the United States, these tips are for you.

Two types of people often harmed by inflation are workers with fixed wages and savers who receive fixed interest rates. Let's look at how to avoid inflation trouble in both instances.

First, let's say you're a worker who is worried about inflation. One way to protect yourself is to avoid committing to long-term wage deals. If you must sign a contract, keep it short in duration. Better yet, include a clause in your contract that stipulates cost of living adjustments (COLAs) that are tied to a price index like the CPI (the Consumer Price Index; see Chapter 11). This way, your wages are hedged against future inflation.

Second, perhaps you're more worried about inflation's effect on your savings or retirement funds. One way to avoid negative returns is to purchase securities or assets that tend to rise in value along with inflation. Stock prices generally go up with inflation, so you may want to invest more of your retirement funds in stocks, rather than bonds. Gold is another asset that tends to appreciate in inflationary times because its value is tied to something real.

However, stocks can be risky, and the long-term returns on gold are historically very low. Thus, you might consider buying Treasury Inflation Protected Securities (TIPS). These are low-risk U.S. government bonds that are indexed to inflation rates. Therefore, if inflation goes up, you get a higher rate of return. These bonds guarantee a particular real rate of return, no matter what the rate of inflation.

Gold is not a great long-term investment unless you really fear inflation.

ANSWERING THE BIG QUESTIONS

What are the tools of monetary policy?

- The Fed has three tools to adjust the money supply: open market operations, the discount rate, and the reserve ratio. Of these tools, the only one used with regularity is open market operations.
- An extreme version of open market operations is quantitative easing, or QE, which involves buying securities in specifically targeted markets.

What is the effect of monetary policy in the short run?

- Expansionary monetary policy can stimulate the economy in the short run, increasing real GDP and reducing the unemployment rate, despite the risk of higher inflation.
- Contractionary monetary policy can slow the economy in the short run, which may help to reduce inflation. The trade-off is lower output and higher unemployment.

Why doesn't monetary policy always work?

- Monetary policy fails to produce real effects under three different circumstances. First, monetary policy has no real effect in the long run, since all prices can adjust. Second, if monetary policy is fully anticipated, prices adjust (and monetary policy works only when some prices are slow to adjust). Finally, the behavior of individuals and banks may not be in sync with the Fed's goals.

CONCEPTS YOU SHOULD KNOW

bond (p. 472)
contractionary monetary policy (p. 477)
discount rate (p. 475)
expansionary monetary policy (p. 477)
monetary neutrality (p. 486)
monetary policy (p. 472)
open market operations (p. 472)
quantitative easing (p. 474)
reserve requirement (p. 475)

QUESTIONS FOR REVIEW

1. How does the Fed increase and decrease the money supply through open market operations?
2. Define quantitative easing. How is it different from standard open market operations?
3. Why is it possible to change real economic factors in the short run simply by printing and distributing more money?
4. Many people focus on the effect of monetary policy on interest rates in the economy. Use the loanable funds market to explain how unexpected contractionary monetary policy affects interest rates in the short run. Also explain the changes in real GDP, the unemployment rate, and the price level.
5. During the economic slowdown that began at the end of 2007, the Federal Reserve used monetary policy to reduce interest rates in the economy. Use what you learned in this chapter to explain why the monetary policy failed to restore the economy to long-run equilibrium.
6. Explain why a stable 5% inflation rate can be preferable to one that averages 4% but varies between 1% and 7% regularly.
7. Who is harmed when inflation is less than anticipated? In what way are they harmed? Who is harmed when inflation is greater than anticipated? In what way are they harmed?

STUDY PROBLEMS (*✱solved at the end of the section*)

1. Determine whether each of the following is considered standard open market operations or quantitative easing:
   a. The Fed buys $100 billion in student-loan-backed securities.
   b. The Fed sells $400 billion in short-term government bonds.
   c. The Fed buys $500 billion in 30-year (long-term) government bonds.

✱ 2. Suppose the Fed buys $1 million in government bonds from a commercial bank. What effect will this action have on the bank's reserves and the money supply? Specifically, by how much will the money supply change? Use a required reserve ratio of 10%, and assume that banks hold no excess reserves and that all currency is deposited into the banking system.

3. Using the model of the loanable funds market, illustrate the change in the interest rate and the change to the amount of investment demand when the Fed decides to buy bonds. How do these effects change if the Fed *sells* bonds?

✱ 4. Suppose the economy is in long-run equilibrium, with real GDP at $17.5 trillion and the unemployment rate at 5%. Now assume that the central bank unexpectedly *decreases* the money supply by 6%. Illustrate the short-run effects on the macroeconomy, using the aggregate supply–aggregate demand model. Be sure to indicate the direction of change in the price level, real GDP, and the unemployment rate.

5. Suppose the economy is in long-run equilibrium, with real GDP at $17.5 trillion and the unemployment rate at 5%. Now assume that the central bank *increases* the money supply by 6%. Illustrate the short-run effects on the macroeconomy using the aggregate supply–aggregate demand model. Be sure to indicate the direction of change in the price level, real GDP, and the unemployment rate.

SOLVED PROBLEMS

2. The immediate result will be that the commercial bank will have \$1 million in excess reserves, since its deposits didn't change. The commercial bank will loan out these excess reserves, and the money-multiplier process begins, leading to a higher money supply. Under the assumptions of this question, the simple money multiplier applies. The money multiplier is $1/rr = 1/0.10 = 10$. Therefore, in the end, \$10 million in additional deposits could be created.

4. Selling bonds is contractionary monetary policy, so the money supply will decrease. As a result, the aggregate demand curve will shift to the left (from AD_1 to AD_2). The result is a decrease in the price level from P_1 to P_2. Real GDP falls from \$16 trillion to GDP_2. Although it isn't shown in the graph, unemployment rises from 5% to a higher rate because with less production more people are out of work.

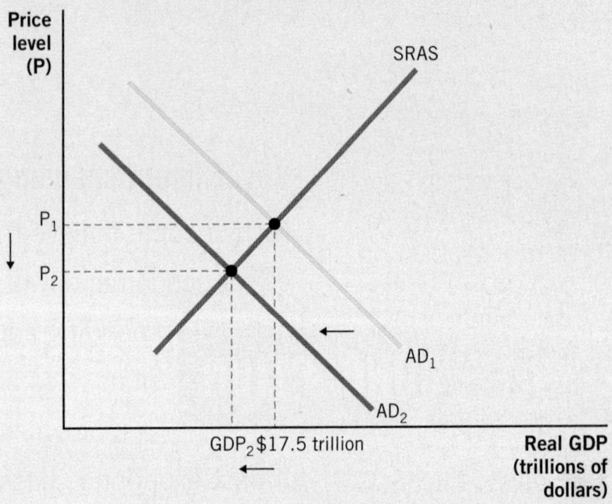

CHAPTER 17

Fiscal Policy and Budget Deficits

MISCONCEPTION

Government spending is a simple tool for fighting recessions.

Many people believe that the government can quickly and predictably offset economic downturns. The belief that the government can increase spending and decrease taxes in order to safely evade recessions is common in the media, among many politicians, and in many historical accounts of past economic troubles. But if past experience has taught us anything, it is that government actions have uneven and unpredictable effects on the economy. While it's true that the government may be able to influence the macroeconomy, it's also true that many of the government's spending initiatives have failed to quickly revive an ailing economy.

In this chapter, we examine the case for fiscal policy, which includes both government spending and taxes. We begin by explaining what fiscal policy is. We then examine expansionary and contractionary fiscal policies. Finally, we look at the consequences and shortcomings of fiscal policy—in particular, the impact of such policies on overall government debt.

The American Recovery and Reinvestment Act, which entailed almost $1 trillion in expansionary fiscal policy, was passed to help the economy recover from the Great Recession.

BIG QUESTIONS

- What is fiscal policy?
- How does the government tax?
- How does the government spend?
- How do budget deficits differ from debt?
- What are the shortcomings of fiscal policy?

What Is Fiscal Policy?

Fiscal policy is the use of government spending and taxes to influence the economy.

When the economy falters, people often look to the government to help reestablish forward momentum. In fact, the government uses many different tools to try to affect the economy. The idea that government should be involved in stimulating the economy was part of the Keynesian revolution we discussed in the Chapter 10 appendix. As we saw in Chapter 16, monetary policy is the use of the money supply by the central bank to influence the economy, but the central bank isn't elected. **Fiscal policy** is the set of tools available to elected officials. It involves the use of government spending and taxes to influence the economy. In the United States, tax and spending changes are implemented through the legislative process, meaning that Congress and the president must work together to pass policy.

While the government can raise money by charging fees for services (for example, admission to national parks), taxes are the government's primary source of income. We address the revenue side of fiscal policy first; but to understand the full implications of fiscal policy, we need to cover both sides of the equation: taxing and spending.

How Does the Government Tax?

People want the goods and services that governments provide. However, when it comes to paying for these things, there is surprising reluctance. The citizens of two countries in Europe are particularly famous for their efforts to avoid paying taxes. In Greece, tax cheats owe the government $266 billion—an amount larger than the entire value of the Greek economy. In Italy, the amount is a robust $388 billion in unpaid taxes. In the United States, unpaid taxes are estimated at $450 billion. Worldwide, the estimate is that over $24 trillion in assets are hiding in tax-sheltered locations.

People the world over seem to have at least one thing in common: they don't like paying taxes. But taxes are the main source of government revenue. Without taxes, the government couldn't provide police or fire departments, national defense, schools, fair courts, Social Security payments, or anything else. In short, taxes provide the money that governments need to provide

services. So how do we strike a balance between too much taxation and too little? To begin, let's take a look at how governments tax.

The government imposes **taxes** to raise money. These revenues fund government operations and enable the government to provide social services. A tax takes money from citizens, companies, and organizations. In the United States, over 9,600 different governmental bodies can collect, or *levy*, taxes. This list of taxing authorities includes not only federal and state governments but also cities, counties, townships, and school districts. You probably pay sales taxes on items that you buy, income taxes on the money that you earn, and property tax on the land, home, and in some cases the car that you own. To understand these taxes a little better, we first have to understand the basis on which taxes are levied.

Governments use **taxes** to raise the money that funds government operations and provides social services.

Who Is Taxed?

One way to understand taxes involves understanding who is taxed. Governments typically decide whom to tax by implementing one of two principles. The first is the **benefits principle**, and it means that the tax is directed toward those who most benefit from the taxed product or activity. An example is the gasoline tax: only individuals who own a car and use roads are taxed through their purchase of gasoline. The federal government taxes gas to help pay for the maintenance and construction of the interstate highway system, and states add an additional tax to help pay for the upkeep of state roads. The federal gasoline tax is 18.4 cents per gallon. State tax rates vary widely, from a low of 14.5 cents per gallon in Alaska to a high of 50.5 cents per gallon in New York.

When taxes are based on the **benefits principle**, taxes are levied on those who most benefit from the taxed product or activity.

The second approach to taxation uses the **ability to pay principle**, which implies that the more money you make, the more taxes you are able to pay. The ability to pay principle manifests itself most clearly in the income tax. With the income tax, not everyone pays the same rate.

When taxes are based on the **ability to pay principle**, those who make more money pay more money in taxes.

A History of the Income Tax

Though taxes may seem like a fact of life now, the U.S. income tax is only about 100 years old. Prior to 1913, there was no income tax in the United States; most tax revenues were generated by taxes on imports. But import taxes were set to decline in the early 1910s, so the government looked to income taxes as another source of revenue.

First, however, a significant obstacle had to be overcome. According to the U.S. Constitution, the federal government did not have the power to tax income. To give itself this power, the federal government presented the Sixteenth Amendment to the Constitution to the states. Congress passed this amendment in 1909 and ratified it in 1913. One of the shorter amendments to the Constitution, it says:

> The Congress shall have power to lay and collect taxes on incomes, from whatever source derived, without apportionment among the several States, and without regard to any census or enumeration.

This means that the Congress can collect income taxes from your wages and other sources of income such as the sale of stocks, bonds, or other financial gains. The levying of the income tax is to occur equitably across the states regardless of the population of any state.

The Income Tax: A Progressive Tax

With a **progressive tax**, the more you earn, the higher your average tax rate.

The **average tax rate** is how much you pay in taxes divided by your income.

The income tax is a **progressive tax**. This means that the more you earn, the higher your average tax rate will be. The **average tax rate** is how much you pay in taxes divided by your income.

The U.S. federal income tax system is based on brackets, or groupings. As you make more money, you might move into a higher tax bracket, which means your tax bill will rise. Each year, the brackets change a little to account for changes in the economy. Table 17.1 shows the tax brackets for 2015. If you made $50,000 in 2015, you would be in the 25% bracket. But this doesn't mean that you pay 25% on all of your income. Rather, your income is taxed in increments. Let's look at an example to illustrate this point.

Upon graduation, you take a job with the Walt Disney Corporation that pays you a salary of $40,000 a year. Assuming that you're single, this salary would put you in the 25% tax bracket. Since 25% of $40,000 is $10,000, you might think that you'll owe $10,000 in taxes, leaving you with $30,000 in *disposable income* (the amount of spendable money left over after paying taxes). But that isn't correct. If it were, you would be better off making $37,450 and falling in the 15% bracket. Your tax burden there would only be $5,617.50, and you would have $31,832.50 in disposable income.

Because the income tax is progressive, you pay the higher rates only on the additional, or marginal, income. Your $40,000 salary is taxed in steps. The first $9,225 is taxed at 10%. The next $28,225 (the difference between the top and bottom of the 15% bracket) is taxed at 15%. Only the remaining $2,550 that takes you up to $40,000 is taxed at 25%. Your federal tax bill is thus $5,793.75, leaving you with disposable income of $34,206.25. This calculation is displayed in column 1 of Table 17.2.

Because tax rates are different for different amounts of income, you need to calculate the average tax rate to see what your overall tax burden is. In this example, your average tax rate is the $5,793.75 divided by your income of $40,000, which is 14.5%. Yes, you're in the 25% tax bracket; but since so

TABLE 17.1

2015 U.S. Federal Tax Rates

Taxable Income	Tax rate*
$0–$9,225	10%
$9,225–$37,450	15%
$37,450–$90,750	25%
$90,750–$189,300	28%
$189,300–$411,500	33%
$411,500–$413,200	35%
Over $413,200	39.6%

*These tax rates are marginal tax rates for those who are unmarried. A marginal rate means that each rate applies only to dollars within the specified income ranges. For example, all income earned between $37,450 and $90,750 is taxed at 25%; but if someone earns $90,751, that last dollar is taxed at the 28% rate.

Source: Internal Revenue Service.

TABLE 17.2

Computing Taxes Owed and Average Tax Rates

Tax Bracket	(1) Salary = $40,000	(2) Salary = $50,000	(3) Salary = $100,000
10%	$9,225 × .10 = $922.50	$9,225 × .10 = $922.50	$9,225 × .10 = $922.50
15%	$28,225 × .15 = $4,233.75	$28,225 × .15 = $4,233.75	$28,225 × .15 = $4,233.75
25%	$2,550 × .25 = $637.50	$12,550 × .25 = $3,137.50	$53,300 × .25 = $13,325.00
28%	—	—	$9,250 × .28 = $2,590
Total Tax	$5,793.75	$8,293.75	$21,071.25
Avg. Tax Rate	14.5%	16.6%	21.1%
Disposable Income	$34,206.25	$41,706.25	$78,928.75

much of your income is taxed in the lower brackets, your average tax rate is much lower than 25%. If you get a raise to $50,000, your average tax rate rises to 16.6% even though you're still in the 25% tax bracket. (See column 2 in Table 17.2.) This is simply the ability to pay principle at work. As you make more, your tax burden rises. Column 3 of Table 17.2 shows what happens when you get a big raise to $100,000 and a move into the next tax bracket.

ECONOMICS IN THE REAL WORLD

Tax Dodging at the Mall

Shop at the Grove City Outlet Mall, and pay less in taxes.

Drive through a parking lot at the Grove City Premium Outlet mall, a large outlet mall in western Pennsylvania, and you'll see many out-of-state license plates. You'll also see many from Canada. The mall is huge, with over 130 stores. There are hotels and restaurants for those who want to spend multiple days wandering the shops, and the mall's web site offers information for tour groups and those wanting to find other area attractions, presumably to break up the shopping day. The biggest draw for the mall is its location. Situated immediately off an interstate highway, the mall is less than three hours south of Canada and an easy drive from Ohio, New York, and West Virginia. The selection of merchandise, the outlet prices, and the lack of sales tax on clothing are enormous draws. In fact, shoppers are frequently reminded of the fact that there is no sales tax on clothing purchases in Pennsylvania.

These low tax rates are a marketing tool for the mall. In the Canadian province of Ontario, the closest to the Grove City Mall, sales tax rates on clothing are 13%. Even after considering the cost of travel, many shoppers find that it makes sense to spend an enjoyable weekend of shopping in Grove City, Pennsylvania, just to save the taxes they would have paid in Canada. ✳

Social Security: A Regressive Tax

With a **regressive tax**, the more you earn, the lower your average tax rate.

The **marginal tax rate** is paid on the individual's next dollar of income.

A **regressive tax** is one in which your average tax rate falls as you earn more. This means that those with larger incomes actually pay less of their income in taxes. The Social Security tax, which is deducted directly from your paycheck, is regressive. This tax is used to pay for the Social Security retirement system. The tax rate is 12.4%, but it is split between you and your employer, with each of you paying 6.2%. The rate is proportional up to a point (that is, everyone pays the same rate up to that point), but beyond that point the tax becomes regressive. After $118,500 (in 2015), the **marginal tax rate** is zero. This means that for every additional dollar you earn above $118,500, you pay no additional Social Security tax.

If you make $40,000 a year, you'll have $2,480 taken out of your pay annually for Social Security taxes. Your average tax rate is thus 6.2%. If you earn $100,000, you'll have $6,200 taken for Social Security taxes—once again, a 6.2% average tax rate. If you earn $118,500, you'll have $7,347 taken out of your pay—still a 6.2% average tax rate. If you make $125,000, you'll have only $7,347 taken out of your pay because you've exceeded the $118,500 limit for Social Security taxes. This means that your average tax rate is 5.9%. If you make $1 million, you still pay only $7,347 in Social Security tax, bringing your average tax rate to 0.73%. In short, the Social Security tax is regressive. As you make more, your average tax rate drops.

Figure 17.1 shows the sources of tax revenue for the U.S. government in 2013. The two largest sources are individual income taxes and social insurance (Social Security and Medicare) taxes. Together, these two categories accounted for 81.6% of all federal tax revenue in the United States in 2013. Because both of these taxes are deducted from workers' paychecks, they're often called payroll taxes. The other major types of taxes produced just 18.4% of the federal revenue. The largest of these is the corporate income tax, which

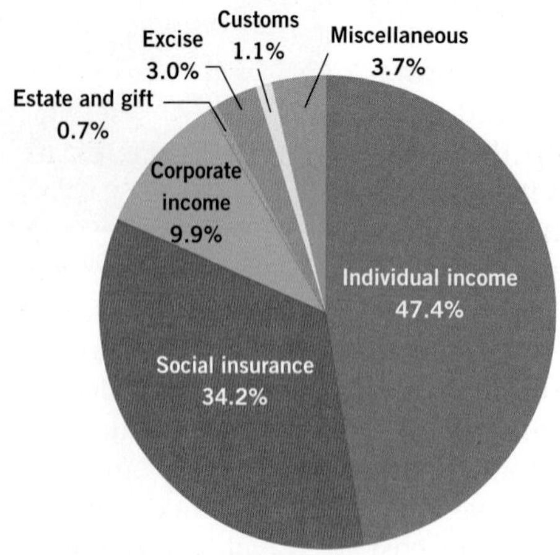

FIGURE 17.1

U.S. Federal Tax Revenue Sources, 2013

The major sources of tax revenue for the U.S. government begin with the two payroll taxes: individual income taxes and social insurance (Social Security and Medicare) taxes. Together, these two categories accounted for 81.6% of all tax revenue in 2013. Total tax revenue in 2013 was nearly $2.8 trillion.

Source: Office of Management and Budget, Historical Budget Data.

PRACTICE WHAT YOU KNOW

Government Revenue: Federal Taxes

Figuring out your income tax bill involves some basic math.

Assume that your taxable income is $150,000. Use the 2015 marginal tax rates from Table 17.1 to determine your taxes.

Question: How would you compute your federal income tax?

Answer: Looking at Table 17.1, keep in mind that the different rates apply only to the income in the specified brackets. For example, the first tax rate of 10% applies only to income up to $9,225. Income between $9,225 and $37,450 is taxed at 15%. Use this pattern to determine the tax paid on all income up to $150,000. Multiply these rates by the income in the respective brackets, and sum these to get the total income tax:

0.10 × $9,225	=	$907.50
+ 0.15 × ($37,450 − $9,225)	=	$4,223.75
+ 0.25 × ($90,750 − $37,450)	=	$13,325.00
+ 0.28 × ($150,000 − $90,750)	=	$16,590.00
Total	=	**$35,071.25**

Question: How would you compute your Social Security tax? (The relevant tax rate is 6.2%.)

Answer: Remember, Social Security tax is paid only on the first $118,500 in income. Thus, you compute your tax as:

$$\$118{,}500 \times 0.062 = \$7{,}347.00$$

yielded $273.5 billion in 2013, or nearly 10% of the total revenue. Estate and gift taxes are levied when property is gifted to others, particularly as an inheritance. **Excise taxes** are taxes on a particular good or service, such as cigarettes or gasoline. The federal excise tax on cigarettes is $1.01 per pack, and as mentioned earlier, the tax on gasoline is 18.4 cents per gallon. Excise taxes yielded $84 billion in tax revenue in 2013. Customs taxes are taxes on imports, and these yielded $31.8 billion in 2013.

An **excise tax** is a tax on a particular good or service.

State and Local Taxes

Some of the most common taxes that people pay are levied by the state or locality in which they live. For instance, most states have a sales tax. These taxes are paid at the time of purchase and are a percentage of the sales price.

However, not all states have sales taxes, and not all states levy them in the same way. Alaska, Delaware, Montana, New Hampshire, and Oregon have no state sales tax. Many states exempt essential items like food or clothing from sales tax, and some (among them Virginia, Illinois, and Utah) have a reduced sales tax rate for food. Other states (including Massachusetts, Minnesota, New Jersey, and Pennsylvania) have no sales tax on clothing.

Many states levy a state income tax. These rates vary widely among states. Some states have flat tax rates, under which everyone pays the same rate regardless of income level. This type of tax is called a **proportional tax.** Others have more progressive systems so that, like the federal income tax, people who earn more, pay more. In 2015, the state with the highest income tax rate was California. In addition to the federal income taxes, residents of California could pay up to an additional 12.3% in state income taxes. This means that if you live in California and are in the highest tax bracket, your combined state and federal income tax would consume 51.9% of your income! However, if you live in Florida, Nevada, South Dakota, Tennessee, Texas, Washington, or Wyoming, you would pay no state income tax at all.

With a **proportional tax**, everyone pays the same tax rate regardless of income level.

Property taxes are another type of tax. Many local governments and school boards use taxes on homes and land to fund school districts. Property taxes are based on the benefits principle. If you live in a particular area, it's assumed that you will benefit from local government services like police, water, and schools. Even if you have no children in school, it is presumed that an excellent school system will benefit you when you put your house on the market.

While every state has some form of property taxes on houses and land, some states extend this tax to vehicles and other forms of property as well. Arkansas, Ohio, South Carolina, Texas, and Virginia are some of the states that levy a car tax. This isn't a sales tax paid at the time of purchase. Rather, it is a separate annual tax on the value of your car.

Table 17.3 summarizes five major tax categories. These different taxes constitute a significant portion of government revenue.

TABLE 17.3

Types of Taxes

Tax	Who levies this tax?	Relationship to income
Income	Federal, state, and a few local governments	Income taxes are progressive in most cases. Some state income taxes are proportional.
Social Security	Federal government	Regressive
Sales/Excise	Federal, state, and local governments	Everyone pays the same rate regardless of income.
Property	State and local governments	The same percentage applies to all payers in a geographic area.
Corporate income	Federal and state governments	Progressive. Higher-earning firms pay higher rates.

ECONOMICS IN THE REAL WORLD

Why Average Is Better: Actor Wesley Snipes Goes to Jail for Not Paying Taxes

The Internal Revenue Service (IRS) prosecutes people who don't pay their taxes. However, finding those who skirt the tax laws can be difficult. For the average taxpayer, the chance of being audited—the process by which the IRS makes sure you were truthful on your taxes—is very low. In 2013, the IRS audited less than 1% of all tax returns filed. This means that for the average person, the chance of being caught cheating is minimal. If you're weighing the costs and benefits of telling a lie to the IRS, it's likely that you'll get away with it (unless you tell a whopper). However, if you aren't an average taxpayer, you should probably be as truthful as possible.

Due to the large number of returns being filed and the lack of resources to audit those returns, the IRS spends its time on bigger fish. For example, Gisele Bundchen, supermodel and wife of football player Tom Brady, was audited in 2012–2013. Because she essentially works for herself, it's more likely that she made a mistake in filing. Also, Ms. Bundchen makes tens of millions of dollars each year. Thus, a mistake on her tax return probably means more tax revenue for the government.

One of the most severely punished celebrity tax cheats in recent memory is actor Wesley Snipes. Mr. Snipes served a three-year sentence for tax evasion after a jury found him guilty of willfully neglecting to file a tax return in 1999, 2000, and 2001. It was estimated that he owed the IRS over $7 million. Snipes isn't the only famous person to run afoul of the IRS, however. Skier Lindsey Vonn was hit with a $1.7 million tax bill, which she promptly paid. The comedy duo Abbot and Costello went bankrupt when audited by the IRS. They owed so much in back taxes that they had to sell their homes and rights to many of their films to pay what they owed the federal government. Singer Willie Nelson owed the IRS over $6 million. He avoided jail time by raising the money over a three-year period. Ty Warner, the creator of Beanie Babies, was perhaps hit hardest of all. He had to serve 500 hours of community service and pay $53 million in fines along with $27 million in back taxes for hiding income in a Swiss bank account.

Many people get away with not paying their taxes. However, if you're caught, the penalties can be very high. The take-away: pay your taxes. ✳

What do Gisele Bundchen, Wesley Snipes, and Lindsey Vonn all have in common? They didn't pay their taxes.

How Does the Government Spend?

When you think of U.S. government spending, your mind probably jumps to goods and services like roads, bridges, military equipment, and government employees. This is the government-spending component (G) of gross domestic product. But as we examine the total government budget, we must also include transfer payments. **Transfer payments** are payments made to groups or individuals when no good or service is received in return. With a transfer payment, the government transfers funds from one group in society to another. These payments include income assistance (welfare) and Social

Transfer payments are payments made to groups or individuals when no good or service is received in return.

TABLE 17.4

2014 U.S. Government Outlays

Category	2014 outlays (billions of dollars)	Percentage of total	
Social Security	$852.3	23.4%	Mandatory outlays (61.8%)
Medicare	519.0	14.2%	
Income assistance	542.2	14.9%	
Other	339.3	9.3%	
Interest	223.4	6.1%	Interest payments (6.1%)
Defense/military	612.4	16.8%	Discretionary outlays (32.2%)
Non-defense/non-military discretionary	561.9	15.4%	
Total	**$3,650.5**		

Source: Office of Management and Budget.

Government outlays are the part of the government budget that includes both spending and transfer payments.

Mandatory outlays comprise government spending that is determined by ongoing long-term obligations.

Entitlement programs are mandatory benefits that some citizens who meet certain requirements are entitled to receive under current laws.

Discretionary outlays comprise spending that can be altered when the government is setting its annual budget.

Security payments to retired or disabled persons. When looking at government budgets, we include both spending and transfer payments in a broader category called government outlays. **Government outlays** are the part of the government budget that includes both spending and transfer payments.

Table 17.4 shows the major divisions in U.S. government outlays in 2014. The table divides the outlays into three groups: mandatory outlays, interest payments, and discretionary outlays. By far the largest portion of the federal budget is dedicated to **mandatory outlays**, which constitute government spending that's determined by ongoing programs like Social Security and Medicare. These programs are mandatory because existing laws oblige the government to provide funding for them. Mandatory outlays are not generally altered during the budget process; changing them requires changing existing laws, which takes a long time to accomplish. Sometimes, these programs are known as **entitlement programs**, since citizens who meet certain requirements are then entitled to benefits under current laws.

Discretionary outlays comprise government spending that can be altered when the government is setting its annual budget. Examples of discretionary spending include monies for bridges and roads, payments to government workers, and defense and military spending. When you think of government spending, you may think of these discretionary items. But total discretionary spending accounts for less than a third of the U.S. government budget.

Another important category in Table 17.4 is interest payments. These are payments made to current owners of U.S. government bonds—the IOUs issued when government borrows to pay for things it doesn't have enough tax revenue to pay for. As we discuss in detail in Chapter 19, borrowing to buy something makes that item more expensive because of the interest you have to pay. Similarly, when government borrows, it has to pay to use someone else's resources. If it fails to repay what it borrowed, its borrowing costs will go up in the future.

We distinguish between mandatory and discretionary spending because it's important to realize that certain categories are pre-determined and not negotiable from year to year. The distinctions also help us understand the recent growth of government spending. It turns out that much of the growth in government spending has been in mandatory spending. Returning to Table 17.4, we see that mandatory spending constituted 61.8% of the U.S. budget in 2014. In fact, if we include interest payments as obligatory, that leaves just 32.2% of the U.S. budget as discretionary. You might remember these numbers the next time you read or hear about budgetary negotiations. While much of the debate focuses on discretionary spending items, like bridges, environmental subsidies or defense/military items, the majority of the budget goes to mandatory spending categories, making it difficult to cut overall spending.

Government spending includes purchases of military equipment.

Spending and Current Fiscal Issues

The U.S. government now spends over $3.6 trillion each year—more than $11,000 for every citizen. Figure 17.2 shows real U.S. government outlays from 1990 to 2014. Notice how the slope of the line begins to get steeper

FIGURE 17.2

U.S. Government Outlays, 1990–2014 (in billions of 2013 dollars)

Total outlays represent the spending side of the government budget. This graph shows real outlays (in billions of 2013 dollars) since 1990. In the decade between 2004 and 2014, real outlays grew by 21.5%. Total outlays are now over $3.6 trillion per year, or $11,000 per U.S. citizen. Data for 2014 is estimated.

Source: U.S. Office of Management and Budget. Figures are converted to 2013 dollars using the GDP deflator for government expenditures from the Bureau of Economic Analysis.

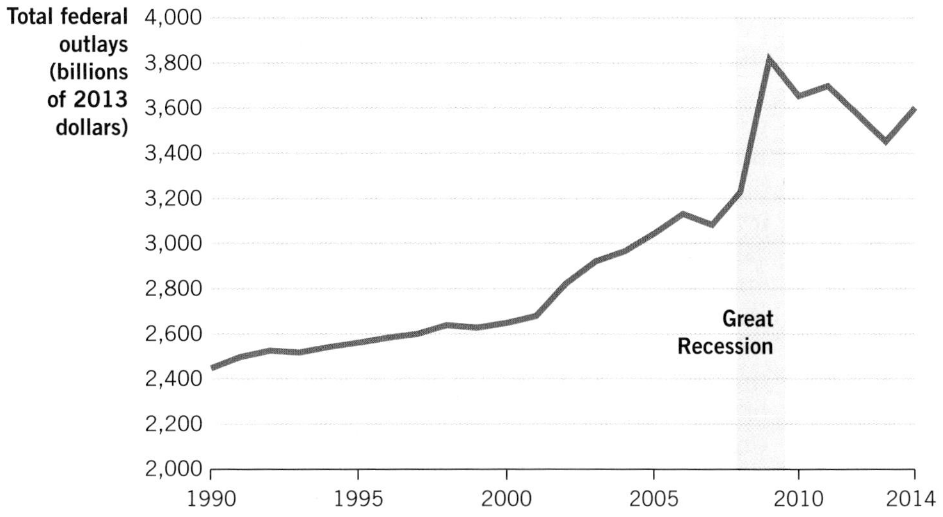

around the year 2000 and then really jumps during the Great Recession period. While there are many reasons for the increased spending, we can identify three major factors:

1. *Increased spending on Social Security and Medicare.* As the population has aged, more people are collecting Social Security. As they live longer, they collect Social Security for a longer period of time. In 2006, prescription drug coverage was added to Medicare, further increasing the overall cost of the program.
2. *Defense and military spending in the wake of the terrorist attacks of September 11, 2001.* Prior to 2001, military spending had consistently declined as a portion of the federal budget since the fall of the Soviet Union in 1991, to just 16.5% by 2001. But by 2010, military spending constituted 19.1% of the federal budget. As the United States wound down its wars in Afghanistan and Iraq, the share of military spending fell to 16.8% of the 2014 federal budget.
3. *Government responses to the Great Recession, beginning with fiscal policy in 2008.* Government outlays increased from $3.1 trillion in 2007 to $3.8 trillion in 2009. Much of this increase was due to the stimulus programs designed to move the economy out of the recession.

The third point above is a perfect place for us to begin looking at the ways Congress and the president use fiscal policy. Government policymakers can design policy to either speed the economy up or slow it down. When things are bad, we want the economy to expand. It is to this situation that we now turn our attention.

Expansionary Fiscal Policy

In the fall of 2007, the U.S. economy was slipping into recession. In the context of the business cycle, the economy had reached a peak, and economic growth as measured by GDP was falling. Many people expected the government to step in to encourage economic growth. With an **expansionary fiscal policy**, the government increases spending or decreases taxes to stimulate the economy.

An **expansionary fiscal policy** increases government spending or decreases taxes to stimulate the economy.

Remember that GDP is composed of four parts: consumption, investment, government spending, and net exports. When private spending (consumption, investment, and net exports) is low, government can increase GDP directly by increasing its own spending, the G component of GDP. Fiscal policy can also focus on consumption (C) by decreasing taxes. Decreases in taxes can increase GDP because people have more of their income left to spend after paying their taxes. If people keep more of their paycheck, the theory goes, they can buy more things, thereby increasing consumption.

When government policymakers engage in expansionary fiscal policy, they are trying to increase GDP and employment. We can show the effects of expansionary fiscal policy with the aggregate demand and supply model. Consider Figure 17.3, which shows the economy in a recession with aggregate demand at AD_1. Here GDP is below the long-run output at equilibrium point A. Policymakers use expansionary policy to try to shift aggregate demand from AD_1 to AD_2. As the economy moves from equilibrium A to B, output rises to GDP* (the long-run level) and employment increases (that

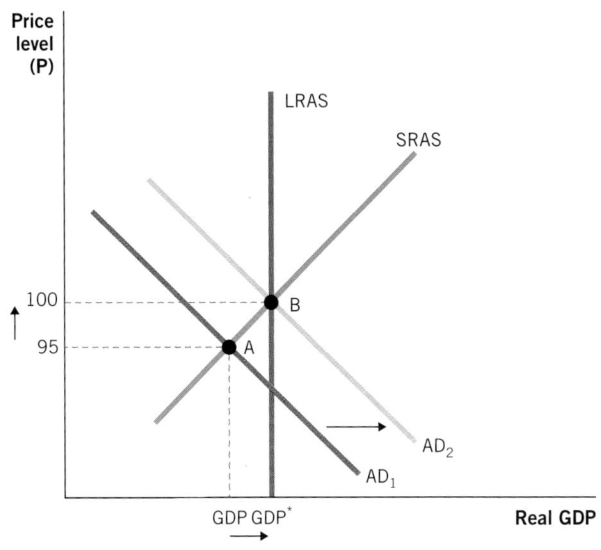

FIGURE 17.3

Expansionary Fiscal Policy

During a recession, when a decrease in aggregate demand has moved the economy to equilibrium point A, there is less than full employment output (GDP < GDP*), and unemployment rises. The goal of expansionary fiscal policy is to shift aggregate demand to AD_2 so that the economy returns to full employment without waiting for long-run adjustments.

is, unemployment decreases to the natural rate). The economy experiences inflation as the price level rises from 95 to 100.

As we discussed in Chapter 12, the economy will return to equilibrium in the long run as expectations adjust. However, policymakers and the public at large may not want to wait for that. In that case, expansionary policy can be used to try to push the aggregate demand curve more quickly back to where it began. Note in Figure 17.3 that AD_2 shows the pre-recession aggregate demand curve and point B is the equilibrium before the recession occurs. Expansionary policy is intended to shift aggregate demand back to AD_2 and equilibrium point B, which is also the long-run equilibrium point at which AD_2 and the long-run aggregate supply curve (LRAS) intersect.

Recent U.S. history offers two prominent examples of expansionary fiscal policy. In the next section, we use these examples to clarify how fiscal policy can use both government spending and taxes.

Fiscal Policy during the Great Recession

In the fall of 2007, the U.S. unemployment rate climbed from 4.6% to 5%. As it became clear that economic conditions were worsening, the government took action. Political leaders decided that fiscal policy could help. Figure 17.4 shows real GDP growth and the unemployment rate in the United States from 2007, through the period of the Great Recession, to the end of 2012. The official period of the recession is shaded blue. The top panel shows quarterly real GDP growth over the period, which fell to –1.8% at the beginning of 2008. The bottom panel shows the monthly unemployment rate, which

FIGURE 17.4

Major Fiscal Policy Initiatives During the Great Recession

The Great Recession began in December 2007. In February 2008, President Bush signed the Economic Stimulus Act of 2008, which introduced tax cuts to stimulate the economy and avoid recession. But during 2008, the economy sunk deeper into recession. In February 2009, President Obama signed the American Recovery and Reinvestment Act of 2009, which focused on government spending programs.

Source: GDP data is from the U.S. Bureau of Economic Analysis; unemployment rate data is from the U.S. Bureau of Labor Statistics.

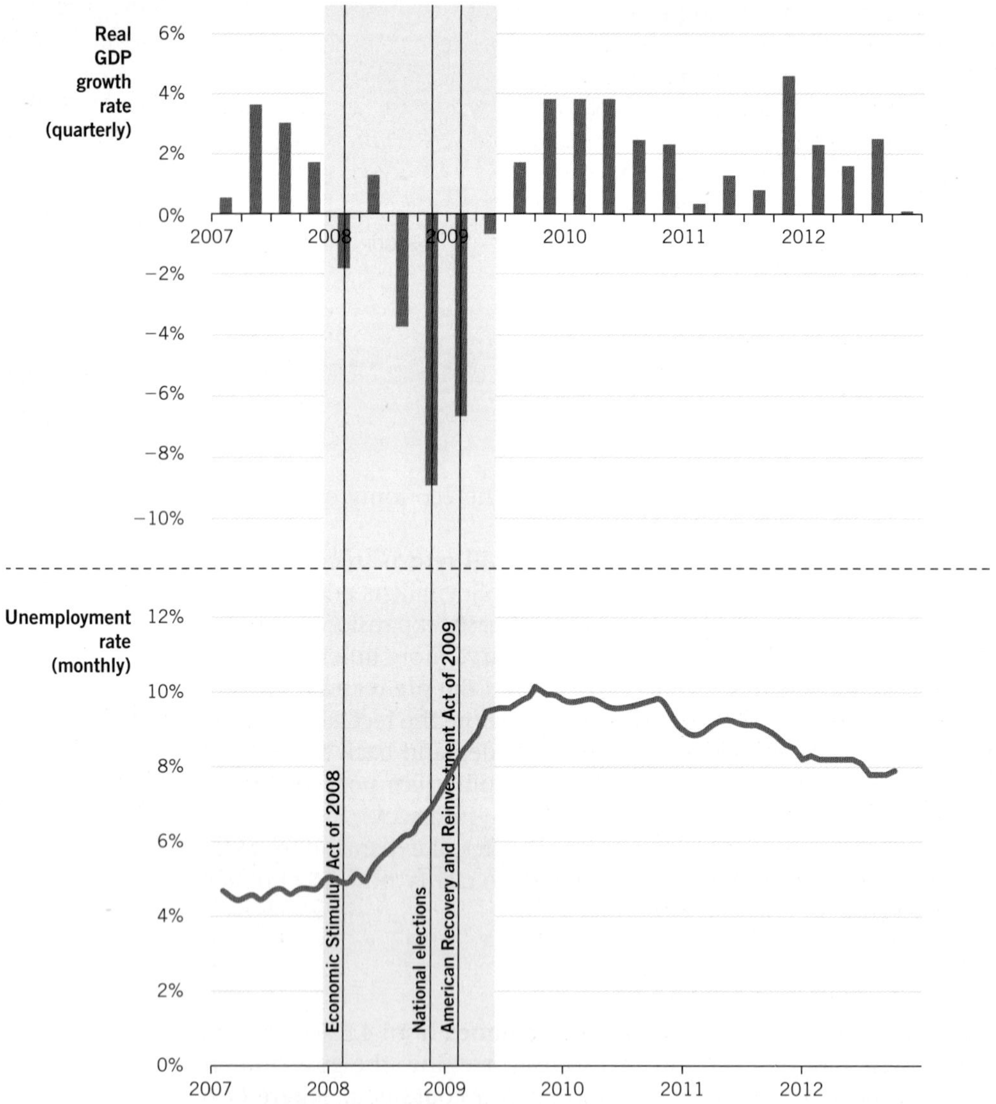

began climbing in late 2007. Although the Great Recession officially ended in June 2009, unemployment did not fall below 8% until September 2012.

Surrounded by congressional leaders, President Bush signed the Economic Stimulus Act of 2008 . . .

. . . and one year later, President Obama signed the much larger American Recovery and Reinvestment Act of 2009.

In this context, the government enacted two significant fiscal policy initiatives. The first, signed in February 2008 by President George W. Bush, was the Economic Stimulus Act of 2008. The cornerstone of this act was a tax rebate for Americans. While citizens had already paid their taxes for 2007, the Stimulus Act included a partial rebate of those previously paid taxes. The government actually mailed rebate checks to taxpayers! These refunds were not insignificant: a typical family of four received a rebate check for $1,800 ($600 per adult and $300 per child). The expectation was that American taxpayers would spend rather than save most of this $168 billion tax rebate, thereby increasing consumption and stimulating the economy.

However, after this first fiscal stimulus was passed, economic conditions worsened. In Figure 17.4, notice that real GDP growth plummeted and the unemployment rate rose significantly in 2008 after the first fiscal stimulus legislation. National elections at the end of 2008 brought Barack Obama to the White House and changed the balance of power in Congress. In February 2009, less than one month after taking office, the new president signed the American Recovery and Reinvestment Act of 2009. The focus of this second act shifted to government spending. In addition, the size of this second fiscal stimulus—$787 billion—was much larger than the first.

These two major pieces of legislation illustrate the tools of expansionary fiscal policy: tax cuts and spending increases. The two acts may seem very different, but both seek to increase GDP.

Contractionary Fiscal Policy

While expansionary fiscal policy attempts to increase GDP during economic downturns, sometimes the government uses contractionary fiscal policy to slow GDP growth. With a **contractionary fiscal policy**, the government decreases spending or increases taxes to slow economic expansion.

A **contractionary fiscal policy** decreases government spending or increases taxes to slow economic expansion.

A government might want to slow GDP growth for two reasons. The first has to do with repaying money the government borrowed. An increase in taxes or a decrease in spending during an economic expansion can help pay off the government's debt. The side effect is that it slows economic growth.

Second, the government might want to slow GDP growth if it believes that the economy is expanding beyond its long-run capabilities. The long-run output is considered the highest level of sustainable output. Recall from Chapter 11 that this is consistent with the natural rate of unemployment. If the unemployment rate falls below the natural rate, output may be too high. Some analysts then worry that the economy may "overheat" from too much spending, which can lead to inflation.

Here again we can observe the impact of policy by using the aggregate demand–aggregate supply model. If the economy is producing beyond its capacity, it would be at a point like equilibrium A in Figure 17.5. Here output is above full employment output and unemployment is below the natural rate. Contractionary fiscal policy would involve raising taxes or cutting government spending in order to push the aggregate demand curve to the left, from AD_1 to AD_2. The resulting equilibrium at point B would be consistent with the long-run aggregate supply (LRAS) and the natural rate of

FIGURE 17.5

Contractionary Fiscal Policy

When policymakers believe the economy is producing beyond its long-run capacity ($GDP_1 > GDP^*$), fiscal policy can be used to reduce aggregate demand. Contractionary fiscal policy moves the economy from short-run equilibrium at point A to the more sustainable equilibrium at point B.

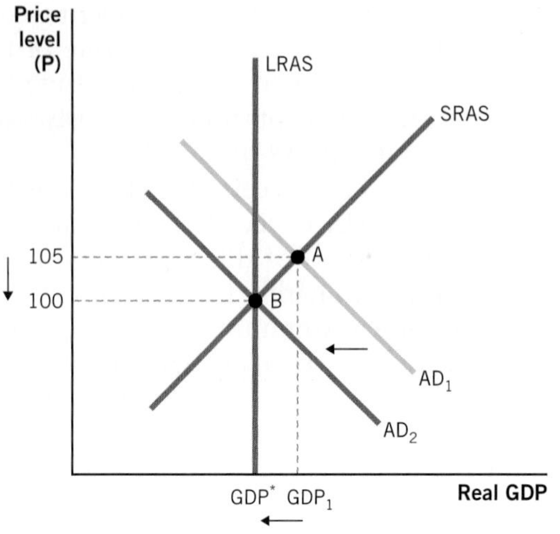

unemployment. This policy has the added benefit of lower prices (the price level drops from 105 to 100).

Together, contractionary and expansionary fiscal policy can help to counteract the ups and downs of business cycles. We examine this combination more closely in the next section.

Countercyclical Fiscal Policy

Other things being equal, people generally prefer smoothness and predictability in their financial affairs. In Chapter 14, we talked about this characteristic in reference to consumption smoothing. Along these lines, an economy that grows at a consistent rate is preferable to an economy that grows erratically. For these and other reasons, politicians generally use fiscal policy to try to counteract the business cycle.

Today, much of fiscal policy is *countercyclical*. To smooth the ups and downs in the business cycle, many economists advocate expansionary policy when the economy is slowing and contractionary policy when the economy is growing. Figure 17.6 illustrates the goals of countercyclical fiscal policy. The natural path of the economy (without countercyclical fiscal policy) includes business cycles during which income and employment fluctuate. The hope is that **countercyclical fiscal policy** can reduce the fluctuations inherent in a business cycle to keep the highs from getting too high (thereby limiting the impact of inflation) and the lows from getting to low (thereby keeping unemployment in check).

Countercyclical fiscal policy is fiscal policy that seeks to counteract business-cycle fluctuations.

Table 17.5 summarizes the tools of countercyclical fiscal policy, including the timing and effects of the policy on GDP.

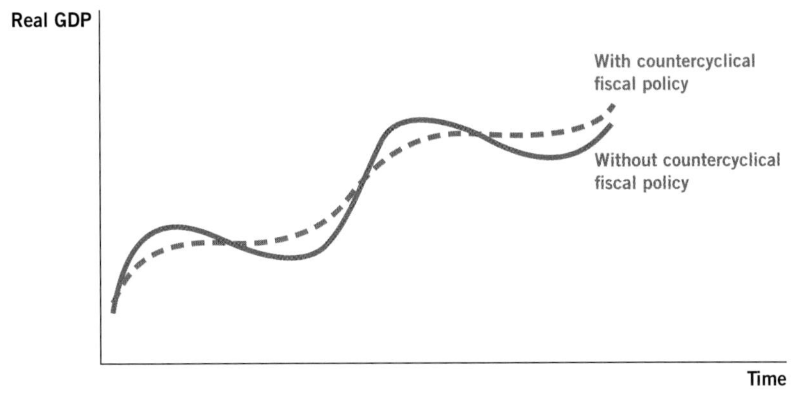

FIGURE 17.6

Countercyclical Fiscal Policy and the Business Cycle

The goal of countercyclical fiscal policy is to smooth out the fluctuations in the business cycle.

TABLE 17.5

Countercyclical Fiscal Policy Tools

Fiscal Policy Timing	Action	Objective: Effects on GDP
When the economy is contracting	↑ Government spending (G)	G is one component of GDP, so increases in G directly increase GDP.
	↓ Taxes (T)	Decreasing T leaves more funds in the hands of consumers, who then spend more on consumption (C). When C rises, GDP rises.
When the economy is expanding	↓ Government spending (G)	Decreases in G directly decrease GDP.
	↑ Taxes (T)	Increasing T leaves fewer funds in the hands of consumers, who then spend less on consumption (C). When C falls, GDP falls.

Multipliers

The tools of fiscal policy are even more powerful than our initial discussion reveals because the initial impact can snowball into additional effects. When fiscal policy is implemented, some effects occur immediately. But a large share of the impact happens later, as spending ripples throughout the economy. To understand how, we need to build on two concepts—one is review, the other is new.

First, the review concept: recall from Chapter 11 that what one person spends becomes income to others. This is true not only for private spending but also for government spending. For example, if the government uses fiscal policy to increase spending on new roads, the dollars spent on these roads become income to the suppliers of all the resources that go into road production.

Now the new concept: increases in income generally lead to increases in consumption. When a person's income rises, he or she can either save it or spend it. The **marginal propensity to consume (MPC)** is the portion of additional income that is spent on consumption. It is a fraction between 0 and 1, and it is an average for all people.

The **marginal propensity to consume (MPC)** is the portion of additional income that is spent on consumption.

(Equation 17.1)

$$MPC = \frac{\text{change in consumption}}{\text{change in income}}$$

Spend or save? What is your marginal propensity to consume?

Let's look at an example to see how the marginal propensity to consume works. Say you earn \$400 in new income, and you decide to spend \$300 and save \$100. Your marginal propensity to consume is then \$300 ÷ \$400 = 0.75. In other words, you spend 75% of your new income. Now let's consider a simple example of how changes in spending affect the economy. For this example, let's say that the government decides to increase spending by \$100 billion and spends all of the funds on salaries for government workers. This government spending becomes new income for the government workers. Assume that these workers spend 75 cents of each

FIGURE 17.7

The Spending Multiplier Process

Assume that MPC = 0.75 and the government increases spending by \$100 billion. In the table, you can see how the spending multiplies throughout the economy. We begin at AD_1. Each subsequent round is 75% of the prior round. In the end, at AD_N, the total spending increase is four times the initial change in government spending.

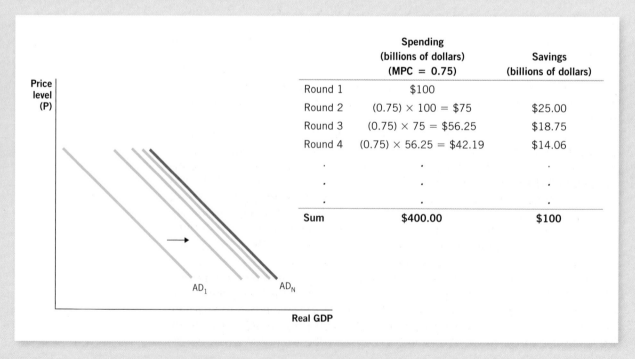

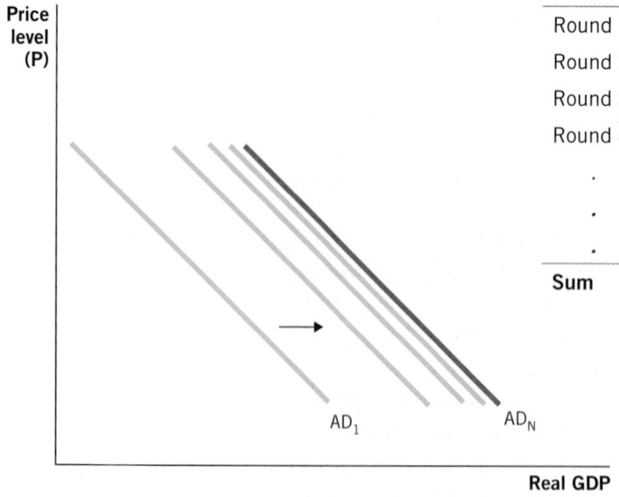

	Spending (billions of dollars) (MPC = 0.75)	Savings (billions of dollars)
Round 1	\$100	
Round 2	(0.75) × 100 = \$75	\$25.00
Round 3	(0.75) × 75 = \$56.25	\$18.75
Round 4	(0.75) × 56.25 = \$42.19	\$14.06
.	.	.
.	.	.
.	.	.
Sum	**\$400.00**	**\$100**

ECONOMICS IN THE MEDIA

The Spending Multiplier

Pay It Forward

In this movie, a drama from 2000, a young boy named Trevor (played by Haley Joel Osment) comes up with an idea that he thinks can change the world. Instead of paying people back for good deeds, Trevor suggests a new approach called "pay it forward." The idea is for him to help three people in some way. According to Trevor, "it has to be really big, something they can't do by themselves."

Then each of those three people helps three more. You can see how this idea leads to a multiplication of people helping other people.

Trevor's scheme is both similar to and different from the spending multiplier at the center of Keynesian fiscal policy. It is similar in that one person's "spending" leads to "spending" by others.

But we have seen that the spending multiplier is driven by the marginal propensity to consume, which is a fraction between 0 and 1, as people generally save part of any new income they earn. So the spending multiplication process slows down and eventually dies out.

However, the multiplier in *Pay It Forward* exceeds 1 because each person can help many people. Mathematically, the multiplier in Trevor's scheme is infinite. So the good deeds continue to expand to more and more good deeds.

Trevor explains his good-deed pyramid scheme.

dollar of their new income—or that their MPC is 0.75. In total, then, the government workers spend \$75 billion and save \$25 billion of their new income. The government workers' spending becomes \$75 billion worth of income to others in the economy. So far, we now have \$175 billion in new income (\$100 billion from government spending and \$75 billion from new consumption). If the recipients of the \$75 billion income also spend 75% of it, they create another \$56.25 billion in new income for others in the economy, for a total of \$231.25 billion.

It's clear that the initial \$100 billion in government spending creates more than \$100 billion in income; this occurs through the "multiplying" effect we just described. The effect continues on, round after round, as new income-earners spend a portion of their income.

The multiplying effect is significant when we focus on GDP. Each time people earn new income, they spend part of it. After all the dust settles, the total impact is a multiple of the original spending created by the fiscal policy. Figure 17.7 illustrates this multiplier process for our current example. It shows how spending becomes income and then how part of the new income is spent. The first round represents the government's initial spending (at AD_1) of \$100 billion. The following rounds represent the new income generated by consumption spending. Since the MPC is 0.75 in this example, each round generates 75% of the income produced in the preceding round. This continues as long as money continues to be spent, all the way to the final round at AD_N.

The **spending multiplier (m^s)** is a formula to determine the total impact on spending from an initial change of a given amount. The formula is 1 divided by (1 – the marginal propensity to consume).

While we could continue to multiply the previous spending by 0.75 to determine the total impact on spending from any initial government expenditures until there's no new income to be spent, there's a much more efficient tool for determining the overall impact of the government spending: the spending multiplier. The **spending multiplier (m^s)** tells us the total impact on spending from an initial government stimulus. The multiplier depends on the marginal propensity to consume: the greater the marginal propensity to consume, the greater the spending multiplier. The formula for this spending multiplier is:

(Equation 17.2)

$$m^s = \frac{1}{(1 - \text{MPC})}$$

Since the MPC is a fraction between 0 and 1, the multiplier is generally larger than 1. For example, if the marginal propensity to consume is 0.75, the multiplier is determined as:

$$m^s = \frac{1}{(1 - \text{MPC})} = \frac{1}{1 - 0.75} = \frac{1}{0.25} = 4$$

Sometimes, this multiplier is called the Keynesian multiplier or the fiscal multiplier.

Note that the multiplier concept applies to all spending, no matter whether that spending is public or private. In addition, there is a multiplier

PRACTICE WHAT YOU KNOW

Some government spending projects are more shovel-ready than others.

Expansionary Fiscal Policy: Shovel-Ready Projects

In early 2009, with the U.S. economy in deep recession, newly elected President Obama vowed to use fiscal stimulus spending on "shovel-ready" projects. These projects had already been approved and were just waiting for funding. The president hoped his stimulus plan would create new jobs with minimal delays.

Question: Assume the economy is in short-run equilibrium with output being less than full employment output. Also assume, for this entire question, that the marginal propensity to consume (MPC) equals 0.50. What is the value of the spending multiplier in this case?

Answer: Equation 17.2 gives us the formula for the spending multiplier:

$$m^s = \frac{1}{(1 - \text{MPC})} = \frac{1}{(1 - 0.5)} = \frac{1}{0.5} = 2$$

Question: Given the size of the multiplier, what would be the potential change in income (GDP) from stimulus spending of $800 billion?

Answer: The total potential impact would be: 2 × $800 billion = $1.6 trillion.

associated with tax changes. A reduction in the tax rate leaves more income for consumers to spend. This spending multiplies throughout the economy in much the same way as government spending multiplies.

The multiplier process also works in reverse. If the government reduces spending, people have less income to spend, causing GDP to fall. The initial decline in government spending leads to subsequent declines as the effects reverberate throughout the economy.

The spending multiplier implies that the tools of fiscal policy are very powerful. Not only can the government change its spending and taxing, but also multiples of this spending then ripple throughout the economy over several periods.

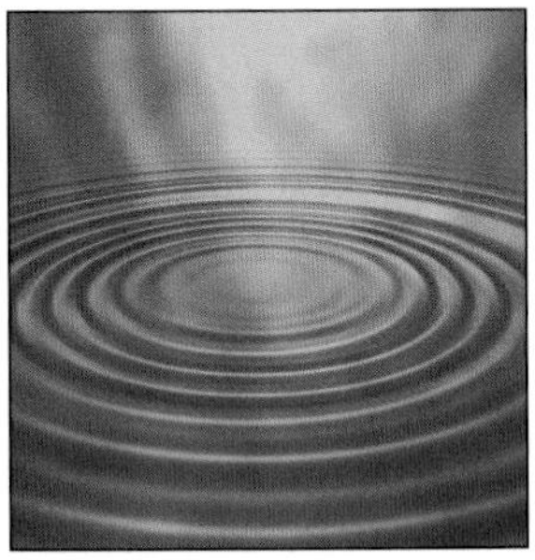

The multiplier effects of fiscal policy on an economy are similar to the rippling effects of a stone thrown into water.

How Do Budget Deficits Differ from Debt?

We have seen that the typical prescription for an ailing economy is to increase government spending, decrease taxes, or both. At this point, you may be wondering how the government pays for all the spending or deals with the shortfall in tax revenue. The answer is through borrowing.

One of the premises of fiscal policy today is that budget deficits are an acceptable part of government spending. A **budget deficit** occurs when government spending exceeds revenue in a particular year. Panel (a) of Figure 17.8 plots real U.S. budget outlays and revenues from 1960 to 2014. As we noted above, outlays (displayed in orange) have grown rapidly. Over the long run, revenue has grown, but there have been periods of decline—for example, during the Great Recession of 2007–2009. You can see that outlays have generally exceeded revenue for much of the recent past. In 2014 total outlays were $3.5 trillion, while revenues were nearly $3 trillion. The difference, around $500 billion, is the budget deficit for that year.

A **budget deficit** occurs when government outlays exceed revenue in a particular year.

It is also possible for the government to have a **budget surplus**, which occurs when revenue exceeds outlays in a particular year. The most recent federal budget surpluses came in the four years from 1998 to 2001. Panel (b) of Figure 17.8 graphs the budget balance from 1960 to 2014. When the budget is in deficit, the balance is negative; when the budget is in surplus, the balance is positive.

A **budget surplus** occurs when government revenue exceeds outlays in a particular year.

Borrowing to Cover the Deficit

If government is running a deficit, how does it pay for operations? After all, government must pay its bills. Soldiers in the military, economists at the Treasury Department, and groundskeepers at the White House need to be paid. The newest jet fighter must be purchased; so must paper for the printers at the Department of Justice. If the government doesn't have the money to make these purchases because expenditures exceed revenues, the government can't say "Too bad!" and refuse to pay people. If it did so, very few people would be willing to deal with or work for the government. So the government borrows the funds it needs to pay the bills.

FIGURE 17.8

U.S. Federal Budget Data, 1960–2014 (in billions of 2013 dollars)

(a) Real outlays are shown in orange, and revenue in blue, for the U.S. federal government budget since 1960. When the outlays exceed revenue, the budget has a deficit for that year.

(b) In the plot of the real budget balance, negative values indicate a deficit. The Great Recession of 2007–2009 and the government's response to it helped to create the 2009 deficit of over $1.5 trillion (in 2013 dollars), the largest in U.S. history.

Source: U.S. Office of Management and Budget.

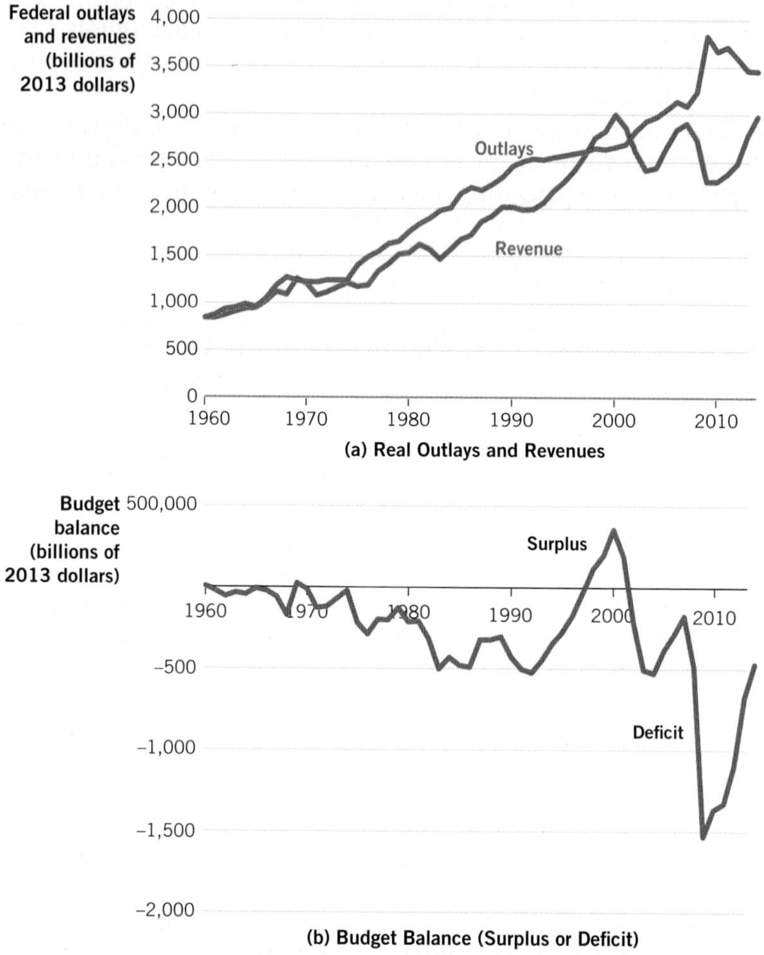

This borrowing occurs when a government issues bonds. A bond is a promise to pay back the purchaser with interest. The U.S. government issues bonds in order to get the money it needs to pay its bills today. Let's take a look at a scenario with which you might be more familiar to see the implications of borrowing.

Deficits versus Debt

When you start college, you're probably spending more than you earn. Take all of your expenses—including tuition, books, room and board, transportation, your cellphone plan, everything you spend money on—and compare it to your income. Most college students' incomes fall far short of their expenditures. In other words, you're running a budget deficit. To cover this deficit, you take out loans, promising to pay them back once you graduate and start working full-time.

Next year, when you return to school and once again find that your income doesn't cover your expenses, you'll have another budget deficit. If you add these two years of deficits together, you have what is all too common among college students: debt.

It's easy to confuse the terms "deficit" and "debt." A **deficit** is a shortfall in revenue for a particular year's budget. A **debt** is the total of all accumulated and unpaid budget deficits. Consider your tuition bill over the course of your time in college. If you borrow $5,000 to help pay for your first year of college, that's your first-year deficit. If you borrow another $5,000 for your second year, you have a $5,000 deficit for each year, and your debt grows to $10,000.

A **deficit** is a shortfall in revenue for a particular year's budget.

A **debt** is the total of all accumulated and unpaid budget deficits.

You can get a student loan because lenders are likely to get repaid. If you don't pay back your loans, you'll get a call from a collection agency; if you still don't pay, there's a negative impact on your credit report. (We discuss individual credit reports in Chapter 19.) A similar thing happens to governments. As we saw earlier in this chapter, one part of the government's budget is the interest it's required to pay on its debt. Interest is a significant expenditure in the government's annual budget. If the country doesn't make its interest payments, it goes into default. If a country defaults, it may have great difficulty borrowing in the future; and even if it can borrow, it will have to pay much higher interest rates. There is also another consequence of defaulting. If the government can't borrow, it can't engage in deficit spending; and if it can't deficit-spend, then its power to deal with the business cycle is severely limited.

Foreign Ownership of U.S. Federal Debt

A good question to ask at this point is: *From whom do governments borrow?* The answer might surprise you. They mainly borrow from you—or, more precisely, from the citizens who live in the country. The vast majority of the U.S. government debt is "owned" by U.S. citizens and institutions. After reading media reports, you might think that the U.S. government is in hock to the Chinese, but this isn't the case at all. Citizens and governments of other countries have lent the U.S. government money, but the percentage of borrowing from these sources is relatively small.

Many people are concerned about foreign ownership of U.S. debt. The concern stems from a fear that foreigners who own U.S. debt will control the country politically as well as economically. However, according to the U.S. Treasury, as of September 2014 about 67% of U.S. national debt was held domestically, and just 33% internationally. China, Japan, and Belgium are the major foreign holders of U.S. debt.

Figure 17.9 shows foreign and domestic ownership of total U.S. debt from 1990 to 2013. Total national debt grew from about $3 trillion to over $17 trillion. However, domestic investors and U.S. government agencies were the holders of most of the new debt. Still, the portion of U.S. government debt that is internationally owned doubled from about 14% to nearly 33% over this period.

While this foreign ownership of U.S. government debt is troubling for many Americans, it's important to realize the importance of the international

FIGURE 17.9

Foreign and Domestic Ownership of U.S. Government Debt, 1990–2013 (in billions of 2010 dollars)

Most U.S. government debt is owned by Americans or by the U.S. government itself. This graph shows total national debt and internationally owned debt. The percentage owned internationally has grown in recent years, but it is still just about one-third of the total.

Source: U.S. Treasury, *Treasury Bulletin*.

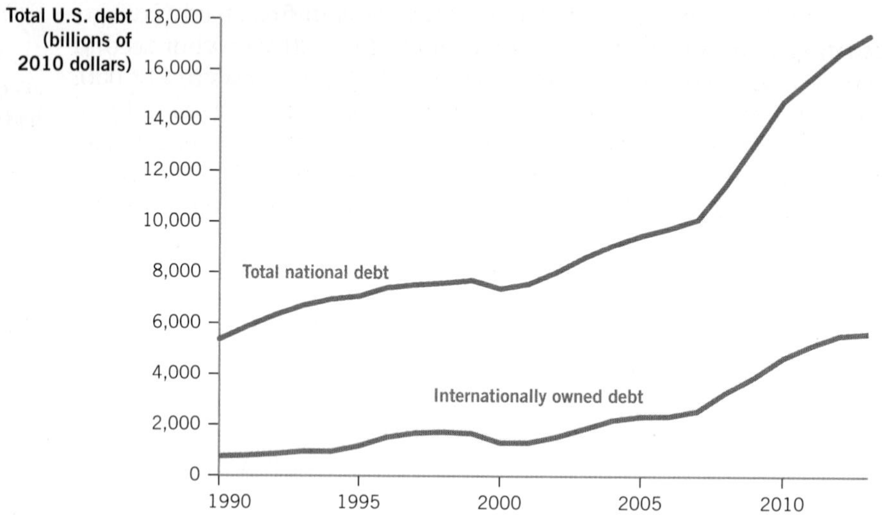

funds in the U.S. loanable funds market. As we discussed in Chapter 14, foreign lending increases the supply of loanable funds in the United States, which helps keep interest rates low. Lower interest rates mean that U.S. firms and governments can borrow at lower cost. Furthermore, the increase in foreign ownership is a natural byproduct of emerging foreign economies—as they get wealthier, they buy more U.S. government bonds.

ECONOMICS IN THE REAL WORLD

Argentina Defaults . . . Again

In August 2014, Argentina failed to make a payment on its debt. Unfortunately, this occurrence is nothing new for the South American nation. Since issuing bonds for the first time in 1824, Argentina has defaulted on its debt eight times. The first default occurred in 1828, only four years after the first bonds became available. After a more recent default, a court-negotiated agreement was reached in 2001 that set out terms in which the bondholders would be repaid, but at a discount. In 2014, Argentina failed to meet these obligations (as well as other obligations).

Argentina's continued failure to repay its lenders has had significant ramifications for the country. *The Economist* detailed these negative consequences in a recent article.* Argentina needs to borrow in order to grow. However, as the article states, "Argentina has been locked out of international capital markets for 13 years." Despite the country's gains in restoring its reputation, the most recent default has the potential to return Argentina to financial pariah status.

What are the possible ramifications for Argentina? If a government cannot borrow, one recourse is to print money. However, printing money to finance budget deficits will spur inflation, thus reducing the purchasing power of existing money. A second problem is consumption. Argentines who bought bonds are now not going to get their money back. Maybe they will someday, but for now it's gone. Thus, their ability to spend and their consumption rate both fall, deepening the recession that Argentina entered in early 2014.

Unfortunately for Argentina, the government's history of failure to repay what it has borrowed will continue to discourage investment from overseas. The risk of lending to a habitual defaulter is likely to prove too great, especially when there are many other safer places where foreign lenders could lend their money. ✷

Former first lady of Argentina Eva Perón was memorialized in the musical *Evita*. In the most memorable song from the show, Perón's character sings "Don't cry for me, Argentina." Today, lenders aren't crying for Argentina; they just want the country to pay its debts.

* "Argentina's Debt Saga: No Movement," *The Economist* August 2–8, 2014, pp. 26–27.

Fiscal Policy and Budget Deficits

What is the connection between fiscal policy and budget deficits? Let's start with a simplified example. Assume that the government is currently balancing the national budget so that outlays equal tax revenue. Then the economy slips into recession, and the government decides to increase government spending by $100 billion. This expansionary policy means that government must borrow to pay for its expenses. To acquire the funds, the government sells $100 billion worth of bonds and the federal budget is in deficit by $100 billion.

But that's only part of the story. In reality, the deficit will rise by more than $100 billion because tax revenue will fall. More than 80% of U.S. tax revenue derives from payroll taxes. In a recession, with income down and unemployment up, the amount of revenue that the government takes in from taxes falls.

It's easy to verify both of these phenomena by looking at recent U.S. recessions. Figure 17.10 shows U.S. federal outlays and tax revenue from 1985 to 2014, with recessionary periods shaded as vertical blue bars. First, look at the period of the Great Recession of 2007–2009. Note how spending (outlays) increased sharply in 2009, the year of the $787 billion fiscal stimulus. But falling income also led to less income-tax revenue. Looking back over the three recessions shown in this graph, we see that spending increased but tax revenue fell during each one.

The bottom line is clear: expansionary fiscal policy inevitably leads to increases in budget deficits and the national debt during economic downturns. This policy prescription may seem odd to you. After all, if you personally fell on rough economic times, you might (reasonably) react differently.

FIGURE 17.10

Real U.S. Outlays and Revenue, 1985–2014 (2013 dollars)

The use of expansionary fiscal policy to counteract economic downturns leads to greater budget deficits. During recessionary periods, outlays increase and tax revenue falls. In 2001, these strategies erased the budget surplus; in 1990 and 2008, these strategies expanded the size of the deficit.

Source: Office of Management and Budget.

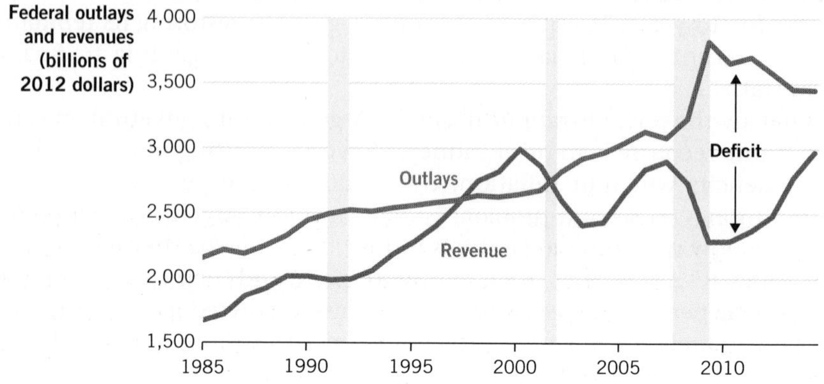

For example, if your employer cut you back to part-time employment, would it seem like a good idea to go on a spending binge? You might feel better while you were out shopping, but it wouldn't help your financial situation much. From a macroeconomic perspective, however, one reason why expansionary fiscal policy might work for the overall economy is that spending by one person becomes income to another, which can snowball into income increases throughout the economy through the multiplier effect.

What Are the Shortcomings of Fiscal Policy?

At this point, you may wonder why fiscal policy doesn't always work perfectly in the real world. If fiscal policy is as simple as tweaking government spending or taxes and letting the multiplier go to work, why do recessions still happen? Unfortunately, the real world isn't so simple. Millions of people make individual decisions that affect the entire economy. How much fiscal policy is enough? How much will people save? Economists can't know the answers to these questions ahead of time. In this section, we consider three shortcomings of activist fiscal policy: time lags, crowding-out, and savings shifts.

Time Lags

Both fiscal policies and monetary policies are intended to smooth out the economic variations that accompany a business cycle. So timing is important. But if the policy isn't implemented at the right time, the impact will be muted. We noted the problem with timing in Chapter 12, where we discussed the idea of a *recognition lag:* it takes time to realize there's a problem. Then there's an *implementation lag*: you need to do something about the problem, and that takes time. Finally, there's an *impact lag* because it takes time to see the effects of the policy.

ECONOMICS IN THE REAL WORLD

Recognizing Lags

It is very difficult to determine instantaneously how the economy is performing. Looking back now, we know that the U.S. economy entered a recession in December 2007. But this development was far from clear at the time. In fact, as Edmund Andrews pointed out in a *New York Times* article in February 2008, the Bush administration wasn't convinced that the economy was in recession. Reporting on February 12, Andrews wrote:

> The White House predicted on Monday that the economy would escape a recession and that unemployment would remain low this year, though it acknowledged that growth had already slowed. "I don't think we are in a recession right now, and we are not forecasting a recession," said Edward P. Lazear, chairman of the White House Council of Economic Advisers . . . . The administration's forecast calls for the economy to expand 2.7 percent this year and for unemployment to remain at 4.9 percent.

It's not inconceivable that this forecast was biased by political considerations, but, according to Andrews, even independent economists were predicting a 1.7% growth rate for 2008. In reality, real GDP fell by 3.5% and the unemployment rate rose to 7.3% by the end of 2008. As this example demonstrates, it is very difficult to accurately recognize current economic conditions. ✷

Crowding-out occurs when private spending falls in response to increases in government spending.

Crowding-Out

The second shortcoming of activist fiscal policy addresses the actual impact of government spending and the multiplier effects. This critique is based on the idea that government spending may be a substitute for private spending. When this is the case, the impact on GDP is smaller than expected. **Crowding-out** occurs when private spending falls in response to increases in government spending.

If the government bought you a new tablet, would you spend your income on another one too?

For example, say the government starts a new program in which it buys a new tablet computer for every college student in America. (Don't get too excited; this example is just hypothetical!) But if the government is buying tablets for students, then students won't buy as many tablets for themselves. They may continue to spend on other items, but they might end up saving that money instead. When private spending falls in response to increases in government spending, we say that crowding-out has occurred. If there is crowding-out, then GDP doesn't increase by as much as planned, and the fiscal policy is less effective than it otherwise would have been.

Let's look more closely at how crowding-out works. Assume that the government has a balanced budget. Then the government increases spending by \$100 billion but doesn't raise taxes. This means that it has to borrow the \$100 billion in the loanable funds market. But, as we know, every dollar borrowed requires a dollar saved. So when the government borrows \$100 billion, the money has to come from \$100 billion in savings.

Figure 17.11 illustrates what happens when the government enters the loanable funds market to borrow \$100 billion. The graph shows that initially the market is in equilibrium at point A with demand for loans designated as D_1 (that is, investment). The initial interest rate is 5%, and at this rate there is \$250 billion worth of savings. This amount of savings funds \$250 billion in private borrowing. The table in Figure 17.11 summarizes these initial values in the column labeled "Before stimulus."

When the government borrows, the demand for loans increases by \$100 billion at all points. This increased demand is indicated on the graph as a shift from D_1 to D_2. But the new demand for loans completely changes the equilibrium in the market. The increased demand drives the interest rate up from 5% to 6%, and the new equilibrium quantity of loanable funds increases to \$300 billion, shown as point B on the graph. The interest rate rises because of the increased demand for loans caused by government borrowing.

FIGURE 17.11

Crowding-Out in the Loanable Funds Market

Initially, at point A, private savings all becomes private investment of \$250 billion. But government borrowing shifts the demand for loans from D_1 to D_2. The new demand for loans leads to equilibrium at point B, with a higher interest rate. At the new equilibrium, there is \$300 billion in private savings (S_B in the table), but \$100 billion goes to the government (G_B) and \$200 billion is left for private investment (I_B).

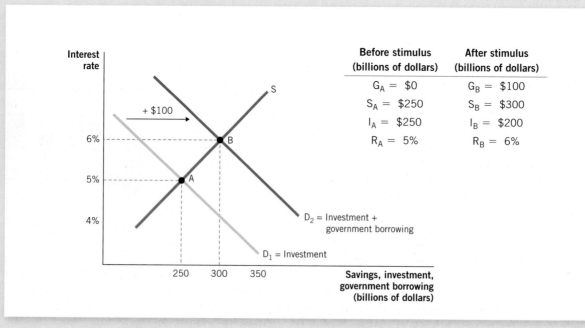

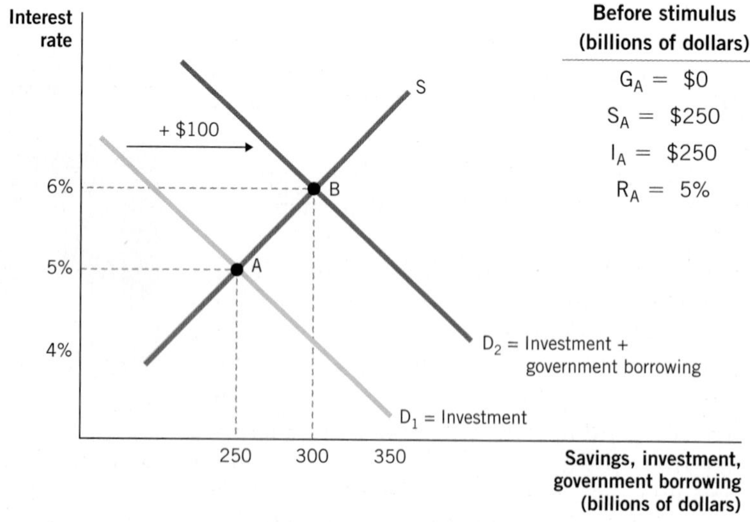

Before stimulus (billions of dollars)	After stimulus (billions of dollars)
G_A = \$0	G_B = \$100
S_A = \$250	S_B = \$300
I_A = \$250	I_B = \$200
R_A = 5%	R_B = 6%

To demonstrate the overall effects of this new government borrowing, the table in Figure 17.11 compares the values of private savings (S) and investment (I) at the two equilibrium points. The new equilibrium quantity of loans is \$300 billion (S_B), but the government has borrowed \$100 billion (G_B). This means that borrowing for private investment spending is only \$200 billion (I_B), \$50 billion less than before (I_A). Essentially, the higher interest rate discourages some private purchases; in other words, the government purchases crowd out private spending.

Finally, note that private savings increases from \$250 billion (S_A) to \$300 billion (S_B)—that is, by \$50 billion—because the higher interest rate (R_B) has caused more individuals to devote more of their income to savings. But if savings rises by \$50 billion, then consumption must fall by \$50 billion. This is a direct relationship because households can only spend or save their income. The end result is that an increase of \$100 billion in deficit-financed government spending leads to \$100 billion less of private spending—\$50 billion from investment and \$50 billion from savings.

In this example, we have complete crowding-out: every dollar of government spending crowds out a dollar of private spending. In reality, crowding-out may be less than complete, but this example does illustrate an important caveat regarding the effects of fiscal policy.

ECONOMICS IN THE REAL WORLD

Did Government Spending Really Surge in 2009?

Economist and *New York Times* editorial writer Paul Krugman is an ardent defender of Keynesian countercyclical fiscal policy. During the course of the Great Recession, Krugman used his column to consistently advocate for more and more government spending.

Yet, after the historically large fiscal stimulus in 2009, many people were baffled as to why the economy struggled with high unemployment rates and slow real GDP growth even through 2012. In a February 14, 2011, post on his blog, Krugman argued that the increase in federal spending was offset by reductions on spending at the state government level. According to Krugman, "Once you take state and local cutbacks into account, there was no surge of government spending."

Why should states build new highways when the federal government offers to do it for them?

In a sense, even though he didn't identify it as such, Krugman was pointing out a variation of crowding-out. Technically, crowding-out occurs when private individuals substitute government (federal, state, and local) spending for their private spending. But Krugman's complaint is that the crowding-out occurred in the government sector. Federal government spending rose, and then state and local government spending fell. Most states were facing crises of their own as a result of the recession. Unlike the federal government, states are legally bound to balance their budgets. Since tax revenues were falling, they had to cut expenditures to make outlays equal revenue. Thus, they substituted federal spending for state spending. This strategy helped them to balance their budgets during the recession. But it also meant that total government spending didn't rise as much as the federal government intended. And this may help explain why the 2009 fiscal stimulus failed to push the U.S. economy back to full employment. ✳

PRACTICE WHAT YOU KNOW

Crowding-Out: Does Fiscal Policy Lead to Higher GDP?

Imagine that the country is in recession and the government decides to increase spending. It commissions a very large statue for $50 million. To pay for the statue, the government borrows all of the $50 million.

After the government borrows the $50 million, the interest rate rises from 3% to 4% and the equilibrium quantity of loanable funds increases from $500 million to $530 million.

Question: How would you sketch a graph of the loanable funds market representing this scenario? Be sure to indicate on this graph all the changes that take place after the borrowing.

Answer: Originally, the market is in equilibrium at point A with an interest rate of 3% and savings and investment being equal at $500 million. Then the demand for loans increases by $50 million at all points when the government borrows $50 million. This change moves the market to a new equilibrium at point B.

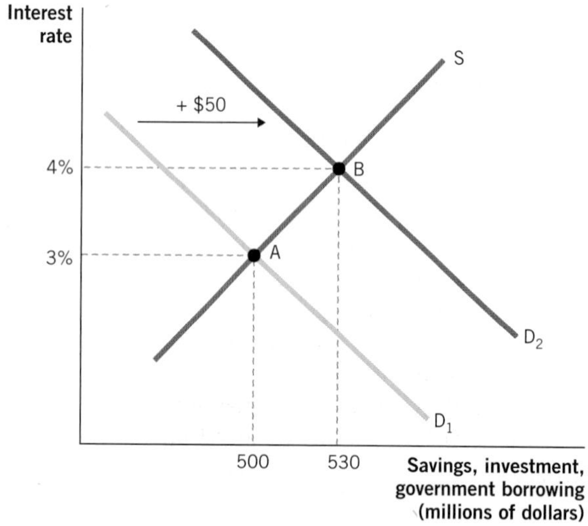

Without crowding-out, a new statue of economist Adam Smith could stimulate the economy.

Question: Using the above information, and assuming complete crowding-out, what would you predict will happen to C, I, G, and total GDP in response to the government's action?

Answer: Government spending (G) will increase by $50 million. Total savings will increase to $530 million, which means that consumption (C) will fall by $30 million—when you save $30 million more, you have to consume $30 million less. But since the government is borrowing $50 million of the savings, private investment (I) will fall to $480 million, a decrease of $20 million. All of this means a net change of zero in GDP (while government spending increases by $50 million, consumption falls by $30 million and investment falls by $20 million). The table below summarizes these changes.

Component	C	I	G	GDP
Change (millions of dollars)	$ −30	$ −20	$ +50	+$0

Savings Shifts

If your new income is temporary, are you more inclined to save it?

Suppose that the government sends everyone a $1,000 tax refund as part of a stimulus package. Anticipating that people will spend some of their refund, policymakers use the multiplier effect to predict the impact of this expansionary fiscal policy. If they assume a marginal propensity to consume (MPC) of 0.8, then the multiplier will be 5:

$$\text{multiplier} = \frac{1}{(1 - \text{MPC})} = \frac{1}{1 - .8} = \frac{1}{.2} = 5$$

However, if the assumed MPC is lower than estimated, the impact of the policy will be much lower than expected. Say that households end up saving more and the MPC falls to 0.4. In this case, the multiplier is only 1.67. When the multiplier drops, the impact of the fiscal policy falls as well, and the policy has a smaller effect than was hoped for. Of course, the MPC could be higher than expected, resulting in a larger multiplier and therefore a more dramatic stimulus, which likely would lead to higher-than-hoped-for inflation.

Table 17.6 summarizes the three shortcomings of fiscal policy.

TABLE 17.6

Summary of Fiscal Policy Shortcomings

Shortcoming	Summary	Result
Time lags	The effects of fiscal policy may be delayed by lags in recognition, implementation, and impact.	If lags are significant, fiscal policy can be destabilizing and magnify business cycles.
Crowding-out	Government spending can serve as a substitute for private spending.	Even partial crowding-out reduces the impact of fiscal stimulus.
Savings shifts	If the wrong MPC is assumed, people will save more or less than expected.	If MPC is higher than expected, there will be too much stimulus. If MPC is lower than expected, the impact of the policy will be muted.

Conclusion

We began the chapter with the misconception that government spending is an infallible tool for fighting recessions—in other words, that government policy can quickly and predictably counteract business-cycle fluctuations. It's certainly true that reductions in GDP accompany economic downturns. It's also true that government can use fiscal policy to increase expenditures or stimulate private spending through tax reductions. But the complete effects are difficult to predict. Recent experiences confirm this difficulty. When conducting fiscal policy, it's important to understand the potential unintended consequences that could result. Just like eating too much candy, too much fiscal policy can lead to some pain. In the case of running budget deficits, this pain is called debt.

ECONOMICS FOR LIFE

Planning for Your Future Taxes

The U.S. national debt is currently over $18 trillion, or more than $56,000 per person. In 2007, the national debt per person was only $30,000. Thus, we can infer that the increase is directly attributable to the Great Recession and the fiscal policy undertaken during that period.

What does this mean for you? It means that your taxes are going to be higher in the future. All Americans will need to contribute to pay down this large national debt. So taxes in the future will surely be higher, and you should plan for this.

In addition, economic growth will likely be lower until the debt is paid down. We know that higher income taxes reduce incentives for production, so it's safe to say that economic growth will be lower until this debt is paid off and taxes can come down again.

Government spending on highway projects was part of fiscal policy legislated during the Great Recession.

However, you can take actions to lower your future tax bills. First, you probably ought to budget for higher taxes. This may mean saving more now than you would have saved otherwise. Second, in terms of personal investments, you might consider buying securities that provide tax-free income. For example, the interest on municipal bonds (state and local government bonds; discussed in Chapter 19) is not federally taxed. These simple steps might turn out to be significant when your future tax bills arrive.

In the next chapter, we turn our attention to the one segment of the macroeconomy that we haven't addressed in detail. Today, more than ever before, international trade and finance are part of how we deal with scarcity. As the world becomes ever more interconnected, it is important to understand the basics of international economics.

ANSWERING THE BIG QUESTIONS

What is fiscal policy?

* Fiscal policy is the use of government spending and taxes to affect the macroeconomy.
* Fiscal policy is conducted through the legislative process.

How does the government tax?

* Governments use taxes to raise money, fund government operations, and provide social services. Federal, state, and local governments all levy taxes. Taxes may be progressive, regressive, or proportional.

- Taxes are levied based on two primary principles: the benefits principle, whereby you pay if you benefit from the service provided; and the ability to pay principle, whereby the more you make, the more you pay.
- The income tax is progressive, meaning the higher your income, the higher your average tax rate. The Social Security tax becomes regressive after a point. If your income exceeds a threshold, your average tax rate falls as your income rises.

How does the government spend?

- The majority of the government budget is spent on mandatory outlays rather than discretionary outlays. Mandatory outlays are required by law, and funding them often requires the government to take on debt.
- With expansionary fiscal policy, the government increases spending or decreases taxes to stimulate the economy. With contractionary fiscal policy, the government decreases spending or increases taxes to slow economic expansion. Countercyclical fiscal policy is designed to counteract business-cycle fluctuations.
- The results of fiscal policy ripple throughout the economy as a result of the spending multiplier, which is calculated by taking the marginal propensity to consume (MPC) into account. The MPC is the portion of additional income that is spent on consumption.

How do budget deficits differ from debt?

- If total government outlays exceed revenue in a given year, the budget is in deficit. When revenue exceeds outlays in a given year, the budget is in surplus.
- Debts are accumulated deficits. Each year with a deficit causes the debt to increase.
- Government borrows money to cover any budget deficits. The majority of the money borrowed by the U.S. government is owed to citizens of the United States.
- Expansionary fiscal policy usually leads to a higher budget deficit.

What are the shortcomings of fiscal policy?

- Fiscal policy is subject to three significant lags: a recognition lag, an implementation lag, and an impact lag.
- In addition, crowding-out can diminish the effects of fiscal policy.
- Finally, savings adjustments by private individuals can further diminish the stimulating effects of fiscal policy.

CONCEPTS YOU SHOULD KNOW

ability to pay principle (p. 497)
average tax rate (p. 498)
benefits principle (p. 497)
budget deficit (p. 515)
budget surplus (p. 515)
contractionary fiscal policy (p. 509)
countercyclical fiscal policy (p. 510)
crowding-out (p. 521)
debt (p. 517)
deficit (p. 517)
discretionary outlays (p. 504)
entitlement programs (p. 504)
excise tax (p. 501)
expansionary fiscal policy (p. 506)
fiscal policy (p. 496)
government outlays (p. 504)
mandatory outlays (p. 504)
marginal propensity to consume (MPC) (p. 512)
marginal tax rate (p. 500)
progressive tax (p. 498)
proportional tax (p. 502)
regressive tax (p. 500)
spending multiplier (m^s) (p. 514)
taxes (p. 497)
transfer payments (p. 503)

QUESTIONS FOR REVIEW

1. Since the 1960s, Social Security and Medicare have grown as portions of U.S. government spending. Has the U.S. budget become more or less flexible as a result of the growth in the mandatory programs? Explain your response.
2. Explain the difference between a debt and a deficit.
3. This question refers to Figure 17.10, which shows U.S. outlays and revenues over the period 1985–2014.
   a. List three periods when the U.S. budget deficit was relatively large.
   b. What historical events were taking place in the United States during these three periods that may have led to these large deficits? Be specific.
4. How are government budget balances affected by countercyclical fiscal policy? Be sure to describe the effects of both expansionary and contractionary fiscal policy.
5. Explain the three types of fiscal-policy lags.
6. In what circumstances would contractionary fiscal policy be recommended? How might you implement this type of policy? Why would you implement this policy—what are the reasons why it might make sense to use government policy to slow the economy?

STUDY PROBLEMS (**solved at the end of the section*)

1. Use the marginal income tax rates in Table 17.1 to compute the following:
   a. tax due on taxable income of \$25,000, \$200,000, and \$500,000
   b. average tax rate on taxable income of \$25,000, \$200,000, and \$500,000
2. Upon graduation, you accept a job with a software development firm. The job will pay you \$60,000. First, use the marginal income tax rates in Table 17.1 to compute your federal income tax owed. Now assume that the United States moves to a flat tax system instead of a progressive system. With a flat tax, everyone pays the same percentage of income in taxes. If the flat tax rate were levied at 20%, which system would you prefer? At what rate would you be indifferent between the systems? (That is, at what rate would you have no preference for one system or the other?)
3. To explore crowding-out, let's set up a simple loanable funds market in initial equilibrium.
   a. Draw a graph showing initial equilibrium in the loanable funds market at \$800 million and an interest rate of 4%. Label your initial supply and demand curves as S_1 and D_1.
   b. Now assume that the government increases spending by \$100 million that is entirely deficit-financed. Show the new equilibrium

in the loanable funds market. (*Note:* there is a range of possible numerical answers for this question. You should choose one number and then be sure the rest of your answer is consistent with this number.)

c. Write the new equilibrium interest rate and quantity of loanable funds in the blanks below:
New interest rate: _______
New quantity of loanable funds: _______

d. If we assume there was no government debt prior to the fiscal stimulus, determine the new quantities for the categories below:
Savings: ______
Investment: _______
Government spending: _______

e. How much did private consumption change as a result of the change in savings?

✳ **4.** Fill in the blanks in the following table. Assume that the MPC is constant over everyone in the economy.

MPC	Spending multiplier	Change in government spending	Change in income
_______	5	\$100	_______
_______	2.5	_______	−\$250
0.5	_______	\$200	_______
0.2	_______	_______	\$1,000

✳ **5.** Congress wants to stimulate the economy by using fiscal policy. What kind of fiscal policy would you recommend? Illustrate the impact of your recommendation in a fully labeled aggregate demand–aggregate supply graph. What does your plan suggest will happen to output, employment, and inflation?

6. Congress decides to try to slow the economy by using fiscal policy. What kind of fiscal policy would you recommend? Illustrate the impact of your recommendation in a fully labeled aggregate demand–aggregate supply graph. What does your plan suggest will happen to output, employment, and inflation?

SOLVED PROBLEMS

4.

MPC	Spending multiplier	Change in government spending	Change in income
0.8	5	\$100	*\$500*
0.6	2.5	−*\$100*	−\$250
0.5	*2*	\$200	*\$400*
0.2	*1.25*	*\$800*	\$1,000

To determine the spending multiplier, take 1 ÷ (1 – MPC).

If you have the spending multiplier, to find MPC take 1 – (1÷ spending multiplier).

If you have the change in government spending, then to get the change in income take the change in government spending times the spending multiplier.

If you have the change in income, then to get the change in government spending take the change in income divided by the spending multiplier.

5. Congress would use expansionary policy to try to stimulate the economy. This policy could entail tax cuts, government spending increases, or some combination of both. As a result, the aggregate demand curve would shift to the right, causing output and employment to increase. GDP moves from GDP_1 to GDP_2. The price level would also rise (from P_1 to P_2). See the graph below.

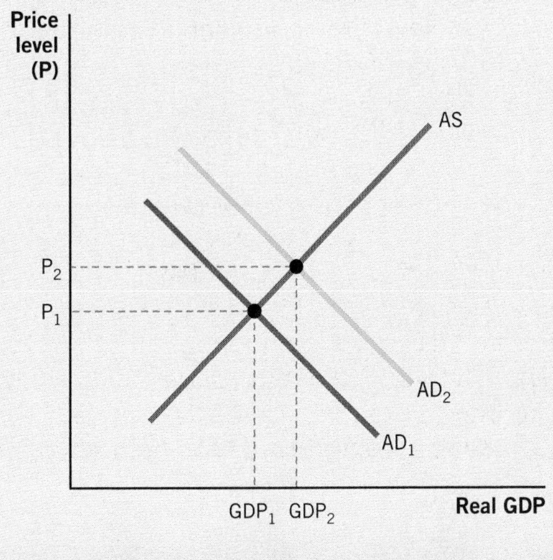

CHAPTER

18 International Economics

MISCONCEPTION

A nation should never trade for goods and services that it can produce itself.

It is generally assumed that nations should try to produce their own goods and services. In particular, it seems intuitive that if the United States can produce a particular good, then the United States should definitely produce that good (rather than import it). But economics helps us understand that we may be better off letting another nation produce the good and then trading for it later. Trading enables us to specialize in the production of goods that we can produce better. In addition, trade is beneficial for all nations, not just the United States.

Over the past few decades, the level of trade among the world's nations has risen dramatically. We begin this chapter by discussing how trade benefits the parties involved. Nevertheless, there are interests within a country that seek to limit trade. We'll examine why that is the case in the second part of the chapter. Finally, trade is not barter. People use money to facilitate international trade just as they use it domestically; however, since most countries have their own money, a second trade is involved when exchanging goods across national borders: the trade of currency. Trading currency adds a layer of complexity that we also must explore to fully understand international trade.

Imports come into the United States from all over the globe. But do the contents of these shipping containers harm our economy?

BIG QUESTIONS

- How does international trade help the economy?
- What are the effects of tariffs?
- Why do exchange rates matter?
- Why do exchange rates rise and fall?

How Does International Trade Help the Economy?

A nation's **trade balance** is the difference between its total exports and total imports.

A **trade surplus** occurs when exports exceed imports, indicating a positive trade balance.

A **trade deficit** occurs when imports exceed exports, indicating a negative trade balance.

In Chapter 11, we defined *net exports* as total exports of goods and services minus total imports of goods and services. The difference between a nation's total exports and total imports is its **trade balance**. If a nation exports more than it imports, it has a positive trade balance, known as a **trade surplus**. However, if a nation imports more than it exports, the trade balance is negative and known as a **trade deficit**. The United States has had a trade deficit since 1975. In 2014 alone, the nation exported \$2.34 trillion in goods and services but imported \$2.88 trillion, leading to a trade deficit of \$538 billion—no small sum.

If you look at the data presented in Figure 18.1, you might notice three patterns. First, in panel (a) you can see that both imports and exports increased significantly over the 50 years from 1965 to 2014. As a share of GDP, U.S. exports grew from a little over 5% to 13.5% of GDP. During the same period, imports rose from a little over 4% to 16.4% of GDP. This vast increase in the volume of trade is a glimpse at the modern trend toward globalization. The world's largest economy—that of the United States—is becoming ever more intertwined with the economies of other nations.

Panels (b) and (c) of Figure 18.1 reveal a little-known fact about U.S. trade: while the trade deficit in goods is large and growing, the United States actually has a service trade surplus. Popular service exports of the United States include financial, travel, and education services. To put a face on service exports, think about students in your classes who are not U.S. citizens (perhaps this even includes you). In 2014, the United States exported over \$30.8 billion worth of education services.

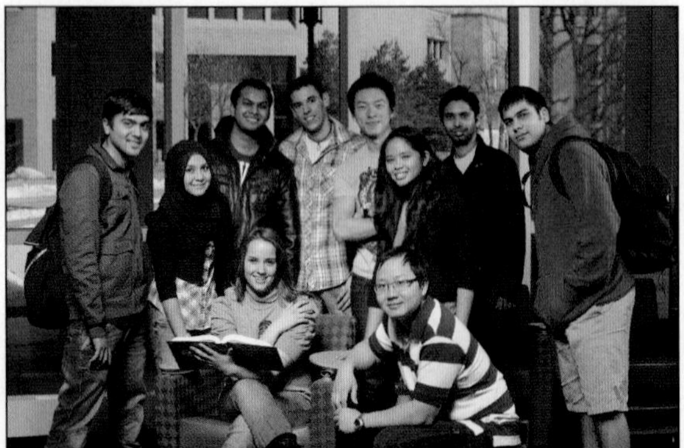
Foreign students who purchase their education in the United States are buying one type of U.S. service export.

Finally, notice how the business cycle affects international trade. During recessionary periods—indicated by the vertical blue-shaded bars in Figure 18.1(a)—imports generally drop. As the economy recovers, imports begin to rise again. In addition, while exports often drop during recessions, the trade

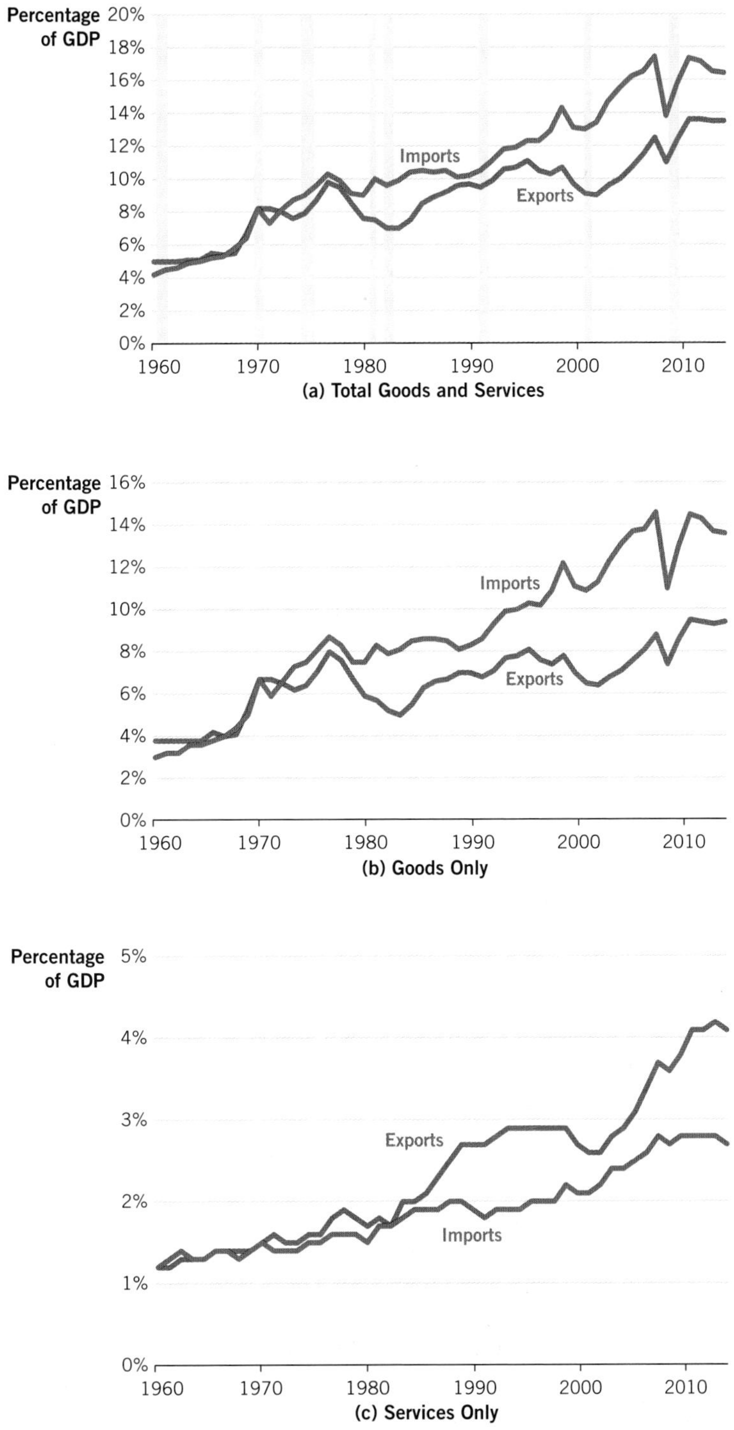

FIGURE 18.1

U.S. Exports and Imports, 1965–2014 (as a percentage of GDP)

(a) Both imports and exports have significantly risen in the United States over time. In addition, the trade balance is becoming more negative over time, as imports are exceeding exports by an increasingly wider margin. This trade deficit grows larger during periods of economic growth and shrinks during recessions (shaded bars).

(b) The trade deficit is driven by a merchandise (goods) deficit, because

(c) the United States enjoys a trade surplus in services.

Source: U.S. Bureau of Economic Analysis, *U.S. International Transactions.*

deficit tends to shrink during downturns. This important point suggests that when things are going well economically, people buy more goods from other countries. This conclusion should make sense. In good economic times, incomes are higher and consumption spending increases, no matter where the goods and services are made.

Major Trading Partners of the United States

So with which countries do we trade? In 2013, the United States imported goods and services from 238 nations. However, 60% of imports came from just seven nations. Figure 18.2 shows the value of imports from and exports to these top seven trading partners of the United States.

In the past, our closest neighbors—Canada and Mexico—were our chief trading partners. From Canada we get motor vehicles, oil, natural gas, and many other goods and services. From Mexico we get coffee, computers, household appliances, and gold. Recently, transportation costs have decreased and we are trading in volume with other countries. For example, total imports from China alone were almost $456 billion in 2013, up from $105 billion (adjusted for inflation) a decade ago. Popular Chinese imports include electronics, toys, and clothing. While we import a lot from China, we don't export as much to China as we would like because of the Chinese government's trade restrictions on imports.

Trade creates value

Now that we have some perspective on trade, let's focus on how trade helps countries by returning to a topic we covered in Chapter 2: comparative advantage. To keep the analysis simple, we'll assume that two trading partners—the United States and Mexico—produce only two items, clothes and food. This simplification enables us to demonstrate that trade creates value in the absence of any restrictions.

FIGURE 18.2

Major Trading Partners of the United States, 2013 (in millions of dollars)

Fully 60% of all U.S. goods imports come from the seven nations shown here. We export more to Canada and Mexico than to other nations, but we import more from China. The U.S. trade deficit with China is almost $300 billion.

Source: International Economic Accounts, U.S. Bureau of Economic Analysis.

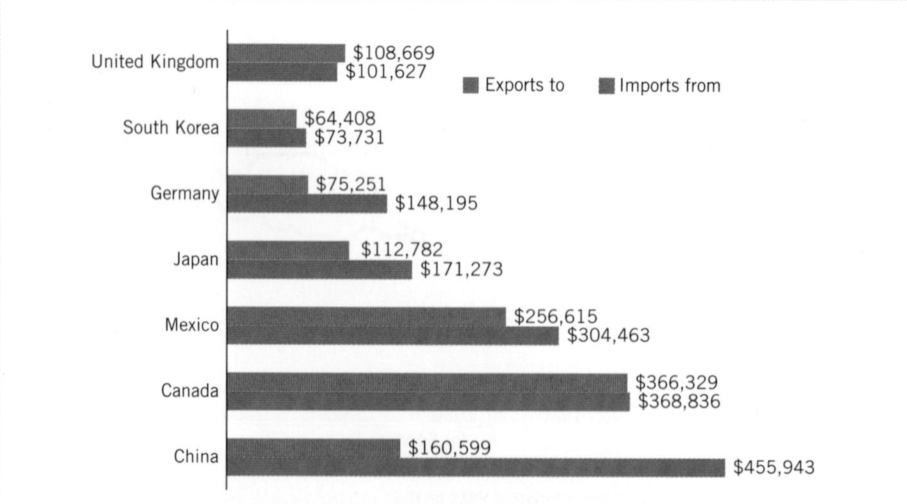

PRACTICE WHAT YOU KNOW

Trade in Goods and Services: Deficit or Surplus?

The United States imports many goods from Japan, including automobiles, electronics, and medical instruments. But we also export many services to Japan, such as financial and travel services. The table below presents trade data between the United States and Japan for 2013. (All figures are in billions of U.S. dollars.)

	Exports to Japan	Imports from Japan
Goods	$67	$141
Services	$46	$30

Video game consoles are a popular U.S. import from Japan.

Question: Using the data shown above, how would you compute the U.S. goods trade balance with Japan? Is the balance a surplus or a deficit?

Answer: The U.S. goods trade balance equals:

$$\text{goods exports} - \text{goods imports} = \$67 \text{ billion} - \$141 \text{ billion} = -\$74 \text{ billion}$$

This is a deficit, since imports exceed exports. As a result, the trade balance is negative.

Question: Now how would you compute the U.S. services trade balance with Japan? Is the balance a surplus or a deficit?

Answer: The U.S. services trade balance equals:

$$\text{service exports} - \text{service imports} = \$46 \text{ billion} - \$30 \text{ billion} = \$16 \text{ billion}$$

This is a surplus, since exports exceed imports. As a result, the trade balance is positive.

Question: Finally, how would you compute the overall U.S. trade balance with Japan, which includes both goods and services? Is this overall trade balance a surplus or a deficit?

Answer: The overall U.S. trade balance equals:

$$\text{goods and services exports} - \text{goods and services imports} = \$113 \text{ billion} - \$171 \text{ billion} = -\$58 \text{ billion}$$

This is a deficit, since imports exceed exports. Consequently, the trade balance is negative.

Data source: Office of the United States Trade Representative.

Comparative Advantage

Trade creates value

Since the beginning of this book, we have seen that trade creates value. Gains arise when a nation specializes in production and exchanges its output with a trading partner. In other words, each nation should produce the good for which it has a comparative advantage and then trade with other nations for the goods in which those countries have a comparative advantage. Trade leads to lower costs of production and maximizes the combined output of all nations involved.

Is anything in this picture *not* produced in China?

For example, assume that the U.S. workforce is generally more skilled than that of Mexico and that the United States has much more farmland. Mexico has a less skilled workforce and tends to produce goods that require more labor than capital. Therefore, Mexico has a comparative advantage in producing labor-intensive goods such as clothing, and the United States has a comparative advantage in producing capital-intensive goods such as food.

In Figure 18.3, we see the production possibilities frontier (PPF) for each country when it does *not* specialize and trade. In panel (a), Mexico can produce at any point along

FIGURE 18.3

The Production Possibilities Frontier for Mexico and the United States without Specialization and Trade

(a) Mexico chooses to operate along its production possibilities curve at 450 million units of clothing and 150 million tons of food. Each unit of clothing incurs an opportunity cost of one-third of a ton of food—a ratio of 3 tons of food to 1 unit of clothing.

(b) The United States chooses to operate along its production possibilities curve at 300 million units of clothing and 200 million tons of food. Each unit of clothing incurs an opportunity cost of two tons of food—a ratio of 2 tons of food to 1 unit of clothing.

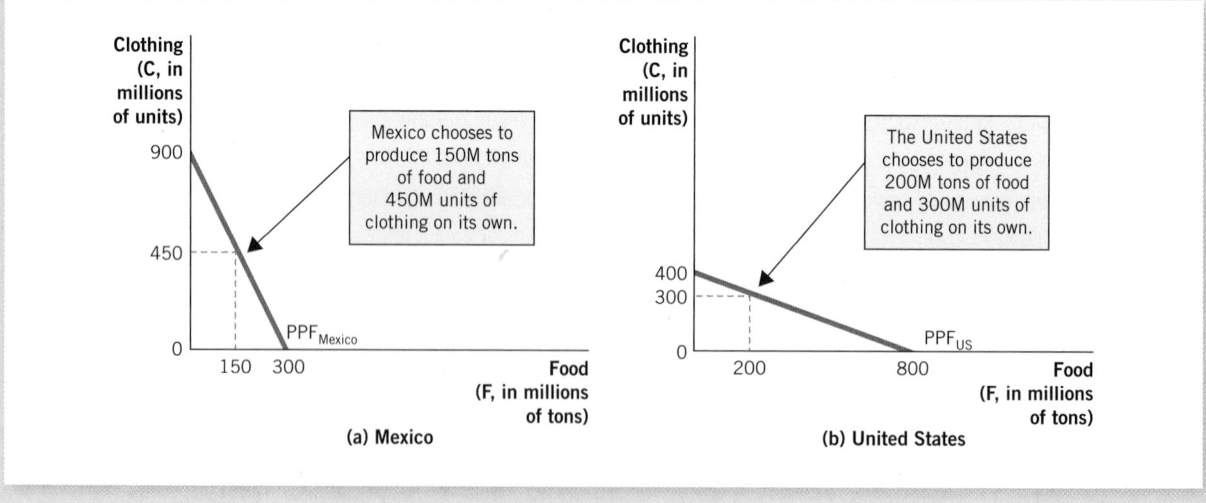

PRACTICE WHAT YOU KNOW

Opportunity Cost and Comparative Advantage: Determining Comparative Advantage

Does China enjoy a comparative advantage in textile production?

U.S. trade with mainland China has exploded in the past decade, with imports from China reaching $456 billion a year and exports up to $161 billion. In this question, we consider a hypothetical production possibilities frontier for food and textiles in both China and the United States.

The table below presents daily production possibilities for a typical worker in both China and the United States, assuming these are the only goods produced in both countries. (The numbers represent units of food and units of textiles.)

Output per worker per day

	Food	Textiles
China	1	2
United States	9	3

Question: What are the opportunity costs of food production for both China and the United States?

Answer: The opportunity cost of food production in China is the amount of textile production that is forgone for a single unit of food output. Since a Chinese worker can produce 2 textile units in a day or 1 unit of food, the opportunity cost of 1 unit of food is 2 textiles.

In the United States, a worker can produce 3 textile units in one day or 9 units of food. Thus, the opportunity cost of 1 unit of food is just $1/3$ textile unit. (If you set up a 3 textile to 9 food ratio, 3:9, divide each side of the ratio by 9 to get the ½ textile to 1 food ratio.)

Question: What are the opportunity costs of textile production for both China and the United States?

Answer: The opportunity cost of textile production in China is the amount of food production that is forgone for a single textile unit produced. Since a Chinese worker can produce 1 unit of food in a day or 2 textile units, the opportunity cost of 1 textile unit is ½ unit of food. (If you set up a 1 food to 2 textile ratio, 1:2, divide each side by 2 to get the ½ food to 1 textile ratio.)

In the United States, a worker can produce 9 units of food in one day or 3 textile units. Thus, the opportunity cost of 1 textile unit is 3 units of food.

(CONTINUED)

(CONTINUED)

Question: Which nation has a comparative advantage in food production? Which nation has a comparative advantage in textile production?

Answer: The United States has a lower opportunity cost of food production (it has to give up only 1/3 versus 2 textile units), so its comparative advantage is in food production. China has a lower opportunity cost of textile production (it gives up only ½ versus 3 units of food), so it has a comparative advantage in textile production.

its PPF. The PPF shows that Mexico could produce 900 million units of clothing if it doesn't make any food, or 300 million tons of food if it doesn't make any clothing. Neither extreme is especially desirable since it would mean that Mexico would have to do without either clothing or food. As a result, Mexico will choose to operate somewhere between the two extremes. Panel (a) shows Mexico operating along its production possibilities frontier at 450 million units of clothing and 150 million tons of food. Panel (b) shows that the United States could produce 400 million units of clothing if it doesn't make any food, or 800 million tons of food if it doesn't make any clothing. Like Mexico, the United States will choose to operate somewhere in between—for example, at 300 million units of clothing and 200 million tons of food.

Since the opportunity costs differ between the two countries, trade has the potential to benefit both. In Mexico, moving along the PPF from making all clothing to making some amount of food means giving up some clothing production. Producing 150 million tons of food means giving up the production of 450 million units of clothing (900 − 450 = 450). If you take the amount given up (450 million units of clothing) and compare it to the 150 million tons of food Mexico gets in return, you have a 3:1 ratio (450 divided by 150, or three units of clothing per one ton of food). Thus, each ton of food incurs an opportunity cost of three units of clothing.

In the United States, producing 200 million tons of food means giving up production of 100 million units of clothing (400 − 300 = 100). Therefore, comparing what the United States gives up (100 million units of clothing) to what it gets (200 million tons of food) yields a 1:2 ratio, or one unit of clothing to two tons of food. Table 18.1 shows the initial production choices and the opportunity costs for both nations.

The key to making trade mutually beneficial in this case is to find a trading ratio between 3:1 and 1:2. For instance, a 1:1 trading ratio means that one

TABLE 18.1

Output and Opportunity Costs for Mexico and the United States

	Chosen output level		Opportunity cost	
	Food (tons)	**Clothing (units)**	**Food (F)**	**Clothing (C)**
Mexico	150	450	3 C	⅓ F
United States	200	300	½ C	2 F

ton of food would trade for one unit of clothing. Since it costs Mexico three units of clothing to produce one ton of food, a trade in which Mexico has to give up only one unit of clothing to get one ton of food would be good for Mexico. The production of food is cheaper when Mexico trades rather than produces its own food.

At the same time, the United States has to give up two tons of food to produce one unit of clothing. But if the United States trades with Mexico at a 1:1 trading ratio, the United States has to give up only one ton of food. Basically, the cost of producing clothes goes down for the United States when it trades with Mexico rather than produces its own clothing.

Figure 18.4 shows how both countries are better off after specialization and trade, each country specializes in its comparative advantage. This means that the United States produces food and Mexico produces clothing. If the trade ratio is 1:1, then Mexico ends up at point M_2 in panel (a) with 500 million units of clothing and 400 million tons of food. The country is able to consume a combination of food and clothing that is impossible for it to produce on its own, because this combination is beyond Mexico's production possibility frontier.

In panel (b), the United States ends up at point US_2 with 400 million units of clothing and 400 million tons of food. We see that with specialization and trade the United States also can consume more than if it produced both goods on its own.

FIGURE 18.4

The Joint Production Possibilities Frontier for Mexico and the United States with Specialization and Trade

(a) After Mexico specializes in clothing and trades with the United States, it is better off by 50 million units of clothing and 250 million tons of food (compare points M_1 and M_2).

(b) After the United States specializes in food and trades with Mexico, it is better off by 100 million units of clothing and 200 tons of food (compare points US_1 and US_2).

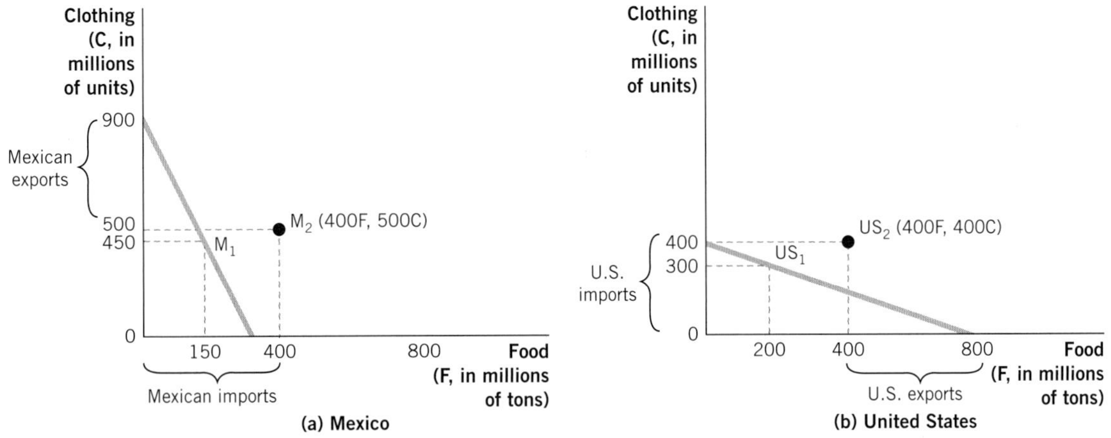

The combined benefits that Mexico and the United States enjoy are even more significant. As we saw in Figure 18.3, when Mexico didn't specialize and trade it chose to make 450 million units of clothing and 150 million tons of food. Without specialization and trade, the United States chose to produce 300 million units of clothing and 200 million tons of food. The combined output without specialization was 750 million units of clothing and 350 million tons of food. However, as we see in Figure 18.4, the joint output with specialization is 900 million units of clothing and 800 million tons of food. Trade is a win-win proposition because each country is able to (1) concentrate on the production of goods for which it is a low-opportunity-cost producer, (2) trade for goods for which it is a high-opportunity-cost producer, and (3) consume more than it could without trade.

Opportunity cost

What Are the Effects of Tariffs?

Despite the benefits of free trade, significant trade barriers such as import taxes often exist. For example, imported peanuts are more expensive than peanuts grown in the United States. Shelled peanuts are subject to a 131.8% tariff (import tax). This means that two $3.00 bags of peanuts, one filled with peanuts grown in the United States and the other containing peanuts grown in India, would sell for significantly different prices in the United States. The price of the Indian peanuts would be $6.95 due to the tariff, while the U.S.-grown peanuts would sell for just $3.00.

Import taxes like those on peanuts are not unusual (although the tariff on peanuts is remarkably high). In this section, we examine these taxes on trade more closely. After we consider the impacts of an import tax, we focus our attention on common economic and political justifications for restricting international trade and determine whether or not they are effective.

Tariffs

Tariffs are taxes levied on imported goods and services.

Tariffs are taxes levied on imported goods and services. The producer of the imported good pays the tariff when the good arrives in a foreign country, and the tariff is usually passed on to the consumer as part of the item's price. Figure 18.5 illustrates the impact of a tariff on foreign shoes (another heavily taxed import). To assess how a tariff affects the market price of shoes in the United States, we observe the relationship between domestic demand and domestic supply.

Panel (a) shows the domestic consumers (demand) and domestic producers (supply) of shoes in the United States. If trade between countries did not happen, the equilibrium price and quantity would be set where the domestic supply ($S_{domestic}$) and the domestic demand ($D_{domestic}$) intersect. Here, price (P_{dom}) is $140 per pair and quantity is 100 million. If free trade is allowed, however, foreign producers enter the market and the supply curve shifts to the right, to $S_{free\ trade}$, which shows supply for all domestic producers and all foreign producers combined. The increase in supply pushes price down to the free-trade price (P_F), which is $100 per pair. At this lower price, the quantity demanded increases to 140 million.

FIGURE 18.5

The Impact of a Tariff

(a) In a world of free trade without tariffs, the domestic market for shoes is dominated by imports. Total quantity demanded is 140 million pairs of shoes, but domestic producers supply only 60 million pairs. Imports equal 80 million pairs and make up any shortage that otherwise would have resulted. With free trade, total surplus in the economy rises as consumers are made better off, but producers are made worse off.

(b) When a tariff is imposed, the price rises and domestic production expands from 60 million pairs to 80 million pairs. At the same time, imports fall to 40 million pairs. Tariffs also cause a reallocation of the consumer surplus. A deadweight loss is created (shaded areas L_1 and L_2), as is revenue for the government (area T). Domestic producers also regain some of their producer surplus (area B).

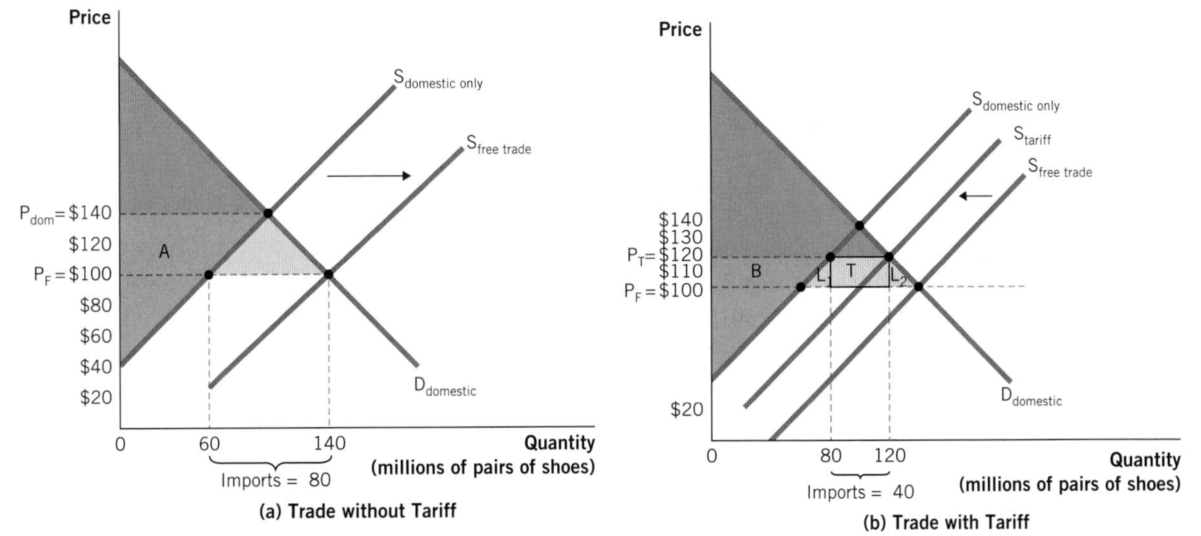

At the free-trade price, though, domestic producers reduce the amount they supply to 60 million pairs. In a normal market, the quantity available to consumers would drop. But with free trade, imports from foreign sources will make up for what would have been a shortage. Foreign producers make up the difference between what domestic producers manufacture and the amount consumers want by sending 80 million pairs of shoes (140 – 60) to the United States.

This trade has another benefit. In Chapter 4, we discussed the concepts of consumer and producer surplus. In Figure 18.5(a), consumer surplus is the area above the price and below the domestic demand curve (shaded in green). Producer surplus is the area below the price and above the domestic supply curve (shaded in red). When the price falls, producer surplus shrinks because domestic producers are selling less. The area marked A goes to consumers, and thus consumer surplus increases. However, consumers gain even more because there is more being bought. The triangle shaded in yellow is now consumer surplus. Before the free trade, this area of consumer surplus didn't exist. This extra surplus is the main reason why economists advocate for free trade. With trade, the total surplus is larger than it was before the trade, meaning the overall economy is better off.

Of course, domestic producers may not see it this way. Trade makes them worse off, and despite the overall macroeconomic benefit from trade, they may seek protection from foreign competition in the form of a tariff. If they succeed in getting a tariff implemented, the market changes, as Figure 18.5(b) shows. The tariff is placed on the foreign producers, raising their costs of doing business in the United States. As a result, the supply curve shifts to the left, from $S_{\text{free trade}}$ to S_{tariff}. Market price climbs from $P_F = \$100$ to $P_T = \$120$. At this higher price, two things happen. First, domestic consumers reduce the number of shoes they want to buy; quantity demanded falls from 140 million pairs to 120 million pairs. Second, the amount of shoes produced domestically increases from 60 million pairs to 80 million pairs. This change has the added effect of reducing the number of shoes imported from 80 million pairs to 40 million pairs (120 – 80).

Let's evaluate the tariff's impact on the market. As the price rises, producer surplus increases at consumers' expense. Area B marks the transfer of consumer surplus back to producers. Consumers lose in another way, too. The areas marked L_1, L_2, and T used to be consumer surplus, but now they are not. The area T (for taxes) reflects gains for the government. Tariffs are taxes, after all, so the government earns tax revenue equal to the size of the tariff times the number of imports. The remaining areas, L_1 and L_2, represent deadweight loss: surplus that existed before the tariff was put in place but that no longer belongs to anyone. This deadweight loss explains why economists are overwhelmingly against trade barriers. It reflects value that could be gained by the economy but that isn't collected by anyone. (For more on deadweight loss, see Chapter 6.)

From a macroeconomic perspective, the allocation of the total surplus isn't particularly important. What matters is that the total surplus is as large as possible. Trade helps to expand the total surplus, which is why economists like trade. Barriers to trade, such as tariffs, reduce those gains. When people argue against free trade, they may have compelling arguments (as we're about to see), but these arguments need to be weighed against the deadweight losses that result from impeding trade.

ECONOMICS IN THE REAL WORLD

Inexpensive Shoes Face the Highest Tariffs

Overall, U.S. tariffs average less than 2%, but inexpensive shoes face a tariff 20 times that amount (or more). What makes inexpensive imported shoes so "dangerous"? To help answer this question, a history lesson is in order.

Just 40 years ago, shoe manufacturers in the United States employed 250,000 workers. Today, the number of shoe workers is less than 3,000—and none of those workers assemble cheap shoes. Most of the shoe jobs have moved to low-labor-cost countries. But the shoe tariff, which was enacted to save domestic jobs, remains the same. Not a single pair of sneakers costing less than $3 is made in the United States, so the protection isn't saving any jobs. In contrast, goods such as cashmere sweaters, snakeskin purses, and silk shirts face low or no import tariffs. Other examples range from the 2.5% tariff on cars, to duty-free (tariff-free) treatment for cell phones, to tariffs of 4% to 8% for guitars.

Shoppers who buy their shoes at Walmart and Payless Shoe stores face the impact of shoe tariffs that approach 50% for the cheapest shoes, about 20% for a pair of name-brand running shoes, and about 9% for designer shoes from Gucci or Prada. This situation has the unintended consequence of passing along the tax burden to those who are least able to afford it, making the shoe tariff easily one of the most regressive taxes.

Why do cheap imported shoes face such a high tariff?

One could reasonably argue that the shoe tariff is one of the United States' worst taxes. First, it failed to protect the U.S. shoe industry—the shoe jobs disappeared a long time ago. Second, consumers who are poor pay a disproportionate amount of the tax. Third, families with children pay even more because they have more feet that need shoes. ✷

Reasons Given for Trade Barriers

Considering our discussion about the gains from trade and the inefficiencies associated with tariffs, you might be surprised to learn that trade restrictions are quite common. In this section, we consider some of the reasons for the persistence of trade barriers. These include national security, protection of infant industries, retaliation for dumping, and favors to special interests.

National Security

Many people believe that certain industries, such as weapons, energy, and transportation, are vital to our nation's defense. They argue that without the ability to produce its own missiles, firearms, aircraft, and other strategically significant assets, a nation could find itself relying on its enemies during times of war. Thus, people often argue that certain industries should be protected in the interest of national security.

On the one hand, it is certainly important for any trade arrangement to consider national security. On the other hand, in practice this argument has been used to justify trade restrictions on goods and services from friendly nations with whom the United States has active, open trade relations. For example, in 2002 the United States imposed tariffs on steel imports. Some policymakers argued that the steel tariffs were necessary because steel is an essential resource for national security. But, in fact, most imported steel comes from Canada and Brazil, which are traditional allies of the United States.

Protection of Infant Industries

Another argument in support of steel tariffs was that the U.S. steel industry needed some time to implement new technologies that would enable it to compete with steel producers in other nations. The **infant industry argument** states that domestic industries need trade protection until they are established and able to compete internationally. According to this argument,

The **infant industry argument** states that domestic industries need trade protection until they are established and able to compete internationally.

ECONOMICS IN THE MEDIA

Free Trade

Star Wars Episode I: The Phantom Menace

The Phantom Menace (1999) is an allegory about peace, prosperity, taxation, and protectionism. As the movie opens, we see the Republic slowly falling apart. Planetary trade has been at the heart of the galactic economy. The central conflict in the movie is the Trade Federation's attempt to enforce its franchise by trying to intimidate a small planet, Naboo, which believes in free trade and peace.

The leader of the Naboo, Queen Amidala, refuses to pursue any path that might start a war. Her country is subjected to an excessive tariff and blockade, so she decides to appeal to the central government for help in ending the trade restrictions. However, she discovers that the Republic's Galactic Senate is ineffectual, so she returns home and prepares to defend her country.

Meanwhile, two Jedi who work for the Republic are sent to broker a deal between Naboo and the Trade Federation, but they get stranded on Tatooine, a desert planet located in the Outer Rim. In the Outer Rim, three necessary ingredients for widespread trade—the rule of law, sound money, and honesty—are missing. As a consequence, when the Jedi try to purchase some new parts for their ship, they find out that no one accepts the credit-based money of the Republic. The Jedi are forced to barter, a process that requires that each trader have exactly what the other wants. This situation results in a complicated negotiation between one of the Jedi and a local parts dealer. The scenes on Tatooine show why institutions and competition matter so much for trade to succeed.

Disruptive, barriers to trade are!

Which of these, the infant or the adult, is a better representation of the U.S. steel industry?

once the fledgling industry gains traction and can support itself, the trade restrictions can be removed.

However, reality doesn't work this way. Firms that lobby for protection are often operating in an established industry. For example, the steel industry in the United States is over 100 years old. Establishing trade barriers is often politically popular, but finding ways to remove them is politically difficult. There was a time when helping to establish the steel, sugar, cotton, or peanut industries might have made sense based on the argument for helping new industries. But the tariffs that protect those industries have remained, in one form or another, for over 100 years.

Retaliation for Dumping

In 2009, the U.S. government imposed tariffs on radial car tires imported from China. These tariffs began at 35% and then gradually decreased to 25% before being phased out after three years. The argument in support of this tariff was that Chinese tire makers were dumping their tires in U.S. markets. **Dumping** occurs when a foreign supplier sells a good below the price it charges in its

PRACTICE WHAT YOU KNOW

Tariffs: The Winners and Losers from Trade Barriers

Why should we penalize Chinese tire imports?

In 2009, the United States imposed a tariff of 35% on radial car tire imports from China. The result of this tariff was a drop in imports of these tires from 13 million tires to just 5.6 million tires in one quarter. In addition, within a year, average radial car tire prices rose by about $8 per tire in the United States. The average price of Chinese tires rose from $30.79 to $37.98, while the average price of tires from all other nations rose from $53.94 to $62.05.

Question: Who were the winners and losers from this tire tariff?

Answer: The primary winners were the producers of tires from everywhere except China. Since this tariff was targeted at a single nation, it did not affect tire producers in other nations. Non-Chinese tire producers realized an average of $8 more per tire. In addition, given that the tire tariff is a tax, it also produced some tax revenue.

The primary losers were U.S. tire consumers, who saw prices rise by about $8 per tire, or $32 for a set of four tires.

Data source: Gary Clyde Hufbauer and Sean Lowry, "U.S. Tire Tariffs: Saving Few Jobs at High Cost," Policy Brief (Washington, D.C.: Peterson Institute for International Economics, April 9, 2012).

home country. As the name implies, dumping is often a deliberate effort to gain a foothold in a foreign market. It can also be the result of subsidies provided to producers by foreign governments.

Dumping occurs when a foreign supplier sells a good below the price it charges in its home country.

In cases of dumping, the World Trade Organization (WTO) allows for special countervailing duties to offset the subsidies. In essence, the United States places a tariff on the imported tires to restore a level playing field. Or, in other words, anytime a foreign entity decides to charge a lower price in order to penetrate a market, the country that is dumped on is likely to respond by imposing a tariff to protect its domestic industries from foreign takeover.

Special Interests

The imposition of trade barriers is often referred to as "protection." This term raises the questions *Who is being protected?* and *What are they being protected from?* We have seen that trade barriers drive up domestic prices and lead to a lower quantity of goods or services in the market in which the barriers are imposed. This situation does not protect consumers. In fact, tariffs protect domestic producers from international competition. Steel tariffs were put in place to help domestic steel producers, and tire tariffs were put in place to help domestic tire producers.

When we see trade barriers, the publicly stated reason is generally one of the three reasons we've already discussed: national security, infant industry protection, or retaliation for dumping. But we must also recognize that these barriers may be put in place as a favor to special interest groups that have much to gain at the expense of domestic consumers. For example, due to sugar import regulations, U.S. consumers pay twice as much for sugar as the rest of the world does. Thus, while sugar tariffs protect U.S. sugar producers from international competition, they cost U.S. consumers nearly $1.4 billion in 2013 alone. This outcome represents a gain for a special interest group at the expense of U.S. consumers.

Why Do Exchange Rates Matter?

Thus far, we have assumed that countries trade goods for goods. Of course, this isn't the case in reality. The United States doesn't trade food to Mexico for clothing. Instead, there are two trades going on. Before you can get clothing from Mexico, you first need to acquire pesos, the currency of Mexico. Workers in Mexico want to be paid in the currency they can use to buy things for themselves and their families. Dollars won't do. So before any trade in goods can take place, there must first be an exchange of money.

Exchange Rates: The Price of Foreign Currency

The **foreign exchange market** is the market in which the currencies of different countries are traded.

An **exchange rate** is the price of foreign currency, indicating how much a unit of foreign currency costs in terms of another currency.

Facilitated by markets, the trading of money is surprisingly easy. The **foreign exchange market** is the market in which currencies—or *foreign exchange*—from different countries are traded. The price of foreign currency is called an **exchange rate**. This price represents how much a unit of foreign currency costs in terms of another currency. For example, the price of a single Mexican peso in terms of U.S. dollars is about $0.06, or six cents. This is the exchange rate between the peso and the dollar: 1 peso = $0.06.

When you're dealing with foreign currency, it's helpful to remember that there are two sides to every trade. Because two different currencies are being traded, you have to examine the market from both perspectives. Think of currency trades as similar to looking in a mirror. The movements of two currencies are reflections of each other.

Table 18.2 shows some actual exchange rates from June 2015. Exchange rates can be viewed from either side of the exchange. For example, the exchange rate between the U.S. dollar and the Mexican peso can be viewed as either of the following:

1. the number of U.S. dollars required to buy one Mexican peso ($ per peso)
2. the number of Mexican pesos required to buy one U.S. dollar (pesos per $)

While these two rates communicate the same information, they aren't usually the same number. Instead, they are reciprocals of each other. (A *reciprocal*

TABLE 18.2

Exchange Rates between the U.S. Dollar and Other Currencies, June 2015

	Units of foreign currency you can buy with one U.S. dollar	Number of U.S. dollars required to buy one unit of foreign currency
Brazilian real	3.12	0.32
Chinese yuan	6.21	0.16
Euro	0.89	1.12
Indian rupee	63.54	0.016
Japanese yen	123.58	0.0081
Mexican peso	15.50	0.065
U.K. pound	0.64	1.57

Source: Google Public Data.

of a number is 1 divided by that number.) How you report the exchange rate depends on what you're trying to buy. If you're trying to buy Chinese yuan and you have dollars, you report the exchange rate as the number of dollars needed to buy a yuan. If you have euros and want to buy Indian rupees, you ask how many euros it will take to buy one rupee.

Exchange rates don't remain the same. In fact, they change regularly. If a currency becomes more valuable in world markets, its price rises. This increase is called an appreciation or a strengthening of the currency. **Currency appreciation** occurs when a currency increases in value relative to other currencies. If the dollar appreciates, it becomes more valuable in world

Currency appreciation occurs when a currency becomes more valuable relative to other currencies.

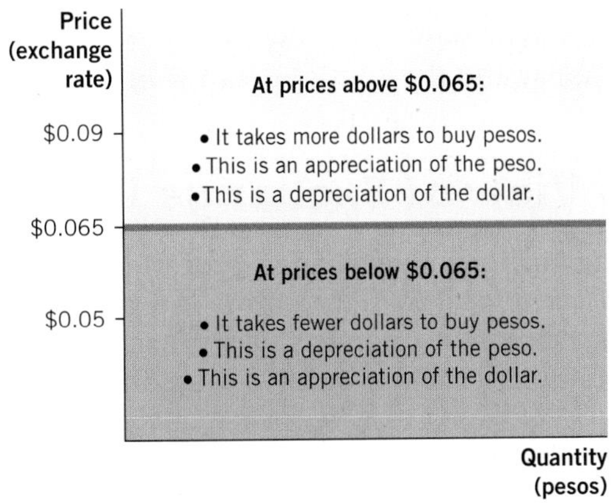

FIGURE 18.6

Exchange Rates and Currency Appreciation and Depreciation

Currency depreciation occurs when a currency becomes less valuable relative to other currencies.

markets. In contrast, **currency depreciation**, or weakening, occurs when a currency decreases in value relative to other currencies. If the dollar depreciates, it becomes less valuable in world markets.

Figure 18.6 illustrates appreciation and depreciation with the exchange rate between the U.S. dollar and the peso. The exchange rate starts at $0.065 for a peso. If the rate rises to $0.09 per peso, it will take more American currency to buy a peso, which signals an appreciation of the peso and a depreciation of the dollar. If, instead, the price falls to $0.05 per peso, it will take less American currency to buy a peso, which signals a depreciation of the peso and an appreciation of the dollar.

Remember the notion of the reflection of currencies that we mentioned earlier. We see these mirror images clearly now. When one currency appreciates, the other depreciates. When an exchange rate changes, one currency always appreciates while the other depreciates.

Derived Demand

People purchase a foreign currency in order to buy goods or services produced in the foreign country that uses that currency. For example, if you head off to Europe for spring break, you'll need to convert your dollars into euros. Don't lose sight of this simple truth, because it is at the core of our entire conversation about exchange-rate determination and why exchange rates matter.

Derived demand is demand for a good or service that derives from the demand for another good or service.

The demand for foreign currency is a derived demand. We talked about the demand for labor as *derived* in Chapter 8. **Derived demand** is demand for a good or service that derives from the demand for another good or service. For example, if you travel to Australia, you may want to buy a boomerang. But first you must buy Australian dollars, which are the currency of Australia. Your demand for Australian dollars isn't for the sake of holding Australian dollars. Instead, your demand for the currency is derived from your demand for the boomerang.

Since you have to buy another currency before you can purchase goods from another country, the price of the currency affects how many goods you can buy. Exchange rates matter because they influence the relative prices of goods and services. Any good that crosses a border has to pass through a foreign exchange market on its way to sale. For example, the price you pay in the United States for a Samsung television built in South Korea depends not only on the supply and demand for televisions, but also on the exchange rate between the U.S. dollar and the South Korean won.

The Macro View of Exchange Rates

Zooming out to the macro view, exchange rates affect the prices of all imports and exports—and, therefore, GDP. The more integrated the world economy becomes, the more closely economists watch exchange rates because they affect both what nations produce and what nations consume. Let's see how this plays out.

If the dollar appreciates (gets stronger), you might think that's a good thing. After all, the dollar is now worth more. As a result, you can buy more of another country's currency. Let's say the dollar appreciates against the Brazilian real. What happens to the real? If the dollar appreciates against the

TABLE 18.3

Summary of Trade as the U.S. Dollar Strengthens against the Brazilian Real

	Trade balance in the United States	Trade balance in Brazil
Exports	U.S. products are relatively more expensive in Brazil.	Brazilian products are relatively less expensive in the United States.
Imports	Goods from Brazil are relatively less expensive in the United States.	Goods from the United States are relatively more expensive in Brazil.
Trade Balance	Exports fall. Imports rise. Trade balance falls.	Exports rise. Imports fall. Trade balance rises.

real, the real depreciates against the dollar. So if you want to buy coffee from Brazil, you can now buy more because you can buy more reals (the plural of "real"). When the dollar appreciates, you can buy more Brazilian currency and thus buy more things from Brazil. But that's not all that is going on.

If you buy more Brazilian coffee, you affect the trade balance. Imports from Brazil are rising, and the trade deficit grows. But wait! Remember, there is the Brazilian side of things to consider, and it's the opposite of what's happening in the United States.

Since the real is now weaker, Brazilians cannot buy as many dollars. They therefore buy fewer U.S.-made cars and everything else from the United States. Thus, U.S. exports to Brazil fall, further increasing the trade deficit. In Brazil, exports increase—more coffee is going to the United States—and Brazil imports less because dollars (and therefore U.S.-made products) are more expensive. As a result, the trade balance improves for Brazil.

Table 18.3 summarizes what occurs when the value of a currency is changing. If the dollar appreciates, it can buy more of Brazil's currency, thus making goods from Brazil relatively cheaper. As a result, people in the United States buy more, and imports rise. At the same time, the Brazilian real is depreciating. People living in Brazil buy fewer U.S. goods, so Brazil's imports fall. Don't forget: one country's imports are another country's exports. When imports from Brazil to the United States rise, Brazilian exports rise. When exports from the United States to Brazil fall, imports from the United States to Brazil fall.

All of this discussion means that a country with a strong currency is more likely to have a negative trade balance. Similarly, a country with a weak currency is more likely to have a positive trade balance. So does a nation want its currency to be strong or weak? It may not actually have much say in the value of its currency. Exchange rates are typically determined in the market, meaning they're subject to the forces of demand and supply.

Why Do Exchange Rates Rise and Fall?

Let's now look at the factors that can affect the foreign exchange market. When we have finished, we'll be able to consider why exchange rates rise and fall.

The Demand for Foreign Currency

In this section, we discuss the factors that affect the demand side of the market for foreign currency. We distinguish three primary factors: the price of the currency (the exchange rate), the demand for foreign goods and services, and the demand for foreign financial assets.

Price of Foreign Currency

Since we're dealing with a market, we also deal with the law of demand. For instance, when the price of the yen falls, goods and services produced in Japan (such as Sony televisions or Toyota SUVs) are less expensive relative to goods and services produced in the United States. Therefore, if the price of the yen falls, the quantity demanded for yen increases. If, instead, the price of the yen rises, it becomes more expensive to purchase Japanese goods, and the quantity of Japanese goods demanded falls. Remember, a change in price causes a move along the demand curve. The curve itself does not change.

Demand for Foreign Goods, Services, and Financial Assets

As we've emphasized, you purchase foreign currency so that you can buy goods or services produced in foreign countries. In fact, no matter what you buy from another country, you need its currency. If you wanted to buy financial assets from a foreign country, such as a Japanese government bond or some stock in Honda, you would need to buy yen. Perhaps you're thinking, "But wait, I buy goods from other countries quite often without purchasing foreign currency." This is true: you can buy imported TVs, cars, fruits, and clothing without ever touching a coin or bill of foreign currency. But in fact those goods were originally purchased with the foreign currency of the nation in which they were produced.

For example, a Sony television is produced in Japan, but you buy it in a retail store here in the United States. The workers and factory owners in Japan are paid in yen. This means that the U.S. company that imports the Sony TV from Japan has to buy yen so it can pay for the product. In short, someone has to buy the foreign currency to pay for the TV, even if it's not you. For this reason, the demand for a nation's currency depends on the demand for its exports.

When the demand for a nation's exports rises, the demand for its currency rises as well. For example, if the U.S. demand for Japanese TVs increases, the demand for yen will increase at all prices. Figure 18.7 illustrates changes in demand for yen. An increase in demand for Sony TVs shifts the demand for yen from D_1 to D_2. If the U.S. demand for Sony TVs decreases, then there is less reason to buy yen, so the demand for yen declines. This decline is illustrated as a shift in the opposite direction—from D_1 to D_3.

If you want to snorkel in Mexico, you'd better buy some pesos.

The Supply of Foreign Currency

In Chapter 15, we talked about modern money, which is fiat currency. This kind of currency is printed and supplied by governments. From a market standpoint, it is fixed in quantity at any one time. Governments increase and decrease the

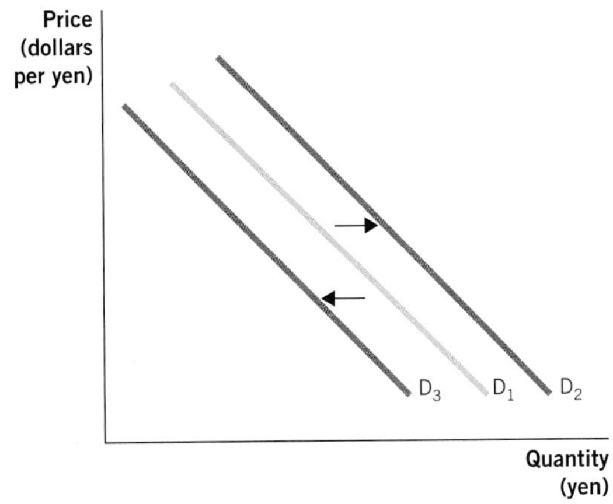

FIGURE 18.7

Shifts in the Demand for Foreign Currency

Increases in the demand for foreign currency derive from an increased demand (D_2) for foreign goods and services and/or foreign financial assets. Decreases in the demand for foreign currency derive from a decreased demand (D_3) for foreign goods and services and/or foreign financial assets. Here we illustrate these relationships with the U.S. dollar and the Japanese yen.

supply of fiat currency very often, and when they do, the supply curve for foreign currency shifts, as Figure 18.8 shows. For example, consider the possible actions of the Bank of Japan (BOJ), which is Japan's central bank, the agency that determines the country's monetary policy. Initially, the supply of yen is vertical at S_1. If the BOJ increases the supply of yen relative to the supply of dollars, the supply curve shifts outward, from S_1 to S_2. If, instead, the BOJ reduces the supply of yen relative to the supply of dollars, the supply curve shifts in the opposite direction, from S_1 to S_3.

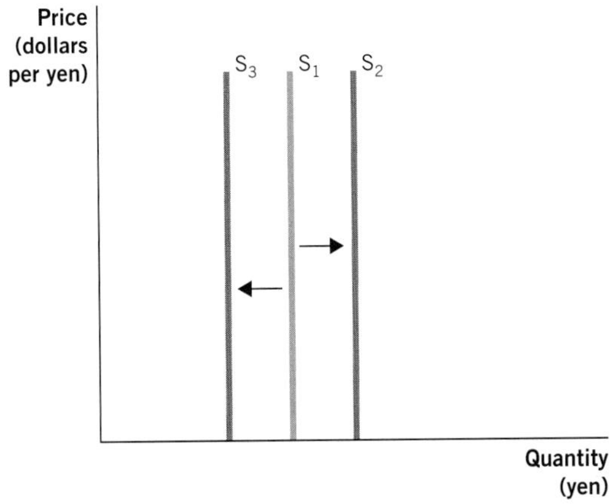

FIGURE 18.8

Shifts in the Supply of Foreign Currency

The supply of any nation's currency is determined by that nation's government. If the Bank of Japan increases the supply of yen relative to the supply of dollars, the supply curve shifts from S_1 to S_2. If the supply of yen decreases relative to the supply of dollars, the curve shifts in the opposite direction, from S_1 to S_3.

Applying Our Model of Exchange Rates

In this section, we consider some applications of our exchange-rate model. In reality, exchange rates fluctuate daily, and these prices affect the prices of all imports and exports. These fluctuations are the result of shifts in demand, supply, or both; however, the majority of the action in the market for foreign exchange occurs on the demand side, so that's where we focus our analysis.

Changes in Demand

In most of the world, car shoppers can choose from many cars; these include Toyotas produced in Japan and Jeeps produced in the United States. In microeconomics, we might study the impact on the auto manufacturers from a shift in consumer preferences away from Jeeps and toward Toyotas. But these kinds of demand changes, which occur quite frequently, also affect the market for foreign currency. For example, if consumer preferences in the United States shift away from Jeeps and toward Toyotas, the demand for yen rises.

How are exchange rates affected when consumers choose Toyotas over Jeeps?

Figure 18.9 shows the results of a shift toward Toyotas. Initially, the market for yen is in equilibrium with supply of S and demand of D_1. The initial equilibrium exchange rate is \$0.010. Then, after U.S. consumers demand more Toyotas, the demand for yen shifts outward to D_2. This shift causes the exchange rate to rise to \$0.012.

If the cause of the shift were an increase in the demand for Japanese financial assets, the result would be the same. For example, if interest rates in Japan rise, investors around the globe will want to

FIGURE 18.9

How Demand Shifts Affect the Exchange Rate

An increase in the demand for foreign currency (yen) leads to an increase in the exchange rate from \$0.010 to \$0.012. The yen appreciates relative to the dollar, and the U.S. dollar depreciates relative to the yen. A decrease in the demand for yen leads to a decrease in the exchange rate from \$0.010 to \$0.008. In this case, the yen depreciates relative to the dollar, and the U.S. dollar appreciates relative to the yen.

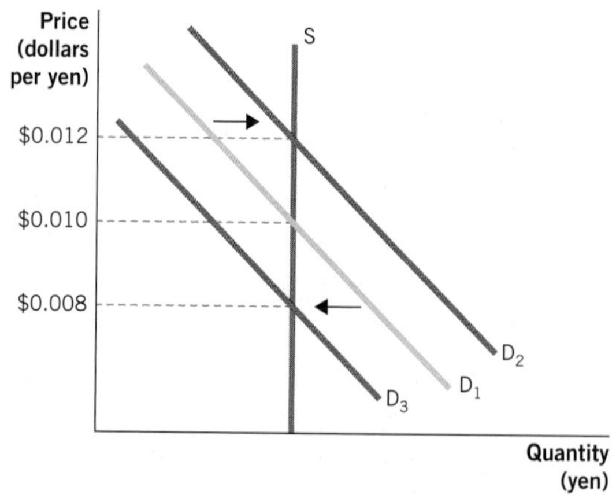

PRACTICE WHAT YOU KNOW

European Vacation

In early 2015, the value of the euro—the currency used in much of Europe—became much weaker against the dollar. This change in the relationship between the two currencies caused tourist companies to begin a heavy advertising campaign, encouraging U.S. citizens to travel to Europe.

Question: Is this a good time to travel to Europe?

Answer: Yes, it is! The strengthening of the dollar means that the euro is relatively cheaper. Not only are goods produced in Europe less expensive for Americans, but also services such as hotel rooms, meals, and tour guides have become relatively less expensive.

Question: How would you graph the market for foreign exchange showing the decline in the value of the euro?

Answer: Since there is no indication that the European Central Bank has altered the supply of euros, the demand for euros must have fallen. This decrease in demand creates a new equilibrium at a lower exchange rate (ER). Notice the label on the y axis. Since this is the market for euros, the label is "Price (dollars per euro)."

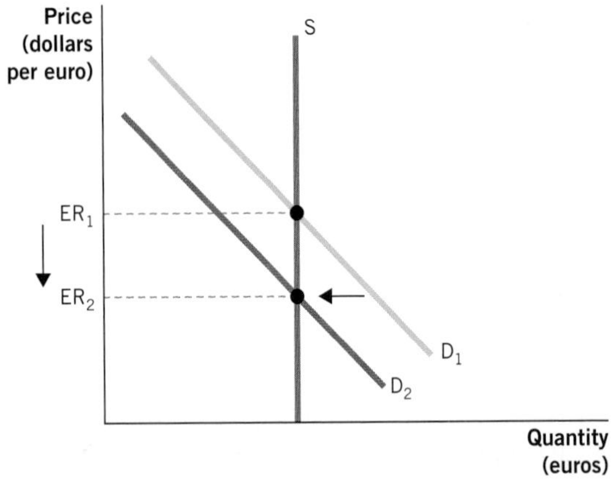

buy Japan's financial assets. The increase in the demand for yen leads to an increase in the exchange rate. The higher exchange rate implies an appreciation of the yen and, by comparison, a depreciation of the dollar. People want more yen, so its value rises in relation to the dollar.

If, instead, global demand for goods, services, and financial assets moves away from Japan and toward the United States, the demand for yen will fall (shifting to D_3) as people move toward dollars. In this case, the exchange rate falls and the yen depreciates, but the dollar appreciates.

TABLE 18.4

Shifts in Demand for Foreign Currency

Cause	Demand for foreign currency	Change in exchange rate
Increase in demand for foreign goods and services or financial assets	Demand increases.	Exchange rate rises.
Decrease in demand for foreign goods and services or financial assets	Demand decreases.	Exchange rate falls.

These shifts in demand occur naturally in a global economy in which consumers across different nations choose among products produced in a wide variety of countries. Even just focusing on cars, we can choose to buy from the United States, Germany, Japan, South Korea, the United Kingdom, Canada, and Italy, to name a few. But as international demanders' product preferences change, exchange rates are affected. Table 18.4 summarizes how shifts in demand affect foreign exchange rates.

Today, it's easier to buy goods in foreign countries because you can often just use your credit or debit card to make foreign purchases; you don't have to physically buy foreign currency. This approach works because your bank or card company is willing to buy the foreign currency for you. To you, it feels like you're paying in U.S. dollars, since you use the same card all over the world and you see deductions from your bank account in dollars. But your bank literally takes dollars from your account and then exchanges them for foreign currency so that it can pay foreign companies in their own currency. Your bank usually charges a fee for this service, but it certainly makes the transaction simpler for you.

Conclusion

We began this chapter with the misconception that nations shouldn't trade with other countries if they can make goods on their own. However, this strategy can lead to higher production costs and reduced consumer surplus. Nevertheless, because trade has microeconomic components, some groups, particularly domestic producers, seek protection from competition. Thus, trade barriers are sometimes put in place despite their deleterious effects.

We also studied exchange rates and considered them as market prices that depend on the supply of, and the demand for, foreign currency. Depreciating a nation's currency makes its exports less expensive relative to other countries'. When a country's currency depreciates, that country is able to increase its exports and decrease its imports. If the nation's currency appreciates, then that country's goods become relatively more expensive. In this case, the nation's exports fall and its imports rise. Thus, the trading of currencies significantly affects the trading of goods.

The Internet Reduces Trade Barriers

ECONOMICS FOR LIFE

You probably don't remember the world without the Internet. People still conducted business, but communications were tedious and were often delayed due to time zone changes and unreliable connections. There were fewer options for firms looking for suppliers of inputs, and a business's customer base was limited by geography because it was more difficult to spread the word about products. The widespread adoption of the Internet has changed all this and in so doing has reduced many barriers to trade. With the click of a mouse, now you can find goods and services from around the world. Businesses can locate suppliers and expand their markets. In fact, the International Trade Administration, a part of the U.S. Department of Commerce, credits the Internet for opening up markets for buyers and sellers alike.

For example, services can be exchanged online, opening the world to small businesses like never before. You can offer tutoring services, graphic design plans, and business advice to clients around the globe almost instantaneously from your home. Doctors can provide assistance to one another in remote locations. Even education is being beamed into homes half a world away through MOOCS—massive open online courses.

Moreover, you can find inputs for whatever you make. Companies like Alibaba, a Chinese Internet company with the tagline "Global trade starts here," help to coordinate orders not only for goods but also for inputs of all shapes and sizes. While you may have to wait a few days for shipping, being able to direct-order from the supplier cuts costs for businesses and reduces prices for consumers.

The Internet also enables consumers to keep track of reputable and disreputable firms. Feedback options on sites like Amazon and eBay provide future customers with the ability to make more informed choices. Web sites like Angie's List offer consumers information about service providers so they can make better choices.

The Internet is more than just Facebook and Twitter. While social media is important for communication purposes, not to mention fun, the Internet's primary benefit to society is economic. By increasing the ability of buyers and sellers to connect, along with providing more information about potential exchanges, the Internet has expanded global trade and helped to make the world a more economically connected place.

ANSWERING THE BIG QUESTIONS

How does international trade help the economy?

* Gains from trade occur when a nation specializes in production and exchanges its output with a trading partner. For this arrangement to work, each nation must produce goods for which it is a low-opportunity-cost producer and then trade for goods for which it is a high-opportunity-cost producer.

What are the effects of tariffs?

* Tariffs are taxes on imports. Tariffs reduce consumer surplus but benefit domestic producers. They also raise revenue for the government.
* Proponents of trade restrictions often cite the need to protect defense-related industries and fledgling firms, and to fend off dumping. But protectionist policies can also serve as political favors to special interest groups.

Why do exchange rates matter?

* An exchange rate is the price of one country's currency in terms of another. If you want to buy the goods and services of one country, you first need to acquire the other country's currency. Therefore, the demand for currency is derived from the demand for the goods and services which that currency can buy.
* If one country's currency gets stronger, it can buy more of another country's currency and thus more of that country's output. If a currency gets weaker, then it can buy less of another country's currency and therefore less of that country's output.

Why do exchange rates rise and fall?

* An increase in the exchange rate indicates an appreciation of the domestic currency. When currency appreciates, it becomes more valuable relative to another country's currency. An appreciation is generally the result of an increase in the demand for the goods, services, and financial assets of the domestic country.
* A decrease in the exchange rate indicates a depreciation of the domestic currency. When a currency depreciates, it becomes less valuable relative to another country's currency. A depreciation is generally the result of a decrease in the demand for the goods, services, and financial assets of the domestic country.

CONCEPTS YOU SHOULD KNOW

currency appreciation (p. 547)
currency depreciation (p. 548)
derived demand (p. 548)
dumping (p. 545)
exchange rate (p. 546)
foreign exchange market (p. 546)
infant industry argument (p. 543)
tariffs (p. 540)
trade balance (p. 532)
trade deficit (p. 532)
trade surplus (p. 532)

QUESTIONS FOR REVIEW

1. What three reasons are often offered in support of trade restrictions?
2. What would happen to the standard of living in the United States if all foreign trade were eliminated?
3. How might a nation's endowment of natural resources, labor, and climate shape the nature of its comparative advantage?
4. Tariffs reduce the volume of imports. Do tariffs also reduce the volume of exports? Explain your response.
5. Is a trade deficit a sign of economic weakness? Why or why not?
6. Which nations are the three largest trading partners of the United States?
7. Who benefits and who loses from a tariff? What is the new outcome for society?
8. What disadvantages exist if your country has a strong currency?

STUDY PROBLEMS (* *solved at the end of the section*)

1. Consider the following table for the neighboring nations of Quahog and Pawnee. Assume that the opportunity cost of producing each good is constant.

Product	Quahog	Pawnee
Meatballs (per hour)	4,000	2,000
Clams (per hour)	8,000	1,000

   a. What is the opportunity cost of producing meatballs in Quahog? What is the opportunity cost of producing clams in Quahog?
   b. What is the opportunity cost of producing meatballs in Pawnee? What is the opportunity cost of producing clams in Pawnee?
   c. Based on your answers in parts (a) and (b), which nation has a comparative advantage in producing meatballs? Which nation has a comparative advantage in producing clams?

2. Let's think about how imports affect official GDP statistics. Recall from Chapter 11 that GDP is computed as:

$$GDP = Y = C + I + G + NX$$

   Assume that originally U.S. GDP is $10 trillion, but that the economy is closed and there are no imports or exports. Now the nation of Bataslava begins selling high-quality automobiles in the United States but charges a very low price—say, $500 each. Assume that U.S. consumers use this opportunity to substitute out of U.S.-produced automobiles and into automobiles from Bataslava, and that spending on other U.S. goods does not change.

   a. What happens to U.S. GDP going forward?
   b. Is this a positive or a negative development for citizens of the United States? Why?
   c. What would be an argument for a tariff on the Bataslavan cars?

3. Suppose that the marginal-cost ratios of two products—mangoes and sardines—are as follows in the hypothetical nations of Mangolia and Sardinia:

   Mangolia: 1 mango = 2 cans of sardines

   Sardinia: 1 mango = 4 cans of sardines

   In what product should each nation specialize? Explain why the terms of trade of 1 mango = 3 cans of sardines would be acceptable to both nations.

✱ 4. Germany and Japan both produce cars and beer. The table below lists production possibilities per worker in each country (for example, one worker in Germany produces 8 cars or 10 cases of beer).

	Labor force	Cars (C)	Beer (B)
Germany	200	8	10
Japan	100	20	14

   Which nation has a comparative advantage in car production? Which one has a comparative advantage in beer production? Explain your answers.

✱ 5. Continuing with the example given in the previous problem, assume that Germany and Japan produce their own cars and beer and allocate half their labor force to the production of each.

   a. What quantities of cars and beer does Germany produce? What quantities does Japan produce?

   Now suppose that Germany and Japan produce only the good for which they enjoy a comparative advantage in production. They also agree to trade half of their output for half of what the other country produces.

   b. What quantities of cars and beer does Germany produce now? What quantities does Japan produce?

   c. What quantities of cars and beer does Germany consume now? What quantities does Japan consume?

6. If demand for clothing made in Haiti rises, how does this change affect the world value of the gourde (the Haitian currency)? Illustrate these effects in the market for gourdes.

✱ 7. Explain why the supply curve for foreign currency is vertical. Let's say you return from a trip to Mexico with 1,000 pesos. If you decide to exchange these pesos for dollars, does your action shift the supply of pesos?

SOLVED PROBLEMS

4. Japan has a comparative advantage in car production since its opportunity cost is less than Germany's (0.7 < 1.2). Germany has a comparative advantage in beer production since its opportunity cost is less than Japan's (0.8 < 1.4).
5. **a.** Germany: (C, B) = (800, 1,000); Japan: (C, B) = (1,000, 700)

   In Germany, each worker can produce 8 cars and 10 beers. If half the workforce of 200 makes cars and half brews beer, you would take 100 × 8 and 100 × 10 to get a total output of 800 cars and 1,000 cases of beer. The same process applies to Japan. Thus, Japan produces 1,000 cars and 700 cases of beer.

   b. Germany: (C, B) = (0, 2,000); Japan: (C, B) = (2,000, 0)

   Now all of the workers in Germany make beer. So 200 workers times 10 beers each gives you 2,000. The same process applies to Japan, resulting in 2,000 cars.

   c. Germany: (C, B) = (1,000, 1,000); Japan: (C, B) = (1,000, 1,000)
7. The supply curve is vertical because the supply is completely controlled by the government and doesn't change with changes in price. Your exchange does not shift the supply of pesos; only the government can do that. Instead, your action signals a reduction in demand for pesos.

Fives
$500
IF THE NUMBERS ON NOTES IN THIS PACKAGE DO NOT RUN IN SEQUENCE, THE SUBSTITUTED NOTES ARE INDICATED BY A "STAR". INQUIRIES SHOULD INCLUDE THE SERIAL NUMBERS OF THE NOTES.
Fives
$500
FEDERAL
JC42448301A
C3
FEDERAL
JC41848301A
C3
THIS NOTE IS LEGAL TENDER FOR ALL DEBTS, PUBLIC AND PRIVATE

APPENDIX

CHAPTER

19 Personal Finance

MISCONCEPTION

There is no opportunity cost to spending found money.

Imagine you get a phone call from your parents with some sad news. A long-lost uncle whom you have never met has passed away. As you wonder what to make of this news, your parents drop the bombshell that for some reason this uncle has left you $100,000 in his will!

Your mind starts racing. What are you going to do with all this money? Surely you'll spend some of it, but an economics-trained voice in your head asks what the opportunity costs of spending that money would be. Then you think, "Why should I worry about opportunity costs? This is free money! What in the world am I giving up by spending money I didn't have before?"

Just because you didn't do anything to earn this money doesn't mean there aren't costs associated with how you spend it. Whenever you make a choice about how to spend money, there is something else that you cannot do with that money. In other words, there is an opportunity cost. If you use the money to buy a car (or two), you can't use it to take a vacation. If you use it to pay off your student loans, you can't put a down payment on a house. If you spend it on a party with your friends (and what a party it would be!), you can't save it for retirement . . . and that might be the most expensive choice of all.

Opportunity cost

Managing money is a difficult and sometimes confusing part of our lives. There are many options when it comes to saving, and the possibility of making poor decisions can be very frightening. Even extremely wealthy people make poor decisions with their money. The Bernie Madoff scandal was just such a situation. Many people, a lot of them multimillionaires, lost large amounts of money when they invested it

with Madoff, a Wall Street stockbroker and investment advisor, only to find that he was essentially stealing from them. In December 2008, Madoff received a 150-year prison sentence for his deception, but by the time of his sentencing most of the money was long gone.

Fortunately, the vast majority of advisors who help people manage their money are honest folks who will guide their clients through the maze of retirement and investment options. Still, if you know something about the saving and investing process, you'll find that you can ask better questions and more likely avoid the kind of disaster that befell those who trusted Bernie Madoff.

In this chapter, we look at issues of personal finance. We begin by examining credit and personal debt. As a whole, Americans have accumulated over $3 trillion in debt. We focus first on credit cards and then move on to home ownership. While credit card debt can be very detrimental to your personal finances, buying a home and paying a mortgage have a significant upside. In the second part of the chapter, we investigate investment options for the present and for retirement. Perhaps you'll get some ideas about where that $100,000 should go.

BIG QUESTIONS

- **What do you need to know about borrowing?**
- **How do interest rates affect borrowers?**
- **Is it better to buy or rent a house?**
- **How do people save for retirement?**

What Do You Need to Know about Borrowing?

As you move through life, you'll likely find yourself borrowing money. You may already be borrowing to attend school. The upside of borrowing is that you can buy the things you want right now. The downside is that at some point you have to pay back the person or institution from which you borrowed. Still, that might not seem like such a bad thing. At least you got the car, house, education, or tablet you wanted when you borrowed the money, right?

Yes, you did, but those things end up costing you more when you borrow than when you pay for them without borrowing. Think about this situation from the lender's perspective. If you were lending money to your brother, you might tell him that he could pay the money back whenever he can and then you would be even. But if you lent money to someone you didn't know, would you be so generous? That person is using your money when you lend it to him. This means *you* can't use it. If you lend your hard-earned money to a stranger, you want to be compensated for making the loan. Thus, you charge an interest rate.

Interest Rates

The **interest rate** is the price a borrower pays to a lender to use the lender's money. If you don't want to find yourself in a position where all you're doing is paying for the privilege of borrowing money, you need to understand something about the effects of interest rates and the dangers of indebtedness. As an example, let's look at credit cards and credit card debt.

An **interest rate** is the price a borrower pays to a lender to use the lender's money.

Is a credit card money? By swiping that card or entering the numbers when you check out at Amazon.com, you take ownership of goods or services. But, as we mentioned in Chapter 15, that doesn't mean that your credit card is money. Actually, when you swipe that card, you're incurring debt. The credit card company is paying for your purchase, and you are promising to pay back the bank that issued your card at some time in the future—usually, next month when your statement arrives.

Let's look at a specific example. You're looking for the newest release from singer Blake Shelton. You find it on Amazon, put it in your cart, and check out. The music download costs you $10.50, which you put on your credit card. You can immediately listen to the music, but you don't have to pay for it until next month when the bill arrives. Unfortunately, you don't have enough in your bank account to cover the bill. So what can you do? Well, the credit card company is happy to take a partial payment; but because it will take you longer than a month to pay off your purchase, the bank is going to charge interest. This means that your $10.50 splurge on Blake Shelton is now going to cost just a little bit more. How much more depends on the price you have to pay for borrowing the bank's money. In other words, how high is the interest rate?

Risk

Before we figure out how much you're going to pay for your music, let's think about the interest rate a little more. If you were the bank, what factors would affect how much you charge someone to borrow from you? Think about this: *Whom would you charge more to borrow from you—your mother or your economics professor's mother?* Most likely, you wouldn't charge your own mother anything at all. However, you probably don't know the first thing about your professor's mother. She might be very sketchy indeed. Maybe she never pays her bills on time, has no source of income, or lives in a foreign country. Since

ECONOMICS IN THE MEDIA

"Neither a borrower nor a lender be"

Shakespeare's Hamlet

Neither a borrower nor a lender be;
For loan oft loses both itself and friend,
And borrowing dulls the edge of husbandry.

Polonius provides this advice to his son Laertes in Shakespeare's *Hamlet* (act 1, scene 3) before Laertes heads back to Paris. These are valuable words of wisdom from Polonius, who typically provides nonsensical suggestions to his children. There are two points to be made here. First, lending money to friends can be a tricky business. If your friend doesn't pay you back, you could lose both your money and your friend. Even if the friend does repay you, tensions can arise over the debt. Second, by borrowing, you may find that you're neglecting to save (the likely meaning of "husbandry" in this case), which Polonius views as an important characteristic of a responsible adult.

Interestingly, this line regarding husbandry was probably a jab at London's upper classes, which during Shakespeare's day were prone to extravagant living. To finance this lifestyle, they would sell off bits of their estates, thereby reducing their property holdings (and the future earnings from those property holdings).

Words of wisdom: "Neither a borrower nor a lender be."

you don't know much about her, she poses more of a risk of not paying you back. Thus, if you're lending money to your professor's mother, you probably should charge her an interest rate.

The credit card company does the same thing with you. It tries to find out something about you when you apply for the card. It wants to know where you live and how long you've lived there. It wants to know about your work history to see if you have a steady enough stream of income to pay your bills. It wants to know your phone number and email address so it can contact you if there's anything wrong with your card (for example, if it gets stolen) and in case you don't pay your bill on time. It may also ask for the name and phone number of a relative, just in case you forget to pay.

A **line of credit** is the maximum amount that a lender is willing to lend to a borrower.

Your income will affect your **line of credit**—the maximum amount that the bank is willing to lend you. Usually, when you get your first credit card this is a very short line of credit. You probably don't have much of a work history, and your income stream is limited because you're in school. Therefore, it's extremely unlikely that the bank would extend you a $10,000 line of credit. There just isn't much chance, based on the information the bank has about you, that you could pay that amount back. A $1,000 credit line is more reasonable. Even if you rang up $1,000 of charges, you could eventually pay that amount back; and if you don't, the bank doesn't lose too much money.

This low credit line helps you, too. You may not be able to buy as many things as you would like, but your low credit line limits how much debt you can get yourself into, and it allows you to begin building up a credit history. Banks look at your **credit history** when you apply for more serious loans, like a car loan or a mortgage. If you pay your bills on time, banks will be more willing to lend to you; and if you're careful about not missing payments, you may also be able to borrow money at lower interest rates.

A **credit history** is a record of an individual's loan and payment history.

ECONOMICS IN THE REAL WORLD

The CARD Act: Limiting Your Ability to Get a Credit Card

In 2009, Congress passed the Credit Card Accountability, Responsibility, and Disclosure (CARD) Act. The Act's many provisions include a requirement of 45 days notice of any interest-rate increases, restrictions on the number and size of over-limit and late fees, and increases in the number of days that credit card users have to pay their balances. Perhaps more important for you, the CARD Act also limits credit card companies' ability to issue cards to college students. Cards cannot be issued to anyone under age 21 who doesn't meet one of two provisions. Either there must be a co-signer on the account—a parent or spouse who will be jointly responsible for any balances on the credit card—or the applicant must provide proof of adequate income to pay for any charges. Additionally, credit card companies are prohibited from using food or other tangible gifts to advertise on college campuses. Card companies can still solicit students on campus, but they must inform regulators. Universities, in turn, are no longer allowed to sell students' contact information without disclosing this behavior.

Does limiting access to credit cards reduce students' debt burden—or prevent them from building a credit history?

All these rules were put in place to protect students from getting credit cards and consequently running up debt. However laudable the Act's goal, there are unintended consequences. Having and using a credit card is a valuable way for students to build a credit history. Limiting access to credit cards, even if the restriction applies only to people under age 21, means that it takes longer to build that history. Also, credit cards are used primarily as a convenience. Using a credit card instead of cash helps to facilitate trade, so restraining their use slows commerce. If financial responsibility is the main concern, there is nothing magical about turning 21. Unless you learn about the dangers of credit card debt at some point, turning 21 doesn't make you any wiser. But taking an economics class might. ✷

Credit Reports

Your credit history—the information about your ability to repay your loans—is captured in a **credit report**.* This is like a financial report card, and on this

A **credit report** is a financial report card that reports your credit history (your ability to repay your loans).

*The web site of the Federal Deposit Insurance Corporation (FDIC) provides a great deal of information about credit scores and how to order your credit report. Go to: http://www.fdic.gov/consumers/consumer/ccc/reporting.html.

evaluation you want the highest score possible. Once you're downgraded, it can be very difficult to raise your score.

A number of companies collect credit information about you. The three largest are Equifax, Experian, and TransUnion. You can order a free copy of your credit report from each of these companies once every 12 months. All these companies collect data about how well you pay your credit card bills, medical bills, student loans, car loans, mortgages, and utility bills. Almost everything you have to pay or repay will show up on your credit report.

Not only does your credit report provide information about whom you pay, but it also discloses if you missed a payment and how much you still owe. From this information, the agencies compile a credit score. The particular scoring system varies by company, but higher scores are better than lower scores. A higher score tells a potential lender that you are a lower risk and therefore more likely to pay your bills on time.

A higher score can also mean that if you need to borrow money you can shop around for better rates. Lower-risk borrowers have more bargaining power because they can usually go to a second lender if the first lender tries to charge them a higher interest rate. A lower credit score means you're a higher risk, which will reduce your borrowing options. Not only will you find it more difficult to find a lender, but when you do find one, you will probably be charged a higher interest rate.

Payday Loans

A **payday loan** is a short-term loan in which the borrower writes the lender a check against an upcoming paycheck. The lender waits until the borrower's payday to cash the check.

When money is particularly tight, some people resort to taking a **payday loan**. The number of establishments making payday loans has grown astronomically since 2008, during the Great Recession. Essentially, the borrower writes a check for the amount he or she wants to borrow, plus a fee for the loan. The lender then gives the borrower the amount of the check, less the fee. The lender then waits to cash the check until the borrower's next payday.

While some states ban payday lenders, others merely limit the interest rate they can charge. In states that do allow them, the interest rates can be extremely high. Payday lenders in Colorado can charge as much as 129% interest for a payday loan. In other states, there are no legal limits. In Idaho, the average (not the highest) payday loan rate is 582%. In South Dakota and Wisconsin, rates are a little better. In these states, the average interest rate on a payday loan is 574%. At these interest rates, you can imagine how quickly someone could get into deep trouble. By borrowing even a small amount, borrowers will be repaying two, three, four, or more times what they borrowed, meaning they may need to take out another loan just to repay their original loan. The result is a vicious cycle of debt that may be impossible to escape. To understand this situation completely, we have to understand how an interest rate affects how much you repay the lender.*

---

*Information about payday loan rates in 2014 comes from: http://www.usatoday.com/story/money/personalfinance/2014/04/20/id-nv-ut-have-among-highest-payday-loan-rates/7943519/.

Loan Sharks

ECONOMICS IN THE MEDIA

Get Shorty

Perhaps you've heard the term "loan shark." A loan shark is someone who is essentially a lender of last resort. People who can't find a lender anywhere might resort to a private individual who charges very high interest rates. There are rules regulating how much interest a legitimate lender can charge. However, loan sharks typically work outside the normal legal system. Thus, they charge rates that far exceed the legal limits. If you have to borrow money from a loan shark, you may end up paying back double or triple what you borrowed in a very short time because of the exorbitant interest rate.

In the movie *Get Shorty* (1995), Chili Palmer is chasing down Leo Davoe to collect on a debt. He also starts chasing Harry Zimm, who owes money to someone else. Chili isn't into breaking legs; rather, he sees the potential to acquire some legitimate money by making a movie about loan sharking.

Time to pay up.

Unfortunately, Chili's boss isn't so forgiving and starts acting like a real loan shark by beating Zimm within an inch of his life. Eventually, all of the bad guys end up in jail, and Chili ends up in the movie business.

How Do Interest Rates Affect Borrowers?

Now we'll return to your credit card bill. Let's say that the **minimum payment**, the smallest amount the credit card company requires you to pay each month so as not to damage your credit score, is $2. "Fine," you say to yourself. "That means it'll take about five months to pay off my $10.50 Blake Shelton music purchase." You calculate that $2 a month for five months equals $10, and if you add 50 cents to the last payment you're free and clear. That would be the case if interest payments weren't included; however, there are interest payments to make, and you need to take that into consideration. But here is where you can get yourself into real trouble if you make only the minimum payment every month: the interest *compounds*. In the context of borrowing, **compounding** means that interest is added to your balance, so you end up paying interest on the increasingly higher balance.

On the saver's side, compounding interest can be a very good thing. When you're saving money, compounding interest helps you save more. (We'll see how this type of compounding works a little later in this chapter.) Unfortunately, when you're borrowing money, compounding interest can cause your repayment plan to drag on and on and on.

The **minimum payment** is the smallest amount that a lender requires a borrower to pay each month so as not to damage the borrower's credit score.

Compounding of interest (in the context of borrowing money) means that interest is added to an account balance so that the borrower ends up paying interest on an increasingly higher balance. In the context of saving, compounding means that interest is added to your total savings: you get paid interest on your savings plus any prior interest earned.

Principal and Interest

Let's assume you pay your credit card bill on the first of the month and make the minimum payment. When you pay the $2 on your bill, that leaves you with $8.50 to repay, plus interest. To start out, assume the interest rate is 12.99% per year—a rate that's at the low end for credit cards. Since you have a balance on your bill, you have to start paying interest on the *entire amount* you borrowed. In other words, even though you paid down the amount of the loan, or the **principal amount**, you still have to pay interest on the entire amount that you borrowed. So in the first month you would pay 11 cents in interest.

The **principal amount** is the total amount of money borrowed.

How is this number calculated? Credit card companies determine your *daily average interest rate.* You take the interest rate you pay, in this case 12.99%, and divide it by the number of days in the year, 365. For this particular loan, that number is .00036 (or .036%). This means that for *every day* you have an outstanding balance, you pay .036% on the average balance for the month. The average balance for last month was $10.50. If there are 30 days in the month, you pay .036% for each day on a balance of $10.50.

(Equation 19.1) $$\text{interest paid} = (\text{amount owed}) \times (\text{daily interest rate}) \times (\text{days in the month})$$

In this case, you can see that the amount of interest you will pay is $10.50 × .00036 × 30, or 11 cents.*

Each month that you leave the loan outstanding, you have to pay interest. If you pay only the minimum required in the second month, you pay interest on the remaining $8.50. This means that in the second month you pay interest of 9 cents. What you may not realize, though, is that you're paying interest not just on the $8.50 but also on the 11 cents of interest you owed from last month. This is the compounding interest. The compounding of the interest means that your balance doesn't fall by $2, but instead by a little bit less than $2, which means that you're paying back a little less than you thought to the lender.

In month three, when you make your minimum payment of $2, your principal amount falls (the balance drops), so you don't pay as much interest as you did in the previous month. Now you're paying interest on the $6.50 balance plus the interest of the previous two months.

This process goes on until you completely pay off the principal amount and all of the interest. When you make your final payment six months after purchasing the music, you've paid a little bit more than $10.50. As the first column of Table 19.1 shows, your grand total for the Blake Shelton download is $10.86.

Notice two things about Table 19.1. First, it takes a month longer to pay off your bill than it would have if there were no interest payments. Second, $0.36 isn't very much. "So," you may ask, "what's the big deal?" First, the 12.99% interest rate we assumed is at the very, very low end of credit card interest rates. Second, not many people put only $10.50 on their credit card each month. Let's first see how things change with a higher interest rate.

The upper limit for interest rates on credit cards is 29.99%. Applying the same formula we used above, what is the difference in the amount you would pay under these two rates? Table 19.1 shows the difference. At the higher interest rate, you pay over 50 cents more in the six months it takes to pay off

---

*Remember, when multiplying a percentage you need to move the decimal point two places to the left. As a result, .036% is the equivalent of .00036.

TABLE 19.1

Interest Paid on a Loan at Different Interest Rates

	(1) Interest Rate = 12.99%		(2) Interest Rate = 29.99%	
Months to repay	**Principal**	**Interest Paid**	**Principal**	**Interest Paid**
0	$10.50	$0.11	$10.50	$0.26
1	$8.61	$0.09	$8.76	$0.22
2	$6.70	$0.07	$6.97	$0.17
3	$4.78	$0.05	$5.15	$0.13
4	$2.83	$0.03	$3.27	$0.08
5	$0.86	$0.01	$1.35	$0.03
TOTAL INTEREST PAID		$0. 36		$0.89
TOTAL PAID		$10.86		$11.39

Note: Calculations are based on a daily average interest rate.

your balance. You may still think that this is a very small amount, but look at it from a percentage viewpoint. At the 12.99% interest rate, you're paying 3.5 percent more for the music than if you had paid cash. When the interest rate rises to 29.99%, you're paying 8.5 percent more for your purchase.

Second, what happens when you have a real-life balance? The average credit card debt for college students is $3,200. How long will it take to pay off this balance if the minimum payment is $98.67* and the interest rate is 25%?

It will take you 55 months, or over four and a half years, assuming you don't add anything to the principal amount—which means you never use the card again during all this time. The grand total that you'll repay is $5,388. Of that, $2,188 will be interest. Remember that paying interest is paying a fee for borrowing money, instead of using money to buy something else. Makes you rethink that Blake Shelton download, doesn't it?

"Better be careful with that credit card . . ."

Credit card debt is unique in that the interest you pay compounds. It's unique in another way, too. Usually, the rate that you pay on a credit card is variable. A **variable interest rate** is one that can change based on market conditions or the borrower's creditworthiness. While you're paying your credit card debt, it might become more or less expensive depending on what happens to interest rates.

A **variable interest rate** is an interest rate that can change based on market conditions or the borrower's creditworthiness.

Other common types of debt—particularly federally funded student loans, car loans, and home loans (mortgages)—have **fixed interest rates**. These are rates that you can "lock in": they won't change during the course of the loan. When mortgage loans hit historic lows of 3.66% in 2012, many people raced to refinance their mortgages. This means that they paid off their original

A **fixed interest rate** is an interest rate that remains in effect for the full term of a loan.

*This is a typical minimum payment on a credit card determined by the interest rate plus 1% of the balance.

mortgage with a different loan at a lower interest rate. The process enabled homeowners to save thousands of dollars a year on lower interest payments, and in many cases also reduced the amount of time they needed to pay back their home loans.

Student Loans

As the price of a college education has risen, so too has the number of students requiring help to pay for college.* You likely don't need to be told this, as you may be one of the nearly 70% of students who borrow money to pay for school. As with credit cards, knowing something about how these loans are repaid will help you understand the true cost of college.

Student loans have some unique aspects that make them unlike other types of debt. Specifically, these loans are backed by the government and, as such, come with lower interest rates. Federally funded student loans are provided via legislation passed by Congress. The interest rates for these loans are also determined by Congress. Depending on what the loan is for (graduate or undergraduate study) and when you receive your first payout, the interest rate will range between 3.86% and 7.21%. Many federally funded student loans also have fees attached to them. The fees are typically deducted directly from the disbursement, so you receive a lower amount than you borrowed. These fees, which are a percentage of the amount borrowed, range from 1.072% to 4.292%. In addition, student loans are not discharged in bankruptcy. That is, even if you declare bankruptcy, you must still repay your student loan.

Repayment Options

While paying on a student loan works very much like paying on a credit card (but with much lower interest), the terms of the loan can be altered to fit your income. Repayment plans are designed to help students as they're getting on their feet after college, but there are significant differences in these plans—differences that can lead to paying a lot more in interest if you don't understand the ramifications.

One option is to pay a flat amount every month until the loan is paid off. This option would involve paying the smallest amount of interest, but it might cause financial hardship if you have difficulty finding a job after graduation. Another option is to pay in graduated steps: you start off paying a smaller amount, and over time your payments increase, presumably making the burden of repayment easier early on, when you have less income. The downside of this arrangement is that smaller initial payments keep the balance of the loan higher for a longer period, and therefore you pay more in interest.

Another option for repayment includes a pay-as-you-earn plan in which your monthly payment is limited to 10% of your discretionary income. As your earnings increase, your payments increase too. The advantage of this plan is that if your earnings fall, so does your payment. The downside is that there is no certainty to how much interest you might end up paying. A simi-

*Calculations in this section were made using the calculators at www.studentloans.gov. At this web site you can see how much you will have to pay on your student loans.

lar plan, an income-based repayment plan, limits your payments to 15% of your discretionary income. With these two options, you're placed on a fixed term of 20 to 25 years. At the end of the term, any outstanding balance is forgiven and treated as taxable income. So if you still have a balance to repay on these plans at the end of your fixed term, that balance is dropped. While this idea may sound appealing, there are a few things to think about. First, if you're carrying student loans for 20 to 25 years, that's a lot of financial burden for a long time. Second, if you haven't been able to repay your loan over this period, you haven't made very much money and perhaps your college degree wasn't worth it. Third, to qualify for these plans, you need to exhibit financial hardship.

Is this going to be enough to pay for college?

A Numerical Example

To quantify our discussion, let's look at some options for repaying student loans. According to many sources, the average student-loan debt approaches $30,000. Let's use this amount as a benchmark to see what it means for repayment. We'll use the lowest federally funded loan interest rate of 3.86% for undergraduate loans to determine how much you'll repay. If your loan has a 10-year term (the standard term for a typical and graduated repayment plan), you'll pay $302 a month on a standard plan and your overall repayment will be $36,277. Thus, you'll pay $6,277 in interest plus the original $30,000 that you borrowed.

A graduated plan will start with a monthly payment of $169 and end with a final monthly payment of $507. Over the 10 years of your payments, you'll pay a total of $37,829. Of this amount, $7,829 is interest. For the pay-as-you-earn and income-based adjustment plans, your payments depend on how much you earn and how many people are in your family. If you have a family of two (just you and one other person) and a job that pays $40,000 a year, you would pay $41,733 under the pay-as-you-earn plan over the course of 15 years. Under the income-based repayment scheme, you would pay $37,902. Table 19.2 details all of these scenarios.

TABLE 19.2

Repayment of a $30,000 Student Loan under Various Plans

Type of repayment plan	Maximum term	Term for this example	Monthly payment or payment range	Amount repaid	Interest paid
Standard	10 years / 120 months	120 months	$302	$36,277	$6,277
Graduated	10 years / 120 months	120 months	$169 – $507	$37,829	$7,829
Pay–as-you-earn*	20 years / 240 months	185 months	$137 – $302	$41,733	$11,733
Income-based*	25 years / 300 months	139 months	$205 – $302	$37,902	$7,902

*Amounts are determined based on a $30,000 loan balance at 3.86% interest, assuming a family of two and employment that pays $40,000 a year.

No matter how you slice it, repaying your debt is a financial burden. You pay a lot in interest even at low rates. The only way to save on the interest payments is to pay down the principal of the loan. The faster you pay off your loan, the less interest you'll have to pay.

Is It Better to Buy or Rent a House?

Many people believe that the American dream is to buy and own a house. Despite this, many people rent homes or apartments rather than buying a house. Are renters failing to take advantage of the American dream? With the current low interest rates for mortgages, it sounds like buying is a no-brainer. Before you jump to that conclusion, though, let's take a look at some of the advantages and disadvantages of buying a house.

Mortgages

When you have a mortgage, the interest that you pay is "baked" into the loan. In fact, your early mortgage payments are made up almost entirely of interest. The principal of the loan falls slowly at first; then, by the end of the loan period, the payments are almost entirely devoted to paying down the principal. Because the rate is fixed, the amount of interest you pay is fixed—and banks want to get that interest early, just in case you decide to refinance the loan.

The primary method that mortgage holders use to reduce their principal is to make extra payments. Under this approach, any amount you pay above the minimum mortgage payment amount goes toward the principal. Paying down the principal can help you pay off the mortgage more quickly and can save you significantly on interest payments over the life of the loan. For example, if you buy a home for $200,000 and borrow for 30 years at 5% interest, you'll pay $1,073.64 a month. Your total payments will be $386,512, meaning you pay $186,512 in interest. Table 19.3 shows how much less you pay, and over how much less *time* you pay, by adding just a little to your mortgage payment each month. This little extra per month goes toward the principal of the mortgage, so the interest is accumulating on a smaller balance. If you

TABLE 19.3

Paying Additional Principal on a 30-Year, $200,000 Mortgage at 5% Interest

Monthly payment	Total repaid	Interest paid	Interest savings	Time cut off the mortgage
$1,073.64	$386,511.57	$186,511.57		
$1,123.64	$365,730.74	$165,730.74	$20,776.37	2 years, 10 months
$1,173.64	$349,438.93	$149,438.93	$37,068.19	5 years, 2 months

Note: The minimum monthly payment is $1,074. The monthly mortgage payment is rounded up slightly for presentation.

pay an extra $50 a month for the life of the loan, you'll save $20,779 in interest payments and cut almost three years off your mortgage. Amazing! If you pay an extra $100 every month, you'll save over $37,000 in interest payments and reduce the life of the mortgage by more than five years!

The Costs and Benefits of Home Ownership

Home ownership is expensive. There is homeowner's insurance to pay and property taxes to pay. If there is damage to your home or property, you have to pay to have it fixed. Leaks in the basement need to be repaired, the driveway needs to be cleared during the winter, the grass needs to be cut, occasional broken windows need to be replaced—and the homeowner pays for (or does) all of this. Homeowners also have to pay for utilities—water, sewer, electric, cable, and trash pick-up. That adds up!

As a homeowner, fixing this is your responsibility.

If you're a renter, many of these headaches go away. You pay a fixed amount for your rent, which may include some of your utilities and almost always provides for snow removal and lawn care. In addition, you don't have to pay property taxes directly (although your rent does pay part of them) or pay for homeowner's insurance (although you might want to buy renter's insurance to guard against theft or fire).

Why do so many people want to own a home when there are so many added costs associated with the purchase? Much of this decision has to do with building equity. There are also tax implications to owning your own home. Let's look at both of these issues.

Equity

Equity refers to the part of an asset that you own. When you own a home and decide to sell it, you first pay off any remaining mortgage. In other words, you pay what you still owe the lender. Whatever is left afterwards belongs to you. If you move out of an apartment, you don't get anything; in fact, if you break your lease agreement early, you may even have to pay a penalty. The longer you stay in your home paying down your mortgage, the more equity you build up. This equity is valuable because it represents how much of the home and property is yours.

Equity refers to the part of an asset that you own. In the case of a house, equity comes down to what part of the selling price you get to keep after paying off the balance on your mortgage.

Equity also allows you to use your home as collateral. If you need to borrow money, perhaps for a home-improvement project, a vacation, or even to attend college, you can take out a second mortgage. This is a loan using your home as a promise that you will repay the lender. A mortgage is a **securitized loan**—that is, a loan that uses an asset as collateral. If you don't repay the loan, the lender can take your house. Since lenders assume that you don't want to lose your house, they accept your equity in your home as security. A securitized loan typically has a much lower interest rate than a non-securitized loan because the lender gets something even if you don't pay back the money you borrowed. Credit cards are non-securitized, which is one of the reasons the interest rates on credit cards are so high.

A **securitized loan** is a loan in which a borrower's asset serves as collateral.

Opportunity cost

So why do people choose to rent? If you can build equity by paying for something (shelter) that you need anyway, doesn't it make more sense to buy? Consider that a mortgage payment is often much higher than a rent payment, especially in cities. In Chapter 4, we talked about rent controls. In cities with rent controls, those price ceilings apply only to renters, not to buyers. For many people living in cities, home ownership is simply too costly. Think about this situation in terms of opportunity cost. Paying on a mortgage might mean that you cannot take a vacation every year, or buy the car you want, or eat at restaurants because you don't have the funds. In addition, young people often don't have the credit history or the income that a lender would require to give them a mortgage of what could be hundreds of thousands of dollars. Buying a home usually involves a down payment as well. You may need 20% or more of the purchase price, and usually it takes some time to save up that amount.

ECONOMICS IN THE REAL WORLD

House Flipping

A home is the largest purchase most people make in their lives. The thought of buying a second home may be an enticing dream, especially if that house is in a desirable location like the beach or the mountains. However, buying multiple houses can be a form of investment. People who can afford to have always bought homes for the purpose of reselling them in the hopes of making a profit. This type of activity, called flipping, became a national story during the early 2000s. Flipping a house means buying a house with no intention of living in it. You buy it, hold on to it for a little while, and then sell again (hoping for a profit). Real-estate prices were rising very quickly during the early 2000s, and banks were making it very easy to borrow money, so many people viewed flipping as a sound investment strategy.

It's very possible that an investor's plans to flip this house turned into a flop when the real-estate bubble burst.

Unfortunately for many flippers, prices in the housing market ran out of steam. When the housing bubble burst, prices fell; in some places, the decline was precipitous. In dramatic cases, people owed the bank more than they could sell the house for because prices had dropped so much. (This situation is referred to as *being underwater.*) In some cases, the owner of the house simply stopped paying the mortgage and walked away. This decision left the bank with a house that was now difficult to sell and no way to recover the money it had lent. While the former homeowner was no longer paying a mortgage, his or her credit score declined considerably. ✳

Tax Advantages

Incentives

A significant incentive to home ownership is that homeowners receive a tax advantage in the United States and in many other countries. You can deduct the mortgage interest that you pay from your gross income when you file your income-tax return. The more interest you pay, the lower your tax bill.

This *homeowner deduction* provides an incentive to buy a house. The tax break stems from the view that ownership creates a sense of permanence. Homeowners become more invested in the community and tend to be more civic-minded. Owners are also more likely than renters to maintain their property. Governments therefore promote home ownership because of the positive externalities that result (see Chapter 9 for a review of externalities). Remember that if a government wants more of an activity that generates positive externalities, it will typically provide a subsidy. Tax breaks act as that subsidy.

How Do People Save for Retirement?

The shelter that a house provides is important, and building equity increases the owner's wealth. However, houses—even when they're being flipped—aren't usually considered an asset that will help you through retirement. You could sell your house and move into something smaller in your retirement years, but you still need shelter. Because people are often tied to their houses for financial, logistical, and/or emotional reasons, many people save for retirement by buying other things that they won't mind selling when they get older. Among these financial instruments are stocks, bonds, and mutual funds.

Stocks

When people talk about personal investing, they often think first of the stock market. Buying stock is the most glamorous of all investment strategies. This belief is reflected in movies like *The Wolf of Wall Street* (2013), *Margin Call* (2011), *The Bonfire of the Vanities* (1990), and, of course, *Wall Street* (1987)—to name just a few. In contrast, there aren't many movies about the excitement surrounding savings accounts. So what is the allure of the stock market, and can you really become rich by trading stocks?

The first thing we have to do is address a simple question: What is a stock? A **stock** is a piece of paper representing a share of ownership in a company. Actually, a stock used to be a piece of paper; today, most stock certificates are virtual. You rarely actually see the paper; instead, a broker holds the paper for you.

A **stock** is a share of ownership in a company.

The important thing is what that piece of paper means. When you buy stock, you are buying a part of a company. Your share of stock makes you a part-owner of the company. If you buy 10 shares of Facebook stock, you become an owner, just like Mark Zuckerberg. (Well, not exactly like Zuckerberg, because he owns a lot more stock than you do.) Still, being an owner of stock entitles you to certain benefits. Otherwise, why buy the stock?

When you buy stock, you receive the right to vote on company matters. One of the most important votes you get as an owner is a say in who will run the company: you get to vote on the membership of the board of directors. If you want to kick

A stock certificate is a paper indicating that someone owns shares in a company.

Zuckerberg off the board of Facebook, you can attempt to do so by using your vote. The problem is that Zuckerberg may not want to be voted out. Therefore, he votes for himself. And he'll win. Why? Because every share of stock is worth one vote. Your 10 votes are never going to overcome Zuckerberg's roughly 443 million votes.

Maybe you want to run Facebook yourself. How can you accomplish this goal? Buy enough stock, and vote yourself in! This is one of the dangers of selling stock. When a company is *publicly traded* (meaning that people can buy and sell stock in that company), there's always a chance that someone else might buy more stock and vote out the directors.

Stockholders also vote on how much to compensate the executives, whether to appoint an accounting auditor, and (sometimes) to authorize the sale of parts of the company. But mainly stockholders vote on the directors—the people who decide how the company should be run. You may be thinking, "Well, voting on a board of directors doesn't sound like much fun." It certainly isn't going to make you rich. So what else can you do with your stock? You can sell it. Selling stocks is one of the primary ways people make money in the stock market, but it isn't the only way. To understand how to make money in the stock market, you must understand the different kinds of stock. Once you have determined your objectives for buying stocks, you can choose stocks that will help you to reach your goals.

Growth Stocks

The old adage in stock trading is "If you want to make money, buy low and sell high." In other words, you can make a great deal of money by buying a company's stock at a low price and then selling that stock after the price has gone up. It isn't any more complicated than that.

How do you know if the stock price is going to go up? That's the tricky part. You don't. Instead, you look for companies with the potential to grow. What kind of product do they sell? Do you think that the consuming public will want to buy what the company is selling? What does the company's future look like? Will it be successful? Will it grow?

A **growth stock** is a stock in a company that is expected to grow and to become profitable.

Investors typically ask these kinds of questions about **growth stocks**—stocks in companies that are expected to grow and to become profitable. As a company grows and its profits increase, more people want to buy the stock. The price goes up, and then you sell. That's how you make money. Buy low and sell high.

There are two ways to make money on growth stocks. You can buy a few shares at a low price and sell them for a higher price. Or you can buy a lot of shares at a given price, and if the price rises, by even just a couple of pennies, you can earn a nice return when you sell.

Growth stocks can be risky. What happens if the price doesn't go up? What if it goes down instead? In this case, you would lose money—but only if you sell the stock. Gains and losses occur in the stock market when the stock is sold. If you sell at a price greater than what you paid, you make money. If you sell at a price below what you paid, you lose money.

Sometimes, it's very difficult to predict if a company will be successful. It took Amazon.com over six years to turn a profit. For years, the company operated its business but lost money. Many such companies fail and are never heard from again. Amazon ultimately became extremely profitable, and the price of its stock went from $23.62 when it listed in May 1997 to $304.64 in May 2014. If you had bought 10 shares of Amazon in 1997 and sold them in 2014, you would have made a 17,509.25% return on your investment.* Now that's making money!

However, if you had bought stock in financial services firm Lehman Brothers, a company whose name is synonymous with the collapse of the financial sector, the value of your stock would be zero. Lehman went out of business in 2008. When a company goes out of business, its stockholders are essentially out of luck. There is no guarantee that you will make money by trading stocks. There is no guarantee that you will even get your money back. As in the case of Lehman Brothers, you may get nothing back at all.

Income Stocks

An **income stock** is a stock that pays a predictable dividend over a relatively long period.

A **dividend** is a cash payment to stockholders for each share of stock owned.

Not all stocks are growth stocks. In fact, the prices of some stocks don't change very much. These stocks are called income stocks. Why would you want to buy such a stock if you can't make money on the variation in the stock price? Well, as a stockholder, you can take advantage of another stockholder right: as a part-owner of the company, you may be paid part of the company's profits in the form of a dividend. Thus, an **income stock** is a stock that pays a predictable dividend over a relatively long period.

Dividends are cash payments made to the owners of a company—that is, the stockholders. Each share of stock receives the same dividend. Dividends are typically paid every three months (quarterly); however, some companies pay dividends more frequently or less often. Some companies pay large dividends, some pay small dividends, and some pay none at all. Dividend payments are made from the firm's profits. So if a firm doesn't make a profit, it won't pay a dividend—even if it paid a dividend in the previous year.

The bull and the bear represent the optimism (bull) and pessimism (bear) of traders in the stock market. Which one are you?

If you own enough shares of stock, the dividend income can be significant. For example, if you owned 100 shares of Coca-Cola stock, you would earn $30.00 per quarter based on the divided payment of $0.30 per share. If you owned more shares, you would earn even more dividend income.

What can you do with dividends? They serve as income for you, so you can do anything you want with them. Use them to buy a new iPhone; use them to buy gas for your car; you can even burn them if you want. Or you could use them to *reinvest*—that is, to buy more stock. Reinvesting dividends enables you to increase the number of shares you own and therefore increase the amount of dividend income you earn. Thus, the opportunity cost of

Opportunity cost

*This price is determined after accounting for stock splits, a situation that occurs when a company gives shareholders multiple shares for each share they hold while dividing the price. For instance, if you have 50 shares of a $100 stock that splits 2 for 1, you will be given an additional 50 shares of stock, resulting in a total of 100 shares. The price of the stock will be divided by 2, yielding a price of $50. Firms sometimes do this to make their stock price lower and therefore more attractive to a wider base of buyers. The adjusted opening price of Amazon.com in May 1997 was $1.73.

spending your dividends on a nice dinner is the number of additional stock shares that those dividends could have purchased.

Both growth stocks and income stocks can be very risky. The increase or decrease of a stock price isn't easy to predict; if it were, there would be a lot more millionaire stock traders. Not only this, but if you do make money by trading stocks, that income is taxable. Specifically, if the price of a stock goes up and you sell, you'll have to report any gains when you file your taxes. Taxes on the proceeds of a stock sale are called capital-gains taxes. In addition, you're required to report any payments you receive from dividend income. In 2015, both of these types of income are taxed at a rate of 15% for an individual reporting income up to $413,200. Above this income level, the rate rises to 20%.

Remember, there are no guarantees with stocks, just as there are no guarantees with any financial product. One way to avoid being taken advantage of is to consider this rule: if someone is promising you a sure thing or claiming they "know" a stock will rise in value, you should proceed with caution. If you're uncomfortable with risk, though, you do have other options. You might try buying bonds instead.

Bonds

A **bond** is an IOU that joins two parties in a contract that specifies the conditions for repayment of the loan. In this case, a firm or government is the borrower and an individual is the lender.

The **maturity date** is the date in the future when a bond will be repaid.

Par value is the value of a bond at maturity—the amount due at repayment; also called *face value*.

Bonds are simply IOUs. Like a stock, a bond is a piece of paper, but the bond does not convey ownership. Rather, a **bond** joins two parties in a contract: the buyer of the bond is lending money to the seller of the bond. The bond itself contains the conditions for repayment of this loan: who will be doing the repaying (the name of the borrower), the repayment or **maturity date**, and the **par value** (how much will be repaid). Even if a company goes bankrupt, it may have to pay its bondholders something.

Notice that the bond does not specify who gets repaid. The reason is simple: it may not be the same person who lent the money in the first place. Like stocks, bonds can be traded. These transactions occur in the bond market. In the *bond market*, there is a demand for and a supply of bonds. A bond's price is based on these conditions. Supply is fairly fixed and is based on the number of bonds sold by the borrowers. Although we're talking here primarily about corporate or business bonds, governments also borrow a lot of money, and they do so by selling a lot of bonds. Government bonds include savings bonds, U.S. Treasury bonds (also called T-bonds) that mature in more than 10 years, U.S. Treasury notes that mature between 1 and 10 years after issuance, and U.S. Treasury bills (T-bills) that mature in less than 1 year. For our purposes here, we'll refer to all bonds as corporate or business bonds; but it's important to remember that governments sell bonds to raise money, too. (For a review of open market operations, where the Fed buys and sells bonds, see Chapter 16.)

How do you make money in the bond market? Well, you could try the buy low/sell high approach. It's possible to make money this way, but in the bond market you mainly make money just the way a bank does when it makes a loan to you. As the lender, you're entitled to interest income paid by the party to whom you lent your money. How often you get paid is dictated by the terms of the bond. Sometimes, you get paid once a month; sometimes, once a year.

How much you get paid is a bit trickier to determine. The amount you receive is based on two factors: (1) the price paid for the bond and (2) the par value. As the bondholder, you're paid a specific interest rate, which is determined with the following formula:

$$\text{interest rate} = R = (\text{par value} - \text{initial bond price}) / \text{initial bond price} \qquad \text{(Equation 19.2)}$$

Let's look at an example. If the airplane maker Boeing wanted to raise \$1,000 to expand its operations, you might be willing to lend the money to the company, but how much would you expect in return? Assume that Boeing will repay you in one year. If Boeing agrees to pay you \$1,100 when the bond matures, what is the interest rate? Putting these numbers into Equation 19.2 reveals that you will earn 10%:

$$R = (\$1{,}100 - \$1{,}000) / \$1{,}000 = \$100/\$1{,}000 = 0.10 = 10\%$$

If the initial bond price drops to \$800, then the interest rate rises to 37.5%:

$$R = (\$1{,}100 - \$800) / \$800 = \$300/\$800 = 0.375 = 37.5\%$$

Equation 19.2 points to an important relationship: as the price of a bond falls, the interest rate rises. The less you pay for a bond of a fixed amount, the better the rate of return will be as signaled by the interest rate.

While the bond tells you the par value, the market for the bond—the supply and demand—alters the price paid for the bond. So what impacts the price? The price is based on a key factor that most people are trying to manage when they save for the future: risk.

Investment-grade bonds pay lower interest rates but are issued by companies that are very likely to repay their creditors.

Junk bonds pay higher interest rates but are considered speculative.

Risk Factors for a Bond

Because bonds are loans, you have to consider the risks involved in purchasing them. When you borrow money, lenders look at your credit history to determine the interest rate they will charge. Similarly, there are credit ratings agencies that evaluate companies' creditworthiness. The two largest of these agencies are Moody's and Standard and Poor's.

Each agency gives a grade to a company (or a country) to alert potential lenders, and bond buyers, to the borrower's creditworthiness. While you get a number score for your credit report, bond sellers get a letter grade. A higher grade means a safer bet that the company will repay the money it borrows, meaning that it will be able to borrow money at a lower interest rate. Table 19.4 lists the letter grades assigned by Moody's and Standard and Poor's.

Some bonds are considered very safe. These **investment-grade bonds** pay lower interest rates, but the issuer of the bond has a solid financial balance sheet and is very likely to repay its creditors. Other bonds are rated much lower and are therefore considered speculative. These **junk bonds** pay a higher rate of interest; but if you lend to a company selling junk bonds, you may find that you don't get repaid as much as you lent.

TABLE 19.4

Letter Grades for Bonds

Moody's	Standard and Poor's
Aaa	**AAA**
Aa	**AA**
A	**A**
Baa	**BBB**
Ba	BBB–
B	BB+
Caa	BB
Ca	B
C	CCC
	CC
	C
	D—in default
JUNK BONDS—below Baa	JUNK BONDS—below BBB

Note: Bold indicates investment grade.

Another risk factor is time: How long will it take to get repaid? Some bonds are very short term; these bonds are less risky. The likelihood of a company suddenly filing for bankruptcy or ceasing to exist in the next six months after issuing bonds is small. Other bonds won't repay the holder for decades; these bonds are more risky. For example, buying a 30-year bond is a long-term commitment. Although you'll collect interest and can sell the bond if you want, the bondholder won't receive the par value until sometime in the future. And, of course, anything could happen in 30 years. A company could file for bankruptcy, inflation could jump to 50%, a terrorist attack could cripple the economy, or a country may cease to exist.

What does all this discussion mean for bonds? If you're going to lend your money to a company for a long time, you need to be compensated for the risks involved. The future in 10, 20, or 30 years is almost entirely unknowable, which means you're taking on more risk. The longer the term of the bond, the more the borrower must pay in interest.

Finally, there are tax risks associated with bonds. Remember that you earn income in the form of interest payments when you buy a bond. This type of income can be taxed, and tax laws can change. What happens if tax rates rise? You would have to pay more of your interest income in taxes, and you would have less to spend on yourself. Due to this risk, interest rates on bonds are higher. *Higher than what?* you might ask. *Don't I have to pay taxes on interest income no matter what?* Actually, the answer is somewhat surprising. Some bonds, called municipal or "muni" bonds, pay interest income that is tax-free.

Municipal bonds are sold by local governments or municipalities, and they are backed by tax dollars. The power to tax the people living in the municipality gives these entities a type of collateral that essentially ensures that the bondholders will be repaid. Municipal bonds are usually sold to raise money for large-scale projects like public schools, hospitals, electric power plants, and other facilities that contribute to the public good.

Bondholders pay no income taxes on the interest income from munis; thus, munis pose no tax risk. Since they have no tax risk, the interest rates on munis are lower than on other types of bonds.

Of course, there's a challenge with buying stocks and bonds when saving for retirement. While both almost certainly pay a larger return than putting money in a savings account, there is still risk involved. What if you pick the wrong company? Perhaps you buy the stock of a solar energy firm, and the next day it goes out of business. What happens if you buy a bond issued by a foreign country's government, and the next day a civil war breaks out and that government defaults on all of its debt? In either case, you could lose everything. Can you protect yourself from such risks, or is the outcome utterly uncertain—like in a Wild West shootout? The bad news is that you can't eliminate all risk. The safest place to put your money is the bank, but you won't earn much there. If you want a larger return than bonds or the bank can provide, without taking quite as much risk as buying stocks, perhaps a mutual fund is the way to go.

Are you feeling lucky? Picking stocks and bonds can be just as risky as taking part in a Wild West shootout.

Mutual Funds

When it comes to saving money, the best advice is to diversify your portfolio. This is essentially the old dictum "Don't put all of your eggs in one basket." A mutual fund helps you to place your eggs in many baskets. Mutual funds have the added advantage of allowing you to turn over the management of your money to a professional who probably knows more about which companies will be profitable than you do.

How does a mutual fund work? Think of a window, one of the old-fashioned kind divided by wood inserts so that the window is really made up of, say, 12 little panes of glass. Back in the day, it was very expensive to make large sheets of glass. If the glass broke or cracked, you would have to replace the entire window. However, if just one pane of glass cracked, you could have that pane replaced at relatively little cost without having to order an entirely new window. That's basically how a mutual fund works—except instead of individual panes of glass making up a complete window, a **mutual fund** comprises different stocks making up a diversified investment portfolio. Figure 19.1 shows a mutual fund made up of twelve different companies. If all of them do well, the value of the mutual fund goes up. If they all do poorly,

A **mutual fund** is an investment program that trades in diversified holdings and is professionally managed.

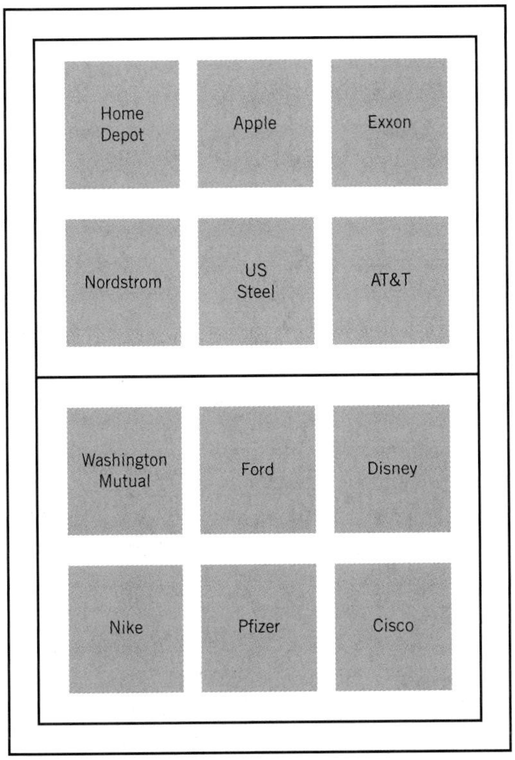

FIGURE 19.1

A Mutual Fund

A mutual fund is like a window in which each pane of glass represents one company. If one pane of glass breaks, the other panes are still intact; if the stock value of one company (or even more than one) in the mutual fund does poorly, the performance of the others helps to cover any losses. Mutual funds help you to diversify your investment portfolio.

the value of the fund goes down. However, it's more likely that some will do well and others won't do so well. The job of the fund's manager is to pick more winners than losers when assembling the fund.

Now let's go back to the window analogy. Let's say that one of your panes of glass is Washington Mutual bank. This company, along with the other 11 shown in Figure 19.1, is a part of your mutual fund. Unfortunately, Washington Mutual was caught up in the financial crisis and filed for bankruptcy in 2008. If Washington Mutual had been the only stock you owned, you would have lost all of the value of your investment. But because you owned the stock as part of a mutual fund, those other 11 companies can cover for you (assuming that the majority do well). All of your eggs are not in one basket; so despite the failure of one company in your mutual fund, you can "replace that pane of glass" with another company without losing your entire investment.

There are many different types of mutual funds, some made up of stocks, some made up of bonds, but they all have the same purpose: diversification and minimization of risk.

Starting Early to Save for Retirement

Retirement might seem to you to be a long way off, but it's never too early to start thinking about that time way in the future. What do you have to think about? For starters, according to the trustees of the Social Security program (the government-run retirement program), by 2033 there will not be enough funds coming into the system at current Social Security tax rates to guarantee the same level of payments being made today. This means that relying on Social Security to fund your retirement is likely to be a losing proposition.

FIGURE 19.2

Savings Growth of $100 per Month with 5% Compounding Interest

This figure shows the result of saving $100 per month over the course of 40 years, with compounding interest of 5%.

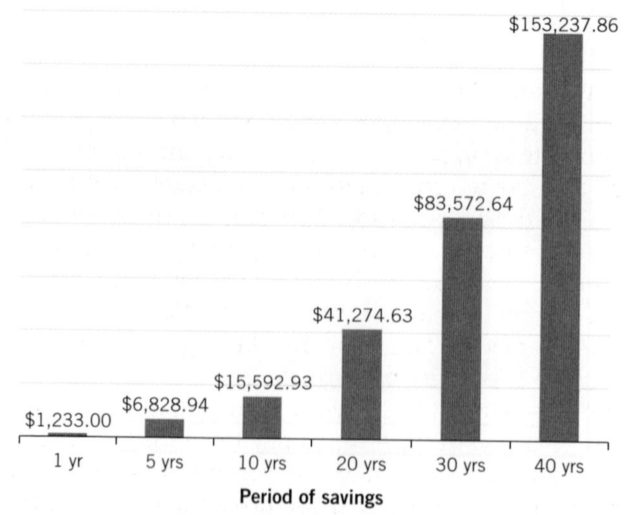

TABLE 19.5

Savings Options

Years of saving	Amount saved per month	Interest rate	Total saved	Balance at end of period
5	$200	4%	$12,000.00	$13,504.00
10	$100	5%	$12,000.00	$15,857.63
20	$100	6%	$24,000.00	$46,866.13
30	$200	5%	$72,000.00	$167,345.28
40	$200	6%	$96,000.00	$400,489.64

So what can you do? There are many options. The key is to start saving early. Why? Recall the idea of compounding interest that we talked about earlier in the chapter. When you save, compounding works in your favor. As you save more and earn interest, the amount you save plus the interest gets paid even more interest. If you keep adding to the pool of money, the pool will grow exponentially. Take a look at Figure 19.2. If you're 20 years old and save $100 a month until you're 60 years old by putting cash in a jar, you'll have $48,000 at retirement. That's not bad; but if you put your money in an account earning 5% interest, you'll end up with $153,237 by age 60. That's quite a difference!

If you put that $100 a month into an account at 5% interest *starting only at age 40*, you'll end up with $41,274 at age 60. That's only one-third as much as you would have if you start saving at age 20. Why? The earlier you start saving, the more time your interest and savings have to compound.

Look at Table 19.5 for some alternative savings options. These include different amounts of saving, time periods, and interest rates. If you want to retire comfortably—maybe even as a millionaire—you'll be much more likely to achieve that goal if you start saving now.

Individual Retirement Accounts (IRAs)

The simplest way to start saving for retirement is through an **individual retirement account (IRA).** An IRA is a retirement savings account that provides tax incentives to promote saving. By writing off your contribution to a "traditional" IRA on your income-tax return, you lower your taxable income for the tax year in which you make the contribution. You can contribute every year, if necessary, up to a certain amount depending on your age. The money accumulates in your IRA fund until you retire. Then you withdraw the money slowly and pay income tax on any increases in the value of the fund. While you are permitted to take withdrawals from your IRA starting at age 59½ without a penalty, you must begin taking them at age 70½.

An **individual retirement account (IRA)** is a retirement savings account that provides tax incentives to promote saving.

A **Roth IRA** allows you to take your savings and earnings from the IRA when you retire, but you don't have to pay taxes on the gains. Instead, you pay the taxes at a younger age, while still working, when you earn the money as part of your paycheck. You pay those taxes today, and in the future you don't have to pay. As with a "traditional" IRA, you can contribute every year up to a certain amount depending on your age and income. A Roth IRA can save you a lot of money that you would otherwise have paid in taxes.

A **Roth IRA** is an individual retirement account in which gains are not taxed at the time of withdrawal.

ECONOMICS FOR LIFE

Long-Run Returns for Stocks, Bonds, and CDs

The best way to save your money depends in large part on how long you have to save. Starting to save early for retirement is ideal, but not everyone can do so. If you find that retirement is only a few years away and you haven't started saving yet, you may think that your best approach is to find the savings options with the biggest return. Before jumping to any conclusions, let's look at how various investments have performed over time.

Stock market returns are historically much higher than returns from bonds. They are also higher than returns on bank certificates of deposit (CDs). A CD is like a short-term bond at a bank. You give the bank a particular amount of money for a fixed amount of time, and the bank pays you interest and returns the amount lent at a predetermined date in the future. The interest rate on a CD is usually better than that on a savings account. The drawback is that if you need the money and withdraw it prior to the CD's maturity date, you have to pay a penalty.

So, while stock returns are higher than those on bonds and CDs, the market is notoriously erratic from year to year. The figure below shows annual returns for four different types of investments during the period 1960–2013. The average return for the S&P 500, an index of 500 company stocks, was 11.29%. But the figure shows some wild swings in stock returns. Stocks were up over 37% in 1995 but down 36.5% in 2008. Compare this performance to that of 10-year Treasury bonds (T-bonds), which are issued by the U.S. government. The average rate of return for the T-bond over the same period was 6.97%, quite a bit lower than the stock market. However, there was still quite a lot of fluctuation in the yearly return. The 10-year T-bond was up as much as 32.8% in 1982 but down over 11% in 2009.

If you want less volatility, you could look at buying a 3-month Treasury bill (a short-term government bond that matures in 3 months). The average rate of return during the period shown was 5.11%. A 6-month bank certificate of deposit (CD) was also much more predictable. The average return for the CD was 5.94%. On average, these two investments yielded much lower returns than stocks, but they didn't experience wild year-to-year swings in value. Neither of them had a negative return.

Annual Returns on the S&P 500, 10-year T-bond, 3-month T-bill, and 6-month CD, 1960–2013

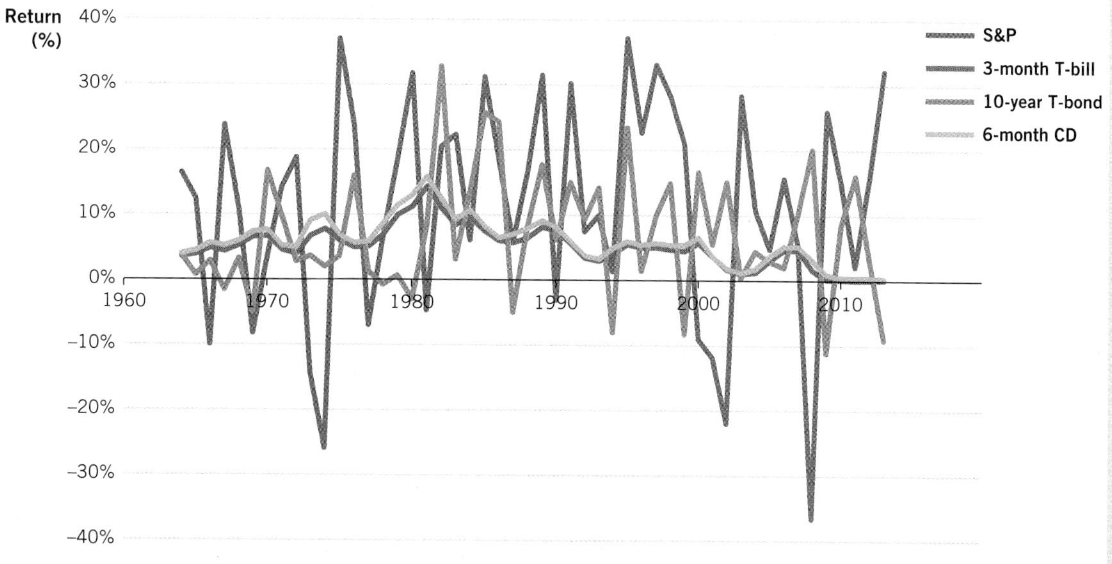

So if you have only a short amount of time in which to save, should you put your money in the stock market? That seems to be where the biggest returns are, but it also has the most risk. If you put your savings in the stock market and the market drops, you might end up with less than you started with. For example, if you had put $100,000 in the market in 2008, the value of your savings would have fallen by 36.5%, leaving you with $63,500 after one year. If you had opened a CD in 2008 with the same $100,000, it would have earned 3.14% and you would have had $103,140 after one year.

Here's the point: by beginning to save early, you can ride out the ups and downs of the stock market and be more likely to earn the stock market average of 11.29%. If you begin saving late, you'll want to seriously consider the risks of volatile markets. In that case, it might make sense to pursue a safer investment to maintain the value of your savings.

Employer Contributions

Some employers help their workers to save for retirement. For example, some jobs come with a **pension**, which is an employer-funded retirement plan. When you retire, you receive a pension paycheck from the company for as long as you live. Government jobs and those that are part of a unionized workforce are the most typical jobs that still offer pensions. However, pensions are becoming much less common because they're very expensive for the company and become more so as people live longer. An increasing problem for firms paying pensions is that in many cases they're paying retired workers for more years than the employees actually worked for the company.

A **pension** is an employer-funded retirement plan.

Instead of offering pensions, many employers are switching to making contributions to individual retirement plans as long as the employee works for the company. A 401(k) plan is a way to save part of your salary toward your retirement. Usually, you choose an amount to be deducted from each paycheck. This amount is invested tax-free (that is, you don't pay income tax on this contribution) into an individual retirement account. Sometimes, the employer will match all or part of your contribution. This is a nice benefit for the employee and a much less expensive retirement package for the company because it stops contributing when the employee stops working for the company. You do have to pay taxes on the money when you begin to make withdrawals.

Conclusion

So what are you going to do with that money your long-lost uncle left you? After you've had a bit of fun, you might want to consider putting some of it away. You can pay off debt to help buoy your credit score and reduce the amount of interest you're paying. Getting out of debt is liberating. Most financial planners suggest that you pay off the debt with the highest interest rate first, which lowers your debt burden in the long run. It does take discipline; but until you pay off your debt, it's difficult to start accumulating wealth. Some studies have shown that indebtedness is a major contributing factor in the wealth gap. People with a lot of debt stay poor, while those without debt are able to move up the economic ladder.

Maybe you could save your inheritance for a down payment on a house, purchase stocks or bonds, buy into a mutual fund, or start an IRA. Remember: the

more you save now, the more you'll have when retirement comes, or the sooner you'll be able to retire. Social Security doesn't provide enough income for most people to retire on, so think ahead and start saving early. Buying a new car today might seem fun, but maybe the money would be better saved in your retirement plan.

ANSWERING THE BIG QUESTIONS

What do you need to know about borrowing?

* To understand the cost of borrowing, you should understand interest rates (the price a borrower pays to a lender to use the lender's money) and risk. Borrowers who are considered risky pay higher interest rates.
* A credit report lists your credit history and helps lenders to assess the risk in lending to you. A higher credit score will give you more borrowing options at lower interest rates.
* Payday loans are extremely high-interest loans that you should avoid; they frequently become a trap from which it is difficult to escape.

How do interest rates affect borrowers?

* When you use your credit card, you must make the minimum payment each month. If you don't pay off the balance, you'll have to pay compound interest on the principal amount until your debt is paid off. Interest can add up very quickly.
* While student loans generally have lower interest rates than credit cards, they still represent significant debt for college graduates. Various plans allow students to customize their payment schedules; but in general, the sooner you pay back your student loan, the less interest you will pay.

Is it better to buy or rent a house?

* People who choose to buy a home are often motivated by the desire for equity as well as the tax advantages. However, owning a home can be costly in terms of the required maintenance, and it may be difficult for young people to qualify for a mortgage.
* Personal circumstances such as where you live and how old you are dictate whether renting or buying is the better choice.

How do people save for retirement?

* To save for retirement, people often buy stocks and bonds. Growth stocks offer the potential for income through an increase in the stock price, while income stocks increase income through dividend payments.
* Bonds are contract-based IOUs. Investment-grade bonds are usually safe investments, while junk bonds entail higher risk.
* Mutual funds can help savers to diversify their savings by spreading the risk among many companies.
* Putting money into an individual retirement account (IRA) can offer many tax advantages.
* The key to a secure retirement is to start saving early.

CONCEPTS YOU SHOULD KNOW

bond (p. 580)
compounding (p. 569)
credit history (p. 567)
credit report (p. 567)
dividend (p. 579)
equity (p. 575)
fixed interest rate (p. 571)
growth stock (p. 578)
income stock (p. 579)
individual retirement account (IRA) (p. 585)
interest rate (p. 565)
investment-grade bonds (p. 581)
junk bonds (p. 581)
line of credit (p. 566)
maturity date (p. 580)
minimum payment (p. 569)
mutual fund (p. 583)
par value (p. 580)
payday loan (p. 568)
pension (p. 587)
principal amount (p. 570)
Roth IRA (p. 585)
securitized loan (p. 575)
stock (p. 577)
variable interest rate (p. 571)

GLOSSARY

ability to pay principle: the principle according to which those who make more money pay more money in taxes

absolute advantage: the ability of one producer to make more than another producer with the same quantity of resources

aggregate demand: the total demand for final goods and services in an economy

aggregate supply: the total supply of final goods and services in an economy

assets: the items that a firm owns

average tax rate: the total tax paid divided by the amount of taxable income

average total cost (ATC): the sum of average variable cost and average fixed cost

balance sheet: an accounting statement that summarizes a firm's key financial information

bank run: an event occurring when many depositors attempt to withdraw their funds at the same time

barriers to entry: restrictions that make it difficult for new firms to enter a market

barter: the trade of a good or service without a commonly accepted medium of exchange

behavioral economics: the field of economics that draws on insights from experimental psychology to explore how people make economic decisions

benefits principle: the principle according to which taxes are levied on those who most benefit from the taxed product or activity

black markets: illegal markets that arise where either illegal goods are sold or legal goods are sold at illegal prices

bond: an IOU that joins two parties in a contract that specifies the conditions for repayment of the loan

bounded rationality: a concept proposing that although decision-makers want a good outcome, either they are not capable of performing the problem-solving that traditional theory assumes, or they are not inclined to do so

budget deficit: a condition occurring when government outlays exceed revenue

budget surplus: a condition occurring when government revenue exceeds outlays

business cycle: a short-run fluctuation in economic activity

cap and trade: an approach used to curb pollution by creating a system of pollution permits that are traded in an open market

capital: the tools and equipment used in the production of goods and services

central bank: the bank for the banks; its roles include controlling the money supply, providing loans to struggling banks, and regulating the banking system

***ceteris paribus*:** the concept under which economists examine a change in one variable while holding everything else constant

checkable deposits: deposits in bank accounts from which depositors may make withdrawals by writing checks

circular flow model: a model that shows how resources and final goods and services flow through the economy

classical economics: a school of thought that stresses the importance of aggregate supply and generally believes that the economy can adjust back to full employment equilibrium on its own

collusion: an agreement among rival firms that specifies the price each firm charges and the quantity it produces

commercial banks: the banks where most people have their checking and savings accounts and where most households would go to get a loan

commodity money: the use of an actual good in place of money

commodity-backed money: money that can be exchanged for a commodity at a fixed rate

common resources: resources that have no legal owner

comparative advantage: the situation in which an individual, business, or country can produce at a lower opportunity cost than a competitor can

compensating differential: the difference in wages offered to offset the desirability or undesirability of a job

competitive market: one in which when there are so many buyers and sellers that each has only a small impact on the market price and output

complements: two goods that are used together; when the price of a complementary good rises, the demand for the related good goes down

compounding: (1) in the context of borrowing, compounding means that interest is added to an account balance so that the borrower ends up paying interest on an increasingly higher balance; (2) in the context of saving, compounding means that interest is added to the total savings the saver gets paid interest on his or her savings plus any prior interest earned

consumer price index (CPI): a measure of the price level based on the consumption patterns of a typical consumer

consumer surplus: the difference between the willingness to pay for a good and the price that is paid to get it

consumption: the purchase of final goods and services by households, excluding new housing

consumption smoothing: behavior occurring when people borrow and save in order to smooth consumption over their lifetime

contractionary fiscal policy: a decrease in government spending or an increase in taxes meant to slow economic expansion

contractionary monetary policy: a central bank's action to decrease the money supply

countercyclical fiscal policy: fiscal policy that seeks to counteract business-cycle fluctuations

CPI: see *consumer price index*

creative destruction: the introduction of new products and technologies that leads to the end of other industries and jobs

credit history: a record of an individual's loan and payment history

credit report: a financial report card that reports an individual's credit history (one's ability to repay one's loans)

crowding-out: a phenomenon occurring when private spending falls in response to increases in government spending

currency: the paper bills and coins that are used to buy goods and services

currency appreciation: a currency's increase in value relative to other currencies

currency depreciation: a currency's decrease in value relative to other currencies

cyclical unemployment: unemployment caused by economic downturns

deadweight loss: the decrease in economic activity caused by market distortions

debt: the sum total of accumulated budget deficits

default risk: the risk that a borrower will not repay the full value of a debt

deficit: a shortfall in revenue for a particular year's budget

deficit spending: borrowing money in order to spend it

deflation: a condition occurring when overall prices fall

demand curve: a graph of the relationship between the prices in the demand schedule and the quantity demanded at those prices

demand schedule: a table that shows the relationship between the price of a good and the quantity demanded

derived demand: (1) the demand for an input used in the production process; (2) the demand for a good or service that derives from the demand for another good or service

diminishing marginal product: a condition occurring when successive increases in inputs are associated with a slower rise in output

discount rate: the interest rate on the discount loans made by the Federal Reserve to private banks

discouraged workers: those who are not working, have looked for a job in the past 12 months and are willing to work, but have not sought employment in the past 4 weeks

discretionary outlays: government spending that can be altered when the government is setting its annual budget

dissaving: behavior occurring when people withdraw funds from their previously accumulated savings

dividend: a cash payment to stockholders for each share of stock owned

dominant strategy: in game theory, a strategy that a player will always prefer, regardless of what his or her opponent chooses

double coincidence of wants: a condition occurring when each party in an exchange transaction happens to have what the other party desires

dumping: behavior occurring when a foreign supplier sells a good below the price it charges in its home country

durable consumption goods: goods that are consumed over a long period

economic contraction: a phase of the business cycle during which the economy is shrinking

economic expansion: a phase of the business cycle during which the economy is growing

economic growth: the percentage change in real per capita gross domestic product (GDP) from one period to another

economic profit: calculated by subtracting both the explicit and the implicit costs of business from a firm's total revenue

economic stability: a condition that occurs when those who wish to work have jobs in an environment where the economy experiences growth and stable prices

economic thinking: a purposeful evaluation of the available opportunities to make the best decision possible

economics: the study of how people allocate their limited resources to satisfy their nearly unlimited wants

economies of scale: a condition occurring when costs decline as output expands in the long run

efficiency: an allocation of resources that maximizes total surplus

elastic: the type of demand condition in which consumers are responsive to a change in price

elasticity: a measure of the responsiveness of buyers and sellers to changes in price or income

entitlement programs: mandatory benefits that some citizens who meet certain requirements are entitled to receive under current laws

entrepreneur: a person who conceives and starts a business

equilibrium: a condition occurring at the point where the demand curve and the supply curve intersect

equilibrium price: the price at which the quantity supplied is equal to the quantity demanded; also known as the *market-clearing price*

equilibrium quantity: the amount at which the quantity supplied is equal to the quantity demanded

equity: (1) the fairness of the distribution of benefits within the society; (2) the part of an asset that an individual owns. In the case of a house, equity is the part of the selling price that the individual gets to keep after paying off the balance of his or her mortgage

excess reserves: any reserves held by a bank in excess of those required

exchange rate: the price of foreign currency, indicating how much a unit of foreign currency costs in terms of another currency

excise taxes: taxes levied on a particular good or service

excludable goods: goods that the consumer must purchase before being able to use them

expansionary fiscal policy: an increase in government spending or a decrease in taxes meant to stimulate the economy toward expansion

expansionary monetary policy: a central bank's action to increase the money supply in an effort to stimulate the economy

expected value: the predicted value of an event; calculated by multiplying each possible outcome by its respective probability and then summing all of these amounts

explicit costs: tangible out-of-pocket expenses

exports: goods and services produced domestically but purchased and used abroad

external costs: the costs of a market activity paid by people who are not participants

externalities: the costs or benefits of a market activity that affect a third party

face value: see *par value*

factors of production: the inputs (labor, land, and capital) used in producing goods and services

fiat money: money that has no value except as the medium of exchange; there is no inherent or intrinsic value to the currency

final good: a good sold to final users

financial intermediaries: firms that act as go-betweens for savers and investors by taking in deposits and extending loans

fiscal policy: the use of government's budget tools, government spending, and taxes to influence the macroeconomy

Fisher equation: an equation stating that the real interest rate equals the nominal interest rate minus the inflation rate

fixed costs: costs that do not vary with a firm's output in the short run

fixed inputs: inputs that cannot be changed in the short run

fixed interest rate: an interest rate that remains in effect for the full term of a loan

foreign exchange market: the market in which the currencies of different countries are traded

fractional reserve banking: a system in which banks hold only a fraction of deposits on reserve

framing effects: a phenomenon seen when people change their answer (or action) depending on how the question is asked

free-rider problem: a phenomenon occurring when someone receives a benefit without having to pay for it

frictional unemployment: unemployment caused by delays in matching available jobs and workers

full-employment output level (y^*): the output level produced in an economy when the unemployment rate is equal to its natural rate

game theory: a branch of mathematics that economists use to analyze the strategic behavior of decision-makers

GDP: see *gross domestic product*

government failure: a situation that occurs when government intervention makes a problem worse

government outlays: the part of the government budget that includes both spending and transfer payments

government spending: spending by all levels of government on final goods and services

Great Recession: the U.S. recession lasting from December 2007 to June 2009

gross domestic product (GDP): the market value of all final goods and services produced within a country during a specific period

growth stock: a stock in a company that is expected to grow and to become profitable

human capital: (1) the skill that workers acquire on the job and through education; (2) the resource represented by the quantity, knowledge, and skills of the workers in an economy

hyperinflation: an extremely high rate of inflation that completely stymies economic activity

impact lag: the time between passing legislation and observing its effectiveness

implementation lag: the delay that occurs when it takes time to decide on a course of action and pass the legislation required to solve a problem in the economy

implicit costs: a firm's opportunity costs of doing business

imports: goods and services produced abroad but purchased and used domestically

incentives: factors that motivate a person to act or exert effort

income stock: a stock that pays a predictable dividend over a relatively long period

individual retirement account (IRA): a retirement savings account that provides tax incentives to promote saving

industry: a group of firms that sell similar products or services

inelastic: the type of demand condition in which consumers are not very responsive to a change in price

infant industry argument: the idea that domestic industries need trade protection until they are established and able to compete internationally

inferior good: a good that consumers buy more of as income falls, holding other things constant

inflation: the growth in the overall level of prices in an economy

inputs: the resources (labor, land, and capital) used in the production process

institution: a significant practice, relationship, or organization in a society

intellectual property: non-physical property such as an idea, invention, or creative work that is a result of someone's intellect

interest rate: a price of loanable funds, quoted as a percentage of the original loan amount; the price a borrower pays to a lender to use the lender's money

intermediate good: a good that firms repackage or bundle with other goods for sale at a later stage

internal costs: the costs of a market activity paid by an individual participant

internalization: a condition occurring when a firm takes into account the external costs (or benefits) to society that occur as a result of its actions

intertemporal decision-making: decision-making that involves planning to do something over a period of time; this requires valuing the present and the future consistently

investment: (1) the process of using resources to create or buy new capital; (2) private spending on tools, plant, and equipment used to produce future output

investment banks: banks that most commonly help firms raise money to invest

investment-grade bonds: bonds that pay low interest rates but that are issued by companies that are very likely to repay their creditors

investor confidence: a measure of what firms expect for future economic activity

junk bonds: bonds that pay higher interest rates than investment-grade bonds but that are considered speculative

Keynesian economics: a school of thought that stresses the importance of aggregate demand and generally believes that the economy needs help in moving back to full employment equilibrium

labor force: those who are already employed or actively seeking work

labor-force participation rate: the percentage of the population that is in the labor force

labor-leisure trade-off: the opportunity costs people entail when choosing between working and not working

laissez-faire: ("allow to do" in French); the view that governments should allow firms to conduct their business without interference

law of demand: the law that, other things being equal, quantity demanded falls when prices rise, and rises when prices fall

law of increasing relative cost: a law stating that the opportunity cost of producing a good rises as a society produces more of it

law of supply: the law that, other things being equal, the quantity supplied of a good rises when the price of the good rises, and falls when the price of the good falls

law of supply and demand: the law that the market price of any good will adjust to bring the quantity supplied and the quantity demanded into balance

liabilities: the financial obligations that a firm owes to others

line of credit: the maximum amount that a lender is willing to lend to a borrower

liquidity: a term that refers to how easily something can be spent

loanable funds market: the market where savers supply funds for loans to borrowers

long run: (1) the period of time that allows consumers and producers to fully adjust to market conditions; (2) a period of time sufficient for all parts of the economy to adjust to economic conditions

loss: the result of total revenue being less than total cost

loss aversion: a phenomenon occurring when individuals place more weight on avoiding losses than on attempting to realize gains

M1: the money supply measure that is essentially composed of currency and checkable deposits

M2: the money supply measure that includes everything in M1 plus savings deposits, money market mutual funds, and small-denomination time deposits (CDs)

macroeconomics: the study of the overall aspects and workings of an economy

mandatory outlays: government spending that is determined by ongoing long-term obligations

marginal cost (MC): the increase in cost that occurs from producing additional output

marginal product: the change in output associated with one additional unit of an input

marginal product of labor: the change in output associated with adding one additional worker

marginal propensity to consume: the portion of additional income that is spent on consumption

marginal revenue (MR): the additional revenue generated by the production and sale of one more unit of output

marginal tax rate: the tax rate paid on an individual's next dollar of income

marginal thinking: the evaluation of whether the benefit of one more unit of something is greater than its cost

margins: incremental changes

market: a system that brings buyers and sellers together to exchange goods and services

market demand: the sum of all the individual quantities demanded by each buyer in the market at each price
market economy: an economy in which resources are allocated among households and firms with little or no government interference
market failure: a condition occurring when the output level of a good is inefficient
market power: the control that any individual firm has over the price that it can charge
market structure: the way the firms in a particular market relate to one another
market supply: the sum of the quantities supplied by each seller in the market at each price
market-clearing price: see *equilibrium price*
maturity date: on a bond, the date on which the loan repayment is due
medium of exchange: what people trade for goods and services
microeconomics: the study of the individual units that make up the economy
minimum payment: the smallest amount that a lender requires a borrower to pay each month so as not to damage the borrower's credit score
minimum wage: the lowest hourly wage rate that firms may legally pay their workers
monetary neutrality: the idea that the money supply does not affect real economic variables like GDP or employment
monetary policy: the government's adjustment of the money supply to influence the macroeconomy
monopolistic competition: a situation characterized by free entry, many different firms, and product differentiation
monopoly: a condition existing when a single company supplies the entire market for a particular good or service
moral hazard: a phenomenon seen when a party that is protected from risk behaves differently from the way it would behave if it were fully exposed to the risk
mutual fund: an investment program that trades in diversified holdings and is professionally managed
Nash equilibrium: in game theory, a phenomenon occurring when a decision-maker has nothing to gain by changing strategy unless it can collude
natural monopoly: a situation in which a single large firm has lower costs than any potential smaller competitor
natural rate of unemployment: the typical rate of unemployment that occurs when the economy is growing normally
negative externality: a situation in which a third party is adversely affected
net exports: exports minus imports of final goods and services
nominal GDP: gross domestic product measured in current prices and not adjusted for inflation
nominal interest rate: the interest rate before it is corrected for inflation
nominal wage: a worker's wage expressed in current dollars
non-durable consumption goods: goods that are consumed over a short period
normal good: a good that consumers buy more of as income rises, holding other things constant
normative statement: an opinion that cannot be tested or validated; it describes "what ought to be"
oligopoly: a condition existing when a small number of firms sell a differentiated product in a market with high barriers to entry
open market operations: the purchase or sale of bonds by a central bank
opportunity cost: the highest-valued alternative that must be sacrificed in order to get something else
output: the production the firm creates
outsourcing of labor: a firm's shifting of jobs to an outside company, usually overseas, where the cost of labor is lower
par value: the value of a bond at maturity—the amount due at repayment; also called *face value*
payday loan: a short-term loan in which the borrower writes the lender a check against an upcoming paycheck and the lender waits until the borrower's payday to cash the check
pension: an employer-funded retirement plan
per capita GDP: gross domestic product (GDP) per person
positive externality: a situation in which a third party is positively affected
positive statement: an assertion that can be tested and validated; it describes "what is"
positive time preference: a condition in which people prefer to have what they want sooner rather than later
preference reversal: a phenomenon arising when risk tolerance is not consistent
price: the market-determined opportunity cost of a good or service; the key determinant of how market economies allocate goods and services
price ceilings: legally established maximum prices for goods or services
price controls: an attempt to set prices through government involvement in the market
price elasticity of demand: a measure of the responsiveness of quantity demanded to a change in price
price floors: legally established minimum prices for goods or services
price gouging laws: temporary ceilings on the prices that sellers can charge during times of emergency
price level (P): the general level of prices for the whole economy; a measure of the average prices of goods and services throughout the economy
price maker: a firm with some control over the price it charges
price taker: a firm with no control over the price set by the market

priming effects: a phenomenon seen when the ordering of the questions that are asked influences the answers
principal amount: the total amount of money borrowed
prisoner's dilemma: a situation in which decision-makers face incentives that make it difficult to achieve mutually beneficial outcomes
private goods: goods with two characteristics they are both excludable and rival in consumption
private property: provision of an exclusive right of ownership that allows for the use, and especially the exchange, of property
private property rights: the rights of individuals to own property, to use it in production, and to own the resulting output
producer surplus: the difference between the willingness to sell a good and the price that the seller receives
product differentiation: the process that firms use to make a product more attractive to potential customers
production function: a description of the relationship between the inputs a firm uses and the output it creates
production possibilities frontier: a model that illustrates the combinations of outputs that a society can produce if all of its resources are being used efficiently
profit: total revenue minus total cost; a negative result is a *loss*
profit-maximizing rule: the rule stating that profit maximization occurs when the firm chooses the quantity that causes marginal revenue to be equal to marginal cost, or MR = MC
progressive tax: a tax under which the more a person earns, the higher his or her average tax rate
property rights: an owner's ability to exercise control over a resource
proportional tax: a tax according to which everyone pays at the same tax rate regardless of income level
public goods: goods that can be jointly consumed by more than one person, and from which non-payers are difficult to exclude
purchasing power: how much a person's money can buy
quantitative easing: the targeted use of open market operations in which the central bank buys securities specifically targeted in certain markets
quantity demanded: the amount of a good or service that buyers are willing and able to purchase at the current price
quantity supplied: the amount of a good or service that producers are willing and able to sell at the current price
real GDP: gross domestic product (GDP) adjusted for changes in prices
real interest rate: the interest rate that is corrected for inflation
recession: a short-term economic downturn that typically lasts about 6 to 18 months
recognition lag: the delay that occurs when it takes time to recognize the existence of a problem in the economy
regressive tax: a tax under which the more a person earns, the lower his or her average tax rate
rent seeking: behavior occurring when resources are used to secure monopoly rights through the political process
required reserve ratio: the portion of deposits that banks are required to keep on reserve
required reserves: the portion of deposits that a bank must have readily available for withdrawal
reserve requirement: the amount of deposits that a bank must hold in reserve as determined by the central bank; this limits the amount of deposits a bank can lend
reserves: the portion of bank deposits that are set aside and not lent out
resources: the inputs used to produce goods and services; also called *factors of production*
risk takers: those who prefer gambles with lower expected values, and potentially higher winnings, over a sure thing
risk-averse people: those who prefer a sure thing over a gamble with a higher expected value
risk-neutral people: those who choose the highest expected value regardless of the risk
rival goods: goods that cannot be enjoyed by more than one person at a time
Roth IRA: an individual retirement account in which gains are not taxed at the time of withdrawal
rule of law: the consistent and trustworthy enforcement of a nation's laws
rule of 70: a rule stating that if the annual growth rate of a variable is x%, the size of that variable doubles approximately every 70 ÷ x years
savings rate: personal saving as a portion of disposable (after-tax) income
scale: the size of the production process
scarcity: the limited nature of society's resources, given society's unlimited wants and needs
school of thought: a cohesive way of thinking about a subject
securitized loan: a loan in which a borrower's asset serves as collateral
service: an output that provides benefits without the production of a tangible product
short run: (1) the period of time in which consumers and producers can partially adjust their behavior; (2) the period of time in which only some parts of the economy adjust
shortage: a market condition when the quantity supplied of a good is less than the quantity demanded
signals: information conveyed by profits and losses about the profitability of various markets
simple money multiplier: the rate at which banks multiply money when all currency is deposited into banks and they hold no excess reserves
social costs: the internal costs plus the external costs of a market activity
social optimum: the price and quantity combination that would exist if there were no externalities

social welfare: see *total surplus*
specialization: the breaking up of a job into tasks and the assignment of those tasks to individuals; also called the division of labor
spending multiplier: a formula to determine the total impact on spending from an initial change of a given amount; the formula is 1 divided by (1 minus the marginal propensity to consume)
stagflation: the combination of high unemployment rates and high inflation
status quo bias: a condition existing when decision-makers want to maintain their current choices
stocks: ownership shares in a firm
store of value: a means for holding wealth
strike: a work stoppage designed to aid a union's bargaining position
structural unemployment: unemployment caused by changes in the industrial makeup (structure) of the economy
subsidy: a payment made by the government to encourage the consumption or production of a good or service
substitutes: goods that are used in place of each other; when the price of a substitute good rises, the quantity demanded falls and the demand for the related good goes up
supply curve: a graph of the relationship between the prices in the supply schedule and the quantity supplied at those prices
supply schedule: a table that shows the relationship between the price of a good and the quantity supplied
supply shock: a surprise event that changes a firm's production costs
surplus: a market condition that occurs when the quantity supplied of a good is greater than the quantity demanded
t-account: a basic balance sheet on which the assets on one side equal the liabilities on the other
tariffs: taxes levied on imported goods and services
taxes: the mechanism that governments use to raise the money that funds government operations and provides social services
technological advancement: the introduction of new techniques or methods that enable firms to produce more valuable outputs per unit of input
technology: the knowledge that is available for use in production
time preferences: the fact that people prefer to receive goods and services sooner rather than later
tit-for-tat: a long-run strategy that promotes cooperation among participants by mimicking the opponent's most recent decision with repayment in kind
total cost: the amount a firm spends in order to produce the goods and services it produces
total revenue: (1) the amount that consumers pay and sellers receive for a good; (2) the amount a firm receives from the sale of the goods and services it produces
total surplus: the sum of consumer surplus and producer surplus; also known as *social welfare*
trade: the voluntary exchange of goods and services between two or more parties
trade balance: the difference between a nation's total exports and total imports
trade deficit: a condition occurring when imports exceed exports, indicating a negative trade balance
trade surplus: a condition occurring when exports exceed imports, indicating a positive trade balance
tragedy of the commons: the depletion of a good that is rival in consumption but non-excludable
transfer payments: payments made by the government to groups or individuals when no good or service is received in return
ultimatum game: an economic experiment in which two players decide how to divide a sum of money
underemployed workers: those who have part-time jobs but who would prefer to work full-time
underground economy: transactions that are not reported to the government and therefore are not taxed; also known as the shadow economy
unemployment: a condition occurring when a worker who is not currently employed is searching for a job without success
unemployment insurance: a government program that reduces the hardship of joblessness by guaranteeing that unemployed workers receive a percentage of their former income while unemployed
unemployment rate: the percentage of the labor force that is unemployed
union: a group of workers that bargains collectively for better wages and benefits
unit of account: the measure in which prices are quoted
value of the marginal product (VMP): the marginal product of an input multiplied by the price of the output it produces; VMP = marginal product of labor × price
variable costs: costs that change with the rate of output
variable inputs: inputs that can be easily changed, thereby altering output levels
variable interest rate: an interest rate that can change based on market conditions or the borrower's creditworthiness
wage: the payment made to labor, including benefits
willingness to pay: the maximum price a consumer will pay for a good
willingness to sell: the minimum price a seller will accept to sell a good or service

CREDITS

TEXT

Chapter 10: "Employment, Italian Style," *The Wall Street Journal* by News Corporation, June 25, 2012. Copyright © 2012 Dow Jones, Inc. Reproduced with permission of Dow Jones Company in the format Republish in a book via Copyright Clearance Center.

PHOTOGRAPHS

Chapter 1: 2 Pancaketom | Dreamstime.com; 5 John Lund / Stephanie Roeser / Getty Images; **6 left** Phang Kim Shan | Dreamstime.com; **6 right** Nguyen Thai | Dreamstime.com; 7 Visions of America, LLC / Alamy; **9 top** Joe Robbins / Getty Images; **9 bottom** Seanyu | Dreamstime.com; **10 top** Yusputra | Dreamstime.com; **10 bottom** TuTheLens / Shutterstock; 12 Jacqueline Larma / AP Photo; 14 Haywiremedia | Dreamstime.com; 16 PARAMOUNT / The Kobal Collection / Art Resource, NY; 17 Stockbyte / Getty Images; 18 Andres Rodriguez / Dreamstime.co

Chapter 2: 23 Wizards of the Coast and Magic: The Gathering are trademarks of Wizards of the Coast LLC; 24 Archive Holdings Inc. / The Image Bank / Getty Images; 27 M.L. Watts / Wikimedia Commons; 32 Lou-Foto / Alamy; 38 Philcold | Dreamstime.com; 39 DREAMWORKS / Album / Newscom; 41 AP Photo / Nick Wass; 42 Charles Islander / iStockphoto.com; 44 © Boeing

Chapter 3: 51 AP Photo / The Day, Sean D. Elliot; **53 left** All Canada Photos / Alamy; **53 right** Getty Images / First Light; 57 Edith Layland | Dreamstime.com; 60 POLYGRAM / WARNERS / SILVER PICTURES / The Kobal Collection / James Bridges / Art Resource, NY; 61 Carolyn Lagattuta / Stocksy; **62 top** Radius Images / Alamy; **62 bottom** Showface | Dreamstime.com; 69 AP Photo / Ted S. Warren; 71 Degtiarova Viktoriia / Shutterstock; 72 Stockbyte / Getty Images; 77 R. Gino Santa Maria / Dreamstime.com; 86 Hugoht | Dreamstime.com; **89 top** Allstar Picture Library / Alamy; **89 bottom** Cobalt88 | Dreamstime.com; 90 Evan-Amos / Wikimedia Commons; **91 top** Wisconsinart | Dreamstime.com; **91 center** Oleksiy Mark | Dreamstime .com; **91 center** Lisa Thornberg / iStockphoto; **91 bottom** IFCAR / Wikimedia Commons

Chapter 4: 95 The Gallery Collection / Corbis; 96 DreamWorks / Courtesy Everett Collection; 102 Dee Cercone / Newscom; 103 Randy Duchaine / Alamy; **104 top** DreamWorks / Courtesy Everett Collection; **104 bottom** Grublee | Dreamstime.com; 105 Chuck Place / istockphoto. com; 106 Jen Grantham / iStockphoto .com; **107 top** Peter Hermann III / / AP / Corbis; **107 bottom** Andres Rodriguez / Alamy; **108 top** Jonathan Larsen / Diadem Images / Alamy; **108 top center** Flairgun / Shutterstock; **108 center** Steve Debenport / Getty Images; **108 bottom center** Peter Hermann III / AP / Corbis; **108 bottom** © Jeffry Konczal; **110 top** copypast.ru; **110 center** AP Photo / Liu Heung Shing; **110 bottom** David J. Phillip / AP / Corbis; 111 Lisa F. Young | Dreamstime.com; 114 Yuri Arcurs | Dreamstime.com; **115 bottom** Steven von Niederhausern / iStockphoto.com; **115 top** Julie Feinstein | Dreamstime.com; **115 center** Chris Graythen / Getty Images; **115 center** Chris Graythen / Getty Images; 116 Anthony Aneese Totah Jr / Dreamstime .com; 117 Peter Booth / iStockphoto.com; 119 FX Networks / Courtesy:Everett Collection; **120 top** EPA / NIC BOTHMA / Newscom; **120 bottom** Robert Churchill / iStockphoto.com; 124 AP Photo / Kathy Kmonicek

Chapter 5: 128 Geoffrey Kidd / Alamy; 131 Marc F. Henning / Alamy; 134 Chip East / Reuters / Corbis; 137 YinYang / iStockphoto.com; 140 blickwinkel / Alamy; 143 San Antonio Express-News / ZUMA Press / Newscom; 148 Stephen Chernin / Getty Images; **149 bottom** Antonio Jodice | Dreamstime.Com; **149 top** NBC Universal, Inc. / Chris Haston / ZUMA Press / Newscom; 150 akg-images / Newscom; 153 Columbia / courtesy Everett Collection

Chapter 6: 159 Graça Victoria | Dreamstime.com; 161 Henry M. Trotter / Wikimedia Commons; **162 top** Neilson Barnard / iStockphoto.com; **162 center lt** Manon Ringuette |Dreamstime.com; **162 center rt** Raine Vara / Alamy; **162 bottom** Russell Shively / iStockphoto.com; 163 Michel Porro / Getty Images; 164 20th Century Fox. All rights reserved / courtesy Everett Collection; 166 Alexandr Mitiuc | Dreamstime.com; 169 CBS-TV / The Kobal Collection / Art Resource, NY; 172 Howard Harrison / Alamy; 174 PARAMOUNT PICTURES / Album / Newscom; 175 Michelle Del Guercio / Photo Researchers / Getty Images; 180 desuza. communications / iStockphoto.com; 183 ONE MAN BAND, 2005. © Buena Vista Pictures / courtesy Everett Collection; **184 top left** AP Photo / Ric Feld; **184 top right** AP Photo / Jessica Hill; **184 bottom** Paul Souders / Corbis; 185 rabbit75 / iStockphoto.com

Chapter 7: 188 John Mutrux / MCT / Newscom; **195** Paramount / Courtesy: Everett Collection., Paramount Pictures; **196** LifesizeImages / iStockphoto.com; **198 top** Filmfoto | Dreamstime.com; **198 bottom** Presselect / Alamy; **199** Westend61 GmbH / Alamy; **203 bottom** Alex Slobodkin / iStockphoto.com; **203 top** Mark Stahl / iStockphoto.com; **206** Eric Gaillard / Reuters / Corbis; **208** MURDER BY NUMBERS, Ryan Gosling, 2002, © Warner Brothers / courtesy Everett Collection; **210** TheCrimsonMonkey / iStockphoto; **211** AP Photo / Sergey Ponomarev; **213** THE DARK KNIGHT, Heath Ledger as The Joker, 2008. © Warner Bros. / Courtesy Everett Collection; **214** Nickilford / iStockphoto; **216** Yuri Arcurs | Dreamstime.com

Chapter 8: 223 Redbaron | Dreamstime.com; **225 top** Ernesto Diaz / iStockphoto.com; **225 bottom** Candybox Images | Dreamstime.com; **226** Daniel Laflor / iStockphoto.com; **228** Columbia Pictures / courtesy Everett Co / Everett Collection; **229** Pzaxe | Dreamstime.com;**230** AP Photo / The Daily Dispatch, Ashley Steven Ayscue; **231** South West Images Scotland / Alamy; **234** EPA / Newscom; **235** The Everett Collection, Inc.; **237** Eric Hood / iStockphoto.com; **239** OUTSOURCED, Josh Hamilton, Ayesha Dharker, 2006 / The Everett Collection, Inc.; **240** AP Photo / Ajit Solanki; **241** pete collins / iStockphoto.com; **242** Barry Brecheisen / Invision / AP; **243** Ljupco / iStockphoto.com; **244** pete collins / iStockphoto.com; **245 top** Matthew Simmons / Stringer / WireImage / Getty Images; **245 table: top** pete collins / iStockphoto.com; **245 table: center top** Stockbyte / Getty Images; **245 center bottom** Natalia Bratslavsky | Dreamstime.com; **245 table: bottom** Matthew Simmons / Stringer / WireImage / Getty Images

Chapter 9: 253 Frederic Prochasson / iStockphoto.com; **256** Christian Heeb / JAI / Corbis; **258** Annie Su Yee Yek | Dreamstime.com; **259 right** http://www.youtube.com/watch?v=hnOPu0_Ywhw; **259 left** Realimage / Alamy; **260** U.S. Navy photo by Mass Communication Specialist 3rd Class John Grandin; **262** kali9 / iStockphoto; **263** Stockbyte / Getty Images; **264 top** Robert Nickelsberg / Getty Images; **264 bottom** Karl Dolenc / iStockphoto; **265** NASA / Goddard Space Flight Center; **267** Ted Wood / Aurora Photos; **268** Christophe Testi | Dreamstime; **269** Charlieb34 | Dreamstime.com; **271 top** Alistair Laming / Alamy; **271 bottom** Sean Locke / iStockphoto.com; **273 left top** Charlieb34 | Dreamstime.com; **273 left center** Steve Lovegrove |Dreamstime.com; **273 left bottom** Stef Bennett | Dreamstime.com; **273 right top** Yarinca / iStockphoto.com; **273 rt center** Jonathan Cohen / iStockphoto.com; **273 right bottom** RiverNorthPhotography / iStockphoto.com; **274** June M Sobrito | Dreamstime.com

Chapter 10: 278 Ocean / Corbis; **282 left** Sailorman | Dreamstime.com; **282 right** Bloomberg via Getty Images; **283** William J. Smith / Associated Press; **285 left** Jhanganu | Dreamstime.com; **285 right** Kristoffer Tripplaar / Alamy; **287** Rivertracks | Dreamstime.com; **289** ROPI / ZUMAPRESS / Newscom; **290** Fotosearch / Getty Images; **291 top** Michael Krinke / iStockphoto.com; **291 bottom** Eliza Snow / iStockphoto.com; **295** ZHU QINGXIANG / Xinhua Press / Corbis; **297** George Peters / iStockphoto.com; **300 left** Russell Lee / Corbis; **300 right** Britta Kasholm-Tengve / iStockphoto.Com

Chapter 11: 305 https://www.youtube.com/watch?v=d0nERTFo-Sk; **306** Photographerlondon | Dreamstime.com; **310** Juice Images / Alamy; **311 left** Joe Biafore / iStockphoto.com; **311 right** Shane Shaw / iStockphoto.com; **312** epa european pressphoto agency b.v. / Alamy; **313** Sipa via AP Images; **315 top** Kelpfish | Dreamstime.com; **315 center** Alexander Kharchenko | Dreamstime.com; **315 bottom** Lezh / iStockphoto.com; **318 bottom** Katja Bone / iStockphoto.com; **319 top** Keith Dannemillet / Alamy; **320** Universal Pictures 2000 / The Everett Collection; **321** Jackstraw22 | Dreamstime.com; **322 top** kristian sekulic / iStockphoto.com; **322 bottom** MBI / Alamy; **328** Maskot / Offset / Shutterstock; **330** Blend Images / Alamy; **332** Ljupco / iStockphoto.com; **333** Blend Images / Alamy; **334 left** alexander kirch / istockphoto.com; **334 right** Manaemedia / Shutterstock; **336** AUSTIN POWERS: THE SPY WHO SHAGGED ME, Mike Myers, 1999, © New Line / courtesy Everett Collection; **340** Courtesy of Daniel D. Lee

Chapter 12: 347 Ashley Cooper / Alamy; **357** EricVega / iStockphoto.com; **358 bottom** Steven Pepple | Dreamstime.com; **358 top** DUMB AND DUMBER, Jim Carrey, Jeff Daniels, 1994. © New Line Cinema / courtesy Everett Collection; **359** Weng lei—Imaginechina / AP Images; **361** Christopher Pillitz / Photonica World / Getty Images; **363** The Kobal Collection / Paramount Television; **365** Courtesy of Lee Coppock; **366** Joseph Sohm / Shutterstock; **367** Frederic Legrand / COMEO / Shutterstock; **369** Danita Delimont / Gallo Images / Getty Images; **372** Adam Dean / Panos Pictures; **375** AP Photo / Jae C. Hong; **377** Peter Kim | Dreamstime.com

Chapter 13: 383 Planet Observer / UIG / Getty Images; **386** Courtesy of Irene Abdou; **390** Mark Sullivan / Getty Images; **391** Courtesy of Lee Coppock; **395** Feiyuwzhangjie | Dreamstime.com; **397 top** studio157 / iStockphoto.com; **397 bottom** MorePixels / iStockphoto.com; **398 bottom left** ClassicStock / Alamy; **398 bottom right** Cobalt88 | Dreamstime.com; **398 top left** Onepony | Dreamstime.com; **398 top right** Sonya Etchison | Dreamstime.com; **398 center left** Martyn Goddard / Corbis; **398 center right** Drive Images / Alamy; **399** Chris Ratcliffe / Bloomberg via Getty Images; **400** Asci Advertising & Publishing | Dreamstime.com; **401** Britta Kasholm-Tengve / iStockphoto.com; **403** Edward Kamau / Wikimedia Commons; **405** Alhovik | Dreamstime.com; **406** Carolyn Cole / Los Angeles Times; **407** Jacom Stephens / iStockphoto.com; **409** Edward Kamau / Wikimedia Commons

Chapter 14: **415** GYI NSEA / iStockphoto.com; **418** Courtesy of Lee Coppock; **419** Patti McConville / Alamy; **424** Tony Burns / Lonely Planet Images / Getty Images; **425** Wesley Thornberry / iStockphoto.com; **426** Horizons WWP / Alamy; **427** Ellen Ozier / AP / Corbis; **430** Andres Rodriguez | Dreamstime.com; **431 top** DeadDuck / iStockphoto.com; **431 bottom** tedestudio / iStockphoto.com; **432** Despicable Me (2010) / The Kobal Collection; **433** SpongeBob Squarepants, 2004, © Paramount / courtesy Everett Collection; **437** Feng Li / Getty Images; **439** Images.com / Corbis

Chapter 15: **445** Yekaterina Rashap / iStockphoto.com; **447** Patti McConville / Alamy; **448 left** Dpenguinman / Wikimedia; **448 right** Scottnodine | Dreamstime.com; **449** DeborahMaxemow / iStockphoto.com; **450 left** Maurice Crooks / Alamy; **450 right** Versluis Photography / iStockphoto.com; **451** iurii / Shutterstock; **452** Massachusetts Historical Society; **453 top** T.J. Kirkpatrick / T.J. Kirkpatrick Photography / Corbis; **453 bottom** Ken Tannenbaum / iStockphoto.com; **455** tomas del amo / Alamy; **459** ANDY RAIN / EPA / Newscom; **460** © 20th Century Fox Film Corp. All rights reserved. / Courtesy Everett Collection; **463** Ted Foxx / Alamy

Chapter 16: **471** Dwight Nadig / iStockphoto.com; **481** Dani Simmonds / Alamy; **484** Bettmann / Corbis; **485** Ho / Reuters / Corbis; **488** AP Photo / Susan Walsh; **490** Oleksiy Mark | Dreamstime.com

Chapter 17: **495** AP Photo / Amy Sancetta; **499** Jhardz1 / Wikimedian Commons; **501** lucky336 / iStockphoto .com; **503 top** Photo Image Press / Splash News / Corbis; **503 center** Caroline Seidel / epa / Corbis; **503 bottom** AP Photo / Armando Trovati; **505** U.S. Navy photo by Andy Wolfe courtesy of Lockheed Martin; **509 top** Gerald Martineau / The Washington Post / Getty Images; **509 bottom** AP Photo / Darin McGregor, Pool; **512** Tetra Images / Corbis; **513** PAY IT FORWARD, Haley Joel Osment, 2000 / Everett Collection; **514** BRIAN KERSEY / UPI / Newscom; **515** Raja Rc | Dreamstime.com; **519** Corbis; **521** Denys Prykhodov / Shutterstock; **524** Ronnie McMillan / Alamy; **525** Edyta Pawlowska | Dreamstime.com; **526** Bohuslav Mayer | Dreamstime.com

Chapter 18: **531** Rafael Ramirez Lee / iStockphoto.com; **532** R. Gino Santa Maria | Dreamstime.com; **535** Anthony Rosenberg / iStockphoto.com; **536** Sanjay Pindiyath | Dreamstime.com; **537** Andrew Rowat / Corbis; **543** AP Photo / Damian Dovarganes; **544 top** Mary Evans / LUCASFILMS / Ronald Grant / Everett Collection; **544 bottom** Anna Bryukhanova / iStocknphoto.com; **545** LARRY LEUNG / FEATURECHINA / Newscom; **550** Patryk Kosmider / iStockphoto.com; **552** Anthony Dunn / Alamy; **560** Andrew Harrier / Bloomburg via Getty Images

Chapter 19: **563** Mega Pixel / Shutterstock; **566** Nat Farbman / The LIFE Picture Collection / Getty Images; **567** Andy Dean Photography / Shutterstock; **569** MGM / Jersey Films / The Kobal Collection; **571** Alamy; **573** Comstock / Getty Images; **575** Zastolskiy Victor / Shutterstock; **576** AP Photo / David J. Phillip; **577** Oneshare; **579** Martin Leissl / Bloomberg via Getty Images; **582** 68 Ocean / Corbis

INDEX

Page numbers where key terms are defined are in **boldface.**